Handbook of Research
in Early Childhood Education

Handbook of Research in Early Childhood Education

Edited by
Bernard Spodek

THE FREE PRESS
A Division of Macmillan Publishing Co., Inc.
NEW YORK

Collier Macmillan Publishers
LONDON

The Free Press
A Division of Macmillan Publishing Co., Inc.
866 Third Avenue, New York, N.Y. 10022

Collier Macmillan Canada, Inc.

Library of Congress Catalog Card Number: 81–71152

Printed in the United States of America

printing number

2 3 4 5 6 7 8 9 10

Library of Congress Cataloging in Publication Data

Main entry under title:

Handbook of research in early childhood education.

  Includes index.
  1. Child development—Addresses, essays, lectures.
2. Education of children—Curricula—Addresses, essays, lectures.   3. Education, Preschool—Research—Addresses, essays, lectures.   4. Child development—Research—Adresses, essays, lectures.   I. Spodek, Bernard.
LB1119.H23   372′.21   81–71152
ISBN 0–02–930570–5   AACR2

CONTENTS

PREFACE

THE DEVELOPMENT of any book requires that choices be made—choices in what to include and exclude. There is no way that everything that everyone might consider relevant can be addressed in a single volume. Authors who have written specific chapters have been forced to select carefully from what might have been included. As editor, I had to make similar choices. Important areas of research and theory have not been included. Although some of this might be the result of oversight, in general it is the result of forced choices in the context of what seemed to be of critical importance at this point in the development of the field. Had this *Handbook* been developed at another time, another set of choices might have been made.

This book is designed to be used by students of early childhood education at all levels of sophistication—mature scholars seeking resources to be further studied in depth as well as others searching for summary statements of various aspects of the field. It should be of use to administrators and policy makers as a source of information to be used in policy determination. It should also be of use to classroom teachers as a way to help them reflect on practice, acquaint them with theories and empirical research to explain classroom occurrences, and provide suggestions for what might become classroom activities.

I had the help of a great many people in compiling this book, more than could easily be acknowledged. Certainly thanks must be given to all those authors who contributed to this *Handbook*. The help and support of the editorial staff at The Free Press must also be acknowledged, especially Ron Chambers who helped to initiate the *Handbook* and Kitty Moore who provided continued support and encouragement toward it's completion. I also wish to thank those colleagues who read and critically reacted to portions of this book, especially Brenda Eheart, Mae Lorber, James Raths, and Marilyn Smith.

BERNARD SPODEK

ABOUT THE CONTRIBUTORS

DON BUSHELL, JR., received his Ph.D. from Washington University and is currently Professor of Human Development and of Curriculum and Instruction at the University of Kansas. He designed the Behavior Analysis Follow Through Program serving disadvantaged children in twelve communities across the country; has been a Fellow of the National Institute of Education; and has written extensively on applying behavioral procedures in schools, including *Classroom Behavior: A Little Book for Teachers*.

BETTYE M. CALDWELL received her Ph.D. from Washington University. She is currently Donaghey Distinguished Professor of Education at the University of Arkansas, Little Rock. She has been active in developing, operating, and evaluating early childhood and day-care programs for the past fifteen years and has published widely in the field. In 1976, she was named Woman of the Year for Educational Leadership by a national magazine. In 1980, she was named the Distinguished Alumna of Baylor University. MARJORIE FREYER serves as Dr. Caldwell's research assistant, and is an information retrieval specialist and day-care consumer for her three-year-old son.

CAROL E. COPPLE received her doctorate from Cornell University in 1973. She is currently an associate research psychologist at the Educational Testing Service in Princeton, New Jersey, where she directs the educational program of the Child Care Research Center. Dr. Copple's publications include *Educating the Young Thinker: Classroom Strategies for Cognitive Growth* (with Irving Sigel and Ruth Saunders) and *Structure and Development in Child Language: The Preschool Years* (with Marion Potts, Patricia Carlson, and Rodney Cocking).

BRYANT J. CRATTY received his Ph.D. from UCLA. Since 1958, he has been Professor of Kinesiology at UCLA. He has directed the Perceptual-Motor Learning Laboratory, and his publications include over fifty books and monographs translated into fifteen languages. He has received grants from the National Science Foundation, the National Institute of Neurological Diseases and Blindness, and the Joseph P. Kennedy, Jr., Foundation. Recent books include *Perceptual and Motor Development in Infants and Children* and *Adapted Physical Education for Handicapped Children and Youth*. He is author of the sensory-motor learning section of the *Encyclopaedia Britannica*.

RICHARD B. DARLINGTON is Professor of Psychology at Cornell University. He received his Ph.D. from the University of Minnesota in 1963. He specializes in psychometric methods and behavioral statistics. He has published several papers in the areas of culture–fair psychological testing and multivariate correlational methods and has written an introductory statistics textbook entitled *Radicals and Squares*.

RICHARD DE LISI received a Ph.D. degree in psychology from the Catholic University of America in 1977. He is currently an Assistant Professor of Educational Psychology at Rutgers University's Graduate School of Education. Dr. De Lisi has conducted research on children's cognitive development within a Piagetian framework. This research has focused on children's spatial–imaginal abilities and sex role development. Dr. De Lisi has served as a Consulting Editor for *Developmental Psychology* and as a member of the Board of Directors for the Jean Piaget Society.

ELLIS D. EVANS is a Professor of Educational Psychology at the University of Washington, Seattle, where he has taught since 1964. He received his Ed.D. from Indiana University. Author of *Contemporary Influences in Early Childhood Education* and *Transition to Teaching*, Dr. Evans is also co-author of *Children and Youth: Psychosocial Development* and *Development and Classroom Learning*. His professional awards include election to Outstanding Educators of America and selection as a Fellow in the U.S. Office of Education Leadership Training Institute for Early Childhood Education.

GRETA FEIN is research scientist at the University of Michigan. A Yale University Ph. D., Fein was formerly Professor of Child Development at the Merrill-Palmer Institute. She is the co-author of *Day Care in Context* and has published widely in the area of children's play. A recently completed review of the research literature on the development of pretend play in young children will be published in *Child Development.*

GEORGE E. FORMAN received his Ph.D. in developmental psychology in 1963 from the University of Alabama. He is currently Associate Professor, Early Childhood Education, at the University of Massachusetts, Amherst, and research associate at Harvard's Project Zero. He is the author of *The Child's Construction of Knowledge* (with David Kuschner), *Cognitive Development* (with Irving Sigel), and *Constructive Play* (with Fleet Hill) and the editor of *Action and Thought* (forthcoming). He also serves on the Jean Piaget Society Board of Directors.

CATHERINE TWOMEY FOSNOT received her M.S. degree in curriculum and instruction from the State University of New York, Albany, in 1976. She is currently a doctoral candidate in Early Childhood Education at the University of Massachusetts, Amherst. In the past, she ran a model Piagetian-based kindergarten for teacher training at the State University of New York, New Paltz, and has served as a workshop leader and consultant on the application of Piagetian theory to education.

EUGENE E. GARCIA received his Ph.D. in 1972 in child development from the University of Kansas. He was a Ford Foundation postdoctral Fellow at Harvard University (1976–1977) and has served on the faculties of the University of Utah (1972–1976) and the University of California, Santa Barbara (1976–1980). He is currently Professor of Early Childhood Education and Director of the Center for Bilingual Studies at Arizona State University. He has published some thirty research/review articles in the area of language acquisition and bilingual development.

CELIA GENISHI received her Ph.D. from the University of California, Berkely, in 1976. She is currently an Associate Professor of Curriculum and Instruction at the University of Texas at Austin. Her research has focused on observing and assessing young children's language in the classroom, including the language of bilingual children. Awards since 1976 include a citation for exemplary dissertation research, University of California, Berkeley; Spencer Foundation Seed Grant, University of Texas, Austin; and an American Psychological Association/National Institute of Education Fellowship for Minority Behavioral Scientists. She is the co-author, with Millie Almy, of *Ways of Studying Children* (revised edition).

MICHAEL J. GURALNICK received his Ph.D. from Lehigh University and is currently Director of the Nisonger Center and Professor of Psychology and Communication at the Ohio State University. A former President of the Division for Early Childhood of the Council for Exceptional Children, Dr. Guralnick's primary research interests include mainstreaming, peer relations, and the social and language development of young handicapped children. He is the author of numerous research and programmatic publications in these areas, including the edited volume, *Early Intervention and the Integration of Handicapped and Nonhandicapped Children.*

LAURA D. GOODWIN received her Ph.D. degree in research methodology, evaluation, and measurement through the Laboratory of Educational Research at the University of Colorado, Boulder (1977). Currently she is assistant professor in the School of Nursing, University of Colorado Health Sciences Center in Denver, where she teaches courses in statistics, research design, and measurement and serves as evaluator for several school health projects. Her prior articles have appeared in various education and nursing journals and, with her husband, she is the co-author of the recent *Handbook for Measurement and Evaluation in Early Childhood Education: Issues, Measures, and Method.*

WILLIAM L. GOODWIN was awarded the Ph.D. degree in educational psychology at the University of Wisconsin, Madison (1965), and was an AERA–USOE postdoctoral fellow in the Laboratory of Human Development, Harvard University (1969–1970). At the University of Colorado since 1970, he now is professor of education. He teaches courses in early childhood education, educational psychology, research methodology, and measurement at the Denver Campus and is affiliated with the Laboratory of Educational Research on the Boulder Campus. His previous publications include several books and numerous articles in educational and psychological journals.

ALICE STERLING HONIG received her Ph.D. in developmental psychology from Syracuse University, where she is currently Associate Professor of Child Development. From 1965–1977 she served as Program Director of the Syracuse University Family Development Research Program and Children's Center. She was chosen as a National Leadership Training Fellow in Early Childhood Education for 1969–1970. Dr. Honig's publications include *Parent Involvement in Early Childhood Education, Infant Caregiving: A Design for Training* (with Dr. J. R. Lally), and three ERIC bibliographies on Infancy, Language Development, and Fathering.

LUIS M. LAOSA is Senior Research Scientist at Educational Testing Service in Princeton. He earned his Ph.D. in psychology and educational psychology at the University of Texas, Austin, in 1971 and completed a post doctoral residency in clinical and community psychology at the University of Texas Medical School, San Antonio. Subsequently, he held the posts of Chief Psychologist and Director of Appraisal at the Edgewood Independent School District, San Antonio, and for several years was on the faculty of the Graduate School of Education, University of California, Los Angeles. His publications include many research articles in psychological and educational journals.

IRVING LAZAR is Professor and Chairman of the Department of Human Service Studies in the New York State College of Human Ecology, Cornell University. He received his Ph.D. from Columbia University and has had a varied career as a clinician and teacher and has been involved in the design, administration, and evaluation of social programs. In the research described in this book's chapter, he served as executive officer of the Consortium for Longitudinal Studies, a voluntary collaborative effort of fourteen investigative groups of child psychologists and early childhood educators.

SHIRLEY G. MOORE is Professor at the Institute of Child Development and Director of the Center for Early Education and Development at the University of Minnesota. She received her Ph.D. from the University of Iowa in 1960. She is co-author of *Contemporary Preschool Education: A Program for Young Children* and co-editor of *Evaluation of Educational Programs for Young Children*. Dr. Moore has published research on aspects of preschool development including peer acceptance, communication factors that have an effect on compliance with prohibitions, and curiosity. Also, she has written and edited numerous reviews of research for practitioner audiences.

GWEN MORGAN is a lecturer at Wheelock College, where she teaches courses in social policy, day care, administration, and regulation. She is also a policy analyst on Project Connections at American Institutes for Research in Cambridge, Massachusetts. For three years, she was Senior Child Care Consultant to the Massachusetts Department for Administration and Finance, the Office of Planning and Program Coordination. She is presently a Vice-President of the Day Care Council of America, Inc., an Advisor to the Association for Regulatory Administration, a member of the Commission on Licensing and Regulation for the National Association for the Education of Young Children, and a member of the Steering Committee of the National Campaign for Child Daycare for Working Parents.

HARRY W. MURRAY is presently working on his doctorate in sociology at Syracuse University. He received his master's degree in regional planning from Cornell University in 1976. His current research interests include phenomenological sociology and the Catholic worker movement.

GARY G. PRICE received his Ph.D. in 1976 from Stanford University, where he concentrated in Child Development and Early Education. He is Assistant Professor of Early Childhood Education in the Department of Curriculum and Instruction at the University of Wisconsin–Madison and a Faculty Associate of the Wisconsin Research and Development Center for Individualized Schooling. His research interests concern the influence of the environment in early childhood on the development of individual differences and the influence of assumptions embedded in data analysis on the thinking of educators and psychologists. He is a 1981 Spencer Fellow of the National Academy of Education.

JACQUELINE M. ROYCE, Project Coordinator for the Consortium for Longitudinal Studies and Research Associate in the Department of Human Service Studies, Cornell University, obtained her Ph.D. from Cornell University in 1979. Her major fields of interest are research methodology, sociology, and policy analysis. She was a collaborating author of publications of the Consortium for Longitudinal Studies, including a recent article in *Science* and a monograph prepared for the *Society for Research in Child Development.*

OLIVIA N. SARACHO is Assistant Professor at the University of Maryland. She completed her Ph.D. in early childhood education at the University of Illinois in 1978. Prior to that, she taught Head Start, preschool, kindergarten, and elementary classes in Brownsville, Texas, and was Director of the Child Development Associate Program at Pan American University. Her current research and writing are in the areas of cognitive style, academic learning, and teacher education in relation to early childhood education.

JUDITH A. SCHICKEDANZ received her Ph.D. degree in 1973 from the University of Illinois, Urbana–Champaign. She is currently Associate Professor of Early Childhood in the School of Education, Boston University. Publications include two texts—*Strategies for Teaching Young Children* and *Toward Understanding Children* (forthcoming)—and numerous articles concerning preschool children, written language acquisition, and instruction.

PAMELA M. SCHWARTZ received her Ph.D. in 1978 from the University of Michigan. She is currently an assistant research scientist at the University of Michigan School of Public Health, working in the area of infant assessment and mother–infant interaction.

IRVING SIGEL received his Ph.D. in Human Development from the University of Chicago in 1951. He is currently a Distinguished Research Scientist at Educational Testing Service. He is a former President, Division of Developmental Psychology, American Psychological Association, and former President of the Jean Piaget Society. He has published numerous books, notably, *Cognitive Development from Childhood to Adolescence: A Constructivist Perspective* (with R. R. Cocking), *New Directions in Piagetian Theory and Practice* (with D. M. Brodzinsky and R. M. Golinkoff, eds.), and *Infants at Risk: Assessment of Cognitive Functioning* (with R. B. Kearsley, eds.).

NANCY R. SMITH, trained as a painter at Bennington College, received an Ed. D. from Harvard University in 1971. She has taught children at The New Lincoln School and The Museum of Modern Art and teachers at Bank Street College of Education, New York University, and Wheelock College. She is currently Chairperson, Art Education, at Boston University. Recent publications include "How a Picture Means," in *New Directions for Child Development*, and "Classroom Practice: Creating Meaning in the Arts," in J. Hausman (Ed.), *Arts and the Schools.* She is co-editor, with M. B. Franklin, of *Symbolic Functioning in Childhood.*

BERNARD SPODEK is Professor of Early Childhood Education at the University of Illinois, Urbana–Champaign. Prior to that he was on the faculty of the University of Wisconsin–Milwaukee. He received his doctoral degree from Teachers College, Columbia University. He has taught nursery school, kindergarten, and elementary school classes. He has also been visiting faculty member at the University of Wisconsin–Madison and at Western Washington State University and has lectured extensively in the United States, Canada, England, Israel, and Australia. He has written extensively in the field of early childhood education, authoring and editing books, chapters in books, and articles in that field. He has also been active in a number of professional associations. From 1976 through 1978 he was president of the National Association for the Education of Young Children.

DORIS SPONSELLER is Dean of the Graduate School at Wheelock College, Boston. She received her Ph.D. from Michigan State University in 1974 and spent 1979–1980 as a National Science Foundation Public Service Science Resident studying the topic of child care policy in Michigan. She has also been co-director of two BEH grants for training teachers of young children with special needs; conducted research on play and development; edited the book, *Play as a Learning Medium;* and published articles on play, child care policy research, and child advocacy.

ROBERT S. SOAR and RUTH M. SOAR both graduated from the University of Minnesota with degrees in psychology, she a BA in 1949, he a Ph.D. in 1952. He is now Professor of Education at the University of Florida in Gainesville. They have collaborated in research on classroom behavior for approximately twenty years, with recent chapters summarizing and conceptualizing their work (Peterson and Walberg, *Research on Teaching*)and discussing the role of systematic observation in education (Orlosky, *Introduction to Education*, forthcoming).

CHARLES E. STRICKLAND, after receiving a Ph.D. from the University of Wisconsin in 1963, accepted a position in the Division of Educational Studies and the Department of History at Emory University, Atlanta, where he currently holds the rank of Associate Professor. He attended the University of Copenhagen, 1953–1954, on a Fulbright fellowship and in 1968–1969 held a Charles Warren postdoctoral fellowship at Harvard University. He has published numerous articles and chapters in books and is co-editor of a volume entitled *Health, Growth, and Heredity: G. Stanley Hall on Natural Education* (with Charles Burgess).

HERBERT ZIMILES, a developmental psychologist, received his Ph.D. in experimental psychology from the University of Rochester in 1956. Since then, he has worked in the Research Division of Bank Street College, where he served as Chairman from 1964–1980. He is the co-author of *The Psychological Impact of School Experience* and has written extensively on eduational evaluation and cognitive and personality development.

INTRODUCTION

EARLY CHILDHOOD EDUCATION is an art that is practiced in nursery schools, elementary schools, day-care centers, homes, and other institutions. Its practitioners are known as teachers, day-care workers, child development specialists, early childhood educators, and by other names. As a field, it serves children ranging in age from birth to about eight years of age; sometimes parents of these children are also viewed as its clients. Its purposes include education, child care, and the nurturing of development.

There are a number of foundations upon which the practice of early childhood education is built. One venerated basis is the intuition of competent practitioners. The experience of these practitioners has been distilled into conceptions of what works with children, how best to organize for their education, and how best to relate to and interact with them. These intuitions are internalized by practitioners into a form of tacit knowledge, transmitted to others in a number of ways through discourse and demonstration at workshops and teachers meetings and even through informal meetings in teachers' lounges. Possibly the best way this form of knowledge can be communicated is through modelling, as the fledgling practitioner works alongside the seasoned veteran in a practicum situation. Although this intuitive knowledge has served the field well, it has its limitations. For one thing, such knowledge is not always generalizable. In addition, it is not subject to critical examination or to validation and replication by others.

Early childhood education practice is also founded on ethical considerations. These relate to what program outcomes should be valued as well as to what constitutes good experiences for young children. This basis for practice is rooted in conceptions of what constitutes the good life for children and adults in our society. Since early childhood education, like education at all other levels, is preparatory in nature, judgments about activities are often made in relation to their expected outcomes. In addition, there are some activities that are considered worthy in themselves and are thus not justified in relation to their outcomes.

In addition to the intuitive and the ethical, there are also rational foundations for early childhood education practice. The body of research and theory within the field of early childhood education and in related fields constitutes this foundation. It is to this body of research and theory that this book is addressed.

The chapters that are included in the first four sections of this *Handbook* present reviews of research and theory within the various areas of early childhood education. The final section of the *Handbook* contains presentations related to discussions of the methods by which research data are collected to address concerns of the field.

Much of the theory and research in early childhood education are derived from the field of child development. Indeed, there are some educators who view the field as one of applied child development. The first section of this *Handbook* presents reviews of research in areas of child development that are of particular significance to early childhood education. Also included is a discussion of the uses of child development knowledge for early childhood education.

In their chapter on cognitive development, Carol E. Copple, Richard De Lisi, and Irving Sigel identify the field's traditional theoretical orientations, including learning theory, psychoanalytic theory, and the measurement of intelligence. More recently the works of Jean Piaget in developmental epistemology, of Noam Chomsky in linguistics, and of researchers in computer science have impacted the field.

The authors focus on four areas in their review. Research on mental imagery indicates how children come to see the world. Research in the area of logical knowledge helps us understand how children think mathematically. Research in symbolic play indicates how children use objects to stand for something else and are able to take on the roles of others. Differences in children's symbolic play are related to maturation as well as to children's social class, culture, and family background. In the area of metacognition, research is indicating the degree of knowledge and control that children have of their own cognitive processes, including information-seeking and information-organizing strategies. Each of these areas of research has implications for the design of early childhood programs and the development of teaching strategies.

Bryant J. Cratty discusses issues and identifies research related to the study of motor development in young children. Among the important areas identified is the relationship of motor behavior to intellectual behavior and especially the issue of whether motor behavior is a precursor to intellectual behavior. Other issues deal with the need to separate factors related to perception from children's motor behavior in research, the problems of awkward children, and concerns for appropriate assessment of motor enrichment programs. The author also identifies possible significant areas of research need, including the study of the relationship between ethnicity, child-rearing patterns, and play environments to motor development in children.

The areas of native language acquisition, second language acquisition, and bilingualism are discussed in Eugene E. Garcia's chapter on language acquisition. Language development is understood in terms of the development of phonology, morphology, syntax, and semantics. The concerns for language variability, especially as it relates to dialect, is also discussed. Reviews are provided of studies of second language acquisition and bilingualism in young children.

The area of prosocial behavior is the focus of the chapter by Shirley G. Moore that relates to social development. Prosocial behavior includes positive acts that benefit others, including altruistic acts that are performed without regard to personal gain. Biological/evolutionary explanations of the development of prosocial behavior along with developmental/learning explanations are presented. The suggestion is made that perhaps by combining both sets of explanations we may come to a better understanding of the etiology of prosocial behavior. Moore reviews the possible antecedents of prosocial behavior, including the development of emotional dependence, or attachment, and the development of an ability to view the world from another person's position, or perspective taking. She related prosocial behavior to child-rearing practices in families as well as to the development of mastery of social interactions within children's peer groups.

The final chapter in this section acts as a bridge between the reviews of research presented in the first section and the theoretical basis of early childhood models included in the second section. Greta Fein and Pamela M. Schwartz discuss the relationship of theories of development to theories of practice. The former, minimalist and passive in their orientation, are concerned with the normal course of development and with identifying the consequences of environmental factors for development. Theories of practice, on the other hand, are concerned with the consequences of changes in behavior to maximize development. Thus they are action oriented and value based.

Fein and Schwartz analyze three strains of child development research to illustrate the difference: research on attachment theory, which has been related to concerns about the consequences of placing very young children in day-care settings; research related to arousal theory, which might suggest what elements in a learning environment might stimulate a child to perform and learn; and research related to mastery and assimilation, which could help teachers understand what constitutes optimum challenge to a child as well as the impact of novelty and familiarity on interest in learning activities. In each case, the authors show that the theories are not specific enough to prescribe practice. They offer clues but few guides in terms of what would make a difference for most children.

The second section of the *Handbook* presents articulated statements of three specific child development theories that have had a significant impact on the way in which early childhood education is conceived. Coupled with these chapters is one on the development of curriculum models in early childhood education.

A number of different curriculum models have been developed for early childhood education, many of them derived, at least in part, from child development theory. Ellis D. Evans' chapter identifies the components of such models. Each has a statement of philosophy or theory that integrates a conception of child development with a statement of aims and assumptions that provide the value base for the model. Models also include a set of administrative policies regarding personnel (staff, clients, parents, and community members), physical settings (the provision and arrangement of space, equipment, and time), and program evaluation (strategies for judging the worth and effectiveness of the model). Statements regarding curriculum content and methods of instruction are also included. This content can include cognitive skills, basic concepts, academics, aesthetics and/or affective/social skills. Models are abstractions; when implemented, their impact can be evaluated both in terms of the model's particular goals as well as of goals shared with other models. Each model, however, has an integrity of its own.

Psychodynamic theories of development have probably had an impact on early childhood education longer than any other theories of development. In his chapter, Herbert Zimiles defines psychodynamic theory as elements of psycho-analytic thought that pertain to psychological development. It is concerned with the interplay of internal and external forces on the child. Early experiences are viewed as seminal to development with the child being involved in resolving conflicts arising from those experiences and his inner forces. This theory is more concerned with how reality is experienced by the child than with objective reality.

Because psychodynamic theory is clinically derived, there are problems with applying traditional research methods to its validation. Psychodynamic theory is wholistic and is concerned with long-term effects. Much of the research is based on observations in naturalistic settings and is longitudinal in nature. Despite the problems of research, this theory has value as a heuristic, as well as being the basis for, clinical practice.

Early childhood educational programs based on this model tend to be process oriented. They accept children's feelings and their vulnerability and sexuality, as well as the potency of parent–child separation. These programs are child centered and individualized and build upon the child's ego strengths. Psychodynamic theory has been used to raise issues relating to the scope of educational interventions, the impact of early group care experiences on children, and the nature of appropriate educational evaluation.

Don Bushnell, Jr., views behavior analysis less as a theory and more as a technology built upon a set of principles. One principle is that behavior is a function of its consequences, and another is that the evaluation of behavior change can use direct and reliable measures of behavior. The techniques include making attention and approval contingent on desirable or improved behavior, making access to desirable activities preferred by students contingent upon desired or improved behavior, and reinforcing appropriate behavior while reducing inappropriate behavior through ignoring, time out, and the denial of preferred activities.

The behavior analysis teacher actively builds new behavior repertoires through the use of hints, cues, instructions, and materials that encourage appropriate desirable behavior. These techniques are combined into a dynamic system to shape students' performance. The goals of the system and its techniques need to be endorsed by the programs clients.

George E. Forman and Catherine Twomey Fosnot present an analysis of Piaget's constructivism as used in early childhood programs. According to Piaget, knowledge is constructed by the individual out of inferences based on information collected. The ways in which children organize knowledge change qualitatively as they mature; these can be characterized as stages. In constructing knowledge, children engage in reflective actions. They resolve discrepancies in how they view and symbolize the world through equilibration, a process which is self-regulating. Developing constructivist-oriented early childhood programs requires the creation of problem-solving environments that allow for failure and self-correction and enable the children to create their own knowledge system.

The authors present four propositions of constructivism that they use to analyze six Piaget-based early childhood programs: (1) The integration of knowledge comes from constraints inherent in action rather than from a culturally based grammatical language. (2) Understandings can occur only when the child generates questions that seek to explain discrepancies in effects resulting from opposite antecedents. (3) Meaningful learning results from the reconciliation of opposites. (4) The basic unit of knowledge is a coherent system of core correspondences and transformations. Each program is shown to be unique in relationship to these criteria.

Research and theory of child development form only one source of knowledge upon which early childhood curriculum decisions are based. Another source is the nature of what is to be learned by children. The third section presents research related to these various curriculum areas: written language, mathematics, science, social studies, the visual arts, and movement. Because so much of the learning activities of early childhood education are embedded in play, a separate chapter is devoted to play.

Doris Sponseller reviews research on play in early childhood education in her chapter. Early studies of young children's play, which occurred in the 1920s and 1930s, paralleled the beginning of the nursery school movement in the United States. These studies were primarily concerned with generating normative data on play, relating different types of play behavior to age and sex. Current research on play tends to be more theoretical in nature. Much of it is concerned with relating different forms of play to cognitive, language, physical, and social development. Other studies are concerned with the effects of the physical and social environment on play and the consequences of modifying that environment. Problems in studying play arise from the difficulty in defining play and in identifying appropriate research methods. Interpretations of the research on play are often related to the theoretical orientation of early childhood educators.

In her chapter on the acquisition of written language in young children, Judith A. Schickedanz reviews research leading to an understanding of reading in terms of basic psychological and linguistic processes. She synthesizes studies that reveal the understandings children bring to reading before they know how to read, including their knowledge of the features of print, the distinctions they can make between letters and words, and their understanding of the reading process. She also reviews studies of the experiences that young children have that contribute to their reading development. Children who grow up in a socially literate environment develop literacy skills early in ways that approximate oral language development. These studies seem to suggest that schools can make use of what children already know about reading and might be able to create environments that contain the critical elements of naturally occurring socially literate environments.

Gary G. Price surveys the research related to young children learning mathematics, science, and social studies. Mathematics research has taken three distinct directions. One attempts to relate Piagetian concepts to the teaching of mathematics to young children. A second has been concerned with describing mathematics education phenomena, including children's number concepts, counting skills, and understanding of addition and subtraction processes and their geometric and spatial concepts. The third, more recently developing direction, is based upon information processing psychology derived from work with computers.

Research in science education has also been concerned with Piagetian conceptions of knowledge. Further, there are descriptive studies of young children's science concepts and the learning strategies used in relation to science. In the area of social studies, research has reflected a concern with a range of such topics as citizenship education, social science and reflective inquiry, and young children's social behavior, including their sociableness, social competence, prosocial behavior, and nonaggression. Young children's social concepts, attitudes, and thinking processes have also been studied.

Nancy R. Smith's review of research on the visual arts focuses on the development and creation of meaning through art. She suggests that the early conceptions of the therapeutic and creative functions of art in early childhood education that restricted the role of the teacher is contrary to the dynamics of child development. Studies of art education for young children today relate to the need to develop an understanding of the physical and visual properties of art materials, as well as to the creation of visual symbols. This research includes studies of central processing, performing processing, and children's emotional status and symbol formation, as well as studies of children's responses to art. Research on cognition, learning style, and individual and cultural differences are viewed as relevant to this curriculum area.

In recent years, increased attention has been given to the relationship of public policy to the field of early childhood education. Decisions by legislative and administrative units of governments at all levels have determined the nature of early childhood services, the availability of these services to various segments of our society, and the limitations to be placed on practitioners in the field. The fourth section of this *Handbook* presents reviews of research and theory related to a number of public policy areas. Issues related to day care, parent programs, the mainstreaming of young handicapped children, the preparation of personnel, and the regulation of programs, as well as the historical and sociocultural context of early childhood education, are addressed in this section.

In attempting to account for the development of early childhood education in the United States and in understanding why early childhood institutions have failed to become a part of the normal experience of all American children, Charles E. Strickland takes us back to pre-Civil War America. Three alternative approaches to early childhood education were attempted during that era. The first was the development of the Infant School modeled on that of Robert Owen in England. The second was the education of young children within the common school. The third, and the one that was not rejected, is characterized by Strickland as "fireside education," the education of young children by their mothers within the family environs. The selection of this third choice has exacted an enormous price from women who have been confined in role and identity as a result and from poor children whose education has been neglected. Early childhood educators today are still compelled to fight those who are convinced that the nature and needs of young children can only be fulfilled within the precinct of the home.

Bettye M. Caldwell and Marjorie Freyer organize their review of research on day care into outcome studies, concerned with the effects of day care on children, families and institutions, and process studies, which inquire into what goes on within day-care programs. Earlier outcome studies primarily dealt with small samples. More recently, larger process studies have been developed that look at characteristics of providers, parent involvement, and the nature of day-care programs and day-care environments. The authors draw a number of implications from the research reviewed.

Gwen Morgan, in her chapter on licensing and regulation of early childhood programs, presents basic assumptions about the nature of regulations and discusses the formulation of standards. She presents a brief history of day-care standards in the United States and a view of licensing and regulation today. She also offers a strategy for regulatory reform and an agenda of needed research related to regulation.

Bernard Spodek and Olivia N. Saracho, in their chapter on the preparation and credentialing of early childhood personnel, identify issues related to professionalism and to the preparation of early childhood personnel at various levels. Certification, credentialing, and accreditation are discussed in relation to the need for quality control in personnel and in the programs that prepare personnel. Research on teaching and teacher education is reviewed as it pertains to early childhood education.

Over the years, parent involvement has come to be viewed as an important ingredient in good early childhood programs. Alice Sterling Honig reviews research related to various kinds of parent involvement programs, including programs of home visitation, education oriented and mental health oriented programs, programs that allow parents to participate as teachers and aides in classrooms, job training programs, programs for abusive parents and for parents of handicapped children, and teenage parenting programs. Conclusions derived from these programs are presented.

In dealing with the relationship between public policy, education/developmental programs, and developmental principles, Michael J. Guralnick presents a model relating studies of feasibility and efficacy to the ecology of programs. The model can be used to identify benefits in terms of product measures, process measures, measures of social integration and attitude, and measures of developmental potential at each of four ecological levels. The microsystem level relates to the person's immediate environment. The mesosystem level identifies relations among various settings involving the developing person. The exosystem embraces the other specific social structures that impinge on the setting in which the person is found. The macrosystem refers to the overarching institutional pattern of the culture. To date, most outcome data on early childhood programs are at the macrosystem level.

Luis M. Laosa discusses the implication of sociocultural diversity and pluralism for educational evaluation and uses Head Start as an illustration. Head Start, conceived as a single program with a basic goal of achieving social competence in young children, represents an administrative framework that allows a wide range of local initiative in interpreting goals and developing means to achieve these goals. Because its programs are geographically diverse and its staff and clients ethnically diverse, this has led to a heterogeneity of interpretations of Head Start's goals and objectives and to wide interpretations of the meaning of social competence. The use of standardized tests for evaluating Head Start raises the issue of population validity. Evaluation needs to be both developmentally and socioculturally valid. Programs can only be judged in the context of specific roles and values of its clients.

Research in early childhood education constitutes a body of knowledge that is growing and changing. New methods for collecting and analyzing data are being developed as more established methods are being refined. New research paradigms are being generated as new questions are asked of the field. Insights are gained through the continued inquiry of scholars and practitioners. In recognition of this, the final section of the *Handbook* is concerned with research techniques in early childhood education.

In their chapter on measuring young children, William L. and Laura D. Goodwin address the questions of why we measure young children, how we can measure them, and what we can measure. They provide a discussion of issues related to each of these questions. In addition, they include a list of sourcebooks of measures for early childhood education.

In her chapter, Celia Genishi presents a discussion of observational methods in studying young children. She discusses the uses of observational techniques and a description of different quantitative and qualitative approaches to observation. She also discusses the issues of validity and reliability of these techniques.

In the chapter on measuring classroom processes, Robert S. and Ruth M. Soar discuss the methodology of classroom observation, the development of observation instruments, and the advantages and disadvantages of various types. They review procedures for combining measures and for estimating reliability and discuss methods of analyzing the relationship of observational measures with outcome measures.

In the final chapter of the book, Jacqueline M. Royce and her colleagues present an overview–placed in the context of evaluation research–of research methods for studying outcomes of early childhood education programs. Issues related to research design are discussed with examples taken from the research of the Consortium for Longitudinal Studies. A number of methodological issues are discussed in relation to studying program outcomes.

PART I

Early Education and Child Development

CHAPTER 1

Cognitive Development

Carol Copple
Richard De Lisi
Irving Sigel

OUR OBJECTIVE in this chapter is to examine elements of research and theory in cognitive development that have bearing on early childhood education. With such a potentially limitless task, it is clear that choices must be made as to what is included. We have elected to begin by looking at how cognitive development is seen within the major theoretical frameworks of twentieth-century psychology. We shall see that ideas have changed and diverged, each shaped by a variety of factors within the field and outside it. Next, we will turn to a consideration of four substantive areas. Each of the selected areas has yielded interesting new findings as well as thorny issues and each has relevance to the field of early childhood education.

Defining cognition or cognitive development is not an entirely straightforward task. Perhaps the best approach is simply to describe what we will be discussing under the heading of cognitive development: changes in children's knowledge and thinking skills and the way these are organized and used in dealing with problems.

It is instructive to consider the conceptions of cognitive development that have loomed large in modern psychology. Among psychologists of the first half of the century two principal theoretical frameworks were in sway: learning theory and psychoanalytic theory. Familiar though they are, it is useful to remind ourselves of the perspective that each has on the development of the intellect.

Learning theory, or stimulus–response theory, approaches intellectual development as it approaches the study of behavior in general. The development of the child is viewed as simply one type of behavioral change. For the learning theorist, intellectual development consists of an accumulation of gradual learnings, of changes in specific behaviors. Differences between a child's and an adult's learning are viewed as quantitative and content-related. Thus, a five-year-old child learns new facts in the same manner as an adult learns a new computer language. The learning theorist does not believe that these changes are qualitatively different. They are both behavioral changes subject to analysis in terms of previous learnings and current environmental factors.

The early learning theories were based on John Watson's behavioristic theory which eschewed such concepts as mind and cognition. This tradition, continued by Clark Hull and others, focused on behavior in relation to environmental contingencies. Children's intellectual development was conceptualized in terms of learning about the world. From this perspective, the environment was seen as the origin of the learner's knowledge. Basically, children learned discriminations and stimulus–response associations. Research carefully specified the environmental stimuli and contingencies and measured resulting behaviors. Questions of what went on in the mind were deliberately rejected as alien to a behavioral science.

Learning theory has had a direct impact on educational enterprises. In retrospect, it is easy to see why learning theory became so popular and influential. Psychology was a young science striving to be as "scientific" as possible, disavowing philosophy for the empirical study of behavior. The United States was a society oriented toward finding technologies for the improvement of virtually everything (as was Russia for that matter). In such a climate all was ripe for the appearance of a few great minds (Pavlov, Watson, Skinner, and others) describing phenomena which became pivotal in establishing the core of a theory and a methodology. All signals were go for the enthusiastic reception of a behavioristic model and methodology. It is an eminently "appliable" theory and directs its primary attention to learning and behavioral change; it was natural that learning theory tools would be used in the classroom, in part or in whole.

In contrast to learning theory, the psychoanalytic system asserts that there are qualitative differences in behavior at different periods of development. Central to psychoanalytic theory is the concept of instinctual drives as the force behind all mental or physical activity. In order to satisfy these instinctual needs the child develops what Freud called the ego. The ego is in touch with reality and operates to satisfy the child's instinctual needs. The ego is in the service of the instinctual drives. Its function is to guide adaptive behavior through realistic and logical processes. In the psychoanalytic tradition, more attention was given to the dynamics of personality development than to specifying what the functioning of the ego is like—what structures and processes could be identified or how these changed over time.

Insofar as education is concerned, the psychoanalytic argument opted for healthy ego development by helping children cope with the conflicts that are inevitable in a family. Children's intellectual growth could flourish through working out these conflicts in play. Since the ego develops through the child's engagements with reality and since the child has to forego his/her pleasure, the child will manifest mastery of these early conflicts through play. Thus, from the psychoanalytic model, the approach in educational terms is not directly cognitive as we know it today. Rather, the idea is to promote ego development so that the ego is free to learn, to solve problems, to know.

A third major tradition of twentieth-century psychology that deals with children's intelligence is the standardized measurement of human abilities. This tradition focuses on individual differences, most notably individual differences in intellectual ability. The beginnings of the intelligence testing movement can be traced to Francis Galton's work in England and to the laboratory of Alfred Binet and Theodore Simon in France in the early 1900s. The task which Binet and Simon were given by the French government was to identify those children who could not benefit from the Parisian educational system, that is, retarded children. With a belief in the existence of a general dimension of brightness or ability, Binet and Simon constructed many items aimed at assessing comprehension, reasoning, and the like. They sought to develop items that discriminated among children at different age levels. For example, the test makers sought items which five-year-olds could answer but four-year-olds and three-year-olds could not. The intelligence test was validated essentially by determining that it was predictive of school success. This validation procedure was consistent with Binet's purpose in developing the test.

Binet's tests were adapted for use in the United States, most notably by Lewis M. Terman who adopted Stern's concept of IQ, the quotient that identified a relationship between the child's chronological age and the mental age based on the levels of children's performance. As was true of their predecessors, current intelligence tests are used to predict success in school. (See Resnick, 1979, for a more complete discussion of current and future uses of IQ tests in education.)

Questions of innate versus environmental determination of performance on these tests have been around as long as the tests have. Standardized testing per se is neutral with respect to this issue. Binet himself contended that a child's intelligence is a function of his environment to a considerable degree. In the United States, a major conflict arose between those who espoused a hereditarian view of intelligence versus those who contended that environmental factors were the determinants (Skodak & Skeels, 1949; Stoddard, 1940; Wellman, 1945). This issue is being hotly debated once again.

Although the term IQ took on the ring of innateness for the layman, the defining characteristic of the testing movement lies in the interest in the individual's standing relative to peers along a quantitative continuum. Questions of thinking processes and the mechanisms of development are not typically raised within this tradition.

In the twentieth century, then, data on children's "cognition" have been obtained from one of these three major traditions within psychology—learning theory, psychoanalytic theory, and the testing movement. Each offered a different perspective on children's thought and knowledge and each had its own methods to study children. Recently, although work goes on in each tradition, some rather different questions have been raised.

As we reflect on the past several decades, we can see certain works which seem watersheds of the change within the study of cognitive development. For example, an accumulation of empirical results on curiosity and exploration in humans and animals was not readily explainable within existing frameworks of motivation (White, 1959). Investigations in the fields of perception and memory added more empirical fuel to the fire. Three additional sources of enormous change should be noted in more detail. First, the work of Jean Piaget, which began in the 1920s, constituted an increasingly formidable body of observations and findings difficult to handle within existing models. Second, Noam Chomsky's theory of transformational grammar began a revolution in linguistics and sparked a generation of psycholinguistic studies which were light-years away from the verbal learning studies of the learning theory tradition. Third, the advent of the computer gave psychologists both a powerful new tool and a new set of analogies for thinking about how the mind works. Other forces have played a role, undoubtedly, but these three can be singled out as prominent in moving the study of cognition toward a great recognition of the complexity of the mind's workings and the legitimacy of talking about what goes on in the mind.

It is interesting to speculate about how it happens that an idea or framework comes to be widely or universally accepted. Is it the discovery of a new phenomenon? If so, why was the phenomenon overlooked previously? Frequently, an individual coming from a different set of premises, biases, or assumptions encounters a phenomenon and sees it in a new way. For example, an anthropologist accustomed to observing primate behavior may see things in the human mother–child interaction that others have missed. This difference of perspective, along with a healthy measure of genius, may account for the very different view of children's cognitive development proposed by Jean Piaget.

Piaget came from a background of biology, philosophy, and European psychology, which rejected the behavioristic tradition. He asked different questions and was intrigued by different phenomena. Piaget worked in the Binet laboratory (after Binet's death) during the refinement of intelligence testing. He became fascinated by children's *wrong* answers. He did not want to know how many answers the child got right at a given age, but why children gave different kinds of incorrect answers at various ages. He became fascinated with the question of different sorts of reasoning operating at different developmental points. Posing such questions, Piaget naturally proceeded in a different manner from Binet and his colleagues. He began to ask children *why* they said what they said and followed up with more questions until he could see what the child's reasoning had been and what his understanding actually was.

This was the beginning of what is known as the clinical interview method—a methodology altogether different from that of standardized testing and with an altogether different purpose. Piaget sought to explain the nature of children's knowledge of the world and the mechanisms of development through which this knowledge changed in character. He maintained that children's thinking changes qualitatively through development and can be described in terms of stages. Concepts that develop in stages include causality, number, quantity, space, and time.

Piaget's perceptions of cognitive development in terms of innate and environmental factors is firmly interactionist and rooted in his biological studies of how organisms develop physical structures in order to adapt to their environments. Beginning with certain biological structures and reflex behaviors, the infant acts in biologically adaptive ways. For example, the infant will attempt to make pleasant and interesting events recur. The infant perceives the results of his action and assimilates this experience in terms of his current structures. Out of such interactions, the infant's structures are progressively elaborated and changed, with the emergent structures the results of the interaction of the way the child is with the way the environment is.

Piaget was interested in seeing what was happening in infants' interactions with the world—how they were adapting, how their behavior was becoming organized. To see this, he needed to watch a few infants closely over an extended period of time, preferably in their natural habitat. Hence, a methodology was used which was entirely different from the laboratory investigations others were doing. The methodology was more like that of the biologist or ethologist because Piaget was asking different questions and making different assumptions. And out of such a radically different methodology and set of assumptions about development came observations and theories of how the infant developed which could never have come from decades of research within the laboratory paradigms of the day.

Infants had been around quite a while by this time. The behaviors Piaget observed were not particularly exotic. Yet, Piaget's observations of such everyday behaviors as direction of gaze, crying, or searching for a missing object were the basis of his conclusion that children only gradually develop the concept of object permanence (that is, they still exist when out of view). In such descriptions of the nature of the knowledge and of *how children develop it,* namely, through active construction, we see the emergence of a theoretical perspective and methodology which unabashedly examines questions of the mind.

The process of old models being shaken by someone asking very different questions or being struck by different phenomena can be seen again in the linguistic revolution of the late 1950s and the 1960s. The landmark event for this revolution was the publication of Noam Chomsky's *Syntactic Structures* in 1957. Chomsky is a linguist, not a psychologist. He was not arguing for a model of the mind as he repeatedly emphasized, yet his impact on cognitive psychology was vast. Chomsky did not think that existing linguistic systems could account for two particularly striking features of human language: the relationship of "deep structure" to "surface structure" (for example, the relatedness of two sentences such as "The boy hit the ball" and "What did the boy hit?") and the fact of linguistic "productivity," the ability speakers have to produce and understand an infinitely large number of sentences that they have never heard before. When taken seriously, these characteristics present a formidable challenge for the development of a psychological theory of language use and acquisition, which in turn places demands on our models of cognition. It was on these two features that Chomsky based the need for a new kind of grammar which he called the transformational grammar. Without elaborating on Chomsky's theory here, we need only say that when Chomsky got through posing both the problems and his system for dealing with them, things were never the same in the study of either language acquisition or cognitive development.

Since then, the work of psycholinguists, especially those investigating child language, has continually provided a challenge to cognitive developmental theory. The focus shifted from grammar, or syntax, to semantics, which is involved with questions of meaning, and more recently to pragmatics, the study of language uses.

One of the many issues raised by the work of Chomsky and those who followed him resembles the old nature–nurture debate (which we saw within the IQ test movement). How much of the course of the child's language development is determined by innate factors? How much by environment? When Chomsky made a compelling case for a grammar that conveyed the enormous complexity of language use, suddenly the rapidity of language acquisition stood out as an astonishing fact. Chomsky and others argued that the organism must be "preprogrammed." Child language researchers began to look for universals in the emergence of language competence (R. Brown, 1973; Fillmore, 1968). Others turned to an examination of the linguistic input in guiding hypotheses about the strategies children might use in acquiring linguistic rules (for example, Phillips, 1973; Snow, 1972; Snow & Ferguson, 1977). Chapter 3 deals with this issue and with current theories and research on language development.

In the history of science there are numerous instances when an invention for one purpose, often a utilitarian one, has an enormous impact on scientific theory and investigation. For example, the telescope, which was developed for navigational purposes, revolutionized astronomy. A twentieth-century example is the computer and its impact on psychological theory and research on cognition.

Kessen has noted that "the computer as a metaphor of mind has dispelled, even for the most dedicated mechanist, the illusion that simple machinery limits our conceptions of man" (1966, p. 57). With such a metaphor we gain new conceptual possibilities, new means of describing complex cognitive processes, as well as a new tool. We now have terms like input, transformation, storage, retrieval, and output, and we have the task of specifying what each of these operations is like in programmable terms. We have a methodology for testing highly specific hypotheses about the way the mind processes information.

The computer-based field of artificial intelligence has provided a dramatic lesson for cognitive theorists. The attempt to simulate human intellectual skills has shown the astonishing complexity, and in some cases the nature, of what has to be "programmed into the computer" of the mind. The difficulties in the simulation of even relatively "simple" perceptual abilities such as decoding handwriting have often put pressures on existing theories. More complex activities such as the comprehension of speech have provided even more of a challenge. At the same time, by giving us a new language for talking about the human mind and a methodology for testing specific hypotheses, the computer has provided a major new approach to studying and describing cognition.

As a result of these developments (Piaget's work, the revolution in language study, and the computer) and the changes they have brought in views of cognition, one finds that in many places within psychology it is now legitimate to ask questions about what is happening in the mind, a legitimacy such questions did not enjoy during the heyday of behaviorism. Each of the areas we will now examine is very much of this sort—"cognitive" rather than strictly behavioral.

We have chosen to examine within each of four areas some of the current answers to the question of what develops during childhood. The areas we have selected are mental imagery, symbolic play, mathematical thinking, and metacognition. In each case, we are interested in the basic developmental trends and whether there are important differences in children's development in these areas which can be linked to environmental influences. In addition, we will briefly consider the relevance of each area of research to early childhood education.

Mental Imagery

Directions in Development

For centuries, images were said to be the direct product of sensation. Thus, to view a leaf falling to the ground was sufficient to form an image (an internal representation) of this flight. A related position maintained that mental imagery is a primitive form of cognition, characteristic of young children, which gives way to more abstract, propositional forms at later ages.

The past two decades of research on mental imagery have convinced some (but not all) psychologists that both views were incorrect. Formation of an image is now described as an active, internal construction similar to perceptual processing (compare Kosslyn, 1978). As for images being "primitive forms of cognition," there are two lines of research that indicate the contrary. On the one hand, the work of Shepard and his colleagues (see Shepard, 1978, for an introductory review) indicates that mental imagery is an analogical thought process used by adults, especially when dealing with spatial arrays and transformations. On the other hand, Piaget and Inhelder's (1971) research indicates that young children's images of spatial movements are remarkably sparse and improve from early to late childhood.

At the present time, psychologists differ in their definitions and techniques for measuring mental imagery. As the examples below will indicate, these differences have led to alternative views as to when children can form and use mental imagery in cognition.

Marmor (1975, 1977) used Shepard's mental rotation paradigm to study young children's kinetic imagery. Children were shown pairs of stimuli which were either identical (for example, teddy bears which had their left paws raised) or different (one bear had its left paw raised, the other its right paw raised). Children were trained to press one button if the pairs were identical and a second button if they were different. Following training, the children were shown the pair of bears with one of the bears rotated (30°, 60°, 90°, or 150°) in the picture plane. They had to judge whether the pairs were the "same" or "different."

Marmor's four-, five-, and eight-year-old subjects showed the same performance patterns as Shepard's adults. That is, the time to respond increased as a linear function of the degree of rotation. These time patterns are used to infer that an internal analog of the overt rotation was performed. In Marmor's studies the differences between younger and older children's imagery were quantitative. Younger children took longer to respond (to rotate the bear mentally) and made more errors than older children and adults. Marmor concluded that children as young as four years old are capable of using and evoking kinetic imagery in problem solving.

Piaget and Inhelder (1971) paint a very different picture of children's mental imagery. It is important to note that Piaget and Inhelder used drawings, gestures, and picture selection instead of reaction time to make inferences about children's imagery. Their general research paradigm involved a state–transformation–state methodology. Children viewed a stimulus array. The experimenter described (or demonstrated) that the array would be transformed in some fashion. The children had to imagine how the array would appear after the transformation was applied and also how the array appeared during the transformation.

For example, a colored tube was balanced on a table edge. The experimenter showed the child how the tube could be made to somersault in one rotation onto the floor. The tube was repositioned on the table and the child was asked to draw how the tube would look as it fell and when it landed on the floor. (These two drawings were done separately.) Piaget and Inhelder identified three levels of performance on this and other state–transformation–state tasks with four- to ten-year-old subjects:

1. Younger children were not successful in depicting either the end state or the transformation. Moreover, their images of end states showed a characteristic error pattern called pseudoconservation. That is, they imagined the end state to appear just like the initial state only in a new location. Thus, they drew the tube on the floor with the colors in the same order as they appeared when the tube was on the table. (The correct answer was to reverse the order of the colors.)
2. At a second level of imagery performance, children successfully depicted the resultant end state but not the transformation which brought it about. Thus, children could imagine the product of a transformation before they could imagine the process of transformation.
3. At the highest level, association with older children, both the process and product were correctly depicted.

Differences in Development

Studies such as those reviewed above indicate that children can form images of objects and can mentally rotate, expand, or contract figures. However, the exact age of onset of successful use of imaginal processes has not yet been specified. Another unresolved issue is the question of individual differences in imaginal abilities. Adults have been found to differ in the degree to which they report their imagery to be vivid and controllable. Future research may try to identify individual differences in imagery and imaginal processes in children. Once reliable findings on individual differences have been documented, questions as to the factors responsible for these differences can be addressed.

Educational Relevance

The research findings on children's use of mental imagery and its development have implications for classroom instruction. Many school activities either implicitly or explicitly involve processes such as mental rotation. If Piaget and Inhelder's (1971) analysis is correct, teachers should probably not assume that their students can "see" things (especially transformations) as depicted or intended by the teacher. For example, telling time is usually taught with reference to the hands on a clock "moving" to a new number. The child is asked, "What time is it when the big hand is on the twelve and the little hand on the two?" Next, the teacher might say, "Suppose the little hand now points to the seven, what time is it?" Over and above difficulties with time and number concepts, a student may have difficulty answering the latter question because he visualizes instead of ! A difficulty in forming mental images of movement may hinder learning to tell time. Similarly, lessons on the motion of the planets (rotating on their own axes and revolving about the sun) may be difficult for younger children to understand and retain, even when presented with props, because of the kinetic imagery required. George Forman and his colleagues (Forman & Kuschner, 1977; Forman & Hill, 1980) have stressed the need for teachers to take into account young children's difficulty in visualizing transformations and have made numerous suggestions for doing so.

Mathematical Thinking

Directions in Development

If one were to observe a roomful of adults solving logic and math problems, one would probably find a great deal of individual variability in degree of enjoyment, success, and so on. We think of mathematics as a subject which only a few people are "good in." Are there aspects of logic and math which almost all adults understand? Instead of differences, is there a common denominator to our human intelligence?

Piaget's research allows us to answer these questions in the affirmative. For example, very few adults would be unable to answer the following questions: (1) Are there more dogs in the world or more animals? (2) If Alan weighs more than Betty, and Betty weighs more than Chuck, who weighs the least? Answers to questions about classes and relations [(1) and (2) respectively] seem so obvious to adults that they sometimes assume that once a child understands language he could answer such questions correctly or could be quickly taught the correct answer.

In order to understand universal categories of logical knowledge in adults, Piaget decided to study its formation in children. To assess children's conceptions of numbers, classes, and relations, Piaget worked with individual children and posed problems using concrete stimuli and a flexible set of verbal probes (Piaget, 1971; Inhelder & Piaget, 1964). Piaget sought to uncover not only how children responded but why they reasoned in a certain manner.

Piaget's research dispels the notion that children are "miniature adults" who simply lack knowledge or experience. Instead, children organize experience on their own terms. They have conceptions of number, for example, that are qualitatively different from those of adults. These conceptions, Piaget contended, have a different structure at each stage of development. The structures derive from overt and internal coordination of actions; they are not fully "mature" right away. Thus, although there are universal categories of adult knowledge, they are constructed over the course of childhood.

Consider Piaget's assessment of knowledge of one-to-one correspondence and number conservation. Children from four to seven years of age were shown six objects, such as checkers, spread out in a row on a tabletop. The child was asked to reach into a bag and select the same number of checkers and to place them in a second row below the original on the table.

Three levels of performance were observed. At level 1, children could not make a second row which had the same number of checkers as the original row. Instead, they matched the end points of the two rows, and thought that this ensured that there was an equal number of checkers in each. So instead of six checkers, some children would squeeze eight together, whereas others might spread out five. As long as the end points matched, the number was judged to be the same. Children at level 2 could make a one-to-one correspondence such that the rows matched in number as well as length. But if the experimenter altered the appearance of one of the rows (spread out or condensed it), the children now judged that one of the rows, usually the longer one, had more checkers. This occurred even though children could count "six" in each row! At a final level of performance, children could form a one-to-one correspondence and conserve the number despite changes in appearance.

This experiment illustrates how young children's conceptions are too closely tied to perceptual appearances. At levels 1 and 2, the child thinks number changes as spatial extension changes even though he can count the checkers correctly. Only the level 3 child is able to mentally reverse the experimenter's action of spreading out or condensing a row and thereby conserve the number "six."

The Piagetian characterization of younger children's thought is often interpreted in "negative" terms, that is, that the child is a nonconserver. In recent years, psychologists have attempted to describe what the preschool child *can* do. What arithmetic and mathematical competencies does the young child have? These questions have been investigated by Ginsburg (1977), Gelman (1978, 1979), and Gelman and Gallistel (1978).

Ginsburg's basic method is to have children solve problems, providing concrete materials where appropriate, and to ask them how they went about getting their answers. He has gained a great deal of information about children's informal knowledge of arithmetic and self-evolved strategies for counting, adding, and subtracting.

Gelman takes a different approach, stripping down old tasks like conservation of number to modified versions. Gelman's versions are intended to control variables that might interfere with the child's belief that number is invariant with changes in spatial arrangement. In Gelman's "magic task," for example, children designate one of two sets of objects "the winner" and the other "the loser." It seems that children do confer such labels spontaneously on the basis of number. At this point in the procedure the children have established an expectancy for two particular numerical values, for example, 3 and 4. The experimenter then surreptitiously changes the displays in one of several ways (adding, subtracting, or displacing objects, changing color). When there are changes in number, the children notice this and even mention the transformation that must have taken place ("You added one here"). When there are changes in the length of a display, color, or identity of the objects, children say that the number of the elements is the same. (The same row is the "winner.") Thus, Gelman finds that children are not totally without the notion of number invariance. She argues that there are aspects of the classic Piagetian conservation task which may give them trouble, for example, watching the transformation of length being performed and then having to ignore its effect. The child's inability to ignore this displacement is not a trivial lack in the young child's competence, as Gelman would readily admit. But through studies designed to uncover the specific extent of children's knowledge and limitations, we gain important information beyond that which Piagetian research has taught us.

Differences in Development

In considering environmental influences on mathematical thinking, we will first examine the evidence for influences on the development of the logical-mathematical knowledge described by Piaget. Then we will look briefly at the development of the numerical and computational knowledge described by Ginsburg (1977).

The evidence relating to logical-mathematical knowledge is of two very different types: (1) studies of children whose experiences differ along some global dimension (schooled versus unschooled, Western versus non-Western in culture, urban versus rural), and (2) training studies.

Most of the first type of studies have investigated conservation. In general, they have found that children acquire conservation, whatever their cultural, social class, or schooling experience (Goodnow, 1962; Mermelstein & Shulman, 1967; Price-Williams, 1961; Vernon, 1965a, 1965b). There is some evidence that the rate of attaining conservation differs with some of these sociocultural differences (Dasen, 1976). This difference in rate is not at all disconcerting for Piagetian theory, which expects "general experience," that is, relatively long-term and global aspects of the environment, to play a role in the rate of development while not affecting its basic pattern.

The training literature is more difficult to summarize. (A review of these studies can be found in Sigel & Cocking, 1977). Many of these studies have been carried out with the idea of disproving Piaget's claim that conservation and other operations cannot be taught overnight. Whether or not they have succeeded is somewhat subject to interpretation. It is clear that children can be taught to make conserving responses within the confines of the experiment. The stability and generalizability of this behavior are not always so clear (Kuhn, 1979).

As for the environmental influences on the development of the sort of counting and computational skills described by Ginsburg, there is evidence that these are acquired outside the school situation. Ginsburg (1977) observed children on the Ivory Coast who were in school and those who were not. He found that rules for counting and doing basic adding and subtracting were developed spontaneously by unschooled children. For children in school, such strategies seem to develop alongside formal instruction. Further work is needed on what is and is not developed spontaneously and under what environmental conditions.

Educational Relevance

Assuming that it were possible to accelerate the development of conservation or other logical-mathematical knowledge, would this acceleration be of educational benefit? Piaget was critical of the idea, which he found a very American notion. He stresses the importance of children consolidating their knowledge at a given point in development rather than being pushed ahead. This does not mean that there are no environmental factors which nourish the development of logical-mathematical knowledge. At the least, it is likely to be valuable for the young child to have ample opportunity to explore concrete materials. In addition, it may be useful for children to have a "mathematically coherent" environment in which to conduct their explorations (cited in Condry, 1977). Although the elements of such an environment require further specification, the general idea is that the environment should be conducive to the perception of regularities in the properties of numbers.

Piagetian theory also points to limitations on when various concepts can be taught because of the developmental characteristics of children's thought. Such implications have been described at numerous points in the literature on Piagetian applications to education (see De Lisi, 1979).

As mentioned above, there is much useful information coming from investigations of children's early mathematical inventions and strategies (Gelman, 1978, 1979; Gelman & Gallistel, 1978; Ginsburg, 1977). It is clear that knowing what children are doing spontaneously with number is important to helping them develop mathematically. Further work is needed on how these self-developed systems interact with the development of mathematical thinking in school and on the use that can be made educationally of children's "practical arithmetic."

Symbolic Play

Directions in Development

What are some of the things children do that make us think that their level of symbolic development is changing markedly during the preschool years? Among the most visible and intriguing manifestations of such change is children's symbolic play activity. It is also likely to be one of the means through which symbolic development takes place. Children's make-believe play has long been fascinating to adults in general and to psychologists in particular. In fact, when compared to developmental phenomena such as metacognition (which will be described in a subsequent section), symbolic play is a well-trodden area of observation and speculation.

Not surprisingly, the richest descriptions of children's symbolic play activity come from those who have watched a few children closely for an extended period of time—Bühler (1935), El'konin (1971), and Piaget (1951). Piaget, in his usual manner, provides a detailed structural description of the levels of symbolic activity. While others have had some points of disagreement or refinement with respect to the particulars of this developmental progression, the same general features of children's symbolic play have been found by most investigators (Bühler, 1935; El'konin, 1971; Nicolich, 1977).

Those interested in the details of the developmental progression which Piaget describes can find them in *Play, Dreams, and Imitation in Childhood* (1951). Here, we will summarize the major directions of development and characteristics of symbolic play from its emergence at about eighteen months to about five or six years of age.

Objects are prominent in the earliest forms of symbolic activity. A child may use an everyday object out of context in a playful manner, as in pretending to drink from an empty cup and laughing about this as a joke. Or she may use one object as another when she clearly knows it is not, as in employing a leaf as a telephone receiver. When the child is younger, she is likelier to enact pretend sequences with objects that bear a considerable resemblance to the real objects depicted, although in some cases she may substitute an object such as the leaf above.

Fein (1975) found that substituting two objects that were less realistic replicas was more difficult than substituting only one along with a more realistic replica. For example, it was easier for a child to pretend to feed a horse from a cup when one or the other of the objects was "highly prototypical"—children could have a very horselike horse eating from a clamshell cup or use a replica of a cup to feed a very stylized horse, but could not manage both unrealistic objects at once. A finding of this sort emphasizes the fact that pretending that one object is another reflects a higher level of symbolic development than the use of realistic objects in imitative actions.

At a later stage, children are able to dispense with objects altogether if they wish (Markey, 1935; Matthews, 1977). The ability to sustain dramatic play without props increases with age. At the same time, children more often take on make-believe roles in their play. Rather than merely imitating mother's action, such as ironing, the child now pretends to be the mother. Children also begin to pretend entire situations or themes, such as playing supermarket or taking an airplane trip. In these extended episodes, the children are now capable of using make-believe to bridge gaps in the action when convenient. For example, if a child is not interested in going through a particular part of the action, she may say, "Pretend I went to the store and bought groceries and now I'm going to make a cake."

Another change in symbolic play is in children's ability to engage in what has been called *collective symbolism* or *sociodramatic play.* Two or three children will share a play premise (for example, that this is a spaceship on its way to the moon). They will each have a role and will act to each other according to these roles. They will have a shared definition of objects in the make-believe episode, for instance, that the hoop is the steering wheel, the small blocks are laser guns, and so on (Fein & Clarke-Stewart, 1973).

To summarize, children apparently begin with symbolic transformations that are suggested to them by the objects themselves and move toward a higher degree of premeditation in their make-believe use of objects and enactment of situations. Their use of objects becomes secondary and optional as they are capable of planning and sustaining a make-believe episode with mental representation alone. More and more, the child is not merely imitating actions she has seen adults do, but she is pretending to *be* the adult. Symbolic transformations of objects, situations, and roles can even be shared by several children as the development of imaginative play activity reaches a high level. In very brief form, these are the major forms of change in symbolic play during the years from one-and-a-half to six. The next question is what difference, if any, the environment makes in this development.

Differences in Development

Differences have repeatedly been found in the quantity and quality of make-believe play among children of different social class, cultural, and family backgrounds (Freyberg, 1973; Pines, 1969; Sigel & McBane, 1967; Smilansky, 1968; Whiting & Child, 1953). Smilansky observed advantaged and disadvantaged Israeli kindergarten children in free-play periods and found striking differences in their dramatic play. Dramatic play activity accounted for 78 percent of the observation periods in the advantaged classrooms and only 10 percent in the disadvantaged rooms. Differences in the level of the play were also marked. The disadvantaged children tended simply to manipulate the realistic props or use them in imitation of adult actions. They were not as likely to use undefined play objects, for example, a block as an iron. The children in the advantaged class-rooms took on roles and enacted extended play sequences. They engaged in interactive dramatic play and sustained such episodes over longer periods of time. On the basis of observations in the United States, it appears that similar differences exist among advantaged and disadvantaged children here (Freyberg, 1973; Mattick, 1965).

So it appears that cultural and socioeconomic differences relate to differences in symbolic play. What specific conditions or variables make a difference? This issue is less clear, but some evidence is available. Studies of specific variables in children's home environments provide some clues, but it is difficult to disentangle various factors to identify which ones play a causal role. Training studies are somewhat more helpful. In a follow-up to her observations of children's play, Smilansky divided children into four groups. One group received an enrichment program centered on play themes; a second group was taught play techniques by teachers intervening in their play (modeling make-believe play behaviors which the children were observed to lack); a third group received training in both themes and techniques; and a fourth group received no intervention.

Smilansky found that exposure to play themes alone was not sufficient to change the level of children's play significantly. She did find considerable effects when the adults used more direct techniques in the course of ongoing play sequences, for example, the modeling of use of make-believe objects. Freyberg (1973) also used this method in her training procedures.

When we consider together the training results (Smilansky, 1968; Freyberg, 1973) and the evidence from home observations and parental interviews (Freyberg, 1973; Pines, 1969; Smilansky, 1968), certain environmental variables emerge as likely candidates in the nurturance of make-believe play. Children who engaged in only limited dramatic play were likely to be from homes where they had little experience with playful and make-believe interactions (such as a parent pretending to be a mouse, feeding a doll, or asking what would happen if we did not have houses). Parents in these homes rarely modeled a fantasy or make-believe attitude. Present evidence suggests that such interactions play a role in the emergence of imaginative play (Freyberg, 1973; Sigel & McBane, 1967; Singer, 1973). It seems from the Smilansky (1968) and Freyberg (1973) intervention studies that direct experiences with models of make-believe play behaviors have a facilitative effect on the development of imaginative play, whether they occur within the home or at school.

Educational Relevance

One might ask why so much effort is being directed toward facilitating children's make-believe play. Smilansky (1968), Singer (1973), and Sutton-Smith (1971), to name a few, have contended that through make-believe play children develop capacities important for later learning. The suggested reasons for this relationship include the claims that make-believe play: (1) increases the capacity and/or tendency to use internal representation; (2) provides a vehicle for active assimilation of new input; (3) strengthens the "as if" mental attitude, the ability to deal with hypothetical or nonpresent situations; and (4) increases social competence through the practice of adult roles and through the interactive opportunities of the play itself (Copple, Sigel & Saunders, 1979).

Although further empirical work is needed to substantiate more directly the claims made for the educational benefits of dramatic play, this is an area of development in which early environmental inputs appear to play a considerable role. As such, it is an important area for the early childhood educator.

Symbolic Play and Language: A Footnote

The child's developing symbolic abilities are, of course, richly manifested in language development as well. We have chosen to consider the reflection of symbolic development in play rather than language because Chapter 3 of this volume discusses language development. Recent work and theory on symbolic play and language development suggest that the relationship between them is close indeed, a link that has considerable implications for early childhood education. For example, it has been found that children who have difficulties with language, while functioning at age level in many other respects, also show delayed or limited development in symbolic play (Brown, Redmond, Bass, Liebergott, & Swope, 1975; Kahmi & Johnston, 1979). A possible implication of this research for intervention is working with the development of children's symbolic abilities rather than specifically with their language (Leonard, 1980).

Metacognition

Directions in Development

The focus on children's competencies throughout the developmental sequence, on what they are capable of rather than where they fail, has also been a notable characteristic of recent work in the area of children's self-monitoring and knowledge about cognition, or metacognition. In keeping with the spirit of this focus, let us note at the outset that although the metacognitive knowledge and strategies of the eight-year-old are superior to those of the four-year-old, the younger child is already doing things of a metacognitive nature. For example, a young child whose mother has misunderstood what he is asking repeats his inquiry. A preschooler who wants to know about the last episode of "Space Gang" asks her friend, but she asks her teacher when she wants to know the name of a flower or the reason that squirrels run away when you try to pet them. A young child who is told that later he will need to remember where an object was in the room after it has been moved, turns to stare intently at the object's location.

The first child has a notion that when someone does not understand a message, that person is more likely to get it on hearing it again. The second child has some ideas about the kinds of information people of different ages or experience are likely to have. The third child seemed to think that he would remember better if he had a good look first. These examples would all qualify as having a metacognitive dimension, although admittedly at a low level. Matacognition refers to knowledge and thought about cognitive phenomena (Flavell, 1979). In all the above cases, a child is operating with some kind of knowledge of people, including himself, as cognitive beings.

If we acknowledge that preschool children have some degree of metacognition, what can we say about what develops in metacognition and the monitoring of cognitive enterprises? Let us begin by noting some metacognitive knowledge and metacognitive experience in an instance of adult task involvement. Suppose you decide to find out about the medical effects of a new drug. In setting this goal you have made a judgment that you need to know more than you currently do in order to undertake the cognitive task of forming an opinion on the subject. Your metacognitive knowledge about a goal of this sort leads you to believe that getting informed on this subject will be moderately difficult to achieve (on the basis of your own abilities and experience and on the basis of the nature of material written about medicine, which you judge to be quite technical). Having some metacognitive knowledge about efficient ways to get medical information at your own level, you get two articles from a reference librarian. Both are in favor of the drug. You realize that you need to know more about the counterarguments and seek further articles. After reading them, you stand back from your task and evaluate whether what you have learned makes sense as a whole. Are there any discrepancies in information which you need to resolve? Is the gist of each set of claims clear to you? Do you know on what points they reject each others' facts, assumptions, and priorities? Would you be able to describe the medical facts on the drug to a friend? If this assessment brings any problems to light, you might go on to try other strategies for information seeking and organization. In any event, you probably form a notion, correct or incorrect, about the extent of your knowledge and understanding of the subject.

From this account of an adult's approach to a cognitive goal (idealized but all within the range of adult information seeking) we recognize aspects of metacognitive functioning and knowledge when they have reached a high degree of development. What specific aspects of the competence undergo development?

One ability employed at various points in the described task is extracting the main idea of a message. Ann Brown and her colleagues have investigated the development of this ability. Brown and Smiley (1977a, 1977b) found the same basic pattern in this tendency across age: whether they consciously intend to or not, subjects extract the main theme of a story and ignore the trivia. Although this tendency may be different with material other than stories, it seems reasonable that some of the same processes are involved. If people get the gist at all ages, what develops? Brown and DeLoache (1978) argue that what changes is the conscious control of the tendency to extract the main idea. With this control comes more efficient information gathering, as the research of Brown, Smiley, and colleagues has indicated.

Children also gain in their knowledge of the features of texts which are crucial (Brown & Smiley, 1977a, 1977b). Thus, they are better able to improve their recall of a passage with extra study time than are younger children. By observing children's study actions, including their note-taking and underlining, Brown and Smiley gained further information about how the children were using this extra time. They concluded that while younger children have a natural tendency to extract main features from text, they cannot improve upon their spontaneous performance because it is not under conscious control. Older children can employ deliberate strategies of noting essential features and thus can subject these to study or analysis. Brown and DeLoache (1978) assert that this is a common pattern in cognitive development: "increasingly conscious control over an early emerging process."

There is a growing literature on developmental changes in metamemory, that is, children's knowledge concerning their own memory. One of the first attempts to look at this dimension of memory development was a study by Flavell, Friedrichs, and Hoyt (1970). Children ranging from nursery school to fourth grade were given two types of predictions to make: (1) their own memory span *before* a memorization experience; and (2) their readiness to recall a series of items *after* the memorization experience. The older children were more accurate on both kinds of predictions. They judged their own memory span with considerable accuracy and they were able to tell the experimenter when their recall was ready to be tested. Younger children were farther off the mark in anticipating how many items they could recall, and their assessment of the point at which they had memorized a series of items was quite poor. The results of this study and others which have followed (e.g., Brown, Campione, & Barclay, 1978; Kreutzer, Leonard, & Flavell, 1975) present a general picture of the child as being far less attuned to his own cognitive processes and knowledge early in the preschool period.

Differences in Development

Is their any evidence that some children or adults are better than others at monitoring their cognitive enterprises? Are there individual differences in metacognitive knowledge or experience? There is a lack of research investigating these questions directly. However, studies conducted for other purposes such as assessing or training children's metacognitive knowledge or strategies (for example, Kreutzer, Leonard, & Flavell, 1975; Meichenbaum & Asarnow, 1979) frequently find considerable variation among children at a given age.

If reliable differences among individuals exist, are they demonstrably related to environmental variables? We know even less about this issue. Training studies tell us what types of planned intervention can influence the use of metacognitive strategies, but they shed little light on the natural development of such abilities and knowledge.

Educational Relevance

For the educator, another issue is the value of cognitive monitoring. Can one have too much metacognition? Flavell has raised these questions and stated his conviction that there is "far too little rather than enough or too much cognitive monitoring in this world" (1979, pp. 9–10). He believes that this is especially true for children and he is convinced that children who do more cognitive monitoring are better learners in and out of school. This seems to be a reasonable view. However, it will be helpful for educators when there is more empirical work about metacognitive knowledge and strategies that are particularly useful in various cognitive enterprises and, of course, research about how they can be developed.

The study of the facilitation of metacognition is in its infancy. Asarnow and Meichenbaum (1979) found that kindergarteners trained in self-instruction showed a consistent level of rehearsal and recall in both an immediate posttest and a follow-up a week later. Brown, Campione, and Barclay (1978) taught educable retarded children to use self-taught strategies for assessing their own readiness for a recall task, as in the Flavell, Friedrichs, and Hoyt study (1970). A follow-up one year later found the children spontaneously using the self-monitoring strategies when they were presented with the same task. Futhermore, they seemed to have adapted the strategies for use on a memory task of a very different nature.

Some children with reading difficulties may be failing to check their own comprehension as they read. Researchers at the University of Illinois Center for Research in Reading (Brown, Campione, and others) are investigating how the metacognitive strategies of these children might be improved by training.

Work relating to the "preventive" or "enriching" environmental inputs that play a role in the development of metacognition is in even shorter supply, though there may be some useful clues in related literatures such as work on cognitive style, self-regulation, and role taking. The training work can serve to point out possible directions for investigations of home and school environments.

Some educational programs have encouraged children to reflect on their own thought processes and thus could be viewed as attempts to develop metacognitive capacities. The program with which we are most familiar emphasizes inquiry strategies intended to encourage children to reflect on how they knew certain things, how they solved problems, how ideas and knowledge of others differed from their own, and so forth (Copple, Sigel & Saunders, 1979).

Summary

Any examination of cognitive development must acknowledge the fact that there are a number of different theoretical conceptions of cognition. We have seen that the study of cognitive development has itself undergone a process of development. We began by briefly reviewing the place of cognitive development within learning theory and psychoanalytic theory. A third significant tradition with yet a different approach to the intellectual development of the child is the testing movement. Against the background of these three major traditions, the emergence of new approaches and of theoretical notions and concerns can be readily discerned from the 1950s to the present time. There were major shifts in views of motivation (see White, 1959) and in the unabashed discussion of the mind rather than simply of behavior. A body of more "cognitive" research and theory became evident, notably the work of Jean Piaget, the psycholinguistic revolution, and the computer-based fields of information processing and artificial intelligence. To varying degrees, these bodies of work have been concerned with the nature of organization of children's knowledge, the strategies and processes of various cognitive enterprises, and the nature of developmental change in knowledge or processes.

Out of the increased interest in children's mental life, there have been a host of contributions to the understanding of cognitive development. We looked at four areas in which there have been productive approaches to answering the question of what is developing during early childhood. There are many others. In selecting a limited number of areas for discussion, we took several factors into account (along with our own interests, or course).

One consideration was the inclusion of areas reflecting prominent current trends within cognitive developmental study, such as the emphasis on young children's competencies rather than their deficiencies or the focus on identifying children's cognitive strategies.

Another consideration in selecting areas for discussion was presenting work from each of the two major types of cognitive developmental investigation: those focusing on the *structure*, organization, or rules characterizing children's knowledge, and those focusing on children's cognitive strategies or *processes*. Structure and process are, of course, closely related. However, there is a real difference in the type of analysis the investigator is making in a structural versus a process description. Of the areas we have included, two seem to be more heavily loaded with issues about emerging structures: the study of mathematical thinking (particularly Piaget's contributions) and the study of symbolic play. The work we report on mental imagery and metacognition is more oriented toward discovering the processes that change with development.

A third factor in our choice of areas was a decision to include some bodies of work that have not been typically linked to early childhood education but that seem to have considerable applicability. The upsurge of interest in metacognition has not as yet received much explicit attention from early childhood educators. Mental imagery, an older area of investigation, is also frequently bypassed in considering research implications for the education of young children. Symbolic play and mathematical thinking are more typically found within the early childhood fold, but in each case there are interesting new areas of exploration with educational relevance.

In such a brief chapter we have had to confine our objectives, but we have stressed the importance of the theoretical framework within which cognitive development is viewed and we have emphasized the changes in theoretical conceptions that have had a major impact on current research. We have also attempted to convey the richness and diversity of the contributions to early childhood education from research and theory in cognitive development.

References

Asarnow, J. R., and Meichenbaum, D. Verbal rehearsal and serial recall: The mediational training of kindergarten children. *Child Development*, 1979, *50*, 1173–1177.

Berlyne, D. E. *Structure and Direction in Thinking*. New York: McGraw-Hill, 1965.

Brown, A. L., Campione, J. C., and Barclay, C. R. Training self-checking routines for estimating test readiness: Generalization from list learning to prose recall. Unpublished manuscript, University of Illinois, 1978.

Brown, A. L., and DeLoache, J. S. Skills, plans, and self-regulation. In R. S. Siegler (ed.), *Children's Thinking: What Develops?* Hillsdale, N. J.: Lawrence Erlbaum Associates, 1978.

Brown, A. L., and Smiley, S. S. Rating the importance of structural units of prose passages: A problem of metacognitive development. *Child Development*, 1977a, *48*, 1–8.

Brown, A. L., and Smiley, S. S. The development of strategies for studying prose passages. Unpublished manuscript, University of Illinois, 1977b.

Brown, J., Redmond, A., Bass, K., Liebergott, J., and Swope, S. Symbolic play in normal and language-impaired children. Paper presented to the American Speech and Hearing Association, Washington, 1975.

Brown, R. *A First Language*. Cambridge, Mass.: Harvard University Press, 1973.

Bühler, C. *From Birth to Maturity*. London: Routledge & Kegan Paul, 1935.

Chomsky, N. *Syntactic structures*. The Hague: Mouton, 1957.

Condry, J. Enemies of exploration: Self-initiated versus other-initiated learning. *Journal of Personality and Social Psychology*, 1977, *35*, 459–477.

Copple, C., Sigel, I. E., and Saunders, R. *Educating the Young Thinker: Classroom Strategies for Cognitive Growth*. New York: Van Nostrand, 1979.

Dasen, P. R. *Piagetian Psychology: Cross Cultural Contributions*. New York: Gardner Press, 1976.

De Lisi, R. *The educational implications of Piaget's theory and assessment techniques* (ERIC TM Report 68). Princeton, N. J.: ERIC Clearinghouse on Tests, Measurement & Evaluation, Educational Testing Service, November 1979.

El'konin, D. Symbolics and its function in the play of children. In R. E. Herron and B. Sutton-Smith (eds.), *Child's Play*. New York: Wiley, 1971.

Fein, G. G. A transformational analysis of pretending. *Developmental Psychology*, 1975, *11*, 291–296.

Fein, G. G., and Clarke-Stewart, A. *Daycare in Context*. New York: Wiley, 1973.

Fillmore, C. The case for case. In E. Bach and R. T. Harms (eds.), *Universals in Linguistic Theory*. New York: Holt, Rinehart, and Winston, 1968.

Flavell, J. H. Metacognition and cognitive monitoring. *American Psychologist*, 1979, *34*, 906–911.

FLAVELL, J. H., FRIEDRICHS, A. G., and HOYT, J. D. Developmental changes in memorization processes. *Cognitive Development*, 1970, *1*, 324–340.

FORMAN, G. E., and HILL, F. *Constructive Play*. Monterey, Calif.: Brooks/Cole, 1980.

FORMAN, G. E., and KUSCHNER, D. S. *The Child's Construction of Knowledge: Piaget for Teaching Children*. Monterey, Calif.: Brooks/Cole, 1977.

FREYBERG, J. T. Increasing the imaginative play of urban disadvantaged kindergarten children through systematic training. In J. L. Singer (ed.), *The Child's World of Make-Believe Play*. New York: Academic Press, 1973.

GELMAN, R. Counting in the preschooler: What does and does not develop. In R. S. Siegler (ed.), *Children's Thinking: What develops?* Hillsdale, N. J.: Lawrence Erlbaum Associates, 1978.

GELMAN, R. Preschool thought. *American Psychologist*, 1979, 34, 900–905.

GELMAN, R., and GALLISTEL, C. R. *The Child's Understanding of Number*. Cambridge, Mass.: Harvard University Press, 1978.

GINSBURG, H. *Children's Arithmetic: The Learning Process*. New York: Van Nostrand, 1977.

GOODNOW, J. J. A list of milieu differences with some of Piaget's tasks. *Psychological Monographs*, 1962, *36*.

INHELDER, B., and PIAGET, J. *The Early Growth of Logic in the Child*. London: Routledge & Kegan Paul, 1964.

KAHMI, A., and JOHNSTON, J. Symbolic and conceptual abilities in language-impaired and MA- and MLU-matched controls. Paper presented to American Speech and Hearing Association, Atlanta, 1979.

KESSEN, W. Questions for a theory of cognitive development. In H. Stevenson (ed.), Concept of development. *Monographs of the Society for Research in Child Development*, 1966, *31*, 55–81.

KOSSLYN, S. M. Imagery and cognitive development: A teleological perspective. In R. S. Siegler (ed.), *Children's Thinking: What Develops?* Hillsdale, N. J.: Lawrence Erlbaum Associates, 1978.

KREUTZER, M. A., LEONARD, C., and FLAVELL, J. H. An interview study of children's knowledge about memory. *Monographs of the Society for Research in Child Development*, 1975, *40*.

KUHN, D. The application of Piaget's theory of cognitive development to education. *Harvard Educational Review*, 1979, 49, 338–360.

LEONARD, L. B. Cognitive development and language impairment: Implications for intervention. Paper presented at the Annual Conference of Piagetian Theory and the Helping Professions, Los Angeles, February 1980.

MARKEY, F. Imaginative behavior in preschool children. *Child Development Monographs*, 1935, *18*.

MARMOR, G. S. Development of kinetic images: When does the child first represent movement in mental images? *Cognitive Psychology*, 1975, 7, 548–559.

MARMOR, G. S. Mental rotation and number conservation: Are they related? *Developmental Psychology*, 1977, *13*, 320–325.

MATTHEWS, W. S. Modes of transformation in the initiation of fantasy play. *Developmental Psychology*, 1977, *13*, 212–216.

MATTICK, I. Adaptation of nursery school techniques to deprived children. *Journal of the American Academy of Child Psychology*, 1965, *4*, 670–700.

MEICHENBAUM, D., and ASARNOW, J. R. Cognitive behavior-modification and metacognitive development: Implications for the classroom. In P. Kendall and S. Hollon (eds.), *Cognitive-Behavioral Interventions: Theory, Research and Procedures*. New York: Academic Press, 1979.

MERMELSTEIN, E., and SHULMAN, L. S. Lack of formal schooling and the acquisition of conservation. *Child Development*, 1967, *38*, 39–52.

NICOLICH, L. Beyond sensorimotor intelligence: Assessment of symbolic maturity through analysis of pretend play. *Merrill-Palmer Quarterly*, 1977, *23*, 89–99.

PHILLIPS, J. R. Syntax and vocabulary of mothers' speech to young children: Age and sex comparisons. *Child Development*, 1973, *44*, 182–185.

PIAGET, J. *Play, Dreams, and Imitation in Childhood*. New York: Norton, 1951.

PIAGET, J. *The Origins of Intelligence in Children*. New York: International Universities Press, 1952a.

PIAGET, J. *The Child's Conception of Number*. London: Routledge & Kegan Paul, 1952b.

PIAGET, J., and INHELDER, B. *Mental Imagery in the Child*. New York: Basic Books, 1971.

PINES, M. Why some three-year-olds get A's—and some C's. *New York Times Magazine*, July 6, 1969.

PRICE-WILLIAMS, D. A. Study concerning concepts of conservation of quantity among primitive children. *Acta Psychologica*, 1961, *18*, 297–305.

RESNICK, L. B. The future of IQ testing in education. *Intelligence*, 1979, *3*, 241–253.

SHEPARD, R. The mental image. *American Psychologist*, 1978, *33*, 125–137.

SIGEL, I. E., and COCKING, R. R. *Cognitive Development from Childhood to Adolescence: A Constructivist Perspective*. New York: Holt, Rinehart, and Winston, 1977.

SIGEL, I. E., and McBANE, B. Cognitive competence and level of symbolization among five-year-old children. In J. Hellmuth (ed.), *The Disadvantaged Child*. New York: Brunner/Mazel, 1967.

SINGER, J. L. *The Child's World of Make-Believe: Experimental Studies of Imaginative Play*. New York: Academic Press, 1973.

SKODAK, M., and SKEELS, H. M. A final follow-up of 100 adopted children. *Journal of Genetic Psychology*, 1949, *75*, 85–125.

SMILANSKY, S. *The Effects of Socio-Dramatic Play on Disadvantaged Preschool children*. New York: Wiley, 1968.

SNOW, C. E. Mothers' speech to children learning language. *Child Development*, 1972, *43*, 549–565.

SNOW, C. E., and Ferguson, C. A. (eds.). *Talking to Children: Language Input and Acquisition*. Cambridge: At the University Press, 1977.

STERN, W. *The Psychological Method of Testing Intelligence*. Baltimore, Md.: Warwick and York, 1914.

STODDARD, G. D. *The Meaning of Intelligence*. New York: Macmillan, 1943.

STODDARD, G. D., and WELLMAN, B. L. *Environment and the IQ*. Yearbook National Social Studies in Education, 1940, *39*(Part 1), 405–442.

SUTTON-SMITH, B. The role of play in cognitive development. In R. E. Herron and B. Sutton-Smith (eds.), *Child's Play*. New York: Wiley, 1971.

VERNON, P. E. Ability factors and environmental influences. *American Psychologist,* 1965a, *20,* 723–733.

VERNON, P. E. Environmental handicaps and intellectual development. *British Journal of Education Psychology,* 1965b, *35,* 1–12 (Part 1), 13–22(Part 2).

WELLMAN, B. IQ changes of preschool and non-preschool groups during preschool years: A summary of literature. *Journal of Psychology,* 1945, *20,* 347–368.

WHITE, R. W. Motivation reconsidered: The concept of competence. *Psychological Review,* 1959, *66,* 297–333.

WHITING, J. W., and CHILD, I. L. *Child training and personality.* New Haven, Conn.: Yale University Press, 1953.

CHAPTER 2

Motor Development in Early Childhood: Critical Issues for Researchers in the 1980s

Bryant J. Cratty

WRITINGS AND WORKS of the first experimentally oriented psychologists, in the late nineteenth century, reflected an interest in the movement capacities of infants and children. The first to construct intelligence tests for children in the 1880s, including Alfred Binet, inserted drawing tasks into their content. During the first decades of this century, motor performance qualities, perhaps because of their visibility and measurability, continued to be vigorously researched by individuals interested in human development. At first, these investigations focused on identifying the stages through which the young pass as they learn to turn over, sit, stand, and walk, and to manipulate objects.

During the decade after World War II, several books appeared which maintained that great change could take place in a variety of motor abilities if one exposed children to various movement tasks. These writings, in turn, inspired programs which still continue. The proponents of this viewpoint suggest that participation by children results in better "neurological organization," perceptual functioning, and academic performance. Reviewers of this research and these programs have not held equally expansive views; nevertheless, these writings and speculations continued to appear into the 1970s. A recent and popular theoretical model, for example, is that advanced by Jean Ayres, promising better sensory integration of youngsters through exposure to activities involving kinesthetic, vestibular, and tactual stimulation (Ayres, 1972, 1977).[1]

In the 1960s, efforts were made to determine just how sensory-motor remediation programs might aid the progress of preschoolers from low socioeconomic backgrounds. In the late 1960s and the 1970s, other investigators began to probe into the processes underlying maturational milestones by using sophisticated research tools, including physiological measures of psychological states, as well as

---

[1] These theories and the supporting evidence for their validity have been reviewed over the years by numerous writers (Cratty, 1979, 1981; Goodman & Hammill, 1973; Mann, 1970; Myers, 1976).

cinematographical methods to study motor behaviors (Bower & Paterson, 1972; Bower & Wihart, 1972; Saida & Mitsumasa, 1979).

Perhaps inspired by the observations of Piaget and others, the subjects of numerous studies have reflected an interest in the ways in which various emerging movement capacities interact with other components of the maturing attribute pattern, including perceptual, linguistic, and cognitive abilities (Bower & Wihart, 1979; Lipsitt & Kaye, 1964; Weiderholt, 1975).

At the present time, the literature displays healthy differences in theoretical viewpoints. These scholarly arguments concern, for example, whether or not sensory-motor functions undergird and lead to conceptual behaviors in infants, or whether perceptual and conceptual behaviors emerge before and independent of the quality and quantity of the motor activities exhibited by the infant and child. Concern about these issues has tended to make interested professionals probe more deeply into just what kinds of content may be placed within programs for preschool children in order to optimize abilities needed for school, play, and life in general. This chapter contains a look at critical issues and problems and a survey of needed research as perceived by this writer.

Critical Issues, Problem Areas

The Movement Base

One critical question holding both theoretical and applied implications concerns whether or not sensory-motor behaviors form an imperative for other emerging components of the child's behaviors. Many, if not most, developmental specialists, perceptual-motor theorists, and other observers and researchers of the developing human personality feel rather dogmatically that indeed Piaget is correct in his view of emerging stages. They cite the distinguished Swiss scholar's writings in which he carefully presented in detail the important six stages within the sensory-motor period, containing movement experiences involving the child's own body, as well as primitive interactions with elements of the environment. Many scholars interpret the placement of these six sensory-motor periods before those reflecting thought and symbolism, as signifying that sensory-motor behaviors are indeed the foundation of later cognitive operations (Piaget, 1926, 1952).

The data and writings of a smaller number of writers, scholars, and researchers seem at variance with the notion that movement behaviors are critical antecedents of cognitive and/or perceptual functions. Citing data published during the past fifteen years by Fantz (1963) and Lipsitt and Kaye (1964), Bower and Paterson (1972) and Siqueland (1967) point out that the human infant seems to engage in a variety of perceptual behaviors before he gains accurate control of his hands and body. Furthermore, they reflect, if one is clever in monitoring subtle responses by the human infant (components of the surprise response are popular), it is possible to obtain data that reflect that within the first weeks in the infant's life he or she is capable of engaging in discriminating visual and auditory perceptual behaviors and that various cognitive operations also seem to take place during these same early days of life. The work they cite seems not necessarily contradictory to some of the speculations of Piaget, but it does suggest that cognitive operations he believed took place at the end of the second year of life may sometimes be assessed during the first week or so of life. For example, Piaget places the beginnings of thought between the eighteenth month and second year of life, as evidenced by his daughter Jacqueline's awareness of object permanence, reflected in searching behaviors indicating her awareness that a pencil hidden in her father's hand still exists and can be retrieved even though it has been hidden from sight.

In contrast, data from work by Bower and his colleagues indicate that infants within the eighth week of age will anticipate movements via visual tracking of moving objects when they disappear behind a screen; this same experimenter has found that surprise reactions in the form of changes in heart rate are observed in infants who expect to view an object again after it has first been covered, made to disappear, and then uncovered.

Numerous other studies since the 1960s have resulted in findings confirming the apparent existence of various cognitive structures which theretofore had been believed by most earlier scholars in child development to have to await the appearance of various movement capacities, in particular manual grasping behaviors (Lipsitt & Kaye, 1964; Siqueland, 1967).

The viewpoint that shortly after birth the infant may be armed with at least rudimentary behaviors of four or five kinds has been presented schematically by this writer (Cratty, 1979). This model suggests that shortly after birth the beginnings of perceptual, verbal, cognitive, and motor behaviors may be recorded and that with maturation these behaviors (1) differentiate and become more diffuse in nature; and (2) combine in various interactions via "behavioral bonds" in intricate and useful ways. Those supporting a "sensory-motor basis" thesis, on the other hand, suggest a model composed of horizontal laminations.

Contemporary cognitive theorists have been interested in the manner in which children and infants classify and categorize objects, events, and relationships in their environment as a function of maturity. Several decades ago, Piaget observed his own children apparently attempting to place various movement experiences into classes.

A thorough review of the writings of Piaget, however, reveals numerous references to early cognitive and perceptual behaviors which have been objectified by more recent experimentally oriented behavioral scientists. For example, during the first stage of the sensory-motor period (within the first fifteen days of life) Piaget observed that the infant engages in modifications of the sucking "schema." He suggests that this apparently reflects a rudimentary kind of hypothesis formation.

Piaget also refers to the existence of the seeking of means–ends relationships by the infant during the second month as the infant reacts to selective cues (the appearance of the mother) before engaging in sucking actions. This same kind of relationship between means and outcomes is a concern of many today who might classify themselves as cognitive rather than sensory-motor theorists.

The drive for novelty, explored in more detail by others later, was seen by Piaget during this same sensory-motor period as he observed that the infant seemed consciously to seek stimulation and new sensations formed by movements and by the feelings obtained from the mouth and lips. Novelty seeking was also seen by Piaget as he observed his children spending long periods of time regarding their hands and the fringes of their cribs while spending less and less time on more familiar objects, after an initial survey. Almost four decades later, these observations were objectified in studies by Fantz and others, individuals who were interested in early motivational and perceptual states of neonates (Fantz, 1963; Bowers, 1974).

From an applied standpoint, if one accepts the ideas that (1) the infant engages in a great deal of perceptual behavior before the onset of accurate movement capabilities; and (2) that human infants also are able to formulate concepts and to engage in rudimentary thought before they can move their hands and body accurately, one will adopt an approach to the early enrichment of the preschool infant that is different from those who believe that movement is the basis of intelligence. The perceptual-motor theorist might, for example, not be as concerned with the quality of movement experiences afforded the young child as with their quantity. He or she also might believe that an awkward child is necessarily impeded intellectually, perceptually, and academically and that remediation of movement problems inevitably improves academic performances.

The cognitive theorist, formulating the contents of a preschool enrichment program might, in contrast, be more concerned with the quality of thought that the various movement experiences might elicit. They might, for example, encourage the child to construct their own obstacle course before moving through it, and they might present materials for manipulation which require hypothesis formation on the part of the youngster (for example, "What noise will be made if I strike these two objects together?). The cognitive theorist might also think it productive if preschoolers are left alone at times to contemplate silently and perhaps manipulate their environment mentally rather than constantly being pressured to cross balance beams, roll down mats, and play angels-in-the-snow.

Numerous research possibilities exist if one wishes to contrast the effect of the two approaches (cognitive versus perceptual-motor) upon various present and future behaviors of the preschool child. Among them would be a model to measure the impact of a movement program in which decision making by the child-participants is encouraged compared with one that is teacher-directed. Another possibility would be to measure the effect of a program containing carefully graded tasks, reflecting increasingly sophisticated cognitive behaviors.

In any case, when formulating programs for youngsters in early childhood, it is believed, one should be prepared to defend a theoretical position of one of the two types indicated. Those in a position to research program effects should likewise attempt to separate the impact of simple teacher-directed movement.

Perceptual versus Motor Behaviors: Their Separation and Assessment

The often indiscriminate use of such terms as perception, sensory-motor, motor-sensory, and perceptual-motor has encouraged the enthusiastic insertion of motor tasks into programs for early childhood. Lay people and researchers alike, however, use these words in many different ways. The inaccurate differentiations have often been made between visual-perceptual problems and motor ineptitude within the younger child. The use of hand–eye drawing tasks in such tests as the Frostig and the Bender Gestalt to evaluate visual-perceptual function has done little to rectify this type of confusion. For example, failure to do well on these figure-copying tests and others, has caused panicky parents to take their children to developmental optometrists, opthomologists, and reading specialists. These individuals might then engage in further remediation and/or diagnostic work reflecting the assumption that something is wrong in the way in which the child sees and perceives the world, despite the fact that his or her ineptitude in either of the above testing instruments may have been caused by a problem in motor control.

A child's inability to copy and/or arrange copied figures well in relation to each other may have its genesis in a problem involving right-hemisphere function (spatial motor qualities) rather than reflect any ineptitude in writing and reading (left-hemisphere functioning). In the 1970s, however, some professionals have recognized the lack of congruence between a child's ability to process and interpret visual information, including letters and words, and their ability to print and to write both letters and geometric figures. Diagnostic tools of increased sophistication have been developed. In 1972, for example, Colarusso and Hammill published a "motor free" test of visual perception, whose scores when obtained from normal or retarded populations failed to correlate with the "traditional" drawing tests of visual perception (Colarusso & Hammill, 1972).

Perceptive diagnosticians realized that if a child failed to draw overlapping squares "correctly," the interpretation of the results should be predicated upon questioning the child as to what he or she saw both in the model to be reproduced as well as in his or her own drawing. Further evaluations of the child's maturity, perceptual capacities, and motor competencies, using assessment tools in which movement and perceptual attributes do not interact should be undertaken.

For example, if a child produces either of the following, after being shown the model, various interpretations might be forthcoming. A production like Copy 1 might indicate that the child actually "saw" the model to be composed of wavy

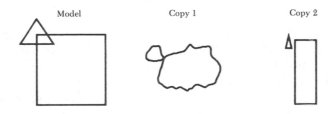

Model   Copy 1   Copy 2

lines or that the child simply cannot control the writing implement well. In any case, the child might be asked, "Is your drawing the same as the one I have shown you?" A negative reply probably indicates that the child has a motor, not a perceptual problem; a positive response may indicate that there is either a combined perceptual-motor problem or a perceptual problem, requiring further diagnostic work.

Failure to overlap the figures might indicate that the child simply wishes to place the figures separately; that he or she may be suffering from a figure ground problem and, wishing to avoid confusion, simply separates the two; or that the child (particularly when young) does not believe that it makes any difference whether or not the figures overlap.

Elongated rectangular figures (Copy 2), may indicate that the child is perceptually immature and has inscribed exactly what has hit the retina (the retinal image) rather than what a perceptually more mature child would produce.

Several writers over the past decades have also indicated that children with balance problems, unable to relate to gravity, will inevitably have visual perceptual problems reflected in classroom tasks including reading. The data supporting this type of perceptual-motor relationship are hard to find, however (Mann, 1970). Thus, valid research findings that lend credence to a close causal and statistical relationship between a child's motor functioning and both auditory and perceptual abilities are hard to locate. Data suggesting that these two facets of the preschooler's function are separable do exist (Goodman & Hammill, 1973; Myers & Hammill, 1976). Future research should be devoted to further unscrambling the perceptual and motor picture. More important, the separability of these two facets of the preschool child's personality should be clearly pointed out to practitioners, both when diagnosing problems and when formulating programs to remedy atypical behaviors or to enrich the movement and perceptual capacities of the normal youngster.

The practitioner who continues to believe in the close causal and statistical relationship between perception and motion will continue to constitute movement education programs to improve the child's ability to form various visual-perceptual and auditory-perceptual discriminations, syntheses, and analyses. Sophisticated practitioners, in contrast, will place carefully sequenced activities in such programs to improve perceptual functions alone, sometimes pairing them with movement tasks for emphasis and motivation.

Early Motor Capacities and Later Intelligence

For decades, child development researchers and theorists have attempted to determine whether or not one was able to predict later intelligence from early indices of maturational signposts, including movement capacities. They attempted to ascertain whether or not the active, physically capable baby was one who later would become intellectually precocious. Was a mature and able nervous system, as reflected in movement capacities, a good predictor of capable adult behaviors including academic achievement and professional success (Bayley, 1968; Honzik, 1948)?

Longitudinal studies carried out on populations from birth to maturity unfortunately did not supply the needed answers. For the most part, the measures which such researchers as Bayley (1968), Kagan and Moss (1962), and others collected did not include scores from an extensive number of movement tasks. Bayley, for example, in her investigation titled "Behavioral Correlates of Mental Growth—Birth to Thirty-Six Years," indicated that male infants who evidenced prolonged visual attention to tasks were those who tended to do well in intelligence tests administered later.

Hofstaetter, evaluating the behavior of infants and young children at various ages, concluded that three separate types of qualities emerged at various times, and thus became measurable, during the first sixteen years of life. Hofstaetter termed the first quality, up to the age of twenty months, "sensory-motor alertness." From forty months on, tests containing this quality contributed "practically nothing" to the variation of mental-age scores obtained later. A factor that Hofstaetter named "persistence" emerged at the twentieth month. This quality reflected the ability to act in accordance with an established set rather than being influenced by interfering situations and stimuli, and continued to be reasonably important until about the fifth or sixth year. The final quality that emerged continued to remain important until late in childhood. This, Hofstaetter suggested, reflects the ability to manipulate symbols and to engage in planning and in abstract thinking. These and more contemporary analyses indicate that whatever is measured early in the child's life, before the age of four or five years, for the most part does not predict well the nature of intelligence test scores obtained later in childhood.

It is possible, however, that some carefully designed tasks, reflecting the infant's notions of object permanency, visual alertness, and/or attentional skills, may be more predictive of later intelligence and of emerging talents than the rather crude measures of movement capacities seen on the traditional developmental scales used throughout the decades.

Language and Speech

Language and speech are critical indices of development which emerge in some ways parallel with movement capacities during the first years of life. Speech, the ability to articulate clearly, requires the same precision of motor planning (praxic) behaviors as are required in the precise movements of the hands and fingers as the child learns to manipulate objects, button his clothes, and handle table utensils. Exploratory studies which have contrasted motor planning involving the larger muscle groups and the planning needed in clear speech have produced moderate correlations within the first twelve to eighteen months of life. These types of praxic behaviors, one involving the mouth, tongue, and associated structures, the other, limbs and hands, tend to become diverse and differentiated abilities within the second and third years (Cratty, 1979). However, among populations of motorically impaired children, it is probable that one will find an inordinate number of children with articulation problems. Studies aimed at factor-analyzing a number of acts requiring motor planning (of the speech apparatus as well as of other muscle groups) might help to clarify this important and interesting type of sequencing behavior (Curran & Cratty, 1979).

Language, on the other hand, reflects vocabulary development, the formation of sentences, and the use of words. Frequently, developmental tasks involving movement activities are combined with those which reflect facility in language. Alexander R. Luria, the Russian child development specialist, has formulated models reflecting the manner in which both language and motor behaviors pair in interesting and important ways. The elements of Luria's model not only afford potentially useful research possibilities, but also have important implications for the enrichment of language in young children. Luria suggests, for example, that initially a child will vocalize, describing a movement which he or she is about to execute. That is, the child may say "Now Johnny is going to throw the ball" before he actually throws the ball, perhaps accompanying the movement with a sentence describing the action. Finally, the child may reflect upon what has occurred by recapitulating the action with words ("Johnny threw the ball").

A second stage occurs when the child may preprogram the movement with vocal utterances, but then does not accompany the movement with words. A subvocal description may accompany the action, however, at this point. The action may or may not be accompanied by a vocal recapitulation able to be heard by those present.

Finally, as the movement is well learned and/or the child matures, the movements are not preprogrammed vocally nor are they accompanied by either covert or subvocal language. In some cases, the actions may be too rapid to be accompanied efficiently with words.

The implications of these sequences are numerous, both for the researcher and for the practitioner. For example, it is not entirely clear just when they occur. The focus and variables which may mold the appearance and disappearance of these language-movement combinations are not well researched. These might include parental stimulation, socioeconomic variables, the language of the family into which the child is born, as well as the quality of the motor behavior which the child is capable of displaying. The presence or absence of verbally mature or immature play companions might also influence the nature of the child's vocalizations before, during, and after various actions.

Acceptance of the general order of these sequences also has implications for the educator interested in enriching the language and/or motor behaviors of preschool youngsters. For example, special encouragement may be given to the youngster evidencing a language delay when exposed to movement tasks. He or she may be encouraged to emit pretask verbal preprogramming behaviors to slow down actions initially so that they may be accompanied by words and to tell the teacher or parent just what occurred. Language enrichment in this manner is and has been attempted by speech pathologists, with reasonable success. Movement tasks present a vivid and motivating type of experience for the preschool child, one whose description is obvious to both the child and to those observing and encouraging him or her.

As one progresses with a child, rational and useful decisions should be made as to (1) when and if to encourage termination of words that accompany movements; (2) whether or not to encourage subvocal behaviors when more rapid movements are executed; and (3) what type of child may be aided or hindered by encouragement to pair verbal behaviors with movement behaviors. This final decision, for example, may rest upon whether or not the child evidences articulation problems, whether there are cultural pressures present which encourage language development, and whether the child possesses the necessary motor, intellectual, social, and emotional characteristics and competencies.

Social Behavior(s)

Social competencies are often associated with movement behaviors in young children. Five of the seven categories on the Vineland Test of Social Maturity (Doll, 1952), for example, contain items which reflect motor competencies (stair climbing, combing hair, and the like). The same kinds of motor items are seen in numerous other tests reflecting the social competencies of the preschool youngster.

In addition, it appears that social behaviors may be blunted if certain manipulative tasks are not mastered "on time." Uzgiris (1967), for example, postulates the existence of a "showing schema" in young children, emerging about the middle to the end of the first year of life. Uzgiris suggests that the apparent wish of the infant to instigate social behavior is reflected in his or her tendency to grasp objects and to hold them up for inspection by a nearby adult.

Researchers interested in social behaviors of the preschool child frequently observe play behaviors, reflecting both the quantity and the quality of the child's early social interactions. These play behaviors may be early indicators of later emotional health, social maturity, as well as of intelligence. They are also indicators of motor development.

The Awkward Child

The physically awkward child has probably always been with us. Although in the 1920s A. Oseretsky formulated his tests for "motor idiots" at the Moscow Neurological Institute, it has not been until recent decades that educators, physicians, psychologists, and parents have become interested in youngsters evidencing "the clumsy child syndrome."

Their physical awkwardness can stem from many sources, including pre- and paranatal insults and postbirth trauma. At times, there is no discernible reason for the child's awkwardness; he or she simply can't move well in certain situations.

Awkward children may evidence other behavioral problems, including hyperactivity, mental slowness, and distorted affective behaviors. Although these problems are found in abundance among children labeled "learning disabled," many children with learning disabilities are free of motor problems, just as some academically gifted children evidence inept physical coordination. For reasons not entirely clear, most awkward children are males. These youngsters are difficult to classify with precision. In an overall sense, they seem to consist of two types. Those whose problem seems to suggest an organic basis may exhibit motor behaviors that resemble mild to moderate forms of the traditional types of cerebral palsy (athetoid, spastic, ataxic, tremor, mixed). Children whose problems seem to reflect a developmental delay at times exaggerate awkward behavior because of "learned helplessness" acquired from parents who overreact to their problems.

Interest in the latter type of youngster has grown since World War II because of the writings of perceptual-motor theorists. In recent years, several books, numerous articles, and many programs in schools and nursery programs have focused upon the discovery and the remediation of the physically less capable child. The evaluation of physical awkwardness poses several problems, and at times it seems as though it may lie in the eye of the beholder. The opinions of teachers may differ from the judgments of a "motor expert." Whether or not a child is judged to have poor coordination may depend upon the peer group with whom she or he must compete rather than upon the measurable abilities they may evidence.[2]

In addition to the problems of identifying the awkward child, there are other important questions: (1) can such children be helped? (2) what variables seem to enhance or detract from efforts to change their physical abilities? (3) what kinds of content should be placed in such programs? (4) what kinds of personnel should take part in the effort to change them? (5) what individual differences in children should be taken into account when devising remedial programs? and (6) how broad should the testing and remediation program be relative to goals? For example, should concern be shown for both large and small muscle activity, and for the identification and control of hyperactive behavior?

Data as to the incidence of the so-called awkward child vary, but in general from 8 to 15 percent of first graders can be so classified. Conceivably, this figure is similar in populations of preschool youngsters. However, in addition to the previously cited problems in evaluation, accurate assessment of the motor competencies of the preschool youngster is made more difficult by the fact that their performance evidences marked intra-individual variability when performing the same task from trial to trial. Children at these ages attempt to discover and to

---

[2] The lack of precise testing instruments does not help in the identification of these children. The best available test, in my opinion, is the Stott Test of Morot Impairment (Stott, Moyes & Henderson, 1972).

employ adequate and consistent "work methods" when confronted with similar tasks, and variations in the manner in which they perform are due to the instability of the approaches they use from time to time.

Variations in attentional behavior also influence the task performance by the preschool youngster. Taken together, the influence of these and other variables makes most difficult the delineation of just who is and who is not awkward within a nursery school-age population. Some of the more useful recent evaluation instruments suggest that a given kind of motor behavior may normally be expected to appear within a range of months rather than at a precise time in the life of the preschool youngster. The Denver Developmental Survey (1970) is an example of this type of scale. This instrument as well as the remedial program developed by Koontz are useful in the evaluation and program planning of the child below the age of five (Koontz, 1978).

The writers promoting the various programs of perceptual-motor education, neurological organization, physiological optics, and sensory-integration, although for the most part too expansive in their claims to remedy academic functioning, have supplied a number of useful strategies with which to correct motor deficiencies. However, there is a surprising lack of well-designed studies which indicate that exposure to programs containing movement experiences really produces measurable changes in motor functioning.

For the most part, reviews by Goodman and Hammill (1973), Myers and Hammill (1976), and others have indicated that exposure to programs advocated by Gerald Getman, Newell C. Kephart, and others have not had a significant influence upon the motor capacities of children. However, the findings from several recent studies (P. Werner, 1974; Hebbelinck, 1978; and Schaney, Brekke, Landry & Burke, 1976) do indicate that exposure to carefully planned programs of motor enrichment exert a positive and significant influence upon the movement behaviors of the preschool child. In an earlier investigation by myself and my staff, we found that prognosis for change was dependent upon the age of the youngster and upon the severity of the problem encountered. Williams's work with "low-birth-weight" infants to whom early stimulation was applied (composed mostly of motor tasks) also indicated that positive changes could occur when employing movement tasks (Scarr Salapatec & Williams, 1973). Thus, the relatively little available evidence seems to indicate that, if one attempts, through the application of a relatively few movement tasks, to modify perceptual and academic qualities, it is unlikely that movement attributes will be significantly affected. However, if one devises a rather comprehensive program of enrichment whose goal is to improve movement for its own sake through exposure of preschool youngsters to a variety of motor tasks, there is some likelihood of success, particularly when working with younger and "less involved" groups of youngsters.[3]

---

[3] Separating the various effects of numerous program components is often difficult. This could be circumvented by designing studies in which various combinations of program content are used. The results could then reflect what combination of activities seems to change youngsters best and what components of the program seem most useful.

Research Problems

The preceding review suggests innumerable research topics; some are related to theoretical issues, while others are of a practical nature. Still others wed the applied and the theoretical.

In the following paragraphs I intend to delineate some possible problem areas. The section concludes with a look at areas of study not directly related to the previous review.

The Movement Base

During the 1970s, a great deal of creative work was carried out to determine the nature of the early underpinnings of the infant's emerging pattern of intellectual, perceptual, verbal, and motor attributes (Bower, 1974). Still to be explored, however, are innumerable complexities, including the delineation of the nature of intelligence itself. For the most part, literature which deals not only with intellectual attributes, but with creative abilities and with talent of various kinds, appears most promising. Studies dealing with the strategies adopted by children within various cultures confronted with complex problems, represents a fruitful new direction for research.

The manner in which motor competencies and movement characteristics interact with these abilities might be further explored by attempting to determine the nature of creative abilities and whether or not creative movement experiences enhance creative tendencies in other contexts. Studies of the manner in which various programs of movement education may contribute to a child's tendency to engage in divergent thought, for example, might be productive. Studies are needed to outline more clearly the nature of the apparent differentiation effect, seen when movement abilities (and other attributes) are factor-analyzed at various age levels. Although there is sketchy evidence that the attribute pattern becomes more complex as one ascends the "age scale" (Cratty, 1979), the exact nature of this proliferation of attributes is not clearly spelled out. Information of this nature would result not only in more valid and useful evaluation instruments but also in programs containing components closely aligned with the number of separate attribute areas (factors) unique to a specified age group.

Perceptual versus Motor Assessment

The beginnings of work which emerged in the 1970s attempting to separate motor versus perceptual functioning was documented in the previous section (Colarusso and Hammill, 1972). This type of investigation needs expansion and continuation. When a child exhibits apraxic behavior, for example, it seems important to determine if the confused motor planning is a result of the child's failure to perceive a demonstrated movement series correctly, whether there is an integration problem, whether proper movement sequences seem difficult to reproduce, or whether some combination of these components troubles the child. The contrasting of a child's praxic behaviors with other data obtained via motor-free perceptual tests and "pure" movement assessments might aid in the clearing up of this kind of problem.

Similarly, it seems important to determine just how an auditory perceptual problem may be interacting with movement abilities. Does a child who cannot adequately perceive verbal directions given by another or internalized self-directions tend to evidence movement deficits? Studies with populations of deaf or hard-of-hearing youngsters might shed some light on this kind of subtle interaction between auditory perception, language, and motor abilities.

Early Motor Capacities and Later Intelligence

As has been pointed out, the early indices of movement capacities are not good predictors of later intelligence (Hofstaetter, 1954). However, the data available from longitudinal studies (Kagan & Moss, 1962) do not include extensive reference to movement attributes. Not only are studies of this nature needed, but, with a more sophisticated approach to the nature of human intelligence, further work could also concentrate upon whether or not children endowed with adequate or superior movement capacities evidence different cognitive styles or strategies than are seen in the motorically less able youngster.

The opportunities for young children to carry out simple behaviors in order to test hypotheses (just *what* floats in the toilet?) seems dependent upon at least average movement capacities. Does the absence or blunting of these capacities lead to other ways of intellectual coping or even to the diminuation of intellectual behaviors later in life? The data are not too clear on this point at the present time.

Language and Speech

Clinicians, including this writer, have often noted that children with speech articulation problems are overrepresented in populations of youngsters evidencing other types of movement problems involving both the larger and smaller muscle groups. Some therapists have suggested that the improvement of head control and of generalized movement capacities causes improvement in speech. Experimental work exploring these interesting suppositions seems warranted.

Language enrichment programs have long contained opportunities for youngsters to play, and to otherwise act out tasks which they are asked to describe in words (Currant & Cratty, 1979). Studies attempting to verify the importance of overt action versus passive listening in programs of this nature would appear useful.

The tendency of younger children to precode movements verbally suggests innumerable studies in both applied and theoretical developmental linguistics (Luria, 1961). Does a movement deficiency signal garbled internal speech? Are totally deaf children, purportedly deficient in internal speech, handicapped when beginning to engage in complex movements? These and similar questions would seem to be fruitful queries to explore.

The Awkward Child

One of the most obvious needs is to obtain data determining just how one may improve movement attributes of children with moderate to severe awkwardness. Current data reflect both sketchy clinical techniques and weak research designs. Most available studies present entire programs of enrichment to a group of children, and separating just what components contribute in what ways to what kinds of improvement is a difficult undertaking.

Further work, combining the insights of the neurologist with those of the developmental psychologist and movement specialists, might identify more clearly the various neuromotor types, as suggested by Cohen (1969). It is apparent that youngsters closely resembling each other in movement characteristics, age, sex, and other morphological parameters, respond differently to the same therapies given for the same duration of time. With a more sophisticated assessment of such youngsters, the design of individualistic programs conforming to various neuromotor types could be a helpful outcome.

Recent theorizing by Schmidt and his colleagues concerning the concept of "generalized motor programs" also suggests innumerable productive studies (Shapiro & Schmidt, 1981). They suggest that movements are not acquired in highly specific ways, but that several types of general patterns of movement seem to be learned and demonstrated by children and adults. However, the breadth of these patterns and the number of more specific types of tasks they may contain is not clear at this point. Further delineation of the breadth of generalized motor programs should prove useful in the design of remedial programs. Pursuing this concept should result in program content which transfers optimum ways to culturally valued sports skills, to self-care tasks, and to basic locomotor activities.

In addition, the results of early stimulation upon motor development should be researched. The results of the study by Zelazo, Zelazo, and Kolb (1972) suggest that perhaps reflex training might hasten the onset of various basic movement patterns.

Other Directions

There are numerous other directions which further research might take with regard to the motor development of the preschool child. Four more topics are (1) the problems of differences in the numerous ethnic-racial subgroups found in the United States; (2) the influence of child-rearing practices upon possible and potential motor development; (3) the components and general nature of the play environment provided for the preschool child; and (4) needed biomechanical analyses of movement behaviors within a developmental framework. These problem areas are not mutually exclusive. For example, child-rearing practices seem to relate, at least moderately, to ethnic-racial elements. A detailed knowledge of the biomechanics of movement tasks, viewed developmentally, is more than useful when attempting to educate parents in how they may contribute to the enrichment of these same behaviors. In addition, the nature of the play environment provided has important ethnic overtones as well as implications for parent education and child-rearing practices.

ETHNIC-RACIAL CONSIDERATIONS

Well-documented and relatively consistent differences in the manner in which infants exhibit motor competencies have been reported in numerous studies. One of the most thorough reviews of this literature was carried out by E. E. Werner (1972). For example, it is a consistent finding that infants reared in pre-industrial societies in the so-called traditional ways (including black infants and children in Africa and those in certain Latin-American tribes) exhibit marked motor precocity. Within the first eight to ten months of life, these children exhibit initial acceleration in head control and in the stages leading to an upright gait, which places them from three to six weeks ahead of the Caucasian infant born in an industrialized society. Often, this early acceleration dissipates, however, as the child from the "primitive" village is weaned. When these same infants are provided adequate diets after weaning, as is true within the industrialized portions of emerging African countries, their development continues to surpass that of white children. These findings do not always parallel racial lines, for the same precocity has been found in Caucasian children reared under primitive conditions in India.

Numerous interacting variables apparently contribute to this early precocity as well as to the advanced development before weaning. These include the previous stresses placed on the young within the ethnic groups studied, including the necessity to quickly gain head control while being carried constantly on the mothers' backs, and to gain locomotion quickly during the end of the first year, so that they do not continue to be a physical burden to the hard-working parent. Moreover, child-rearing practices which include feeding and toileting on demand, constant tactile stimulation from the mother's body day and night, as well as frequent handling by others in the village, further seem to contribute to early success in physical tasks.

Studies from other cultures seem to indicate that undue physical restriction in the form of clothing, studied in both a Japanese population and a primitive Mexican tribe, can delay the emergence of movement attributes; as can too little attention (E. E. Werner, 1972).

These findings suggest a number of research directions. Among the first, barely begun, is to ascertain just what kinds of racial-ethnic differences exist between and among the numerous and varied sub-groups in the United States and the degree to which these differences are reflected in intragroup consistencies in child-rearing practices, which in turn may reflect in the manner in which the infants born to these groups evidence either delay or precocity in motor development. The findings of this kind of survey would also suggest the possible influence of racial-ethnic genotypes emanating from the part of the world from which various groups have their origins. Upon gaining this kind of information, further steps taken might include ethnic-specific programs of motor development intended to either enhance the normals or enrich the delayed within each subpopulation. Moreover, parental training programs might be tied into the characteristic manner in which that ethnic-racial group rears its children, as well as to the motor characteristics evidenced by children born to the racial-ethnic subgroup under consideration.

CHILD-REARING PRACTICES

Studies could be carried out based upon the evidence gained from apparently helpful child-rearing practices found in so-called primitive societies. These studies, perhaps employing institutionalized infants as subjects, could attempt to replicate those practices which appear to aid in the acceleration of motor capacities found within populations of children who have been traditionally reared in pre-industrial societies.

The research by Sears et al. (1957) could be extended to determine how restrictions imposed upon young children may influence their motor development. Two types of restriction are geographical restriction within the neighborhood and constraint of body movements through clothing, which have been found to associate with delayed motor development.

Even more subtle practices may influence motor development and could be explored as possible causal variables. For example, the frequency with which the infant is placed on the stomach by mothers in Westernized cultures, in contrast to other cultures, may serve to restrict manipulative behaviors.

Linguists might give clues as to the degree to which various cultures value assistive behaviors in parents as they work with their children's physical development. For example, many African languages are rich with words of this nature, reflecting various techniques and an interest in accelerating motor development. The incidence and the type of assistance given to the child as it matures motorically varies from home to home within a similar ethnic group in the United States. A survey of these practices, as related to the emerging motor abilities of the children within these various households, would seem a fruitful direction for further studies (Curran & Cratty, 1979).

A final type of research involving the parent–child interaction could consist of teaching the mother and father to optimize the environment and/or their child-rearing practices with the intent to hasten physical development. Possible influencing variables such as parent attitudes, controls, personality, and liking for the child, as well as mother-father feelings and attitudes might be explored to determine just what kinds of personal-social qualities need to be present in order to promote the best home program for the enhancement of physical attributes.

PLAY ENVIRONMENTS

Preschool children, when placed in environments containing various kinds of equipment, surrounded by an emotionally supportive staff, usually engage in high levels of productive physical activity, reflective of promoting social, emotional, and intellectual growth. Throughout the years, numerous researchers have attempted to ascertain just what components of the play environment seem to promote the most productive kind of exploratory motor activity.

Often, sorting out just what components of a multifaceted situation promote what attributes is a difficult undertaking. However, at the present time it seems that the presence of an optimum amount of toys, including wheeled vehicles, elicits high levels of social interaction. Children apparently prefer privacy at times and like to retreat into opaque boxes rather than into transparent ones to achieve this privacy. These enclosures at times promote social interactions as two or more children "club up" in a box, cave, or other enclosure which permits them to cut off extraneous stimuli. As they communicate, however, optimum motor activity reflective of other processes seems to be dependent upon how easily the child itself modifies the components of the play situation. The "Junk Playground" movement in England is a testament to this; vacant lots containing junk permit children to explore, imagine, manipulate and otherwise have an effect upon the facilities and equipment with which they are surrounded. In contrast, the typical playground whose equipment is set in cement, elicits interest and exploration for brief periods, but then is abandoned, as the youths turn to more challenging endeavors.

Within this type of research, play environments could be presented as having varying degrees of modifiability; posttests could include those which evaluate not only possible modifications in motor competencies, but such cognitive and perceptual abilities as divergent thought and perceptual flexibility.

BIOMECHANICAL ANALYSES

Since the 1930s, filmed analyses of children's movement behaviors have appeared in the literature. Halverson's look at prehensive behaviors is only one example (Halverson, 1931). These studies, however, are not numerous nor have they encompassed a wide variety of basic movement attributes. Wickstrom's text has summarized some of the more useful of these (Wickstrom, 1970).

Additional work in this important area is needed. A look at gait characteristics, including walking, running, landing, and jumping as well as other locomotor behaviors, would be useful from several standpoints. A thorough look at the torques, forces, and spatial parameters of walking as a function of age would afford an important insight into the manner in which therapists might work best with pathological gait problems. Norms of this type, carried out with neurologically intact children, would afford comparative tools with which a child evidencing some kind of developmental lag might be compared to ascertain (1) whether the problem involves simply a delay but is otherwise a normal type of walking behavior; or (2) whether the gait seen in the problem child is pathological and perhaps reflective of some mild to moderate form of the traditional types cerebral palsy (for instance, lower limb ataxia).

Additional analyses of this kind, particularly those geared to uncover the causes of sex differences in both pre- and post-pubescent children and youth, would be valuable.

References

AYRES, A. J. *Sensory Integration and Learning Disorders.* Western Psychological Services, Los Angeles, California, 1972.

AYRES, A. J. Cluster analyses of measures of sensory integration. *The American Journal of Occupational Therapy,* 1977, *31,* 363–366.

BAYLEY, N. Behavioral correlates of mental growth—Birth to thirty-six years. *American Psychologist,* 1968, *23,* 1–17.

BOWER, T. G. R. *Development in Infancy.* San Francisco, Calif.: W. H. Freeman & Co., 1974.

BOWER, T. G. R. The development of object performance: Some studies of existence constancy. *Perception and Psychophysics,* 1967, *2,* 411–418.

BOWER, T. G. R., BROUGHTON, J. M., and MOORE, M. K. The development of the object concept as manifested by changes in the tracking behavior of infants between 7 and 20 weeks of age. *Journal of Experimental Child Psychology,* 1971, *11,* 182–193.

BOWER, T. G. R., and PATERSON, J. R. Stages in the development of the object concept. *Cognition,* 1972, *1,* 47–56.

BOWER, T. G. R., and WIHART, J. G. The effects of motor skill on object permanence. *Cognition,* 1972, *1,* 165–172.

COHEN, L. A. Manipulation of cortical motor responses by peripheral sensory stimulation. *Archives of Physical Medicine and Rehabilitation,* 1969, *50,* 495–505.

COLARUSSO, R., and HAMMILL, D. *The Motor Free Visual Perception.* San Rafael, Calif.: Academic Therapy Publication, 1972.

CRATTY, B. J. Perceptual-motor theories in the 1980's: A new look. *Proceedings,* International Congress in Psychomotor Behavior, University of Quebec, Trois Rivières, Quebec, 1979.

CRATTY, B. J. *Perceptual and Motor Development in Infants and Children.* Englewood Cliffs, N.J.: Prentice-Hall, 1979.

CRATTY, B. J. *Adapted Physical Education for Handicapped Children and Youth.* Denver, Col.: Love Publishing Co., 1980.

CRATTY, B. J. Sensory-motor and perceptual-motor theories and practices: An overview and evaluation. In Walk, R., and Pick, H., eds., *Perception and Experience,* New York: Plenum Press, 1981.

CRATTY, B. J., KEDO, M., MARTIN, M. M., JENNE, H. C., and MORRIS, M. *Movement Activities, Motor Ability and the Education of Children.* Springfield, Ill.: Charles C. Thomas, 1970.

CURRAN, J., and CRATTY, B. J. *Speech and Language Problems in Children*. Denver, Col.: Love Publishing Co., 1979.

DOLL, E. A. *Measurement of Social Competence*. American Guidance Service, Inc., Circle Pines, Minn., 1952.

FANTZ, R. L. Pattern vision in newborn infants. *Science*, 1963, *140*, 296–297.

FRANKENBURG, W. K., DODDS, J. B., and FANDAL, A. W. *Denver Developmental Screening Test*, University of Colorado Medical Center, 1970.

FROSTIG, M. *Developmental Test of Visual Perception*. Palo Alto, Calif.: Consulting Psychologist Press, 1964.

GOODMAN, L., and HAMMILL, D. The effectiveness of the Kephart-Getman activities in the developing perceptual-motor and cognitive skills. *Focus on Exceptional Children*, 1973, *4*, 121–126.

HALVERSON, H. M. An experimental study of prehension in infants by means of systematic cinema records. *Genetic Psychology Monographs*, 1931, *10*, 107–286.

HEBBELINCK, M., and BOREMS, T. A multidisciplinary longitudinal growth study. *Proceedings*, Introduction of the Project LLEGS. 21st International World Congress of Sports Medicine, Brasilia, Brazil, September 1978.

HOFSTAETTER, P. R. The changing composition of "intelligence": A study in T-technique. *Journal of Genetic Psychology*, 1954, *85*, 159–164.

HONZIK, M. P., MacFARLANE, J. W., and ALLEN, L. The stability of mental test performance between two and eighteen years. *Journal of Experimental Education*, 1948, *17*, 309–324.

JOHNSON, D. L., BREKKE, B., and HARLOW, S. D. Appropriateness of the motor-free visual perceptual test when used with the mentally retarded. *Education and Training of the Mentally Retarded*, 1977, *10*, 312–315.

KAGAN, J., and MOSS, H. A. *Birth to Maturity: A Study in Psychological Development*. New York: Wiley and Sons, 1962.

Koontz, C. W. *Koontz Child Developmental Program*. Western Psychological Services, Los Angeles, Calif., 1978.

LIPSITT, L. P., and KAYE, H. Conditioned sucking in the human newborn. *Psychonomic Science*, 1964, *1*, 29–30.

LURIA, A. R. *The Role of Speech in the Regulation of Normal and Abnormal Behavior*. London: Pergamon Press, 1961.

MANN, L. Perceptual trainings mis-directions and re-directions. *American Journal of Orthopsychiatry*, 1970, *40*, 18–23.

MYERS, P. I., and HAMMILL, D. *Methods for Learning Disorders*, 2d ed., New York: Wiley and Sons, 1976.

PIAGET, J. *The Language and Thought of the Child*, trans. M. Gabain. London: Routledge & Kegan Paul, 1926.

PIAGET, J. *The Origins of Intelligence in Children*, trans. M. Cook. New York: International Universities Press, 1952.

PIKLER, E. Data on cross motor development of the infant. *Child Development and Care*, 1972, *3*, 297–310.

SAIDA, Y., and MITSUMASA, N. Development of fine motor skill in children: Manipulation of a pencil in young children aged 2–6 years old. *Journal of Human Movement Studies*, 1979, *5*, 104–113.

SCHANEY, Z., BREKKE, B., LANDRY, R., and BURKE, J. Effects of a perceptual-motor training program on kindergarten children. *Perceptual and Motor Skills*, 1976, *43*, 428–430.

SCARR-SALAPATEC, S., and WILLIAMS, M. L. The effects of early stimulation on low birth-weight infants. *Child Development*, 1973, *44*, 94–101.

SEARS, R. R., MACCOBY, E. E., and LEVINE, H. *Patterns of Child Rearing*. Evanston, Ill.: Row Peterson, 1957.

SHAPIRO, D. C., and SCHMIDT, R. A. The schema theory: Recent evidence and developmental implications. In Kelso, J. A. S., and Clark, J. (eds.), *The Development of Motor Control and Coordination*. New York: Wiley and Sons, 1981.

SIQUELAND, E. R. Continued sucking and visual reinforcers with human infants. Unpublished Paper, Brown University, February 1967.

STOTT, D. H., MOYES, F. A., and HENDERSON, S. A. *Test of Motor Impairment*. Brook Educational Publishing, Ltd. P.O. Box 1171, Guelph, Ontario, Canada, 1972.

UZGIRIS, I. C. Ordinality in the development of schemas for relating to objects. In J. Hellmuth (ed.), *Exceptional Infants*, 1967, *1*, 315–334.

WEIDERHOLT, J. L. Historical perspectives on the education of the learning disabled. In Mann, L., and Sabatino, D. A. (eds.), *The Second Review of Special Education*. Philadelphia: Grune and Stratton, 1975.

WERNER, E. E. Infants around the world: Cross-cultural studies of psychomotor development from birth to two years. *Journal of Cross-Cultural Psychology*, 1972, *3*, 111–134.

WERNER, P. Education of selected movement patterns of pre-school children. *Perceptual and Motor-Skills*, 1974, *39*, 795–798.

WICKSTROM, R. L. *Fundamental Motor Patterns*. Philadelphia: Lea and Febiger, 1970.

ZELAZO, P. R., ZELAZO, N. A., and KOLB, S. Walking in the newborn. *Science*, 1972, *176*, 314–315.

CHAPTER 3

Language Acquisition: Phenomenon, Theory, and Research

Eugene E. Garcia

THE STUDY OF LANGUAGE continues to expose more and more complex problems in theories of linguistics, cognition, and socialization. What was once a study of linguistic structure has become today an interlocking study of linguistic, psychological, and social domains, each important in its own right, but together converging in broader attempts to construct and reconstruct the nature of language. These converging perspectives acknowledge the multifaceted nature of social interaction.

Within the last few years, research in language acquisition has shifted from the study of one native language (Brown, 1973; Gonzalez, 1970) to the comparative study of children from diverse linguistic societies (Bowerman, 1975; Braine, 1976). This chapter deals with the study of young children acquiring the native language of English. Yet, for many children, multilingual acquisition is the norm. Therefore, the present treatment of language acquisition will include the phenomena of second language acquisition and bilingual acquisition in early childhood.

Native Language Acquisition: A Task Analysis

Within the last few decades, interest in language acquisition has been intense and has consistently resulted in a multiplicity of methods, terms, and, of course, research publications. I will in no way attempt to do justice to this immense body of literature, but I will attempt to summarize and discuss major trends in this field inasmuch as they relate to the basic topic of interest here. For more detailed reviews of monolingual language acquisition, several other publications (some technical, others not as technical) are recommended: Menyuk, 1971; Cazden, 1972; Brown, 1973; Lenneberg and Lenneberg, 1975; Braine, 1976; Bloom, 1978; and de Villiers and de Villiers, 1978.

When we consider the observation and documentation of language, it seems appropriate to conclude that "languages are composed of speech sounds, syllables, morphemes and sentences, and meaning is largely conveyed by the properties and particular use of these units" (Menyuk, 1971, p. 21). Therefore, language can be seen as a regularized system. Native speakers of a language can make judgments concerning this regularity by considering whether or not any utterance makes "sense." Although the emphasis has been placed on languages' structural regularity, additional evidence (Bloom, 1978) clearly indicates that structure cannot stand alone. That is, the meaning of an utterance is conveyed by both its formal structure and the specific environment in which it occurs. Therefore, for any verbal signal to make "sense," we must also consider the physical and social characteristics of the surrounding environment.

Moreover, particular physical characteristics of the utterance itself (the intonation, stress, speed, and so on, of the utterance) are important. These characteristics become more and more significant during the study of early language acquisition when the structure of the child's utterance is limited yet functioning of verbal communication is quite complex. In sum, the effect of any verbal signal depends on its linguistic, physical character in conjunction with its social context.

Children's acquisition of their native linguistic competence can be characterized as a continuum, moving from simple one-word utterances to more complex word combinations (syntax). If one ignores the functional use of crying as the beginning of communicative competence, then single word utterances, usually very idiosyncratic (for example, "papa" for food), mark the first distinguishable stage for formalized language development. To move beyond this early stage, the child faces developmental tasks associated with phonology, morphology, syntax, and semantics.

Phonology

This form of information available to the infant is characterized by articulatory and acoustic features of speech sounds. Therefore, any word's (or utterance's) basic physical constituent is the sound or combination of sounds which make it distinguishable from another sound or combination of sounds. The specific distinctive features and the "rules" for using these features are not evident at this time and are a source of continuous investigation. Evidence of phonological discrimination in infants four to six weeks of age is available (Morse, 1974) although the exact nature of such discrimination as it is related to linguistic development is unclear (Morse, 1974; Eimas, 1974; Fergusen and Garnica, 1975). An international alphabet of phonemes categorizes the various individual speech sounds which are found throughout the world. Phonologists can therefore transcribe or code the sounds of language and in some cases mechanically duplicate these sounds. It is the task of the child to differentiate between the sounds in his environment, much like the phonologist, and then duplicate and structure these sound systems into communicative networks. At this level, it seems crucial for the child to receive phonological input; he does not come preprogrammed for any one class of sound systems.

Morphology

Morphemes can be considered the smallest meaningful unit of speech (Cazden, 1972). "Free" morphemes are the first to occur in early language. These units can stand alone: "mommy," "daddy." "Blend" morphemes are developed later and cannot occur alone but must be attached to other morphemes. These include verb inflections like *ed* and *ing* and noun inflections like *s* (for pluralization and possession). Extensive studies which have traced the development of certain morphemes longitudinally in the same children have detailed a reliable order of development for specific morphemes in English speakers (Brown, 1973; de Villiers and de Villiers, 1973). The use of morpheme development as an index of developmental language complexity is best exemplified by work with the now famous Cambridge children: Adam, Eve, and Sarah (Brown, 1973). Of significance in this detailed longitudinal study was the clear rise in linguistic ability as measured by the Mean Length of Utterance (MLU) over time and the individual differences across subjects in this rise.

Syntax

Syntactic rules identify sequential relationships of verbal units and in doing so describe one further systematic regularized character of language. In English we are accustomed to word strings beginning with a subject (a noun or noun phrase), followed by a verb or verb phrase, and terminated with an object (a noun or noun phrase related to the verb). Of course, this description is only an ideal mapping of pieces we call sentences. Utterances in typical human discourse frequently exclude one or more of these units and rely on the context of the utterance to convey the proper meaning. For example, the utterance "Bill" under particular circumstances may be restated as one of a number of fully formed sentences. "Come in the house, Bill"; "Bill, look at me"; "Bill, open the door"; and so on.

Of interest in the study of syntax has been the development of transformational strategies (Chomsky, 1965). Transformational rules, by operations such as addition, deletion, permutation, and substitution among strings of words, act to change the meaning of that string (Menyuk, 1971). Through the use of relative clauses and conjunctions, indefinitely long sentences can be produced by any speaker consciously or unconsciously aware of transformation operations.

Semantics

The semantic component of language might best be characterized as an individual or community dictionary of a specific individual's language or of the language of several individuals. Just as I have attempted to define phonology, syntax, and semantics in these pages, each unit of speech must be defined in order to serve any meaningful function. Definitions of any linguistic unit may not be formalized in the spoken language of young children yet they are as important to the functioning of language as formal definitions are in written prose. For instance, a child's utterance of "cucu" may be defined both for him and his audience by its function, "asking for a cookie." Confusions in definition often occur due to the differential experience with a particular unit of speech. It is clear that this same sort of definitional confusion is also operating among adults. (The term "coffee regular" in most regions of the United States indicates the absence of cream or sugar; in parts of New England and in New York City this same term specifies the addition of cream.) Countless examples such as these are readily available to each of us.

Therefore, interpretation of a sentence such as "the girl jumped rope" requires knowledge concerning the properties of each constituent part, "girl," "jumped," and "rope." Yet, the string of these parts placed together in the sentence are just as important a facet of the sentence as its individual parts. That is, the *syntagmatic* relationship of these parts (how they are placed in sequence) reveals significant information concerning the relationship of those parts.

Linguistic Variability

Two terms are frequently used to describe the major diversity of language: *idiolect* and *dialect*. The first term is used to recognize each person's unique linguistic experiences and how they shape that person's individual language. A group of similar idiolects that differs from other groups with respect to phonology, morphology, and so on, identifies a dialect. It is therefore the case that "similar" dialects usually make up an identifiable language group. This in turn suggests the nonexistence of a "pure" language. Theoretically, "nonstandard" dialects can be assumed to be equally well developed and systematic. Independent of its theoretical validity, the notion of dialect equivalence with regard to development and regularization receives empirical support from the extensive research on black dialect patterns (Labov, 1970). Labov and his colleagues have pointed out several systematic differences between black english and what is normally identified as the dialect of standard English. The research describes the verb form *be* "to indicate generally repeated action, or existential state in sentences such as 'He be with us'; 'They be fooling around' " (Labov and Cohen, 1967, p. 76). An additional study by Henrie (1969) found that urban black children used unconjugated *be* ("he always be there") to express habitual meaning in a task requiring them to retell a story they had heard in standard English.

Physical, geographic separation is one variable that accounts for such linguistic diversity. Although this is a common and clearly observable explanation, dialects occur under other circumstances. For instance, the speech of parents (or any adult) to young children differs significantly from adult speech. Snow and Ferguson (1977) have documented and discussed this interesting and consistent form of linguistic differentiation as more simple and more redundant. In fact, the overall speech of young children might be considered a dialect as it is presently defined here. (It is important to note that the term dialect is usually constrained to the description of adult, fully mature speech competencies.) Of major significance is that speakers develop diverse linguistic repertoires and that this is the norm not the exception.

Due to its importance in the investigation of social class differences in speech usage, another concept related to linguistic diversity needs to be raised here: speech code. Historically, the concept of speech code can be traced to the early work of Basal Bernstein, an English sociologist who was concerned with the different linguistic styles of middle class and working class children in English (Bernstein, 1961). The speech of these children was reportedly classified into "restricted codes" and "elaborated codes." Restricted code was characterized by indexical speech, speech that presumes some high degree of shared knowledge. Therefore, this speech was described as usually much shorter (in terms of utterance length) and less specific in character. The elaborated code, on the other hand, was more formal in the sense that no shared knowledge was presumed. This speech made use of more adjectives, adverbs, and clauses. Lower class children were described as using only a restricted code while middle class children could switch between codes depending on the environmental demands. Although these formulations are clearly still a major focus of controversy, they are discussed here to serve as an introduction to the form of linguistic diversity later referred to as "codes."

For children who are acquiring more than one language, the issue of codes is one of great importance. That is, since these individuals have two topographically distinct forms of language, how, when and why does language switching (typically referred to as code switching) occur? Is this yet another linguistic attribute which the bilingual person must be concerned with in terms of acquisition? This issue is discussed briefly here with reference to monolingualism to stress the linguistic reality that all speakers (monolingual or bilingual) most probably are immersed in social environments that control the form of their linguistic behavior. Hymes (1974) has explicitly detailed some of the variables which must be considered in determining the code or style of the speaker and the ability of the listener to "make sense" of variations:

SETTING

This represents where and when the speech act is taking place. Children are generally allowed to be louder outside than in, for instance, and may already have learned they are supposed to whisper (or not talk at all) in church.

PARTICIPANTS

Age, sex, kinship, social class, education, or occupation may make a difference. An English speaker would seldom have difficulty identifying the listener in a conversation with a young child by the speaker's grammar, word choice, and intonation (although the same style is sometimes used with pets). Many languages have different pronominal forms to indicate social distance, and the sex of a speaker, to some extent, determines appropriate word choice.

ENDS

Style sometimes depends on purpose, whether the speech act is a request, demand, query, warning, or more a statement of information.

ACT SEQUENCE

This refers to the prescribed form a speech act takes when it is closely controlled by the culture, as is usually the case with prayers, public speeches or lectures, and jokes. It also refers to what may be talked about in each—what can be appropriately prayed about in contrast to what can be appropriately joked about.

KEY

The same words may express various tones, moods, manner (serious, playful, belligerent, sarcastic). The signal may be nonverbal, such as a wink or gesture, or conveyed by intonation, word choice, or some other linguistic convention.

INSTRUMENTALITIES

Different verbal codes may be selected. Even a monolingual will have a choice of registers (varieties along a formal–informal continuum). Many speakers are able to choose among regional and social dialects as well. The choice is usually an unconscious one and may indicate respect, insolence, humor, distance, or intimacy.

NORMS

Norms of interaction and interpretation in a speech act include taking turns in speaking (if appropriate in the speaker's culture), knowing the proper voice level to express anger, and sharing understandings about such things as what to take seriously and what to discount. It includes knowing polite greeting forms and other "linguistic manners," like what not to talk about at the dinner table.

GENRES

Some speech acts may be categorized in formal structures: poem, myth, tale, proverb, riddle, curse, prayer, oration, lecture, editorial. Even children are often expected to know a few of the forms appropriate to their culture, including the "Once upon a time . . ." of middle-class English (Hymes, 1974, pp. 47–48).

Native Language Acquisition: Theoretical Perspectives

It is this multifaceted nature of language that the developing child comes face to face with when achieving communicative competence. It is possible to conclude that by a very early age, children have mastered a large segment of their linguistic environment. That is, without little seemingly systematic effort on the part of parents, a child has developed a significant portion of linguistic and social interaction competency within the first five to six years of his life. The child is able to understand and produce complex forms of language at this time. Complexity is defined here in terms of the linguistic features discussed earlier: phonology, morphology, syntax, and semantics. In addition, the child is capable of code switches, or shifts which serve to clarify his speech productions and his understanding of his social interactions.

How does he tackle this myriad of tasks? Chomsky (1965) considers language as dichotomous in nature consisting of linguistic *competence* and linguistic *performance*. The first attribute of language is concerned with the speaker's linguistic knowledge; the second, with the speaker's actual linguistic productions. Chomsky relegates the duties of the child to that of a linguist: the child must determine from relevant linguistic information in his environment the underlying systems of rules in order to generate appropriate linguistic performances. As indicated earlier in the chapter, it does not seem appropriate to restrict our interest in language to a pure structural analysis. Yet, Chomsky's definition served as a theoretical base for much of the research presently available on young children. The structure of children's speech and their ability to perform transformations has been of prime interest. It is true that any analysis of language acquisition must account for the almost miraculous performance of young children with respect to generative speech. That is, any theoretical or conceptual treatment of language acquisition must account for the clear performance of children in understanding and producing utterances which they themselves have never heard. As Cazden (1981) has argued, acquisition of language does not seem to be related to environmentally oriented interactions which focus on the mechanisms of modeling or speech correction. This theoretical perspective would hold as most important the genetic base for language development and is reflective of a larger nativistic perspective represented in Chomsky's view of language.

An alternative environmental assistance, "learning" perspective, has concentrated on the mechanism of modeling and environmental feedback in considering the acquisition of language (Miller and Dollard, 1941; Skinner, 1957; Sherman, 1971; Baer, 1976). This conceptualization of language has had a significant effect on research that is clinically concerned with language training of language-deviant and -deficient populations (Garcia and DeHaven, 1974). This research has indicated the effectiveness of training specific instances of morphology and syntax using a training package that includes (1) shaping; (2) fading;

and (3) differential reinforcement. Central to these training efforts has been the use of imitation of "correct" speech forms and generalized use of trained speech beyond the specific stimulus/response parameters receiving attention during training. For instance, Guess (1968) trained a speech-deficient child first to imitate singular and plural labels, then, to label specific singular and plural instances of stimulus arrays without the aid of a model. As training progressed to various singular and plural sets, the subject was able to label correctly never-before-trained plural stimulus arrays. Training on a series of plural arrays produced a generalized plural response class. Similar demonstrations have been made available with preschool children (Garcia and Batista-Wallace, 1977) across various morphemes (Whitehurst, 1971, 1972; Sherman, 1971; Baer, 1976; Bricker and Bricker, 1974).

In contrast to the linguistic and learning conceptualization of language, a third environmental assistance alternative has recently received research attention. Within the developmental area, there exists an ongoing controversy over whether language influences cognition or whether cognition influences language. Piaget (1952) has long recognized that complex cognitive functioning occurs in young children who have yet to develop only the simplest of linguistic skills. He has proposed that language is a subset of cognitive and symbolic functioning. (Morehead and Morehead [1974] have directly related Piaget's cognitive development conceptualization to the process of language acquisition.) Vygotsky (1962), on the other hand, argues that higher levels of cognition originate in language. He proposed that certain concepts cannot be developed until language has "developed the capacity" to deal with these concepts. He holds that after the age of two years, emotions, perceptions, and social behavior are intimately related with linguistic experience. Independent of the locus of control (that is, whether language influences cognition or cognition influences language), there is a growing agreement that the two symbolic processes are intricately related (de Villiers and de Villiers, 1978).

Prutting (1979) selectively reviewed literature related to this cognitive-language interaction perspective. She summarized and organized the development of phonological, morphological, syntactic, and pragmatic communication behaviors in six stages from prelinguistic to the adult level. She argues that the ontogeny of linguistic behavior is directly related to the cognitive processes which the child is capable of at various stages of development. Although such a conclusion leaves unresolved the specific causal relationship between cognition and language, it clearly provides a conceptualization of language development cognizant of the relationship. Moreover, much like Piaget (1952), this stage-process position holds that the child is an active participant in his own development. Linguistic development is not as determined by some predetermined genetic code or selective schedule of reinforcement. Instead, language seems to be determined by the forces of maturation, cognitive development, and the environment. This last statement best characterizes the "majority" vote of those researchers who are presently active in the field of language acquisition.

In sum, native language acquisition must presently be considered within several conceptual domains. It seems most appropriate to acknowledge at least three major theoretical orientations: (1) linguistic; (2) learning; and (3) cognitive. It seems just as appropriate to emphasize that each position has its supporters and detractors. However, empirical research generated by each position has clearly advanced our understanding of language acquisition by emphasizing the empirical phenomena and the alternative processes that account for these phenomena. It seems evident that language acquisition is systematic. It can be described as a developmental phenomenon, with its present character dependent on its past character, and its development significantly related to environmental interaction. Although the descriptive account of its developmental character is unfolding, the exact causal relationship between environmental, cognitive, and linguistic parameters continues to be explored from the three theoretical perspectives.

Second Language Acquisition

The study of second language acquisition must be considered here due to its applicability both theoretically and methodologically to the issue of language acquisition. This form of research has been concerned with those variables operating in the acquisition of a second language after the native language has been acquired. Investigations of young children undergoing the process of second language acquisition have been completed only recently. Research in this area has borrowed extensively from the work in first language acquisition. That is, the same linguistic features have been of interest within the same methodological framework. Specifically, the procedure for accumulating data on second language acquisition has taken on two forms: (1) samples of spontaneous speech of the individual are gathered in his second language during periods of early, middle, and late exposure to the second language; and (2) cross-sectional investigations of individuals exposed for varying amounts of time to the second language are undertaken. Typically, investigations of the second type make use of specific language measurement instruments designed to maximize the probability of the occurrence of certain linguistic features.

In addition, second language acquisition research has made much use of contrastive analysis. This technique calls for the comparative analysis of Language 1 (L_1) with Language 2 (L_2) so as to identify phonological, morphological, and syntactic differences and similarities (Stockwell & Bowen, 1965). This form of analysis is used to predict the relative probability of linguistic errors due to the differences between L_1 and L_2. Therefore, if a speaker of Spanish is learning English, errors in adjective-noun syntactic placement may be frequent due to the differences in rules governing this syntactic relationship. Furthermore, it attempts to predict areas of positive transfer. For instance, plurals in Spanish and English are formed similarly by addition of an *s* or *es* inflection to singular noun. (This is an oversimplification, since there are other allomorphs in each language.) In this case, we might expect the L_2 learner to be able to transfer positively his past experiences with this morphological form due to previous experience with this inflectional derivative in L_1.

Dulay and Burt (1972, 1973) have used the above methodology to investigate the type of errors made by children who are second language learners. This extensive research effort has made use of cross-sectional administration of a speech elicitation instrument, *The Bilingual Syntax Measure* (BSM), in order to study the development of specific morphological classes. The BSM attempts to elicit production of target morphemes by combining the presentation of several cartoon pictures and strategic tester dialogue. Subjects' scores are determined by considering the number of utterances in which fully formed, partially correct morphemes are either present or absent in obligatory context. Morpheme order is determined by listing scores from highest percentage of occurrence to lowest percentage of occurrence. For experimental purposes, rank orders such as these are then used to compare morpheme development from one group of subjects (say, Spanish speakers learning English) to a second group of subjects (say, Chinese speakers learning English).

These studies with the BSM have led Dulay and Burt to make the following conclusions:

1. There is an invariant order of acquisition among second language learners with respect to grammatical morphemes (as measured by the BSM).
2. Fewer than 5 percent of all English errors are directly traceable to "interference" errors, errors related to L_1 forms.
3. Children learn a second language via a creative construction process: "they gradually reconstruct rules for the speech they hear guided by a universal innate mechanism" (Dulay & Burt, 1972; 1973).

The theoretical and applied implications seem clear from this conclusion. Theoretically, it would seem that L_2 acquisition is very much like L_1 acquisition. In fact, Dulay and Burt (1973), in a detailed analysis of the few errors which were observed during BSM administration, assigned responsibility for those errors to the "creative construction process" rather than previous L_1 rule-governing experiences. That is, observed errors were related more to language learning than to the influence of L_1–L_2 structure differences.

Several methodological and empirical considerations leave doubt in the conclusions drawn by the above researchers. First, the studies reported have used two techniques of considerable questionability with respect to measurement. The BSM is designed to elicit particular morpheme constructions under semicontrolled testing situations. The influence of "demand" characteristics posed by the tester, the stimuli, and the multitude of administration variables has been documented experimentally (Olmedo, 1977). Larson-Freeman (1976), in a comparative study of typical methods of collection of L_2 data, presents evidence indicating the differential influences of these methods on the number of specific L_2 errors. In addition, Hakuta (1974) has reported a different morpheme acquisition order than that reported by Dulay and Burt. His investigations considered the acquisition of English in a Japanese five-year-old but did so by collecting spontaneous speech samples on a longitudinal basis.

Even more recent are data by Rosansky (1976) detailing particular L_1 effects on L_2 acquisition for Spanish-speaking children and adults acquiring English. These data strongly suggest that morpheme acquisition order in L_2 is related to L_1 morpheme similarities. Garcia (1977), in a series of studies aimed at an experimental analysis of L_2 acquisition in three- to four-year-old children, showed a clear transfer effect due to L_1 language training manipulations. Moreover, in a detailed comparative study of L_2 acquisition using several language assessment techniques, including the BSM, Larson-Freeman (1976) found differences in morpheme orders of acquisition with measures other than the BSM. Given these series of empirical results, it is impossible to conclude validly that an invariant ordering of morphemes presently occurs during L_2 acquisition. (See Bailey, Madden & Krashen, 1974; Larson-Freeman, 1976; and Rosansky, 1976; for a more detailed review of L_2 acquisition.)

It is probably best to conclude that several theoretical formulations are presently available to account for the process and form of L_2 acquisition. McLaughlin (1978) best summarized the incongruencies in theoretical positions by admitting the unavailability of firm information pertaining to L_2 acquisition. He explicitly does so by detailing the following five unsubstantial beliefs widely held with respect to L_2 acquisition and language acquisition in general during early childhood.

1. The young child acquires a language much more quickly and easily than an adult because the child is biologically programmed to acquire languages, whereas the adult is not.
2. The younger the child, the more skilled in acquiring a second language.
3. Second language acquisition is a qualitatively different process than first language acquisition.
4. Interference between first and second language is an inevitable and ubiquitous part of second language acquisition.
5. There is a single method of second language acquisition instruction that is most effective with all children (McLaughlin, 1978, pp. 197–205).

Such beliefs have been generated through extensions of previous work with children acquiring their native language and adults acquiring a second language. Only recently has a major research effort begun to emerge with children acquiring a second language during the ages of two to five. Therefore, it is not justifiable at present to provide an unclouded single view concerning this important developmental phenomenon. Instead, various views, each worthy of consideration, emerge. A similar representation evolves in the consideration of early childhood bilingualism.

Bilingual Development

Certainly, one of the most impressive characteristics of child development is related to language acquisition. It seems remarkable that within the first few years of life, drastic changes in linguistic competence can clearly be identified

(Menyuk, 1971). Although the exact variables influencing this development are still not evident, research in this field has been voluminous and theoretically varied (Lenneberg and Lenneberg, 1975; de Villiers and de Villiers, 1978). The main focus of this research has centered on single language acquisition (Brown, 1973) although more recent research has employed cross-linguistic analysis with children who are learning different languages (Bowerman, 1975; Braine, 1974). Compared to these bodies of literature, very little systematic investigation is available regarding children who are acquiring more than one language, simultaneously, during the early part of their lives.

It does seem clear that a child can and does learn more than one linguistic communicative form in many societies throughout the world. Sorensen (1967) describes the acquisition of three to four languages by young children who live in the northwest Amazon region of South America. Although the Tukano tribal language serves as the lingua franca in the area, there continue to exist some twenty-five clearly distinguishable linguistic groups in this Brazilian-Columbian border region. In the United States, Skrabanek (1970) reports the continued acquisition and support of both English and Spanish language systems among preschool children of the Southwest for the last hundred years with no indication that this phenomenon will be disrupted. Although not apparent from a cursory scanning of linguistic literature, research with bilinguals is not a recent subarea of linguistic or psychological inquiry. Ronjat (1913) reports the development of French and German in his son. Finding little deleterious effects of bilingual development, he attributed such positive outcomes to the separation of the languages. In this particular case, one parent consistently spoke French and the other German. Pavlovitch (1920) also reports the development of two languages, French and Serbian, in his son. Similarly, languages were separated across individuals. The languages reportedly developed simultaneously with minimal confusion. Geissler (1938) reports, anecdotally, that as a teacher of foreign languages he had observed young children acquire up to four languages simultaneously without difficulty. It is only Smith (1935), in a study of missionary families who spoke English and Chinese, who reports difficulty during simultaneous acquisition. This difficulty was most apparent in the language-mixing character of the children's speech.

One of the first systematic investigations of bilingual acquisition in young children was reported by Leopold (1939, 1947, 1949a, 1949b). This author set out to study the simultaneous acquisition of English and German in his daughter. These initial descriptive reports indicate that as the subject was exposed to both languages during infancy, she seemed to weld both languages into one system during initial language production periods. For instance, early language forms were characterized by free mixing. Language production during later periods seemed to indicate that the use of English and German grammatical forms developed independently.

More recent studies have systematically addressed several issues relevant to bilingual acquisition. Carrow (1971, 1972) has restricted her study to the receptive domain of young bilingual Mexican-American children in the Southwest.

Children (ages three years 10 months to 6 years 9 months) from bilingual Spanish-English home environments were administered the Auditory Test for Language Comprehension. This test consists of a series of pictures representing referential categories that can be signaled by words, morphological constructions, grammatical categories, and syntactical structures. These include verbs, adjectives, adverbs, nouns, pronouns, morphological endings, prepositions, interrogatives, and syntactic complexity in both languages. A comparison of English and Spanish comprehension on this task for bilinguals revealed (Carrow, 1971) that: (1) linguistically, children were very heterogeneous; some scored better in one language than another, others were equal in both; (2) a greater proportion of children scored higher in English than in Spanish; (3) older children scored higher on these measures in both languages (this was the case even though Spanish was not used as a medium of instruction for children who were in educational programs).

In a cross-sectional comparison of English comprehension among monolingual English and bilingual Spanish-English children (ages three years ten months to six years nine months), Carrow (1972) reports a positive developmental trend for both Spanish and English in bilingual children. In addition, bilingual children tended to score lower than monolingual children on English measures during ages three years ten months to five years nine months; but for the final age comparison group (six years nine months), bilingual and monolingual children did not differ significantly on these same English measures. These combined results seem to indicate that at the receptive level, Spanish-English bilingual children were: (1) progressing (increasing their competence) in both Spanish and English; (2) heterogeneous as a group, favoring one language (typically English) over another; and (3) lagged behind monolingual children in their acquisition of English but eventually caught up. Although there are obvious constraints to the specific conclusion reported above and to their generalizations to other populations of bilingual children, they do offer some empirical information relevant to the study of early childhood bilingual development.

With respect to expressive development, Padilla and Liebman (1975) report the longitudinal analysis of Spanish-English acquisition in two three-year-old bilingual children. These researchers followed the model of Brown (1973) in recording linguistic interactions of children over a five-month period. Through an analysis of several dependent linguistic variables (phonological, grammatical, syntactic, and semantic characteristics) over this time period, they observed gains in both languages although several English forms were in evidence while similar Spanish forms were not. They also report the differentiation of linguistic systems at phonological, lexical, and syntactic levels. They conclude:

> The appropriate use of both languages even in mixed utterances was evidence, that is, correct word order was preserved. For example, there were no occurrences of "raining está" or "a es baby" but there was evidence for such utterances as "está raining" and "es a baby." There was also an absence of the redundance of unnecessary words which might tend to confuse meaning [Padilla and Liebman, 1975, p. 51].

Garcia (1981a) reports developmental data related to the acquisition of Spanish and English for Spanish-English bilingual preschoolers (three- to four-years-old) and the acquisition of English for a group of matched English-only speakers. The results of that study can be summarized as follows: (1) acquisition of both Spanish and English was more advanced based on the quantity and quality of obtained morphological and syntactic instances of language productions; and (2) there was no quantitative or qualitative difference between Spanish-English bilingual children and matched English-only controls on English language productions.

Huerta (1977) has provided a report of a longitudinal analysis for a Spanish-English bilingual two-year-old child. She reports a similar pattern of continuous Spanish-English development, although identifiable stages appeared in which one language forged ahead of the other. Moreover, she reports the significant occurrence of mixed language utterances which made use of both Spanish and English lexicon as well as Spanish and English morphology. In all such cases, these mixed linguistic utterances were well formed and communicative. Garcia (1981b), in a national study of bilingual children four, five, and six years of age, found regional differences in the relative occurrence of switched language utterances. That is, bilingual Spanish-English children from Texas, Arizona, Colorado, and New Mexico showed higher (15-20 percent) incidence of language-switched utterances than children from California, Illinois, New York, or Florida, especially at pre-kindergarten levels. These findings suggest that some children may very well develop an "interlanguage" in addition to the acquisition of two independent language systems later in development.

The above "developmental" findings can be capsulized succinctly but not without acknowledging their tentative nature:

1. The acquisition of more than one language during early childhood is a documented phenomenon.
2. The acquisition of two languages can be parallel but need not be so. That is, the qualitative character of one language may lag behind, surge ahead, or develop equally with the other language.
3. The acquisition of two languages may very well result in an interlanguage, incorporating the aspects of both languages.
4. The acquisition of two languages need not hamper, developmentally, the acquisition of either language.

Of course, these conclusions are very broad in character. The specific nature of bilingual development and its causal links to environmental and/or biological variables remains unavailable.

Conclusion

Research in the area of language acquisition continues to flood the market place of theoretical and empirical inquiry. Such enthusiam reflects both the commonality of the language acquisition experience and the magic of language itself. It is difficult to assess the significance of recent research due to the voluminousness of its character. This chapter has attempted to describe the common linguistic character in terms of the task set before a child in becoming a proficient speaker. Second, it has attempted to acknowledge three basic conceptualizations of language which have generated research excitement in the last decade. Last, it has incorporated research which has focused on second language acquisition and bilingual acquisition because of both theoretical and educational interest recently generated in multilingual populations.

The chapter can best be understood as a selective review of those issues surrounding language acquisition. This statement is not meant as an apology for such selectivity. Instead, it acknowledges the broad base of interest in language acquisition and its relationship to other aspects of human development.

References

ARENAS, S. Bilingual/bicultural programs for preschool children. *Children Today*, 1975, July and August.

BAER, D. M. The organism as host. *Human Development*, 1976, *19*, 87–98.

BAILEY, N., MADDEN, L., and KRASHEN, S. Is there a "natural sequence" in adult second language learning? *Language Learning*, 1974, *24*, 233–243.

BERNSTEIN, B. Social class and linguistic development: A theory of social learning. In A.H. Halsey, J. Floud, and C.A. Anderson (eds.), *Education, Economy and Society*. New York: Free Press, 1961.

BLOOM, L. *Readings in Language Development*. New York: Wiley, 1978.

BOWERMAN, M. Crosslinguistic similarities at two stages of syntactic development. In E. Lenneberg and E. Lenneberg (eds.), *Foundations of Language Development*. London: UNESCO Press, 1975.

BRAINE, M. D. S. Children's first word combinations. *Monographs of the Society for Research in Child Development*, 1976, *41*.

BRICKER, W., and BRICKER, D. An early language training strategy. In R.L. Schiefelbush and L. Lloyd (eds.), *Language perspectives: Acquisition, Retardation and Intervention*. Baltimore, Md.: University Park Press, 1974.

BROWN, R. A. *A First Language: The Early Stages*. Cambridge, Mass.: Harvard University Press, 1973.

CARROW, E. Comprehension of English and Spanish by preschool Mexican-American children. *Modern Language Journal*, 1971, 55, 299–306.

CARROW, E. Auditory comprehension of English by monolingual and bilingual preschool children. *Journal of Speech and Hearing Research*, 1972, *15*, 407–457.

CAZDEN, C. B. *Child Language and Education*. New York: Holt, Rinehart and Winston, 1972.

CAZDEN, C. B. Language development and the preschool environment. In C. B. Cazden (ed.), *Language in Early Childhood Education*. (rev. ed.) Washington, D.C.: NAEYC, 1981.

CHOMSKY, N. *Aspects of the Theory of Syntax.* Cambridge, Mass.: M.I.T. Press, 1965.

DE VILLIERS, J. G., and DE VILLIERS, P. A cross-sectional study of the acquisition of grammatical morphemes. *Journal of Psycholinguistic Research,* 1973, *2,* 267–278.

DE VILLIERS, J. G., and DE VILLIERS, P. *Language Acquisition.* Cambridge, Mass.: Harvard University Press, 1978.

DULAY, H. C., and BURT, M. K. Goofing: An indication of children's second language learning strategies. *Language Learning,* 1972, *22,* 235–252.

DULAY, H.C., and BURT, M.K. Should we teach children syntax? *Language Learning,* 1973, *23,* 245–258.

EDELMAN, M. The contextualization of school children's bilingualism. *Modern Language Journal,* 1969, *53,* 179–182.

EIMAS, P. D. Linguistic processing of speech by young infants. In R. L. Schiefelbush and L. L. Lloyd (eds.), *Language Perspectives.* Baltimore, Md.: University Park Press, 1974.

EVANS, J. S. Word-pair discrimination and imitation abilities of preschool Spanish-speaking children. *Journal of Learning Disabilities,* 1974, *7,* 573–584.

FERGUSON, C. A., and GARNICA, O. K. Theories of phonological development. In E. Lenneberg and E. Lenneberg (eds.), *Foundations of Language Development.* London: UNESCO Press, 1975.

GARCIA, E. The study of early childhood bilingualism: Strategies for linguistic transfer research. In J. L. Martinez, Jr. (ed.), *Chicano Psychology.* New York: Academic Press, 1977.

GARCIA, E. Mother–child bilingual interaction: A developmental analysis. *Journal of Discourse Behavior* (in press, 1981a).

GARCIA, E. Language switching in bilingual children: A national perspective. In E. Garcia and M. Sam Vargas (eds.), *The Mexican American Child: Language, Cognitive and Social Development.* Tucson: University of Arizona Press, 1981b.

GARCIA, E., and BATISTA-WALLACE, M. Parental training of the plural morpheme in normal toddlers. *Journal of Applied Behavior Analysis,* 1977, *10,* 505.

GARCIA, E., and DeHAVEN, E. Use of operant techniques in the establishment and generalization of language: A review and analysis. *American Journal of Mental Deficiency,* 1974, *79,* 169–178.

GARCIA, E., and TRUJILLO, A. A developmental comparison of English and Spanish imitation between bilingual and monolingual children. *Journal of Educational Psychology,* 1979, *21,* 161–168.

GEISSLER, H. *Zweisprachigkeit deutscher Kinder im Ausland.* Stutgart: Kohlammas, 1938.

GONZALEZ, G. The acquisition of grammar by native Spanish speakers. Unpublished doctoral dissertation, University of Texas, Austin, 1970.

GUESS, D. An experimental analysis of linguistic development: The productive use of the plural morpheme. *Journal of Applied Behavior Analysis,* 1968, *1,* 297–306.

HAKUTA, K. Prefabricated patterns and the emergence of structure in second language acquisition. *Language Learning,* 1974, *24,* 287–297.

HENRIE, S. N., JR. A study of verb phrases used by five-year-old nonstandard English-speaking children. Unpublished doctoral dissertation, University of California, Berkeley, 1969.

HUERTA, A. The development of codeswitching in a young bilingual. *Working Papers in Sociolinguistics*, No. 21, June 1977.

HYMES, D. Models of the interaction of language and social setting. *Journal of Social Issues*, 1967, *23*, 8–28.

HYMES, D. *Foundations in Sociolinguistics: An Ethnographic Approach.* Philadelphia: University of Pennsylvania Press, 1974.

LABOV, W. *The study of Nonstandard English.* Urbana, Ill.: National Council of Teachers of English, 1970.

LABOV, W., and COHEN, P. Systematic relations of standard and nonstandard rules in grammars of Negro speakers. *Project Literacy Reports No. 8.* Ithaca, N.Y.: Cornell University, 1967.

LARSON-FREEMAN, D. An explanation for the morpheme acquisition order of second language learners. *Language Learning*, 1976, *26*, 125–134.

LENNEBERG, E. H., and LENNEBERG, E. *Foundations of Language Development*, Vol. I and Vol II, London: UNESCO Press, 1975.

LEOPOLD, W. F. *Speech Development of a Bilingual Child: A Linguist's Record. Vol. I, Vocabulary Growth in the First Two Years.* Evanston, Ill.: Northwestern University Press, 1939.

LEOPOLD, W. F. *Speech Development of a Bilingual Child: A Linguist's Record. Vol. II, Sound Learning in the First Two Years.* Evanston, Ill.: Northwestern University Press, 1947.

LEOPOLD, W. F. *Speech Development of a Bilingual Child: A Linguist's Record. Vol. III, Grammars and General Problems in the First Two Years.* Evanston, Ill.: Northwestern University Press, 1949(a).

LEOPOLD, W. F. *Speech Development of a Bilingual Child: A Linguist's Record. Vol. IV, Diary from Age Two.* Evanston, Ill.: Northwestern University Press, 1949(b).

LINDHOLM, K. J., and PADILLA, A. M. Child bilingualism: Report on language mixing, switching and translations. *Linguistics*, 1979, *211*, 23–44.

McLAUGHLIN, B. *Second Language Acquisition in Childhood.* Hillsdale, N.J.: Lawrence Erlbaum Associates, 1978.

McNEILL, D. Developmental psycholinguistics. In F. Smith and G. Miller (eds.), *The Genesis of Language: A Psycholinguistic Approach.* Cambridge, Mass.: M.I.T. Press, 1966.

MENYUK, P. *The Acquisition and Development of Language.* New York: Prentice-Hall, 1971.

MILLER, N. E., and DOLLARD, J. *Social Learning and Imitation.* New Haven, Conn.: Yale University Press, 1941.

MOREHEAD, K. M., and MOREHEAD, A. From signal to sign: A Piagetian view of thought and language during the first two years. In R. L. Schiefelbusch and L. L. Lloyd (eds.), *Language Perspectives: Acquisition, Retardation and Intervention.* Baltimore, Md.: University Park Press, 1974.

MORSE, P. A. Infant speech perception: A preliminary model and review of literature. In R.L. Schiefelbusch and L.L. Lloyd (eds.), *Language Perspectives: Acquisition, Retardation and Intervention.* Baltimore, Md.: University Park Press, 1974.

OLMEDO, E. L. Psychological testing and the Chicano: A reassessment. In J. L. Martinez, Jr. (ed.), *Chicano Psychology.* New York: Academic Press, 1977.

PADILLA, A. M., and LIEBMAN, E. Language acquisition in the bilingual child. *The Bilingual Review/La Revista Bilingue*, 1975, *2*, 34–55.

PAVLOVITCH, M. *Le Langage Enfantin: Acquisition du Serve et du Français par un Enfant Serbe.* Paris: Champion, 1920.

PIAGET, J. *The Origins of Intelligence in Children.* New York: Norton, 1952.

PRUTTING, C. A. Process/ 'pras/,ses/n: The action of moving forward progressively from one point to another on the way to completion. *Journal of Speech and Hearing Disorder*, 1979, *26*, 185–198.

RONJAT, J. *Le Développement du Langage Observé Chez un Enfant Bilingue.* Paris, Champion, 1913.

ROSANSKY, E. Second language acquisition research: A question of methods. Unpublished doctoral dissertation, Harvard University, 1976.

SAVILLE, M. R. Interference phenomenon in language teaching: Their nature, extent, and significance in the acquisition of standard English. *Elementary English*, 1971, *48*, 396–405.

SHERMAN, J. Imitation and language development. In H. W. Reese and L. P. Lippset (eds.), *Advances in Child Development and Behavior.* New York: Academic Press, 1971.

SKINNER, B. F. *Verbal Behavior.* New York: Appleton-Century-Crofts, 1957.

SKRABANEK, R. L. Language maintenance among Mexican-Americans. *International Journal of Comparative Sociology*, 1970, *11*, 272–282.

SLOBIN, D. Developmental psycholinguistics. In W.O. Dingwell (ed.), *A Survey of Linguistic Science.* College Park, Md.: University of Maryland Linguistics Program, 1971.

SMITH, M. D. A study of the speech of eight bilingual children of the same family. *Child Development*, 1935, *6*, 19–25.

SNOW, C. and FERGUSON, C. *Talking to Children.* Cambridge: At the University Press, 1977.

SORENSEN, A. P. Multilingualism in the Northwest Amazon. *American Anthropologist*, 1967, *69*, 670–684.

STOCKWELL, R. P., BOWEN, J. D., and Martin, J. W. *The Grammatical Structures of English and Spanish.* Chicago: University of Chicago Press, 1965.

VYGOTSKY, L. S. *Thought and Language.* Cambridge, Mass.: M.I.T. Press, 1962.

WHITEHURST, G. J. Generalized labeling on the basis of structural response classes. *Journal of Experimental Child Psychology*, 1971, *12*, 59–71.

WHITEHURST, G. J. Production of novel and grammatical utterances by young children. *Journal of Experimental Child Psychology*, 1972, *13*, 502–515.

ZENTELLA, M. Codeswitching in elementary level Puerto Rican children. *Working Papers in Sociolinguistics*, #43, 1978.

CHAPTER 4

Prosocial Behavior in the Early Years: Parent and Peer Influences

Shirley G. Moore

EVERY PARENT AND TEACHER looks for signs that children are becoming "human." Is the child they care about developing a repertoire of friendly social behaviors, acquiring a conscience and a sense of social responsibility, showing signs of becoming helpful; is he/she cooperative and considerate of others? As adults, we are expected to display such behaviors as part of our daily interactions with others, particularly with the young, the old, and the disabled who cannot adequately care for themselves. At times, we may be called upon to display altruism or heroism under conditions of considerable sacrifice or danger to ourselves. Although we do reward people for such acts of consideration and selflessness, we are expected to perform them for their own sake because someone else is in need, without regard for external reinforcement or recognition.

During the past decade or more, psychologists have shown an increased interest in the conditions under which people perform acts of altruism and in the development of such behaviors in children. Research with school-age children and adults has included studies of helping behavior, charitable donations to the needy, and "rescue" paradigms in which a judgment must be made (hypothetical or real) to react under conditions that involve social risk or danger to the helper. Investigators have studied the personality and background of Civil Rights activists of the 1960s (Rosenhan, 1969) and of German citizens during World War II who helped Jews escape Nazi Germany (London, 1970).

Psychologists and others have speculated about the etiology of such behaviors in humans. What causes people to perform behaviors that, on the surface at least, are not in their own best interest? Two major theoretical perspectives have been considered, each of which is capable of explaining some data but each of which is inadequate to account for the varied array of altruistic behaviors displayed by humans. One perspective is a biological/evolutionary approach in which it is assumed that humans are genetically programmed to care for others and to reduce the distress of those in need even at the risk of their own comfort and safety. Strong protective bonds between mothers and their young among members of a social unit are well documented in lower animal species and clearly lead to the survival of such units through the mutual interdependence and occasional sacrifice of one or more of its members (Wilson, 1975). A similar predisposition in humans would tend to assure the survival of the family in particular and the society in general.

In many animal species, affection and affiliation between a mother and infant are predetermined by primitive instincts evident from birth or emerging shortly after birth ("imprinting", for example) that assures the care of the infant by the mother. The current emphasis on "bonding" directly after the birth of human infants is based, to some extent, on the importance of this initial contact as a determinant of parental commitment to the infant (Klaus & Kennell, 1976). To the extent that banding together for protection has survival value, selection over a period of thousands of years could have favored individuals with a strong predisposition to become empathetically aroused over the distress of others (Clark, 1980) and with the capacity to do something to relieve that distress.

A second rationale to account for those prosocial behaviors that involve self-sacrifice and personal risks is a developmental/learning perspective in which prosocial behaviors are seen as an outgrowth of maturation and socialization. As children become capable of understanding the needs of others and acquire the repertoire of skills needed to perform helpful altruistic acts, they are expected, at times, to put the needs of others above their own. The family that encourages its seven-year-old to collect money for UNICEF on Halloween instead of collecting candy is getting that point across to their child.

Perhaps the best working hypothesis is the one that takes into account the interaction of biological/evolutionary factors and socialization factors in accounting for social responsibility and altruism. Biology presents the organism with a sensitive nervous system and a predisposition to adapt to environmental conditions in its own best interest; socialization endows the child with the common wisdom of the society, including the social values that are espoused and rewarded in the particular culture in which the child lives.

Although humans are biological creatures, subject to the constraints of mind and body, they clearly have the most advanced, complex nervous system of any animal and hence are capable of generating an almost infinite variety of cultural milieus within which socialization can occur. One of the unique features of humans is the capacity to *think* about the social values we hold. No other creature on earth can contemplate its own fate to such an extent nor can any other creature do as much to change its fate through the instruction of its young. We consciously shape the behavior of our children through direct instruction, reinforcement, and modeling. If we are concerned about our children's failure to show consideration for others, we speculate about the causes of such a state of affairs. Psychologists and others are doing just that. In a recent discussion of aggression in American culture, Leonard Eron (1980) describes his position with regard to our social values in this domain of behavior.

> To reduce the level of aggression in our society, it is essential that we intervene early in the socialization of children so that they learn alternative ways of solving problems and do not have to rely on aggressive techniques to gain their ob-

jectives. Although in general girls demonstrate less aggressive behavior of all types than boys do, there are some girls who have been socialized like boys, who behave as aggressively as boys do. This article proposes that boys be exposed to the same training that girls have traditionally received in our society, and that they be encouraged to develop similar kinds of socially positive, tender, cooperative, nurturant, and sensitive qualities, which are antithetical to aggressive behavior [Eron, 1980, p. 244].

What Do We Mean by Prosocial Behavior?

Psychologists have defined prosocial behavior, in its narrowest sense, as those acts which (1) benefit another; (2) are done without regard for external rewards or punishments; and (3) involve some sacrifice or danger to the self. Broadly defined, however, prosocial behaviors include all of those behaviors that are regarded positively by another (such as friendly approach, helping another, sharing resources, nurturing another) whether or not the behaviors are, or could be, motivated by a desire for approval from others and whether or not they could be said to involve self-sacrifice.

We have good reason to define prosocial behavior broadly when applying the label to the behavior of young children since children under seven or eight rarely voluntarily show behaviors that threaten their sense of well-being and safety for the sake of another; nor should they be expected to do so given their lack of mastery of the prerequisite and instrumental skills involved, to say nothing of their lack of judgment in such matters.

In this chapter, attention will be given to those aspects of prosocial behavior that are the most relevant to young children up to about eight years of age. Discussion of some of the more profound prosocial behaviors—acts of danger and self-sacrifice—will be limited to their potential roots in early childhood. Consideration will be given to child-rearing practices that appear to influence the onset and incidence of prosocial behavior during the early years of life and that predict altruism in older children. The role of peers in eliciting and supporting prosocial behaviors will also be considered.

Developmental Overview: The Antecedents of Prosocial Behavior

Major developmental theorists have shared the view that the young child is preoccupied with the self. Piaget (1959) describes the child as egocentric—not only unable to take the perspective of another but also inclined to attribute his or her own perspective to all others. In the view of Freud (1933), the young child is unable to separate the self from the other, is motivated by the "pleasure principle," and lacks a conscience. Erikson (1968) discusses the child's narcissism and "sense of omnipotence." When do we begin to observe prosocial behavior in the young child?

Given such a preoccupation with the self, certainly one of the first truly *social* behaviors to be observed is the smile. Early in the first year of life the child is capable of a smile that indicates pleasure in the presence of a caregiver. By mid-year, the child will be able to display a complex repertoire of social behaviors, including vocalizations and laughs, that indicate a desire to be near others, to be attended by them, "play" with them, imitate them, and generally be one of them.

Two companion processes unfold during these early months of life, one of which can best be seen as serving the child's needs, and one, the mother's and society's needs. The first is *attachment,* an aspect of the caregiver–child relation which, under the best of circumstances, allows the child to feel secure in the primary caregiver's ability and willingness to meet the child's basic needs. An early expression of this security is the child's assertiveness in conveying mood states to the adult, smiling, cooing, and generally being winsome when things are going well, and crying, fussing, or showing anger when things are not. Further, the child appears to expect a sensitive reciprocal response from the caregiver and may register indignation if one is not forthcoming. As the child becomes mobile and object-oriented, the caregiver becomes a secure base of operation from which to move out and explore the social and physical milieu. The child comes back to the adult for protection and consolation under conditions of threat or frustration, and then ventures out again.

The second socialization process that unfolds during the early months of life is the development of an *emotional dependence,* a phenomenon identified by social learning theorists to account for the child's growing need for affection and approval from the caregiver (Sears, Maccoby & Levin, 1957). Through the constant association of the caregiver with pleasure-producing and stress-reducing experiences, that person takes on secondary reward value for the child. The gentle physical contact, smiles, and pleasant affectionate interactions that at first are associated specifically with caregiving become rewarding for their own sake, apart from the caregiving context. The child seeks out ways to elicit and maintain the adult's nurturant attentions even in the absence of a need for physical care. In fact, the desire for love and approval from the caregiver will eventually compete successfully with the child's dedication to prompt and unqualified self-gratification. Avoiding disapproval will be a motivating force during toilet training, in teaching the child to resist touching things that are forbidden, and eventually in motivating sharing, helping, and consideration for others.

One of the ironies of early socialization is that the child no sooner becomes dependent on significant adults for love and approval than the adults begin to make their nurturance contingent on the child's giving up some autonomy and self-gratification. Social learning theorists have referred to a discipline technique called "withdrawal of love" to describe the use of the mother–child relation to motivate compliance in the child (Sears et al., 1957).

But more is needed than the desire to maintain the nurturant attention of the caregiver. Before a child can display altruistic behavior in response to another's need, certain milestones of development must take place. First, the child must have at least minimal perspective-taking abilities that allow him or her to recognize the plight and circumstances of another. Given the egocentric predispositions of young children and their inability to take the perspective of another, it is not surprising that altruism is a relatively infrequent behavior in the child's repertoire. Secondly, the child who wishes to help another must possess the instrumental problem-solving skills to select and perform a behavior that is appropriate to the situation; it is not often that a toddler or preschooler possesses either the ability or the resources to help another who is in trouble even if the child knows what should be done. A twenty-month-old, for example, can understand that his brother has just broken his favorite toy but does not know either how to fix it or replace it. A mother reported that her twenty-month-old, in this situation, presented his five-year-old brother with his own nighttime bottle, a true gift of love.

In addition to the perspective-taking abilities and instrumental know-how, affectionate arousal—that is, empathic emotional arousal in response to the knowledge of another's distress—is presumed by some to be a necessary antecedent to altruistic behavior or at least to increase greatly the likelihood of such behaviors occurring. Even though very young children do show evidence of empathic emotional arousal in the presence of the distress of others, their limited role-taking abilities reduce the likelihood of the appropriate motivating affect being elicited by the distressing event. Young children, for example, at times interpret a distressing event as humorous, and vice versa. Despite the preschooler's neophyte status as an altruist, three- and four-year-olds are surprisingly capable of interpreting the needs of others from facial expressions and situational cues (Shantz, 1975) and of selecting appropriate reparative acts in situations in which the child is familiar with the setting and may have experienced a similar source of distress sometime in the past (Yarrow, Scott & Wapler, 1973).

How do parents and other agents of socialization teach children to show prosocial behaviors that, on the surface at least, appear to be contrary to the child's self-serving, egocentric interests? How do they build on the foundation of basic trust and emotional dependence to establish for the child a "norm of responsibility"?

Child-rearing Practices and Prosocial Behavior

Hoffman (1963, 1975a, 1975b) has contributed as much as any other researcher to the study of child-rearing practices as they relate to altruistic behavior in children. In 1963, this investigator conducted a study of "consideration for others" in a sample of middle and workingclass nursery school children. The mothers of the children were interviewed about their child-rearing practices, and their children were observed in a nursery school setting for indicators of a general sociability with peers and consideration for the feelings and needs of others. Hoffman was interested in the extent to which the mothers of the children used "victim-oriented" discipline, calling the child's attention to the consequences of misbehavior for the victim and expecting the child to make restitution for misdeeds. He hypothesized that children whose mothers used such techniques would show higher levels of consideration for others than other children their age.

With some qualifications, the results of this study supported Hoffman's position. There was a positive relation between the use of victim-oriented discipline and consideration for others, but only for the children whose mothers used relatively nonpunitive, rational (inductive) forms of discipline including high use of reasons and explanations in support of disciplinary demands and expectations. The relation did not hold for the children of parents who used what Hoffman called "power assertive" techniques stressing high use of threats against the child and force without explanations. Hoffman had not predicted this particular interaction, although it fits the theory well inasmuch as the children of high-power-assertive mothers could be expected to be more concerned about their own plight at the hands of a punitive parent than that of their victim even if their mothers had stressed reparations. Also, the high-power-assertive mother presents a more aggressive interpersonal model of social problem solving to her child than the rational, nonpunitive mother. The children of power-assertive mothers would not be likely to think of their mothers as "considerate" of them.

In this study, Hoffman also assessed the frequency of everyday nurturant interactions between the mothers and children in the sample. Although maternal nurturance was positively related to general sociability in the nursery school, nurturant mother–child relations did not predict consideration for others unless the nurturant mother also stressed victim-oriented discipline. In other words, mothers who were nurturant with their children, but who did not make a special effort to instill in their children a sensitivity to the needs of others had children who were friendly and sociable, but were no more likely than others to help, share, or show consideration.

Hoffman (1975a) tested a similar hypothesis with older children and their parents. He predicted that the more altruistic children among a group of fifth graders would have parents who, during the time that the child was five or six years of age, had been particularly nurturant to their children and had made frequent use of victim-oriented discipline. Hoffman also asked the parents to discuss their present attitudes about altruism and consideration for others, both in and out of the home, on the assumption that parental commitment to altruistic values would provide an altruistic model for the child. Parental practices and values were scored from separate interviews with mothers and fathers. Altruism in the children was assessed by administering a sociometric questionnaire in which the classmates of the children were asked to nominate members of their class who (1) care about how other kids feel; (2) stick up for kids who are being made fun of; and (3) follow rules even when the teacher is not around.

Although the results of this study varied across measures, and for boys compared with girls, in general, the evidence supports a relation between each of the child-rearing variables and peer-assessed altruism. Altruistic children more often had at least one parent who had stressed victim-oriented discipline when the child was young and at least one who presently espoused altruistic values. Nurturance in child rearing during the early years was related to altruism only for the boys in this sample; the degree of parental nurturance did not significantly predict altruism in girls. In discussing this sex difference, Hoffman points out that both mothers and fathers reported, in their interviews, having expressed more nurturance during the early years to their daughters than to their sons, suggesting that the girls may generally have enjoyed enough parental nurturance to feel secure in considering the needs of others whereas, for at least some of the boys, the level of early nurturance may have been so low as to interfere with the development of altruistic feelings for others.

Of the three parent variables measured in this study, the most powerful predictor of altruism in the children was the espousal of altruistic values by their parents. Parents who presently held altruistic values had children who were judged by their classmates to be more considerate of others.

Needless to say, for altruistic parental values to have an impact on child behavior, the parent must convey the value to the child through his or her own behavior and through interactions with the child concerning the child's behavior. The research of Olejnik and McKinney (1973) is relevant to this issue. These investigators studied the children of parents who favored *prescriptive* rewards and punishments (with an emphasis on the *good* behaviors that were to be performed and not avoided) and those of parents who favored *proscriptive* rewards and punishments (emphasizing primarily the bad behaviors that were to be avoided). Generosity in their four-year-old children was studied by giving the children a supply of candies and inviting them to give (anonymously—and only if they wished) some of their candies to "poor children." The data indicate that the children of parents with a prescriptive orientation—in which they direct the child's attention to doing good versus avoiding being bad—were more generous than the children of parents with a proscriptive orientation. Whether or not the parent preferred control through rewards or punishments did not relate to generosity in these children. This study, too, suggests that parents who convey their altruistic values—in this case by setting positive behavioral goals for their children—have children who behave more altruistically.

Presumably, one of the advantages of a prescriptive emphasis in child rearing is that the discipline and value inculcation often leads directly to a prosocial behavior, whether it is spontaneously offered or performed to make restitution. In either case, the emission of the behavior provides an opportunity for the parent to reinforce the response with approval, pride in the child's performance, and—in the case of reparation—reduction of guilt for the child. All of these behavioral outcomes should help to strengthen the tendency to perform such behaviors in the future.

Baumrind (1966, 1967, 1971) has conducted a number of studies on the relation between parent–child interaction styles and social responsibility in young children, a construct that broadly samples the child's prosocial behavioral repertoire. Data on one sample of children studied by Baumrind (1971) were obtained from observations carried out over a three- to five-month period in a nursery school setting and in a test situation when the children were approximately four to five years of age. The measure of social responsibility was a composite score for each child from ratings on three behavioral dimensions—friendly/hostile, cooperative/resistive, and achievement-oriented/non-achievement-oriented.

Data on the parents' child-rearing attitudes and practices were obtained through home observations conducted during the dinner hour and early evening and through separate interviews of mothers and fathers. To preserve in-dependence, the home measures were obtained by individuals other than those who were observing and rating the children in the nursery school and test situa-tions.

Baumrind identified three major child-rearing orientations: authoritarian, authoritative, and permissive. Authoritarian parents particularly valued obe-dience from their child and did not believe in verbal give and take in such matters. They favored forceful discipline and sought to preserve traditional values and orderliness in their interactions with their children. Some, but not all, of these parents were also hostile and rejecting to their children.

Authoritative parents were those who preferred rational, issue-oriented discipline (similar to the rational, inductive child-rearing style identified by Hoff-man), encouraged verbal exchanges with their child, recognized the child's needs and desires but also the adult's rights and responsibilities, and set standards for the future conduct of their child. Permissive parents, in contrast to the other two groups, made few demands on their child for household responsibilities, allowed the child to regulate his or her own activities, and did not expect the child to show high conformity to externally defined standards.

The results of this study are numerous and complex, but some generalizations can be made concerning the child-rearing practices of parents whose children—especially boys—are high in social responsibility. Of the three major patterns of child rearing, authoritative parents had sons who scored highest on social responsibility, although their daughters did not score higher than others on the measure. Permissive parents, on the other hand, had sons (but not daughters) who lacked social responsibility compared with the sons of other parents. Authoritarian parents had boys and girls with intermediate social responsibility scores—neither high nor low overall compared with others. Again, it appears to be the case that parents who set standards for their children—at least for their sons—have children who take more social responsibility than the children of very permissive parents. In discussing the findings of this study and related research on social responsibility, Baumrind states that "firm enforcement policies in which behavior desired by the parent is positively reinforced and behavior regarded as deviant by the parent is negatively reinforced, facilitate the development in the child of socially responsible behavior" (Baumrind, 1971, p. 95).

Information on the effects of parental demands is also available from an earlier study of child-rearing practices and child behavior reported by Baldwin (1948). On the basis of parent behavior ratings made by home visitors, Baldwin identified a child-rearing style called "democratic" that resembles Hoffman's ra-tional, inductive discipline and Baumrind's authoritative child-rearing pattern. Democratic child rearing was characterized by high levels of verbal exchange with the child, the giving of reasons for family rules, consultation with the child about policy decisions, support for the child's initiative and curiosity, and restraint on family emotionality. Among parents in the Baldwin study who favored democratic child-rearing practices, some also scored moderate to high on a second variable labeled "control." These parents modulated their child-oriented democratic practices with the firm establishment of limits and expectations. Restrictions, however arrived at, were clearly conveyed to the child, and there was a lack of friction in these homes over disciplinary decisions.

The children in Baldwin's study were rated, at age four, on an extensive battery of social and task-oriented behaviors based on observations in their homes and in a nursery school setting. In assessing the effects of the democratic and control child-rearing dimensions independent of each other, it was found that parents who favored democratic practices had children who were high in activity level and who showed leadership and initiative in the nursery school. However, they also were high in aggressiveness, cruelty, and fearlessness. The control dimension had effects that appeared to be quite different. Parents high in the use of control had children who were low in quarrelsomeness, negativism, and disobedience, but they also were low in initiative and tenacity.

As might be expected from these behavioral constellations, parents who emphasized democratic principles at the expense of control risked having children who were prone to pursue their own purposes without regard for the consequences to others. On the other hand, parents who favored control at the expense of democratic practices, had children who were quiet, well-behaved, and nonresistant but restricted in curiosity and originality.

In combination, the democratic and control orientations appeared to strike a balance. Parents who were high in the use of democratic principles but who also maintained reasonably high levels of control over their children, had children who were appropriately assertive without showing too little conformity to cultural demands and expectations.

In discussing these findings, Baldwin cautions against an interpretation in which democratic practices are dismissed as fostering rebellious, nonconforming children. He suggests that during the preschool years, children respond to social stimulation in a generalized and undifferentiated manner and are not yet able to discriminate adequately between prosocial and antisocial forms of activity. With support for spontaneity and exploration during the early years, the child will have the necessary experiences to learn acceptable behavioral standards and adequate self-control. In the meantime, the child may be somewhat rambunctious and inconsiderate.

Others are not so sanguine about the future of children who, by age four, are aggressive and uncooperative with authority figures. Although neither Hoffman nor Baumrind specifically recommend some child-rearing techniques over others, there is a tacit assumption in their work that the preferred child outcome is one in which children are spontaneous, confident, and creative yet well-behaved, kind, and considerate. Such outcomes appear to be facilitated by rational, nonpunitive discipline techniques combined with clear enforcement of demands and expectations.

There is more to be said, however, concerning the effects of demands and expectations on the behavior of children. Apparently, the methods by which parents implement their demands for good behavior is a critical factor in the extent to which their children will develop a prosocial orientation toward others. Parents who are dedicated to the use of severe physical punishment, hostile rejection, and harsh criticism to enforce their demands clearly do not have children who show consideration and caring for others. In fact, it is often the children of such parents who themselves become child abusers (Steinmetz & Straus, 1974). Highly punitive parents do not usually appear in large numbers in most studies of child rearing unless either the parents or the children are selected on the basis of their aggressiveness and hostility. When this population is studied, the data are persuasive; hostile parents are more likely than others to have hostile children (Bandura & Walters, 1959; Becker, 1964; Martin, 1975)—and this despite the fact that the harsh punishment is often justified by the parent as necessary to curb the antisocial behavior of the child. Any parenting technique will work some of the time, but as a general rule, using harsh punishment to curb high levels of aggression does not work. Highly punitive parents not only provide their children with aggressive interpersonal models to emulate but they also risk undermining their child's sense of personal worth, frustrating and embittering the child and orienting the child toward his or her own misery rather than to the plight of another.

It does seem to be the case that there are risks and limitations to virtually all child-rearing techniques pushed to the extreme or used in isolation. A strong emphasis on the nurturant aspects of the parent–child relation appears to provide the child with a prerequisite sense of personal security (Rutherford & Mussen, 1968) yet nurturance alone does not instill a norm of responsibility in the child without the added indoctrination of altruistic values through modeling and victim-oriented discipline. From the limited data we have on sex differences, the emergence of prosocial tendencies in boys may be governed more systematically by their parents' child-rearing practices than that of girls. As Eron (1980) suggested in his earlier statement concerning the socialization of aggression in our society, nurturance and caring are behaviors that may be seen by the young boy as antithetical to the masculine sex role and may not be readily incorporated into the boy's behavioral repertoire without special attention from adults—both mothers and fathers. Apparently, if we want children, especially boys, to show moderate to high levels of nurturance and consideration for others, we will have to work at it.

Prosocial Behavior in the Peer Group

From the time children are three or four years of age, they spend a significant part of their time interacting with other children, especially with age mates. The young child's play companions provide the first social interactions that are truly egalitarian, in which sharing and cooperation are carried on among equals and in which status must be earned through the quality of interpersonal relations. The peer group can be thought of as a mini-society in which children try out their social repertoire. For the young child, it is a time to practice and gain mastery. The significance of the peer group during early childhood looms large when one considers the evidence from longitudinal studies of social development. It is clear from such studies that poor social adjustment to peers during the early school years is a realiable predictor of social maladjustment in middle childhood, adolescence, and young adulthood (McCord, McCord & Howard, 1963; Roff, Sells & Golden, 1972). But are preschool children a "good influence" on each other? Do they help each other acquire the repertoire of social behaviors that will serve the child well upon entering the elementary school?

In addressing these questions, consideration will be given first to what we know about two broad categories of social behavior in the early childhood peer group, *friendly interaction* and *aggression*. Both have been studied extensively using naturalistic observations during free play or in semistructured play sessions in nursery schools, day care centers, camp settings, and Head Start classrooms. Although category systems vary from one investigator to another, generally friendly behavior includes such things as smiling, conversing, inviting another to join, complying with another's request, imitating, offering help, praise or approval, giving affection, willingly cooperating or sharing, and giving tokens of friendship. Aggressive behavior includes verbally or physically attacking, threatening, rejecting, criticizing or disapproving, damaging property, and refusing to cooperate or share.

One important question to ask concerning the young child's social interactions with peers is the relative frequency of these two broad categories of behavior. Consistently, studies addressing this question indicate that preschoolers show higher frequencies of friendly behaviors than of aggressive behaviors toward their companions (Moore, 1978). Different studies indicate ratios of from three to seven or eight friendly interactions occurring for every aggressive interaction. From about three years of age on, boys consistently show more aggression than girls, but they also show a preponderance of friendly behaviors.

Despite the overall positive orientation of the children, socially active preschoolers, as Baldwin suggested, seem to lack the ability and experience to discriminate acceptable from unacceptable social behaviors in their repertoire and consequently perform both. Several investigators have confirmed that, in general, the children who are generous in their use of friendly interaction also fight more than their share or attempt to dominate their companions. In a study by Muste and Sharpe (1947), for example, pairs of preschoolers were observed in play sessions, each child playing several times, with a different companion each time. In this study, *sharing materials* and *fighting over materials* yielded a low positive correlation (r = .39), indicating that the children who shared also did more than their share of fighting. Barrett and Yarrow (1977), studying five- to eight-year-old children in a camp setting, found that among those children who were good perspective-takers, "assertive" children (those exerting high levels of control over companions, although not physical coercion) were also high in prosocial behaviors such as comforting, sharing, and helping. Finally, in an early observation study of sympathy behavior in young preschool-age children, Murphy (1937) found, ironically, that children who scored high on *comforting others* also *pushed and pulled others;* those who *defended others from attack* also *joined in the attack of another;* and those who *helped children out of painful situations* also *pummeled children who fell accidentally.*

The impression one gets from these studies is that young children do, indeed, try out different approaches in interacting with peers, some of which are friendly and some of which are aggressive. It is well to keep in mind, however, that although the correlation between friendly behavior and aggressive behavior is generally positive in direction, it is low in magnitude, leaving room for those children in a group who strongly favor one mode of interaction over another.

Generally, observational data indicate that both friendly behaviors and aggressive behaviors increase in frequency during the preschool years but friendly interactions increase at a faster rate than aggression (Green, 1933; Walters, Pearse & Dahms, 1957). That is, friendly behaviors account for a larger proportion of the social interaction of older preschoolers than of younger ones. The older children also play in larger groups and show more complex forms of play involving cooperation and sharing (Barnes, 1971; Parten, 1932). There is evidence to suggest that the strength of friendships increase during these years. In a study by Green (1933), there was an increase in the number of different children a child played with from age two to three; after three, however, the increase in social interaction was due to greater time spent with special friends.

The complexity of play groups and the intensity of friendships among the older preschoolers no doubt put some strain on the children's limited social skills. Observations indicate that children are more likely to fight with their friends than with others in their group (Green, 1933). Yet, they also do their share in encouraging their companions to be friendly rather than aggressive. They give positive social reinforcement for friendly behaviors and generally respond in negative ways to discourage aggression and selfishness (Hartup, Glazer & Charlesworth, 1967). They accord high sociometric status to the more socially competent children (Vaughn & Waters, 1980) and to the friendlier children (Moore, 1967), selecting them as "liked" or as preferred playmates. And they show their dislike for highly aggressive children (Moore, 1967) although moderately aggressive children are often among those who are liked.

When disagreements among peers arise during play, the older preschoolers, compared with the younger ones, clearly handle the situation with more sophistication. The four- and five-year-olds are more likely to use verbal scolding and argument as an alternative to physical assault (Shure, 1963; Walters, Pearse & Dahms, 1957) and more of their aggression is retaliation for a rule infraction or aggressive act rather than unprovoked attack (Green, 1933).

One milestone in the development of consideration for others is the understanding of property rights; one does not confiscate things that belong to others! A study by Eisenberg-Berg, Haake, Hand, and Sadalla (1979) indicates that older preschoolers are able to make a distinction between a toy in the nursery school setting that belongs to the "class" and one that belongs to themselves, and that they share the jointly owned things to a greater extent than those things that are theirs.

Although most of the investigators studying social interactions in early childhood settings have been interested in the general category of friendly behavior, a few researchers have studied specifically help giving and nurturance giving in young children. Observations indicate that young children do perform such behaviors, but they account for a very small proportion of all friendly initiations or responses and are much less frequent than *seeking* help or nurturance. Stith and Connor (1962), for example, observed instances of help seeking and help giving and found that, at all age levels from three to six, help seeking was more frequent than help giving. The youngest children sought help about six times as often as they gave it, but the older children had a ratio of approximately two instances of seeking for every one of giving. The change in the ratio from the youngest to the oldest children was due to both an increase in giving help to others and a decrease in seeking help from adults—but not from peers. In fact, help seeking from peers actually increased slightly from the youngest to the oldest children, but the decrease in help seeking from adults by the older children was sufficient to cause an overall decline in that category.

This last finding, although tenuous, is an interesting one that has implications for help giving among young children. If, as children mature, a larger proportion of their help seeking is addressed to peers rather than to adults, their companions will have increased opportunities to respond in helpful ways. An observation study by Heathers (1955) provides evidence of a similar trend toward involving one's peers as sources of help and support. Heathers observed a group of twenty two-year-olds and twenty four- to five-year-olds in a nursery school free-play setting recording instances of seeking affection, attention, or approval from adults and from peers. There were marked age differences among the children. The younger children displayed more affection seeking than the older ones and addressed more of their seeking to adults than to peers. The older children, on the other hand, displayed more attention and approval seeking and, compared with the two-year-olds, addressed more of their seeking to peers. Again, the older preschoolers seemed to be turning to their companions for support.

In a similar study, Hartup and Keller (1960) observed for instances of six categories of *seeking nurturance* from others: physical affection, physical proximity, reassurance, positive attention, help, and negative attention. They also observed four categories of *giving nurturance:* giving affection, positive attention, reassurance, and protection. As in the Stith and Connor study, these investigators found that children seek significantly more than they give. Hartup and Keller also addressed the interesting question of the relation between seeking and giving in the same children. To what extent are the seekers also givers? If seeking nurturance is considered a self-serving, egocentric behavior, one would not expect seekers to be concerned enough about others to be givers as well. If, on the other hand, seeking and giving are both expressions of general sociability, the two should be related. In fact, they found that the children who scored high overall on nurturance giving were also likely to score high on two seeking categories, seeking physical affection (p < .10) and seeking help (p < .02). Only one nurturance-seeking category—seeking physical proximity—was related negatively to giving nurturance to others (p < .01). This last result suggests that the more passive children who "hang around" others but are reluctant to interact with them may also be too shy to express their affection for others.

An interesting study by Einiger and Hill (1969) also addresses the relation between seeking and giving nurturance. For this study, teachers were asked to identify preschool girls whom they judged to be primarily seekers of affection (more inclined to seek affection than attention) or primarily seekers of attention (more inclined to seek attention than affection). The girls then participated individually in a brief play session with a large doll and some other toys. A speaker was enclosed in the body of the doll and, with the help of the experimenter, the doll told the child that her name was "Julie." The experimenter explained that Julie had been sick but was feeling better now and asked if the child would "take care" of Julie for her while she left the playroom for a short time. The child was observed for instances of physical affection (hugging, kissing, patting the doll), verbal affection (telling Julie "I love you"), and instrumental attention (giving Julie a blanket or bottle). Nondoll behavior, including play with the other toys, was also recorded. On the basis of social role-taking theory, Einiger and Hill hypothesized that affection seekers, who are often the recipients of affection from others, would have had more opportunities than attention seekers to learn the role of giver of affection and hence would be better at assuming that role. Attention seekers, on the other hand, would presumably be better at instrumental help (such as covering or feeding the doll) than at giving affection. The data indicate that affection seekers were, indeed, significantly more likely to give both physical and verbal affection than were attention seekers. Attention seekers, on the other hand, became more involved with other things and did not give Julie either attention or affection.

It is not clear why children who tend to seek help or affection also behave nurturantly toward others. Such children may feel secure enough from the nurturance they have received to give generously to others, or they may simply be imitating the nurturance of the adults around them. It is also possible that children who have strong needs for affection from others learn early that one way to get affection is to give it. Finally, it is clearly not the case that all seekers are also givers. In the Hartup and Keller study, for example, of the twenty-one children who were above the median in seeking physical affection, only fourteen were also high in total nurturance giving, but seven were not. Some of these children who were high seekers but low givers may have been egocentric and socially immature; others may have lacked a sense of responsibility to care about others. We need a more in-depth study of individual differences in patterns of seeking and giving help and nurturance.

Unfortunately, we know virtually nothing about the influence of teacher behaviors on children's prosocial development in early childhood settings such as day-care centers and nursery schools. One would suspect, however, that some of the same factors of importance in child rearing would apply to adult–child relations in these settings as well, including conveying to children a sense of the importance of helping and nurturing others, being alert to opportunities for children to perform such behaviors, reinforcing them when they occur, and modeling consideration in the interactions the adults have directly with the children. Clearly, more research needs to be done in this area.

In summary, young children are just beginning to master the art of social interaction in the peer group. Great strides are made during the preschool years, from about age two to five. Positive behaviors outnumber negative ones by a healthy margin, fights and arguments become more "civilized," and the more profound prosocial behaviors involving true consideration for others—giving help and giving nurturance—are creeping into the child's repertoire. The capacity to maintain a friendship is taking shape; children expect to be treated decently by their companions and object when they are not.

The family and the peer group each clearly make their respective significant contributions to prosocial development and to the acquisition of friendliness, social responsibility, cooperativeness, consideration of others, and altruism. These, in turn, help define our humanness.

References

BALDWIN, A. L. Socialization and the parent–child relationship. *Child Development*, 1948, *19*, 127–136.

BANDURA, A., and WALTERS, R. H. *Adolescent Aggression*. New York: Ronald, 1959.

BARNES, K. E. Preschool play norms: A replication. *Developmental Psychology*, 1971, *5*, 99–103.

BARRETT, D. E., and YARROW, M. R. Prosocial behavior, social inferential ability, and assertiveness in children. *Child Development*, 1977, *48*, 475–481.

BAUMRIND, D. Effects of authoritative parental control on child behavior. *Child Development*, 1966, *37*, 887–907.

BAUMRIND, D. Child care practices anteceding three patterns of preschool behavior. *Genetic Psychology Monographs*, 1967, *75*, 43–88.

BAUMRIND, D. Current patterns of parental authority. *Developmental Psychology Monographs*, 1971, *4*, 1–103.

BECKER, W. C. Consequences of parental discipline. In M. L. Hoffman and L. W. Hoffman (eds.), *Review of Child Development Research, Volume I*. New York: Russell Sage Foundation, 1964.

CLARK, K. B. Empathy: A neglected topic in psychological research. *American Psychologist*, 1980, *35*, 187–190.

EINIGER, M. A., and HILL, J. P. Instrumental and affectional dependency and nurturance in preschool children. *Journal of Genetic Psychology*, 1969, *115*, 277–284.

EISENBERG-BERG, N., HAAKE, R., HAND, M., and SADALLA, E. Effects of instructions concerning ownership of a toy on preschoolers' sharing and defensive behaviors. *Developmental Psychology*, 1979, *15*, 460–461.

ERIKSON, E. H. *Identity, Youth and Crisis*. New York: W. W. Norton, 1968.

ERON, L. D. Prescription for reduction of aggression. *American Psychologist*, 1980, *35*, 244–252.

FREUD, S. *New Introductory Lecture on Psycho-Analysis*. New York: W. W. Norton, 1933.

GREEN, E. H. Friendship and quarrels among preschool children. *Child Development*, 1933, *4*, 237–262.

HARTUP, W. W., GLAZER, J. A., and CHARLESWORTH, R. Peer reinforcement and sociometric status. *Child Development*, 1967, *38*, 1017–1024.

HARTUP, W. W., and KELLER, E. D. Nurturance in preschool children and its relation to dependency. *Child Development*, 1960, *31*, 681–689.

HEATHERS, G. Emotional dependence and independence in nursery school play. *The Journal of Genetic Psychology*, 1955, *87*, 37–57.

HOFFMAN, M. L. Parent discipline and the child's consideration for others. *Child Development*, 1963, *34*, 573–588.

HOFFMAN, M. L. Altruistic behavior and the parent–child relationship. *Journal of Personality and Social Psychology*, 1975a, *31*, 937–943.

HOFFMAN, M. L. Moral internalization, parental power, and the nature of parent–child interaction. *Developmental Psychology*, 1975b, *11*, 228–239.

KLAUS, M. H., and KENNEL, J. H. *Maternal-Infant Bonding*. St. Louis: Mosby, 1976.

LONDON, P. The rescuers: Motivational hypotheses about Christians who saved Jews from the Nazis. In J. Macaulay and L. Berkowitz (eds.), *Altruism and Helping Behavior*. New York: Academic Press, 1970.

McCORD, J., McCORD, W., and HOWARD, A. Family interaction as antecedent to the direction of male aggressiveness. *Journal of Abnormal and Social Psychology*, 1963, *66*, 239–242.

MARTIN, B. Parent–child relations. In F. D. Horowitz (ed.), *Review of Child Development Research, Volume IV*. Chicago: University of Chicago Press, 1975.

MOORE, S. G. Correlates of peer acceptance in nursery school children. *Young Children*, 1967, *22*, 281–297.

MOORE, S. G. The social interaction of young children: Friend and foe. In J. Shick and J. Klayman (eds.), *Research Reviews for Practitioners and Parents*. Minneapolis, Mn.: Center for Early Education and Development, University of Minnesota, 1978, *No. 1*, 11–23.

MURPHY, L. B. *Social Behavior and Child Personality: An Exploratory Study of Some Roots of Sympathy*. New York: Columbia University Press, 1937.

MUSTE, M. J., and SHARPE, D. F. Some influential factors in determination of aggressive behavior in preschool children. *Child Development*, 1947, *18*, 11–28.

OLEJNIK, A. B., and McKINNEY, J. P. Parental value orientation and generosity in children. *Developmental Psychology*, 1973, *8*, 311.

PARTEN, M. B. Social participation among preschool children. *Journal of Abnormal and Social Psychology*, 1932, *27*, 243–269.

PIAGET, J. *The construction of reality in the child*. New York: Basic Books, 1959.

ROFF, M., SELLS, S. B., and GOLDEN, M. M. *Social Adjustment and Personality Development in Children*. Minneapolis: University of Minnesota Press, 1972.

ROSENHAN, D. Some origins of concern for others. In P. Mussen, J. Langer, and M. Covington (eds.), *Trends and Issues in Developmental Psychology*. New York: Holt, Rinehart & Winston, 1969.

RUTHERFORD, E., and MUSSEN, P. Generosity in nursery school boys. *Child Development*, 1968, *39*, 755–765.

SEARS, R. R., MACCOBY, E. E., and LEVIN, H. *Patterns of child rearing*. Evanston, Ill.: Row, Peterson, and Co., 1957.

SHANTZ, C. U. *The Development of Social Cognition*. Chicago: University of Chicago Press, 1975.

SHURE, M. B. Psychological ecology of a nursery school. *Child Development*, 1963, *34*, 979–992.

STEINMETZ, S. K., and STRAUS, M. A. (eds.). *Violence in the family*. New York: Dodd, Mead & Co., 1974.

STITH, M., and CONNOR, R. Dependency and helpfulness in young children. *Child Development*, 1962, *33*, 15–20.

TRAUSE, M. A., KLAUS, M. H., and KENNELL, J. H. Maternal behavior in mammals. In M. H. Klaus and J. H. Kennell (eds.), *Maternal-Infant Bonding*. St. Louis: Mosby, 1976.

VAUGHN, B. E., and WATERS, E. Social organization among preschool peers: Dominance, attention and sociometric correlates. In D. R. Omark, F. F. Strayer, and D. G. Freedman (eds.), *Dominance relations: An Ethological View of Human Conflict and Social Interaction*. New York: Garland S.T.P.M. Press, 1980.

WALTERS, J., PEARSE, D., and DAHMS, L. Affectional and aggressive behavior of preschool children. *Child Development*, 1957, *28*, 15–26.

WILSON, E. O. *Sociobiology: The new synthesis*. Cambridge, Mass.: Harvard University Press, 1975.

YARROW, M. R., SCOTT, P. M., and WAPLER, C. Z. Learning concern for others. *Developmental Psychology*, 1973, *8*, 240–260.

CHAPTER 5

Developmental Theories in Early Education

Greta Fein
Pamela M. Schwartz

A THEORY OF DEVELOPMENT is not the same as a theory of practice, but the two types of theories interact with each other in provocative ways. In this chapter, we will discuss three developmental theories with respect to implications for a theory of practice. The theories we have chosen for discussion are derived from Bowlby's work on attachment, Berlyne's on arousal, and Piaget's on mastery and assimilation. Our purpose is not to review the extensive literature these theories have yielded, but rather to select issues that illustrate the relationship between theories of development and theories of practice. Before we discuss these theories, some general observations about theories of development and theories of practice are in order.

Quite generally, theories of development and practice differ in their orientation to the developing individual. The orientation of practice is necessarily activist. It assumes that some aspects of behavior or some types of knowledge are more or less desirable than others. A corollary is that these require certain environmental conditions which a skilled practitioner can bring about. Should children know how to fight, read, think, imagine, or love? If the answer is "yes," the task of a theory of practice is to describe what a practitioner must do to cultivate that know-how.

By contrast, a theory of development is passivist in orientation. The core assumption is that behavior changes as a function of encounters present in most environments. Suppose a behavior (for example, crying upon separation from the mother) ordinarily increases and then decreases during the early years. In explaining this pattern of change, the theory might state that the increase in crying is a by-product of the child's social awareness, a welcome mark of growing maturity. True, the intensity of distress may be related to the child's previous experiences or to the setting in which separation is occurring. A theory of development will offer general statements identifying experiential and setting factors and why they work the way they do. It will not offer principles for modifying or generating these factors.

These theories differ in other ways as well. Theories of development are universalistic rather than particularistic, and, with respect to environmental forces, they are minimalist rather than maximalist. By the former, we mean that theories of development describe what is considered the "normal" course of growth and change. Even when developmental theories expand to consider individual differences, they deal with types of individuals and situations rather than with a particular individual at a particular moment in time. By the latter, we mean that developmental theories tend to view the environment as a set of minimal core features, the presence of which is necessary for development to occur. In developmental theories, the environment enters into serious theoretical discussions when it fails to provide the minimum support needed for growth. Even in the study of individual differences, the goal of developmental theory is to specify the minimum band of environmental variation required to produce a given individual variation. By contrast, a theory of practice is concerned with the practitioner's perception of particular individuals. More important in view of its activist orientation, a theory of practice is concerned with maximizing beneficial environmental variations. One goal of such a theory is to formulate strategies for constructing environments that ensure the greatest beneficial impact on the greatest number of individuals.

Finally, a theory of development views the changing individual as a product of the multiple practices of multiple practitioners. By contrast, a theory of practice adopts the perspective of one type of practitioner, and this perspective defines a theory of teaching, parenting, or policy making. The theory builds on what is known about the child, but it uses only that part which pertains to the environmental conditions controlled by the practitioner of interest in the theory. It is in this respect that a theory of practice may have its most significant impact on a theory of development. A theory of practice must inevitably specify the realizable context in which development occurs. Although developmental theorists have recently called for an "ecology of child development" (Bronfenbrenner, 1979), the emergence of useful ecological constructs may be dependent on the formulation of theories capable of providing rules for producing developmentally consequential contexts. The maximalist orientation of a theory of practice requires far more information about environmental arrangements than theories of development typically provide. If the task of a theory of practice is to construct rules for generating realizable arrangements which influence the actual occurrence of desirable child development outcomes, a theory of practice may need to map the malleability of the environment in which children are reared.

John Bowlby's attachment theory is a useful beginning point for a discussion of the interplay between theories of development and practice. Although it serves to underscore the importance of care-giving environments for young children, it stops short of adopting an activist orientation and it fails to address issues of central importance in a theory of practice. The theory's accomplishments and failures nicely illustrate the relationship between a theory of development and a theory of practice as this relationship might be rather than as it is.

Attachment Theory

Formulations developed by Bowlby (1969, 1972) to account for the growth and maintenance of children's initial social ties have a variety of philosophical roots. His explanation contains strands from ethology, psychoanalysis, control systems theory, and Piaget's structural approach to cognition. The resultant combination can best be described as an evolutionary-ethological model of attachment.

From ethology, Bowlby incorporated the view of attachment as an instinctual, species-characteristic behavioral system. According to this view, human infants are born with a predisposition to display various social behaviors such as smiling, sucking, clinging, following, and crying which act as signals bringing the infant into contact with the mother and eliciting nurturant behaviors from her. This evolution of this system of behaviors resulted from its contribution to the survival of the human infant during the long period of relative helplessness.

Throughout the first few years of life, the behaviors which make up the attachment "system" undergo change and modification in response to the current situation, past experiences, and the development level of the child. Control systems theory and the concept of "goal directed" behaviors were adopted by Bowlby to explain the process by which a child comes to employ a variety of strategies to maintain proximity to the mother. Developmental changes in the system are explained through Piaget's cognitive structural theory. Bowlby postulated four stages in the development of the attachment system. The first stage refers to the period soon after birth when instinctual signals such as eye contact, rooting, and sucking maintain maternal contact. During the second period, the infant learns to orient and signal to one or more discriminated figures. The third stage occurs along with person permanence when the infant becomes capable of internally representing the parent who is no longer in view. At this point, active behaviors on the part of the child to regain proximity and contact first occur. This stage lasts from around ten months to three or four years of age. Developmental changes within this stage are marked by the child's gradually increasing ability to maintain elaborated internal representations of the parents during their absences, representations which serve to reduce concern over separation. Also, the child acquires continually more sophisticated signals to obtain the parent's attention. Bowlby characterizes the fourth and final stage as a "goal directed partnership." Separations at this stage are less problematical as the child develops the ability to ascribe purpose to the parent's absence and eventual return.

Most investigations of attachment have focused on the third phase when the presence of an attachment figure appears critical to the infant's sense of wellbeing. The child at this stage has been described as using this figure—whether mother, father, or regular caregiver—as a secure base from which to launch exploratory forays into the environment.

Observing Children's Behavior

To picture the developmental process, one can imagine a circle around the child and mother. Under stress the circle becomes smaller and the child moves closer to the mother. Older children's circles become much larger as they use distal signals to "check in." Under stress the circle may contract but not as severely as before. Thus, as long as the child can maintain optimal proximity, the mother serves as a secure base from which the child can explore the environment. Anderson (1972) described this behavior in one- and two-year-olds at play in the park. Children would wander from the mother as they became absorbed with toys or other children. Once a certain distance was exceeded, however, the children reestablished contact with the mother before returning to play.

Attachment research has identified ways in which children use discrete behaviors to signal their need for reassurance and proximity to adults. Sensitive adults observing these behaviors can use them as a guide to the feelings of the child. An understanding of these signals can help a caregiver respond in ways that assist the child in dealing with separations from home and parents. For example, attachment theory suggests that a young child who bursts into tears when the mother enters the center is signaling his need for comfort and contact with the mother, not displeasure or rejection of the classroom teacher. Similarly, a child approaching the teacher to show a toy or standing silently by her side may be displaying variations of the "check in" behavior described by Anderson. Rather than viewing these behaviors as expressions of excessive dependency, teachers might view them as the child's way of using the teacher as a secure base.

The unique aspect of Bowlby's attachment paradigm is its explanatory focus on the development of social ties from the child's point of view. As a result of the intertwining of ethological and cognitive approaches, observed behaviors of the infant and child can be interpreted as indicators of the child's construction of a social reality. But individual children may differ considerably in the affective aspect of these constructions. Studies of individual differences have identified fairly refined behavioral patterns in children who may require special attention.

Individual Differences

Bowlby's attachment theory has provided a fruitful framework for examining the growth of a child's social world. This work has proved useful not only in establishing expected age norms for particular behaviors but in determining patterns of individual differences as well. Perhaps the most productive work of this kind has been carried out by Mary Ainsworth and her colleagues (Ainsworth, Blehar, Waters & Wall, 1978).

In a longitudinal study of mothers and infants, home observations were made at three-week intervals over the course of the first year. At one year, a laboratory session was designed to determine the infant's reaction to several short separations from the mother. Qualitative differences in the infant's responses were recorded. The largest group of infants responded to these separations much as attachment theory would predict. They actively engaged the mother on her return, signaling for pickup and comfort if upset, or using distal behaviors if the separation had been less stressful. The next two groups of infants were not as successful in using the mother for comfort and reassurance on her return and generally required a longer period to return to active play. One group of infants, referred to as "avoidantly attached," responded to reunion by withdrawing or by ignoring the mother. Another group, referred to as "ambivalently attached," responded to reunion with a mixture of both approach and resistant behaviors. Infants in this group displayed the greatest amount of distress over separation but were not comforted by maternal contact. Examination of home observation data indicated qualitative differences in the interactions of the mothers and infants in these groups. During the first year of life, the mothers of ambivalent and avoidant infants had responded less frequently or appropriately to bids for attention from their infants.

These individual differences (that is, secure, avoidant, and ambivalent patterns of behavior) have been found among samples of infants ranging in age from twelve to twenty-four months of age (Marvin, 1970; Waters, 1978). Moreover, these patterns have been found to be stable over time (Waters, 1978). But changes from secure to anxious attachment patterns do occur. Interestingly, these are related to stressful changes in the mother's life likely to effect interactions with the child (Vaughn, Waters, Egeland & Sroufe, 1979).

Attachment and Day Care

The study of individual differences in the organization of the attachment behavior illustrates the contribution and limitations of developmental theories for a theory of practice in early education. Consider, for example, two complementary issues: the impact of short-term separation on the maintenance of a secure attachment bond to the mother, and the structure of a child-care experience that supports the child's sense of security.

Bowlby's theory predicts that child care occurring before the fourth phase of attachment will involve a special emotional strain for the child. This strain will be greater when the child is younger and will reflect deficits in the child's rudimentary ability to represent the mother in her absence. A variety of factors, including familiarity with the caregiver and the surroundings, the presence of interesting toys, and duration of the separation, also determine the extent of the infant's distress (Rheingold, 1969). However, attempts to apply the theory to practical problems often ignore theoretically significant issues.

Most attempts at examining the effects of separation due to child care have focused primarily on the fact of the child's enrollment, without attention to the multitude of other factors affecting the child's experience such as age of entrance, length of care, or nature of the care. In one of the earlier studies, Blehar (1974) reported that thirty-month-old day-care children were more avoidant and forty-month-olds more resistant than their age-matched, home-reared controls. These results have not been replicated by other researchers (Roopnairene & Lamb, 1978; Portnoy & Simmons, 1978). The assessment situation used in these studies, however, was developed for use with twelve- to twenty-four-month-olds and so may be inappropriate for assessing attachment in older children. Since the strange situation procedure was inappropriate for the age group examined, these discrepant results are difficult to interpret.

In view of Bowlby's analysis, an important issue concerns the influence of day care on the formation of the attachment relationship during the first year of life. Schwartz (1978) examined attachment in eighteen-month-old full-time, part-time, and non–day-care infants. The day-care children had been placed in day-care homes before six months of age. When the three attendance groups were compared, only 9 percent of the part-time children were classified as anxiously attached (avoidant or ambivalent) compared to 30 percent of the non–day-care children and 40 percent of the full-time day-care children. Similar group differences were also noted when ratings of avoidant and resistant behaviors were examined. Full-time day-care infants displayed more avoidant behavior than did their non–day-care or part-time peers. Further, there was a tendency for part-time children to display fewer resistant behaviors than non–day-care children. Thus, day-care attendance as such did not affect the likelihood that an infant would develop an anxious attachment relationship with the mother. Early enrollment on a full-time basis, however, did result in a greater frequency of behaviors that have been interpreted as signs of suppressed anger at the mother (Ainsworth et al., 1978; Main, 1977). By contrast, part-time care appears to support the child's bond to the mother. For middle and upper middle class women like those in the present study part-time employment may serve to support their mothering role by offering periods of outside adult contact without the time constraints of full employment. These findings certainly have implications for mothers interested in returning to work or for policy makers concerned with scaling down the age of children receiving care. The merits of full versus part-time employment and the social costs of full versus part-time child care are issues that have personal as well as public ramifications. A broader issue concerns optimal or nonoptimal periods for entry into care. On a basic level this might involve determining which forms of substitute care are appropriate to children in various age groups. A more subtle issue is whether certain ages, such as ten months of age when attachment behaviors initially appear or eighteen months when there is a sudden reappearance of intense separation protest, might represent crisis points when abrupt introduction to strange surroundings may be disruptive to the child's sense of security. Alternatively, these transitional periods may represent times when the child is ready to make developmental progress and the introduction to day care may facilitate the formation of secondary attachments.

Attachment theory also provides a powerful but as yet unrealized analytical tool for studying children's relationships with significant adults other than primary attachment figures. For example, the children in Schwartz's study attended day-care homes with a single alternate caregiver. Infants under one year of age placed with a single adult caregiver have been found to display less resistant behaviors toward the mother than infants cared for in group settings (Hock, 1976). Children at this age may not be able to use multiple and changing caregivers effectively as sources of security. Further work needs to be conducted to determine whether various child-care parameters, such as center care, number of substitute caregivers, and group size, differentially affect an infant's ability to deal with separation and to form secondary attachments to nonparental adults. Our point is that attachment theory provides a suggestive framework around which applied research can be organized. Although currently the gap between the theory and practical problems is immense, numerous bridging opportunities are available.

While the issue of whether repeated daily separations affect the children's tie to the mother needs further exploration, the inverse, that is, whether the preexisting attachment tie affects adjustment to day care and interactions with peers or caregivers, has received slim attention. A few recently completed studies have examined the relationship between the quality of the attachment bond and later social behaviors with peers. These studies indicate a relationship between secure attachment and subsequent social competence. As part of a longitudinal study, securely attached children were found to display greater task persistence and longer periods of exploration at twenty-four months (Matas, Arend & Sroufe, 1978). These children were rated higher on scales of peer competence and ego strength at age three and a half (Waters, et al., 1979) and scored higher at ages four and five on measures of curiosity (Arend, Grove & Sroufe, 1979). In another sample, securely attached three-year-olds displayed more signs of peer competence than their anxiously attached peers (Lieberman, 1977). Even though secure attachment may promote social competence in laboratory settings or at later ages in school, it is unclear whether a similar relationship holds for younger children in day care where other factors such as the stress of separation might be expected to affect behavior as well. Further, the implications for anxiously attached children's adjustment to day care needs to be explored. On the one hand, separations from the mother are thought to heighten anxiety in these children. On the other, day-care experience has been found to promote peer competence (Fein and Moorin, 1980). In the long run, day care may be beneficial for anxiously attached children if the setting promotes satisfying relationships with adults and peers.

Investigations of individual differences in the quality of attachment might consider the process by which children use the substitute caregiver as a secure base as well as the quality of that relationship. Similar inquiries might also examine whether anxious or secure attachment relationships with the mother are mirrored in the relationship with the caregiver. Apparently, children are able to use substitute caregivers for security when under stress in new situations (Arsenian,

1943) and may even do so with a stranger (Maccoby & Jacklin, 1973). Although there is a good deal of information on the conditions under which infants form secure attachment bonds to the mother, little is known about the formation and the nature of attachment bonds with new caregivers and the conditions under which these attachments optimally occur. For a theory of practice, information about such issues is essential.

Environmental Variation

The process by which young children are introduced to child care may have a major influence on their ability to perceive the setting as a secure environment. Early childhood educators have long struggled with the issue of initial adjustment periods and methods to bring about a sense of familiarity. Using a minimalist approach, Schwatz and Wynn (1971) found that an initial visit to the center by the mother and child had little effect on later adjustment, but the visit was brief and exposure to the new adult was minimal. A maximalist approach would frame the issue somewhat differently. Suppose maternal presence in the center provides the child with a secure base to explore and become familiar with other children and adults. Suppose also that some of these individuals eventually become able to function as supports for the child when the mother leaves. A maximalist approach might attempt to identify the time span within which most children are able to form sufficiently robust secondary attachments to facilitate the transition. A teacher who has visited the child at home several times, a familiar peer, or a sibling may, separately or in combination, serve to smooth the transition period. Numerous other factors such as the level of cooperation and understanding between mother and caregiver, the mother's way of managing the separation, or the warmth and skill of the caregiver probably contribute in some measure to ameloriating distress. Our point is simply that a theory of practice must identify controllable aspects of the environment which in various combinations make a difference for most children. As currently formulated, attachment theory offers some clues but few guides for what these aspects might be.

Curiosity and Exploration

Children spend a substantial amount of time and energy exploring their environment. But this environment is not a neutral force. Some environments are relatively barren and offer little enticement. Others are excessively stimulating and overwhelm children rather than entice them. Although Berlyne's (1966) arousal theory of curiosity and exploration is less well developed than attachment theory, it provides a useful framework for considering the influence of the physical environment on child behavior. If attachment theory implies that a secure base facilitates exploratory behavior, arousal theory implies that some environments are more explorable than others.

According to Berlyne, there are at least two types of exploratory behavior, specific and diversive, that differ in the way they are tied to environmental events. Specific exploration occurs when the individual is disturbed by a "lack of information, and thus left prey to uncertainty and conflict" (1966, p. 26). A lack of information occurs when the individual encounters stimulation that is novel, surprising, ambiguous, incongruous, complex, or in other ways too difficult to assimilate easily. Specific exploration supplies the "precise information" that the individual misses. Berlyne uses the term "curiosity" to describe the condition of discomfort that motivates specific exploration.

By contrast, diversive exploration occurs when the environment is too familiar, too predictable, and too easy to assimilate. Under these conditions, individuals seek out stimulation to alleviate boredom. But sometimes stimulation is in excess; the environment is too novel, too ambiguous, too complex, or too unpredictable. Instead of eliciting approach and contact, these environments may elicit fear and withdrawal.

The glue binding these behaviors is provided by the construct of arousal, a motivating state that can be too low, too high, or just right. When the individual's level of arousal departs from a comfortable optimum, the individual engages in exploration or avoidance until the optimum is restored. The concept of an optimum is conceptualized by Berlyne as a transient state defined by the absence of uncertainty, boredom, or fear (Fein, 1981). Some of the problems posed by a definition "by absence" will be discussed below. First, however, it is helpful to examine how Berlyne's theory pertains to problems in early education.

Exploring Play Materials

Several studies have examined children's behavior with materials varying in complexity. Two of these seem especially informative with respect to the physical characteristics of early childhood environments likely to sustain children's interest.

In one study, the investigators (Scholtz and Ellis, 1975), constructed two play settings varying in complexity. The low-complexity setting consisted of two large trestles, one medium-sized trestle, a balance beam, four mats, a slide, a bench, and a chair. The high-complexity setting included all of the above and, in addition, a metal ladder and a rope spanning the two large trestles, five wooden panels and three ropes attached to each of the trestles, and two wooden boxes and four wooden cubes arranged underneath the trestles. Over a period of three consecutive weeks, two groups of ten children were exposed to each setting for fifteen minutes a day. The investigators asked, first, whether children would prefer the more complex setting to the less complex one and, second, whether this interest would be sustained over successive days. The results were relatively straightforward. The children showed a higher level of engagement with the more complex apparatus. Over the three-week period, their engagement with each type of apparatus dropped, but at the end of three weeks, the children still preferred the more complex apparatus. Clearly, with repeated exposure, children's interest in even attractive play equipment will diminish. There is also evidence that children's waning interests can be recharged. In one study (Mendel, 1965), changing half the items in a toy set increased children's interest in the toys. Berlyne's theory and the findings that follow from it suggest that a theory of practice might need to include rules for producing complexity and variation in the classroom setting. But the level of complexity and variation that is attractive will depend on the age of the child.

Exploratory Behavior and Age

Properly speaking, Berlyne's theory is not a theory of development. There are no specific provisions in the theory for statements about developmental change either in the form of exploratory behavior or in elements of the environment likely to attract children at different ages. However, the theory does suggest that as children encounter stimulation, their ability to process environmental information will improve. Older children are expected to prefer higher levels of novelty, complexity, or surprise than younger children, to become bored more rapidly, and to be less likely to be fearful of new or complex events. However, for any particular event, preference, boredom, or avoidance will depend on the child's prior experiences. Unfortunately, the theory has not developed to the point of being able to identify in advance which events are likely to be more or less familiar or understood. However, the idea that children's response to such events will vary as a function of age is consistent with the evidence.

For example, there is some evidence that young children may avoid excessive complexity. In one study, children were presented two-dimensional vinyl shapes varying in complexity according to the number of turns on the edges (Switsky, Haywood & Isett, 1974). In two-year-olds, exploratory behavior increased from low to moderate levels of stimulus complexity but then declined. By contrast, in four- to seven-year-olds, exploratory behavior reached its highest level with the most complex objects. The message of the study is that a level of complexity that encourages exploration in older children may discourage it in younger children. An activity that intrigues a four-year-old may overwhelm a two-year-old.

Observing Children's Behavior

Although the study of exploratory behavior has been far less richly detailed than the study of attachment behavior, it nonetheless offers some clues for the interpretation of young children's behavior. Consider, for example, a three-year-old's first day in a group program. It is play time and block buildings are being built and toppled, several children are playing a game with the slide, others are working puzzles, finger painting, or just moving from activity to activity watching what the others are doing. The room is noisy and the 15 children are active and engaged:

> Sally clings to her mother. But her eyes scan the room. She watches a group modeling with clay. In one corner of the room, two children have a tussle, and one of them cries. Sally watches the teacher settle the dispute with intense interest. Her eyes move to a corner of the room where a group of children have knocked over a tower. She smiles in response to their laughter. Her mother whispers something in her ear and gets up as if to leave. Sally clutches her mother's dress and protests. Her mother sits down. Sally and her mother stay for the rest of the morning but Sally never leaves her mother's side.
>
> Over the next few days Sally gingerly begins to explore the environment, but always with a watchful eye on her mother. The teacher is able to interest her in play dough or a toy, and she begins to wander around the room pausing to observe various activities. At first, these tours are brief followed by hasty returns to her mother. Gradually, they become longer, but distress appears at the slightest sign of the mother's departure.

Attachment theorists might say that Sally's problem is in separating from the parent. Yet, she has little difficulty staying with babysitters or relatives, in her own home or in other homes, even in those that are relatively unfamiliar. But in the classroom, she seems to be under considerable stress.

Arousal theorists might say that the source of stress is in the classroom environment not in the child. The group setting is not only novel (so is the home of a new babysitter) but excessively complex. Fifteen children and three adults offer more behavioral possibilities than the child can possibly predict; too many things happen too unexpectedly. There is more information in the environment than the child can process and so she clings to the mother, a source of stability and predictability. The child's observing behavior, her tentative, exploratory jaunts, serve to reduce the uncertainty. But the process of uncertainty reduction takes time; it is facilitated by a secure and predictable source of comfort.

This argument has some provocative and verifiable implications for a practical theory of environmental transitions. For example, a new child might be introduced to something like a decompression chamber. This chamber might be simply a protected play vestibule near the door of the class room, a space richly equipped with attractive toys, a friendly teacher, and only a few children. The purpose of the decompression chamber is to contain the uncertainty of a new environment by presenting it in more manageable chunks. Children introduced to the group setting in such a way might be expected to explore more freely, to leave the mother sooner, and to protest less when the mother departs.

Consider another type of child, one who has been attending a group program for almost two years. The following is not an unusual observation.

> Len sits down at the painting table. He picks up a brush and quickly dabs color on the paper. Then he gets up and wanders over to the housekeeping area, pausing briefly to put a pot on the stove before moving on to the blocks. There he takes a car away from Jimmy who cries "No." Len smiles and puts the car behind his back. Jimmy grabs for the car and the two begin to wrestle. The teacher breaks it up and returns the car to Jimmy. Len moves along looking for something else to do.

The teachers describe Len's behavior as restless and aimless. They feel that he is easily distracted and that his attention span is short. He frequently disrupts other children's activity and initiates rough-and-tumble or running games. One day, the teacher brings a water table into the room. The new material has a striking effect on Len's behavior; the restlessness, aimlessness, and seemingly undirected behavior disappear. He is totally absorbed in the water activity, systematically examining the varied objects and exploring the effects produced by combinations of water with things. Len's behavior on the first day involved largely sensory-motor manipulations. By the third day, pretend play appeared, and the ideational quality of Len's behavior changed.

According to arousal theorists, Len's aimless wandering can be interpreted as a response to boredom. The tussle with Jimmy offered a source of relief, except that it was not a permitted activity. The water table provided a pleasant level of novelty and the possibilities it offered sustained Len's interest for several days. In an attempt to refine arousal theory, Nunnally and Lemond (1973) proposed a sequential model of exploratory behavior. According to this model, an interesting event produces heightened attention followed by specific exploration. The object is explored or manipulated until uncertainty concerning its physical properties is reduced. Uncertainty reduction is followed by pretense or some other form of play identified with autistic thinking. Finally, boredom sets in, the individual sets off in search of stimulation, and the sequence repeats itself. The advantage of the Nunnally and Lemond model is that it introduces a role for play as distinct from exploration, but for the most part, the behavioral categories employed by arousal theorists are fairly global. Neither the stimulus properties that attract children's interest nor the behaviors they engage in have been sufficiently specified to offer more than a suggestive framework for a theory of practice. The theory's limitations do, however, illustrate the need for a developmental theory of attractive environments.

Mastery and Play

In Berlyne's theory of exploratory behavior, individuals seek out objects or experiences for their own sake rather than for rewards arbitrarily associated with such activity. According to this view, the motivation for activity is built into the activity itself. If intrinsic motivation were part of a theory of practice, emphasis would be more on the inherently appealing activities or materials practitioners might offer children than on systems of external rewards or inducements. In Berlyne's theory, intrinsic motivation is conceptualized as the alleviation of aversive states (for example, uncertainty or boredom). For a more positive perspective, it is necessary to turn to White's (1959) notion of mastery motivation which owes much to the work of Piaget.

Suppose an infant notices the movement of a toy parrot suspended above his crib. Soon after, the infant discovers that deliberate body movements will control the toy's movements. According to Berlyne, the moving parrot provokes the child's curiosity; he explores the parrot until sufficient information is gained and uncertainty is reduced. But this explanation does not account for the seeming goal-orientedness of the behavior. The baby's exploration is not haphazard and exploration is not a simple matter of visual or tactile contact. Rather, something special happens when the child discovers the contingency between his behavior and an event. This discovery seems to have its own special reward. According to Piaget, the infant has a special capacity to detect such contingencies and to perceive them as causally connected. The child interprets the contingency as evidence of control and derives a feeling of efficacy from successful efforts to control the environment.

According to this view, children not only are motivated to recognize a challenge when it is presented to them, but they also seek out optimally challenging situations (Harter, 1978). Suppose children are presented a range of problems, some easy, some middling, and some hard. Which problems will children choose, and which will give them the most pleasure? Recent evidence suggests that children will choose moderately difficult problems, even when more difficult problems can be solved (Harter, 1978). Moreover, they derive more pleasure from mastering the moderately difficult problems, as if the frustration, energy, and uncertainty associated with excessively difficult challenges undermine the feelings of pleasure that comes with mastery. These findings highlight what we already know; survival in a harsh world may enhance one's feeling of competence without necessarily bringing joy and pleasure. The evidence suggests that in a theory of practice, there may be a need for statements about the diversification of challenges and the child's freedom to choose those best matched to his or her ability. Unfortunately, the research has not clarified how the relation between ability and problem might be specified in advance. And although Piaget's theory has provided much of the basis for the concept of mastery, its structural account of developmental stages has not been used to specify the types of problems likely to be optimally challenging at different developmental levels. As we indicated earlier, the minimalist orientation of developmental theory tends to reduce the importance of such a specification. By contrast, a theory of practice requires rules for assessing children's level of ability with respect to different types of challenges. In this case, the requirements of a theory of practice may exert an independent force for the extension and, perhaps, revision of developmental theory.

Individual Differences

Research on intrinsic motivation has yielded additional information of interest to a theory of practice. On the one hand, much of what children do is done because they derive intrinsic pleasure from activity. But on the other, adults often add external rewards in the form of approval, gold stars, or special treats. What happens when intrinsic and extrinsic rewards are mixed? Not surprisingly, the effect depends on the particular children involved. Suppose, for example, that preschool children are divided into two groups who have either a high or a low spontaneous interest in drawing (Lepper, Greene & Nisbett, 1973; Loveland & Olley, 1979). Now suppose that half the children in each interest group are offered a prize for drawing and the other half are not. Even though the experimental session is brief, rewarded children who initially had a high interest in drawing will, a week later, show less interest than high-interest children who received no extrinsic reward. Children who find an activity intrinsically challenging "turn off" when given prizes for doing what they ordinarily do for its own sake. Moreover, during the reward sessions, the quality of the children's drawings decrease, as if the intrinsic pleasure of combining lines and colors had been replaced by another source of excitement.

A strikingly different effect appeared in children who initially showed little spontaneous interest in drawing. A week after the reward session, these children demonstrated an increased interest in drawing during the free-play period. Changes in the behavior of these children seemed to follow the rule that extrinsic reinforcement will increase the behavior upon which it is contingent. But changes in the behavior of the high-interest children suggest that this rule does not always apply. According to Lepper et al. (1973), extrinsic reward may undermine children's intrinsic motivation because the basis of the activity changes from the intrinsic "I do it because it's fun to make nice pictures" to the extrinsic "I do it because it will get me a prize." The shift to extrinsic reward also leads to less complex, less creative, and less refined drawings, as if the introduction of external rewards also undermines the internal standard of excellence so essential to the pursuit of mastery.

In sum, a number of theoretical formulations have been developed to account for children's response to aspects of the environment such as novelty, complexity, or challenge. These formulations advance a common notion, namely, that much human activity is sustained by satisfactions inherent in an individual's transactions with the environment. These formulations also clarify differences in the way intrinsic motivation might be conceptualized. Arousal theory points to general features of the environment, whereas mastery theory points to the availability of developmentally appropriate problems. A theory of practice, especially in early education, might require statements about each of these environmental domains. It may even be that rules about the provision of developmentally appropriate problems will help to specify more precisely the meaning of novelty, complexity, and similar variables.

Play as Assimilation: Galumphing

The concept of mastery motivation is addressed to the general problem of why children acquire skills and learn to solve problems in the absence of social or appetitizing pressures. But interesting things happen after a skill has been acquired. A young child learns to go down a slide with much effort; each steep step is slowly mounted, and during the first few trips, the child holds tightly and apprehensively to the sides. Within a few days, the same child goes down the slide in all sorts of complicated ways; rocking, clapping, kicking, singing, back-ways, belly-ways, head first, with a friend, a toy, or some combination of these. These ways of maneuvering an inclined plane are repeated, elaborated, recombined, and varied.

Piaget (1962) uses the term practice play to designate activities in which the child creates deliberate complications and seems to make things purposefully difficult. In a mastery activity under the control of a goal, means are marshaled in the service of an end. But in play, means are repeated, elaborated, and become a source of interest in their own right. Miller (1973) refers to these elaborations of means as "galumphing." According to Miller, behavior oriented toward ends becomes efficient and streamlined over time; the child can go up and down the slide with few unnecessary or wasted movements. But after mastery, what next? In developing Piaget's notion of play as a postmastery behavior, Miller argues that its pleasure comes neither from environmental challenge nor from arousal stimulated by a novel or unknown object. Rather, the pleasure comes from the child's control over arousal through the production of diversity, regardless of its particular form. Play involves a relative autonomy of means which implies a degree of autonomy for the player. Miller's notion of "galumphing" as a "patterned, voluntary elaboration or complication of process, where the pattern is not under the dominant control of goals" is entirely in keeping with Piaget's notion of play as assimilation. In Piagetian theory, assimilation refers to the process whereby the child imposes his own way of thinking on the world. Accommodation, by contrast, refers to the process whereby the child's organization is adjusted to meet the world's demands. In mastery activities, assimilation and accommodation operate synchronously—the child behaves according to what he understands; if the behavior doesn't produce a desired goal, it will be adjusted until a better fit between behavior and goal is attained. In the example given earlier, the infant might smile at the parrot to make it move; if smiling does not work, some other behavior will be tried until behaviors which reliably move the parrot are found. Assimilation refers to previously acquired action patterns brought to bear on the current problem; accommodation refers to the behavioral adjustments needed to solve the problem.

In play, assimilation dominates accommodation; there is asynchrony rather than synchrony. Action patterns are produced and varied without much regard to a particular goal. According to Piaget, "play proceeds by the relaxation of the effort at adaptation" (1962, p. 89). The pleasure comes from a feeling of supermastery, a "feeling of virtuosity or power" (ibid.). Play, then, represents a special type of challenge. It is not a type of challenge presented by the environment nor is it a type of challenge sought in the environment. Play represents challenge produced by the child, and as such it offers a special type of developmental opportunity.

As one of the authors has noted elsewhere, pretend play illustrates this assimilative mode at a symbolic level (Fein, 1979a,b). Symbolic play extends the sensory-motor play of an earlier period. Rather than actually going down the slide a hundred ways, the child may make a toy animal go down in ways that for the child would be physically impossible or even disastrous. The toy animal can hop down, leap down, or even fall down. The child can slide down hugging a "frightened" baby doll, turn the slide into a hill for cars, or initiate numerous other activities which transcend the literal meaning of a solid object on an inclined plane.

Pretend play as assimilation also implies that means/ends relations have been temporarily severed. *What at an earlier period were means are now meanings.* During the sensory-motor period, going down the slide head-first was just that: a novel, challenging, slightly scary way of doing a familiar activity. Now, the same behavior might represent a down-hill ride on a sled, a plane coming in for a landing, or a trip to the moon. At an earlier level of development, the slide was a slide, the child was his real self, and the activity occurred in a world of tangible objects. Now, either the slide, the child, or any other feature of the environment can be transformed. According to Piaget (1962), the special pleasure of symbolic play comes from the child's ability to manipulate and vary meanings as well as means.

Observing Play

In discussing attachment theory, we noted that one of its values for teachers and parents is that it marks behaviors that reveal how children feel about people and social situations. The theory offers an interpretive framework within which behaviors such as smiles, eye–eye contact, and proximity along with their opposites—frowns, gaze avoidance, and distance—hold privileged positions as indicators of children's affectional ties and feelings of comfort and security. In discussing theories of arousal and mastery, we argued that these formulations had more to say about the quality of children's environments than about the quality of their behavior.

The notion of galumphing, especially if placed in the context of Piagetian theory, returns us once again to behavior. At a sensory-motor level of behavior, play activities develop from activities with a single object to those involving combinations of two or more objects (Fein & Apfel, 1979a). The overall patterning of object behavior changes as well. Between the ages of eighteen and twenty-four months, children contact more diverse elements of the environment, and as they do so, the tendency to get stuck on one particular object diminishes (Fein & Apfel, 1979a).

Pretense, too, changes in systematic ways. Initially, the child produces the motions of sleeping without intending to sleep or the motions of eating without intending to eat. These activities seem to take place outside their customary context and seem divorced from their customary functions of rest and nourishment. Over the next year and a half, these ephemeral gestures become elaborated and enriched. At first, a doll is simply an object to be touched, moved, or banged. Somewhat later, the doll (rather than the child) is used as the recipient of food and eventually is made the recipient of a complex array of care-giving activities: it is put to bed, dressed, patted, and spanked (Fein & Apfel, 1979b). The child's voice quality might change to sound like a parent; gestures, clothing, and other elements might combine to indicate that a role enactment is occurring.

At first, the objects used in pretense tend to be similar to the things used in the real life situations that pretend activities mimic (babylike dolls and cuplike cups). Gradually, the need for verisimilitude weakens and assorted objects (sticks and shells) can be used as substitutes in pretend enactments. Eventually, the child can create the semblance of a physical entity (hand holding cup or arms rocking absent doll).

Initially, pretend play is a solo activity. Adults may participate and organize it, but children under three years of age rarely share pretend sequences with one another except, perhaps, in brief, imitative, parallel exchanges (Parten, 1932). By two-and-a-half years of age, the beginnings of sociodramatic play appear and, by the age of five years, what began as a few simple gestures encompasses intricate systems of reciprocal roles, ingenious improvisations of materials, increasingly coherent themes, and weaving plots.

Sociodramatic play also demonstrates a systematic pattern of developmental change. At first, children communicate primarily about their own roles ("I'm the mommy"). Later, they discuss others' roles and the activities that will be engaged in during the play (Garvey & Berndt, 1977). There are also changes in the types of role relationships enacted. At first, role relationships tend to be those in which the children have participated in real life (parent–child, sibling), and only later do these encompass the role relationships observed in others (husband–wife, storekeeper–customer). The social organization of the play changes as well (Iwanaga, 1973). At three, children are more likely to engage in complementary role play in which differentiated roles are assigned (for instance, conductor and passengers), but in the play these roles are enacted independently (for example, conductor starts and stops the train, the passengers get on and off, but each child develops the role without reference to one another). Older children are more likely to produce integrative role structures in which the activity of each player is tied to the activity of the others and the roles are constituted through reciprocal relationships between the players.

Enhancing Play

Information about the development of play behavior and sensitive observation of behavior provide clues to children's level of cognitive and social maturity. More important, this information can serve as the basis for attempts to enhance or elaborate the play. A major contribution to a theory of teaching practice can be found in Smilansky's (1968) detailed analysis of how teachers might proceed from a careful assessment of children's current level of play to a set of systematic strategies for enriching the thematic context of the play and children's skills at using play techniques.

Play is also enhanced by features of the physical environment. With respect to a theory of practice, several of these features are under the practitioner's control. Depending on the children's developmental level, realistic props might be more supportive of play than abstract materials. According to Nunnally and Le-mond (1973), novelty might enhance exploratory behavior, but familiarity might enhance play. A play space protected from unpredictable intrusions, familiar peers, and unpressured time are other factors likely to enhance play (see Fein, 1981, for a discussion of these issues). Further progress toward a theory of practice will require more intensive study of how teachers and others can create optimal conditions for play. As this issue is addressed, abstractions such as novelty or familiarity will require rules for their actual production, rules which then might yield examples of environmental variation currently unavailable to theories of development.

The Function of Play

Is it important to have play as part of the preschool curriculum? Must play be part of a theory of practice in early education? So far, the evidence favors a positive response to both questions. Pretend play, for example, is associated with the com-binatorial flexibility that characterizes creative thinking (Dansky, 1980). Although children must have some skills in taking the perspective of others in order to engage in sociodramatic play, there is evidence that these skills are con-solidated when children engage in such play. Numerous studies indicate that sociodramatic play has a positive influence on perspective taking and cooperation (for example, Burns & Brainerd, 1979; Smith & Syddall, 1978; Rosen, 1974). Although the process responsible for this influence is not understood, the evidence indicates that activity in an assimilative mode deepens children's grasp of physical and social phenomena. If creativity and social sophistication are considered desirable developmental outcomes, play becomes a practical means whereby these outcomes can be promoted.

Some Concluding Observations

Developmental theory provides a rich source of information about the remarkable intricacies of human growth. Most certainly, respect for the child's special qualities is a necessary starting point for a theory of practice. But the relationship between a theory of development and a theory of practice may be more intimate. Indeed, the relationship may be one of reciprocity and mutual dependence. In the previous sections, we discussed three distinctively different developmental theories and the different issues they set out to address. In this section, we offer some summary conclusions suggested by that discussion.

Minimums and Maximums

Earlier, we characterized theories of practice as inherently maximalist, with the qualification that maximizing factors fall within the controllable domain of the practitioner. As Bronfenbrenner (1979) astutely noted, a theory of practice creates a demand for an ecological theory of human development. According to our analysis, such a theory will assume the maximalist orientation traditionally adopted by theories of practice and traditionally rejected by theories of development. Bronfenbrenner's proposal in effect requires a massive revision of the form of developmental theory.

Consider, for example, the way attachment theory has dealt with affectional relations. For numerous reasons, the focus of the theory has been consistently on the child's developing relationship with the particular person (usually the mother), who functions as the primary caregiver during the first year of life. In a theory of practice, this focus must expand. For a theory of parenting, for example, the focus must shift to the parent's developing relationships with the child (rather than the child's relationship with the parent), and include the parent's perception of the social and material resources that impinge upon that relationship. Put another way, a theory of parenting must consider the parent's perceptions of the child's perceptions of significant social and material resources. But such a theory must also consider the parent's perceptions of a broader domain, along with rules for mobilizing that domain to serve the best interests of the developing child as determined by the values held by the parent.

At the heart of a theory of practice are statements about how controllable resources are to be obtained and allocated. These statements have enormous implications for an ecologically sensitive and valid theory of development. At one time, developmental theory rested almost exclusively on studies in which the experimental situation was rigged so as to demonstrate almost any possibility (Parke, 1979). These situations have been properly criticized as artificial, first, because they are likely to be perceived as ersatz even by children, and, second, because they often bizarrely distort physical and social events. More recently, there has been a shift in emphasis from rigged to actual environments. But actual environments are inherently opaque because the rigging is obscure. To the extent that principles derived from a theory of practice permit conceptions of *actualizable* environments, developmental theory will be able to consider *realizable* possibilities.

Universals and Particulars

Attachment theory offers one illustration of the pressure of practice forcing maximalist expansion in a theory of development. Theories of exploration and play illustrate a different type of pressure. In the case of arousal theory, concepts of complexity or novelty are too general to serve the needs of practice without additional elaboration. In a theory of development, it is necessary to formulate rules for reducing the immense diversity and variability of the world into general categories; when applied, these rules transform particulars into potentially universal dimensions. These rules make it possible to define complexity as the number of movable parts in a climbing apparatus or as the number of turns in a vinyl object. But in a theory of practice, universal dimensions must be transformed into particulars; the rules of practice are generative rather than reductive.

These rules will be restricted to the particular domain of resources controlled by a given practitioner, but they will be stated so that within the domain an immense variety of concrete examples can be generated. If complexity and novelty are crucial physical dimensions governing the exploratory behavior of children and if this behavior is deemed a desirable goal for practice, then a theory of practice must contain rules for generating environments that are appropriately complex or novel.

The theory of mastery motivation illustrates another problem. To date, this theory has not taken full advantage of the developmental theory from which it was derived. The theory is unnecessarily overgeneralized, omitting the voluminous literature specifying qualitative changes in the nature of children's thinking. From the perspective of practice, this omission offers an instance in which developmental theory has not taken full advantage of its own potential. A proper theory of mastery requires evidence of the way in which children in the natural environment define and solve problems as a function of their level of cognitive development. With this evidence in hand, a theory of practice can construct procedural statements based on the practitioner's identification of children's cognitive level and the specification of developmentally appropriate challenges.

Generative Systems

Finally, there is the message offered by Piaget's notion of play as assimilation. Although the notion of assimilation in this special sense has had its strongest application to the play of young children, it has implications for adult thought that have yet to be explored. According to Piaget (Piaget & Inhelder, 1971), personal and imaginal symbolism is required by adults to concretize abstract thought. In Piaget's words: "The minds which are best able to control abstractions are those which succeed in embodying them in concrete examples . . . which then serve as symbolic springboards without introducing any limitations" (1971, p. 11).

In the division of labor implied by the separation of theories of development from theories of practice, it may fall to the practitioner to generate concrete examples from developmental abstractions. If this is so, a major task of a theory of practice is to consider formulations about the creative and imaginative potential of the practitioner. But Piaget's insight also suggests that the current radical separation between these types of theory might operate to the disadvantage of progress in each. At the very least, a deliberate recognition of mutual dependency may contribute to more adaptive theories in each domain.

References

AINSWORTH, M., BLEHAR, M., WATERS, E., and WALL, S. *Patterns of Attachment.* Hillsdale, N.J.: Lawrence Erlbaum Associates, 1978.

ANDERSON, J. W. Attachment behavior out of doors. In B. Jones (ed.), *Ethological Studies of Child Behavior.* Cambridge: At the University Press, 1972.

AREND, R., GROVE, F. L., and SROUFE, L. A. Continuity of individual adaptation from infancy to kindergarten: A predictive study of ego-resiliency and curiosity in pre-schoolers. *Child Development*, 1979, *50*, 950–959.

ARSENIAN, J. M. Young children in an insecure situation. *Journal of Abnormal and Social Psychology*, 1943, *38*, 225–249.

BERLYNE, D. E. Curiosity and exploration. *Science*, 1966, *153*, 25–33.

BLEHAR, M. C. Anxious attachment and defensive reactions associated with day care. *Child Development*, 1974, *45*, 683–692.

BOWLBY, J. *Attachment and Loss, Vol. 1: Attachment*. London: Hogarth Press, 1969.

BOWLBY, J. *Attachment and Loss, Vol. 2: Separation*. London: Hogarth Press, 1972.

BRONFENBRENNER, U. *The Ecology of Human Development*. Cambridge, Mass.: Harvard University Press, 1979.

BURNS, S. M., and BRAINERD, C. J. Effects of constructive and dramatic play on perspective role taking in very young children. *Developmental Psychology*, 1979, *15*, 512–521.

DANSKY, J. L. Make believe: A mediator of the relationship between free play and associative fluency. *Child Development*, 1980, *51*, 576–579.

FEIN, G. G. Play and the acquisition of symbols. In L. Katz (ed.), *Current Topics in Early Education*. Hillsdale, N.J.: Ablex, 1979(a).

FEIN, G. G. Echoes from the nursery: Piaget, Vygotsky and the relationship between language and play. *New Directions in Child Development*, 1979b, *6*, 1–14.

FEIN, G. G. The physical environment: Stimulation or evocation? In R. Lerner and H. Busch (eds.), *Individuals as Producers of Their Own Development: A Life Span Perspective*. New York: Academic Press, 1981.

FEIN, G. G., and APFEL, N. The development of play: Style, structure and situation. *Genetic Psychology Monographs*, 1979a, *99*, 231–250.

FEIN, G. G., and APFEL, N. Some preliminary observations on knowing and pretending. In M. Smith and M. B. Franklin (eds.), *Symbolic Functioning in Childhood*. Hillsdale, N.J.: Lawrence Erlbaum Associates, 1979b.

FEIN, G. G., and MOORIN, E. Group care can have good effects. *Day Care and Early Education*, 1980, *7*, 14–18.

GARVEY, C., and BERNDT, R. Organization of pretend play. *Catalogue of Selected Documents in Psychology*, 1977, I(no. 1589), American Psychological Association.

HARTER, S. Pleasure derived from challenge and the effects of receiving grades on children's difficulty level choices. *Child Development*, 1978, *49*, 788–799.

HOCK, E. Alternative approaches to child rearing and their effects on the mother–infant relationship. Final Report to the Office of Child Development, Washington, D.C., 1976.

IWANAGA, M. Development of interpersonal play structures in 3, 4, and 5 year old children. *Journal of Research and Development in Education*, 1973, *6*, 71–82.

LEPPER, M. R., GREENE, D., and NISBETT, R. E. Undermining children's intrinsic interest with extrinsic rewards: A test of the overjustification hypothesis. *Journal of Personality and Social Psychology*, 1973, *28*, 129–137.

LIEBERMAN, A. F. Preschoolers competence with a peer: Influence of attachment and social experience. *Child Development*, 1977, *48*, 1277–1287.

LOVELAND, K. K., and OLLEY, J. G. The effect of external reward on interest and quality of task performance in children of high and low intrinsic motivation. *Child Development*, 1979, *50*, 1207–1210.

MACCOBY, E. E., and JACKLIN, C. N. Stress activity and proximity seeking: Sex differences in the three year old child. *Child Development*, 1973, *44*, 34–42.

MAIN, M. Analysis of a peculiar form of reunion behavior seen in some day care children: Its history and sequelae in children who are home reared. In R. Webb (ed.), *Social Development in Day Care*. Baltimore, Md.: Johns Hopkins University Press, 1977.

MARVIN, R. S. Attachment and reciprocity in the two year old child. Unpublished masters thesis, University of Chicago, 1970.

MATAS, L., AREND, R. A., and SROUFE, L. A. Continuity of adaptation in the second year: The relationship between quality of attachment and later social competence. *Child Development*, 1978, *49*, 547–556.

MENDEL, G. Children's preferences for differing degrees of novelty. *Child Development*, 1965, *36*, 453–465.

MILLER, S. Ends, means and galumphing: Some leit-motifs of play. *American Anthropologist*, 1973, *75*, 87–98.

NUNNALLY, J. C., and LEMOND, L. C. Exploratory behavior and human development. In H. Reese (ed.), *Advances in Child Development and Behavior, Vol. 8*. New York: Academic Press, 1973.

PARKE, R. D. Interactional design and experimental manipulation: The field-lab interface. In R. B. Cairnes (ed.), *Social Interaction*. Hillsdale, N.J.: Lawrence Erlbaum Associates, 1979.

PARTEN, M. B. Social participation among preschool children. *Journal of Abnormal and Social Psychology*, 1932, *27*, 243–269.

PIAGET, J. *Play, Dreams and Imitation in Childhood*. New York: Norton, 1962.

PIAGET, J., and INHELDER, B. *Mental Imagery in the Child*. New York: Basic Books, 1971.

PORTNOY, C. F., and SIMMONS, C. H. Day care and attachment. *Child Development*, 1978, *49*, 239–242.

RHEINGOLD, H. L. The effect of a strange environment on the behavior of infants. In B. M. Foss (ed.), *Determinants of Infant Behavior, IV*. London: Methuen, 1969.

ROOPNAIRENE, J. L., and LAMB, M. The effects of day care on attachment and exploratory behavior in a strange situation. *Merrill-Palmer Quarterly*, 1978, *24*, 85–96.

ROSEN, C. E. The effects of sociodramatic play on problem-solving behavior among culturally disadvantaged preschool children. *Child Development*, 1974, *45*, 920–927.

SCHOLTZ, G. J. L., and ELLIS, M. J. Repeated exposure to objects and peers in a play setting. *Journal of Experimental Child Psychology*, 1975, *19*, 448–455.

SCHWARTZ, P. The Effects of separations due to child care on attachment behavior of 18 month old infants. Unpublished doctoral dissertation, University of Michigan, 1978.

SCHWATZ, J. C., and WYNN, R. The effect of mother presence and previsits on children's emotional reaction to starting nursery school. *Child Development*, 1971, *42*, 871–881.

SMILANSKY, S. *The Effects of Sociodramatic Play on Disadvantaged Pre-school Children*. New York: Wiley, 1968.

SMITH, P. K., and SYDDALL, S. Play and non-play tutoring in preschool children: Is it play or tutoring which matters? *British Journal of Educational Psychology*, 1978, *48*, 315–325.

SWITZKY, H. N., HAYWOOD, C. H., and ISETT, R. Exploration, curiosity, and play in young children: Effects of stimulus complexity. *Developmental Psychology*, 1974, *10*, 321–329.

VAUGHN, B., WATERS, E., EGELAND, B., and SROUFE, L. A. Individual differences in infant–mother attachment at 12 months and 18 months: Stability and change in families under stress. *Child Development*, 1979, *50*, 971–975.

WATERS, E. The reliability and stability of individual differences in infant and mother attachment. *Child Development*, 1978, *49*, 483–494.

WATERS, E., WIPPMAN, J., and SROUFE, L. A. Attachment, positive affect and competence in the peer group: Two studies in construct validation. *Child Development*, 1979, *50*, 821–829.

WHITE, R. W. Motivation reconsidered: The concept of competence. *Psychological Review*, 1959, *66*, 297–333.

PART II

Developmental Theories and Early Education

CHAPTER 6

Curriculum Models and Early Childhood Education

Ellis D. Evans

A CURRICULUM MODEL provides an ideal representation of the essential philosophical, administrative, and pedagogical components of a grand education plan (Evans, 1975; Spodek, 1973). It constitutes a coherent, internally consistent description of the theoretical premises, administrative policies, and instructional procedures presumed valid for achieving preferential educational outcomes. Ultimately, this abstraction can serve as the basis for educational decision making. As decisions are translated into action, we can speak of model implementation, thus enabling the empirical study of models.

This chapter has two related purposes. The first is to explore major components or characteristics of early childhood education models with reference to selected conceptual issues that permeate the literature on models development. Second, various concepts and issues about model analysis and evaluation are reviewed, with emphasis upon some recent developments important for improved evaluation practice.

Background to the Discussion

Curriculum models have appeared in one form or another since the advent of formal education for young children. But focus upon the utility of early education curriculum models has sharpened considerably in recent years. Perhaps the most notable force in this sharpening process is the Planned Variation experiment first integrated into Project Follow Through, later extended on a limited basis to Project Head Start (Zigler & Valentine, 1979). Selected educational authorities were encouraged to propose conceptual alternatives for controlled application in educational settings for children ages four to eight. The result was a widely ranging set of curricular activities and instructional strategies to operationalize preferred philosophies or theories of child development, learning, and education. At its zenith, as many as twenty-two alternative educational plans, called models, were considered for Planned Variation (Goodwin & Driscoll, 1980).

Implicit in this thrust to develop, implement, and evaluate models were two fundamental assumptions: no one best way exists to educate all children in all social contexts, and different curriculum models are variously well suited for different children (and staff) in different social contexts. This move to develop alternative curriculum models was consistent with the value of pluralism in education, conceivably to provide the citizenry with choices among legitimate and comparable educational designs.

Serious students of early childhood education theory and practice will note many important questions about the alternative models ideal, three of which are addressed here. The first question concerns model building—that is, which model characteristics or components are functional and relevant as a framework for developing curriculum models in the original sense? Once determined and used for model building, these characteristics or components should be further useful for the comparative analysis of alternative models. Such analysis normally will concern a specification of similarities and differences among models at the theoretical-descriptive level.

As for similarities, a prime issue is the extent to which models agree upon certain fundamentals (for example, educational goals, principles of curriculum design, conditions for learning) even though these models may emerge from diverse theoretical wellsprings and represent "different roads to Rome." Authentication of similarities may result in the identification of a basic core of principles and conditions: to represent the best of educational thought about early childhood curricula, and to serve as the point of departure for the creation of new curriculum models.

A parallel issue is the extent to which model rationales may differ in substance or design. From these differences will flow implications about children's educational welfare, cost to society, suitability to various social contexts, and so on. Differences among early educational curriculum models are certain to reflect value commitments about what is more or less important for young children and their families. Presumably, these differential commitments will affect educational practices and, in turn, educational outcomes. It is incumbent upon model builders clearly to identify these commitments at the theoretical-descriptive level so that analysts and consumers can determine distinctiveness.

A second major question about curriculum models goes beyond a conceptual analysis of similarities and differences at the theoretical-descriptive level. To wit, how clearly are these theoretical model similarities and differences revealed in actual educational practices? It is one thing to state distinctive curriculum components on paper; to validate such components by way of empirical observation is quite another. Validation requires a set of procedures for measuring model implementation, often referred to as process evaluation (Morris & Fitz-Gibbon, 1978). Process evaluation involves an assessment of the presence and merit of program components (for example, instructional methods and materials) antecedent to or theoretically functional for attaining model objectives.

The third major question about curriculum models is to what extent various models when implemented competently, are effective in producing their intended educational outcomes? This question usually draws attention first to any changes in children's behavior and development that are associated with model implementation. But outcome assessment will often include the evaluation of changes among teachers, parents, and even community services that follow model implementation. In practice, curriculum model guidelines can vary markedly in relation to impact evaluation. One set of guidelines may be geared to intrinsic or criterion-based evaluation. This means that the acid test for model implementation is how well or how completely stated goals are achieved. A contrasting orientation to evaluation is based upon model comparisons. Here, the effectiveness of two or more models is compared on the basis of common goals, usually for the purpose of selecting the most powerful or cost-efficient alternative.

A bias for intrinsic or criterion-based model evaluation may make comparative evaluation irrelevant. If an advocate accepts the goals and methods of a given model as inherently worthy and evidence can be marshaled to demonstrate the model's capacity to "deliver," it may matter little how the favored model compares to others. However, many consumers (as well as model advocates) are understandably intrigued by questions about which models are more or less efficient and effective for achieving generic outcomes. This implicit competitive aspect of model development and implementation may be masked by the idea that different models are more or less effective for different outcomes. So the issue of comparative model effectiveness lingers on.

To summarize, a clear conception of model characteristics is relevant for several important tasks. Such characteristics can serve as analytical criteria useful for model selection. Those characteristics also provide a basis from which to plan model improvements and even create new models. An understanding of model characteristics is relevant to educational researchers. Many characteristics can be considered as independent variables to guide model implementation and impact research. Eventually, this research may provide a clearer picture of what model characteristics are most important for facilitating different outcomes among children whose needs and learning styles differ. In fact, research along these lines may disclose that some characteristics have little, if any, bearing on children's educational development while others are critical for this development. As model features are empirically validated, much of the speculation or guesswork about model development and implementation should be reduced, if not eliminated.

Curriculum Model Components

A careful examination of the literature suggests that program models can be analyzed for three major categories of program components: theoretical foundations, administrative policies, and curriculum content and methods. In this section, each category of components is explained with reference to illustrate conceptual and evaluation research issues.

Theoretical Foundations

Theoretical foundations for curriculum models typically reflect a mix of philo-sophical and psychological thought about educational aims. This mix will include value statements about the basic purpose(s) of education in concert with assump-tions about children's learning and development. Thus, "should's" and "ought's" about education to promote the good life are focal. These statements of good usually link with convictions about what are the essential conditions of learning and development for instructional design.

The interrelationships of educational ideology and psychological theory are at best complex and intricate. At worst, these interrelationships are obscure, con-fusing, or conspicuously absent. Over time, however, certain bodies of consistent, integrated thought about philosophy and psychology have come to dominate cur-riculum models for early childhood education. These bodies of thought are iden-tified by various labels, such as the behaviorist, dynamic, and constructivist ap-proaches (see Chapters 7, 8, and 9; also Franklin & Biber, 1977, and Murray, 1979).

Goal Orientations

Model philosophies and educational aims are diverse, but much of their concep-tual diversity can be reduced to a relative emphasis upon one or another of two broad goal orientations for children: to nurture general socialization or to achieve specific learnings, usually in the academic realm (Spodek, 1977). Also associated with this emphasis are differences in interpretation of ideas about education as preparation for the future (J. Anderson, 1947). One interpretation is a claim that young children's education should be designed on the basis of requisites for success in adult society. Children's momentary or transitory needs and interests are sub-servient to adult beliefs about what achievements and skills are essential for socio-economic self-sufficiency. Applied to early childhood curriculum models, this view includes support for "continuity in the educational enterprise as it currently exists" (Miller, 1979, p. 199). A foremost priority is solving the problem of se-quencing preschool educational demands to better prepare children for successive demands in the kindergarten and primary grades. This means that educational planning is essentially a "top down" experience. Broadly defined adult roles and values form the basis of a formal K–12 span of educational requirements. Early childhood curricula, as preschool-kindergarten, are conceived to facilitate suc-cessful adaptation to existing primary programs, and so on.

Although all formal educational programs are to some extent "preparatory," the issue is one of degree or emphasis. Education as preparation for the future may too easily result in a "cold storage" concept of learning. Should educators not be forced to justify the worth of learning experiences for children in terms of some projected scholastic or socioeconomic value? It is argued that such thinking diverts attention from young children's interests and unique learning thinking styles, especially as expressed in play. Instead, their uniqueness should be nurtured to stimulate balanced affective and cognitive development.

Protagonists for a nurturance view of early education claim that the best insurance for successful adulthood is fully enriched, day-to-day, child-centered experience. From this, children will best develop a secure sense of competence and selfhood. Curriculum planning begins with an analysis of children's developmental characteristics, consistent with their unique needs, interests, and modes of thinking—a "bottom up" design. In this way, a strong foundation for subsequent growth and development is achieved. Concomitantly, ideal early childhood education may promote both social and educational reform (Lazerson, 1972). This is because the educational system would accommodate *to* children instead of requiring the conformity dictated by top-down curriculum development.

VIEWS OF DEVELOPMENT

This philosophical difference in curriculum aims and purposes is paralleled in the fields of developmental psychology: a schism between proponents of "naturalistic, indigenous growth" theories of development and the "cultural competence" or "environmental determination" viewpoint (Evans, 1975). The schism aggravates contentions about desirable conditions of learning. These contentions, in turn, link to preferences about curriculum methods.

Advocates of the natural growth or maturationist view argue that the best education will be achieved by providing children with an enriched, benign, accepting, permissive, and relatively informal environment. High value is placed upon children's need for creative expression. Through such expression, self-development is best nurtured; developmental or maturational sequences provide whatever cues may be important for realizing individual growth potentials.

In contrast, supporters of the "cultural competence" school emphasize more the shaping power of experience and necessity for social adaptation. Systematic and direct tuition thus figure more prominently in socialization practice. Skill development for mastery of cultural demands is the key to maximum growth achievement. Accordingly, the structure and continuity of environmental events will largely determine children's patterns of learning and development.

This schism in thinking about the nature of human development has been adroitly couched in terms of *context-free* versus *context-sensitive* theories of development (Bruner, 1972). Early childhood educators sympathetic to the universals of child development, especially stage-sequence interpretations from genetic psychology, will claim that basic principles of developmental education apply to all children. These principles should provide the basis for common educational experiences at successive age levels. Though differences in developmental level are carefully accounted for, differences associated with socioeconomic status, racial-ethnic identity, and other demographics do not figure strongly in thinking about goals or aims. From this it can be argued that development per se is the fundamental aim of education (Kohlberg & Mayer, 1972). Philosophies that are context-specific or context-sensitive will, in contrast, accentuate the role of cultural variables in promoting or impeding children's skills acquisition. Thus, educational aims may emerge from an analysis of any learning deficiencies allegedly rooted in social background experience.

Schisms in educational philosophy and psychological theory represent, of course, degrees of emphasis, not conceptual dichotomies. Thus, curriculum model philosophy and aims can be viewed in relative position along a given continuum of thought. For example, the applied behavior analysis approach (see Chapter 8) leans more in the direction of a cultural-competence, context-sensitive viewpoint than do constructivist approaches (Chapter 9), which have more in common wth a natural growth, context-free position. Even so, pure applications of educational philosophy and developmental theory are not easily observed in everyday, practical experience (Goodlad, Klein & Novotney, 1973).

Theoretically based differences *can* become a reality, however, as indicated by various model demonstration programs (for example, Miller & Dyer, 1975) and the planned variation experiments within Projects Head Start and Follow Through (Stallings, 1975; Zigler & Valentine, 1979). Among the clearest theory-based differences are extent of child-centeredness in educational planning, nature or type of learning sequences, accent on basic academics, incentive systems, and explicitness in seeking affective outcomes (Evans, 1975). These differences are generally consistent with values and assumptions of alternative philosophies and theories. However, in the final analysis shorter-term objectives and methods for achieving them seem more vocally disputed among early childhood educators than are longer-range educational aims. In fact, efforts to promote unification of purpose have been called for under the banner of social competence (for instance, Zigler & Trickett, 1978).

In sum, one's philosophical view of education and human development is the foremost model component from which statements about curriculum goals, content, and method will emanate. For a conceptual analysis of models, the issue for this component is twofold: comprehensiveness and internal consistency. A comprehensive, internally consistent statement will articulate the theoretical basis from which a model is conceived to clarify the logical interrelationships of philosophy and psychology. It will also clarify assumptions about educational purpose, conditions of human learning, and the nature of human development. It will further show how assumptions are integrated with other basic model components, especially curriculum content and method. Coherence of philosophy and aims is a matter of both degree and kind. This necessarily requires a careful study of curriculum in concept as well as in implementation.

Administrative Policies

A second major category of curriculum model components concerns policies and procedures for overall program administration or management. In contrast to philosophical discourse about education and child development, specific literature about administrative variables of early education models seems less extensive. Consequently, much information about this topic must be extrapolated from more general educational administration literature. It is perhaps significant that specific administrative concerns are being addressed more and more by early childhood professionals (Hewes, 1979; Stevens & King, 1976).

There seems to be no definitive consensus about how best to categorize administrative policy variables for the conceptual analysis of curriculum models. Some administrators prefer a human relations approach to administrative policy. Their focus is staff and community involvement for policy development and implementation. Other administrators work from a more technical orientation to management, dealing especially with the economics of a program, including fiscal policy and cost efficiency studies. Still others take an ecological stance, stressing the study of political, sociological, and legal forces that influence or dictate administrative decision making.

Acknowledgment of different orientations need not distract attention from the point that administrative variables represent decision-making points about how best to insure the success of an educational program. Accordingly, it is convenient to group administrative policy variables into three interrelated categories upon which is superimposed a method for establishing program budget (determining costs, revenue sources, allocating resources). These are policy about personnel, the physical setting for model implementation, and program evaluation.

PERSONNEL

Personnel specifications for early education curriculum models include nature of the population to be served, identification of staff to deliver basic services, and community participation or involvement, especially parents or primary caregivers. Criteria should be present to define pupil eligibility for a given model or population characteristics useful for determining the suitability of a model. These criteria may include age, cultural-linguistic background, socioeconomic status, clinical health status, ethnicity, and even sex. Some models claim their suitability for all children of a particular age group or developmental stage, regardless of cultural background. Others are designed specifically for special populations as, say, a bilingual program for limited English-speaking children. In addition, a pupil personal services policy should address the following topics: health, safety, nutritional standards, individual pupil assessment practices (diagnostic testing, measuring pupil progress), procedures for reporting pupil progress to parents, referral procedures for children with special problems (at risk for social adjustment or mental health), guarantees for children's rights (Feschbach & Feschbach, 1978), and general ethical guidelines for program quality (Katz, 1980).

Program staff, a second major category for personnel policy considerations, concerns teachers, aides, administrators and supervisors, and adjunct service personnel (nurse, dietician, psychometrist). Minimal staff qualifications, hiring policies, in-service training provisions, staff evaluation procedures, staff–pupil ratio designations, grouping practices, and extent of staff involvement in curriculum decision making are common sources of personnel staff variation. To illustrate, one sorely argued difference in early education staff function is the extent to which teachers are trained to implement a fixed or "teacher-proof" curriculum versus developing competence in the management of one that is more fluid, flexible, informal. Standards or requirements for preservice credentials, staff training, selection, and evaluation will be influenced substantially by one's position on this issue (Spodek, 1972; Stevens & King, 1976).

A third major category of policy considerations deals with forms of community involvement in early education programs. These forms usually vary according to the age of the children for whom benefits are sought (Nedler, 1973). Models developed for infants or toddlers, for example, present a set of staff–parent relationships and responsibilities somewhat different from those designed for older children. If a model's major thrust is home-based education, then parental involvement policies—including parent education—are of paramount importance. Strategies for securing involvement can be described along a continuum from none-to-minimal to nearly complete parental control of an educational program. Some models (for instance, Florida Parent Education Program, Gordon, 1969) are founded upon principles of parent involvement. Others (classical Montessori method) exclude direct parent participation. Either way, policies can be traced to a model's theoretical foundations and should generate testable assumptions about the relationship of parental involvement to children's developmental education (Clarke-Stewart & Apfel, 1978). These policies may also extend to decision making about parent education (see, for example, Fine, 1980).

PHYSICAL SETTING

Inextricably bound to administrative considerations are physical setting requirements for model implementation. This calls for attention to space and equipment needs and their arrangements, juxtaposed with health and safety standards. Existing programs vary remarkably in the degree to which ideal physical facilities and space use are tied consistently to model philosophy or theoretical rationale. Well-developed models (for example, Hohmann, Banet & Weikart, 1978) often provide explicit graphics, as floor plans, to guide appropriate implementation. Minimum square footage for classroom and playground space may also be recommended.

These considerations are significant in view of two broader issues about the physical environment for early education: first, *the place* where children's formalized early education is best conducted (as home, home-school combination, institutional setting only) (Evans, 1975); and second, *what effects* physical space variables may have on children's behavior (Gump, 1980; Phyfe-Perkins, 1980; C. S. Weinstein, 1979). Space considerations are closely bound to time use as well. Time use—meaning allotments for specific learning activities—anticipates a forthcoming discussion about curriculum methods. But administrative policy issues are also involved in decisions about full- or half-day programming, definition of a "school year," and so on. Incredible as it may seem, little is known about the effects of different time arrangements on children in formal educational programs.

PROGRAM EVALUATION POLICY

The third and final major category of curriculum model administrative policy explored here involves provisions for ongoing program evaluation: determining the worth of integral model components and, ultimately, the model as a whole. These provisions can be classified into formative and summative evaluation tasks (Scriven, 1967). Formative evaluation—instrumental during the early stages of model development and implementation—addresses the extent and quality of intended services. In contrast, summative evaluation addresses the overall worth of a model program at some terminal or critical decision point (end of program, time for a "go–no go" decision). Program administrators may also find it desirable—even necessary in an increasingly economics-minded society—to apply principles of cost analysis to program evaluation. If so, summative model impact is studied in terms of cost efficiency, cost–benefit, cost utility, or cost effectiveness (Halpern, 1979). A cost-effectiveness approach will involve evaluation for the purpose of gaining maximum results for the lowest or most reasonable expenditure.

Both formative and summative evaluation procedures demand careful attention to the selection of appropriate measurement and data-analysis techniques. Also important for this aspect of administrative policy are personnel qualifications, authority, and responsibilities for evaluation. Generally speaking, insiders familiar with the workings of a model have both an advantage and a vested interest in "trouble-shooting" their program and providing constructive feedback to other staff for program improvement. In contrast, qualified and disinterested external evaluation specialists are usually better situated to provide objective summative evaluation. In either case, administrative guidelines to justify the role definition and selection of evaluation personnel are at issue (Anderson & Ball, 1978).

Administrative policies comprise a major category of curriculum model characteristics. These policies encompass practical decision making about personnel, physical facilities, and program evaluation. Ideally, policies are consistent with, if not determined directly by, overall model philosophy. Any set of model administration policies must be accompanied by a master fiscal policy, usually to include cost-accounting procedures. Fiscal concerns will be model-specific, though general principles for budgeting and accounting can apply. Interested readers may consult Candoli et al. (1978) for further information.

Curriculum Content and Method

The joint issues of what and how best to educate young children have persisted unabated since the earliest days of formal educational thought. Neither issue is easily divorced from model philosophy and aims nor conveniently isolated from administrative policy decisions. For present purposes, however, content concerns the *what* of learning and its general arrangement in a curriculum; method concerns presentation strategies—the *how* of curriculum delivery.

CONTENT

Generally speaking, model philosophy and content selection go hand in hand. For example, a model based upon a philosophy of essentialism (Brameld, 1956) will be defined in content by a selected body of knowledge to which all children are exposed, ecological variables notwithstanding. Key issues associated with this philosophical stance include justifying the essentials and determining valid means for securing their achievement. Fixed or uniform levels of mastery or minimum competence for children in advance of instruction are compatible with this position. Content selection for a second model, in contrast, may spring from a moral imperative. This means that, to whatever extent possible, children should have freedom to exercise their own learning styles, choose their own content, and determine their own competence standards. Given this imperative, neither uniform content nor fixed ideas about pedagogy figure strongly in educational planning. Somewhere in between essentialism and the moral imperative for self-determined education may emerge a moderate, child-centered position to emphasize opportunity for content choices from among a varied but limited set of options.

Some Basic Content Distinctions. Curriculum content emphases vary even among moderate positions. One long-standing content distinction in early education concerns learnings for cognitive-intellectual achievement on the one hand and affective-social growth on the other. Cognitive–affective distinctions, of course, can easily strike a false or artificial dichotomy when, in truth, such learnings are highly interrelated. Yet, the distinction is important, especially for scrutiny of content priorities within a curriculum model. It is instructive to note that educational applications of integrated cognitive and social development theory have been proposed (for instance, Enright, 1980).

A second, related distinction for curriculum model analysis is academic skills or subject matter proficiency versus intellectual content or cognitive skills proficiency (Katz, 1970; Rohwer, 1971). A primarily academic emphasis concerns acquisition of predetermined factual material along traditional subject matter lines. Intellectual content, however, is concentrated more upon the heuristics of learning: general inquiry skills, elaboration skills, and problem-solving strategies. Theoretically, a cognitive-intellectual skills approach is independent from (but may involve some) academic content. If so, academic content is seen as a means to an end, not as an end in itself.

It seems fair to say that uncertainty, if not confusion and wariness, pervades decision making about content for early childhood education. Research has not yet confirmed much about what program contents are best for successive levels of early education. Promising rationales for content selection have been proposed (Rohwer, 1971), but they are infrequently applied in practice.

Perhaps the most basic content issue for educators to address concerns a functional taxonomy for classifying educational content and objectives. To date, no standard, consensual taxonomy permeates early childhood educational model building; nor is consensus likely in view of theoretical foundation differences among models. A constructivist approach, for example, may use the Piagetian categories of physical, social, and logical knowledge (Kamii & DeVries, 1977). Curriculum models for intellectually precocious children are frequently governed by Guilford's (1967) structure of intellect theory to emphasize figural, symbolic, semantic, and behavioral content. Still other taxonomies are used for educational planning and evaluation (Bloom et al., 1956; Gagne, 1978; Hoepfner et al., 1971; Steinaker & Bell, 1979) despite nagging questions about their empirical validity (Seddon, 1978).

Some Integral Content Components.   The taxonomy issue prompts a further specification of three integral content components important for the conceptual analysis of curriculum models: scope, priorities, and structure. Scope refers to the breadth or variety of content and skill values built into a curriculum model (Parker & Day, 1972). One model may incorporate content across a broad spectrum, such as *aesthetics* (art, music, creative drama, dance), *cognitive-intellectual skills* (classification and seriation skills, logical-reasoning skills, problem-solving skills), *basic concept acquisition* (concepts of space, time, number), *academics* (reading, arithmetic computation, handwriting), and *social-affective skills* (prosocial behavior, self-control, achievement motivation). Other models may emphasize fewer skill domains, even to exclude certain content areas such as academics or aesthetics.

Closely related to scope are the relative priorities assigned to content within a curriculum model. One clear indicator of priorities is amount of time allocated for content exposure. The variable *time of exposure* is critical for estimating children's opportunities for both acquisition and rehearsal or practice as well as practicing learnings. Exposure time can be operationalized in various ways, as, for example, by "time on task" or sheer duration of learning events. Either way, important links to curriculum method surface here, especially pacing and intensity of stimulation. Multiple interactions between and among content and method variables can thus be proposed for empirical study. Such interactions are particularly notable in the brouhaha surrounding basic language training and remediation for young children (Bricker, 1980; Evans, 1975).

A third major content component variable is content *organization* or *structure* with accompanying rationales about sequencing content for different modes of instruction. Again, theoretical foundations (or their lack) are at least implicit in prescriptions for structuring content. One model, for example, may reflect armchair analysis of the structure of knowledge (Bereiter & Engelmann, 1966). Another may draw upon experimental task analysis procedures (White, 1973). Still another may base content organization and structure upon broad developmental sequences of cognition, as disclosed by longitudinal and cross-sectional research with children. However it may be conceptualized, content structure provides another continuum insofar as analysis is concerned. At one extreme of this continuum are tightly organized, immutable content sequences prescribed for all children (maximum conformity). At the other extreme are content structures supported by the moral imperative (maximum individuality). These latter structures may be arbitrarily determined or, conceivably, based upon comprehensive assessment of individual readiness for learning.

There is some degree of consensus among theoreticians that much of human learning and development is hierarchical in nature (Evans, 1975). Consensus is lacking, however, about the precise nature of hierarchical learning and the conditions or forces that influence hierarchical progression. At issue is a basis for structuring educational content over time for most effective learning, retention, and transfer. Controversy along these lines seems most pointed in the extent to which model advocates believe that *external* organization of content and general learning activities is desirable or necessary for given learning outcomes (see, for example, Strauss, 1972).

Some additional content variables relevant to this discussion are *continuity* and *stability* or *regularity* in curriculum experience (Lay & Dopyera, 1971; Parker & Day, 1972). To the extent that thematic content is introduced, built upon, sustained, and integrated during a given instructional day, one can speak of continuity. To illustrate, consider a teacher who introduces selected grammatical structures during formal language training and then integrates these same structures with other lessons later in the day, such as musical songs, poetry, and arithmetic story problems. A common learning can thus be reinforced while simultaneously providing the occasion for generalization or transfer of learning. Stability refers to the extent to which a particular pattern of curriculum encounters recurs with predictable regularity, as daily, weekly, and so on. Model content high in stability will be revealed by specific curriculum routines. A model may prescribe that each day open with a group planning activity and close with a group evaluation of things accomplished. The interim period would be filled with an established order of content-related activities. Presumably, stability is important for children as an aid to time perspective development, sequential thinking, and general emotional security. If so, curriculum stability may be more or less important, depending upon age and experiential background of the children involved. But a compulsive regularity, with few breaks from routine, conceivably could result in boredom and fatigue among some children. By the same token, insufficient regularity could breed anxiety and frustration among others. These ideas are relatively untested but appear together with other related hypotheses about the psychology of the open classroom (Horwitz, 1979).

Specification of Program Objectives.   A final content variable is how content and skill emphases are translated into program objectives. One feature of curriculum objectives readily culled from model analysis is the extent to which objectives are explicit and operationalized for appropriate assessment. In general, model objectives most suited to reliable measurement are specific, precise, and stated in terms of observable behavior. The objective will state what a learner should be able to do, under what circumstances of assessment, and at what level of competency (Morris & Fitz-Gibbon, 1978b).

A rich literature on the characteristics and application of behavioral objectives has accumulated together with many attendant issues about their utility and effects (Duchastel & Merrill, 1973; Melton, 1978). Some content domains (for example, basic academic skills) have been more amenable to behavioral phraseology than others (especially affective learning). Consequently, models may present varying degrees of specificity and precision across content domains. Models are far from uniform in their affinity for behavioral objectives and choice of measurement strategy. At the theoretical level, any set of content or skill objectives, however operationalized, should flow consistently from the overall goals or global, long-range aims as revealed in curriculum philosophy. Unfortunately, rationales for translating broad, general program goals into specific objectives for instructional design are obscure, if extant, in many contemporary models.

The clarity, relevance, and appropriateness of curriculum content objectives surface as basic criteria for decisions about pupil progress assessment and model program evaluation. Still larger educational issues surface as well, including program accountability functions, how a curriculum model for young children may fit into broader developmental perspective (as preschool-kindergarten-primary-intermediate-secondary), and measurement philosophy (the product–process distinction in learning, criterion versus norm-referenced assessment strategies, and whether formal or systematic measurement has any place at all in curriculum evaluation).

To summarize, six major curriculum content variables have been identified: scope (including variety and breadth), priorities, organization (including structure and sequence), continuity, stability, and operationalization of content objectives.

METHOD VARIABLES IN CURRICULUM MODELS

As with curriculum content, methods are conceptualized and described in many different ways. Standard designations of general methods come immediately to mind—tutorial, discussion, recitation, lecture, laboratory demonstrations—each of which has its own strengths and limitations insofar as establishing conditions for learning is concerned (Gagne, 1978). More basic for conceptual analysis, however, is a set of methodological dimensions or processes that can be described as didactic versus prepared and group versus individual (Miller, 1979).

Basic Methodological Distinctions.   A didactic versus prepared method dimension concerns the extent to which teachers engage in expository teaching in contrast to more indirect means for preparing or arranging the learning environment (including materials and activities) to facilitate children's active involvement and self-initiated discovery learning. At issue are the how's and why's of alternative teacher–learner role enactment, that is, role definition in relation to curriculum objectives. Likewise, the group versus individual dimension involves a relative preference for group-based activities common for all learners or the desires of individualized learning experiences. Group-based activity usually emphasizes uniform presentation and teacher-controlled recitation strategies. Although groups may range in size, adult–child interactions typically dominate with varying degrees of freedom for child–child interactions. Programs that emphasize individualized experiences can also present a wide range of adult–child interactions with considerable attention to tutorial relationships, self-pacing, varied-child materials, and ample peer interactions. In practice, model programs rarely show an exclusive preference for one or the other methodological format. Dominant patterns of experience are common, however, and different combinations of method may vary through time. Thus, there are model differences in *pacing*, wherein the frequency and rapidity of alternative individual–group and prepared–didactic experiences are salient concerns. Decisions about pacing various combinations of experience imply beliefs about what means (methods) are more or less suitable for what ends (program objectives). For example, small-group activities may be preferred to promote children's cooperative behavior; individualized discovery methods may be introduced to promote autonomous problem-solving; and so on. Such beliefs or preferences about means–end relations provide a rich source of research hypotheses for field research.

Some Further Method Variables.　However basic the covarying dimensions of didactic-prepared and group-individual methods are, additional variables further illustrate the methods' substructure of curriculum models. For example, *formal assessment strategies* to determine children's program entry behavior ("readiness for learning") usually figure prominently in any diagnostic-prescriptive instructional design, regardless of whether the learning tasks in question are introduced at a group or at an individual level. *Motivational strategies* also come into play. Curriculum models frequently differ in their emphasis upon activating and nurturing intrinsic motives (as epistemic curiosity) or incentive systems that constitute extrinsic sources of motivation (as token-economy systems). The issue of relations between intrinsic motivation and extrinsic rewards has intensified in recent years, partly because of strong behavioristic influences in early childhood education. Current research issues, by no means resolved, include the study of how various reward systems may undermine or enhance young children's desire to learn for learning's sake (Bates, 1979). A related motivational strategy variable under study is classroom goal structure: the relative emphasis placed upon cooperative and competitive activity as the antecedent to group versus individual rewards and recognition, respectively (Michaels, 1977).

A method dimension closely tied with motivational psychology is the preferred style of teacher–child interaction (as the familiar Flanders, 1965, notion of indirect-to-direct influence) to include corrective feedback strategies. Some research issues here are teacher's question-asking strategies and their effects (Sigel &

Saunders, 1979), how best to deal with the wrong response (Blank, 1975), the role of different types and schedules of reinforcement for different kinds of learning (Travers, 1977), and nonverbal communications in teaching (Smith, 1979). A second class of human interaction variables in model development concerns peer tutorial methods and cooperative team learning strategies. This class of variables reflects a growing research interest in the *Learning Through Teaching* (LTT) movement (Gartner, Kohler & Reissman, 1971). Recent methods and results of various peer-tutoring and group-investigation strategies are reviewed by Sharan (1980).

Still another class of instructional methods important for model analysis includes procedures for facilitating *retention and positive transfer* of learning. As for enhancing retention, especially long-term effectiveness of learning, several instructional design variables are noteworthy: procedures for generating meaningfulness of children's new learning, assisting children to develop coding strategies for effective memory storage and retrieval, and appropriate practice and review tactics (Bugelski, 1979; Kail, 1979; C. S. Weinstein, 1979). In turn, securely retained learnings are a necessary, though insufficient, condition for *positive transfer*. By this is meant the extent to which school learnings facilitate later performance and learning, both in and out of the school context.

It is tempting to argue that transfer is what school is all about. Theoretically, models designed to prepare children for successful adaptation to future schooling should show a strong commitment to vertical transfer: early, simpler learnings are purported to facilitate learning of later, more complex, and subordinate learnings (Gagne, 1968). Models that stress acquisition of problem-solving strategies or "learning how to learn" imply a bias for skills that serve children well in an unpredictable and changing world. In any case, methods to promote transfer will have in common a focus on rules or principles that have broad generality, varied application of these rules and principles, explicit procedures to establish a set to transfer, and so on (Travers, 1977). A problem for model analysis is the extent to which a formal theory of transfer guides the process of instructional design (Royer, 1979).

A final method component to be discussed here is the orchestration of *instructional media and materials*: how sensory equipment, audio-visual resources, simulation games, autotelic devices, kits, workbooks, and other resources are coordinated and used. Variety in instructional media and materials is basic to any system of individualized instruction and enables a flowing of stimulation across different sensory modalities to maintain children's attention and reinforce learning (Travers, 1977). Appropriately scheduled, the novelty effect of various media theoretically can also sustain motivation for learning. It is important, of course, to distinguish among the mere presence of alternative media sources, their quality, how these sources are used, and their effects on educational development.

Much has been learned about the impact of instructional media variables on learning that is useful to model builders (Jamison, Suppes & Wells, 1974). But with the possible exception of television studies (see Palmer & Dorr, 1980), media research with preschool children seems to have lagged behind that with older learners. Given young children's natural propensity for play, there seems to be a strong potential for games approaches to learning. These include physical activities to reinforce academic skills (Cratty, 1971) and group games for coordinated human development (Kamii & DeVries, 1980). Research possibilities seem especially promising for the media component of early childhood curriculum models.

In sum, the curriculum methods dimension of curriculum models can be defined in terms of certain basic criteria. These criteria include the didactic-prepared, individual-group distinction as well as preassessment strategies, motivational procedures, interaction style, feedback procedures, provisions for transfer, and instructional resources. Choice of instructional methods is tied directly to beliefs about the conditions of learning. That is, methods comprise means to manipulate the ways in which children receive, process, and act upon information from the environment. Thus, any set of prescribed methods presumably will reflect hypotheses about what conditions are essential for learning efficiency and effectiveness. In short, a theory of instruction is at issue. These collective ideas may be more or less well-founded in the empirical studies about children's learning. This foundation itself is an important point for scrutiny in model analysis; and a scrutiny of the methods component brings us back full cycle to the theoretical foundations component as a basis for decision making in model implementation.

A Point of Transition

Discerning readers may have noted that, excepting a brief reference to interaction style, nothing explicit has been written about the general social-affective climate for learning as a model component. Few would challenge the importance of this variable, however elusive its operationalization. Certainly the variable has a longstanding educational research interest as indicated by the literature on teacher personality (warmth–coldness), teaching style (restrictive–supportive) (Bidwell, 1973; Getzels & Jackson, 1963). From humanistic perspectives, education rhetoric supports the value of a warmly responsive, benevolent learning environment as best for young children (Rogers, 1969). Humanists may call for the nurturant emotional climate primarily on moral grounds; but empirical data, such as a negative relationship between teacher's use of hostile criticism and children's achievement and attitudes toward school (Rosenshine, 1971) are also germane to this point.

However passionate any rhetoric, the research issue here is how well an intended emotional climate occurs in model implementation. Both administrative and instructional personnel are key factors in this aspect of implementation. Children themselves also contribute to classroom climate in several ways: the attitudes and expectancies they bring initially to the formal setting, their responses to attempts by others to influence their behavior, peer modeling and reinforcement that occurs in the classroom, and so on (Kounin, 1970; Patterson, Littman & Bricker, 1966).

In larger perspective, though curriculum models may be analyzed on conceptual grounds independent of any social context, their implementation and effectiveness cannot. And both the implementation and the impact of a given model may vary with the context in which implementation occurs (House & Hutchins, 1979). Eventually, then, the validity of a model must be determined from the observation of real events. This prompts a shift from the conceptual blueprint stage of model analysis to issues and procedures of model implementation and impact evaluation research.

Evaluation of Curriculum Models

The basic technical thrust for curriculum model evaluation is determining how, when, and from what sources information will be gathered and analyzed for decision-making purposes. Thus, evaluation contributes to decisions about model development, modification, replication, contamination, expansion, certification, and installation (Anderson & Ball, 1978). Accordingly, a systematic approach to model evaluation will begin by clarifying the purpose(s) of evaluation (Rossi & McLaughlin, 1979). Once the purpose is clarified, problem solving about suitable evaluation methodology follows (Perkins, 1977). Decisions about model program development and improvement, for example, call for the application of formative evaluation procedures (see earlier section on administrative policy). Decisions about program continuation or adoption will call for evidence of program impact or total effectiveness. Hence, summative evaluation procedures are necessary. Both kinds of procedures may be combined to promote understanding of basic psychological or social processes, depending upon the extent to which this kind of information is central to the evaluation effort (Anderson & Ball, 1978).

A specification of procedures for both formative and summative evaluation, or model implementation and impact evaluation, will comprise an *evaluation design*. The main components of an evaluation design are the conditions, schedule, and type of data collection and analysis, details of which are discussed elsewhere (for example, Popham, 1975). Model impact or outcome evaluation has been dominated by applications of experimental and quasi-experimental research methods. Although the feasibility of such methods is usually limited in field settings, these methods have earned an important place in educational evaluation (Cook & Campbell, 1979). The literature on formative evaluation procedures is less extensive, but nonetheless important for students of curriculum models (see, for example, Fitz-Gibbon & Morris, 1978). Moreover, conceptual systems for determining the adequacy of comprehensive evaluation designs (Sanders & Nafziger, 1976) are noteworthy for study.

Model Implementation and Impact Evaluation

Traditionally, decision making about early childhood model evaluation has been dominated by summative or outcome evaluation research, especially to seek immediate, short-term evidence of model impact on children. The merit of curriculum models typically has been assessed according to how clearly models produce desired or intended changes among children exposed to them. Support or opposition to a model, then, is rallied on the basis of evidence about children's progress (gains) in academic achievement and other valued goal areas.

Requisite Assumptions for Meaningful Impact Evaluation

However preoccupied evaluators have been with summative impact evaluation, a meaningful empirical test of any model clearly requires that certain basic assumptions be met. A first is that stated outcomes are (can be) attainable through educational processes. This calls forth again the rationale by which realistic and worthwhile goals and objectives are selected, formulated, judged, and linked to instructional design (Morris & Fitz-Gibbon, 1978a; Stake, 1972).

A second requisite assumption for meaningful model impact evaluation is that valid, reliable measures are available to assess goal achievements. The assumption of technically respectable measurement has been difficult to meet fully in practice. Satisfactory assessment of young children's educational progress poses peculiar challenges to evaluation. Not only have measurement strategies been limited in scope and technique, but evaluators have also tended to place ease of measurement above quality control. Evaluation has been heavily dependent upon the use of spurious testing procedures. Such problems and challenges to evaluation are discussed elsewhere (Bradley & Caldwell, 1974; Evans, 1974; Goodwin & Driscoll, 1980) as are the matters of measurement availability, construction, selection, and evaluation (Hoepfner et al., 1971; Johnson, 1976). Few will deny, however, that model impact data are only as valid as the procedures used to gather them. Associated issues for model outcome evaluation are determining what effects are worth assessing and how they shall be assessed (Bracht, 1975; Cooley, 1975).

The third assumption for meaningful model impact evaluation is that a model is, in fact, implemented as prescribed or intended. The importance of this condition cannot be overemphasized. A given model can easily be jeopardized on grounds of "no effects" or "poor results" in the absence of data about how adequately, completely, or competently it was implemented. The alleged early failure of Project Head Start illustrates this problem. That is, data from a limited range of generic, short-range measurements were taken virtually at face value to judge the effectiveness of compensatory intervention before any semblance of implementation quality could be determined. Premature and narrowly conceived evaluation seriously threatened Head Start's existence; and controversy about Head Start models impact has continued to persist still short of adequate implementation data (Bentler & Woodward, 1978; Magidson, 1978).

A Word about Process Evaluation

The Head Start object lesson, among others, has contributed to a greater appreciation of process evaluation: assessing the merit of program variables antecedent to and presumably related in a causal way to program outcomes. Process variables encompass curriculum methods and materials, teacher personality or style, emotional climate, and characteristics of the physical environment. In conventional experimental research parlance, process variables collectively constitute the "treatment," that is, the independent variable(s) to which subjects are exposed and upon which predictions about change are based. Process evaluation, then, is concerned with the problem of insuring that the treatment has occurred.

The importance of this insurance for valid impact evaluation has already been stressed. But process evaluation is more and more valued for its own sake (Zimiles, 1977). For one thing, overall program quality is at issue. For another, process evaluation is well suited to questions about what instructional methods and materials are best tailored to or most preferred by given program personnel. For still another, explicit process-outcome linkages are probably best understood through the careful examination and systematic manipulation of treatment variables (Soar & Soar, 1972).

Process approaches to curriculum model evaluation depend heavily upon, but are not limited to, observational techniques. Consequently, a basic problem for process evaluation is selecting or developing an appropriate system for taking and recording observational data. Child development and early education researchers have provided a wealth of observational systems and procedures (Gordon & Jester, 1972), many of which are aptly illustrated by curriculum model implementation and impact studies (see, for example, Leinhardt, 1977; Miller & Dyer, 1975; Stallings, 1975). Interview and questionnaire methods figure prominently in innovative approaches to determine the level of program implementation in specific educational settings (Hall & Loucks, 1977). Systematic process evaluation procedures for measuring domains of instruction have also been proposed, the most detailed of which concern variations on the theme of mastery learning and prescriptive teaching (Leinhardt, 1980). Arguments for integrating ethnographic techniques into model research and evaluation activity have appeared with increasing frequency during the past several years as well (see, for example, Wilson, 1977). For evaluators who fear that use of such techniques undermines objectivity in evaluation research, strategies for dealing with the issue of subjectivity can be recommended (Goodrich, 1978).

Further Developments in Early Education Evaluation Research

As progress in process evaluation continues, so does thinking about how to broaden the scope of impact evaluation for a better understanding of educational processes. One practice championed for this purpose is the multivariate analysis of model programs (Messick & Barrows, 1972). Conventional evaluation practice has usually been limited to documenting average gains for groups of children involved in one or another model program. Multivariate analysis seeks to disclose interactions between child and program characteristics, that is, to determine which program characteristics are more or less important in accounting for variations in children's responses to programs. This sort of analysis has been slow in application to routine evaluation methodology but it figures prominently for questions about why some children may flourish in a given program while others may not (Evans, 1979). The more basic line of scholarly inquiry involved here, of course, is the increasingly popular aptitude- or trait-treatment interaction research (Cronbach & Snow, 1977). Practical applications of this form of inquiry are yet uncertain. Conceptually, however, this inquiry seems pertinent to solving problems about matching children to treatment, that is, finding the "best fit" between programs and their participants.

A second, related idea for improved curriculum model evaluation concerns adaptations of longitudinal research methodology to better monitor long-term program effects on children, parents, and staff. Much of the impetus for this "cumulative impact" approach to evaluation emanates from exemplary programs, as the Perry Preschool Project (Weikart, Bond & McNeil, 1978), and the consortium for longitudinal studies (Lazar & Darlington, 1978). The push for standard longitudinal evaluation is, in part, a reaction to swarms of skeptics who question the values of early education. Broadly conceived longitudinal evaluation seems now recognized as essential for a more complete understanding of education and development. Fundamental questions concerning type of intervention programs, duration and intensity of intervention, and amount of family involvement can all be dealt with at a more sophisticated level through longitudinal evaluation (Palmer & Anderson, 1979).

Some authorities (for instance, Takanishi, 1978) advocate that evaluation should be planned and conducted from a truly developmental perspective. Though cumulative, long-term impact is important from this perspective, more critical for ongoing evaluation are program quality and participant response to it. Qualitative change among both children and staff, especially in terms of realizing human potentials, becomes more central to evaluation than the conventional behavioral assessment of child outcomes. Still other authorities (Cronbach et al., 1980) call for fundamental reformation in evaluation practice. Among other things, reformation would require a softening of demands for technical purity in evaluation and greater commitment to progressive enlightenment, that is, a more complete understanding of program operations within their sociopolitical contexts. Relevance and credibility, not scientific quality, become principal standards from which evaluations are planned, executed, analyzed, and disseminated (Crombach et al., 1980).

Broadened perspectives on evaluation can often be clarified or enhanced by reference to one or another *conceptual framework* from which to chart essential evaluation tasks. Thus, conceptual frameworks are available for planning formative-summative procedures, determining accountability to clientele, identifying deficiencies in staff training, determining the effectiveness of innovative programs and assessment, evaluating the context in which a model program may be implemented, evaluating unintended or unanticipated model outcomes, and other purposes (Gephart, 1976; Goodwin & Driscoll, 1980; Perkins, 1977). Such frameworks, usually called evaluation models, show still another use of the term "model."

Use of an evaluation model appropriate to the various purposes of curriculum model evaluation is inherently sensible for any systematic, logical, and consistent approach to decision making about the worth of program processes and outcomes. Among the more sensitive areas of decision making applied to early education is economics (Halpern, 1979). Economic theory holds that continual investment in a given enterprise or opportunity is warranted insofar as that enterprise or opportunity shows or continues to yield "better returns" than alternatives would. In the context of early education, this theory guides a variety of cost-analysis procedures that concern measuring costs in relation to program effectiveness, efficiency, benefits to participants, and so on. Methodological problems abound in this approach to evaluation; but impressive instances of cost analysis can be cited (for example, Weber, Foster & Weikart, 1978) to indicate that the expense incurred by competently implemented model programs may be compensated by long-term benefits to society. Interested readers should consult the technical literature for details (Rossi, Freeman & Wright, 1979; Thompson, 1980).

A final issue for curriculum model evaluation concerns the external validity of a model program, or the power of a model to produce similar effects across a wide variety of specific settings. Models are implemented in particular environmental contexts. Evaluation proceeds to validate their implementation, goal achievements, and even cost efficiency or effectiveness. But this documentation is insufficient to conclude that a given curriculum model will be equally effective under different environmental conditions and with different populations of consumers. There is a need for replicative evaluation research to better understand any intersite variation in model processes and outcomes. Needs, resources, personnel competencies, and support services are but a few potentially significant factors in intersite variation. The Project Follow Through evaluation is ample precedent for showing that the same model may "work" better in some contexts than in others, even when instructional procedures are comparable across sites (House & Hutchins, 1979). Since much remains to be learned about such variation, caution against any premature generalization of model effects is advised. Models, even when refined to the point of high exportability, seem subject to subtle social forces. It appears that staff commitment to a model and the extent to which the values of a particular community are met through that model are among the most critical of these forces (Egbert & Brisch, 1979; Weikart, 1972).

Comprehensive curriculum model evaluation will include both process and impact assessment in a longitudinal perspective with an eye toward reconciling cost with benefits to individuals and the larger society. Considerable progress has been made in the methodology for this purpose, a study of which is a requisite for genuine professionalism in early childhood education.

Summary

A curriculum model is an ideal conceptual structure for decision making about educational aims, administrative policies, curriculum content, and instructional methods. Educational philosophy and psychological theory combine to form the core of a comprehensive curriculum model. From this core are generated policy guidelines for the selection of curriculum goals and objectives. Goals and objectives normally indicate degrees of emphasis upon education for cultural competence, naturalistic growth, and preparation for the future. At issue is a rationale or justification for taking any value stance about the functions of organized education for young children.

Internally consistent administrative policies are also governed by theory in a thoroughly formulated curriculum model. Administrative policies have been classified into three interrelated categories. A first category—personnel specification—involves criteria for the target population of learners, program staff, and community involvement (especially parents). Considerations about the physical setting for curriculum model development comprise a second category of administrative policy. The third is program evaluation policy. This category calls for decisions about formative-summative evaluation and may be juxtaposed with cost-accounting procedures.

Curriculum content and method were discussed in terms of distinctions among academic skills, cognitive-intellectual development, and affective growth. The issue of a functional taxonomy for defining content emphasis was highlighted along with decision points about content priorities and the organization of content sequences. Arrangements for continuity–stability in content delivery and the issue of operational statements of curriculum model objectives were also discussed. Method variables in curriculum models were examined in relation to two interlocking dimensions: didactic versus prepared, and group versus individual methods. Implications of these choices were framed against selected research issues that embrace still further method variables: motivational strategies, procedures for securing retention and transfer of learning, and the use of instructional media and materials. Content-method issues were couched more broadly in the trend to study early education from an ecological perspective.

Examining curriculum models from the standpoint of formal evaluation involves a series of decisions about evaluation purpose(s), design and analysis, and the application of results. Evaluation for level or fidelity of implementation was distinguished from evaluation for cumulative model impact. Needs and trends in model evaluation research were also reviewed. These include more sophisticated process evaluation to establish process-outcome linkages, the longitudinal-multivariate analysis of model impact, cost-utility applications, and the quest to establish external validity for innovative models.

References

ANDERSON, J. The theory of early childhood education. In N. Henry (ed.), *Early Childhood Education*. Chicago: University of Chicago Press, 1947.

ANDERSON, S. B., and BALL, S. *The Profession and Practice of Program Evaluation*. San Francisco, Calif.: Jossey-Bass, 1978.

BATES, J. C. Extrinsic reward and intrinsic motivation: A review with implications for the classroom. *Review of Educational Research*, 1979, 49, 557–576.

BELLER, E. K. Research on organized programs of early education. In R. M. W. Travers (ed.), *Second Handbook of Research on Teaching*. Chicago: Rand McNally, 1972.

BENTLER, P. M., and WOODWARD, J. A. A Head Start reevaluation: Positive effects are not yet demonstrable. *Evaluation Quarterly*, 1978, 2, 493–510.

BEREITER, C., and ENGELMANN, S. *Teaching the Culturally Disadvantaged Child in the Preschool*. Englewood Cliffs, N.J.: Prentice-Hall, 1966.

BIDWELL, C. E. The social psychology of teaching. In R. M. W. Travers (ed.), *Second Handbook of Research on Teaching*. Chicago: Rand McNally, 1973.

BLANK, M. *Teaching Learning in the preschool: A Dialogue Approach*. Columbus, Ohio: Charles E. Merrill, 1975.

BLOOM, B. S. (ed.). *Taxonomy of Educational Objectives, Handbook I: Cognitive Domain*. New York: David McKay, 1956.

BRACHT, G. H. Planning evaluation studies. In R. A. Weinberg and S. G. Moore (eds.), *Evaluation of Educational Programs for Young Children*. Washington, D.C.: Child Development Associate Consortium, 1975.

BRADLEY, R. H., and CALDWELL, B. M. *Issues and Procedures in Testing Young Children*. Princeton, N.J.: Educational Testing Service, 1974.

BRAMELD, T. *Philosophies of education in cultural perspective*. New York: Dryden Press, 1956.

BRICKER, D. (ed.). *Language Intervention with Children*. San Francisco, Calif.: Jossey-Bass New Directions Series, 1980.

BRUNER, J. S. Poverty and childhood. In R. K. Parker (ed.), *The Preschool in Action*. Boston: Allyn and Bacon, 1972.

BUGELSKI, B. R. *Principles of Learning and Memory*. New York: Praeger, 1979.

CANDOLI, I. C., HACK, W. G., RAY, J. R., and STOLLAR, D. H. *School Business Administration: A Planning Approach* (2nd ed.). Boston: Allyn and Bacon, 1978.

CLARKE-STEWART, K. A., and APFEL, N. Evaluating parental effects on child development. In L. S. Shulman (ed.), *Review of Research in Education*, Vol. 6. Itasca, Ill.: F. E. Peacock, 1978.

COOK, T. D., and CAMPBELL, D. T. *Quasi-Experimentation: Design and Analysis Issues for Field Settings*. Chicago: Rand McNally, 1979.

COOLEY, W. W. Evaluation of educational programs. In R. A. Weinberg and S. G. Moore (eds.), *Evaluation of Educational Programs for Young Children*. Washington, D.C.: Child Development Associate Consortium, 1975.

CRATTY, B. J. *Active Learning: Games to Enhance Academic Abilities*. Englewood Cliffs, N.J.: Prentice-Hall, 1971.

CRONBACH, L. J., and SNOW, R. E. *Aptitudes and Instructional Methods*. New York: Irvington, 1977.

CRONBACH, L. J., AMBRON, S. R., DORNBUSCH, S. M., HESS, R. D., HERNICK, R. C., PHILLIPS, D. C., WALKER, D. F. and WEINER, S. S. (eds.). *Toward Reform of Program Evaluation: Aims, Methods, and Institutional Arrangements*. San Francisco, Calif.: Jossey-Bass, 1980.

DUCHASTEL, P. C., and MERRILL, P. F. The effects of behavioral objectives on learning: A review of empirical studies. *Review of Educational Research*, 1973, 43, 53–70.

EGBERT, R. L., and BRISCH, M. E. G. The advantages of educational models. *High/Scope Report*, 1979, 4, 30–32.

ENRIGHT, R. D. An integration of social cognitive development and cognitive processing: Educational applications. *American Educational Research Journal*, 1980, *17*, 21–41.

EVANS, E. D. Measurement practices in early childhood education. In R. W. Colvin and E. M. Zaffiro (eds.), *Preschool Education*. New York: Springer, 1974.

EVANS, E. D. *Contemporary Influences in Early Childhood Education*. New York: Holt, Rinehart, and Winston, 1975.

EVANS, E. D. Reflections on the long-term effects of early intervention. Urbana, Ill.: ERIC, ED 171 423, 1979.

FESHBACH, N. D., and FESHBACH, S. (eds.). The changing status of children: Rights, roles, and responsibilities. *Journal of Social Issues*, 1978, *34*, 196 pp.

FINE, M. J. (ed.). *Handbook on Parent Education*. New York: Academic Press, 1980.

FITZ-GIBBON, C. T., and MORRIS, L. L. *How to Design a Program Evaluation*. Beverly Hills, Calif.: Sage Publications, 1978.

FLANDERS, N. A. *Teacher Influence, Pupil Attitudes, and Achievement*. Washington, D.C.: U.S. Government Printing Office, 1965.

FRANKLIN, M. B., and BIBER, B. Psychological perspectives and early childhood education: Some relations between theory and practice. In L. G. Katz (ed.), *Current Topics in Early Childhood Education*, Vol. 1. Norwood, N. J.: Ablex, 1977.

GAGNE, R. M. Contributions of learning to human development. *Psychological Review*, 1968, *75*, 177–191.

GAGNE, R. M. *The conditions of learning* (3rd ed.). N.Y.: Holt, Rinehart and Winston, 1978.

GARTNER, A., KOHLER, M., and REISSMAN, F. *Children Teach Children*. New York: Harper and Row, 1971.

GEPHART, W. J. *Evaluation: Past, Present and Future*. Bloomington, Ind.: Phi Delta Kappa, 1976.

GETZELS, J. W., and JACKSON, P. W. The teacher's personality and characteristics. In N. L. Gage (ed.), *Handbook of Research on Teaching*. Chicago: Rand McNally, 1963.

GOODLAD, J., KLEIN, M., and NOVOTNEY, J. *Early Schooling in the United States*. New York: McGraw-Hill, 1973.

GOODRICH, T. J. Strategies for dealing with the issue of subjectivity in evaluation. *Evaluation Quarterly*, 1978, *2*, 631–645.

GOODWIN, W. L., and DRISCOLL, L. A. *Handbook for Measurement and Evaluation in Early Childhood Education*. San Francisco, Calif.: Jossey-Bass, 1980.

GORDON, I. J. *The Florida Parent Education Model*. Gainesville, Fla.: Institute for Development of Human Resources, 1969.

GORDON, I. J., and JESTER, R. E. Techniques of observing teaching in early childhood and outcomes of particular procedures. In R. M. W. Travers (ed.), *Second Handbook of Research on Teaching*. Chicago: Rand McNally, 1972.

GUILFORD, J. P. *The Nature of Human Intelligence*. New York: McGraw-Hill, 1967.

GUMP, P. V. The school as a social situation. *Annual Review of Psychology*, 1980, *31*, 553–582.

HALL, G. E., and LOUCKS, S. F. A developmental model for determining whether the treatment is actually implemented. *American Educational Research Journal*, 1977, *14*, 263–276.

HALPREN, R. The economics of preschool education. *High/Scope Report*, 1979, *4*, 14–18.

HEWES, D. W. (ed.). *Administration: Making Programs Work for Children and Families*. Washington, D.C.: National Association for the Education of Young Children, 1979.

HOEPFNER, R., STERN, C., and NUNMEDAL, S. G. (eds.). CSE–ECRC *preschool-kindergarten test evaluations*. Los Angeles: UCLA Graduate School of Education, 1971.

HOHMANN, M., BANET, B., and WEIKART, D. P. *Young Children in Action: A Manual for Preschool Educators*. Ypsilanti, Mich.: High/Scope Educational Research Foundation, 1979.

HOROWITZ, F. D., and PADEN, L. Y. The effectiveness of environmental intervention programs. In B. M. Caldwell and H. N. Ricciuti (eds.), *Review of Child Development Research*, Vol. 3. Chicago: University of Chicago Press, 1973.

HORWITZ, R. A. Psychological effects of the "open classroom." *Review of Educational Research*, 1979, *49*, 71–86.

HOUSE, E. R., and HUTCHINS, E. J. Issues raised by the Follow-Through evaluation. In L. G. Katz (ed.), *Current Topics in Early Childhood Education*. Vol. 2. Norwood, N.J.: Ablex, 1979.

JAMISON, D., SUPPES, P., and WELLS, S. The effectiveness of alternative instructional media: A survey. *Review of Educational Research*, 1974, *44*, 1–68.

JOHNSON, O. G. *Tests and Measurements in Child Development: Handbook II*. Vols. I and II. San Francisco, Calif.: Jossey-Bass, 1976.

KAIL, R. *The Development of Memory in Children*. San Francisco, Calif.: W. H. Freeman, 1979.

KAMII, C., and DEVRIES, R. Piaget for early education. In M. C. Day and R. K. Parker (eds.), *The Preschool in Action* (2nd ed.). Boston: Allyn and Bacon, 1977.

KAMII, C., and DEVRIES, R. *Group Games in Early Education: Implications of Piaget's Theory*. Washington, D.C.: National Association for the Education of Young Children, 1980.

KATZ, L. G. *Four Questions on Early Childhood Education*. Urbana, Ill.: ERIC Clearinghouse on Early Childhood Education, 1970.

KATZ, L. G. Ethics and the quality of programs for young children. In S. Kilmer (ed.), *Advances in Early Education and Day Care*. Vol. 1. Greenwich, Conn.: JAI Press, 1980.

KOHLBERG, L., AND MAYER, R. Development as the aim of education. *Harvard Educational Review*, 1972, *42*, 449–496.

KOUNIN, J. W. *Discipline and Group Management in Classrooms*. New York: Holt, Rinehart, and Winston, 1970.

LAY, M., and DOPYERA, J. *Analysis of Early Childhood Programs: A Search for Comparative Dimensions*. Urbana, Ill.: ERIC Clearinghouse on Early Childhood Education, 1971.

LAZAR, I., and DARLINGTON, R. B. Lasting effects after preschool. Report of the Consortium for Longitudinal Studies to the Education Commission of the States.

Washington, D.C.: U.S. Department of Health, Education, and Welfare, Grant 90C-1311, 1978.

LAZERSON, M. The historical antecedents of early childhood education. In I. J. Gordon (ed.), *Early Childhood Education*. Chicago: University of Chicago Press, 1972.

LEINHARDT, G. Program evaluation: An empirical study of individualized instruction. *American Educational Research Journal*, 1977, *14*, 277–293.

LEINHARDT, G. Modeling and measuring educational treatment in evaluation. *Review of Educational Research*, 1980, *50*, 393–420.

MAGIDSON, J. Reply to Bentler and Woodward: The .05 significance level is not all-powerful. *Evaluation Quarterly*, 1978, *2*, 511–519.

MELTON, R. F. Resolution of conflicting claims concerning the effect of behavioral objectives on student learning. *Review of Educational Research*, 1978, *48*, 291–302.

MESSICK, S., and BARROWS, T. S. Strategies for research and evaluation in early childhood education. In I. J. Gordon (ed.), *Early Childhood Education*. Chicago: University of Chicago Press, 1972.

MICHAELS, J. W. Classroom reward structures and academic performance. *Review of Educational Research*, 1977, *47*, 87–98.

MILLER, L. B. Development of curriculum models in Head Start. In E. Zigler and J. Valentine (eds.), *Project Head Start: A Legacy of the War on Poverty*. New York: Free Press, 1979.

MILLER, L. B., and DYER, J. L. Four preschool programs: Their dimensions and effects. *Monographs of the Society for Research in Child Development*, 1975, *40*, No. 162, 170 pp.

MORRIS, L. L., and FITZ-GIBBON, C. T. *How to Measure Program Implementation*. Beverly Hills, Calif.: Sage Publications, 1978a.

MORRIS, L. L., and FITZ-GIBBON, C. T. *How to Deal with Goals and Objectives*. Beverly Hills, Calif.: Sage Publications, 1978b.

MURRAY, F. B. The generation of educational practice from developmental theory. *Educational Psychologist*, 1979, *14*, 30–43.

NEDLER, S. *Parent Education and Training: Literature Review*. Austin, Texas: Southwest Educational Development Laboratory, 1973.

PALMER, E. L., and DORR, A. (eds.). *Children and the Faces of Television: Teaching, Violence, Selling*. New York: Academic Press, 1980.

PALMER, F. H., and ANDERSON, L. W. Long-term gains from early intervention findings from longitudinal studies. In E. Zigler and J. Valentine (eds.), *Project Head Start*. New York: Free Press, 1979.

PARKER, R. K., and DAY, M. C. Comparisons of preschool curricula. In R. K. Parker (ed.), *The Preschool in Action: Exploring Early Childhood Programs*. Boston: Allyn and Bacon, 1972.

PATTERSON, G. W., LITTMAN, R. A., and BRICKER, W. Assertive behavior in children. *Monographs of the Society for Research in Child Development*, 1966, Serial No. 113.

PERKINS, D. N. T. Evaluating social interventions: A conceptual schema. *Evaluation Quarterly*, 1977, *1*, 639–656.

PHYFE-PERKINS, E. Children's behavior in preschool settings: A review of research concerning the influence of the physical environment. In L. G. Katz (ed.), *Current Topics in Early Childhood Education*, Vol. III. Norwood, N.J.: Ablex, 1980.

POPHAM, W. J. *Educational Evaluation.* Englewood Cliffs, N.J.: Prentice-Hall, 1975.

ROGERS, C. R. *Freedom to Learn.* Columbus, Ohio: Charles E. Merrill, 1969.

ROHWER, W. D., JR. Prime time for education: Early childhood or adolescence? *Harvard Educational Review,* 1971, *41,* 316–341.

ROSENSHINE, B. *Teaching Behaviors and Student Achievement.* London: National Foundation for Educational Research in England and Wales, 1971.

ROSSI, R. J., and MCLAUGHLIN, D. H. Establishing evaluation objectives. *Evaluation Quarterly,* 1979, *3,* 331–346.

ROSSI, P. H., FREEMAN, H. E., and WRIGHT, S. R. *Evaluation: A Systematic Approach.* Beverly Hills, Calif.: Sage Publications, 1979.

ROYER, J. M. Transfer of Learning. *Educational Psychologist,* 1979, *14,* 53–69.

SANDERS, J. R., and NAFZIGER, D. H. *A Basis for Determining the Adequacy of Evaluation Designs.* Bloomington, Ind.: Phi Delta Kappa, 1976.

SCRIVEN, M. The methodology of evaluation. In *AERA Monograph Series on Curriculum Evaluation: Perspectives on Curriculum Evaluation, Vol. 1.* Chicago: Rand McNally, 1967.

SEDDON, G. M. The properties of Bloom's taxonomy of educational objectives for the cognitive domain. *Review of Educational Research,* 1978, *48,* 303–323.

SHARAN, S. Cooperative learning in small groups: Recent methods and effects on achievement, attitudes, and ethnic relations. *Review of Educational Research,* 1980, *50,* 241–272.

SHELLY, M., and CHARLESWORTH, R. An expanded role for evaluation in improving the quality of educational programs for young children. In S. Kilmer (ed.), *Advances in Early Education and Day Care,* Vol. 1. Greenwich, Conn.: JAI Press, 1980.

SIGEL, I. E., and SAUNDERS, R. An inquiry into inquiry: Question-asking as an instructional model. In L. G. Katz (ed.), *Current Topics in Early Childhood Education,* Vol. II. Norwood, N. J.: Ablex, 1979.

SMITH, H. A. Nonverbal communication in teaching. *Review of Educational Research,* 1979, *49,* 557–576.

SOAR, R. S., and SOAR, R. M. An empirical analysis of selected Follow-Through programs: An example of a process approach to evaluation. In I. J. Gordon (ed.), *Early Childhood Education.* Chicago: University of Chicago Press, 1972.

SPODEK, B. Staff requirements in early childhood education. In I. J. Gordon (ed.), *Early Childhood Education.* Chicago: University of Chicago Press, 1972.

SPODEK, B. Curriculum models in early childhood education. In B. Spodek (ed.), *Early Childhood Education.* Englewood Cliffs, N.J.: Prentice-Hall, 1973.

SPODEK, B. Curriculum construction in early childhood education. In B. Spodek and H. J. Walberg (eds.), *Early Childhood Education.* Berkeley, Calif.: McCutchan, 1977.

STAKE, R. *Priorities planning.* Los Angeles: Instructional Objectives Exchange, 1972.

STALLINGS, J. Implementation and child effects of teaching practices in Follow Through classrooms. *Monographs of the Society for Research in Child Development,* 1975, *40,* Serial No. 163.

STEINAKER, N. W., and BELL, M. R. *The Experiential Taxonomy: A New Approach to Teaching and Learning.* New York: Academic Press, 1979.

STEVENS, J. H., JR., and KING, E. W. *Administering Early Childhood Programs.* Boston: Little, Brown, 1976.

STRAUSS, S. Learning theories of Gagne and Piaget: Implications for curriculum development. *Teachers College Record*, 1972, 74, 81–102.

TAKANISHI, R. Evaluation of early childhood programs: Toward a developmental perspective. In L. G. Katz (ed.), *Current Topics in Early Childhood Education*, Vol. II. Norwood, N. J.: Ablex, 1979.

THOMPSON, M. S. *Benefit-Cost Analysis for Program Evaluation*. Beverly Hills, Calif.: Sage Publications, 1980.

TRAVERS, R. M. W. *Essentials of Learning* (4th ed.). New York: Macmillan, 1977.

TRAVERS, R. M. W. Taxonomies of educational objectives and theories of classification. *Educational Evaluation and Policy Analysis*, 1980, 2, 5–23.

WEBER, C., FOSTER, P., and WEIKART, D. P. *An Economic Analysis of the Ypsilanti Perry Preschool Project*. Ypsilanti, Mich.: High/Scope Educational Research Foundation, 1978.

WEIKART, D. P. Relationship of curriculum, teaching, and learning in preschool education. In J. C. Stanley (ed.), *Preschool Programs for the Disadvantaged*. Baltimore, Md.: Johns Hopkins University Press, 1972.

WEIKART, D. P., BOND, J., and McNEIL, R. *The Ypsilanti Perry Preschool Project: Preschool Years and Longitudinal Results through Fourth Grade*. Ypsilanti, Mich.: High/Scope Educational Research Foundation, 1978.

WEINSTEIN, C. E. Elaboration skills as a learning strategy. In H. F. O'Neil, Jr. (ed.), *Learning Strategies*. New York: Academic Press, 1978.

WEINSTEIN, C. S. The physical environment of the school: A review of the research. *Review of Educational Research*, 1979, 49, 577–610.

WHITE, R. T. Research into learning hierarchies. *Review of Educational Research*, 1973, 43, 361–375.

WILSON, S. The use of ethnographic techniques in educational research. *Review of Educational Research*, 1977, 47, 245–266.

ZIGLER, E., and TRICKETT, P. K. IQ, social competence, and evaluation of early childhood intervention programs. *American Psychologist*, 1978, 33, 789–798.

ZIGLER, E., and VALENTINE, J. (eds.). *Project Head Start*. New York: Free Press, 1979.

ZIMILES, H. A radical and regressive solution to the problem of evaluation. In L. Katz (ed.), *Current Topics in Early Childhood Education*, Vol. I. Norwood, N.J.: Ablex, 1977.

CHAPTER 7

Psychodynamic Theory of Development

Herbert Zimiles

Psychodynamic theory may be regarded as one offering among an array of alternative theoretical approaches from which early educators may choose, or it can be viewed as the main point of departure for most thinking about how children should be cared for. There is a measure of truth to both perspectives; that is, psychodynamic theory is not the only theoretical framework guiding the planning of early childhood education. On the other hand, it is by far the most well developed and comprehensive. Many alternative perspectives exist only as a negation of this influential point of view or as narrowly defined frameworks exclusively concerned with a particular facet of child development. Because psychodynamic theory has its roots in clinical psychotherapeutic practice—it is based on experience in actual dealings with children and relates to them—it has a breadth and substance that are especially helpful to the educator.

The Nature of Psychodynamic Theory

Psychodynamic theory of development is a term without precise meaning that describes a body of theory incorporating the common elements of most schools of psychoanalytic thought as they pertain to psychological development. It retains much of the theoretical perspective of psychoanalysis without embracing some of its specific constructs. Derived from the efforts of clinicians to understand psychopathology, it is concerned with the sources of irrational fear and feelings of vulnerability in people and their costly efforts to defend against and retreat from dangers which they sense but cannot understand. Foremost among its sources are Sigmund Freud's theory of psychoanalysis (1933), psychoanalytic theory concerned with the development of characterological trends leading to individuality (see, for example, Abraham, 1927, and Adler, 1927), the ego psychology of Hartmann, Kris and Lowenstein (1946), the interpersonal theory of psychiatry of Sullivan (1953), the epigenetic theory of development formulated by Erikson

(1963), and the adaptation of psychoanalytic theory to child development by Anna Freud (1935, 1965, 1968), Isaacs (1932), Winnicott (1958a, 1958b), and many others.

Origins of the Theory

The basic tenets of psychoanalytic theory lie at the core of a dynamic theory of development—the concept of unconscious motivation, the omnipresent role of conflict with family members over unacceptable wishes and impulses, the decisive influence of early childhood and its intense emotional life, a genetic view of development that describes an uneven path of progress through qualitatively different stages of development associated with specific developmental tasks and the resolution of particular areas of emotional conflict, the overriding importance of the need to resolve emotional conflicts and find socially acceptable ways of dealing with forbidden impulses, and recognition of the fact that access to the nether world of primitive and unacceptable impulses is an essential condition for the expression of creativity.

Many specific theoretical constructs originating in psychoanalysis are not typically included in the formulation of a psychodynamic theory of development although the themes they convey have been incorporated. For example, although the details of the libido theory—the theory of infantile sexuality and psychosexual development along with the associated constructs of the Oedipus complex and castration fear—are usually not specifically included, psychodynamic theory takes into account recognition of the prominence of sexual feelings and the conflicts they generate in young children and the powerful rivalries and emotional conflicts that arise among family members.

Originally formulated on the basis of a reconstruction of adult memories and the interpretation of the meaning and origin of unconscious thoughts and pathological trends among adults, psychodynamic theory of early childhood was in effect created to explain the origin of maladaptive patterns in adults. The theory begins with the premise of the continuity of psychic functioning from birth on and focuses on the enduring impact of early experience. Its early formulations were reconstructive and inferential; direct study of early experience from a psychodynamic view came later.

The Role of Early Experience

The term psychodynamic connotes the interplay of forces; it emphasizes the interactive element in psychological functioning. Behavior in the child is propelled and goal-oriented, not merely elicited. From the very earliest days, the child acts on the environment to obtain gratification. With the passage of time, he gradually learns to accommodate his pattern of needs and appetites to the opportunities for gratification which exist in his environment. The child's individuality is shaped by the manner in which he resolves the inevitable conflicts that arise between his needs and expectations, on the one hand, and the responsiveness of the environment, on the other.

In conceiving of the child's behavior from the very first moments of life as urgently concerned with gratifying impulses and avoiding pain, the full intensity of the child's relation to the caring person is brought clearly into focus. Capable of the most intense emotional experience and expression from the beginning of life, the very young child becomes deeply emotionally invested in those who provide gratification. The intensity of the infant's emotional attachments and the vigor of his needs are such that he reacts with rage and despair at the apparent loss of love objects and the frustration of impulses to gratification.

The infant's experience may be characterized as one of feeling powerful needs and discomforts, having a limited repertoire of responsiveness to a largely undifferentiated environment, associating pleasure and the reduction of pain with the presence of particular faces and people and activities, and lacking a conceptual grasp of the contingencies of events and the organizational arrangements that govern their occurrence. The child's earliest impressions of how gratifying and frustrating the world is are shaped by the juxtaposition of events and experiences which are in part determined by systematic features of the caretaking environment and in part by the vagaries of day-to-day living.

The inchoate experiences may be only dimly understood but they are intensely felt. The young infant's earliest experiences are no less important because they occur during a developmental stage of exceedingly limited awareness and understanding of reality. On the contrary, their limited accessibility to the ordered thought which later develops in conjunction with language renders them more potent because they are not easily correctable or modifiable by the cumulative impact of subsequent, language-mediated occurrences.

According to psychodynamic theory, the child's earliest experiences, especially those which revolve around being fed, cared for, and loved, have enduring impact. They become the foundation of experience upon which new differentiations and adaptations are based. Therefore, such factors as the physical health of the child, physiological impediments to feeding or the reduction of pain or stress, or traumatic experiences which cause physical or emotional stress, loom large in importance. Similarly, early styles of feeding and caretaking contribute to the base of experience which guides the formation of tastes, preferences, aversions, areas of sensitivity, anxiety, frustration tolerance, and patterns of emotional arousal and expression. Not all of the influences which impinge on the young child are necessarily systematic and coherent. Unexpected absences, interruptions, accidents, coincidences, and all other aspects of the moment-to-moment flow of events may come to have a decisive impact on the developing child's expectations and anxieties. Thus, one of the distinctive features of psychodynamic theory is that it is genetic, that is, it takes a historical view of patterns of behavior that are seen as evolving from the child's earliest experiences. In attributing great influence to the earliest experiences, it regards them as potent in and of themselves and also as providing the framework for experiencing and interpreting succeeding events.

The Interpersonal Focus

Psychodynamic theory is primarily concerned with interpersonal relationships and how they are impaired and distorted. It focuses on the nuclear relationship between the child and the primary caretakers and the events and circumstances that threaten their integrity. Thus, it is concerned with separation and loss of love objects, with experiences of apparent or real rejection or abandonment, and with the conflicts that are aroused by the threat of loss of love. It deals with primitive wishes; feelings of helplessness and wishes to be taken care of and, at the the same time, to dominate and be all-powerful, "to be the only one"; and with the rivalries and competition that are aroused in the family and the rage and fear evoked by such unacceptable feelings. It examines the interpersonal events that arouse unconscious fear and/or damaged self-esteem and their long-term consequences. It is primarily concerned with issues of relatedness, their derivatives, and their consequences.

A person's feelings of well-being are dependent on the appraisals and judgements of those in whom he is emotionally invested. At the same time, the child's relationships with those about whom he cares most gradually arouse conflict because of his strong dependence on them and their consequent ability to disappoint and frustrate him. Thus, the impetus to growth and the development of competence is both supported and undermined by the child's close emotional ties. The pain and discomfort aroused by his emotional dependence provide an incentive to grow and become more autonomous. But in gaining independence, the child faces the terrifying prospect of losing a caring and protective relationship. As the child becomes aware of his vulnerability, he comes to resent his dependence on loved ones; at the same time, paradoxically, the realization of his vulnerability may serve to intensify feelings of dependency.

Form and Scope of the Theory

As may be inferred, psychodynamic theory is phenomenological, concerned less with the objective reality of an event than with how it is experienced. The level of analysis of the theory is molar. Of central importance is the idea of the existence of an organized monitoring agent usually termed the ego or the self. The theory is concerned with a person's integrative capacity and how it is impaired by the repression or dissociation of emotionally stressful experiences. The different levels of awareness and the distinctive patterns of selective attention and repression induced by conflict or anxiety contribute to the development of a unique intelligence with individual patterns of learning and thinking, curiosity and creativity, and feelings of competence.

Psychodynamic theory is hospitable to a stage theory of development, to the idea that the developmental needs and tasks of children undergo qualitative changes that are associated with particular developmental landmarks and transitions. The theory embraces variations of Freud's theory of psychosexual development, as formulated by Erikson (1963), as well as other efforts (see, for example, Sullivan, 1953) to correlate distinctive patterns of psychological growth and conflict with particular developmental stages.

Psychodynamic Theory and Normal Development

First established to explain psychopathology by identifying impediments to growth and development, concepts of psychodynamic theory of development have only recently been reformulated to explain normal aspects of child development. Among those who have made a significant contribution to the difficult task of defining positive mental health and effectiveness of psychological functioning are Erikson (1963), Jahoda (1958), Smith (1959), Haan (1963), and White (1959, 1963, 1972). In order to go beyond traditional discussions of personality development that dwell on maladaptive patterns, on forces of inhibition and distortion, and feelings of vulnerability and helplessness, White has called attention to the efficacy and versatility of adaptation. White hypothesizes that the impulse to achieve the feeling of efficacy is as basic as that of the instincts and has devised the term effectance to describe the energy entailed in putting forth efforts to influence the environment. He regards self-esteem and ego strength as phenomena closely associated to what has become for him a central theme—the feeling of competence.

The task of assessing normal psychological development in children has been pursued most systematically by Murphy (1937, 1962) and by Murphy and Moriarty (1976). In a recent discussion of more than forty years of study of the development of nondeviant samples of children, Murphy outlines the main categories of investigation which need to be included in order to achieve a comprehensive study of development. Adapted from the work of numerous psychodynamic theorists, Murphy's (1976) roster of major dimensions of developmental study includes the following topics:

- *environment* (social institutions with their supporting and threatening aspects, the family and other persons involved with the family)
- *constitution and equipment in infancy and childhood* (body build, sensory thresholds and affective responses in different zones, orienting, coping and learning capacities from birth, general drive tendencies, consistency or ambivalence of contact needs, erotic reactions, motor drives, aggression, narcissism, mastery drive, and coping capacities)
- *mother–child relation and other object relationships* (viability of mother–child relations in terms of mutual tempos, needs, resources, gratifications, selective and changing patterns of identification in the child)
- *experiences significant at successive stages and their interaction with development at that stage* (major recurrent gratifications, frustrations, deprivations, separations, losses, illness, operations, accidents, other traumas, special gratifications, and integrating events)

- *ego and drive integration* (Emergent ego structure and coping tendencies in successive stages of psychosocial development and stages in the development of aggression)
- *coping patterns and defense mechanisms* (coping with the environment, coping with fantasies, wishes, needs, anxieties, conflicts; ways of using coping devices and defense mechanisms and their efficiency in discharging tension and preventing stress).

In order to provide a framework that could serve parents and professionals who deal with children in normal situations, Anna Freud (1965) began to formulate some of the most salient features of the psychological organization of children. As a point of departure, she cites four distinguishing characteristics of children which predispose them to misinterpret parents' words and actions: (1) the child's egocentricity, the degree to which children persist in viewing their parents' behavior and feelings entirely from the vantage of the children's own needs; (2) the immaturity of children's sexual development, which impairs their ability to learn and understand information about sexual functioning and leads to misinterpretations of the nature of adult sexual behavior; (3) the comparative weakness of a child's grasp of reality in comparison to the strength of his impulses and fantasies, leading to a failure to understand sanctions and prohibitions imposed by parents for the sake of the child's own welfare; and (4) the child's lesser capacity to evaluate time objectively, resulting in failure to tolerate even short delays and to distort the length of time periods that are related to important events.

In another effort to summarize important themes of normal development, Anna Freud introduced the concept of developmental lines—transitions that are characterized by a combination of a decline in "dependent, irrational, id- and object-determined attitudes, and by an increasing ego mastery of the internal and external world" (A. Freud, 1965, p. 63). Included among such developmental lines are the transitions from dependency to emotional self-reliance and adult object relationships, from suckling to rational eating, from irresponsibility to responsibility in body management, from egocentricity to companionship, from the body to the toy, and from play to work. Anna Freud emphasizes that children vary widely in their patterns of growth rate along different developmental lines.

Research Issues in Psychodynamic Theory

Most theoretical constructs in social science gain their currency by means of extensive citation in the research literature. One of the obstacles to more widespread acceptance of psychodynamic theory, especially in academic circles, is the relative paucity of research generated by the theory. Various aspects of psychodynamic theory do not easily fit into the current operational framework of research. Psychodynamic theory is holistic in orientation whereas research proceeds by means of analysis and fragmentation. The microscopic orientation of most researchers cannot be easily accommodated to the breadth of focus required by psychodynamic theory. Many of the basic theoretical propositions hypothesize relationships between events occurring in infancy and early childhood and personality characteristics manifested in adulthood. To investigate such phenomena requires a longitudinal study that would span the length of a researcher's full career. The investment of time, money, and emotional energy required make it impossible for this type of research to proceed on a large scale.

An additionally vexing (to the researcher) characteristic of psychodynamic theory is that it posits so complicated and guarded a set of predictions and dynamic interconnections between events that the theory is capable of accounting for any and all findings. The dialectical character of psychodynamic theory, with its belief in the unity of opposites, enables it to explain and explain away seemingly contradictory and inconsistent results. Since the theory appears to defy empirical validation, it tends to be shunned by many researchers. From the standpoint of research, the theory does not measure up to current standards of verification and validation. On the other hand, from the perspective of the theory's advocates, the fact that it does not conveniently fit the constraints and limitations of current research methods has little bearing on the heuristic value of the theory, its explanatory power, and its clinical usefulness.

Despite its complexity, psychodynamic theory has stimulated a variety of research, including efforts to validate the basic tenets of the theory. Systematic investigations of the validity of psychoanalytic theory in the light of existing research evidence have been periodically conducted since Sears's early work (1944) and as recently as the work of Fisher and Greenberg (1977). The results of such assessments tend to be equivocal. Some studies produce findings congruent with the expectations of psychoanalytic theory, whereas others stand in contradiction. Although the research that is cited bears on the theory, much of it was not specifically designed to serve as a critical test of the validity of psychodynamic hypotheses; few, if any of the studies, may be regarded as definitive. In the past, the principal effect of such assessments has been to deepen the chasm between clinician and researcher.

Of greater relevance to this discussion are studies of children based on psychodynamic theory. When psychoanalytic theory first appeared, the psychological influence it attributed to the earliest years seemed astounding in light of the near-universal predilection for viewing early childhood as dormant and inconsequential. Persuasive and masterful as the new theory of psychodynamics appeared to be, it was derived from adults' memories and reconstructions of traumas and distortions that were ostensibly experienced in the early years. Given the configuration of pathology observed in the adult, it was possible to identify the strands of early influence from a retrospective analysis of childhood experience. The basis for endowing the early years with such enduring impact was highly inferential. Once the psychologically potent aspects of early childhood were identified, some investigators turned to the direct study of early childhood for the purpose of elaborating and clarifying the nature of such antecedent conditions. Psychodynamic theory was applied to the prospective study of the hypothesized impact of early experience.

Foremost among such investigations were those concerned with maternal deprivation in early childhood. Following upon the observations made by Burlingham and Freud (1942, 1944), who noted the adverse effect of maternal separation on young children's capacity to endure the stresses of war, Spitz (1945) and Spitz and Wolf (1946) studied infants cared for by their mothers in a penal institution who were subjected to a three-month period of separation from their mothers during the latter part of their first year of life. The pattern of withdrawal and depression they observed in the separated infants was termed "anaclitic depression." It provided new documentation of separation phenomena.

A landmark in the examination of research literature and the theoretical interpretation of the effects of maternal deprivation was established by Bowlby in a series of papers that culminated in a report entitled *Attachment and Loss* (1969, 1973). Combining psychoanalytic theory with the findings and theoretical constructs of ethology, Bowlby put forth a new theoretical analysis of attachment phenomena. Reaffirming the singular importance of the problem of separation, he maintained that many forms of psychopathology characterized by varying patterns of anxiety and extreme fearfulness in adults as well as children may be traced to impaired attachment experiences.

Largely stimulated by the work of Bowlby, a growing body of research spearheaded by the studies of Ainsworth and her colleagues (1973, 1978) has recorded the development of attachment behavior. However, there continue to be differences among social scientists with regard to how these data should be interpreted (see, for example, Katkin, Bullington & Levine, 1974). In a recent review of the mounting research literature on maternal deprivation, Rutter (1979) raises new questions about the presumed influences of early experience. Pointing to the difficulty of demonstrating the long-term effects of attachment, he calls attention to the multiplicity of factors, other than those currently thought to interfere with attachment behavior, which also contribute to the adverse effects of maternal deprivation. He also reviews new evidence pertaining to the issues of critical periods of development and emphasizes the need to recognize the variability of children's vulnerability to stress and disadvantage.

Based on her observations of symbiotic psychosis in childhood, Mahler and her associates have focused on the separation-individuation phase of normal development (1968, 1975). This painstaking, theoretically significant program of research has identified the factors that affect the child's growing awareness of separateness and the manner in which the individuation process is linked to various forms of psychopathology.

In addition to identifying new areas of study, as in the case of the problems of separation and individuation, psychodynamic theory of development has influenced research by broadening the range of methodology and providing a conceptual framework for describing and ordering the psychological functioning of children. Most child development research has been limited to phenomena that are easily measurable because of a longstanding preference for quantitative methods of investigation. The use of quantitative methods calls for every segment of behavior that is to be counted to be obtained under uniform and, therefore, controlled conditions of study. As a result, most research data have been gathered from standardized tests or experimental situations. In order to facilitate statistical analysis, it has also been desirable to study large numbers of children. These constraints have led to a pattern of research in which only brief samples of behavior are collected from each child under controlled conditions. Most investigators who use psychodynamic theory reject this prevailing methodological framework. In order to achieve greater depth of investigation and to arrive at a more differentiated view of the child, they rely more heavily on a method of naturalistic observation that is more intensive and sustained and that is guided by a holistic theoretical perspective.

The work of Escalona and Heider (1959) and Escalona (1968) illustrates the distinctive character of both the content and method of research generated by psychodynamic theory. In her statement of research objectives for the study of infant development, she empasizes the organized, striving, whole-person quality of the child. Escalona has sought to identify developmental landmarks associated with the separation between the self and the environment, the development of a relationship with another human being, and the emergence of volitional behavior, including such functions as anticipation, memory, and goal striving.

While committed to the process of ordered inquiry demanded by research, Escalona resists the oversimplification and fragmentation that it usually entails. Her sensitivity to the need to respect the complexity of human development and to take into account the full interplay of forces at work in psychodynamics is reflected in the following comments.

> The failure to establish a relationship between any one specific aspect of child care and any later personality characteristic (of those that have been studied up to this point) can be interpreted in either of two ways: It can be concluded that child-rearing techniques and parental attitudes are in fact of little consequence, at least for development during the preschool years; or it can be concluded that the same child-rearing (such as relaxed or rigid feeding schedule, or an indulgent versus a controlling mode of dealing with the baby) may be applied in totally different ways by different parents and may occur as part of widely different family atmospheres. In that case, what is important is not so much the particular child-rearing technique as the manner in which it is implemented, and perhaps also the total pattern of parental practices of which it is a part [1968, p. 14].

Escalona's interest in capturing the organic quality of complex interactions led her to avoid what she terms "constrained conditions of investigation" (experiment or interview or test) in favor of direct observation for prolonged periods of time. Unlike most researchers who adopt a strategy of assessing the role of each factor separately in order to identify the antecedents of a particular developmental outcome, Escalona invokes the phenomenological construct of "experience" as intervening between the hypothesized factors of influence and the developmental outcomes. Because the effect of any single factor is modified and obscured by all other intrinsic and extrinsic factors impinging on the child, it needs to be viewed as one source of influence among many, all of which are integrated to form a complex matrix of "experience patterns." Without such a strategy, the researcher simply examines directly the relation between factor A or B and outcome C and, more often than not (because of the failure to observe how the influence of factor A filters through each individual child's experience), finds a relatively low relationship between the independent and dependent variables of the study. By introducing "experience patterns" as an intervening variable, Escalona acknowledges the role of interactive and integrative processes in the dynamics of development.

Implications of Psychodynamic Theory for the Education of Young Children

Included among the major points of influence of psychodynamic theory on education are the following interrelated areas: (1) basic orientation to children; (2) formulation of educational goals; and (3) development of educational practices.

Basic Orientation to Children

It is at this level that psychodynamic theory is especially potent. It presents a conception of the child that is at once rich and elaborate in theoretical constructs and strikingly at variance with prevailing conventional wisdom and surface impressions. In contrast with the traditional view of the young child as largely unformed and having shallow emotions, psychodynamic theory begins with the premise that each child has had a history of active striving and intense emotional life since birth and is therefore already complexly organized to function according to a particular mode defined by the dynamics of his individual needs, envrionmental pressures, and previous interpersonal relationships. Instead of viewing the young child's relation to his family as passive and uneventful, the child is seen as embroiled in a struggle to overcome feelings of dependence and vulnerability that leave him ambivalent about his closest emotional ties. These feelings of ambivalence will be projected onto the new adults whom the child meets away from home.

The orientation to children fostered by psychodynamic theory has both formal and content aspects. Psychodynamic theory adopts a holistic view of the child; child behavior is seen as coherent and purposive. Although child growth is marked by inconsistent and asynchronous patterns, there is a unity and organization to psychological functioning. The development of competence and mastery takes place by virtue of the child acting on the environment. At the same time, child growth is seen as governed by a set of lawful transitions that define a series of developmental tasks and avenues of development which are mediated by interaction with the environment. Thus, child behavior is regarded as fundamentally interactive and it is viewed from a developmental perspective. Psychodynamic theory further assumes that the child's interpersonal relations develop within a context of conflict and ambivalence. The investments, conflicts, and distortions that characterize the emotional life in turn shape the course of cognitive development.

As to the substantive content of child development, psychodynamic theory describes an intricate network of patterns of adaptation and associated areas of conflict in relation to each developmental stage that identifies for the educator salient themes and categories of child behavior. Among such themes is an image of omnipotence which young children first project onto themselves and then to their parents and other adults. The wish to be all-powerful is in direct proportion to the child's overwhelming feelings of vulnerability. The omnipotence/vulnerability constellation of feelings and fantasies identifies opposite poles of a theme that pervades early childhood.

Another, egocentricity, refers to young children's tendency to view the world exclusively from their own perspective. Since their own needs, and the gratification/frustration thereof, are all that they experience during the earliest months of life, it is natural for very young children to regard all events as though they were set in motion solely for the purpose of serving them. Similarly, caretakers are seen as existing only in order to serve the child. Only gradually does the child develop the cognitive competence and independence of spirit to abandon an egocentric attitude. Closely associated with the very young child's egocentricity is narcissism, a form of self-love that is a forerunner to interpersonal attachments. The gradual transition from an exclusive investment in the self to the capacity for emotional investment in others is a major developmental task.

Of central importance to the earliest developmental stage is the theme of helplessness and dependency which Freud linked to the oral psychosexual stage and which Erikson amplified as the stage when there develops a posture of basic trust or mistrust. The depth of feelings of helplessness, their mode of expression and ways of dealing with them, along with the manner in which a child is able to invest in and rely on another person are issues associated with the earliest stage of development.

Stemming in part from what is likely to be experienced by the child as arbitrary and powerful pressure to control his biological functions, the themes of stubbornness and resentment of authority and a concern with issues of control become important in the lives of young children as they grow old enough to have their behavior regulated. Elaborating Freud's second (anal) psychosexual stage of development, Erikson asserts that anal-neuromuscular maturation brings into prominence the themes of holding on and letting go and may lead to the formation of either hostile or benign attitudes or expectations with regard to issues of control. Observing the issues which surround conflict resolution during this stage of development, Erikson describes it as the stage of autonomy versus shame and doubt.

As previously noted, the pervasiveness of strong emotion during early childhood, especially feelings of anger and fear, are emphasized in the psychodynamic perspective. Without embracing every aspect of Freud's theory of infantile sexuality, the prominence of sexuality in young children is also acknowledged. Psychoanalytic theory explains the onset of many important psychological themes—exhibitionism and intense curiosity as well as the ambitious striving, rivalry, and competitiveness of preschool children—in terms of the intensified sexuality of the phallic stage that generates the Oedipal conflicts. Noting the assertiveness of this stage of development and the early phases of moral awareness that manifest themselves, Erikson describes the dynamics of this period as one concerned with initiative versus guilt.

At about the time when children start elementary school, they begin to identify with like-sex parent figures. This trend helps to resolve conflicts with family members and fortifies children in their growing quest for power and independence. Children attempt to move away from the dominance of their parents, while at the same time striving to emulate them and thereby to gain their magical power. During the middle years of childhood, their perspective broadens and extends beyond the family. It is with relief and curiosity that the child turns from a concern with the family to an exploration of the workings of the outside world. In order to gain greater control over his own impulses and emotions and to find guidelines for interacting with his expanding social environment, the child becomes interested in abstract issues of morality. Erikson describes this era as one concerned with industry versus inferiority.

In sum, the individual who works with children within a psychodynamic framework is sensitized to the vulnerability of children, their sexuality, the potency of separation, the intensity of their fearfulness and capacity for anger, their ambivalent striving for autonomy, and their inevitable manifestations of regression. Psychodynamic theory helps to identify issues, pathways, and consequences of development. Because of its focus on the organic nature of growth and the integrative aspects of development, the theory is especially helpful in identifying overarching concerns, but it also contributes to the roster of specific goals and procedures of educators.

Educational Goals

A wide variety of functional considerations—economic, cultural, political, aesthetic, and moral—guides the formation of educational goals. Education is variously concerned with producing literacy, providing knowledge and skills requisite for assuming a useful occupational role, maintaining a foundation for artistic and cultural cultivation that will sustain and renew elements of refinement in society, and socializing people into a rule-governed, law-abiding, bureaucratically run community. There are strong elements of rites of passage in the design of traditional education. Each grade level is seen as a self-contained packet of skill production, socialization process, and stepping stone in a series of hurtles and landmarks that lead the way to adult competence, responsibility, and privilege.

Psychodynamic theory addresses itself to the psychological and developmental processes that underlie educational experience. The psychodynamic perspective, however, goes beyond pointing to the mediating role of psychological events;

it leads to a reassessment of traditional objectives. The main difference is that a psychodynamic perspective focuses not on the skills and knowledge that a child acquires, *per se*, but on how a child is strengthened psychologically. It is concerned with the coping capacity of a child, with the level of competence and sense of well-being; its main goal is best described as building the child's ego strength.

Since acceptance and enhancement of the self are regarded as essential to the development of ego strength, it is primary to help each child to appreciate the self. Moreover, since each child's concept of self is largely defined by the fact that he or she is a child, education must be centrally involved in the celebration of childhood. Such a posture, consonant with the formulations of John Dewey (1902, 1916), calls for a shift in focus of educational objectives from that of helping children to advance to adult status to that of enhancing and intensifying their experience as children.

The main goals of a psychodynamic approach to education are long-term. Education is viewed as a continuous process rather than as a series of discrete, grade-related training sessions. In order to reinforce the principle that any given age should be regarded as a transitional stage in childhood rather than as a focal point for a circumscribed set of educational objectives, Anna Freud (1968) cautions against having a teacher work exclusively with a single age group. The main goals are not a definable aggregate of knowledge and skills but a growing capacity to function effectively. In addition, whereas the focus of the traditional educator is on socializing the child, on helping the child to achieve a group standard, the psychodynamically oriented educator is equally concerned with strengthening the child's individuality.

From the standpoint of psychodynamic theory, early education is a vehicle for providing a group experience for young children, for enabling the young child to interact with the peer group after a lifetime dominated by adults and almost exclusive emotional investment in parents. It allows the child to interact with people his own size and capacity, thereby providing some relief from ever striving to keep up with ominpotent giants. In addition, it gives a child the chance to interact with a new adult, one who is shared with the other children, under circumstances in which ownership is less exclusive and the emotional bond less intense. In school, the child meets adults with other values, standards, and styles of behaving. While still enmeshed in the intense drama of family life, the child is helped to develop some distance from the family and to form new associations and relationships, and thereby to experience and experiment with a measure of autonomous functioning. These considerations are reflected in the way in which Biber, Shapiro, and Wickens (1971) have formulated the goals for preschool education:

> to serve the child's need to make an impact on the environment through direct physical contact and maneuvers;
>
> to promote the potential for ordering experience through cognitive strategies;
>
> to advance the child's functioning knowledge of his environment;
>
> to support the play mode of incorporating experience;
>
> to help the child internalize impulse controls;

to meet the child's need to cope with the conflicts intrinsic to this stage of development;

to facilitate the development of an image of self as a unique and competent person;

to help the child establish mutually supporting patterns of interaction [1971, p. 10].

Educational Practices

The child-centered education advocated by Dewey's philosophy of education as well as by the psychodynamic theory of development begins with the premise that children should be actively engaged in learning rather than be passive recipients of knowledge. Classrooms are designed to encourage children to take the initiative by arranging for them to select what and how they learn from an array of options. The criteria for determining which options are to be offered are based less on a concern with bridging the gap between child-related ignorance and the knowledge demands of adulthood than with meeting children's own interests and needs for information and exploration, though the two are not unrelated. In a traditional, teacher-directed educational program, it is as though there is a stigma associated with childhood, as though education is a prescribed treatment for a condition, a malady, stemming from childhood status. Yet, the treatment has the paradoxical effect of reinforcing the child's sense of powerlessness by requiring conformity to a rigid classroom regimen imposed from without. In effect, the child is told that the only way to overcome his sense of impotence and vulnerability is to abandon childhood and thereby himself. In contrast, the choices and initiative offered in child-centered education are directed toward affirming and reinforcing the child's own quest for autonomy and power.

The specific teaching strategies and choice of curricula are also guided by child-centered considerations. They take into account what the child is interested in, whether the material to be learned is related to the child's experience, whether the child has the surround of knowledge to assimilate the new information, and whether the conceptual demands of the material to be learned are consonant with the child's level of conceptual functioning. The focus is on enabling the child to feel his own strength by allowing him to build on what he already knows and to choose the realms over which he wishes to extend mastery.

The classroom regimen is planned according to children's needs and preferred style of behavior. It is recognized that children have a need to move about and speak out. They learn by actively exploring and coordinating information derived from a multiplicity of sense modalities. Play is valued as the work of children, as a prime vehicle for generating and expressing fantasy and a way of symbolizing complex events. Block building and other construction activities are emphasized because they provide occasions for joint planning and executing, dealing with problems of spatial orientation, and learning to work with models and to develop analogues. Unlike traditional curricula which catalogue a disconnected aray of facts and skills to be learned in rote fashion, the child-centered curriculum focuses on the interrelatedness of knowledge in order to support the child's own growth of integrative functioning. Coherence and depth of learning are achieved by choosing a unifying, age-appropriate theme that serves as the context for multiple avenues of exploration—constructions, art projects, classroom plays, trips, group discussion, and problem solving—throughout which is interwoven the study of subject matter and academic skills.

Greater value is assigned to cultivating creative functioning in children. In exploring an educational strategy for fostering creativity, Biber (1959) cautions against the undermining influence of premature structuring. Jones (1968) calls for the synthesis of methods of instruction and therapy in order to achieve greater coordination among cognitive, emotional, and imaginal skills. In examining the implications of psychodynamic theory for education, Kubie (1958, 1959) emphasizes the importance of preconscious functioning in creative thought. He deplores the ritualistic mode of instruction and control that characterizes traditional education, viewing it as an institutionalized mechanism for reinforcing the neurotic process.

Because educational goals guided by psychodynamic theory focus on the growth of individual ego functioning rather than on meeting group standards of academic achievement, it is necessary for educational practice to be more individualized. Since children vary widely in their interests, backgrounds, learning styles, and modes of expression, the educator faces the task of helping to develop a sense of competence and an investment in learning within the framework of each child's pattern of skills and interests. Toward these ends, the educator needs a conceptual scheme for ordering variations in learning styles and configurations of cognitive skills, methods of diagnosing such patterns of variation, and a repertoire of teaching strategies that can be responsive to such variations, as well as a mode of classroom organization that makes possible individualized instruction. At the same time, the child's cognitive style is but one dimension of his individuality. The depth of interpersonal sensitivity and relatedness that is entailed in understanding individuality and in communicating this understanding is described by Biber and Franklin (1967).

> The child's self-image does not only incorporate the assessing stance of the adult with respect to his relative brightness or effective functioning; it is built as much around the meaning the child has, as an individual, to the adult. The cues are transmitted to the child not merely through vague warmth of feeling but more particularly through the detailed awareness and prizing of his particularities, powers, and failures, and through empathy with his feelings [1967, p. 14].

I have already mentioned that the educator guided by a psychodynamic perspective is concerned with the interpersonal climate of the classroom, with the extent to which children are relaxed and free to express themselves, question, exchange, explore, and in general feel free from the forces of intimidation of the teacher or the peer group. The teacher needs to provide structure and direction without being dictatorial and punitive. The teacher's main goal is to help children to overcome their feelings of powerlessness and vulnerability by arranging for them to become invested in learning. Each child needs to feel accepted without expending excessive energy to gain the friendship and support of the teacher. On the other hand, the teacher needs to be sufficiently neutral and objective to discourage children from focusing on their special needs for reassurance and love.

In examining some of the errors that teachers make in relating to children, Anna Freud (1968) observes that teachers work so closely with children that they sometimes lose the ability to distinguish between the perspective of the child's world and that of the adult's. Some teachers may form such close attachments to particular children that they lapse into a relation of rivalry with the children's mothers that may lead to a pervasive attitude of antagonism toward mothers. In cautioning against becoming overidentified with particular children, Anna Freud recommends that teachers should form a relationship with childhood rather than a feeling of closeness to certain kinds of children.

Current Issues in the Application of Psychodynamic Theory to Education

Defining the Scope of Educational Intervention

Anna Freud's basically conservative description of the task of the educator as that of finding a middle ground between too little and too much instinctual gratification is often mistakenly interpreted to mean that schools should become permissive. Similarly, when educators become sensitized to the emotional conflict of childhood, they often call for the schools to serve as quasi-therapeutic environments. Exposure to psychodynamic theory frequently gives rise to unrealistic assumptions regarding the limitless plasticity of childhood. Given the current posture of extreme environmentalism, the human potential movement, and the general mood of rising expectations, the psychodynamic theory of development is often interpreted as indicating that early childhood is entirely malleable and modifiable through effective educational intervention. Yet, such a viewpoint is at variance with the tenets of psychodynamic theory.

Nor is the school life of a child regarded by psychodynamic theory as coequal to and continuous with the home environment. Anna Freud reminds teachers that the child's relation to school and teacher is different from his relation to family and mother, that children want to be loved by their mothers but not necessarily taught by them (1968). On the other hand, because children's relationship to the teacher is farther removed from drive activity, they are more willing to give and to take in. In this regard, Anna Freud states, "It is the privilege of the teacher to introduce the child to a new experience, to life within a social community, not merely to duplicate his experiences within the family" (1968, p. 504).

In assessing the relative influence of home and school, most psychodynamic theorists believe that the factors which decisively affect personality development reside within the nuclear family relationships and that these dynamics are established and solidified before the child begins school. School is viewed as a powerful instrument for lessening stress, providing support, exposing the child to new adult modes and relationships, and presenting opportunities to develop and use skills that allow the child to feel more competent and independent. Life in school builds upon and solidifies earlier experience, but it is regarded as having but limited capacity to reverse or undo the perceptions and patterns of interpersonal relationships that develop out of the dynamics of the nuclear family. Educators often fail to see the basically conservative stance of psychodynamic theory with regard to the thresholds and vehicles of behavioral change.

Extending Group Care Downward in Age to Younger Children

Having been the first to recognize the formative influence of the earliest years and having provided much of the conceptual framework for early childhood education, advocates of psychodynamic theory might be expected to be at the forefront of the current interest in expanding group care for very young children, including infants. Yet, their response to this trend has been restrained and questioning. They favor improving and expanding group day care for very young children where it is needed, but it is not a service that they recommend for all children. Many proponents of psychodynamic theory, most notably among them Fraiberg (1977), are opposed to group care for very young children if their mothers are available to care for them. Their reservations are based on a developmental analysis of the different roles played by family members and other persons in the life of the child. They regard the main developmental task of the earliest years to be that of forming object relations. The transition from being exclusively concerned with the self to becoming emotionally invested in another person, the mothering one, is seen as the cornerstone of the child's capacity to relate to others. The earliest emotional bonding forges the capacity for future emotional bonding; it establishes a framework that shapes the pattern of later love relationships. If the initial bonding is fragile or uncertain or marked by tension, then the capacity for future attachment is impaired. The depth of feeling and stability evinced by the infant's caretaker is assumed to influence the quality of the bonding. From this standpoint, any child-care arrangement that introduces stress to the vulnerable young child or interferes in other ways with the establishment of a full bonding between mother and child is to be avoided.

Those who favor universal day care for young children call for reassessment of the attachment and separation theory. They ask whether it is not possible to provide stable, consistent, and loving caretaking within a framework of individualized, institutional care, and question whether the long-term effects of early maternal deprivation are as clearly established as is claimed. The research directed at assessing the effects of day care, as recently reviewed by Belsky and Steinberg (1978), reveals an inconsistent pattern of findings further beclouded by deficiencies in experimental design and measurement. Their survey included evaluation studies that examined the impact of day care on attachment to mother. Here, too, findings varied according to the design of the study and the background of the children.

Even though systematic studies of the effects of early group care may be illuminating, it is important to distinguish between researchers' efforts to measure indices of attachment and to examine their correlates, and clinicians' observations of the long-term effects of early separation traumas. The emotional disturbance derived from separation trauma is frequently a private matter; it may even be unknown to the afflicted person until its nature and source are identified in the course of psychotherapy. Such effects are not likely to be tapped by routine assessments conducted in large research surveys. The overriding importance of separation phenomena has been discovered by clinicians; researchers have only a very limited capacity to record the intricate details of early separation experiences and to assess their impact. The validity of psychodynamic propositions derived from clinical insight cannot yet be definitively probed and verified by research methods. The dilemma posed by the differing perspectives of the clinician and the researcher comes sharply into focus in the following section on evaluation.

Coping with the Demands of Evaluation

The new reliance on cost-effective considerations in administering education and the growing influence of educational evaluation threaten to erode the influence of psychodynamic theory. Psychodynamic theory fosters a complicated vision of the child and of the task of education that is difficult to reconcile with current methods of evaluation. With the advent of massive federal support of education in the 1960s, the need for accountability led to large-scale investment in educational evaluation. Such programs of compensatory education as Project Head Start were so costly that it became obligatory to assess their effectiveness. A technology of evaluation gradually evolved that was based on traditional educational criteria and measures of academic achievement.

On the one hand, evaluations based on achievement tests were regarded as too crude and irrelevant to constitute valid assessments of the programs' major educational objectives. Although these programs were activated in response to evidence of widespread academic failure, many were guided by psychodynamic concerns with the development of trust, self-esteem, communicativeness, and ego strength. Aimed at changing the psychological climate of the classroom, such programs produced a new awareness of the importance of factors other than academic achievement. On the other hand, the evaluator felt constrained to limit his assesment to the gathering of achievement test data. Such data seemed to satisfy the bureacracy and to disarm potential critics.

Once published, the evaluation data came to have an aura of definitiveness. Educators began to be guided by the content of evaluation measures in planning their programs—partly because they inferred that evaluators were wise formulators of educational objectives and possessed scientific information regarding what children should be taught, and partly in order to ensure that their programs would score high in evaluation. Paradoxically, then, indices of evaluation, acknowledged by the evaluators themselves to be deficient and only marginally relevant, began to serve as guideposts for educational planning.

In addition to distracting educators from principles of child development to indices of academic progress, evaluation methods tend to generate findings that are biased against programs guided by psychodynamic theory. Such programs are primarily directed at fostering ego strength and supporting development; they are less explicitly concerned with the content and the style of responding associated with academic achievement testing. Less exposed to fragmentation of knowledge and rote learning, and less conditioned to respond to the pressuring demands of standardized testing, children who are taught by these methods tend to perform less well (Zimiles, 1968). Yet, the results are treated as though they reflect the quality of the program rather than the method of evaluation. Thus, the growing power of evaluation raises the prospect that an educational psychology based on constructs that are easily measureable will gradually supplant a frame of reference based on psychodynamic theory. It remains to be seen, however, whether the indices used to assess educational progress have sufficient substantive content to guide the day-to-day deliberations of educators. It is more likely that the map of childhood and of the issues and variables which need to be reckoned with in dealing with children will continue to be plotted largely from psychodynamic theory. As in the past, the borrowing of these concepts will be informal and haphazard, with their source not always acknowledged, and their validity challenged by measurement-oriented researchers.

References

ABRAHAM, K. The first pregenital stage of the libido (1916). In *Selected Papers on Psychoanalysis*. London: Hogarth Press, 1927.

ADLER, A. *Understanding Human Nature*. New York: Greenberg, 1927.

AINSWORTH, M. The development of infant–mother attachment. In B. Caldwell and H. Ricciuti (eds.), *Review of Child Development Research*, Vol. 3. Chicago: University of Chicago Press, 1973.

AINSWORTH, M., BLEHAR, M., WALTERS, E., and WALL, S. *Patterns of attachment*. Hillsdale, N.J.: Lawrence Erlbaum Associates, 1978.

BELSKY, J., and STEINBERG, L. D. The effects of day care: a critical review. *Child Development*, 1978, *49*, 929–949.

BIBER, B. Premature structuring as a deterrent to creativity. *American Journal of Orthopsychiatry*, 1959, *29*, 280–290.

BIBER, B., and FRANKLIN, M. B. The relevance of developmental and psychodynamic concepts to the education of the preschool child. *Journal of the American Academy of Child Psychiatry*, 1967, *6*, 5–24.

BIBER, B., SHAPIRO, E., and WICKENS, D. *Promoting Cognitive Growth: A Developmental-Interaction Point of View*. Washington, D.C.: National Association for the Education of Young Children, 1971.

BOWLBY, J. *Attachment and Loss: Attachment*. New York: Basic Books, 1969.

BOWLBY, J. *Attachment and Loss: Separation*. New York: Basic Books, 1973.

BURLINGHAM, D., and FREUD, A. *Young Children in War-Time*. London: Allen & Unwin, 1942.

BURLINGHAM, D., and FREUD, A. *Infants without Families*. London: Allen & Unwin, 1944.

DEWEY, J. *The child and the Curriculum*. Chicago: University of Chicago Press, 1902.

DEWEY, J. *Democracy and Education*. New York: Macmillan, 1916.

ERIKSON, E. H. *Childhood and Society* (1950), 2d ed. New York: W. W. Norton, 1963.

ESCALONA, S. K. and HEIDER, G. M. *Prediction and Outcome*. New York: Basic Books, 1959.

ESCALONA, S. K. *Roots of Individuality: Normal Patterns of Development in Infancy*. Chicago: Aldine, 1968.

FISHER, S., and GREENBERG, R. P. *The Scientific Credibility of Freud's Theories and Therapies*. New York: Basic Books, 1977.

FRAIBERG, S. H. *Every Child's Birth Right: In Defense of Mothering*. New York: Basic Books, 1977.

FREUD, A. *Psychoanalysis for teachers and parents*. Boston: Emerson Books, 1935.

FREUD, A. *Normality and Pathology in Childhood*. New York: International Universities Press, 1965.

FREUD, A. Answering teachers' questions. In *The Writings of Anna Freud: Indications for Child Analysis and Other Papers*, Vol. 4. New York: International Universities Press, 1968. (Originally published, 1952).

FREUD, S. *New Introductory Lectures in Psychoanalysis*. New York: W. W. Norton, 1933.

FREUD, S. *A General Introduction to Psychoanalysis* (1917). New York: Permabooks, 1953.

HAAN, N. Proposed model of ego functioning: Coping and defense mechanisms in relation to I.Q. change. *Psychological Monographs*, 1963, 77, 1–23.

HARTMANN, H., KRIS, E., and LOWENSTEIN, R. M. Comments on the formation of psychic structure. *The Psychoanalytic Study of the Child*. New York: International Universities Press, 1946.

ISAACS, S. *Childhood and After*. New York: International Universities Press, 1932.

JAHODA, M. *Current Concepts of Positive Mental Health*. New York: Basic Books, 1958.

JONES, R. *Fantasy and Feeling in Education*. New York: New York University Press, 1968.

KATKIN, D., BULLINGTON, B., and LEVINE, M. Above and beyond the best interests of the child: An inquiry into the relationship between social science and social action. *Law & Society Review*, 1974, Summer.

KUBIE, L. S. *Neurotic Distortion of the Creative Process*. Lawrence: University of Kansas Press, 1958.

KUBIE, L. S. Are we educating for maturity? *NEA Journal*, 1959, 48, 58–63.

MAHLER, M. S. *On Human Symbiosis and the Vicissitudes of Individuation, Vol. 1, Infantile Psychosis*. New York: International Universities Press, 1968.

MAHLER, M. S., PINE, F., and BERGMAN, A. *The Psychological Birth of the Human Infant.* New York: Basic Books, 1975.

MURPHY, L. B. *Social Behavior and Child Personality.* New York: Columbia University Press, 1937.

MURPHY, L. B. *The Widening World of Childhood: Paths Toward Mastery.* New York: Basic Books, 1962.

MURPHY, L. B., and MORIARTY, A. E. *Vulnerability, Coping, and Growth: From Infancy to Adolescence.* New Haven, Conn.: Yale University Press, 1976.

RUTTER, M. Maternal deprivation, 1972–1978: New findings, new concepts, new approaches. *Child Development,* 1979, *50,* 283–305.

SEARS, R. R. Experimental analysis of psychoanalytic phenomena. In J. McV. Hunt (ed.), *Personality and the Behavior Disorders.* New York: Ronald Press, 1944.

SHAPIRO, E., and BIBER, B. The education of young children: A developmental interaction approach. *Teachers College Record,* 1972, *74,* 55–79.

SMITH, M. B. Research strategies toward a conception of positive mental health. *American Psychologist,* 1959, *14,* 673–681.

SPITZ, R. A. Hospitalism: An inquiry into the genesis of psychiatric conditions in early childhood. *The Psychoanalytic Study of the Child,* 1945, *1,* 53–74.

SPITZ, R. A., and WOLF, K. Anaclitic depression: An inquiry into the genesis of psychiatric conditions in early childhood. II. *The Psychoanalytic Study of the Child.* New York: International Universities Press, 1946.

SULLIVAN, H. S. *The Interpersonal Theory of Psychiatry.* New York: W. W. Norton, 1953.

WHITE, R. W. Motivation reconsidered: The concept of competence. *Psychological Review,* 1959, *66,* 297–333.

WHITE, R. W. Ego and reality in psychoanalytic theory. *Psychological Issues,* 1963, *3,* no. 3 (monograph 11).

WHITE, R. W. *The Enterprise of Living: Growth and Organization in Personality.* New York: Holt, Rinehart & Winston, 1972.

WINNICOTT, D. W. Pediatrics and psychology. *British Journal Medical Psychology,* 1948, *21,* 229–240. Reprinted in *Collected Papers* by D. W. Winnicott. London: Tavistock Publications, 1958a.

WINNICOTT, D. W. Transitional objects and transitional phenomena. *International Journal Psycho-Analysis,* 1953, *34,* 1–9. Reprinted in *Collected Papers* by D. W. Winnicott. London: Tavistock Publications, 1958b.

ZIMILES, H. Problems of assessment of academic and intellectual variables. Paper read at the American Educational Research Association Meetings, Symposium on "Problems of Educational Evaluation Confronted in Head Start," Chicago, February 1968.

CHAPTER 8

The Behavior Analysis Model for Early Education

Don Bushell, Jr.

THE BEHAVIOR ANALYSIS MODEL for early education is not a theory but a young technology built from a few principles. During the past decade, these principles have guided teachers and behavior analysts in the development of teaching strategies that are making classrooms more fun, and more effective, for young children and their teachers. Although the principles are few, the model has many parts. Each part is an experimental study. Consequently, the model *is* the sum of the parts that scores of collaborating teachers and researchers have published.

The tables of references that follow are the substance of the behavior analysis model for early education as it now exists, and they provide the foundation for its future development. They outline the empirical basis of an approach that begins with techniques for measuring instructional goals. Several ways to increase and refine student behavior are then described—first with consequences that follow and then with prompts that precede behavior. Finally, the dynamics of the approach—the techniques that promote and accommodate change and growth— are examined.

Decide What Behaviors to Teach and How to Measure Them

Applied behavior analysis is distinguished by its reliance on a principle (that behavior is a function of its consequences) and by its preoccupation with direct and reliable measurement. That preoccupation unites goal setting and measurement development as the first step in behavior analysis teaching.

Instructional goals need to be endorsed by the clients of the school or program. Clients are the people influenced by the daily operation of a school:

teachers, students, and parents. Goals can be vague and ephemeral things subject to misinterpretation and misunderstanding until they are stated in terms of how they will be measured. The goal statement that reads, for example, "to reduce a child's dependence on the teacher," can acquire so many meanings it has none. Described by a measurement procedure, the same goal might read: "to reduce a child's frequency of saying, 'Teacher! Teacher! Look at what I did!' from twenty-three times an hour to four per hour." Now clients can understand the goal well enough to decide if that is what they really want. When they understand and agree with the measures, they are likely to agree with the goals.

Behavior analysis measures are designed to be used repeatedly to describe how performance changes over time in relation to goals. Since there are many goals and measures in every classroom, simple measures are necessary—and possible. Simple measures are available whenever the behavior of interest leaves evidence of its occurrence on an easel, in a block construction, or in a workbook or test. Behaviors that leave products do not have to be witnessed as they occur (as does speech that is uttered and gone), because the evidence remains to be counted or classified later. Worksheets and workbooks readily yield daily counts of correct and incorrect responses; and, when a year-end goal can be stated in terms of the number of pages to be completed, a weekly record of the page on which a student is working creates a graphic account of that student's rate of progress (Table 8–1). Even easier is the practice of teaching students to measure and record their own behavior (Table 8–2). The practice provides clerical help for the teacher, and it has instructional benefits for the students. The reliability of student-produced records cannot, of course, be assumed, but it can be assured when the teacher

TABLE 8–1.   Techniques for Measuring Instructional Goals

TOPIC/REFERENCES	COMMENTS
1. Repeated placement recording	
Bushell, Jackson & Weis, 1975	weekly progress
Filipczak, Archer, Neale & Winett, 1979	weekly progress
2. Students measure and record their own behavior	
Schwarz & Hawkins, 1970	"personal dignity"
Broden, Hall & Mitts, 1971	study behavior
Bolstad & Johnson, 1972	disruptive behavior
Glynn, Thomas & Shee, 1973	on task
Knapczyk & Livingston, 1973	reading assignments
Santogrossi, O'Leary, Romanczyk & Kaufman, 1973	conduct
Van Houten, Morrison, Jarvis & McDonald, 1974	writing
Van Houten, Hill & Parsons, 1975	writing
Farnum & Brigham, 1978	social studies
3. Reliability established by intermittent checking	
Salzberg, Wheeler, Devar & Hopkins, 1971	writing
McLaughlin & Malaby, 1972b	talking out
Wood & Flynn, 1978	room cleaning

TABLE 8-2. Techniques for Increasing Appropriate Behavior with Consequences

TOPIC/REFERENCES	COMMENTS
1. *Contingent attention and approval*	
a. *Teacher attention and approval*	
Harris, Wolf & Baer, 1964	preschool skills
Johnston, Kelley, Harris & Wolf, 1966	motor skills
Buell, Stoddard, Harris & Baer, 1968	motor skills
Thomas, Becker & Armstrong, 1968	classroom conduct
Schutte & Hopkins, 1970	following instructions
Hasazi & Hasazi, 1972	digit reversal
Goetz & Baer, 1973	novel block building
Kazdin & Klock, 1973	attention to task
Kazdin, Silverman & Sittler, 1975	attention to task
b. *Principal attention and approval*	
Brown, Copeland & Hall, 1972	school conduct
Copeland, Brown, Axelrod & Hall, 1972	attendance
Copeland, Brown & Hall, 1974	attendance & achievement
c. *Peer attention and approval*	
Evans & Oswalt, 1968	academic performance
Graubard, Rosenberg & Miller, 1971	improved interaction
Solomon & Wahler, 1973	peer reinforcement
Strain & Timm, 1974	improved interaction
Strain, Shores & Timm, 1977	isolate behavior
d. *Self-evaluation and appropriate self-approval*	
Stokes, Fowler & Baer, 1978	preschool academic work
Wood & Flynn, 1978	room cleaning
2. *Contingent access to preferred activity*	
a. *Direct and embedded access*	
Homme, deBaca, Devine, Steinhorst & Rickert, 1963	attending
Hart & Risley, 1968	descriptive speech
Reynolds & Risley, 1968	verbal rate
Jacobson, Bushell & Risley, 1969	academic tasks
Hopkins, Schutte & Garton, 1971	printing & writing
Hart & Risley, 1975	compound sentences
b. *Access to free time*	
Lovitt, Guppy & Blattner, 1969	spelling
Baer, Rowbury & Baer, 1973	instruction following
Long & Williams, 1973	classroom conduct
c. *Access by contract*	
Cantrell, Cantrell, Huddleston & Woolridge, 1969	classroom conduct
MacDonald, Gallimore & MacDonald, 1970	attendance
Williams, Long & Yoakley, 1972	conduct
d. *Access by token exchange*	
Staats, Staats, Schutz & Wolf, 1962	reading
Birnbrauer & Lawler, 1964	general instruction
Birnbrauer, Wolf, Kidder & Tague, 1965	general instruction
Staats & Butterfield, 1965	reading

(Continued)

TABLE 8–2. *(Cont.)*

TOPIC/REFERENCES	COMMENTS
O'Leary & Becker, 1967	adjustment
Whitlock & Bushell, 1967	reading
Bushell, Wrobel & Michaelis, 1968	general instruction
Clark, Lachowicz & Wolf, 1968	general instruction
McKenzie, Clark, Wolf, Kothera & Benson, 1968	general instruction
Tyler & Brown, 1968	general instruction
Wolf, Giles & Hall, 1968	general instruction
O'Leary, Becker, Evans & Saudargas, 1969	classroom conduct
Zimmerman, Zimmerman & Russell, 1969	instruction following
Miller & Schneider, 1970	handwriting
Chadwick & Day, 1971	general instruction
Ayllon & Kelly, 1972	general instruction
Brigham, Frinfrock, Breunig & Bushell, 1972	handwriting
McLaughlin & Malaby, 1972a	general instruction
Ayllon & Roberts, 1974	reading
Lahey & Drabman, 1974	reading
Robertson, DeReus & Drabman, 1976	classroom conduct
Barber & Kagey, 1977	attendance

3. *Increasing appropriate and reducing inappropriate behavior*
   a. Approval combined with ignoring
      Zimmerman & Zimmerman, 1962
      Allen, Hart, Buell, Harris & Wolf, 1964
      Harris, Johnston, Kelley & Wolf, 1964
      Johnston, Kelley, Harris, Wolf & Baer, 1964
      Becker, Madsen, Arnold & Thomas, 1967
      Hall, Lund & Jackson, 1968
      Madsen, Becker & Thomas, 1968
      Ward & Baker, 1968
      Wasik, Senn, Welch & Cooper, 1969
      Skiba, Pettigrew & Alden, 1971
      Sajwaj, Twardosz & Burke, 1972
      Pinkston, Reese, LeBlanc & Baer, 1973
   b. Approval combined with time-out
      Pendergrass, 1972
      Clark, Rowbury, Baer & Baer, 1973
      Porterfield, Herbert-Jackson & Risley, 1976
      Foxx & Shapiro, 1978

   c. Delay or deny access to preferred activity

Barrish, Saunders & Wolf, 1969	Good Behavior Game
Osborne, 1969	free time
Schmidt & Ulrich, 1969	free time
Surratt, Ulrich & Hawkins, 1969	selected activity
Schwarz & Hawkins, 1970	selected activity
Ramp, Ulrich & Dulaney, 1971	free time
Kaufman & O'Leary, 1972	token loss
Medland & Stachnik, 1972	Good Behavior Game
Harris & Sherman, 1973a	Good Behavior Game

TABLE 8–3.   Techniques for Increasing Appropriate Behavior with Prompts

Topic/References	Comments
1. *Prompting by others*	
a. Teacher guidance	
Schutte & Hopkins, 1970	instructions
Herman & Tramontana, 1971	instructions
Scott & Bushell, 1974	contact duration
Carnine, 1976	pacing
Rowbury, Baer & Baer, 1976	guidance
Carnine & Fink, 1978	pacing
b. Other students as examples	
Broden, Bruce, Mitchell, Carter & Hall, 1970	adjacent student
Kazdin, 1973	adjacent student
Strain & Timm, 1974	adjacent student
Christy, 1975	reinforce peers
Kazdin, Silverman & Sittler, 1975	adjacent peers
Strain, Shores & Kerr, 1976	"spillover"
c. Augmented staffing	
Staats, Minke, Goodwin & Landeen, 1965	add aides
Sanders & Hanson, 1971	subtract students
Ringer, 1973	add token helper
Loos, Williams & Bailey, 1977	add aides
d. Student tutors	
Hamblin, Hathaway & Wodarski, 1971	peer tutors
Willis, Crowder & Morris, 1972	peer tutors
Harris & Sherman, 1973b	peer tutors
Greenwood, Sloane & Baskin, 1974	peer tutors
Johnson & Bailey, 1974	cross-age tutors
Robertson, DeReus & Drabman, 1976	hire a tutor
Dineen, Clark & Risley, 1977	peer tutors
Schwartz, 1977	college students
Trovato & Bucher, 1980	peer tutors
2. *Self-prompting (self-evaluation)*	
Lovitt & Curtiss, 1968	talk out math
Bolstad & Johnson, 1972	record disruptions
Kaufman & O'Leary, 1972	rate disruptiveness
Glynn & Thomas, 1974	record writing
Bornstein & Quevillon, 1976	talk out task
Jones, Trap & Cooper, 1977	record handwriting
Stokes, Fowler & Baer, 1978	evaluate own work
Wood & Flynn, 1978	evaluate own work
3. *Prompts by materials*	
Birnbrauer, Bijou, Wolf & Kidder, 1965	programmed materials
Staats & Butterfield, 1965	programmed materials
Gray, Baker & Stancyk, 1969	task analysis
Brigham, Finfrock, Breunig & Bushell, 1972	programmed materials

(Continued)

TABLE 8-3. *(Cont.)*

TOPIC/REFERENCES	COMMENTS
Corey & Shamow, 1972	fading
Resnick, Wang & Kaplan, 1973	task analysis
4. *Prompts by status and progress reports*	
Bailey, Wolf & Phillips, 1970	daily home reports
Van Houten, Morrison, Jarvis & McDonald, 1974	post highest score
Bushell, Jackson & Weis, 1975	weekly progress
Fink & Carnine, 1975	graph error rate
Van Houten, Hill & Parsons, 1975	post highest score
Todd, Scott, Bostow & Alexander, 1976	home reports
Saudargas, Madsen & Scott, 1977	home reports
Schumaker, Hovell & Sherman, 1977	home reports
Filipczak, Archer, Neale & Winnett, 1979	weekly progress

checks the accuracy of individual entries on an intermittent and unpredictable schedule (Table 8-3).

When goals and their associated measures are established at the outset, and the teacher, parents, and students understand and endorse them, the stage is properly set.

Increase Appropriate Behavior with Consequences

Behavior is maintained or changed by its consequences (the events that follow it). Teaching is the art of changing the behavior of students. Thus, one focus of behavior analysis teaching is the systematic management of the consequences of student behaviors. Of particular interest are reinforcers, those consequences that strengthen behaviors they follow. Teachers and other analysts of classroom behavior have devised a large array of procedures for increasing appropriate student behavior with consequences, but all these procedures can be grouped under three headings, the first of which (functionally and historically) is contingent attention and approval.

Contingent Attention and Approval

The importance of teacher attention and approval is now commonly understood, but it is best practiced by the teachers of younger students. White (1975) observed that "in Grades 1 and 2, teacher approvals occur more frequently than the teacher disapprovals. But in every grade thereafter, the rate of total teacher disapproval is higher than the rate of approval" (1975, p. 369). In contrast to these negative patterns, behavior analysis teaching is preoccupied with the positive.

Contingent attention and approval involves withholding attention until a student displays a desirable or improved behavior and then quickly giving approving attention to that student. Approval can occur in the form of conversation, compliments, praise, or nonverbal signs of affection including pats and hugs. The consistent effectiveness of contingent teacher approval has been demonstrated so often with so many behaviors and so many children that it is a key component of almost every behavior analysis procedure (Table 8–2). Similarly, the contingent use of the principal's attention, although somewhat more formal, has been found comparably effective (Table 8–2). Perhaps the most potent source of social approval, however, are the students themselves. The trick here, of course, is to teach students to deliver their complimentary attention to classmates contingent on behaviors admired by the teacher. It does depart from students' apparent tendency to lavish particular approval on behaviors the teacher would prefer ignored (Solomon & Wahler, 1973), but students can be, and have been, taught to give their attention and approval to the appropriate behavior of their peers (Table 8–2).

Appropriate self-approval is undoubtedly a skill that all educators wish to teach all students. In this case, as with peer approval, the objective is to teach students how to evaluate their own performances and to distinguish what is well done from what is not. Stokes, Fowler, and Baer (1978) taught preschool children to "do good work, then evaluate the quality of that work, and, when the quality was good, cue the trainer to evaluate that work" (1978, p. 288). The similarity between this strategy and that of Wood and Flynn (1978), who taught adolescents to evaluate their own room cleaning by applying the same measurement criteria used by their house parents, suggests the beginning of a technique for systematically teaching appropriate self-approval (Table 8–2), the ultimate form of social approval. Presumably, a first step in teaching appropriate self-approval involves teaching students to observe and record their own performance as previously discussed (Table 8–1).

Contingent Access to Preferred Activities

Variations on a principle advanced by Premack (1965) make up the second category of reinforcing consequences. Premack established that preferred (high probability) activities can reinforce other (lower probability) behaviors if they are properly arranged. If a child would rather play dress-up than do math, the probability of doing math is increased if the opportunity to play dress-up is contingent on the completion of ten math problems. It is a familiar strategy. "As soon as your room is clean, you may go out to play." "As soon as you finish the next four problems, you can go to the reading corner." It is a strategy that has many classroom applications.

Hart and Risley (1968, 1975) have embedded this kind of reinforcement contingency into the activities of a preschool program that has had a continuing interest in the language development of its students. Rather than responding to requests that are linguistically limited, these researchers have improved children's speech production by, for example, providing a toy only when the request for it included its name, color, and even a description of how it would be used.

Free time can also serve as a reinforcer. Daily classroom schedules are punctuated by recess, play periods, lunch breaks, and dismissal. Teachers and researchers have skillfully exploited these intervals by holding them contingent on the prior completion of necessary, but less preferred, tasks. Providing a couple of minutes of extra recess for good work is an easily managed and effective reinforcer for developing skills (Table 8–2).

Exchanging a preferred activity for a desirable behavior is an easy and effective procedure, but it is limited if the preferred activity interrupts the desirable behavior. Performance contracts avoid interruption and can support longer and more complex performances on the way to the preferred activity. These formal agreements between student and teacher specify how much work, of high quality, the student will complete in a given amount of time in student-selected preferred activities. Initially, small amounts of work can be contracted for brief periods of free time, but successive contracts can become progressively more complex and sustain long periods of uninterrupted performance. Research on contracts has emphasized good conduct (Table 8–2), but contracts have clear implications for a wide range of performance skills.

Classroom token systems have been widely used and extensively researched since Staats, Staats, Schutz, and Wolf (1962) used tokens in a laboratory setting to teach elemental reading responses. Tokens are typically given to students (along with praise and encouragement) for correct or improved responding as they are working. Students then exchange their accumulated tokens for the opportunity to engage in an activity of their own choosing. A "menu" that changes often allows students to choose from a list of several available activities that are priced according to popularity. Tokens do not interrupt ongoing study behavior; they can be presented for any behavior the teacher admires; and they can be used to support very long study periods (Table 8–2).

Reinforcing Appropriate While Reducing Inappropriate Behavior

Behavior analysts have been invited into classrooms most often to help solve some sort of problem. Consequently, they have developed a variety of procedures in response to concerns about disruptive or inappropriate behavior. These are the same basic procedures already described, but they increase appropriate behavior while simultaneously reducing inappropriate behavior.

APPROVAL COMBINED WITH IGNORING

If approving attention is a reinforcer, and it usually is, then its absence reduces behavior. The result is extinction. The decrease is very rapid if an alternative behavior results in reinforcement. Some of the most persuasive demonstrations of behavior analysis teaching have resulted from the simple combination of praising the appropriate behavior while ignoring the inappropriate (Table 8–3). To avoid any confusion, this does not mean that a teacher should praise a "good" child and ignore a "bad" child. It is a single student's behavior that is of interest. The message is to praise a child's good behavior and to ignore that child's inappropriate behavior.

APPROVAL COMBINED WITH TIME-OUT

Time-out from positive reinforcement (although sometimes misunderstood) is a direct and humane procedure for eliminating inappropriate behavior. As the name indicates, time-out is a brief period during which no reinforcement is provided. In a setting rich in reinforcement for appropriate behavior, it is an effective consequence for inappropriate behavior. It is not effective in a setting that does not provide much reinforcement for appropriate behavior. The procedure might work as follows:

> A group of students are doing handwriting worksheets at a table while the teacher moves from one child to another offering suggestions, praising accurate work, and dispensing tokens that will later be exchanged for more and less preferred seats at a film showing. Suddenly, one girl grabs another's paper, tearing it in the process, saying, "Let's see how you're doing." The teacher quickly moves the offending child's chair two feet back from the table, while saying, "Remember, the rule is we don't bother people who are working. Sit here for a moment." The teacher then resumes the lesson with the other students. After two minutes, the offending child is invited to pull up to the table, and resume her work. After she has made three or four writing responses, the teacher compliments her on "the shape of those 'a's" and places a token on her paper before moving to another child.

Contingent on an inappropriate behavior, the student encountered a two-minute period during which neither praise nor tokens were available. That's time-out. Beyond the reminder of the rule that was violated, there was no scolding, no recriminations, no lectures about morality or the importance of being "a young lady." Time-out has nothing to do with being sent to the hall, standing in the corner, or in any way being made the object of ridicule or scorn. Perhaps it is because time-out has often been misunderstood that Porterfield, Herbert-Jackson, and Risley (1976) emphasized the topography of the procedure by renaming it "contingent observation."

DELAYING OR DENYING ACCESS TO PREFERRED ACTIVITY

If access to preferred activities is a reinforcer, then a delay of access will reduce any behavior that produces it. Disruptive behavior is quickly reduced when it results in less free time, fewer tokens, a delay in the opportunity to exchange tokens, or any consequence that is a loss of reinforcement. Most of these procedures are carried out by teachers, but some investigators have used electronic devices that automatically respond to too much noise by turning down lights or turning off background radio music (Wilson & Hopkins, 1973).

Behavior analysts have also developed a number of procedures for dealing with severe forms of dangerous, destructive, and self-destructive behaviors. Such behaviors are rarely found in early childhood classrooms, but they are discussed by Zeiler (1978).

Prompt More Behavior to Reinforce

Behavior analysis teachers do not just wait for a response to occur so they can reinforce it. They actively build new behaviors with hints, cues, instructions, and materials that encourage and support appropriate behavior. Events that come before, and increase the probability of, an appropriate behavior are called prompts (Bushell, 1973). Effective prompting pre-empts errors and disruptive behavior by increasing the likelihood that a student will respond appropriately. Prompts gather effectiveness to the extent that they promote behaviors that are reinforced. Instructions, for example, become prompts if following them results in reinforcement (Schutte & Hopkins, 1970). If instruction following did not result in reinforcement, following instructions would extinguish (instructions would no longer be prompts). Prompting strategies are many and varied, but all have the same objective: to encourage more appropriate behavior that can be reinforced.

Prompting by Others

Rowbury, Baer, and Baer (1976) collected many kinds of prompts under the single heading "teacher guidance." It includes most of the things teachers know best: giving instructions, making suggestions, providing assistance, asking questions, giving examples, and even, in some cases, modeling the correct response. Much of the research accumulating on teacher guidance seems to indicate that it is most effective when it is brief, direct, and frequent (Table 8–3).

Prompts need to be clear so that there is no doubt about what behaviors will be reinforced. Posted classroom rules meet this requirement if they are supported by consequences. Madsen, Becker, and Thomas (1968) demonstrated that merely posting rules has little effect. Even when the rules are clear, teachers have sometimes found it helpful to provide gentle reminders. Praising a child who is working has been used to remind an adjacent off-task student to resume studying (Table 8–3), but this technique has been misused. The teacher's announcement from the front of the room in a loud voice, "I like the way Jimmy is working quietly!" has been aptly dubbed "sledgehammer praise" by Hopkins (1978). Announcements and direct instructions should not be veiled by invidious praise.

Lowering the ratio of learners and teachers permits more individualized prompting (Table 8–3). Sanders and Hanson (1971) set a performance standard and allowed students to go to a play area when they met that standard. As more able students left for the play area, the remaining smaller group of students received more frequent teacher guidance. Others have increased the density of prompts (and consequences) by creating teaching roles for paraprofessional aides, by letting older students tutor younger students, or by devising peer tutoring procedures within the classroom (Table 8–3).

Not all instructions, questions, and suggestions are prompts. Only those that lead to student responses that can be reinforced qualify. Instructions that are not followed and questions that cannot be answered are not prompts. Consequently, it is not good teaching to repeat a question that is not answered the first time. Instead, that question needs to be reformulated to be a prompt.

"How much is 4 times 3?"	no correct response
"How much is 3 times 3?"	"9."
"Right; add 3 more."	"12."
"Perfect! How much is 4 times 3?"	"12."
"You're a genius." "Very good."	

The dialogue is not closed until the correct answer to the original question is obtained and praised.

SELF-PROMPTING

Students can be taught to provide many helpful prompts for their own behavior. Mnemonic devices are easily taught and long remembered self-produced prompts for correct responses (for example, i before e, except after c; 30 days hath September; Every Good Boy Does Fine). Lovitt and Curtiss (1968) conducted a series of experiments that demonstrated that students' math performance improved if they verbalized the problem before writing their answer. Fink and Carnine (1975) gave feedback to first-grade students on the number of errors on their arithmetic worksheets. The feedback alone had little effect, but when the students began to graph the feedback information themselves, the number of errors declined. Unquestionably, many of the student self-recording techniques listed in Table 8–1 function as prompts for appropriate behavior. It is also likely that the most helpful kind of self-prompt involves, or leads to, appropriate self-evaluation (Table 8–2).

Prompts by Instructional Materials

A major purpose of instructional materials is to prompt student responses that can be reinforced. Consequently, curriculum materials can be judged effective to the extent that they prompt frequent correct responses (Table 8–3). Good sequencing and frequent response requirements prompt lots of appropriate student behavior; bad sequencing and infrequent response requirements do not. For example, a beginning reading series that is constructed for use with a reading group of six students who read aloud to the teacher, one at a time, provides only one sixth of the prompts of a series that requires every student to make every response.

Good sequencing is the product of good task analysis, the logical process of determining the most favorable order in which related skills should be learned. The observed effectiveness of programmed instruction can be attributed to the fact that it combines good sequencing with frequent response requirements. Sequencing also involves associating an established response with a new prompt. It is easier, and therefore better sequencing, to teach a child to read the word "dog" if that word is already part of the child's vocabulary. It was easier, in the earlier illustration, to teach 4 times 3 to the child who already knew 3 times 3 and 9 plus 3. The art of teaching depends a great deal on techniques that can attach an established behavior to a new prompt; and the technique of gradually fading the form of the old prompt into the form of the new one (itself an artistic process) has produced several promising demonstrations.

Prompts by Status and Progress Reports

Progress reports to clients can be valuable prompts. Unlike report cards that mark the end of an association with a teacher, behavior analysis reports, like behavior analysis measures, are designed for repeated use. Such reports have been called "feedback," but feedback is functional only when it promotes subsequent behavior that is reinforced. For that reason, there is no need to introduce another word. The objective is to devise reports that function as prompts.

Once the student's entering performance level and individual year-end goal in each area are established, they can be presented in a take-home report that is likely to prompt the attention and discussion of parents and student alike. Each subsequent monthly, or even weekly, report describing the student's progress toward the year-end goal can encourage behavior that leads to praise and approval, encouragement, or some discussion between parents and teacher.

Several investigators have used simple daily home reports to improve student performance. Because they only require the teacher to check "Yes" or "No" beside a few descriptive phrases ("completed all assignments," "was attentive"), they require little effort and can provide both objective and subjective evaluations. Even less effort is required for a reporting system devised by Saudargas, Madsen, and Scott (1977) in which the teacher prepared home reports for seven to nine randomly selected children each day (rather than weekly reports for 26 third-graders). The resulting variable interval reporting proved more effective than the weekly fixed interval, and the teacher liked it better! Remembering that students are also clients, Van Houten and his colleagues (1974, 1975) prompted appropriate student behavior by posting records that displayed each student's highest score to date on recurrent assignments.

Develop a Dynamic System

Thus far, behavior analysis teaching techniques have been considered individually. The total effect, however, is best appreciated by observing the product that results when they are skillfully used in combination. The product most admired in education, particularly in early childhood and elementary education, is the "self-motivated independent learner."

Young children begin school with limited skills. They are physically, behaviorally, and emotionally dependent on adults, and they are not expected to be otherwise. The objective is to teach each child to become progressively more independent in successive school situations—situations that provide relatively weak and infrequent reinforcers. As a student progresses through school, more and more skills are required to contact the available reinforcers.

The transformation from dependent to independent learner is neither automatic nor sudden. It is the gradual result of a series of events that expand the student's abilities and array of reinforcers. Artistic teachers have always taught both. Although artistic behavior may be hard to explain, several elements of the artist's discipline can be specified; and the skillful use of a good technique is a key element of every art.

The teacher who can identify a student's beginning skills, specify an objective, control the occurrence of prompts, and manage the delivery of reinforcers can shape new student skills *and* new reinforcers.

Shaping Student Performance

Shaping consists of reinforcing improvements in student behavior. If small improvements go undetected, and therefore unreinforced, they will become less likely (extinction). If reinforcement is held contingent on large improvements when only small ones are available, the student never experiences reinforcing consequences (ratio strain). Both extinction and ration strain stop progress.

Shaping has to focus on improvement. Repeatedly reinforcing the same form of a behavior will restrict its natural variability (including variations that are improvements). Kazdin (1977), for example, found that praising students for short intervals of "attending" resulted in less attending than when reinforcement was contingent on progressively longer intervals of attending. Students frequently praised for ten minutes of work are also learning to stop working after ten minutes (whether or not they can tell time). Similarly, students who are always reinforced for finishing one page of work are learning to stop at the end of each page. From a teacher's point of view, shaping consists of delivering frequent, but unpredictable, reinforcement for successive small improvements in student performance.

The first requirement is to detect those small improvements so that reinforcement can be properly delivered. Holland (1958) called this kind of detection "human vigilance." The measurement and token procedures discussed earlier have both been found to be aids to teacher vigilance. When teachers must observe closely enough to record the occurrence of a behavior or to award a token, they become more responsive to it. Once again, however, a number of studies indicate that students themselves can be taught to improve the teacher's vigilance by appropriately prompting teacher attention (Tables 8–4, p. 170).

The second requirement for shaping involves gradually raising the requirements for reinforcement. Hopkins, Schutte, and Garton (1971), for example, shaped higher work rates by reducing the amount of time available to complete assignments that earned time in the playroom. Others have emphasized improvement by holding reinforcement contingent on a new or novel form of a behavior or by providing differential (more or speedier) reinforcement for extensions or elaborations of a behavior.

Behavior change is most rapid when reinforcement is continuous—when every appropriate response is reinforced. However, behavior is steadiest and most persistent when reinforcement is intermittent and variable. Although continuous and intermittent are different, they are not incompatible. The appearance of incompatibility is removed by re-emphasizing the word improvement. Even when every detected improvement is reinforced (continuous reinforcement, apparently), reinforcement is, in fact, intermittent and variable because the occurrence of improvements is intermittent and variable. For each variation that is an improvement, there are instances of the behavior that are no more, or are even less, proficient than the one last reinforced. In a classroom, reinforcing every observed improvement in a student's performance will inevitably produce a kind of intermittent and variable schedule of reinforcement. It is a blessing.

A few studies are noteworthy because they have deliberately devised schedules of consequences that become more intermittent and variable as a student's skill improves. Such designs suggest how intermediate steps can be a bridge between the more frequent consequences available during the early years of schooling and the less frequent consequences available in later years (Table 8–4).

Shaping New Reinforcers

It is helpful to know that approval and access to preferred activities are reinforcers. The reinforcers of the classroom, however, are not always the same as those established at home and in other nonschool settings. Consequently, it is also helpful to know how to teach new reinforcers. It may, at first, seem an unusual notion, but reinforcers are learned. Teaching them is as important as teaching reading.

Adult attention and approval are established reinforcers for most children long before they enter school. Going to the circus and playing in the sandbox are preferred activities for most children before they reach school. Doing math worksheets and waiting quietly in line are not. Skillful teaching includes transforming necessary activities into preferred activities.

Teaching new reinforcers is not difficult for the teacher who understands that activities that consistently lead to reinforcement become reinforcing them-

TABLE 8-4.   Techniques for Developing Dynamic Systems

Topic/References	Comments
1. Shaping student performance	
a. Improving teacher vigilance and attention	
Cooper, Thomson & Baer, 1970	feedback to teacher
Mandelker, Brigham & Bushell, 1970	token delivery
Graubard, Rosenberg & Miller, 1971	students prompt teacher
Klein, 1971	students prompt teacher
Cossairt, Hall & Hopkins, 1973	feedback to teacher
Knapczyk & Livingston, 1974	students ask questions
Sherman & Cormier, 1974	students prompt teacher
Breyer & Allen, 1975	token delivery
Van Houten & Sullivan, 1975	audio cues
Polirstok & Greer, 1977	students prompt teacher
Stokes, Fowler & Baer, 1978	students prompt teacher
b. Expanding the criteria for reinforcement	
Staats & Butterfield, 1965	more reading
Johnston, Kelley, Harris & Wolf, 1966	more climbing
Risley & Hart, 1968	saying and doing
Gray, Baker & Stancyk, 1969	more reading
Lovitt & Esveldt, 1970	more arithmetic
Packard, 1970	longer attention
Hopkins, Schutte & Garton, 1971	faster printing
Brigham, Graubard & Stans, 1972	more complex writing
Dietz & Repp, 1973	DRL for misbehavior
Goetz & Baer, 1973	novel block building
Maloney & Hopkins, 1973	more complex writing
Kazdin, 1977	longer attending
c. Intermittent and variable consequences	
Lindsley, 1958	variable grading
Wolf, Hanley, King, Lachowicz & Giles, 1970	variable timer
Salzberg, Wheeler, Devar & Hopkins, 1971	variable grading
Clark, Rowbury, Baer & Baer, 1973	variable time-out
Saudargas, Madsen & Scott, 1977	variable home reports
Van Houten & Nau, 1980	variable lottery prizes
2. Shaping new reinforcers	
a. Getting started	
Ayllon & Azrin, 1968	reinforcer sampling
Betancourt & Zeiler, 1971	tokens alter choices
b. Shifting to natural reinforcers	
Staats & Butterfield, 1965	reading skill
Martin, Burkholder, Rosenthal, Tharp & Thorne, 1968	appropriate conduct
Walker & Buckley, 1968	attending
Baer & Wolf, 1970	natural reinforcers
Walker & Buckley, 1972	tokens to natural
Coleman, 1973	school to home
Knapczyk & Livingston, 1973	student teacher
Koegel & Rincover, 1974	individual to class
Bornstein & Quevillon, 1976	individual to class
3. Maintaining social validity	
Foxx & Shapiro, 1978	acceptable time-out
Wolf, 1978	social validity
Trovato & Bucher, 1980	reading program

selves. Betancourt and Zeiler (1971), for example, demonstrated that when preschool children were given tokens for doing least preferred classroom tasks, those tasks became preferred. For students who are consistently and lavishly reinforced for reading improvements, reading becomes reinforcing. The opposite is equally true. Activities that seldom or never result in reinforcement become least preferred and are avoided.

A second technique for teaching new reinforcers is called reinforcement sampling (Ayllon & Azrin, 1968). When a teacher thinks a particular event could be an effective reinforcer, but it is outside the experience of the students, they are given access to it that is noncontingent. Once sampled, the activity may become preferred and, thereafter, used as a reinforcer. Actual contact with potential reinforcers is essential if they are to function.

Reinforcement Systems

Behavior analysis teaching is dynamic along many dimensions. Prompts change, the source and nature of reinforcers change, schedules of reinforcement change, and, because of these changes, students' behaviors change. Such changes will occur whether or not they are controlled by the teacher because any social environment is dynamic. However, the probability of appropriate and desirable change is quite low unless the key dimensions are well managed. The "well-motivated independent learner" is not an accident but the product of careful analysis and thoughtful classroom management.

The goal of early education is to develop students capable of operating effectively in a conventional school situation. Such students respond to prompts of many kinds: teacher instructions and suggestions, instructions in texts and workbooks, the examples of others, time and setting characteristics, and self-evaluations. These students' reinforcers, available after varying intervals of good performance, are those considered "natural" to the school situation: the attention and approval of teachers and peers, self-approval, recognition awards (grades, certificates, merit badges, trophies), instructional activities (reading, solving math problems, discovering the rules of nature, turning a colorful phrase), demonstrating proficiency, holding positions of responsibility, and helping others.

A three-stage strategy can be used to transform the dependent beginning child into an independent learner. Passage from stage to stage is not related to age or grade, but to the teacher's skill in using the techniques already discussed.

The beginning stage is entirely teacher-directed. The teacher sets the rules, determines the daily schedule of activities, is the source of instruction, monitors all performances, and is the source of reinforcement. No matter how effervescent, vigilant, and energetic, however, only the very remarkable teacher can prompt, monitor, and respond to the cascades of behavior displayed by twenty-five energetic children. Some kind of help is needed. Vigilant and energetic aides, however desirable, are too costly for most schools. The Sanders and Hanson (1971) strategy, which reduced class size by releasing students to a free-time area as they completed assignments, requires some degree of student independence. Still, it allows more concentrated instruction for the students who need it most.

Some teachers have found classroom token systems helpful; others object to them because they are not "natural" to the classroom and "what is added, must be withdrawn." That, however, is true for all motivation systems. It is neither more nor less true for tokens. A system built on frequent teacher prompts and praise must be phased into systems that provide less adult attention and approval in later years.

The advantage of tokens is that they can serve as a bridge between the earliest stages which provide abundant adult attention and later stages which depend on materials and intermittent social reinforcement. Just as tokens acquire their reinforcing properties through their association with adult praise and approval, so do they subsequently impart reinforcing properties to the activities with which they are associated, such as reading, doing math, completing spelling lessons, helping peers, and cooperating with the teacher.

Thus, in the beginning stage, tokens (the new reinforcer) are delivered along with praise (the established reinforcer) for every detected performance improvement in the basic school skills of instruction following (including compliance with classroom rules), attention to assigned tasks, classroom courtesies, cooperation with peers, well-kept records of own performance, and any other behavior the teacher admires. Inappropriate behavior is ignored whenever possible or results in less free time. Time-out (two minutes of contingent observation during which no tokens may be earned) is the consequence of last resort for inappropriate behavior.

In the middle stage, the teacher still sets the assignments and all performance criteria, but the requirements for reinforcement are more advanced. The general rule is that the density of reinforcement varies inversely with the student's skill. Consequently, the basic school skills of the beginning stage are now maintained by relatively infrequent and variable reinforcement, while praise and tokens are presented frequently for academic improvements. The objective, of course, is to provide consistent reinforcement for the activities of reading, arithmetic, and spelling so that they will become reinforcing themselves.

Even in academic areas, however, reinforcement intervals are gradually lengthened as skill improves. Intervals must be long enough to teach sustained effort, but not so long as to risk ratio strain. Maintaining the appropriate balance is aided by the records students keep of their own rate and accuracy of pages or problems completed. Where rate and accuracy are high, reinforcement intervals can be lengthened; if accuracy or rate declines, the interval can be shortened temporarily to get things going again. Once students begin working in published curriculum materials, it is safe to assume that accurate performance on subsequent pages represents improvement. Consequently, there is little difficulty in detecting performances that should be reinforced.

The backup activities, picked for entertainment value alone in the beginning stage, now include a variety of instruction activities (the naturally available reinforcers of school). The reinforcing value of reading is evident when students elect to exchange accumulated tokens for a book in preference to a once attractive game. The intervals between exchange periods become progressively longer and more varied during this stage. Misconduct results in reduced participation in exchange periods or brief time-out as before. The students maintain most of their own progress records during this stage, and the teacher's reliability checks on the accuracy of those records become more intermittent if accuracy is high and more frequent if accuracy is low.

The objective of the third stage is to match, as nearly as possible, the characteristics of middle and upper grades. The teacher still sets assignments and performance criteria but is less often the direct source of reinforcement. Teacher approval is still important, but tokens and contract procedures need to be replaced by such naturally available school reinforcers as contingent access to free time and preferred subjects, by recognition symbols (personal progress records, certificates, merit awards), and by appropriate self-approval. All of this is easier, of course, if students are now practiced at praising one another for diligence, progress, and accomplishment.

Assignment lengths at this stage can be expected to cover as much as two weeks of work in some cases; and students should become practiced at determining for themselves how to use unrestricted study periods. To strengthen the generalizability of appropriate independent study behavior further, it is desirable at this stage to introduce substitute teachers to the classroom. The regular teacher can subsequently check student-kept records to ascertain if appropriate performance generalizes to other teachers.

Students cannot be expected to progress smoothly through these three stages. One should expect that a student working in the middle stage will, at some point, encounter difficulty (as shown by his or her own records) and be returned to the first stage for a time. The student working in the third stage is expected to hold independence as a reinforcer. Consequently, if unacceptable or inappropriate performance at that stage results in a one-week required return to the middle stage, it doubles as a period of additional training and a delay of reinforcement well designed to reduce further inappropriate behavior (Bushell & Bushell, 1976).

Because students progress at different rates, a single class will probably have students working in all three stages at the same time. That fits nicely with the Sanders and Hanson (1971) strategy whereby the teacher gives more guidance to students who need it without neglecting or reducing the progress of others.

Maintain Social Validity

Wolf (1978) has recently offered a valuable lesson: a program, such as the behavior analysis model for early education, is socially valid to the extent that its clients endorse its goals, approve of its procedures, and value its results. If the appropriate judges of the acceptability and effectiveness of a program are the consumers or clients of that program, mechanisms must be built that allow clients to render their judgments clearly and often. Instructional goals and their measures need to be described in reports that are sent home and call for some kind of response. Successive take-home progress reports function as prompts for praise, approval, encouragement, or some discussion between parents and teacher. Such informational reports to clients are necessary to the maintenance of social validity but are not sufficient by themselves. Putting the clients of a program in a position to provide continuing quality control over that program requires that they be well informed, that they have a way to express their opinions, and that their opinions function as prompts for the behavior of the program's custodians. Meeting these requirements appears to call for an unconventional but uncomplicated procedure: soliciting and publishing the results of periodic client satisfaction ratings.

Questionnaires (SCALE, 1978) have been used to rate the three areas of social validity: the goals, the procedures, and the effects of a program. Separate questionnaires for parents, teachers, and students allow each group to express its opinions about the importance of and its satisfaction with the specific aspects of all three areas. These judgments are compiled and the results are returned to all clients to prompt appropriate program behavior. Because all results are returned to all clients, individuals can see how widely their opinions are shared by others; parents can become familiar with the opinions of teachers; and the teachers are more likely to be influenced by strong majority opinions than by the vociferous declarations of a few.

Because social validity is assessed repeatedly (for example, twice a year), such questionnaires can support and sustain practices that are valued, identify areas where change is needed, and describe the extent to which attempted changes are successful in improving client satisfaction. Although reports of client satisfaction measures are still few in number (Table 8–4), there is reason to hope that they will become a standard practice for all work that claims the label "applied." That reason is that they generate progressive program improvements—even in the behavior analysis model for early education.

The preparation of this manuscript was supported in part through a grant from the U.S. Department of Education (G 0075 072 26) to the University of Kansas Support and Development Center for Follow Through. The opinions expressed herein are those of the author and should not be construed as representing the opinions or policy of any agency of the United States Government. The author is grateful for the thoughtful and helpful suggestions of Trudylee G. Rowbury and Sherrill A. Bushell.

References

ALLEN, K. E., HART, B. M., BUELL, J. S., HARRIS, F. R., and WOLF, M. M. Effects of social reinforcement on the isolate behavior of a nursery school child. *Child Development*, 1964, *35*, 511–518.

AYLLON, T., and AZRIN, N. Reinforcer sampling: A technique for increasing the behavior of mental patients. *Journal of Applied Behavior Analysis*, 1968, *1*, 13–20.

AYLLON, T., and KELLY, K. Effects of reinforcement on standardized test performance. *Journal of Applied Behavior Analysis*, 1972, 5, 477–484.

AYLLON, T., and ROBERTS, M. D. Eliminating discipline problems by strengthening academic performance. *Journal of Applied Behavior Analysis*, 1974, 7, 71–76.

BAER, A. M., ROWBURY, T., and BAER, D. M. The development of instructional control over classroom activities of deviant preschool children. *Journal of Applied Behavior Analysis*, 1973, 6, 289–298.

BAER, D. M., and WOLF, M. M. The entry into natural communities of reinforcement. In R. Ulrich, R. Stachnik, and J. Mabry (eds.), *Control of Human Behavior*, Vol. II. Glenview, Ill.: Scott, Foresman, 1970.

BAILEY, J. S., WOLF, M. M., and PHILLIPS, E. L. Home-based reinforcement and the modification of pre-delinquents' classroom behavior. *Journal of Applied Behavior Analysis*, 1970, 3, 223–233.

BARBER, R. M., and KAGEY, J. R. Modification of school attendance for an elementary population. *Journal of Applied Behavior Analysis*, 1977, 10, 41–48.

BARRISH, H. H., SAUNDERS, M., and WOLF, M. M. Good behavior game: Effects of individual contingencies for group consequences on disruptive behavior in a classroom. *Journal of Applied Behavior Analysis*, 1969, 2, 119–124.

BECKER, W. C., MADSEN, C. H., JR., ARNOLD, R., and THOMAS, D. R. The contingent use of teacher attention and praise in reducing classroom behavior problems. *Journal of Special Education*, 1967, 1, 287–307.

BETANCOURT, F. W., and ZEILER, M. D. The choices and preferences of nursery school children. *Journal of Applied Behavior Analysis*, 1971, 4, 299–304.

BIRNBRAUER, J. S., BIJOU, S. W., WOLF, M. M., and KIDDER, J. D. Programmed instruction in the classroom. In L. Ullmann and L. Krasner (eds.), *Case Studies in Behavior Modification*. New York: Holt, Rinehart & Winston, 1965.

BIRNBRAUER, J. S., and LAWLER, J. Token reinforcement for learning. *Mental Retardation*, 1964, 2, 275–279.

BIRNBRAUER, J. S., WOLF, M. M., KIDDER, J. D., and TAGUE, C. E. Classroom behavior of retarded pupils with token reinforcement. *Journal of Experimental Child Psychology*, 1965, 2, 219–235.

BOLSTAD, O. D., and JOHNSON, S. M. Self-regulation in the modification of disruptive behavior. *Journal of Applied Behavior Analysis*, 1972, 5, 443–454.

BORNSTEIN, P. H., and QUEVILLON, R. P. The effects of a self-instructional package on overactive preschool boys. *Journal of Applied Behavior Analysis*, 1976, 9, 179–188.

BREYER, N. L., and ALLEN, G. J. Effects of implementing a token economy on teacher attending. *Journal of Applied Behavior Analysis*, 1975, 8, 373–380.

BRIGHAM, T. A., FINFROCK, S. R., BREUNIG, M. K., and BUSHELL, D., JR. The use of programmed materials in the analysis of academic contingencies. *Journal of Applied Behavior Analysis*, 1972, 5, 177–182.

BRIGHAM, T. A., GRAUBARD, P. S., and STANS, A. Analysis of the effects of sequential reinforcement contingencies on aspects of composition. *Journal of Applied Behavior Analysis*, 1972, 5, 421–429.

BRODEN, M., BRUCE, C., MITCHELL, M. A., CARTER, V., and HALL, R. V. Effects of teacher attention on attending behavior of two boys at adjacent desks. *Journal of Applied Behavior Analysis*, 1970, 3, 199–203.

BRODEN, M., HALL, R. V., and MITTS, B. The effect of self-recording on the classroom behavior of two eighth-grade students. *Journal of Applied Behavior Analysis*, 1971, *4*, 191–199.

BROWN, R. E., COPELAND, R. E., and HALL, R. V. The school principal as a behavior modifier. *Journal of Educational Research*, 1972, *66*, 175–180.

BUELL, J., STODDARD, P., HARRIS, F. R., and BAER, D. M. Collateral social development accompanying reinforcement of outdoor play in a preschool child. *Journal of Applied Behavior Analysis*, 1968, *1*, 167–173.

BUSHELL, D., JR. *Classroom Behavior: A Little Book for Teachers.* Englewood Cliffs, N.J.: Prentice-Hall, 1973.

BUSHELL, D., JR., JACKSON, D. A., and WEISS, L. C. Quality control in the behavior analysis approach to project Follow Through. In W. S. Wood (ed.), *Issues in Evaluating Behavior Modification.* Champaign, Ill.: Research Press, 1975.

BUSHELL, D., JR., WROBEL, P. A., and MICHAELIS, M. L. Applying "group" contingencies to the classroom study behavior of preschool children. *Journal of Applied Behavior Analysis*, 1968, *1*, 55–61.

BUSHELL, S. A., and BUSHELL, D., JR. A dual contingency procedure to support student self-determination and performance. In T. A. Brigham, T. F. McLaughlin, J. W. Scott, and R. Hawkins (eds.), *Behavior Analysis in Education: Self-Control and Reading.* Dubuque, Iowa: Kendall/Hunt Publishing Co., 1976.

CANTRELL, R. P., CANTRELL, M. L., HUDDLESTON, C. M., and WOOLRIDGE, R. L. Contingency contracting with school problems. *Journal of Applied Behavior Analysis*, 1969, *2*, 215–220.

CARNINE, D. W. Effects of two teacher-presentation rates on off-task behavior, answering correctly, and participation. *Journal of Applied Behavior Analysis*, 1976, *9*, 199–206.

CARNINE, D. W., and FINK, W. Increasing the rate of presentation and use of signals in elementary classroom teachers. *Journal of Applied Behavior Analysis*, 1978, *11*, 35–46.

CHADWICK, B. A., and DAY, R. C. Systematic reinforcement: Academic performance of under-achieving students. *Journal of Applied Behavior Analysis*, 1971, *4*, 311–319.

CHRISTY, P. R. Does use of tangible rewards with individual children affect peer observers? *Journal of Applied Behavior Analysis*, 1975, *8*, 187–196.

CLARK, H. B., ROWBURY, T., BAER, A. M., and BAER, D. M. Timeout as a punishing stimulus in continuous and intermittent schedules. *Journal of Applied Behavior Analysis*, 1973, *6*, 443–455.

CLARK, M., LACHOWICZ, J., and WOLF, M. M. A pilot basic education program for school dropouts incorporating a token reinforcement system. *Behaviour Research and Therapy*, 1968, *6*, 183–188.

COLEMAN, R. G. A procedure for fading from experimenter-school-based to parent-home-based control of classroom behavior. *Journal of School Psychology*, 1973, *11*, 71–79.

COOPER, M. L., THOMSON, C. L., and BAER, D. M. The experimental modification of teacher attending behavior. *Journal of Applied Behavior Analysis*, 1970, *3*, 153–157.

COPELAND, R. E., BROWN, R. E., AXELROD, S., and HALL, R. V. Effect of a school principal praising parents for student attendance. *Educational Technology*, 1972, *12*, 56–59.

COPELAND, R. E., BROWN, R. E., and HALL, R. V. The effects of principal-implemented techniques on the behavior of pupils. *Journal of Applied Behavior Analysis*, 1974, *7*, 77–86.

COREY, J. R., and SHAMOW, J. C. The effects of fading on the acquisition and retention of oral reading. *Journal of Applied Behavior Analysis*, 1972, *5*, 311–315.

COSSAIRT, A., HALL, R. V., and HOPKINS, B. L. The effects of experimenter's instructions, feedback, and praise on teacher praise and student attending behavior. *Journal of Applied Behavior Analysis*, 1973, *6*, 89–100.

DIETZ, S. M., and REPP, A. C. Decreasing classroom misbehavior through the use of DRL schedules of reinforcement. *Journal of Applied Behavior Analysis*, 1973, *6*, 457–463.

DINEEN, J. P., CLARK, H. B., and RISLEY, T. R. Peer tutoring among elementary students: Educational benefits to the tutor. *Journal of Applied Behavior Analysis*, 1977, *10*, 231–238.

EVANS, G. W., and OSWALT, G. L. Acceleration of academic progress through the manipulation of peer influence. *Behaviour Research and Therapy*, 1968, *6*, 189–196.

FARNUM, M., and BRIGHAM, T. A. The use and evaluation of study guides with middle school students. *Journal of Applied Behavior Analysis*, 1978, *11*, 137–144.

FILIPCZAK, J., ARCHER, M., NEALE, M., and WINETT, R. Issues in multivariate assessment of a large-scale behavioral program. *Journal of Applied Behavior Analysis*, 1979, *12*, 593–613.

FINK, W. T., and CARNINE, D. W. Control of arithmetic errors using informational feedback and graphing. *Journal of Applied Behavior Analysis*, 1975, *8*, 461.

FOXX, R., and SHAPIRO, S. T. The timeout ribbon: A nonexclusionary timeout procedure. *Journal of Applied Behavior Analysis*, 1978, *11*, 125–136.

GLYNN, E. L., and THOMAS, J. D. Effect of cueing on self-control of classroom behavior. *Journal of Applied Behavior Analysis*, 1974, *7*, 299–306.

GLYNN, E. L., THOMAS, J. D., and SHEE, S. M. Behavioral self-control of on-task behavior in an elementary classroom. *Journal of Applied Behavior Analysis*, 1973, *6*, 105–113.

GOETZ, E. M., and BAER, D. M. Social control of form diversity and the emergence of new forms in children's blockbuilding. *Journal of Applied Behavior Analysis*, 1973, *6*, 209–217.

GRAUBARD, P. S., ROSENBERG, H., and MILLER, M. B. An ecological approach to social deviancy. In E. A. Ramp and B. L. Hopkins (eds.), *A New Direction for Education: Behavior Analysis 1971*. Lawrence: The University of Kansas Support and Development Center for Follow Through, 1971.

GRAY, B. B., BAKER, R. D., and STANCYK, S. E. Performance determined instruction for training in remedial reading. *Journal of Applied Behavior Analysis*, 1969, *2*, 255–263.

GREENWOOD, C. R., SLOANE, H. N., JR., and BASKIN, A. Training elementary aged peer-behavior managers to control small group programmed mathematics. *Journal of Applied Behavior Analysis*, 1974, *7*, 103–114.

HALL, R. V., LUND, D., and JACKSON, D. Effects of teacher attention on study behavior. *Journal of Applied Behavior Analysis*, 1968, *1*, 1–12.

HAMBLIN, R. L., HATHAWAY, C., and WODARSKI, J. Group contingencies, peer tutoring and accelerating academic achievement. In E. A. Ramp and B. L. Hopkins (eds.), *A New Direction for Education: Behavior Analysis 1971*. Lawrence: The University of Kansas Support and Development Center for Follow Through, 1971.

HARRIS, F. R., JOHNSTON, M. K., KELLEY, C. S., and WOLF, M. M. Effects of positive social reinforcement on regressed crawling of a nursery school child. *Journal of Educational Psychology*, 1964, *55*, 35–41.

HARRIS, F. R., WOLF, M. M., and BAER, D. M. Effects of adult social reinforcement on child behavior. *Young Children*, 1964, *20*, 8–17.

HARRIS, V. W., and SHERMAN, J. A. Use and analysis of the "Good Behavior Game" to reduce disruptive classroom behavior. *Journal of Applied Behavior Analysis*, 1973a, *6*, 405–417.

HARRIS, V. W., and SHERMAN, J. A. Effects of peer tutoring and consequences on the math performance of elementary classroom students. *Journal of Applied Behavior Analysis*, 1973b, *6*, 587–597.

HART, B. M., and RISLEY, T. R. Establishing use of descriptive adjectives in the spontaneous speech of disadvantaged preschool children. *Journal of Applied Behavior Analysis*, 1968, *1*, 109–120.

HART, B., and RISLEY, T. R. Incidental teaching of language in the preschool. *Journal of Applied Behavior Analysis*, 1975, 8, 411–420.

HASAZI, J. E., and HASAZI, S. E. Effects of teacher attention on digit-reversal behavior in an elementary school child. *Journal of Applied Behavior Analysis*, 1972, 5, 157–162.

HERMAN, S. H., and TRAMONTANA, J. Instructions and group versus individual reinforcement in modifying disruptive group behavior. *Journal of Applied Behavior Analysis*, 1971, *4*, 113–119.

HOLLAND, J. G. Human vigilance. *Science*, 1958, *128*, 61–67.

HOMME, L. E., DEBACA, P. C., DEVINE, J. V., STEINHORST, R., and RICKERT, E. J. Use of the Premack principle in controlling the behavior of nursery school children. *Journal of the Experimental Analysis of Behavior*, 1963, *6*, 544.

HOPKINS, B. L. Personal communication, May 1978.

HOPKINS, B. L., SCHUTTE, R. C., and GARTON, K. L. The effects of access to a playroom on the rate and quality of printing and writing of first and second-grade students. *Journal of Applied Behavior Analysis*, 1971, *4*, 77–87.

JACOBSON, J. M., BUSHELL, D., JR., and RISLEY, T. Switching requirements in a Head Start classroom. *Journal of Applied Behavior Analysis*, 1969, *2*, 43–47.

JOHNSON, M., and BAILEY, J. S. Cross-age tutoring: Fifth graders as arithmetic tutors for kindergarten children. *Journal of Applied Behavior Analysis*, 1974, *7*, 223–232.

JOHNSTON, M. K., KELLEY, C. S., HARRIS, F. R., and WOLF, M. M. An application of reinforcement principles to development of motor skills of a young child. *Child Development*, 1966, *37*, 379–387.

JONES, J. C., TRAP, J., and COOPER, J. O. Technical report: Students' self-recording of manuscript letter strokes. *Journal of Applied Behavior Analysis*, 1977, *10*, 509–514.

KAUFMAN, K. F., and O'LEARY, K. D. Reward, cost, and self-evaluation procedures for disruptive adolescents in a psychiatric hospital school. *Journal of Applied Behavior Analysis*, 1972, 5, 293–309.

KAZDIN, A. E. The effect of vicarious reinforcement on attentive behavior in the classroom. *Journal of Applied Behavior Analysis*, 1973, 6, 71–78.

KAZDIN, A. E. The influence of behavior preceding a reinforced response on behavior change in the classroom. *Journal of Applied Behavior Analysis*, 1977, 10, 299–310.

KAZDIN, A. E., and KLOCK, J. The effect of nonverbal teacher approval on student attentive behavior. *Journal of Applied Behavior Analysis*, 1973, 6, 643–654.

KAZDIN, A. E., SILVERMAN, N. A., and SITTLER, J. L. The use of prompts to enhance vicarious effects of nonverbal approval. *Journal of Applied Behavior Analysis*, 1975, 8, 279–286.

KLEIN, S. S. Student influence on teacher behavior. *American Educational Research Journal*, 1971, 8, 403–421.

KNAPCZYK, D. R., and LIVINGSTON, G. Self-recording and student teacher supervision: Variables within a token economy structure. *Journal of Applied Behavior Analysis*, 1973, 6, 481–486.

KNAPCZYK, D. R., and LIVINGSTON, G. The effects of prompting question-asking upon on-task behavior and reading comprehension. *Journal of Applied Behavior Analysis*, 1974, 7, 115–121.

KOEGEL, R. L., and RINCOVER, A. Treatment of psychotic children in a classroom environment: I. Learning in a large group. *Journal of Applied Behavior Analysis*, 1974, 7, 45–59.

LAHEY, B. B., and DRABMAN, R. S. Facilitation of the acquisition and retention of sight-word vocabulary through token reinforcement. *Journal of Applied Behavior Analysis*, 1974, 7, 307–312.

LINDSLEY, O. R. Intermittent Grading. *The Clearing House: A Journal for Modern Junior and Senior High Schools*, 1958, 32, 451–454.

LONG, J. D., and WILLIAMS, R. L. The comparative effectiveness of group and individually contingent free time with inner-city junior high school students. *Journal of Applied Behavior Analysis*, 1973, 6, 465–474.

LOOS, F. M., WILLAMS, K. P., and BAILEY, J. S. A multi-element analysis of the effect of teacher aides in an "open"-style classroom. *Journal of Applied Behavior Analysis*, 1977, 10, 437–448.

LOVITT, T. C., and CURTISS, K. A. Effects of manipulating an antecedent event on mathematics response rate. *Journal of Applied Behavior Analysis*, 1968, 1, 329–333.

LOVITT, T. C., and ESVELDT, K. A. The relative effects on math performance of single-versus multiple-ratio schedules: A case study. *Journal of Applied Behavior Analysis*, 1970, 3, 261–270.

LOVITT, T. C., GUPPY, T. E., and BLATTNER, J. E. The use of free-time contingency with fourth graders to increase spelling accuracy. *Behaviour Research and Therapy*, 1969, 7, 151–156.

MACDONALD, W. S., GALLIMORE, R., and MACDONALD, G. Contingency counseling by school personnel: An economical model of intervention. *Journal of Applied Behavior Analysis*, 1970, 3, 175–182.

MCKENZIE, H., CLARK, M., WOLF, M. M., KOTHERA, R., and BENSON, C. Behavior modification of children with learning disabilities using grades as token reinforcers. *Exceptional Children*, 1968, *34*, 745–752.

McLaughlin, T. F., and Malaby, J. Intrinsic reinforcers in a classroom token economy. *Journal of Applied Behavior Analysis*, 1972a, *5*, 263–270.

McLaughlin, T. F., and Malaby, J. Reducing and measuring inappropriate verbalizations in a token classroom. *Journal of Applied Behavior Analysis*, 1972b, *5*, 329–333.

Madsen, C. H., Jr., Becker, W. C., and Thomas, D. R. Rules, praise, and ignoring: Elements of elementary classroom control. *Journal of Applied Behavior Analysis*, 1968, *1*, 139–150.

Maloney, K. B., and Hopkins, B. L. The modification of sentence structure and its relationship to subjective judgments of creativity in writing. *Journal of Applied Behavior Analysis*, 1973, *6*, 425–433.

Mandelker, A. V., Brigham, T. A., and Bushell, D., Jr. The effects of token procedures on a teacher's social contacts with her students. *Journal of Applied Behavior Analysis*, 1970, *3*, 169–174.

Martin, M., Burkholder, R., Rosenthal, T., Tharp, R., and Thorne, L. Programming behavior change and reintegration into school milieu of extreme adolescent deviates. *Behaviour Research and Therapy*, 1968, *6*, 371–383.

Medland, M. B., and Stachnik, T. J. Good-behavior game: A replication and systematic analysis. *Journal of Applied Behavior Analysis*, 1972, *5*, 45–51.

Miller, L. K., and Schneider, R. The use of a token system in project Head Start. *Journal of Applied Behavior Analysis*, 1970, *3*, 213–220.

O'Leary, K. D., and Becker, W. C. Behavior modification of an adjustment class: A token reinforcement program. *Exceptional Children*, 1967, *33*, 637–642.

O'Leary, K. D., Becker, W. C., Evans, M. B., and Saudargas, R. A. A token reinforcement program in a public school: A replication and systematic analysis. *Journal of Applied Behavior Analysis*, 1969, *2*, 3–13.

Osborne, J. G. Free-time as a reinforcer in the management of classroom behavior. *Journal of Applied Behavior Analysis*, 1969, *2*, 113–118.

Packard, R. G. The control of "classroom attention": A group contingency for complex behavior. *Journal of Applied Behavior Analysis*, 1970, *3*, 13–28.

Pendergrass, V. E. Timeout from positive reinforcement following persistent, high-rate behavior in retardates. *Journal of Applied Behavior Analysis*, 1972, *5*, 85–91.

Pinkston, E. M., Reese, N. M., LeBlanc, J. M., and Baer, D. M. Independent control of a preschool child's aggression and peer interaction by contingent teacher attention. *Journal of Applied Behavior Analysis*, 1973, *6*, 115–124.

Polirstok, S. R., and Greer, R. D. Remediation of mutually aversive interactions between a problem student and four teachers by training the student in reinforcement techniques. *Journal of Applied Behavior Analysis*, 1977, *10*, 707–716.

Porterfield, J. K., Herbert-Jackson, E., and Risley, T. R. Contingent observation: An effective and acceptable procedure for reducing disruptive behavior of young children in a group setting. *Journal of Applied Behavior Analysis*, 1976, *9*, 55–64.

Premack, D. Reinforcement theory. In D. Levine (ed.), *Nebraska Symposium on Motivation* (Vol. 13). Lincoln: University of Nebraska Press, 1965.

Ramp, E., Ulrich, R., and Dulaney, S. Delayed timeout as a procedure for reducing disruptive classroom behavior: A case study. *Journal of Applied Behavior Analysis,* 1971, *4,* 235–239.

RESNICK, L. B., WANG, M. C., and KAPLAN, J. Task analysis in curriculum design: A hierarchically sequenced introductory mathematics curriculum. *Journal of Applied Behavior Analysis,* 1973, *6,* 679–710.

REYNOLDS, N. J., and RISLEY, T. R. The role of social and material reinforcers in increasing talking of a disadvantaged preschool child. *Journal of Applied Behavior Analysis,* 1968, *1,* 253–262.

RINGER, V. M. J. The use of a "token helper" in the management of classroom behavior problems and in teacher training. *Journal of Applied Behavior Analysis,* 1973, *6,* 671–677.

RISLEY, T. R., and HART, B. Developing correspondence between the verbal and nonverbal behavior of preschool children. *Journal of Applied Behavior Analysis,* 1968, *1,* 267–281.

ROBERTSON, S. J., DeREUS, D. M., and DRABMAN, R. S. Peer and college-student tutoring as reinforcement in a token economy. *Journal of Applied Behavior Analysis,* 1976, *9,* 169–177.

ROWBURY, T. G., BAER, A. M., and BAER, D. M. Interactions between teacher guidance and contingent access to play in developing preacademic skills of deviant preschool children. *Journal of Applied Behavior Analysis,* 1976, *9,* 85–104.

SAJWAJ, T., TWARDOSZ, S., and BURKE, M. Side effects of extinction procedures in a remedial preschool. *Journal of Applied Behavior Analysis,* 1972, *5,* 163–175.

SALZBERG, B. H., WHEELER, A. J., DEVAR, L. T., and HOPKINS, B. L. The effect of intermittent feedback and intermittent contingent access to play on printing of kindergarten children. *Journal of Applied Behavior Analysis,* 1971, *4,* 163 171.

SANDERS, R. M., and HANSON, P. J. A note on a simple procedure for redistributing a teacher's student contacts. *Journal of Applied Behavior Analysis,* 1971, *4,* 157–161.

SANTOGROSSI, D. A., O'LEARY, K. D., ROMANCZYK, R. G., and KAUFMAN, K. F. Self-evaluation by adolescents in a psychiatric hospital school token program. *Journal of Applied Behavior Analysis,* 1973, *6,* 277–287.

SAUDARGAS, R. A., MADSEN, C. H., JR., and SCOTT, J. W. Differential effects of fixed- and variable-time feedback on production rates of elementary school children. *Journal of Applied Behavior Analysis,* 1977, *10,* 673–678.

SCHMIDT, G. W., and ULRICH, R. E. Effects of group contingent events upon classroom noise. *Journal of Applied Behavior Analysis,* 1969, *2,* 171–179.

School Clients' Annual Local Evaluation (SCALE), 1978. Available from SCALE, Inc., 825 Missouri St., Lawrence, Kansas 66044.

SCHUMAKER, J. B., HOVELL, M. F., and SHERMAN, J. A. An analysis of daily report cards and parent-managed privileges in the improvement of adolescents' classroom performance. *Journal of Applied Behavior Analysis,* 1977, *10,* 449–464.

SCHUTTE, R. C., and HOPKINS, B. L. The effects of teacher attention on following instructions in a kindergarten class. *Journal of Applied Behavior Analysis,* 1970, *3,* 117–122.

SCHWARTZ, G. J. College students as contingency managers for adolescents in a program to develop reading skills. *Journal of Applied Behavior Analysis,* 1977, *10,* 645–655.

SCHWARZ, M. L., and HAWKINS, R. P. Application of delayed reinforcement procedures to the behavior of an elementary school child. *Journal of Applied Behavior Analysis*, 1970, *3*, 85–96.

SCOTT, J. W., and BUSHELL, D., JR. The length of teacher contacts and students' off-task behavior. *Journal of Applied Behavior Analysis*, 1974, *7*, 39–44.

SHERMAN, T. M., and CORMIER, W. H. An investigation of the influence of student behavior on teacher behavior. *Journal of Applied Behavior Analysis*, 1974, *7*, 11–21.

SKIBA, E. A., PETTIGREW, L. E., and ALDEN, S. E. A behavioral approach to the control of thumbsucking in the classroom. *Journal of Applied Behavior Analysis*, 1971, *4*, 121–125.

SOLOMON, R. W., and WAHLER, R. G. Peer reinforcement control of classroom problem behavior. *Journal of Applied Behavior Analysis*, 1973, *6*, 49–56.

STAATS, A. W., and BUTTERFIELD, W. H. Treatment of non-reading in a culturally deprived juvenile delinquent: An application of reinforcement principles. *Child Development*, 1965, *36*, 925–942.

STAATS, A. W., MINKE, K. A., GOODWIN, W., and LANDEEN, J. Cognitive behavior modification: 'Motivated learning' reading treatment with subprofessional therapy-technicians. *Behaviour Research and Therapy*, 1965, *5*, 283–299.

STAATS, A. W., STAATS, C. K., SCHUTZ, R. E., and WOLF, M. M. The conditioning of textual responses using "extrinsic" reinforcers. *Journal of the Experimental Analysis of Behavior*, 1962, *5*, 33–40.

STOKES, T. F., FOWLER, S. A., and BAER, D. M. Training preschool children to recruit natural communities of reinforcement. *Journal of Applied Behavior Analysis*, 1978, *11*, 285–303.

STRAIN, P. S., SHORES, R. E., and KERR, M. M. An experimental analysis of "spillover" effects of the social interaction of behaviorally handicapped preschool children. *Journal of Applied Behavior Analysis*, 1976, *9*, 31–40.

STRAIN, P. S., SHORES, R. E., and TIMM, M. A. Effects of peer social initiations on the behavior of withdrawn preschool children. *Journal of Applied Behavior Analysis*, 1977, *10*, 289–298.

STRAIN, P. S., and TIMM, M. A. An experimental analysis of social interaction between a behaviorally disordered preschool child and her classroom peers. *Journal of Applied Behavior Analysis*, 1974, *7*, 583–590.

SURATT, P. R., ULRICH, R. E., and HAWKINS, R. P. An elementary student as a behavioral engineer. *Journal of Applied Behavior Analysis*, 1969, *2*, 85–92.

THOMAS, D. R., BECKER, W. C., and ARMSTRONG, M. Production and elimination of disruptive classroom behavior by systematically varying teacher's behavior. *Journal of Applied Behavior Analysis*, 1968, *1*, 35–45.

THOMAS, J. D., PRESLAND, I. E., GRANT, M. D., and GLYNN, T. L. Natural rates of teacher approval and disapproval in grade-7 classrooms. *Journal of Applied Behavior Analysis*, 1978, *11*, 91–94.

TODD, D. D., SCOTT, R. B., BOSTOW, D. E., and ALEXANDER, S. B. Modification of the excessive inappropriate classroom behavior of two elementary school students using home-based consequences and daily report-card procedures. *Journal of Applied Behavior Analysis*, 1976, *9*, 106.

TROVATO, J., and BUCHER, B. Peer tutoring with or without home-based reinforcement for reading remediation. *Journal of Applied Behavior Analysis*, 1980, *13*, 129–141.

TYLER, V. O., and BROWN, G. D. Token reinforcement of academic performance with institutionalized delinquent boys. *Journal of Educational Psychology*, 1968, *14*, 413–423.

VAN HOUTEN, R., HILL, S., and PARSONS, M. An analysis of a performance feedback system: The effects of timing and feedback, public posting, and praise upon academic performance and peer interaction. *Journal of Applied Behavior Analysis*, 1975, *8*, 449–457.

VAN HOUTEN, R., MORRISON, E., JARVIS, R., and McDONALD, M. The effects of explicit timing and feedback on compositional response rate in elementary school children. *Journal of Applied Behavior Analysis*, 1974, *7*, 547–555.

VAN HOUTEN, R., and NAU, P. A comparison of the effects of fixed and variable ratio schedules of reinforcement on the behavior of deaf children. *Journal of Applied Behavior Analysis*, 1980, *13*, 13–21.

VAN HOUTEN, R., and SULLIVAN, K. Effects of an audio cueing system on the rate of teacher praise. *Journal of Applied Behavior Analysis*, 1975, *8*, 197–201.

WALKER, H. M., and BUCKLEY, N. K. The use of positive reinforcement in conditioning attending behavior. *Journal of Applied Behavior Analysis*, 1968, *1*, 245–250.

WALKER, H. M., and BUCKLEY, N. K. Programming generalization and maintenance treatment effects across time and across settings. *Journal of Applied Behavior Analysis*, 1972, *5*, 209–224.

WARD, M. H., and BAKER, B. L. Reinforcement therapy in the classroom. *Journal of Applied Behavior Analysis*, 1968, *1*, 323–328.

WASIK, B. H., SENN, K., WELCH, R. H., and COOPER, B. R. Behavior modification with culturally deprived school children: Two case studies. *Journal of Applied Behavior Analysis*, 1969, *2*, 181–194.

WHITE, M. A. Natural rates of teacher approval and disapproval in the classroom. *Journal of Applied Behavior Analysis*, 1975, *8*, 367–372.

WHITLOCK, C., and BUSHELL, D., JR. Some effects of "back-up" reinforcers on reading behavior. *Journal of Experimental Child Psychology*, 1967, *5*, 50–57.

WILLIAMS, R. L., LONG, J. D., and YOAKLEY, R. W. The utility of behavior contracts and behavior proclamations with advantaged senior high school students. *Journal of School Psychology*, 1972, *10*, 329–338.

WILLIS, J., CROWDER, J., and MORRIS, B. A. A behavioral approach to remedial reading using students as behavioral engineers. In G. Semb (ed.), *Behavior Analysis and Education*. Lawrence: The University of Kansas Support and Development Center for Follow Through, 1972.

WILSON, C. W., and HOPKINS, B. L. The effects of contingent music on the intensity of noise in junior high home economics classes. *Journal of Applied Behavior Analysis*, 1973, *6*, 269–275.

WOLF, M. M. Social validity: The case for subjective measurement *or* how applied behavior analysis is finding its heart. *Journal of Applied Behavior Analysis*, 1978, *11*, 203–214.

WOLF, M. M., GILES, D. K., and HALL, R. V. Experiments with token reinforcement in a remedial classroom. *Behaviour Research and Therapy*, 1968, *6*, 51–64.

WOLF, M. M., HANLEY, E., KING, L., LACHOWICZ, J., and GILES, D. K. The timer game: A variable interval contingency for management of out-of-seat behavior. *Exceptional Children*, 1970, *36*, 113–117.

WOOD, R., and FLYNN, J. M. A self-evaluation token system versus an external evaluation token system alone in a residential setting with predelinquent youth. *Journal of Applied Behavior Analysis*, 1978, *11*, 503–512.

ZEILER, M. Principles of behavior control. In A. C. Catania and T. A. Brigham (eds.), *Handbook of Applied Behavior Analysis: Social and Instructional Processes.* New York: Irvington Publishers, 1978.

ZIMMERMAN, E. H., and ZIMMERMAN, J. The alteration of behavior in a special classroom situation. *Journal of the Experimental Analysis of Behavior*, 1962, *5*, 59–60.

ZIMMERMAN, E. H., ZIMMERMAN, J., and RUSSELL, C. D. Differential effects of token reinforcement on instruction-following behavior in retarded students instructed as a group. *Journal of Applied Behavior Analysis*, 1969, *2*, 101–112.

CHAPTER 9

The Use of Piaget's Constructivism in Early Childhood Education Programs

George E. Forman
Catherine Twomey Fosnot

SINCE the progressive education movement in the thirties, and even before that when children learned through the apprenticeship method, educators hailed as truth the axiom: learn by doing. Now, in the name of Jean Piaget (1896–1980), educators are advising us that children must actively manipulate tangible objects in order to learn. In just what sense has Piaget's work brought new understanding to this long-standing axiom? We will try to answer that question in this chapter. The difficulty will appear when it becomes obvious that not everyone accepts the same definition of doing. What is doing, what is an experience, and how does the child construct knowledge on the basis of his or her doings? We need to place Piaget's work in perspective in order to understand his theory of doing and knowledge.

The Importance of Piaget in General Psychology

The Man and His Mission

Jean Piaget, at an early age, became intrigued with the possibility that intelligence develops through processes that are common to cell development, anatomical development, and, for that matter, the development of any viable living system. The development of one person's intelligence does not occur exclusively as a product of particular experiences but is, rather, an extension of biological processes begun eons ago. But Piaget realized that intellectual development was not preprogrammed through genetic codes. Only the modes of interacting with the environment, along with certain physical constraints of the person (two arms, two legs, and so on) and the environment (gravity, gaseous at- **185** mosphere, terra firma), were predetermined. He recognized that his task was a difficult one: to account for the elegant compatibility between two things, the person and the environment, two things that are not directly derivative of each other the way that the oak tree is derivative of the acorn. In other words, how is it that our knowledge of the world works? Piaget's answer, as we will state again and again, was that we learn more and more about how we know what we think we know. We develop a more explicit awareness of what constitutes certainty.

This awareness of how we know and how we become certain in our knowledge is gradually constructed through processes of organization. To accentuate the gradual nature of this awareness and its departure from a naïve realism, Piaget's theory of knowledge is known as *constructivism*. Unlike a naïve realism that assumes that knowledge is a direct product of making better mental copies of an external world, constructivism assumes that we have no direct accessibility to an external world and therefore have to construct representations that have more to do with the act of knowing than they do with the external object per se. To Piaget, what we represent is our own mental activity and not some static external object. We then externalize this mental activity as if it were a static external object (see Furth, 1972). The role of activity in the construction of knowledge was no less than Piaget's life's mission.

The Nature of Development

By the time most children are seven years old, they can distinguish two types of knowledge: that which is true most of the time and that which is necessarily true by deduction. Before this point in their development, children can only consider the first type of knowledge. How do we account for this development? Piaget believes that it is impossible to account for the understanding of deductive necessity, for example, the truth of a transitive relation, by saying that it is no more than an additional component to prior knowledge. We can say this of some things, such as learning that states have capitols is an additional component to an earlier concept of the political state. The understanding of transitivity, however, is not so much learning a new component as it is learning how to relate components known in themselves for some time. This shift in understanding is from knowing what is *probably* there to knowing what is *necessarily* true about the relations among objects that are given as there. In the state capitol example, it may be only probable that the largest city in a state is the center of government but it is a logical deduction, once the child is given the phrase "Boston is the capitol of Massachusetts," that he knows for certain that the first is a smaller geographic region than the second. He knows this even though he has seen neither on a map. Somehow the child reaches a stage at which he/she can enter the facts into a set of relations that make such certainty possible. We would not say that the child has learned new facts, but the child has developed new schemes of organization of facts already known.

It is Piaget's interest in changing schemes of organization that makes him talk about qualitative changes in development or stages. Once he realized that one stage could not be a simple extension of the previous stage, he had to find some more complicated mechanism for development. Development was a case of reorganization rather than of accretion. Some would say that feedback from the environment guides the reorganization, but Piaget had seen hundreds of cases where the children's answers to questions were highly organized but completely at odds with feedback that their adult environment would have given them. Reorganization of the facts was not a simple case of listening closely or looking closely. The errors that children made had their own "logic" and were very similar across hundreds of children. Therefore, Piaget concluded that there were definite laws of reorganization, endogenous to our species, that accounted for the consistency in these stages of development. He called these endogenous laws of reorganization *equilibration*.

The importance of the stage concept in Piaget's theory was not that it explained a wide range of behavior. Rather, the stage concept justified the search for endogenous regulation of intellectual development as opposed to a more environmental, exogenous regulation. Without qualitative changes in the manner that data are related, a theory based on quantitative extension of reflexes would do (for example, Bijou & Baer, 1965). But if the developing system undergoes a revolution in spite of the fact that the organization of the environment remains forever "there as is," the revolution must be constructed by laws of the organism. To paraphrase Piaget, the child does not *discover* invariants in the world, the child *invents* representations of the world that themselves contain invariants. Development is not a case of learning more; in fact, it is a case of having to remember less as we develop the ability to make inferences from partial data.

Equilibration Theory

If the child processes data in different ways across his/her lifespan we can say that the processes themselves change. But what governs the manner in which these processes change? What are the regulations on the regulators of data? Certainly, the environment does not demand that we think deductively instead of inductively. In fact, demands are made clear to us through the same thought processes that we use to answer these demands. The environment does not literally hit us over the head, but, rather, we extend our curiosity to it. Piaget takes as a biological given that the human intellect is a question-seeking organ and not an answer-reacting organ. What we have inherited, evolutionarily speaking, is our ability to feel the force of questions we have generated, to feel the lack of closure when facts do not fit, to be moved to reduce the tension if two thoughts contradict each other. This built-in need to eliminate contradiction regulates the regulators and accounts for the transition from stage to stage.

Inhelder, Sinclair and Bovet (1974) demonstrated how children reorganize their thoughts in the face of continuous self-contradiction. By presenting a measurement problem in a manner that alternately highlighted overall length versus numbers of units, these researchers discovered that children eventually taught themselves how to construct equal lengths with different sets of units, for example, four long matches can equal the length of five short matches.

Without applying the specific terms of equilibration theory, we can analyze the child's acquisitions from the equilibration perspective. Initially, the child did not sense the contradiction. Sometimes it takes five, sometimes four to make a row the length of the standard. Probably at the point that the child realized that he was using the same size matches to get different answers and that the standard row was always the same number regardless of its spatial arrangement, he/she sensed that a problem existed. The contradiction itself depended on the child's construction of the relevance of these parameters to what was being asked. The experimenter cannot really tell the child that the size of the smaller matches makes a difference. The child has to assimilate that parameter as an important question to consider. When the experimenter did attempt to orient the children to the parameter of size, children would listen but would not know how to enter size into a set of deductions or they would, so to speak, go outside the system of relations by breaking a match to make the two rows equal. They could not solve the problem within the system of relations given unless they themselves had considered size as a relevant variable.

To summarize, the child is confronted with a situation that causes him to say discrepant things. Later, he understands that these statements are indeed contradictory. Finally, he constructs first a partial resolution and then a new way of thinking about these types of situations such that both answers are coordinated into a single system of relations. The importance of equilibration theory to general psychology rests in its analysis of self-regulated learning as opposed to programmed or teacher-directed learning.

The Extension of Piaget to Education

Success versus Understanding

Piaget made us aware that a child might have success on some task but not really understand the concepts fully. The best example Piaget gives us is the difference between successful counting versus understanding number relations. Even a child who can count two rows of objects accurately may still think that the spread out row of seven has more than the compact row of seven. In essence, Piaget gave educators a better insight into rote learning versus meaningful learning. Meaningful learning requires that the child understand the implications between certain correspondences (such as two rows of seven) and certain transformations (such as spreading out one row as opposed to adding an object to one row). Knowledge of the correspondences alone, as, for example, this A is also a B, can be learned by rote, but the integration of these facts with rules of transformation is more difficult and is necessary for understanding.

When educators became aware of this, there was a flurry of activity in curriculum redesign, particularly in mathematics. Children were asked to transform the rote numeral sequence into different bases and then to transform them back again into base ten. Children were taught complex procedures for grouping and regrouping in hopes that they would learn the premises upon which mathematics was founded. But somewhere along the way we lost sight of the child in the glint of our shiny new curriculum packages. Perhaps our mistake was in applying Piaget's results without applying his method. His method, called the *méthode clinique*, was a highly skilled procedure for interviewing individual children.

A New Respect for Errors

Piaget used the méthode clinique because he wanted to understand the child's errors. When educators read the detailed protocols from these interviews they realize that the child's error often is a logical extension of certain firmly believed assumptions. More important, Piaget helped us figure out what some of these assumptions are, for example, that the number five is the name of the fifth object and if you move the fifth object to first place then it still should be called "five." Our increased respect for errors came because now we know more about their origin and how to enter the child's world in order to facilitate the child's construction of an improved understanding of number.

There are many other areas of early childhood education in which Piaget's work has given us a new respect for errors. In the social realm, Piaget distinguished between egoism and egocentrism. Egoism is the deliberate and fully conscious decision to put one's own interests ahead of others. Egocentrism is the inability to consider a point of view that is different from one's own current point of view. An example of egocentrism would be a child who sincerely thinks that his mother would like an all-day sucker for Valentine's Day. A three-year-old simply has not yet developed the ability to consider two opposing wishes simultaneously, his own and his mother's, any more than the six-year-old in the earlier example could integrate both the number of matches in the row with the relative size of the two sets of matches. The preschool teacher who understands Piaget's concept of egocentrism is more likely to see the child's behavior as a partial system to be reorganized rather than as an absolute mistake that must be eliminated. Herein lies the respect for errors.

Not only do errors give the educator good clues regarding what the child does know, but errors also serve the same function for the child. Errors are the contradictions we mentioned earlier under the discussion on equilibration theory. The child first makes errors but only eventually understands them as contradictions and after that point makes some attempts to eliminate the contradictions by restructuring his/her approach to the problem. Unlike the errorless learning objectives of programmed learning, instruction derived from Piaget's work would value errors. The value of errors does not rest in the fact that errors tell us what something is not. A good programmed text could do this. But only errors can disconfirm our own, self-generated questions. It is the high priority of self-generated questions that, in turn, gives errors a new respect in education (see Forman & Kuschner, 1977).

Action versus Activity

Self-generated questions are the result of mental activity. They may be accompanied by observable actions, but one can be mentally active yet physically passive. The dictum in education that we learn by doing should be qualified to read that we learn by doing in response to our own self-generated and self-regulated questions. The action itself will have no meaning unless it is in response to some guess or some theory about the events yielded during action (see Karmiloff-Smith and Inhelder, 1975). If the child is asked a series of questions, rather than tests a series of her own questions, she may be engaged in a small amount of mental activity, but the answers to each individual question are likely to remain independent of the other answers. However, if the child constructs a series of questions herself, each one in turn emerges organically from the current knowledge base and the whole sequence has a better chance of being interrelated as a meaningful system of relations.

This distinction between action and activity also refers to Piaget's emphasis on reflection. The child can make a physical movement without reflection and is not likely to learn much from that movement. Alternatively, he/she can reflect on the movement as it occurs and assimilate the results of that action to some specific goal or general purpose. Piaget reminds us that since there is a myriad of purposes to which any single act could be assimilated, the importance of that act must always be constructed by the child. In other words, feedback is not an automatic consequence of an act, but, like every other event in the world, has to be constructed as relevant to the task at hand through reflection on the act. There is no built-in wire loop that guarantees that the physical consequences of an act will be treated as information. Thus, the thermostat or simple cybernetic model of human learning grossly oversimplifies our open system of interaction with the environment.

The activity that underlies action very often involves some sort of inference, some method of going beyond the observable acts. For example, a child sees his pull wagon go behind a box and emerge on the other side without its teddy bear rider. The child then infers that the teddy bear bounced out when the wagon was behind the box. The child, in this instance, has made a relation among discrete acts, each independently observable, but meaningful as a closed group of relations only as a result of the child's construction of the inference.

We can also use this example to drive home the point made above about feedback. Had the child's parent informed her where the bear was or had the child found the bear accidentally and not as the result of a deliberate guess, the actual sight of the bear would not have the status of information about the closed system of movements (one completely unobserved) among the bear, wagon, and box. The child may have *discovered* the missing teddy bear but would not have *invented* the closed system of spatial relations nor *understood*, in spite of her *success*, the manner of the teddy bear's disappearance. Piaget's influence on education has been to give teachers a good reason to (1) put a bump in the rug behind the box; and (2) support the child in her attempts to figure out what happened to Pooh.

Rethinking Readiness

Many educators have taken Piaget's stages of cognitive development as a new psychometric for academic readiness. The transition from preoperational to concrete operational intelligence has almost become the equivalent of the GRE for entrance into the first grade. Children from kindergarten to third grade are being given number conservation and class inclusion tasks to assess their readiness for, or the successful passage through, the curriculum sequence.

In a recent essay, Duckworth (1979) challenges the concept of readiness as a diagnostic. She defines the dilemma of the readiness concept to be "either we're too early and they can't learn it or we're too late and they know it already." What she means is that the search for a task that is matched to the child's level is in practice futile. Instead of trying to measure where the child is, as if the child were "in" a particular and widely defined stage, it would be better to observe how the child deals with problems that are themselves very rich with implications. If we can provide children with rich, open-ended materials that allow for multiple levels of entry, we do not have to diagnose the child in advance of presenting the material. It is neither too early nor too late to offer the child rich material as long as we also remember to allow the child to ask her own questions of the material. Readiness becomes a problem only if we are prescribing the questions.

Four Propositions of Constructivism

If we are to move beyond how Piaget's theory has been rather unsystematically applied to early education, we need to identify a set of essentials that can then be used as criteria for evaluating programs that claim to be based on Piaget. We have identified four propositions of constructivism that seem essential at least within the context of an educational extension of the theory. Each proposition is defined, elaborated, and followed by a brief section that cites research substantiating the proposition. In the next major section, we will then apply these four propositions to six early childhood education programs.

Action, Not Language, Is the Source of Deductive Thinking

As we have said, somewhere around the age of six or seven the child can reason from the perspective of certainty rather than probability. Given that Grandma's house is nine miles down Route 101 and that one passes Herbie's house first, the child knows it is ridiculous to think Herbie's house is more than nine miles down Route 101. It is easy to conclude that the child's knowledge is completely "contained" in the knowledge of our language, but Piaget insists that the language is itself submitted to a process of construction and assimilation to action schemes. Knowing the independent meanings of the individual words does not guarantee understanding the relations, and understanding the relations involves submitting the words to a set of active transformations quite analogous to practical actions, albeit that these practical actions have taken on a general form and are independent of specific content.

This proposition has implications for education, to be sure. Yet, we should not be quick to assume that the proposition implies that one cannot teach by telling. Children learn a great deal by being told. Piaget's point is that if they do learn from being told it is because they can submit the words to an integrated set of transformations, the latter a previously learned and much more general level of knowledge. The main message of this proposition is that teachers should not confuse vocabulary learning with an integrated comprehension of relation sets. The knowledge is not "in" the words, but is a result of the constructive and inventive processes applied to words, including questions, inferences, tests, and new inferences.

In a well-known study by Sinclair (1967), children who could not conserve liquid quantity were taught to use comparative terms in pairs, such as "taller yet skinnier" and "shorter yet wider." Although these terms are often used by children who do understand the conservation concept, the verbal training was not sufficient to induce understanding in the nonconservers. The facts, as represented by the words, did not close into a set of relationships.

A more recent study on the language and thought question was done by Rice (1980). She trained preschoolers to identify objects by color names. After consistent reinforcement, children could correctly name the color of an object pointed to by the experimenter. However, when the children were asked to give the experimenter "the green one" for example, they became confused and were frequently in error unless they had previously used color in a classification scheme (sorting). Rice interpreted the data as indicating that finding "the green one" is more complicated than being able to provide the verbal label. The implication here is that knowing the name of something is not sufficient for eliminating objects that are not of that name.

Several other studies attempting to train complex thinking through language enrichment have been done. Boepple (1977) found that silently modeling conservation had longer-lasting effects than either verbal explanations alone or verbal explanation plus modeling. Spiro (1973), on the other hand, trained children in reversibility using only words and found progress in conservation. Actually, Spiro's findings were similar to Boepple's on the immediate posttest, but since Spiro did not provide a delayed posttest it is hard to assess the depth of the training effects. These studies are just two among hundreds of conservation studies (see Modgil & Modgil, 1976); many of these studies do suggest that verbal training improves conservation. What we need is a broader framework to interpret their relevance to the language versus action proposition.

If Piaget is correct in believing that the schemes of action formed during the sensory-motor period (birth to about age two) are the foundation for the logic of later years, then educators need to look at these action schemes as a system of quasi-logic. The actions are first symbolized by the child during the preoperational period (between ages two and five), and later the symbols are entered into a closed deductive system making true logic possible. The relevance of the language and action question for educators becomes manifest in how they interpret sand play, block play, and other action schemes during the preschool years.

In short, the test of the language versus action question should be a reversal of how it has usually been designed. Instead of trying to verify that telling a child does not lead to comprehension, we should attempt to verify that action does lead to comprehension. The work of Beilin (1975), Greenfield and Smith (1976), and Edmonds (1975) are investigations of the parallel and interactive development of intelligent action and intelligent speech. These types of studies are more germane to Piaget's position and therefore carry with them more information about what it is about action that serves as the foundation of deductive thought. Such things as the separation of agent of action from object of action, the understanding of practical negations and reciprocals in action, all give the early childhood educator a new and useful perspective on the significance of free play in the classroom. The peek-a-boo games of the toddler and the symbolic play of the two-year-old all have a structure that can be understood as precursors to good grammar.

Understanding Results from Self-Regulated Activity

This proposition has a more familiar form, to wit, to understand is to invent (Piaget, 1973). In an attempt to be more specific, we emphasize the role of self-regulation. We have already distinguished success from understanding. For example, a child may successfully put backspin on a ping pong ball to make it move forward and then return, yet not understand that the ball is scooting forward while rotating backward (Piaget, 1976). In the social world, the child may be successful in her attempts to get the attention of an adult but fail to understand that this attention follows more from the adult's acquiescence than from the child's native power. Understanding is more likely to result if the child, *in spite of success*, continues to try various actions.

Take the case of a child who thinks that anything made out of wood will float. Say this prediction is upheld with four pieces of pine board that she places in the water. Yet, to understand that the material alone is not sufficient to account for floating, she must think of other variations such as a wooden bead or a tree branch. Another common mistake children make is to add superfluous causes, such as assuming that both lemon and sugar make the ice tea tart when it is the lemon alone. If they are successful in making the tea tart each time they add lemon and sugar they naturally assume both are necessary (Kuhn & Phelps, 1979). If one day she adds lemon alone, she will be surprised to learn that the lemon alone yields tart tea. She is surprised because she has been successful in two different ways, in fact, from the child's point of view, these two ways are opposite (sugar versus no sugar). The point here is that the child does not need to learn to discriminate stimuli that do versus stimuli that do not lead to tart tea; she needs to understand why two opposite stimuli both create the same effect. Discrimination learning, a concept from mechanistic models of behaviorism, may account for the acquisition of success, but self-regulated questioning, a concept from organismic models of constructivism, better account for the development of understanding.

A study by Kuhn and Ho (1977) gives evidence of the importance of self-regulated activity. Preadolescents were asked to discover which chemical or combination of chemicals caused a precipitate to form in a clear solution. Half the subjects generated their own guesses (the experimental group) while the other half were given these guesses as questions (the yoked control group). On the surface, it can be said that the two groups had the same "experience."

The experimental group made more progress on the difficult tasks than did the yoked control group. Kuhn and Ho reason that only in the experimental group were subjects in a position to have an expectation disconfirmed. Since the question came from some assumption, the failure as well as the success served as information about that assumption. The yoked control subjects were not testing their own assumptions so the results of the teacher-directed tests were not information in the functional sense.

Note that the teacher did ask questions in the experimental group, but these questions were general probes for justification of knowledge rather than direct orientation to facts. There is a great difference between a teacher asking, "Can you be sure what makes a difference?" versus "Could it be C in addition to B?" The first question causes the child to think about how she is thinking, the second question causes the child to think about specific facts. If our objective as educators is to improve general strategies of thinking, we need to know what types of questions in combination with what types of materials facilitate these objectives. The conditions found in the Kuhn and Ho experimental group seem to give us one good example, at least for ten- to twelve-year-olds.

Studies with younger children by and large have not been controlled as well as the Kuhn and Ho (1977) study. Sylva (1976) did find that children allowed to play with sticks and clamps solved a two-stick problem better than children who received specific training or who received dramatized training. Watching an adult solve the problem was generally effective, but the free-play group was more systematic and made better use of hints. Sylva concluded that these differences occurred because only the children in the free-play group initiated their own solutions. They had had the opportunity to explore alternative steps in the process and had also gained a more relaxed attitude toward the task. Yet, the question remains: can a well-written programmed text also give these children the necessary exposure to alternatives? The message of constructivism is not that self-regulation exposes the child to more alternatives, but rather that the alternatives to which the self-regulating child is exposed have resulted from his/her own theories and consequentially are better understood. Sylvan's study has no clear relation to constructivism, since even an empiricist would predict that an exposure to more alternatives is better than an exposure to fewer. To test the tenets of constructivism we need a measure of relative benefits of self-generated assimilatory schemes versus other generated questions. This test, in effect, reduces to a much clearer definition what we mean by "exposure."

Meaningful Learning Results from Conflict Resolution

Piaget depicts development as a spiral of knowledge, small at its base, more encompassing as it goes upward. The higher levels of understanding integrate the ad hoc parts of the lower levels. But why does the child ever leave the sometimes more comfortable lower levels? It is too simplistic to say that the child is goaded into a reconstruction of piecemeal concepts into an integrated whole. It is too simplistic to say that the child is "exposed" to conflict and that the tension therein motivates the child to learn more comprehensive concepts. Development, in Piaget's theory, is more complicated than the proverbial child who learns to avoid the heated stove. The reaction to heat is reflexive, automatic, and built into our physiology as a consequence of species evolution. The same cannot be said about a subjective feeling of conflict that exists when one simultaneously holds contradictory beliefs.

Research on the role of conflict in meaningful learning has been plagued with this confusion between exogenous conflict versus a felt contradiction. As Kuhn (1974) points out, we cannot assess the avowed importance of the endogenous form until we have a measure of felt contradiction that is independent of the exogenous conflict staged by the experimenter. Take as an example a study by Charbonneau and Robert (1977). First grade children were asked to make a prediction about the conservation of continuous quantity after which their nonconserving answers were contradicted by an adult model. Other children had to give not only their own answer but were also asked to predict the adult's answer. This latter situation allegedly maximized the conflict between the child's predictions and the actual adult's answers. The experimenters found no differences in improvement on conservation across several of these types of conflict-inducing procedures. But what independent evidence do we have that the discrepancy between the child's answer and the adult's answer was assimilated by the child as a contradiction on one and the same problem?

Contrast the Charbonneau and Robert study with the earlier cited study by Inhelder, Sinclair, and Bovet (1974). Children in this set of studies were contradicting their own answers and the verbatim transcripts gave independent evidence that the children were experiencing tension in regard to these contradictions. Instead of defining the presence of contradiction in terms of the treatment conditions, Inhelder, Sinclair, and Bovet used the méthode clinique, following the child's lead in an individual fashion and defining contradiction in terms of response protocols rather than predetermined treatment conditions.

What do these studies that take a closer and more qualitative view of the child tell us about the nature of contradiction? Duckworth (1979) cites an interesting example of a six-year-old named Didier who was freely playing with a set of Russian nesting dolls. He had discovered that, by working only with the bases in an inverted position and by beginning with the biggest proceeding through to the smallest, he could make a tower instead of a nested set. He then approached the heads with this same intention to build a tower. The heads were also inverted but he unwittingly began with the smallest and proceeded through to the biggest, which to his surprise led to a nested set instead of a tower. Then he undid the heads, turned them all open side up, and began with the biggest through to the smallest, getting a nesting again! Eventually he discovered that to make a tower with the heads he must invert them open side down and proceed from the biggest to the smallest.

The fact that Didier experienced contradiction between his expectation that the heads would yield a tower and the fact that they initially yielded a nest, was most probably because he understood enough about these objects to feel strongly that the heads were in many ways just like the bases. That is, the new set of objects were no more than a similar set. Thus the fact that the heads did not yield a tower created more than surprise, it created paradox. The coordination of the similarities with the differences may be essential before a true contradiction or paradox is felt. Thus, in cases where adults disagree with children, as in many of the studies on conflict inducement, the child may hear the adult's answer as different but does not assimilate that answer as a different answer to the same question.

The Coordination of Correspondences and Transformations

In order for us clearly to distinguish different levels of knowing we need a more precise description of a "unit" of knowledge. Take, for example, the difference between "surprise" and "paradox" introduced in the preceding section. Surprise can be defined as an unexpected event that does not challenge a general principle; paradox is an unexpected event that does challenge a general principle. A balloon that bursts on the third or fourth blow may surprise us, but it does not challenge our view of balloons in general. This particular balloon just had a weak spot. However, a balloon that never gets larger than, say, six inches in diameter, in spite of our continued huffing and puffing additional air into it, would indeed challenge our understanding of a leakless balloon, additional air needing more space, yet no new space being created by expansion. The second case is paradoxical because it violates a deductive system of relations. These two cases can help us identify what a knowledge unit is in terms of correspondences and transformations.

In Figure 9–1 we see that the child expects that when transformation Theta (θ) is applied to object A (the deflated balloon) the result will be state A' (the expanded balloon). However, when Theta is actually applied to A (the observed event), A is changed into A'', an explosion and also a variation on expansion (thus the symbol A'' instead of some new symbol). In a paradox, the child expects Theta to yield A', but in this instance Theta yields the negation of A' ($\overline{A}'$, the absence of any expansion of the balloon). The observed consequence of Theta applied to A is more than a consequence different from the one expected; the consequence observed is actually opposite to the one expected. The opposition of expected and observed results sets up a paradox that must be resolved by further exploration to check the initial premises that the observed A corresponds to other A's the child has

Figure 9-1.

$$\text{Expected A} \xrightarrow{\ominus} \text{A}' \qquad\qquad \text{Expected A} \xrightarrow{\ominus} \text{A}'$$

$$\text{Observed A} \xrightarrow{\ominus} \text{A}'' \qquad\qquad \text{Observed A} \xrightarrow{\ominus} \bar{\text{A}}'$$

Surprise   Paradox

known and that the observed Theta corresponds to the type of transformation the child assumes it to be. The final "unit" of knowledge will be the reconstruction of the relations between these correspondences and transformation once again into a closed system of deductions, say, perhaps by discovering that A' need not be a consequence of Theta if more air can create greater density of air instead of greater volume of the balloon. In other words, the child discovers the reciprocal relation between greater density and greater volume, and this accounts for the apparent paradox. At that point, the balloon that fails to expand is understood only as a surprise because now greater density is seen as a variation on great volume and not the negation of A' as was initially believed by the child.

Children continually face the need to coordinate correspondences with transformations. Questions that deal with the difference between one object seen twice versus two identical objects seen at different times are, in essence, problems of coordinating correspondences with transformations. For a child to think, "this looks like my cup, therefore it is my cup," is a good example of thinking only in terms of correspondences. To decide correctly, the child needs to know how the observed cup got to be where it rests. Did someone move his cup from its previous resting place or did someone bring in a new cup from the outside? In this example, the child needs to reconstruct the transformation that she did not witness. Alternatively, the cup could look quite different than before (accidentally dunked into paint) and still be the child's personal cup. In this case, the child might see the entire transformation, yet erroneously conclude that the lack of physical correspondence between the clean and dirty cup implies a lack of conserved identity. Our main point here is that the coordination of correspondences and transformations can profitably be used as a definition of the unit of knowledge.

What research exists that bears on teacher behavior that facilitates the coordination of correspondences and transformations? In an interesting study by Rovet (1976), eight-year-old children were asked to judge if two objects were rotations of each other or different shapes altogether. Children who could not do this mental rotation task were given different types of training. Some children were given more practice on judging static pictures, others watched a series of practice films where one shape was gradually rotated into a final perspective, and a third group watched a series of practice films in which the animation of the rotation was discontinuous. In this third group, the children watched the beginning and the final portion of the rotation. This last form of practice, the discontinuous transformation, worked best in improving the children's ability to perform the complete mental rotations in the posttest.

This study by Rovet makes two statements about the coordination of correspondences and transformation. First, the correspondence (same or different) between two objects can be improved if the transformation, one into the other, is modeled for the child (in this case, via animated film). Second, the child seems to think more about that transformation if it is incomplete. Rovet reasons that the partial demonstration caused the children to think more than did the complete rotation demonstration. These results fit out earlier comments about self-regulation in that the partial rotation group had to imagine for themselves the continuation of a rotation begun but interrupted.

Other studies have successfully improved conservation abilities in children by highlighting the nature of the transformations that change initial states to final states, as well as the reversal of that change. Denney, Zeytinoglu, and Selzer (1977) successfully trained four-year-olds to conserve number and length by demonstrating both transformations that change quantity and those that do not. Zimmerman and Lanaro (1974) offer a further qualification on the importance of transformations. In a conservation of length task, these experiments found that four-year-olds who watched a model both transform and then reverse that transformation to justify his judgment learned more than those children who merely watched a model say the two lengths were the same as before the transformation. As we indicated earlier, the coordination of correspondences with transformations requires the child to distinguish changes in kind from changes in degree (for instance, the change from volume to density in the case of the balloon). The effectiveness of demonstrating both the initial transformation and its reversal may rest in its power to help the child make this type of distinction.

Consciousness

Rather than list a fifth proposition of constructivism, let us mention an aspect that is common to the four that we have already discussed: consciousness. Cognitive development in Piaget's theory is no less than a growth of consciousness, the awareness of the role of the self in what appear to be external facts. The four propositions mentioned this aspect in different forms such as reflection on action, understanding rather than rote learning, meaningful learning that results from looking at how one looks at a problem (conflict resolution), and, in the last proposition, reflection on the transformations that lead to what seem to be static givens of an external world. Development involves taking a view of how one views a problem, a more explicit consciousness of one's own thinking processes. For example, a child with a stocking cap down over his ears may erroneously conclude that the volume on the phonograph is low. An adult raised in an Anglo culture may erroneously conclude that the Hispanic child, taught not to make eye contact with his teacher, is being defiant. A seven-year-old girl explains to the new milkman that her grandmother lives next door to Mr. Tinker in full expectation that the milkman now knows exactly where that is. Each of these examples suggests that the person needs to reflect on the assumptions he is making about the external object and how he is externalizing self without being aware of that process of externalization. As we proceed now to an analysis of six early childhood education programs based on Piaget we will pay attention to how each program deals with the development of consciousness. Of course, we will also analyze each program according to the four specific propositions mentioned above.

An Analysis of Piaget-Based Early Childhood Education Programs

Whenever someone tries to identify the essentials of Piaget's theory, others disagree (see, for example, Banet's rejoinder to Kaufman, 1976). The analysis that follows may elicit rejoiners as well. We have tried to generate a theory of learning and instruction from Piaget's epistemology and we will look at how each program maps onto those theoretical principles. We have chosen not to discuss empirical evaluations of classroom practice, since what we desire is a better understanding of what a Piaget-based program would actually do. Clear specifications of teacher behavior and a clear explanation of how these specifications derive from Piaget's theory are so difficult in themselves that they will hold our focus exclusively.

Each of the Piaget-based programs reviewed is a dynamic system refining its curriculum and instruction. But to apply our criteria of what constitutes a Piaget-based program we have to look at some set of statements and prescriptions made by each program. We have chosen the statements made in the following books: Lavatelli (1970), Furth and Wachs (1975), Forman and Kuschner (1977), Forman and Hill (1980), Kamii and DeVries (1978), Hohmann, Banet, and Weikart (1979), and Copple, Sigel, and Saunders (1979).

The Priority of Action over Language

All of these programs state that new knowledge cannot be abstracted from words but rather from a system of actions that are marked by words. Lavatelli (1970, p. 65) distinguishes between learning vocabulary and learning a new system of relations, such as conservation. Lavatelli states that children should go beyond mere naming properties of objects (p. 88); they should also learn to coordinate two properties at once ("this is a round yellow bead"). Children are given colored beads and are asked to classify them, to state whether there are more wooden beads than red beads. There is no mention of action precursors to these verbal operations,[1] so the reader is not given help in identifying action schemes that are gradually "reconstructed" by language markers into a, say, class inclusion operation. The reader is left only with a reliance on the child's reaction to the teacher's language.

---

[1] Whenever we say "there is no mention" of something in one of these books, we also recognize that the authors themselves might be able to identify in their text those things we could not find.

The priority of action over language does not imply that we refrain from teaching by telling, but that we learn to recognize the structure of action precursors to operations possible only in language, so that we can assure that children have opportunities to engage in actions with this structure. For example, in block play a child may be attempting to line up four blocks: two big ones then two smaller ones. Upon looking closer, the teacher observes that as the child is moving the two small blocks, one in each hand, toward the two larger ones already in place, he is simultaneously moving the two small ones together in the air. The motion of the small ones together is a single action that is indeed a "subset" of the broader objective of moving the pair of small blocks next to the pair of large blocks.

It would be more in line with Piaget's constructivism to teach teachers to recognize the structure of play and then add language to that structure, rather than to begin with a language instruction and ask the child to react. In this way, the priority of action over language would be preserved. Forman and Hill (1980, pp. 22–23) gave this principle the expression "classify with good causation." Classification should be taught in the context of cause and effect relations, such as all the objects that roll or all objects that can be changed from fat to skinny by some transformation (Theta). Kamii and DeVries (1978, p. 70) are also very sensitive to the need to embed classification operations within a rich cause and effect context.

Both Hohmann et al. (1979) and Copple et al. (1979) seem to be somewhere between the above positions. For example, in the chapter on classification in Hohmann et al. (pp. 191–216), children are encouraged to sort toys into bins so they can find them the next day (classification with a causal context) and to sort toy animals into classes simply because the teacher stages this as a game (a more impoverished context). In the second example, the functional consequence of these actions are virtually nonexistent. The child does what the teacher suggests simply as an act that corresponds to a verbal instruction. Although these actions may teach the child something about language, they probably teach the child nothing about the complex relations mapped by language.

Representational competence, the ability to re-present the nonpresent object or event symbolically, is a stated objective of both Hohmann et al. and Copple et al. The latter conclude that using symbols to make the remote more proximal, such as bringing the past and future to the present, can play a mediating role in the child's construction of knowledge. The teacher's role is to be a "distancing agent," to encourage children to think about remote objects and events. The teachers in Hohmann et al. serve a similar role in that they continually ask the children to plan, to state in words what they will shortly do in the future. Even though these teacher strategies do benefit the children, perhaps it would be best if we designated representational competence in the sense defined by Hohmann et al. and Copple et al. as an aspect of these programs that was not necessarily derived from Piaget's theory.

Representation in Piaget's theory, at least as we interpret it, is only in small measure a case of making the nonpresent object present symbolically. The more important task of representation is to make the present object (A′) a variation on its prior state (A), that is, to compare the present with a special case of the nonpresent. For example, whether the child perceives the ceiling as over himself or himself as under the ceiling depends on an implicit beginning point of "movement" between self and object. For Piaget, representation is the externalization of those implicit relations that may not take the form of making the nonpresent object present. In constructivism, reversing the present rather than recalling the nonpresent occupies more of the purpose of representation. State A' is understood only when it is explicitly compared to A (via representation). Although A may be a nonpresent object, to say only this underdetermines the importance of representing state A as a transformation of A'.

Representation is necessary not only to reverse the present but also to negate the present. Sometimes, the represented comparison takes the form of non-A instead of A which is the reversal of A'. For example, to say that something is dead implies that it is not living any longer. We would not say that a sidewalk is dead because sidewalks, no matter what their condition, cannot be conceived of as the negation of life. Constructivism emphasizes the very special nature of A–A' and A–non-A relations which is insufficiently captured in a more general emphasis on almost any nonpresent object or event. Strict recall and anticipation definitely play a role in the construction of a knowledge unit, but the implicit actions of reversal and the implicit operation of negation identify more clearly the priority of action as a means to create representational structures. Although some examples of representation in Copple et al. do highlight transformations on A', for example, changing the eensy-weensy spider from angry to sleepy (p. 31), many examples leave the relationship between the representation and the experience up to the child. It is, of course, entirely possible that emphasizing representation will facilitate a conscious awareness of relations. Our point is only that Piaget emphasizes action primarily.

Of all the programs reviewed, Furth and Wachs (1975) place the strongest emphasis on action. The fact that the activities are identified according to their structure leads us to believe that Furth and Wachs deliberately intend to have language map actions rather than have language direct actions.

The Importance of Self-Regulated Activity

The differences among the programs in regard to this criterion occur according to how deliberately the teaching staff facilitate self-regulated activity beyond the obvious technique of setting the stage for free play.

Furth and Wachs place a heavy emphasis on the role of the teacher in choosing an appropriate task. In fact, the activities mentioned often appear to be drills. Children are told to walk wooden beams, to copy the design the teacher drew on the chalkboard, and to make arm and leg movements like angels in the snow. These activities seem like motoric patterning, indicating a pedagogy that advocates to get a child to make coordinated actions which will then pattern coordinated thinking. Yet, Furth and Wachs insist that these activities create "high level thinking." They emphasize that their constant aim is to have the child think and reflect on how he/she is doing in a particular task. It is not clear what causes the children to reflect on their actions. We have distinguished success from understanding. Doing something well may not necessarily lead to a reflection on the doing. Perhaps performance of activities designed by the children based on their own assumptions about body, time, and space would create greater reflection than games dictated by a teacher.

Kamii and DeVries (1978) use an approach diametrically opposed to the didactic games of Furth and Wachs. Kamii and DeVries give children material that have many possibilities, such as boards and rollers, and allow them to invent activities. Teachers observe and occasionally make comments such as "We're stuck. What shall we do now?" (p. 72) and less frequently provide structure by saying something like, "Maybe Mark wants us to give him a ride in this." The teachers in Kamii and DeVries give general problem domains to the children; the materials and sometimes the comments orient the children toward a set of related problems, but teachers limit comments that take away the child's initiative in setting his/her own problem.

Forman and Kuschner (1977) and Forman and Hill (1980) cite the value of open-ended activities, but some of the activities in Forman and Hill do not have many degrees of freedom (pp. 142, 177). Others are quite open-ended and child-directed, such as sand play and block play. In these activities, the child is allowed to explore and freely invent while the teacher either makes declarative sentences to summarize the structure of the child's act ("You made a hole while building the mound") or slips in a new item to see if and how the child incorporates that item into his/her spontaneous play.

Lavatelli describes in detail only the didactic lessons between teacher and child, but she advises teachers to facilitate the generalization of classification and seriation to free play activities. Unfortunately, Lavatelli does not give the reader directions to carry out this advice.

In Hohmann et al., the initial choices of the children are self-directed, but is this the same as self-regulated? In some cases, the chosen activity is structured by a teacher (p. 230); in others, the activity is open-ended (p. 242). This balance seems very reasonable both in Hohmann et al. and in Copple et al. Some activities require a degree of structure before the child knows enough about the medium to generate enough hypotheses to keep him going on his own.

The important issue here is not how much structure is good, but rather how do we best facilitate reflection. Certainly, there are situations in which children can be presented a problem of the teacher's design and still learn a great deal, as long as the teacher uses subtle questioning to assure that the child is reflecting on his assumptions. Hohmann et al. do it nicely (p. 231) by asking the child to justify an answer or to predict the consequence of an action in advance of an actual test. The use of prediction typifies Forman and Kuschner (Chapter 9) and is a hallmark of Copple et al. Nevertheless, most educators persuaded by Piaget feel better when the child justifies an answer to his own questions or predicts the consequences of an action he thinks to make. In the latter case, not only is the answer assimilated to the question, but also the question is assimilated to similar problems. In the former case, we run the risk of having children understand the answers to questions that do not relate to other such questions. As long as the child keeps concepts he/she learns isolated from each other, conflict that is so necessary for constructing an integrated system of concepts will not occur.

The Importance of Conflict Resolution

Knowledge is the conversion of a negation into a variation. At first, two events may seen unrelated to the child; later, these two events appear to be the negation of each other; and still later, when the contradiction is resolved, the two events are reconciled as variations on some common theme. Piaget's equilibration theory is a model of these stages of conflict resolution. The six early childhood programs that we are reviewing vary widely in their use of equilibration theory.

In several places in Lavatelli's book, children are confronted with another person's point of view. For example, two children sit on opposite sides of a table and look at a common tableau and choose a picture that portrays a view of the other child (p. 122). When child A is given the picture chosen by child B, assumed by B to be A's view, child A begins to realize that views are relative to position. The conflict exists because child B more often than not presents A with B's own view, an egocentric choice. Child A then realizes that he too had made an egocentric choice when presenting child B with A's own view. Other examples emphasizing conflict, however, are rare in Lavatelli's book. In general, she appears not to highlight conflict inducement.

Forman and Kuschner take a bolder stance on conflict inducement and even identify the role of the teacher as a "troublemaker" (p. 114). They recommend that the teacher parallel plays near a self-directed child for awhile, get a sense of the child's objectives, give the child sufficient opportunity for a run of successful variations in his/her spontaneous play, and then slip the child a comment or an implement that, when incorporated by the child in the child's play, creates surprise or paradox. A good example of conflict inducement is presented in Forman and Hill (p. 156). A child is pulling the top span of a clothesline pulley making a basket attached to the top span come toward himself. When the basket gets about halfway to the child the teacher quickly switches the basket from the top span to the lower span. As the child pulls a bit more, he notices that now the basket is moving away from himself, the opposite of what he desires. He pauses, looks things over, and then switches his hands to the lower span and begins to pull again. The basket now resumes its passage toward the child. Here is a good example of how a teacher can induce a mild degree of conflict without disrupting the child's self-set goals. The child, in this example, probably advanced one step closer to understanding the opposite (the basket moving away) as no more than a variation on the circular movement of the closed loop of rope.

Conflict experienced by the child—endogenous conflict—can help the teacher identify how advanced a child's thinking is in a particular set of tasks. Forman and Kuschner (p. 112) discuss the use of conflict as a diagnostic and devote an entire chapter to the benefits of conflict inducement as compared to the benefits of behavior modification.

Kamii and DeVries also encourage teachers to stage mild conflicts for children to solve. In one example (p. 141), the teacher plays the troublemaker role by placing a target outside the swing of a tether ball suspended from the ceiling. It is interesting that the child tries to compensate for missing the target by pushing the tether ball harder and harder. After a bit, the child moves the target to her favorite position, but it is not apparent that she has understood that the earlier position was an impossible task. So the teacher asks, "Why did you move the target up?" The teacher wants the child to become conscious of what she has done. The child answers, " 'Cause I don't want him way over there." It seems that the child has "solved" the problem without any greater understanding of the physical constraints of a nonelastic rope and a determinant arc of swing. Nevertheless, the teacher's behavior, both in staging the conflict and in encouraging the child to reflect on her actions, are very consistent with equilibration theory.

Copple et al. often confront the children with information or perspectives that are inconsistent with their previous knowledge. For example, in a discussion of airplanes one child insisted that an airplane could land in his backyard, others insisted that airplanes could not. The teacher asked all the children to imagine how airplanes took off and landed. Eventually, the children made the distinction between conventional aircraft and helicopters (p. 31). Using a strictly linguistic mode of representation, the children began to understand that a helicopter was but a variation on conventional aircraft; but this achievement, no doubt, requires children to be sufficiently advanced to learn about real objects while using only a linguistic mode of representation. Copple et al. present other examples that are not so language-bound, such as a child named Josh experimenting with a spot of sunlight on the wall (pp. 129–132). Josh is curious about why the spot appears and disappears (as his own body occludes the sunrays from the window). The teacher asks Josh to put his hand "over" the light. Josh is surprised to discover that the light is not under his hand, but shining on his hand. This creates more curiosity and Josh continues to explore, even trying to grasp the light in mid-air. Even though the learning encounter did not lead to an understanding of why the spot disappears, it did lead Josh further toward understanding that the light was a ray from the window and not just a spot on the wall. The teacher's suggestion seemed to work in that the child's expectations were not confirmed and the resulting conflict led to more exploration.

Conflict inducement and the child's experience of conflict does not appear to be a central theme in Hohmann et al.'s program. They do repeatedly mention the importance of the child experiencing other points of view and being exposed to alternatives that the child might not have considered (pp. 91, 245). Their pedagogy seems to derive from the principle that concepts are formed by identifying many different things as instances of the same concept, much as Bruner, Goodnow, and Austin (1956) have defined concept formation. But there is little attention, that we can see, to the reciprocal relations between affirmations and negations and the construction of a closed set of relations, such as the functional relations of a clothesline pulley or tether ball. And without a deliberate search in the free play of the child for this type of structure, teachers will only accidentally pose conflicts that lead the child to a more broadly based understanding of his/her physical and social world.

Furth and Wachs place little emphasis on conflict inducement. They seem to believe that conflict is inherent in any challenging situation and that there is no need to create conflict situations deliberately by the teacher. They suggest, for instance, that conflict (high level thinking) can result when a child tries to walk an I-beam, falls, and has to rethink his/her approach to the beam. However, without more detailed specification of the learning process in Furth and Wachs, we are left with the impression that even this type of "conflict" leads only to an increase in mental effort and not necessarily to the reconciliation of an apparent opposition. For example, movement games could have been staged with the contradiction structure in mind, such as designing a set of stairs that the child can by degrees change into a slide, like a large Venetian blind. The discontinuous set of steps are opposite to the continuous slide. The conversion of one into the other creates correlated changes in how the child negotiates each, and in the gradual transformation of steps into slide the child may construct these opposite moves into variations on each other.

Piaget emphasized that conflict occurs spontaneously and is a natural consequence of the child's attempts to extend his/her schemes, but what is the role of the teacher? Furth and Wachs present one option, that of designing a graded sequence of activities that increase in difficulty. For example, they suggest (p. 141) that children first make parquetry block designs in the presence of a photographed design and later in the presence of a line drawing. Still later the children are asked to construct reversals of the presented design. The distance, psychologically speaking, from the stimulus and the response is increased. These activities do increase the challenge for the child but it is not clear that this sequence will increase the coherence of mental schemes. The challenges at each level require the child to do more work at translating the blocks into the requested design but there seems to be no emphasis on the closure of a scheme into a set of implications. The coherence of the whole, the scheme as a system, is the sine qua non of Piaget's theory of knowledge construction. The example of the stairs that convert into a slide has a higher likelihood of yielding a coherent structuration of thoughts during the child's spontaneous interaction with the object and each other. The opposite states of the object can be reconciled, thereby yielding a more coherent scheme that can then be applied with greater understanding of the functional relations among the variables. This emphasis on schemes as closed systems of implication needs to be emphasized in education more than the psychological distance of the stimulus from its response or the symbol from its referent.

Knowledge as the Coordination of Correspondences and Transformations

The comparison of similarities and differences has been a stated objective in early education. Attribute blocks and lotto boards call upon children to put together the ones that are the same and to tell how things are different. Often, however, the elements that are being compared are static states and no attempt is made to have the child transform a circle into a square, or to transform my view into yours, or to transform a conventional aircraft into a helicopter by some procedure. Forman and Kuschner explain why the more dynamic approach of relating correspondences via the transformations that produce them has pedagogical advantages (pp. 47–65). Not only does the child come to realize that what a static state means depends on the assumed procedures that lead to that state, but also attention to transformations reduces the amount of isolated, ad hoc associations that the child has to remember by rote in order to make sense of his physical and social world.

Here is an example from Forman and Hill. They noticed that children like to roll a toy bowling ball at plastic pins. Sometimes, because a ball was too light, it would not knock over the pins. Usually, the children would exchange the light ball for a heavy ball. In this fashion, they "learned" that the heavy ball was the one to use and the light ball was "a bad ball." When questioned, the children did not clearly relate the weight of the ball to its effect on the pins. They may have used weight as a discriminative stimulus or they could have used other stimuli such as size or color. In other words, they could discriminate which ball worked but they did not understand that weight was the critical factor.

The teachers could have provided the children with a variety of balls: large and heavy, small and light, large and light, small and heavy. This is a conventional method of facilitating the child to isolate critical variables. But Forman and Hill chose another tactic. They made it possible for the children to change the weight of a given ball. By using a hollow plastic ball the children themselves could transform the one ball from heavy to light and from light to heavy by subtracting or adding tennis balls from or to the inside of the ball. Forman and Hill reasoned that by giving the child control over the transformation of the one object the child would more likely understand the relation between weight and impact. The event A (pin doesn't fall) could then be changed into event A′ (pin does fall) by some procedure (Theta, or adding balls) which makes it clearer to the child that A′ is a variation on A via procedure Theta. The discovery of this pedagogical principle led Forman and Hill to apply it in many different contexts and to coin an axiom used throughout their program: *change without exchange* (p. 21). Whenever possible, children were encouraged to transform an object or event rather than to search for a completely different object or event. Through these techniques, Forman and Hill hoped that they were helping children to conserve one system of understanding while incorporating new variations, rather than learning two unrelated systems (this ball works, that ball does not).

Because this pedagogical principle is somewhat specialized and represents the bias of Forman and Kuschner and Forman and Hill, it is not reasonable to expect that other programs can be evaluated in exactly these terms. Nevertheless, many of the programs reviewed do express the value of having children transform objects, views, and events rather than make comparisons between static, preformed states. Hohman et al. (p. 139) advise teachers to talk to children about what they are doing: "Oh, I see. You're taking a straight pipe cleaner and bending it into a circle and then twisting the ends together." Here, both the initial and final states are labeled as well as the procedure of transformation. Other good examples are found in Hohmann et al. on pages 244–247. Copple et al. emphasize the importance of mental rotation, an imagined transformation (p. 88) and cite other examples of transformations (pp. 31, 36, 58, and 81). Kamii and DeVries give clear evidence of their appreciation of transformations (pp. 77 and 149) with a particularly nice example (p. 92) of a child coordinating changes in the position of a catapult with changes in the effects created. Lavatelli describes some of Piaget's classic research tasks and emphasizes the necessity for children to relate the type of transformation with the initial and final states of a change. For example, children were asked to put their right and left hands over a fork and knife respectively while another child slowly rotated the place mat (and consequentially the utensils) underneath by 180 degrees. Through this procedure of slowly rotating the fork and knife, the children were prompted to think about the fact that their left side is the right side of the person across the table (p. 119). Granted the children in these situations are exposed to the transformations of static states, but how confident can we be that they are assimilating transformations to correspondence? Let's look at another version of our knowledge unit.

$$\text{Previous experience} \quad A_1 \xrightarrow{\theta} A_1{}'$$
$$\text{Current experience} \quad A_2 \xrightarrow{\theta} \text{?}$$

If we have been effective as teachers, the child will not only learn some specific relation between Theta applied to A_1 but also recognize a set of $A_2{}'$s that correspond in kind to the initial task defined by A_1. The recognition of the correspondence between A_2 and A_1 makes it possible for the child to predict that if Theta is applied to A_2, the result will be some version of $A_1{}'$, called $A_2{}'$. In other words, a working knowledge of a concept involves the ability to relate a transformation to a class of initial states that are similar or, as Piaget would say, are morphisms (Piaget, 1979).

We need to know if a previous exposure has been assimilated to the point that it can be used generatively in current experience. To assure that exposure becomes assimilated, we need techniques that encourage the child to reflect on the relation between the transformations and the static states. Slowing the transformation down, as Lavatelli did, and as Inhelder, Sinclair, and Bovet (1974) did, may be one such technique. Having the child discuss transformations, as Copple et al. do, is another. Having the teacher make declarative statements about the relation between action and states, as do Hohmann et al. and Forman and Kuschner/Forman and Hill, is a third. Making the transformation discontinuous, as did Rovet (1976) when she edited the animated films to show only the beginning and end portions of a block rotation, is yet another technique that might improve the child's consciousness of transformations. Forman and Hill present still another strategy called "freezing motion." For example, instead of a tether ball hanging from the ceiling for knocking over targets, they suspended a plastic ketchup bottle that leaked dry sand everywhere it moved (pp. 110–113). If the child missed a target, they could see the motion of the ketchup bottle "frozen" in the trace left by the draining sand. Furth and Wachs give commands to children to reverse their direction of movement in an attempt to have the child experience a transformation of their more usual direction of movement (p. 100) and copy reversals of patterns using parquetry blocks (p. 141). These techniques all share the common intent of making the child more conscious of the procedures by which static states are transformed, but we need some close experimental testing of the relative effectiveness of these techniques. Which techniques are more effective in helping the child abstract the transformation so that he/she might apply it to current experience? Do some of these techniques lead to greater dissociation of Theta from A_1 and thereby greater ability to see A_2 as a recipient of Theta? Indeed, it is the child's sense that A_2 can be the recipient of Theta that defines the correspondence of A_1 and A_2. The physical similarity between A_1 and A_2 is in most cases irrelevant. Thus, we see that a knowledge unit is the coordination of correspondences and transformations and we would like to know which type of pedagogical techniques best facilitates this coordination.

Summary

To Piaget, knowledge is an ever expanding awareness of how what we assume is in the world is in actuality a construction of our own inference making. The input from the environment itself must be interpreted as relevant to some self-selected problem before that input can have any impact on the construction of knowledge. This construction is most likely to occur when the child knows enough to sense that what he/she has just observed is a complete contradiction of what was expected. Piaget would have us believe that this sense of contradiction, or what we have herein termed a sense for the paradoxical, is not learned but is inherent in the function of intelligence, itself on a continuum with biological systems that already have internal laws of self-regulation.

The belief in endogenous laws of self-regulation has many implications for education. For one, we need to place as much emphasis on understanding as we do on success. The constructivist epistemology treats knowledge as a coherent system, and therefore ad hoc successes are not sufficient for the education of our children. Errors are not seen as failures but rather as gaining useful information about why a problem was solved. The child is encouraged to explore alternative solutions to a problem long after an initial success so that the child will understand the principle behind the success.

Action was distinguished from activity. Only the latter includes reflection on the form of the action and therefore only the latter can yield new knowledge. The overt or covert nature of this action is not the issue; rather, what one makes of the observed or imagined action is the issue. Reflection eventually leads to a closed system of relations that allows the child to think inferentially and go beyond personal experience in his/her understanding of the physical and social world. Given this emphasis on knowledge as the construction of closed systems of relations that allow for inferential thinking, it becomes obvious that children need rich problem-solving environments in which to explore interrelations among complex systems. Thus, the curriculum expert no longer searches for the better diagnostic instrument to help improve the match to some prescribed sequence of instruction. Rather, the expert designs problem-solving environments that allow for multiple levels of entry and enough room for failure and self-correction so that the child constructs these implicatory systems spontaneously.

After defining four propositions of constructivism, we discussed six Piaget-based preschool programs in reference to these propositions. The first proposition stated that the integration of knowledge came from the constraints inherent in action and not through cultural transmission of a grammatical language. The second proposed that understanding can occur only when the child generates his/her own questions, particularly questions that seek to explain why the same effect can result from antecedents that appear to be diametric opposites. The third proposition, an extension of the second, stated that meaningful learning results from the reconciliation of opposites, such as Didier's gradual awareness that a tall tower of graduated containers versus a nested collection of the same containers was merely a matter of which container was placed down first. The fourth proposition defined the basic unit of knowledge as a coherent system of correspondences and transformations, whereby the child knows not only what is but also the procedure by which it became that way and, equally important, the procedures that can yield the original condition.

If one accepts these propositions as the essence of Piaget's theory, they form a reasonable set of criteria for evaluating Piaget-based educational programs. The first three propositions have direct implications for educational techniques; the fourth defines an overarching objective since it states the form of a knowledge unit.

All six of the preschool programs reviewed had a unique profile when submitted to analysis by these four propositions of constructivism. The priority of action over language is obvious in Furth and Wachs and also clearly emphasized in Kamii and DeVries, Forman and Kuschner, and Forman and Hill. In the case of Forman and Hill and Forman and Kuschner, this emphasis was due in part to the young age (ages two to five years) of the children. The importance of self-regulated questioning was most obvious in Kamii and DeVries, least so in Furth and Wachs. Other programs were mixed on this criterion. Hohmann, Banet, and Weikart had particularly nice examples of how the teacher can encourage children to reflect on their answers, which is after all the main issue in knowledge construction.

The programs differed widely on the third and fourth criteria. The value of conflict inducement was the hallmark of Forman and Kuschner and Forman and Hill, was mentioned sometimes in the other programs, and was only implicit in Furth and Wachs. We distinguished once again the difference between conflict that could be resolved without demanding the construction of new knowledge and conflict that is truly constructive. The fourth proposition is about the basic unit of knowledge being the coordination of correspondences through the application of particular transformations. Almost all the programs contained some games that clearly dealt with the coordination of correspondences through transformation, and Forman and Kuschner and Forman and Hill organized their curricula explicitly around this proposition. We organized this chapter around this proposition also.

The reader must judge the merits of the criteria themselves by some acceptable strategy. This strategy should be not only a case of empirical evaluation of what works but, in the spirit of Jean Piaget, also a case of seeking to understand our successes in education by extending a theory of knowledge into the classroom.

References

BEILIN, H. *Cognitive Basis of Language Development.* New York: Academic Press, 1975.

BIJOU, S. W., and BAER, D. M. *Child Development. Volume 2: The Universal Stage of Infancy.* New York: Appleton-Century-Crofts, 1965.

BOEPPLE, E. D. Relationship of language ability to symbolic operations in the conservation concept. *Dissertation Abstracts,* 1977, *38,* 3 (1380-B).

BRUNER, J. S., GOODNOW, J. J., and AUSTIN, G. *A Study of Thinking.* New York: Wiley, 1956.

CHARBONNEAU, C., and ROBERT, M. Observational learning of quantity conservation in relation to the degree of cognitive conflict. *Psychological Reports,* 1977, *41,* 975–986.

COPPLE, C., SIGEL, I. E., and SAUNDERS, R. *Educating the Young Thinker: Classroom Strategies for Cognitive Growth.* New York: Van Nostrand, 1979.

DENNEY, N. W., ZEYTINOGLU, S., and SELZER, S. C. Conservation training in four year old children. *Journal of Experimental Child Psychology.* 1977, *24,* 129–146.

DUCKWORTH, E. Either we're too early and they can't learn it or we're too late and they know it already. *Harvard Educational Review,* 1979, *49,* 297–312.

EDMONDS, M. Language acquisition and sensory-motor development: A longitudinal analysis of the evolution of language and its relation to the evolution of cognition. *Dissertation Abstracts,* 1975, *36,* 8 (4129-B).

FORMAN, G. E., and HILL, D. F. *Constructive Play: Applying Piaget in the Preschool.* Monterey, Calif.: Brooks/Cole, 1980.

FORMAN, G. E., and KUSCHNER, D. S. *The Child's Construction of Knowledge: Piaget for Teaching Children.* Monterey, Calif.: Brooks/Cole, 1977.

FURTH, H. *Piaget and Knowledge: Theoretical Foundations.* Englewood Cliffs, N.J.: Prentice-Hall, 1972.

FURTH, H., and WACHS, H. *Thinking Goes to School: Piaget's Theory in Practice.* New York: Oxford University Press, 1975.

GREENFIELD, P. M., and SMITH, J. H. *The Structure of Communication in Early Language Development.* New York: Academic Press, 1976.

HOHMANN, M., BANET, B., and WEIKART, D. *Young Children in Action.* Ypsilanti, Mich.: High/Scope Educational Research Foundation Press, 1979.

INHELDER, B., SINCLAIR, H., and BOVET, M. *Learning and the Development of Cognition.* Cambridge, Mass.: Harvard University Press, 1974.

KAMII, C., and DEVRIES, R. *Physical Knowledge in Preschool Education: Implications of Piaget's Theory.* Englewood Cliffs, N.J.: Prentice-Hall, 1978.

KARMILOFF-SMITH, A., and INHELDER, B. If you want to get ahead, get a theory. *Cognition*, 1975, *3*, 192–212.

KAUFMAN, B., and BANET, B. Will the real Jean Piaget please stand up: A critique of three Piaget-based curricula and a rejoinder. Urbana, Ill.: Publications Office, University of Illinois, 1976.

KUHN, D. Inducing development experimentally: Comments on a research paradigm. *Developmental Psychology*, 1974, *10*, 590–600.

KUHN, D., and HO, V. The development of schemes for recognizing additive and alternative effects in a "natural experiment" context. *Developmental Psychology*, 1977, *13*, 515–516.

KUHN, D., and PHELPS, E. A methodology for observing the development of formal reasoning strategies. In D. Kuhn (ed.), *Intellectual Development Beyond Childhood.* San Francisco, Calif.: Jossey-Bass, 1979.

LAVATELLI, C. S. *Piaget's Theory Applied to an Early Childhood Curriculum.* Boston: Center for Media Development, 1970.

MODGIL, S., and MODGIL, C. Piagetian Research, Volumes 1–8. Windsor, England: NFER Publishing Company, 1976.

PIAGET, J. *To Understand Is to Invent.* New York: Grossman Publishers, 1973.

PIAGET, J. *The Grasp of Consciousness: Action and Concept in the Young Child.* Cambridge, Mass.: Harvard University Press, 1976.

PIAGET, J. Correspondences and transformations. In F. Murray (ed.), *The Impact of Piagetian Theory.* Baltimore, Md.: University Park Press, 1979.

RICE, M. *Cognition to language categories, word meanings, and training.* Baltimore, Md.: University Park Press, 1980.

ROVET, J. F. Can audio-visual media teach children mental skills? Paper presented at the Annual Meeting of the American Education Research Association, San Francisco, Calif., April 1976.

SINCLAIR, H. *Langage et Operations*, Paris: Dunod, 1967.

SPIRO, R. H. Language and thinking in the child: A cognitive developmental approach. *Dissertation Abstracts*, 1973, *35*, 1 (525-B).

SYLVA, K. Play and learning. In B. Tizard and D. Harvey (eds.), *The Biology of Play.* Philadelphia: Lippincott, 1976.

ZIMMERMAN, B., and LANARO, P. Acquiring and retaining conservation of length through modeling and reversibility cues. *Merrill-Palmer Quarterly*, 1974, *20*, 145–161.

PART III

Early Childhood Classroom Processes

CHAPTER 10

Play and Early Education

Doris Sponseller

DURING THE LATE 1920s and the 1930s, many studies of childhood play were conducted. This interest in play research coincided with the growth of the child study and progressive education movements and the beginnings of the nursery school movement. The studies focus primarily on white middle class children attending laboratory nursery schools. Early research on play followed a normative pattern similar to most of the child study projects: researchers objectively and systematically described how children of various ages play in various settings with a variety of materials. There was no attempt to relate results to theories of child development or education. Although early theories of play motives exist (Gilmore, 1966b), early play research was not related to these constructs.

The first major linkage of research on play to theory began with an interest in the Freudian view of childhood, prominent in the late 1930s and 1940s. The clinical model of research using play therapy techniques to reflect deep emotions provided research literature stressing doll play (Levin & Wardwell, 1962).

Because play was not viewed as a basic survival response related to primary reinforcers, early behaviorists ignored it or stated that behaviors called "play" could be explained by behaviorist constructs such as the drive deficit model or reinforcement motivation. However, later works in the behaviorist vein cite behaviors unexplainable by these constructs (Harlow, 1950). Berlyne (1966, 1970) designates these "unexplained" behaviors as "diversive exploration" or play. He indicates that although the stimulus-response theory can explain specific exploration, it cannot explain play. This conjecture, together with research demonstrating that certain play behaviors are learned and culturally influenced, has led to interest in the studies of play by learning and behavior theorists (Roberts & Sutton-Smith, 1962).

Research linking cognitive development to play began in the 1950s when the writings of Jean Piaget gained prominence in the United States. Piagetian theory describes play as an assimilative process related to intellectual development. **215**

Piaget describes three levels of play (practice play, symbolic play, and games with rules) in play development along with various stages of cognitive development. His work provides a base for much research, in particular, the relationship of symbolic play to cognitive and language development. In addition, research on language acquisition stressing self-initiated practice and the semantic aspects of language development are linked with play (Bloom, 1970; Weir, 1962). Special education researchers are also focusing on play's influence on the development of handicapped children (Guralnick, 1978).

The body of research on play is increasing rapidly and indicates relationships between play, development, and early learning. Much of the evidence is mixed or unclear, and methodological problems may make generalizations unwarranted. However, a study of the research and its results should provide some guidance to educators as they view the child and the school.

Research in the Relationship of Play to Children's Development

Early Research

Research on play during the 1920s and 1930s primarily attempted to describe the characteristics of children's play in the setting of the nursery school. No intervention strategies are proposed and no effects measured. This research simply describes the content of play, seeking to establish developmental norms of play. Much of the normative data provided by these early studies are supported in later studies: sensory-motor play in infancy (Shirley, 1931); dramatic play beginning in the second year (Furfey, 1930); and imaginative play peaking in kindergarten (Arlitt, 1930). The work of Blatz and Bott (1929) distinguishing common forms of social play and Parten's (1932) work showing a high correlation between age and social participation are basic to later research and are noted often in child development texts.

The early play therapy session, reported in clinical observation studies during the 1940s and 1950s, attempts to relate research to theory and serves as a prototype for later investigations. Erikson's study (1951) on sexual differences in block play has prompted recent studies of the different approaches boys and girls take to play space (Clance & Dawson, 1974). Research by Barker, Dembo and Lewin (1941), analyzing the effects of frustration on play behavior, has also influenced later play research.

Other seminal studies during this early period are observations of play-revealed aggression (for example, Sears, 1951; Gewirtz, 1950; Levin & Sears, 1956). Early interest in the relationship of play to development is evident in the *Bibliography of Research in Education* which lists over fifty studies of young children's play for the period between 1926 and 1940. Hurlock's review (1934) of the early normative studies lists 128 references to play research. Attempts to develop observational techniques are reported in these early studies, and much attention is given to the reliability and validity of the instruments. Many of the early studies are carefully done and methodologically sound in terms of the research practices of that period. Present researchers have a renewed interest in these early works, and some are attempting to replicate the results (Barnes, 1971). At the same time, they are linking these results to present theoretical interests (Rubin, 1977).

Recent Research

Recent studies linking play to development focus more on theoretical considerations. Areas of interest in current research are:

1. the relationship of symbolic play to cognitive development
2. the relationship of social level of play to cognitive development
3. the relationship of language play to language development
4. the relationship of active motor play to social and physical development.

These developmental studies are correlational rather than causal. A major portion of current research examines the relationship of symbolic play to cognitive development in the light of Piagetian theory or by comparing Piagetian theory to that of Russian theorists such as Vygotsky and El'konin. Another theoretical thrust grows from neo-Freudian theory and emphasizes the role of fantasy play in ego development and mastery.

Recent research demonstrates that although the early levels of symbolic play follow Piaget's predicted developmental sequence, later sequencing levels are less clear (Nicholich, 1977; Sinclair, 1970).

Golomb (1977) challenges Piaget's description of the "lawless" character of symbolic play substitutions. Her study shows symbolic play as having rule-governed characteristics. Other researchers have investigated similar Piagetian questions (Elder & Pederson, 1975; Fenson, Kagan, Kearsley, Zelazo, 1976). For instance, there seems to be some evidence that symbolic play practice by older children can enhance the development of conservation (Golomb & Cornelius, 1977) and the ability to solve problems (Sylva, 1977).

Nicolich (1977) and Fein (1979) verify a relationship between symbolic play and early language levels. Fein concurs with Vygotsky (1962) that language comprehension (the development of inner speech) is a factor in advanced symbolic play, while also supporting Piaget's view that play and early language both serve an expressive function. Other research also correlates symbolic play with cognitive and language development (Becher & Wolfgang, 1977; Rubin & Maioni, 1975; Goodson & Greenfield, 1975).

Researchers focusing on the meaning of symbolic play in terms of neo-Freudian theory take their impetus from the work of Erikson (1940) who stresses the function of play as a way for children to gain mastery of their environment.

Their position differs from early psychoanalytic views of fantasy as catharsis because they see fantasy play as a useful cognitive skill assisting in cognitive development and emotional mastery.

Several developmental studies of fantasy play take this perspective. The Singers (1974a and b, 1978), designing methods for observing and categorizing imaginative play, discuss projective techniques and self-report measures useful in studying symbolic play and fantasy levels. Pulaski (1970) concludes that by the age of five a child's predisposition to fantasy is established and, further, that high fantasy children have greater cognitive flexibility or creativity. Pulaski also shows that low-structure play materials elicit a greater number of symbolic play themes. Effectance, defined as children's independent effective interaction with people and things, has been studied by Borowitz (1970). These researchers conclude that the behaviors leading to optimal learning in school—organization, involvement, and interpersonal responsiveness—correlate with the psychosexual content of symbolic play.

Researchers presently studying the relationship of social levels of play to cognitive development either replicate or elaborate the social participation level categories explored in early studies of play or attempt to link social play, especially role taking or cooperative play behavior, to levels of cognition. In an attempt to replicate Parten's (1932) study, Barnes (1971) fails to replicate Parten's results. He has concluded that play behavior changed during the forty-year interim, with children now less socially oriented. He attributes this to the influence of mass media and the use of more solitary toys. Rubin, Maioni, and Hornung (1976) challenge Barnes's conclusion, using a technique which combines the levels of social participation designed by Parten with levels of cognitive play outlined by Smilansky (1968). This study concludes that socioeconomic factors may be related to the level of social play. Other researchers also note that lower quantity and quality levels of sociodramatic play are often found in lower socioeconomic groups (Smilansky, 1968; Rosen, 1974).

Sponseller and Jaworski (1979), in a longitudinal study of both toddlers and preschoolers, found a significant relationship between social complexity level as measured by scaled Parten categories and chronological age, with age predicting social complexity of play.

Rubin, Watson, and Jambor (1978), comparing kindergarten and preschool children, find that preschoolers engage in significantly more solitary play than kindergarteners although the amount of parallel play is similar. This result differs from that of an earlier study (1976) in which Rubin et al. (1976) conclude that solitary play might reflect a higher level of play development than indicated by Parten.

Roper and Hinde (1978) also state that solitary play does not necessarily mean that a child lacks social ability. They state that "it may mean that he has the confidence to play so" (p. 577). There may be two types of solitary play related to different levels of cognitive development. Further refinement of the categories may yield more information about the levels and sequence of social play.

The interface of prosocial behaviors in play such as cooperation and children's ability to put themselves in another's role (empathy) are explored by Levine and Hoffman (1975) and by Marcus et al. (1978). Zscheye (1976) investigates the relationship between kindergarten children's scores on four self-concept measures and their types of play activities. Children low on self-concept measures engage in more solitary play, with less energy and with less variety of activity. However, their play is of a higher cognitive level. Whether the earlier study by Rubin, Watson, and Jambor (1978) accounts for this finding is unclear. Much of the recent research on social play raises as many questions as it answers.

Research on the relationship of language play to language development has only recently appeared. The importance of language as play material is stressed by Cazden (1974), who describes play as assisting metalinguistic awareness, and by El'konin (1969), who cites Pavlov's view that the word is a stimulus which is perceived initially in its acoustic qualities. In order to develop metalinguistic awareness, that is, the ability to think about and talk about language, play is important. Both confirm that just as a mastery of objective reality requires activity with objects, mastery of language requires activity with language as the play material.

Weir (1962) and Keenan (1974) explore their own children's use of language sounds, syntax, and meaning as play material, finding that self-initiated language play serves as a systematic linguistic exercise. Schwartz (1977) has collected language samples of 149 children in the age range of six months to ten years, finding evidence not only of solitary verbal play with sounds and syntax, but also of cooperative verbal games-with-rules. Garvey (1977) reports on language as a facilitative device to further social and symbolic play and games: play with noises and sounds, play with the linguistic system, and social play with language, including spontaneous rhyming and word play, play with fantasy and nonsense, and play with conversation.

A study by Martlew, Connolly, and McLeod (1978) concludes that role taking during play facilitates the development of social language, flexible and expressive tones, and the recognition of rules underlying the voice or dialogue patterns of the assumed role.

Smilansky (1968) demonstrates that sociodramatic play is greatly facilitated by the use of language which allows words to "take the place of reality" (p 8), with language in play serving to

- change personal identity
- change object identity or action
- substitute for action
- describe context of pretend action.

Language also provides planning and sustaining functions.

The relationship of active motor play to social and physical development is of interest to researchers coming from ethological and interactionist perspectives. Drawing on ethological methods used in studying animal play, Aldis (1975) describes the characteristics of children's motor play and compares it to animal play. Through analysis of films of children in a variety of natural settings, he finds these types of motor play in children: wrestling for superior position (observed primarily in boys); fragmentary wrestling; hitting and kicking; swimming pool dunking and splashing; chasing; vestibular reinforcement such as sliding, swinging, spinning, and acrobatics; and play-fear reinforcement such as peekaboo. He states that the prime human play signal is laughter, serving two functions: distinguishing play from nonplay and serving as a general arousal stimulus which increases playfulness. Screams and an open or smiling mouth are other human play signals. Humans engage in more water play, vestibular reinforcement play, and object play than animals and do not usually engage in mouthing play. Their chasing play is similar to that of animals.

Blurton-Jones's (1976) studies of rough-and-tumble play among nursery school children aged three to five use ethological research methods. She describes both agonistic (dominant and hostile) behavior and rough-and-tumble play. She states:

> Most of the rough-and-tumble play consists of behaviours which on the surface looks very hostile: violent pursuit, assault and fast evasive retreat. . . . [a]lthough rough-and-tumble looks like hostile behaviour it is quite separate from behaviour which I call hostile because of its effects, i.e. involving property ownership and separation of individuals [Blurton-Jones, 1976, p. 356].

She observes that some children seem "permanently unable to join in and take the rough-and-tumble 'in fun'" (p. 356), and speculates there may be a critical period, from about eighteen months to three years in which this type of play develops. Boys typically are observed more than girls in this type of play. Blurton-Jones indicates that both adults and some children respond to this play as if it were hostile. Most players, however, seem to know the difference and the effect of the play is usually to increase friendship rather than lose it.

Ellis and Scholtz (1978) describe a number of studies that focus on the influence of setting manipulation and physiological processes on activity patterns, stereotyped behaviors, and peer or object preferences in play. Recordings with a fisheye camera which photographs a play room with a coordinate grid floor, show that locomotor activity patterns of five-year-olds are greater than for four-year-olds and that within those groups they are greater for boys than for girls (Wuellner, 1970).

Manipulation of the setting by addition of a novel object reduces the activity level of the more active groups. The researchers speculate that the propensity on the part of males to be motorically active if their attention is not captured by novel objects may be "the root of the hyperactivity problem—a male child problem" (Ellis & Scholtz, 1978, p. 67).

Other studies using similar methods report that Down's Syndrome children operate at a slower pace than normal children (Linford et al., 1971), that hyperactive children's activity levels are affected by context rather than by biological factors (Karlsson, 1971), and that children's activity levels show periodicity influenced by habituation/boredom and activity/rest (Wade, Ellis & Bohrer, 1973).

Recent research investigates a variety of aspects of children's play from a range of theoretical perspectives and demonstrates relationships between play and development. Although the relationships seem evident, the question whether play is a causal factor of developmental progress or a behavior accompanying other evidences of developmental progress cannot yet be answered.

Research on the Facilitation of Play

Early Research

Early studies during the 1920s and 1930s focused on the interplay between children and equipment during free play. Many describe children's toy preferences (for example, Bott, 1928); social interactions induced by equipment and materials (Van Alstyne, 1932); and amount of play material (Johnson, 1935).

In general, the early studies indicate that children of different ages play differently and that the materials in the environment can affect the quantity and quality of social interaction. For example, Bott reports that unstructured raw materials such as clay, sand, and blocks are chosen by two- to four-year-olds, but that structured toys gain appeal as children grow older. Van Alstyne (1932) states that between the age of three and four, children begin to use raw materials more constructively.

There are fewer observational reports of toy and material preferences during the 1940s and 1950s. Instead, the focus is on personality variables and parental influences rather than on setting effects.

Recent Research

Recent studies on facilitating play are of two types:

1. investigations of the physical environment and its effect on play, including studies of environmental manipulation
2. investigations of the social environment and its effect on play, including methods used by teachers or parents to facilitate play directly or indirectly.

Current research along physical environment dimensions measure effects of classroom spatial features, equipment use of placement, and ecological patterns (Phyfe-Perkins, 1979). Density of space, arrangement of equipment in space, division of spatial areas, private and common space boundaries, and noise level are topics of research by Loo, 1972; Smith and Connolly, 1972; McGrew, 1970; and others. Some researchers suggest categories or schemata to assist teachers in analyzing and arranging space. Witt and Gramza (1969), reporting on their manipulation of equipment between center and corner positions, indicate that center-positioned equipment receives more usage and encourages more interactive play. Brenner (1976), studying the spatial areas of a preschool classroom, discusses his findings in terms of an "optimal make-believe" environment, which may differ for boys and girls. Most of these studies on space and play conclude that large spaces increase social and rough-and-tumble play and that small enclosed areas encourage solitary and quiet play.

Recent studies on objects within the play space consider the variety, complexity and amount, and type of materials. Prescott and Jones (1967) and Kritchevsky and Prescott (1969) have designed criteria to analyze the complexity levels of a piece or constellation of equipment. A study by Peck and Goldman (1978) determines the effects of increasing the complexity of play material. Quilitch and Risley (1973) note differences in the amount of time devoted to cooperative play when either "social" toys or "isolated" toys are available. Smith and Connolly (1972) report that when only large apparatus is available there is an increase in verbal, physical, and cooperative play. Analyzing the social play of toddlers, Howes and Rubenstein (1978) describe two day-care environments: family day care, with more movable, simple toys, and center care, with more complex, fixed toys. Social play was highest in family day-care homes when children were using no toys; peer interaction in center care was highest when the toddlers were using the complex, fixed equipment.

A number of ecological studies look at level of use, complexity of play organization, and level of social participation. Rubin and Seibel (1979) claim that levels of social and cognitive play are related to types of materials. Tizzard, Philips, and Plewis (1976) find that provision of numerous art activities negatively correlates with amount of symbolic play, suggesting that a wide range of alternatives within classrooms contributes to short attention spans. Sponseller and Jaworski (1979) also document lower-than-expected levels of cooperative play in a rich environment conducive to construction. Weinstein (1977), by separating some of the confounding variables of materials, spatial arrangement, and usage patterns, demonstrates that children's space usage and selection of play activities can definitely be modified by changes in the environment. Shapiro (1975) notes that teachers' and children's preferences for areas are not congruent, suggesting that teachers need to study their own preferences and activity patterns to determine if and how it affects the preference activity patterns of the children. Phyfe-Perkins (1979) suggests that "perhaps the skill of arranging the early childhood environment to support the maximum involvement of children with materials and with each other is a skill that can and should be taught" (pp. 44–45).

Much of the recent research on play facilitation attends to effects of the social environment: the interaction of parents, teachers, and peers. Another aspect, television viewing (a noninteractive process), is also receiving research attention. Learning theorists who view play as a learned rather than a spontaneous activity support these studies. El'konin (1966) discusses children's learning of symbolic play from observing adult models. Social learning theorists, such as Bandura (1973), demonstrate the effects of observational learning on children's aggressive play behavior. Other theorists describe culturally learned differences in play behavior (Millar, 1968; Roberts & Sutton-Smith, 1962).

Many researchers focus on the importance of the first two years of life as the basis for learning how to play. Studies showing very young infants responsive to social stimulation include Brazelton, Koslowski, and Main, 1974, and Clarke-Stewart, 1973.

Believing that parent–infant interaction patterns may be the basis of an ability to play, Bruner and Sherwood (1976) describe the basic rule patterns of parent–infant games such as "peekaboo" by structural analysis from videotapes of infant–mother dyads. Play interactions influence other aspects of development. According to Smith and Lloyd (1978) there is a very early emphasis and encouragement of physically active gross motor play for young males. Downs and Langlois (1977) also demonstrate differential sex reinforcement by mothers of perschool age children who tend to interfere verbally when children play with inappropriate sex-type toys. Reflecting on the interaction patterns of toddlers with their mothers and fathers, Vandell (1978) concludes that a programmed group experience does not affect their differential interaction patterns, but that toddlers in group programs showed more social interactions with parents.

Researchers with a Piagetian orientation have looked at effects of adults on toddlers' symbolic play ability. In some studies adults make specific verbal play suggestions (Fein, Robertson & Diamond, 1975), model symbolic play acts (Fein, 1975; Watson & Fisher, 1977), or "present" toys without actual intervention (Fein & Apfel, 1979; Nicholich, 1977). Hrncir (1980), noticing that higher symbolic play occurs when adult play suggestions are used and that suggestions are most facilitative with low representational objects, is still not clear on whether adult play suggestions are necessary. She hypothesizes that play suggestions are only a catalyst for a naturally developing pretend progression.

Methods for teacher enhancement of prosocial behavior of children have also been suggested (Wolfgang, 1977; Marton & Acker, 1977). Studies of this type have often been concerned with assisting passive or isolated children to become involved in play activity, increasing certain prosocial behaviors such as expression of affection, and decreasing aggression. These prosocial studies, which use a variety of modeling techniques, contrast with Bandura and Walter's (1963) work showing that aggression is increased by modeling.

The sex-role learning effects of differential feedback by male and female teachers on children's play behavior is studied by Fagot and Patterson (1969). Later studies indicate that experienced teachers reinforce more feminine preferred behaviors than inexperienced teachers (Fagot, 1978b) and that male preschool teachers reinforce feminine and masculine behaviors equally (Lee & Walinsky, 1973). Another study by Fagot (1978b) of sex role behavior in play records the feedback consequences of masculine, feminine, and androgynous play behavior.

The bulk of studies of adult facilitation of symbolic play gives evidence that adult suggestions, modeling, or direct training do have effects on children's symbolic play. It is not clear from the research whether the adult functions as a teacher of specific skills or as an elicitor of skills which the child already possesses.

Although the researchers assume that ability to play at more advanced social and symbolic levels is related to intellectual growth and academic success, most studies do not demonstrate a causal effect in these variables.

The question whether a causal link exists between teacher facilitated play and developmental or academic outcomes has been studied by only a few researchers. These studies have measured the effects of a play experience or training procedure on later performance in problem solving or rote learning tasks.

An influential study on play and problem solving was that conducted by Sylva, Bruner, and Genova (1976). They conclude that children who play with problem-solving task materials before attempting problem solving do better because they show self-initiated action and motivation and have an opportunity to order the necessary tools and tasks; the anticipated stress of success or failure is also reduced. Other studies drawing on this approach have been that of Vandenberg (1978) and Smith and Dutton (1978). This line of research suggests that play opportunities may have a causal effect on problem solving, although many variables are as yet unexplored.

A comparison of playful and nonplayful teaching of rote learning has also been studied. Scott and Goetz (1978) compare the effects of a gamelike learning activity (rhyming mnemonic) to rote memorization of telephone numbers. Their results indicate that children's rote memorization methods result in fewer errors and larger memory span than the methods of children learning through the game. Antkoviak (1972), teaching primary number concepts to kindergarteners through role playing or non-role-playing methods, reports that children using role playing learned less. Both researchers indicate that information overload or attention to irrelevant information may have hindered the playful learning of this basic task. A question needing further study is whether play affects higher developmental processes more than basic skills. The present data suggest this. Recent research on effects of play facilitation suggest that play may enhance certain types of learning, particularly those requiring higher cognitive processes and self-motivation.

Studies of peer play facilitation focus on children who do not seem to be playing at the normative levels described in naturalistic research including "disadvantaged" children from low socioeconomic or minority populations and handicapped children. Some studies look primarily at what the adults working with handicapped children can do (Shores, Hester & Strain, 1976); others look at effects of child–child interaction (Peterson & Haralick, 1977).

Direct teacher modeling or training to increase play behaviors has been used primarily with retarded children who are less likely to imitate the behaviors of peers in a play setting. Some studies show that retarded children in integrated programs have not substantially increased their levels of peer imitation and interaction (Allen, Benning & Drumond, 1972). Peck et al. (1978) promote a direct training strategy that awards retarded preschoolers for imitating nonretarded peers. The minimal level of play behavior imitated and the specificity of the responses call into question whether this behavior is play or imitation.

Knapczyk and Peterson (1976), integrating normal children into trainable, but mentally retarded, groups during free play, report an increase in the cooperative and parallel play of the retarded children when mainstreamed with children of the same chronological age, but no change occurs when they are mainstreamed with children of similar mental age. Guralnick (1978) also reports that mildly handicapped children and nonhandicapped children interact well with each other, but that nonhandicapped children seldom interact with moderately or severely retarded children. All of these studies suggest that peer influence is an important variable interacting with sex, developmental level, and setting.

Some researchers attempt to increase sociodramatic play in children from low socioeconomic groups. This type of symbolic play seems to be related to cognitive, language, and social development. Smilansky (1968) describes an intervention technique which consists of analyzing a child's level of sociodramatic play and of providing any of six missing components through adult interaction in the play activity. Working with disadvantaged children, she reports significant improvement when adults interject or stimulate the appropriate element of "pretend." Improvement is most evident in language, that is, length of sentence, contextual speech, and vocabulary range. Saltz, Dixon, and Johnson (1977) promote fantasy play training (fairy tales) as superior to sociodramatic play training because it both raises the empathy level of the players and encourages an understanding of cause and effect.

Freyberg (1973) suggests that a short dose of concentrated training in dramatic play can significantly affect the imagination, concentration, and affect of lower socioeconomic children. However, most studies conclude that the lower socioeconomic children still do not reach levels of imaginative play comparable to middle class children. Marshall and Hahn (1967) find that middle class children, who are already able to play in pretend roles, are also able to improve role playing after training.

Peer interaction without adult intervention is also receiving attention in current literature. Male peers more often ridicule or punish other boys for sex-inappropriate play, according to a study by Downs and Langlois (1977). While studying peer relationships among toddlers, Mueller and Brenner (1977) noticed that parallel play with a similar toy produces social interaction. Abramovitch and Grusec (1978) report on peer imitation during free play: more verbal than motor acts are imitated at all ages. Children judged dominant in both teacher and peer ratings are imitated more often than shyer, quieter classmates. The studies on peer interaction show that other children are often a major influence on a child's play behavior.

Singer and Singer (1974) use Mister Roger's Neighborhood as a television stimulus and analyze the imaginative play of children assigned to no television, television only, television with an interacting adult, and no television but with an adult interacting in fantasy play. The children involved with both sets of interacting adults show more subsequent imaginary play. Singer and Singer (1978), studying children's television habits as logged by their parents, report effects of assigning parents to one of three intervention conditions: one designed to stimulate children's language and cognitive development, one to stimulate children's imaginative play, and one to control the frequency and pattern of their children's television watching. The research suggests that aggression and hyperactivity may be related to family patterns where there is less control by parents over television and fewer alternative family interaction patterns and interests.

Other studies of television's effect on imagination are reported. Using parental reporting techniques, Caldeira, Singer, and Singer (1978) observe that children with imaginary playmates view television less often than children without imaginary playmates. Tower et al. (1977) document that watching a slow-paced children's television program such as Mister Roger's Neighborhood results in greater imagination of play, concentration, and social interaction than that induced by a fast-paced program such as Sesame Street.

Two similar studies, both correlating television and aggression, demonstrate opposite effects. Bandura (1973) states that children who view highly aggressive cartoons show more aggressive free play. Cameron et al. (1971) show no difference in play between that of children who view either high or low aggression cartoons. Whether quality or quantity of television is responsible for differences in children's play behavior is unclear. Further studies are needed to differentiate among other parental and setting variables before the effects of television on play can be clearly demonstrated.

Recent research on facilitating play demonstrates parental, teacher, peer, and television effects on children's play. Because of the number of related variables, however, the effect on specific types and levels of play is as yet not clearly demonstrated. Further studies which systematically vary these social dimensions may offer clarification. If play facilitation is to be a goal of the school, the body of research does stress that attention to adult and peer feedback and the early childhood setting are essential.

Problems in Defining and Researching Play

The studies reported in this chapter differ greatly in approach and in the definition of play used by the researcher. Validity problems are common to all research in child development and education, but there are problems specific to research on play:

1. Definitional problems: what is play and how is it defined as behavior?
2. Methodological problems: should the defined behaviors be studied in the natural or in the experimental environment? When does direct manipulation change the behavior from play to something else?
3. Meaning problems: what do the results mean theoretically and practically?

Research on play may encounter difficulty because of the inherent nature of play. Many behaviors can be observed without the necessity of attributing intent. However, no set of specific motor or verbal behaviors equal play. Almost any observable (and many unobservable) types of behavior are playful, depending on the subject's intention. Blurton-Jones shows, for example, how fighting and play-fighting have observable behaviors which can be confused. Rather than two clear-cut categories—play and nonplay—there is a continuum of behavior with a point on this continuum where playful fighting ends and read fighting begins. Teachers face this continuum question when using a game to teach skills. At what point is the game play and when does it become "work disguised as play?" This question is crucial as researchers focus more and more on play in experimental situations.

Definitional Problems

Play is defined many ways, often by alluding to what is not play. It is sometimes defined very narrowly: play is what is left after all other behavior is explained or, very broadly, play is all the behavior not explainable by the stimulus-response theory—Gilmore's "wastebasket" category (1966b).

In discussing play research, some writers differentiate between exploration and play (Hutt, 1971; Aldis, 1975), others talk about "exploratory" play (Millar, 1968); some sharply differentiate play from imitation (Piaget, 1962), others include imitative play (Millar, 1968) or use imitation to teach play (Yawkey and Silvern, 1979); some define play as a process specific to childhood (Piaget, 1966), and others define it as a lifelong activity (Sutton-Smith, 1971).

Although definitions vary, the construct "play" does have observable elements; however, these elements are not discrete but continuous. For example, Neumann (1971) observes three essentials to playful behavior: internal control, internal reality, and internal motivation, which must be present at some level. When control, reality, and motivation are totally external, outside the actor, the activity is not play. At exactly what level of internal/external balance an activity ceases to be play and becomes work is hard to substantiate. Certain observable signals may indicate playfulness. Lieberman (1977) lists physical, social, and cognitive spontaneity, joy, and a sense of humor as criteria.

Ellis (1973) points out that play is defined either in terms of its motive, "Why does play occur?," or its content "What does play consist of?." He maintains that the way researchers approach the task of studying play depends on whether they are looking at functional questions, structural questions, or both, and he concludes that "play, then, is a plastic construct which has yet to be satisfactorily operationalized in a way that satisfies all" (1973, p.22). What is essential is that researchers on play clarify the criteria they are using and operationalize their studies in a way that is consistent with these criteria.

MOTIVE-BASED RESEARCH

Researchers who define play through motive include the early classical theorists such as Groos (1901) who considers play instinctual, Lazarus (1883) who claims it is initiated by the need to replenish energy, and Schiller (1875) who states that play is caused by a surplus of energy. Present researchers with this perspective are also interested in studying the external and internal conditions under which play occurs.

Thus, play antecedents and consequences are topics of behaviorist research, in studies of the environmental factors and of biological processes which invite or reinforce play. The studies by Ellis and Scholtz (1978) extend understanding of environmental and biological factors influencing gross motor play. Hutt (1971) pursues a study differentiating diverse exploration, or play, from specific exploration, in terms of motive and consequences. Hutt states that children first wonder "what can the object do?"; then they move to the question, "what can I do with the object?" Whereas exploration is "stimulus-referent," play is "response-referent" (Hutt, 1971, p. 246). Hutt also indicates that play may be considered low in the motivational hierarchy because it is overshadowed and inhibited by basic drives. McCall (1974), in a series of studies on infant exploratory behavior, has found that exploratory manipulation increases as the responsiveness of the stimulus object increases. Gilmore (1966), testing the interplay between novelty and anxiety to determine if an antecedent emotional state affects toy choice, observed hospitalized children. He concludes that children's preferences for novel toys is only minimally related to anxiety level. Children generally prefer novel toys; however, the presence of anxiety affects specific toy choice, insofar as children prefer toys related to their anxiety, if their anxiety level is moderate.

Other studies with a behaviorist orientation investigate the effects of extrinsic reinforcement on desired play behavior. Since inner motivation and control are thought to be essential elements of play, researchers question whether reinforcement will increase or decrease spontaneous play. A number of studies report that interest in a play activity decreases if the play is rewarded for some time period and the reward is subsequently withdrawn (Lepper & Greene, 1975). This decrease is sometimes explained in terms of self-perception theory; that is, the child who initially plays for a self-motivating reason no longer perceives the rewarded activity as play. The decrease is also explained in terms of interference: stress related to reward expectation. Perry, Bussey, and Redman (1977) tested an alternative hypothesis: that the activity itself acquires aversive properties associated with frustration and anticipated loss. Studies related to this question are especially important for teachers wishing to facilitate play.

Research on play facilitation often has a motivational question as a basis of the study. If the question why play increases or decreases can be answered, facilitation of play could become a more effective teaching strategy.

CONTENT-BASED RESEARCH

Research defining play through content includes the early normative studies and present descriptive and structural studies. Sometimes, these studies are based on theories positing a motivational hypothesis for play, such as Freud's psychoanalytic theory or the Piagetian cognitive theory. Of interest to these researchers, however, are content issues: how the play theme or content reveals underlying emotional motives, whether the content of play can be classified or sequenced, and how the organizing shemata or structures of play can be used to understand developmental processes.

Much of the Piagetian-based research investigates structural questions (Nicolich, 1977; Fein, 1979). Ethnographic researchers are also interested in structural questions (Aldis, 1975; Blurton-Jones, 1972). Studies on the social level of play are also primarily a content issue, although these researchers have also investigated some of the social elicitors of play.

A structural study from the psychoanalytical perspective is that of Druckner (1979) who observed toddlers interacting with their parents. Play behavior was designated as related to three developmental tasks: drive gratification, mastery, and developing object relations. A socialization study concerned with both content and levels of structured activity is that of Carpenter et al. (1978). The study claims that participation in highly structured activities may teach compliance. Some language play studies also use a content approach; Davison (1974) determines the structural components of toddlers' linguistic play.

Sutton-Smith and Rosenberg (1961) and Roberts and Sutton-Smith (1962) study game preference from a content perspective. These studies categorize three types of games and suggest that the classifications are culture-related. Hunting cultures encourage games of physical skill; agricultural societies encourage games related to chance; and industrial societies encourage games of strategy.

Every researcher who wishes to study play must first define play and then operationalize that definition. Teachers concerned about the implications of play research for educational practice must also decide whether content or motive questions are important and make a reasoned selection from the relevant research. Teachers must be aware of the definitions of play used by researchers and the questions underlying their research methods. The relevance of the research questions and the appropriateness of the particular research methods are determined by the educational decisions that are to be made.

Methodological Problems in Play Research

Once the researcher adequately defines play, a methodological approach must be selected. The early studies use descriptive, naturalistic methods; that is, data were collected through observing and recording naturally occurring events in a natural setting. Although naturalistic research methods are still used, an experimental approach is becoming more common. In an experimental mode, the majority of variables are held constant while a few are manipulated. Presumably, this allows the researcher to be more aware of the actual variables influencing behavior and to draw conclusions of a cause/effect nature.

To decide which approach is better—natural or experimental—is especially difficult for researchers cognizant of the nature of play. For example, at what point in experimental studies does the manipulation of the setting take away the self-motivated or self-controlled aspects of play? The difficulties are not only in experimental approaches. In naturalistic studies, at what point is the observed play behavior affected by natural developmental levels and at what point is it affected by the features of the natural environment? Can these variables be separated?

Some researchers on play stress that a refined, systematic examination of all variables is needed (Fein, 1978b). Fein urges that controlled studies be the major research approach. On the other hand, ethnographic researchers such as Aldis (1975) urge extensive detailed descriptive work because "premature quantification based on classifications that are too broad or too crude can be misleading or meaningless" (1975, p. 8).

Both approaches to studying play can be useful as long as researchers are aware of the kinds of questions answered by each approach and the methodological difficulties involved. For example, naturalistic methods may have the following problems:

1. An attempt to "reinvent the wheel." Because researchers are unfamiliar with earlier data, they may ignore its potential contribution.
2. Little comparability across studies. Because instruments for observation are difficult to design and make specific to each study, they may not be easily adapted or understood by other researchers.
3. Overwhelming amounts of data. Because a method or instrument collects a great deal of data in a short time, analysis of the amount of data is time-consuming.
4. Obscured results. Because reporting this type of study is difficult if reported descriptively, it may not be considered worthy of publication. Or, if it is statistically analyzed by quantitative methods, assumptions about the data categories may be unwarranted.
5. Inability to generalize from the results. Because naturalistic studies cannot control many coexisting variables, confounding variables may make generalization impossible.

Experimental studies, however, have their problems too:

1. A focus on something other than "play." Because the focal variables are observed in a contrived play setting, the behavior occurring may not be play, even though the setting is designated as a "play" situation.
2. An effect of experimental setting on results. Because factors such as novelty or stress in the experimental setting itself may affect the quantity or quality of play, the level, range, or type of play observed may differ from that which would be seen as a naturally occurring play setting.
3. A focus on less complex types of play. Because there are more time and setting constraints in experimental settings, simpler and more easily observed types of play may draw disproportionate focus.
4. Inappropriate methods of analysis. Because quantifiable classification schemes may force behavior into prescribed categories for statistical analysis, behavior may be related more to the available procedures than to appropriateness for the data.
5. Difficulty in making causal assumptions. Because the setting is contrived, assumptions that the observed effects will translate themselves into

similar behavior in the natural environment or that they can be effected in the regular classroom by teachers using similar methods are often not warranted.

Both researchers and readers of research on play must be aware of the various research options. They must choose a method which will provide answers for the kinds of questions they are asking; then, they must consider the drawbacks in researching play from that particular methodological approach and minimize as many of these problems as possible in the design of their study.

Meaning Problems

Play helps children to make their lives meaningful. Research on play can help adults to understand the meanings children give to their experiences and can give guidance to adults in their desire to facilitate children's play. Although early studies are not linked to theoretical constructs, they do provide a base of information about children's spontaneous play that is standing the test (and retest!) of time. Studies of recent years seek to delve deeper into questions of meaning and to link observations of children's play to learning theories. The purpose of a "theory" is to organize and structure thought in a way that permits the researcher to find the problems and questions worthy of inquiry. Finding the problem is the essential first step in problem solving—"the method of inquiry" (Dewey, 1938).

For teachers, the significance of research on play is that it allows them to adopt an organizing schema through which to view children's play. The meaningfulness of this research for teachers is its potential to assist them in forming their own questions about the play of the children they teach.

Teachers may be unsure of how play research will affect their day-to-day classroom behavior. Because of definitional problems, methodological problems, and the fact that reported results often conflict or lack clarity, teachers may feel that play research has little practical meaning. To translate research into practice, teachers need to decide on their goals for play facilitation: the types of play they wish to encourage and the developmental and/or learning processes they wish to influence. They also need to become researchers themselves in the sense that they should monitor the effect on children of whatever tactic they implement.

It is clear that play and learning activities are interrelated and that certain types of learning are facilitated by certain types of play. A continuum of play and learning developed by Sponseller (1974) shows the relationship ranging from activites requiring minimal adult direct intervention to activities that are highly structured by adults.

Impact of Play Research on Views of the Child and of School

As the body of research on play increases, its impact on educators is debatable. Overall, the particular aspects of research that draw a national interest should influence educators most; yet, it is a common human trait to acknowledge research confirming personal expectations and positions.

First, the philosophical orientation of teachers is an important factor in determining the impact of play research on actual education. Many classrooms today are not supportive of playful behavior. Imaginative and playful responses to problems are often discouraged and social interaction with friends is considered disruptive. If play-oriented views of the child as self-motivated and self-directed are to prevail, teachers must change their view of children and themselves. They must begin to see young children as needing to assimilate new information through actual concrete experiences. They must begin to view themselves as facilitators. If teachers are uncomfortable being less directive while teaching, they may not be open to the facilitating methods suggested by play research literature.

Second, even if individual educators become aware of the developmental and learning outcomes that might be generated through play as curriculum, they still may view the role of the school as one of socialization to and preparation for the world of work. Requiring children to "work" is often seen as a basic duty of the school. Approval of schools where children play has never been extensive in American society.

If educators elect to design a play curriculum for their school, they will need a strong foundation of play research in order to communicate to administrators, school boards, and parents the value of play in early childhood education.

Summary

Play as a topic of research has been of variable interest, with many studies during the 1920s and 1930s and a subsequent slackening of inquiry until the 1960s. Play is currently interesting to researchers who are investigating the relationship of play to cognitive, language, social, and gross motor development, and to researchers who are becoming aware of an ability to manipulate the quality and quantity of certain types of play through environmental adjustments.

Studies of play's relationship to development have provided evidence that:

1. Symbolic play is related to cognitive operations, language, creativity, and the performance of some academic skills.
2. Play with the structures, sounds, and meaning of language is related to language acquisition.
3. Gross motor play is related not only to physical development but also to social and sex role development.
4. The level of social play has implications for cognitive and language development.
5. The development of a child's play ability parallels development in all developmental areas; thus, observation of a child's play can give insight to an overall developmental status.

Studies of facilitating play through the manipulation of physical and social factors have provided evidence that:

1. The physical factors of the play space affect social play, sex role learning, and activity level and quality.
2. A child's interaction with parents affects the ability to play.
3. A child's interaction with peers influences social play, sex role learning, play level and quality, and assists with the decentering process.
4. A teacher's direct or indirect facilitation of play affects the type, quantity, and quality of play. It signals the appropriateness or inappropriateness of play in the school.
5. Training or experience in certain types of play can affect play behavior in the classroom and it may improve the learning of academic skills, especially ones requiring higher cognitive processes.

Research can have an important impact on the child and the school if educators will allow the results of these serious inquiries on play to penetrate their thinking and their teaching strategies.

References

ABRAMOVITCH, R., and GRUSEC, J. R. Peer imitation in a natural setting. *Child Development*, 1978, *49*, 60–65.

ALDIS, O. *Play Fighting.* New York: Academic Press, 1975.

ALLEN, K. E., BENNING, P., and DRUMOND, T. Integration of normal and handicapped children in a behavior modification preschool: A case study. In G. Semb (ed.), *Behavior Analysis and Education.* Lawrence: University of Kansas Press, 1972.

ANTKOVIAK, B. M. *Role-Play and Characterization as Techniques for Teaching Primary Level Number Concepts.* Lewisburg, Pa.: Bucknell University, 1972 (ERIC Document Reproduction Service No. ED 061 098).

ARLITT, A. H. *The Child from One to Six.* New York: McGraw-Hill, 1930.

BANDURA, A. *Aggression: A Social Learning Analysis.* Englewood Cliffs, N.J.: Prentice-Hall, 1973.

BANDURA, A., and WALTERS, R. H. *Social Learning and Personality Development.* New York: Holt, Rinehart & Winston, 1963.

BARKER, R. G., DEMBO, L., and LEWIN, K. Frustration and regression: An experiment with young children. *University of Iowa Studies in Child Welfare*, 1941, *18*, No. 386.

BARNES, K. E. Preschool play norms: A replication. *Developmental Psychology*, 1971, *5*, 99–103.

BECHER, R., and WOLFGANG, C. An exploration of the relationship between symbolic representation in dramatic play and art and the cognitive and reading readiness levels of kindergarten children. *Psychology in the Schools*, 1977, *14*, 377–381.

BERLYNE, D. E. Curiosity and exploration. *Science*, 1966, *153*, 25–33.

BERLYNE, D. E. Novelty, complexity, and hedonic value. *Perception and Psychophysics*, 1970, *8*, 279–286.

BLATZ, W. E., and BOTT, H. *Parents and the Preschool Child*. New York: William Morrow and Co., 1929.

BLOOM, L. *Language Development: Form and Function in Emerging Grammars*. Cambridge, Mass.: M.I.T. Press, 1970.

BLURTON-JONES, N. G. (ed.). *Ethological Studies of Child Behavior*. Cambridge: At the University Press, 1972.

BLURTON-JONES, N. G. Categories of child-child interaction. In J. Bruner, A. Jolly, and K. Sylva, (eds.), *Play: Its Role in Development and Evolution*. New York: Basic Books, 1976.

BOROWITZ, G. H. *Play in the Study of Personality Development of Black Ghetto Four-Year-Olds*. Chicago: Kenneth F. Montgomery Charitable Foundation, 1970 (ERIC Document Reproduction Service No. ED 103 540).

BOTT, H. Observations of play activities in a nursery school. *General Psychology Monographs*, 1928, No. 4, 44–48.

BRAZELTON, T. B., KOSLOWSKI, B., and MAIN, M. The origins of reciprocity: The early mother–infant interaction. In M. Lewis, and L. A. Rosenblum, (eds.), *The Effect of the Infant on Its Caregiver*. New York: Wiley, 1974.

BRENNER, M. *The Effects of Sex, Structure, and Social Interaction on Preschoolers' Make-Believe in a Naturalistic Setting*, 1976 (ERIC Document Reproduction Service No. ED 128 103).

BRUNER, J., JOLLY, A., and SYLVA, K. (eds.). *Play: Its Role in Development and Evolution*. New York: Basic Books, 1976.

BRUNER, J., and SHERWOOD, V. Peek-a-boo and the learning of rule structures. In J. Bruner, A. Jolly, and K. Sylva, (eds.), *Play: Its Role in Development and Evolution*. New York: Basic Books, 1976.

CALDEIRA, J., SINGER, L. L., and SINGER, D. G. Imaginary playmates: Some Relationships to preschoolers' television-viewing, language and play. Paper presented at the Eastern Psychological Association, May 1978.

CAMERON, S. M., ABRAHAM, L., and CHERNICOFF, J. *The Effect of Exposure to an Aggressive Cartoon on Children's Play*, 1971 (ERIC Document Reproduction Service No. ED 055 297).

CARPENTER, C. J., HOUSTONSTEIN, A., and BAER, D. *The Relation of Children's Activity Preference to Sex-Typed Behavior*, 1978 (ERIC Document Reproduction Service No. 170 052).

CAZDEN, C. Play with language and metalinguistic awareness: One dimension of language experience. *International Journal of Early Childhood*, 1974, *6*, 12–24.

CLANCE, P. R., and DAWSON, F. B. *Sex Differences in Spatial Play Behavior of Six-Year-Olds*, 1974 (ERIC Document Reproduction Service No. ED 160 952).

CLARKE-STEWART, K. A. Interactions between mothers and their young children: Characteristics and consequences. *Monographs of the Society for Research in Child Development*, 1973, *38*, No. 153.

COOKE, T., APOLLONI, T., and COOKE, S. Normal preschool children as behavioral models for retarded peers. *Exceptional Children*, 1977, *43*, 531–532.

DAVISON, A. Linguistic play and language acquisition. *Papers and Reports on Child Language Development*, No. 8. Stanford University, California, Committee on Linguistics, 1974 (ERIC Document Reproduction Service No. ED 102 829).

DEWEY, J. *Logic: The Theory of Inquiry.* New York: H. Holt and Company, 1938.

DOWNS, A. C., and LANGLOIS, J. H. *Mother and Peer Influences on Children's Sex-Role Play Behaviors.* Austin, Texas: Hogg Foundation for Mental Health, 1977 (ERIC Document Reproduction Service No. ED 146 475).

DRUCKER, J. Toddler play: Some comments on its functions in the developmental process. *Psychoanalysis and Contemporary Science*, 1975, *4*, 479–527.

ELDER, J., and PEDERSON, D. Preschool children's use of objects in symbolic play. *Child Development*, 1975, *16*, 33–47.

EL'KONIN, D. B. Symbolics and its functions in the play of young children. *Soviet Education*, 1966, *8*, 35.

EL'KONIN, D. B. Some results of the study of the psychological development of preschool-age children. In M. Cole and I. Maltzman (eds.), *A Handbook of Contemporary Soviet Psychology.* New York: Basic Books, 1969.

ELLIS, M. *Why People Play.* Englewood Cliffs, N.J.: Prentice-Hall, 1973.

ELLIS, M., and SCHOLTZ, G. *Activity and Play of Children.* Englewood Cliffs, N.J.: Prentice-Hall, 1978.

ERIKSON, E. H. Studies in the interpretation of play. Part I, Clinical observations of play description in young children. *Genetic Psychology Monograph*, 1940, *22*, 557–671.

ERIKSON, E. H. Sex differences in the play configuration of American pre-adolescents. *American Journal of Orthopsychiatry*, 1951, *21*, 667–692.

FAGOT, B. Reinforcing contingencies for sex-role behaviors: Effect of experience with children. *Child Development*, 1978a, *49*, 30–36.

FAGOT, B. *The consequences of same-sex, cross-sex, and androgynous preferences.* Bethesda, Md.: National Institutes of Health, 1978b (ERIC Document Reproduction Service No. ED 160 967).

FAGOT, B., and PATTERSON, G. An in vivo analysis of reinforcing contingencies for sex role behaviors in the preschool. *Developmental Psychology*, 1969, *1*, 563–568.

FEIN, G. A transformational analysis of pretending. *Developmental Psychology*, 1975, *11*(3), 291–296.

FEIN, G. *Play and the Acquisition of Symbols.* Washington, D.C.: National Institution of Education, 1978a (ERIC Document Reproduction Service No. ED 152 431).

FEIN G. Social and cognitive development in children's play: A critique. Paper presented at the Annual Meeting of the American Educational Research Association, 1978b.

FEIN, G. Echoes from the nursery: Piaget, Vygotsky, and the relationship between language and play. In E. Winner, and H. Gardner (eds.), *Fact, Fiction and Fantasy in Childhood.* San Francisco: Josey-Bass, 1979.

FEIN, G., and APFEL, N. Some preliminary observations on knowing and pretending. In N. Smith and M. Franklin (eds.), *Symbolic Functioning in Childhood.* Hillsdale, N.J.: Lawrence Erlbaum Associates, 1979.

FEIN, G., ROBERTSON, A. R., and DIAMOND, E. *Cognitive and Social Dimensions of Pretending in Two Year Olds.* New Haven, Conn.: Yale University, 1975 (ERIC Document Reproduction Service No. ED 119 806).

FENSON, L., KAGAN, J., KEARSLEY, R. B., and ZELAZO, P. R. The developmental progression of manipulative play in the first two years. *Child Development*, 1976, *47*, 232–235.

FREYBERG, J. T. Increasing the imaginative play of urban disadvantaged kindergarten children through systematic training. In J. L. Singer (ed.), *The Child's World of Make-Believe*. New York: Academic Press, 1973.

FURFEY, P. H. *The Growing Boy*. New York: Macmillan, 1930.

GARVEY, C. *Play*. Cambridge, Mass.: Harvard University Press, 1977a.

GARVEY, C. Play with language. In B. Tizzard and D. Harvey (eds.), *Biology of Play*. London: Heinemann, 1977b.

GEWIRTZ, J. L. An investigation of aggressive behavior in the doll-play of young Sac and Fox Indian Children and a comparison to the aggression of midwestern white preschool children. *American Psychologist*, 1950, *5*, 294–295.

GILMORE, J. B. The role of anxiety and cognitive factors in children's play behavior. *Child Development*, 1966a, *37*, 397–416.

GILMORE, J. B. Play: A special behavior. In R. N. Haber (ed.), *Current Research in Motivation*. New York: Holt, Rinehart & Winston, 1966b.

GOLOMB, C. Symbolic play: The role of substitutions in pretense and puzzle games. *British Journal of Educational Psychology*, 1977, *47*, 175–186.

GOLOMB, C., and CORNELIUS, C. B. Symbolic play and its cognitive significance. *Developmental Psychology*, 1977, *13*, 246–252.

GOODSON, B. D., and GREENFIELD, P. M. The search for structural principles in children's manipulative play: A parallel with linguistic development. *Child Development*, 1975, *46*, 734–746.

GROOS, K. *The Play of Man*. New York: Appleton, 1901.

GULLIET, C. Recapitulation and education. *Pedagogical Seminary*, 1900, *7*, 397–445.

GURALNICK, M. J. *Integrating handicapped and nonhandicapped preschool children*. Final report. Washington, D.C.: Bureau of Education for the Handicapped, 1978 (ERIC Document Reproduction Service No. ED 162 472).

HARLOW, H. F. Learning and satiation of response in intrinsically motivated complex puzzle performance by monkeys. *Journal of Comparative and Physiological Psychology*, 1950, *43*, 289–294.

HERRON, R. E., and SUTTON-SMITH, B. *Child's Play*. New York: Wiley, 1971.

HOWES, C., and RUBENSTEIN, J. Peer play and the effect of the inanimate environment. March, 1978 (ERIC Document Reproduction Service No. ED 163 323).

HRNOIR, E. Adult facilitation of the pretend play of two-year-olds. Paper presented at the Annual Meeting of the American Educational Research Association, Boston, 1980.

HURLOCK, E. *Experimental Investigations of Childhood Play*. New York: McGraw-Hill, 1934.

HUTT, C. Exploration and play in children. In R. E. Herron and B. Sutton-Smith (eds.), *Child's Play*. New York: Wiley, 1971.

JOHNSON, M. W. The effect on behavior of variations in the amount of play equipment. *Child Development*, 1935, *6*, 56–68.

KARLSSON, K. A. Hyperactivity and environmental compliance. Unpublished doctoral dissertation, University of Illinois, 1971.

KEENAN, E. Conversational competence in children. *Journal of Child Language*, 1974, *1*, 163–183.

KNAPCZYK, D. R., and PETERSON, N. L. Social play interaction of retarded children in and integrated classroom environment. *Research and the Retarded*, 1976, 3, 104–112.

KRITCHEVSKY, S., and PRESCOTT, E. *Planning Environments for Young Children: Physical Space*. Washington, D.C.: National Association for the Education of Young Children, 1969.

LAZARUS, M. *Concerning the Fascination of Play*. Berlin: Dummler, 1883.

LEE, P. C., and WOLINSKY, A. Male teachers of young children: A preliminary empirical study. *young Children*, 1973, 28, 342–353.

LEPPER, M. R., *and* GREENE, D. Turning play into work: Effects of adult surveillance and extrinsic rewards on children's intrinsic motivation. *Journal of Personality and Social Psychology*, 1975, 31, 479–486.

LEVIN, H., and SEARS, R. R. Identification with parents as a determinant of doll play aggression. *Child Development*, 1956, 27, 135–153.

LEVIN, H., and WARDWELL, E. The research uses of doll play. *Psychological Bulletin*, 1962, 59, 27–56.

LEVINE, L. E., and HOFFMAN, M. L. Empathy and cooperation in 4 year olds. *Developmental Psychology*, 1975, 11, 533–534.

LIEBERMAN, J. N. Playfulness and divergent thinking: An investigation of their relationship at the kindergarten level. *Journal of Genetic Psychology*, 1965, 107, 219–224.

LIEBERMAN, J. N. *Playfulness*. New York: Academic Press, 1977.

LINFORD, A. C., JEANRENAUD, C. Y., KARLSSON, K. A., WITT, P., and LINFORD, M. D. A computerized analysis of characteristics of Down's Syndrome and normal children's free play patterns. *Journal of Leisure Research*, 1971, 3, 44–52.

LOO, C. M. The effects of spatial density on the social behavior of children. *Journal of Applied Social Psychology*, 1972, 2, 372–381.

McCALL, R. B. Exploratory manipulation and play in the human infant. *Monographs of the Society for Research in Child Development*, 1974, 39, Serial No. 155.

McGREW, P. L. Social and spatial density effects on spacing behavior in preschool children. *Journal of Child Psychology and Psychiatry*, 1970, 11, 197–205.

MARCUS, R. F., TELLEEN, S., ROKE, E., and McCARTHY, M. *A reinvestigation of the relationship between cooperation and empathy in young children*, 1978 (ERIC Document Reproduction Service No. ED 154 935).

MARSHALL, H., and HAHN, S. Experimental modification of dramatic play. *Journal of Personality and Social Psychology*, 1967, 5, 119–121.

MARTLEW, M., CONNOLLY, K., and MCLEOD, C. Language use, role and context in a five-year-old. *Journal of Child Language*, 1978, 5, 81–99.

MARTLEW, M., SMITH, P., and CONNOLLY, K. A perspective on nursery education. In W. B. Dochrell and D. Hamilton (eds.), *Rethinking Educational Research*. London: Hodder and Stoughton.

MARTON, J. P., and ACKER, L. E. *Measurement and facilitation of affectionate behaviour in the play of young children*. 1977. (ERIC Document Reproduction Service No. ED 143 428).

MILLAR, S. *The Psychology of Play*. Harmondsworth, England: Penguin, 1968.

MUELLER, E., and BRENNER, J. The origins of social skills and interactions among playgroup toddlers. *Child Development*, 1977, 48, 854–861.

NEUMANN, E. A. The elements of play. Unpublished doctoral dissertation, University of Illinois, 1971.

NICOLICH, L. M. Beyond sensorimotor intelligence: Assessment of symbolic maturity through analysis of pretend play. *Merrill-Palmer Quarterly,* 1977, *23,* 89–99.

NICOLICH, L. M. *Methodological Issues in Studying Symbolic Play,* 1978 (ERIC Document Reproduction Service No. ED 161 547).

PARTEN, M. B. Social participation among preschool children. *Journal Abnormal and Social Psychology,* 1932, *27,* 243–269.

PECK, C., APPALONI, T., COOKE, T., and RAVER, S. Teaching related preschoolers to imitate the free-play behavior of nonretarded classmates: Trained and generalized effects. *The Journal of Special Education,* 1978, *12,* 195–207.

PECK, J., and GOLDMAN, R. *The Behaviors of Kindergarten Children under Selected Conditions in the Social and Physical Environment,* 1978 (ERIC Document Reproduction Service No. ED 152 436).

PERRY, D. G., BUSSEY, K., and REDMAN, J. Reward-induced decreased play effects: Reattribution of motivation, competing responses or avoiding frustration? *Child Development,* 1977, *48,* 1369–1374.

PETERSON, N., and HARALICH, J. Integration of handicapped and nonhandicapped preschoolers: An analysis of play behavior and social interaction. *Education and Training of the Mentally Retarded,* 1977, *12,* 235–245.

PHYFE-PERKINS, E. *Children's Behavior in Preschool Settings: A Review of Research Concerning the Influence of the Physical Environment,* 1979 (ERIC Document Reproduction Service No. ED 168 722).

PIAGET, J. *The Language and Thought of the Child* (M. Gabain, trans.). New York: World Publishing, 1955.

PIAGET, J. *Play, Dreams and Imitation in Childhood.* New York: Norton, 1962.

PIAGET, J. Response to Brian Sutton-Smith. *Psychological Review,* 1966, *73,* 111–112.

PRESCOTT, E., and JONES, E. *Group Day Care as a Childrearing Environment: An Observational Study of Day Care Programs.* Pasadena, Calif.: Pacific Oaks College, 1967.

PULASKI, M. A. Play as a function of toy structure and fantasy predisposition. *Child Development,* 1970, *41,* 531–537.

QUILITCH, H. R., and RISLEY, T. The effects of play materials on social play. *Journal of Applied Behavioral Analysis,* 1973, *6,* 575–578.

ROBERTS, J., and SUTTON-SMITH, B. Child training and game involvement. *Ethnology,* 1962, *1,* 166–185.

ROPER, R., and HINDE, R. A. Social behavior in a play group: Consistency and complexity. *Child Development,* 1978, *49,* 570–579.

ROSEN, C. E. The effects of sociodramatic play on problem-solving behavior among culturally disadvantaged preschool children. *Child Development,* 1974, *45,* 920–927.

RUBIN, K. H. The social and cognitive value of preschool toys and activities. *Canadian Journal of Behavioral Science,* 1977, *9,* 382–385.

RUBIN, K. H., and MAIONI, T. L. Play preference and its relationship to egocentrism, popularity, and classification skills in preschoolers. *Merrill-Palmer Quarterly,* 1975, *25,* 171–179.

RUBIN, K. H., MAIONI, T. L., and HORNUNG, M. Free play behaviors in middle and lower class preschoolers: Parten and Piaget revisited. *Child Development*, 1976, *47*, 414–419.

RUBIN, K. H., WATSON, K. S., and JAMBOR, T. W. Free play behaviors in preschool and kindergarten children. *Child Development*, 1978, *49*, 534–536.

RUBIN, K. W., and SEIBEL, G. G. The effects of ecological setting on the cognitive and social play behaviors of preschoolers. Paper presented at the Annual Meeting of American Educational Research Association, San Francisco, 1979.

SALTZ, E., DIXON, D., and JOHNSON, J. Training disadvantaged preschoolers on various fantasy activities: Effects on cognitive functioning and impulse control. *Child Development*, 1977, *48*, 367–380.

SCHILLER, F. *Essays, Aesthetical and Philosophical.* London: George Bell, 1875.

SCHOLTZ, G. J. L., and ELLIS, M. J. Repeated exposure to objects and peers in a play setting. *Journal of Experimental Child Psychology*, 1975, *19*, 448–455.

SCHWARTZ, J. I. *Metalinguistic Awareness: A Study of Verbal Play in Young Children*, 1977 (ERIC Document Reproduction Service No. ED 149 852).

SCOTT, L. C., and GOETZ, E. M. *Memorization Tasks: Rote Learning vs. "Fun" Learning.* Washington, D.C.: Office of Education, 1978 (ERIC Document Reproduction Service No. ED 174 357).

SEARS, P. S. Doll-play aggression in normal young children: Influence of sex, age, sibling status, father's absence. *Psychological Monographs*, 1951, *65*, No. 6.

SHAPIRO, S. Preschool ecology: A study of three environmental variables. *Reading Improvement*, 1975, *12*, 236–241.

SHIRLEY, M. M. *The First Two Years.* Minneapolis: University of Minnesota Press, 1931.

SHORES, R., HESTER, P., and STRAIN, P. The effects of amount and type of teacher–child interaction on child–child interaction during free play. *Psychology In the Schools*, 1976, *13*, 171–175.

SINCLAIR, H. The transition from sensorimotor to symbolic activity. *Interchange*, 1970, *1*, 119–126.

SINGER, J. L. *The Child's World of Make-Believe.* New York: Academic Press, 1973.

SINGER, J. L., and SINGER, D. G. Fostering imaginative play in preschool children: Effects of television viewing and direct adult modeling. Paper presented at the Annual Meeting of the American Psychological Association, New Orleans, 1974.

SINGER, J. L., and SINGER, D. G. Television-viewing and imaginative play in preschoolers: A developmental and parent-intervention study. Progress Report #2. New Haven, Conn.: Yale University, 1978 (ERIC Document Reproduction Service No. 168 576).

SMILANSKY, S. *The Effects of Sociodramatic Play on Disadvantaged Preschool Children.* New York: Wiley, 1968.

SMITH, C., and LLOYD, B. Maternal behavior and perceived sex of infant: Revisited. *Child Development*, 1978, *49*, 1263–1265.

SMITH, P., DALGLIESH, M., and HERZMARK, G. *A comparison of "play" and "skills" tutoring in nursery classes.* New York: Social Science Research Council, 1978 (ERIC Document Reproduction Service No. ED 167 282).

SMITH, P. K., and CONNOLLY, K. J. Patterns of play and social interaction in preschool children. In N. B. Jones (ed.), *Ethological Studies of Child Behavior.* Cambridge: At the University Press, 1972.

SMITH, P. K., and CONNOLLY, K. J. Social and aggressive behavior in preschool children as a function of crowding. *Social Science Information*, 1976, *16*, 601–620.

SPONSELLER, D. *Play as a Learning Medium*. Washington D.C.: National Association for the Education of Young Children, 1974.

SPONSELLER, D., and JAWORSKI, A. Social and cognitive complexity in young children's the Annual Meeting of play: A longitudinal analysis. Paper presented at the Annual Meeting of the American Educational Research Association, San Francisco, 1979.

SUTTON-SMITH, B. A syntax for play and games. In B. Horton and B. Sutton-Smith (eds.), *Child's Play*. New York: Wiley, 1971.

SUTTON-SMITH, B., and ROSENBERG, J. Sixty years of historical change in games of American children. *Journal of American Folklore*, 1961, *74*, 17–46.

SYLVA, K. Play and learning. In B. Tizard and D. Harvey (eds.), *Biology of Play*. Philadelphia: Lippincott, 1977.

SYLVA, K., BRUNER, J., and GENOVA, P. The role of play in the problem-solving of children 3–5 years old. In J. Bruner, A. Jolly, and K. Sylva (eds.), *Play and Development*. New York: Basic Books, 1976.

TIZZARD, B., PHILIPS, J., and PLEWIS, I. Play measures and their relation to age, sex, and I.Q. *Journal of Child Psychology and Psychiatry*, 1976, *17*, 251–264.

TOWER, R. B., SINGER, B., SINGER, T., and BIGGS, A. Differential effects of television programming on preschoolers' cognition, imagination and social play, 1977 (ERIC Document Reproduction Service No. ED 153 713).

VAN ALSTYNE, D. *Play Behavior and Choice of Play Materials of Preschool Children*. Chicago: University of Chicago Press, 1932.

VANDELL, D. L. *The effects of a play group experience on mother–child and father–child interaction*. Bethesda, Md.: National Institute of Mental Health, 1978 (ERIC Document Reproduction Service No. ED 153 726).

VANDENBERG, B. The role of play in the development of insightful tool-using strategies. Paper presented at the Annual Meeting of the American Psychological Association, 1978 (ERIC Document Reproduction Service No. ED 102 761).

VYGOTSKY, L. S. *Thought and Language*. Cambridge, Mass.: M.I.T. Press, 1962.

VYGOTSKY, L. S. Play and its role in the mental development of the child. *Soviet Psychology*, 1967, 5, 6–18.

WADE, M. G., ELLIS, M. J., and BOHRER, R. E. Biorhythms in the activity of children during free play. *Journal of the Experimental Analysis of Behavior*, 1973, *20*, 155–162.

WATSON, M., and FISCHER, K. A developmental sequence of agent use in late infancy. *Child Development*, 1977, *48*, 828–836.

WEINSTEIN, C. S. Modifying student behavior in an open classroom through changes in physical design. *American Educational Research Journal*, 1977, *14*, 249–262.

WEIR, R. *Language in the Crib*. The Hague: Mouton, 1962.

WITT, P. A., and GRAMZA, A. F. Position effects in play equipment preferences of nursery school children: Springfield: Illinois State Department of Mental Health, 1969 (ERIC Document Reproduction Service No. ED 045 185).

WOLFGANG, C. *Helping Aggressive and Passive Preschoolers Through Play*. Columbus, Ohio: Charles E. Merrill, 1977.

WUELLNER, L. H. Gross activity of children at play. Internal report, Motor Performance and Play Research Laboratory, Children's Research Center, University of Illinois, 1970.

YAWKEY, T., and SILVERN, S. An investigation of imaginative play and language growth in five, six, and seven-year-old children. Paper presented at the Annual Meeting of the American Educational Research Association, San Francisco, 1979.

ZSCHEYE, R. C. The interaction between play and self-concept in young children. Unpublished doctoral dissertation, University of California, 1976.

CHAPTER 11

The Acquisition of Written Language in Young Children

Judith A. Schickedanz

PERHAPS NOTHING has been discussed and debated as frequently or as fervently in educational circles as the topic of how children come to comprehend and create written language, that is, how they learn to read and write. The time and space devoted to this topic indicate its importance in the goal structure of our schools and society as well as its failure to yield to simple probes into its mysteries.

Much research in the area of reading has investigated the effects of various instructional methods used in beginning reading: the language experience approach versus phonics, linguistic readers versus basals, the initial teaching alphabet versus the standard alphabet, and so on. These investigations, however, have yielded little information about the best way to teach children to read: "Regardless of the quantity of research . . . there are no definitive answers to the question of the best program because the results of various studies support different programs, and nothing conclusive can be shown about which programs are superior" (Farr & Roser, 1979, p. 426).

It should be acknowledged, however, that several large studies, in which many individual studies of instructional methods have been surveyed or in which their results have been analyzed as a group, have found small but significant differences in favor of methods emphasizing some kind of systematic phonics instruction (Chall, 1967; Bond & Dykstra, 1967; Guthrie & Tyler, 1978). A recent study of this type also found the sound-symbol method to be superior over other methods (Pflaum et al., 1980). In addition, however, the study found that experimental treatments *regardless of method* produced higher achievement than control methods. The researchers urged caution about their results. The significant effect found for sound-symbol methods could have been "due to chance in the testing of many effects" (Pflaum et al., 1980, p. 18). Others (Guthrie, 1981) have pointed out that competing explanations were not adequately discounted and that the results could have been due to higher learning time for students in some programs, unusual teacher characteristics, a better match between teaching and testing in experimental programs, and differences in pace and task selection.

It appears, then, that this line of inquiry is beset with problems and yields conflicting results. Because the question of which method is best has generally proved to be an unproductive one, this review will not provide any discussion of research specifically aimed at comparing instructional methods used in beginning reading. Instead, I will concentrate on research and clinical observations that have attempted to understand reading in terms of basic psychological and linguistic processes and/or have tried to determine what concepts about written language young children bring with them to formal reading instruction and what experiences contribute to their development.

Young Children's Knowledge about the Features of Print

It has often been assumed that children know little or nothing about written language before they receive formal instruction in school. Evidence indicates, however, that children do have extensive knowledge of some aspects of written language.

Many preschoolers have knowledge about the graphic features of print. They know that the features of lines used in print are different from lines used to make pictures or other nonprint configurations. The features contrasted in one study of three- to six-and-one-half-year-olds were pictures versus writing, linear versus nonlinear arrangement of units, internally varied versus repetitive sequences of units, and multiple units versus single units (Lavine, 1977). Still other displays contained Roman or cursive letters and words, artifical letters (configurations with the features of real letters, but not real letters), Hebrew letters, a Mayan design, and Chinese characters.

Even the youngest children distinguished between pictures and writing, though they often labeled as writing nonpictorial displays that were not writing, basing judgments on gross features of the displays, such as linearity, variety of units, and multiplicity of units. The older children tended to base judgments on actual features of individual units within a display rather than on features of the total display. Thus, the more that units in the display resembled actual letters occurring in the child's environment, the greater the tendency for the display to be labeled as writing, regardless of the display's general characteristics.

A similar developmental trend has been found in studies of preschool children's productions of writing. Two early studies found roughly four stages of development (Hildreth, 1936; Legrun, 1932). First, scribbles became horizontal rather than aimless or basically circular. Then displays became linear and jagged, suggesting knowledge of both linearity and multiplicity of units as features of writing. In stage three, features of real letters, such as straight, curved, or intersecting lines, but no actual letters, were found. Stage four was characterized by

Figure 11-1.   Illustration of Early Understandings of Print by Children Exposed to Different Orthographics.

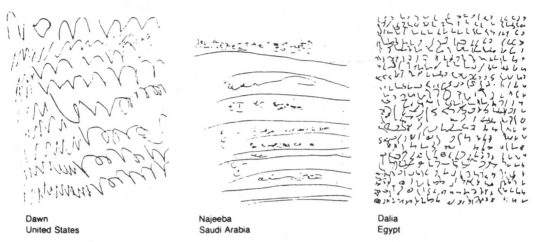

| Dawn | Najeeba | Dalia |
| United States | Saudi Arabia | Egypt |

Source: Harste and Carey (1979), p. 7. Reprinted by permission of the authors and Indiana University, School of Education.

the appearance of actual letters, or good approximations to these. In summary, development moved from representation of overall characteristics of print to representations of the distinctive features of letters.

In a recent study (Harste & Carey, 1979), four-year-olds were instructed to "write everything you can write." The productions of three children are shown in Figure 11-1. Each child's scribble resembled the writing system to which the child had been exposed most frequently, even though no child's sample contained real units of print. Nejeeba, the child attempting to write Arabic, told the researcher that Arabic uses "a lot more dots than English" (1979, p. 6).

This research indicates that before children receive formal instruction in reading and writing, and often before they accurately name letters or recognize words, they abstract features of writing from the print they encounter from exposure to print provided in their everyday environments (Gibson & Levin, 1975).

Knowledge of Reading Processes and Functions

Young children may, of course, differentiate among graphic displays, that is, determine visually some of its properties, but not understand how to use it or what purposes it serves. For example, children who can detect differences in pictorial and print displays and label one writing and not the other may point to pictures rather than print in a storybook when indicating what the reader looks at. In short, children may recognize print versus nonprint but know nothing of the reading process.

Some research has indicated that young children know little about what a reader does or what the reading process entails. Two studies of five-year-olds

(Reid, 1966; Downing, 1970), for example, demonstrated that many children did not know what adults do when they read or that words rather than pictures in books are what one reads. Research by Hiebert (1981), however, suggests that many preschoolers may know more than earlier research has revealed. Early studies posed questions in abstract situations rather than in more concrete contextualized situations where children could show rather than tell what they know. In addition, the children studied previously may not have been provided opportunities to interact with print in their daily lives.

In Hiebert's study, understanding of the reading process was measured by three tasks. In one, the researcher read silently and orally from a book and also stared silently at an object. Children were asked to name each activity performed by the researcher. The second task asked children to read a "secret message" (a page of text). This stimulus was used to ask children about their reading ability and to infer their understanding of the reading process if they attempted to "read" the page. The third task used several books: (1) one with pictures and text; (2) one with pictures only; (3) one with text only; and (4) one with blank pages. Children were asked if each book could be read by someone who could read and if yes, what such a reader would look at. These tasks were designed to reveal children's basic ideas about reading, such as whether reading requires speaking while looking at a book or can be done silently and whether print versus pictures are what one looks at to read.

Hiebert (1981) also investigated preschoolers' understanding of the functions of writing. Story situations were used. For example, children were shown Christmas packages and asked how one would know to which family member each package was to be given. Each package was tagged with a name label. If the child did not refer to this label, he or she was asked who it was for. Three stories used a model town complete with buildings, street signs, road signs, and toy cars. One of these presented two cars approaching an intersection. Children were asked how the drivers would know what to do to avoid a crash. A fifth story used materials and directions for a children's game. The experimenter explained that children wanted to play this new game but did not know how. Was there a way they could find out?

Between three and five years of age, children's concepts about reading processes and functions increase significantly, and in this middle class sample greater gains occurred between three and four than between four and five. These changes apparently occurred as a result of informal encounters with print in the course of everyday events. While all sixty subjects were enrolled in a nursery school or daycare center, neither offered any formal reading instruction.

Additional evidence that preschool children develop knowledge about reading processes or about what one does while reading comes from studies of children's story-reading behavior. Doake (1979) and Rossman (1980), for example, found that the preschool children they studied (very small numbers in both cases) increased their awareness over time that readers look at the text when they read, and that reading involves looking at print in a book, not just saying words of a story that you know while looking at the pictures.

Knowledge of Characteristics of Words

Young children may know that one looks at words (that is, print) to read and that reading serves a variety of purposes, but not what characteristics distinguish a word from other segments of print, or how to determine if a print display shown to them is a word or something that does not qualify as a word.

In a study by Pick et al. (1978), children were presented print displays on white cards. Word displays included single-letter words (I, a), long letter strings (hippopotamus), short letter strings likely to be unfamiliar to the children (obtuse, bias), and fifteen five-letter words (field, tooth, color). Nonword displays included single letters (e, u); two long letter strings (dgobrcifhtp and federabilia); fifteen five-letter pronounceable clusters (teank, tason); ten four-letter consonant clusters (mptc, hywv); ten strings of misoriented letters, of which five could be words (ᴘoꟻM) and five that could not (ᴄꞮⱶ); four groups of meaningful initials (ABC, USA); four vowel clusters (aiue); and five pronounceable clusters that sounded like real words (teer, fre). Variables contrasted were length of a letter string, whether a string was an actual word, vowel and consonant strings only versus strings with both consonant and vowels, letter orientation, and meaning. The subjects were twenty-three three- and four-year-old nursery school children, eighteen five-year-old nursery school children, seventeen kindergarten children, older by one-half year than the oldest nursery school children; sixteen first-grade children, and thirteen second and third grade children. Children were asked to sort the cards into those that had words and those that did not.

Younger nursery school children were significantly more likely than older nursery school children to accept single letters as words, whether they were words or not. The preschool children also accepted a higher percentage of the very long letter strings as words. This tendency decreased with age, with the oldest children accepting very long strings only when these were real words. The percentage of vowel-only and consonant-only clusters accepted as words decreased with age, with significant differences occurring both between nursery school and kindergarten and kindergarten and first grade. Acceptance of strings containing misoriented letters as words was high in the youngest nursery school children, but declined significantly between the nursery and kindergarten groups and again between kindergarten and first grade groups. Acceptance of pronouncable nonwords that sounded like meaningful words decreased between nursery school and kindergarten and between first and second grade, but even the oldest children still accepted a large percentage of them as words (51 percent were accepted by first graders). Acceptance of pronounceable clusters that were not meaningful declined with age, with sharp declines between kindergarten and first grade and between first grade and second grade.

These results indicate that before the beginning of formal instruction in reading, children begin to understand something about word structure. Between kindergarten and first grade when formal instruction has still been somewhat minimal, substantial gains are also made. The youngest children were more likely to classify both single letters and letter strings as words. But by five, children knew that words generally are composed of several letters and that letters and words are different entities. Older children also rejected very long strings, unless they were real words, indicating that they knew a word is not defined simply by a string of letters, but by internal characteristics of the string as well, such as the arrangement of the letters and whether when sounded out they result in a meaningful word. Similarly, by kindergarten age, children more and more rejected strings that were all vowels or all consonants, indicating again that they knew that wordness is determined by characteristics within the letter strings—that there are permissible strings and nonpermissible strings. A letter string by itself does not constitute wordness. Finally, as children got older, particularly between kindergarten and first grade, they rejected letter strings that were pronounceable but meaningless, as well as pronounceable nonwords that were meaningful, with the former showing the stronger decline. Apparently, as children get older they use their ability to sound out strings, as well as their knowledge of how words look (what combinations of letters are permissible), to judge wordness. If sounding out results in a meaningful word, they are likely to judge that the letter string is a word.

Other studies and clinical observations have yielded similar results. When matching speech to print in storybooks, for example, the youngest and/or least experienced preschoolers often point to individual letters as if each were a word or syllable (Schickedanz, 1981).

Frosty the Snowman (print display in book)

Fros ty the Snow man (child's verbalization and finger-pointing)

Older or more experienced preschoolers more often attempt to read by responding to clusters of letters marked by space (words), although a word, as distinct from a syllable, *in speech* may still not be known to them (Doake, 1979; Schickedanz, 1980; Morris, 1980).

Frosty the Snowman (print display in book)

Fros ty the Snow man (child's verbalization and finger-pointing)

Additional evidence comes from a second study by Hiebert (1978) in which children between three and four-and-one-half, shown cards in context (slides of words on food containers, traffic signs, and so on) and out of context (the same words printed on cards which were then photographed), were asked, "What might this say?" Confusion between letters and words should have caused children to respond to single word displays with multiword responses. Yet, a high percentage of the responses for both in-context and out-of-context displays consisted of single words. Most children knew how to make correct printed word to spoken word correspondences, indicating that they knew, at minimum, that words consist of letter clusters—single letters are not words.

Even kindergarten and first grade children, however, cannot accurately determine what a printed word is when asked to respond to various print displays. Meltzer and Herse (1969) asked kindergarten and first grade children to use scissors to cut off words from printed sentences. Children sometimes cut off one word, sometimes two, and sometimes only part of a word, indicating that they did not judge words in a line of print as clusters of letters set off from other clusters by space. The difference between the performance of these children and younger children who accurately point to individual printed words when reading storybooks could be due to their inability to monitor the print by using knowledge of what it said. In short, being able to detect individual words in print or in speech may be facilitated when the child knows what the print presented says. Getting the match between speech (what the child knows the print says) and print (what says it) to come out right (using both simultaneously) can serve as a monitor to judge what constitutes a word in both speech and print.

Support for this hypothesis comes from a study of children just finishing the first month of school (Morris, 1980). Children were first taught a short poem orally. Then the researcher read the first line aloud and pointed along each word. Then the child was asked to finger-point and read the second, third, and fourth lines, which were framed with index cards. After each line was read, the examiner pronounced two target words within the line and asked the child to locate these. Next, the examiner and the child read the entire poem together twice as the examiner pointed to each word. The examiner then pointed to individual words within the poem and asked the child to pronounce them. Finally, the printed poem was taken away, and the child was asked to pronounce six words isolated from the text, one at a time. The four measures of word concepts were ability to: (1) point to words as one reads aloud; (2) recognize specific words within one line; (3) recognize specific words anywhere in the poem; and (4) recognize sight words. Although there was a wide range in success on these tasks, many children performed well, indicating that they could isolate words in both speech and print.

Still other evidence of young children's understanding of word structure comes from their attempts to create words with manipulative alphabet materials or by writing rather than from their judgments about wordness in terms of displays of print presented to them. Research and clinical observations reveal that preschool children may at first string letters together at random to make words. Such behavior often occurs spontaneously as children play with alphabet materials. The child tells the adult that the creation is a "word" and even labels it, or the child may ask the adult, "What does this word say?" (Schickedanz, 1979; Pick et al., 1978). At this stage, the child seems to know that words are composed of more than one unit (words are made of letter strings), but not that such strings are organized in specific ways internally. Absent are visual criteria for permissible letter combinations, as well as any notion that the sequence of letters in a printed word must be related to the sequence of sounds in the spoken word. When the letter realization dawns on children, they may give up visual criteria of wordness used earlier and rely on phonetic relationships when creating words even if knowledge of letter-sound relationships is limited to only one element of the word.

Henderson (1980) has designated a preliterate phonetic stage of spelling in which *dog* is spelled D or DJ, and candy, K or KDE, by different children. What is common to all spellings for a given word at this stage is that letters selected to spell it must bear some phonetic relationship to the spoken word. What is different about various spellings is that at times children have used just one letter to spell the word, while at other times they have used more than one letter.

It is impossible to know from Henderson's data if different children consistently used one strategy and not the other of if the same children used both strategies on different occasions. If they did not know how to represent more than one sound, they may have used only one letter rather than violate their knowledge that when making words, letters must be selected with this criterion in mind. Instead, they may have violated their knowledge that words consist of more than one letter.

Children lacking knowledge of phonetic relationships may use longer letter strings to make words because they judge wordness on the basis of characteristics they have obtained merely from seeing words: words are letter strings. Without phonetic constraints as a guide, stringing may get out of hand. In addition, if the child does not know that words in a line of print are surrounded by space, then exposure to printed text, as opposed to single words such as names or traffic signs, may lead them to believe that words can be very long. In addition, the number of letters used to make a particular word may be influenced by knowledge of the object whose name is spelled. Papandropoulou and Sinclair (1974) and Berthoud-Papandropoulou (1978), for example, found that preschool children often justified a word's length in terms of characteristics of its referent, not in terms of the necessity to match print to length of utterance. *Crocodile* is longer than *cat* because crocodiles are longer than cats. *Typewriter* is long because typewriters have lots of letters. Children who make judgments based on these criteria must know a little about the actual determinants of word structure, particularly that a printed word is related to its spoken counterpart.

Apparently, knowing that a printed word is related to the spoken word in a specific way—that letters used to make a word must represent sounds in the spoken word—is a late development for many children. Henderson (1980) has suggested that the preliterate phonetic stage (D or DJ is used to spell dog) emerges by late kindergarten or beginning first grade. The second stage, called letter name strategy stage (a phonetic strategy which includes the use of letters whose names say a phoneme to represent that phoneme), emerges by mid-first grade. More complicated and sophisticated phonetic strategies appear by grade two and beyond. However, Read (1975) has reported preschool children as young as three-and-one-half using phonetic strategies. Bissex (1980), in a case study of her son, reports such behavior beginning at five. (Before this age, her son used letter strings not phonetically organized to create messages.)

The early emergence of phonetic strategies to create words in some preschool children seems to be related to the print-rich environments these children were reared in (Read, 1975; Bissex, 1980). The ingredients for precocious development seem clear: printed materials of various kinds; materials for creating print of one's own; adult mediation of print in the environment such as naming letters, writing the child's name, and modeling reading and writing; reading to children; answering the child's questions; and allowing the child wide latitude in exploring how words are created.

Variations in documentation of children's knowledge of wordness appear to have two major sources: (1) variations in the populations studied; and (2) differences in definitions or aspects of wordness and methodologies used to study these. In summary, we can say only that some older preschool and kindergarten children seem to know something about what distinguishes words from non-words, using both visual and meaning criteria (with meaning judged by sounding out letter sequences to determine if it is familiar), and that some older preschool and kindergarten children have general notions about criteria one must use to create words. But many children do not have such knowledge even upon entry into, or completion of, first grade. They do not know a letter from a word or how words are constructed either by visual criteria or in relation to the spoken words they represent. Without it, they are likely to be confused by reading instruction.

Knowledge of Speech at the Level of the Phoneme

Speech may be represented in writing in a number of ways, for example, at the word or syllable level. English orthography is based on representation of smaller segments: it is alphabetic. The linguistic unit represented by letters is the individual phoneme or sound. To use such a system, a reader must be able to segment and analyze oral language at the phonemic level. Researchers have tried to determine if young children can do this. The research indicates that analysis at the phonemic level is extremely difficult for the preschool and kindergarten age child.

Liberman et al. (1974) asked nursery, kindergarten, and first grade children to repeat a word or sound spoken by the researcher and to tap on the table with a dowel the number of segments contained in the stimulus item. Nursery school children could not segment stimuli into phonemes, although about half could segment words into syllables. About one fifth of the kindergarten children could segment by phonemes, while about half could segment by syllables. About 70 percent of the first graders (completing first grade) could segment by phonemes, and 90 percent could segment by syllables.

Other researchers have also indicated that young children cannot analyze speech at the phonemic level (Calfee, Chapman & Venezky, 1972; Savin, 1972) and that this inability is related to difficulty in learning to read (Savin, 1972; Golinkoff, 1978; Fox & Routh, 1975; Morris, 1980; Singer, 1979). Without the ability to segment at the phonemic level, that is, to hear three segments in *bat*, it would be difficult to know how speech is mapped onto an alphabetic orthography that provides one letter for each sound.

The major difficulty in segmenting speech into phonemes seems to arise because there is no distinct acoustic segment which marks phonemes. "In *bat*, for example, the initial and final consonants are, in the conversion to sound, folded into the medial vowel, with the result that information about successive segments is transmitted more or less simultaneously on the same parts of the sound" (Liberman et al., 1974, p. 203–204). Syllables, in contrast, are marked by a "peak of acoustic energy" (Liberman et al., 1974, p. 204). Our perception that words consist of distinct sounds is not as much a matter of perceptual reality (Savin & Bever, 1970) as it is of conceptual development. We come to *think* of words in terms of individual sound segments, though they do not exist in "physical" reality. Although some children arrive at this basic insight before they receive formal reading instruction, most children develop it only after exposure to formal reading instruction (Ehri & Wilce, 1979; Golinkoff, 1978). The insight escapes a few children even after considerable instruction, and many of these children have great difficulty in learning to read.

The absence of this insight is not due to faulty auditory or speech perception (Savin, 1972). A child who detects that the words *bad* and *bat* sound different, may not be able to segment each into three parts and say in which segment the difference occurs (Liberman et al., 1974). The problem is centered more on becoming aware of analysis in speech at a level that is tied to printed letters: it involves knowing how to map speech to print (Menyuk, 1976). Conscious analysis at this level would not be necessary or useful if our orthography were not alphabetic. Experience with speech alone, even speech organized to highlight differences at the phoneme level (exercises involving rhyming words, alliteration, or substitutions of initial consonants), may not be enough. The idea of phonemes may not emerge in any concrete way unless the child is confronted with print and must find a use for all of the letters that make up the child's name or the words in a line of text in a favorite storybook.

> Print freezes the continuous stream of speech into perceptually manipulable blocks and begins to pull a child's tacit knowledge about words to the surface where an explicit understanding can begin to develop.
>
> Print appears to play a crucial but paradoxical role in turning the transparency of spoken language into the opaqueness of an object that can be studied—paradoxical because print is supposed to be a second order abstraction from reality, with spoken language being a first order abstraction. Logically, it would appear that print would be more difficult to grasp conceptually than spoken language. If we assume that to understand print entails a fairly elaborate explanation of its characteristics and function, then print may indeed be more difficult. If on the other hand we admit the virtues of tacit knowledge, then we see where print, by being a common and fairly stable symbolic system in the environment, draws the young child's attention toward the abstract symbolic structure of language [Templeton, 1980, p. 30].

The same monitoring of speech used to find word segments corresponding to each letter cluster marked by space when following along a known story or poem text could lead ultimately to monitoring of speech to find segments that correspond to each letter within the cluster making a word. Solving this puzzle, or realizing that it is a puzzle needing a solution, would seem to lead a child to the needed discovery.

In Morris's (1980) study, there was a significant correlation between locating individual words in a poem known orally and performing successfully on a phoneme segmentation test. Knowing what words in print are and locating them were related to the ability to segment speech into phonemes. We can only speculate that being able to match words in speech to words in print is a necessary step in the development of the ability to segment speech into phonemes and match these to letters within a word.

Oral knowledge of the text may be able to force changes in our understandings about print (for example, that more than one letter must be used to form words), and understandings of print (knowing that space separates letter clusters that are words) may be able to force changes in understandings about language (all syllable-length segments are not words; all of the letters within each word must correspond to speech segments smaller than the syllable).

Ability to Read Unfamiliar Text

This review would be incomplete without a brief discussion of children who learn to read before they begin formal instruction. Reports of these children have been provided by Durkin (1966), Plessas and Oakes (1964), Sutton (1964), Krippner (1963), Torrey (1969), Forester (1977), Doake (1979), and Witty and Coomer (1955). For the most part, parents of such children did not set out to teach their children to read. (This is why we see labels such as "spontaneous" and "natural" used to designate these children.) In virtually all cases, however, children have come from print-rich environments. Being read to frequently was an experience common to almost all of these children. In addition, environmental print (traffic signs and food containers, for instance) was interpreted by parents and read to the children. These children were also given materials such as paper and pencils or crayons, chalkboards, and manipulative alphabet materials. Finally, their parents responded to questions and requests. Parents also read the same stories over and over, pointed out words when the child asked "Where does it say——?," provided appropriate demonstrations when children asked, for example, "How does an 'e' go?," and provided the letters when asked "How do you spell——?" While not setting out to teach children to read and not doing so in a formal way, the parents, nevertheless, provided essential experiences.

Implications of Research for Practice

It is difficult to translate research findings into suggestions for practice. Most of the research tells us what children can and cannot do, but little about what determines these abilities. In addition, we know little about how some of these concepts and abilities are related to each other or what other concepts and abilities, as yet unknown, are also critical. Despite these limitations, some tentative decisions can be made about practices that may be promising, and related issues can be considered.

The Use of Formal versus Informal Methods

Because some preschool and kindergarten children have considerable knowledge about written language before receiving formal instruction, some researchers have claimed that learning to read is "natural," as natural as learning to speak (Smith, 1971, 1974, 1977; Goodman & Goodman, 1977; Huey, 1908). Others (Samuels, 1976; Gleitman, 1979; Gleitman & Rozin, 1977) claim that learning to read is not "natural" because most children become readers only after specific tutoring. Learning to speak is natural, but learning to read is different, they claim. Perhaps both views are incorrect: perhaps learning to read is not different from learning to speak, and perhaps neither occurs "naturally."

The frequency with which a behavior occurs does not necessarily indicate anything about the basis for its development. We cannot assume, simply because oral language acquisition is almost universal, that it is innate or "natural," developing without environmental supports, or even instruction of a sort. Assuming that environmental supports for language are virtually universal—robust and redundant—the universality of language acquisition may depend not only on characteristics of the child but also on the environment. Because these characteristics have become commonplace, we fail to recognize their contribution and believe that language acquisition is "natural."

An instructive illustration of this point is provided by Fraiberg's (1975) work with blind infants with retarded motor development.

> In normal development when control of the trunk is achieved in stable sitting posture, there is a smooth transition to bridging and creeping. In our sample, most of our babies achieved stability in sitting well within the range of sighted babies. Most of our babies demonstrated the ability to support themselves on hands and knees within the range for sighted babies. Then, something that should appear on the developmental timetable did not appear. The baby did not creep!
>
> Since locating and reaching a toy on sound cues are the only ways in which the blind child can find equivalence for reaching and attaining an object on sight, there was no motive for reach. The sighted child, in the same posture, will reach for the out-of-reach toy which propels him forward. It is the visual incentive that initiates the creeping pattern. . . .
>
> At every point where vision would normally intervene to promote a new phase in locomotor development we had to help the baby find an adaptive solution. The prone position, for example, is not an "interesting" position for the blind baby. The sighted baby spends long periods in prone, with head elevated, "just looking around." The blind baby, without such incentives, may resist the prone position. We build in "interest" in prone through speaking to the baby, through dangle toys or other devices. . . .
>
> Practicing pulling to stand and cruising will be "more interesting" in the familiar space of a playpen with favorite toys offering sound-touch incentives [Fraiberg, 1975, p. 48].

Even motor development, typically thought to be controlled by genetic or maturational factors, is dependent on objects and people that are approached with the guidance of vision in sighted children. These supports are so abundant in most children's environments that it takes a study of visually impaired children to make us aware of their role.

Extensive research has recently been conducted on the effects of adult language on infant language development (Snow & Ferguson, 1977). Adult linguistic input is often extensive, and the quality of the adult language (responsiveness to the infant, appropriateness of the adult's language to the infant's level of development, and so on) influences the infant's language development.

Evidence that written language acquisition occurs without formal instruction only when appropriate social and physical environments are provided comes from almost every study of children who have learned to read before they received formal instruction in school. Most of these children had extensive experience with print and tools for creating it, as well as interactions with parents who answered their children's questions, modeled reading, and read to them frequently. The fact that parents did not set out to teach their children to read and to write, and were often not aware that they were doing so, does not mean that they did not provide crucial experiences and supports. The evidence suggests that they did.

The term "natural" is not very useful. We might be wiser to think of the "given" characteristics of children as "invariant functions," to borrow an idea and terminology from Piaget (1954). What is "given" are modes of adaptation or particular orientations to circumstances. The structure of intelligence, or what we come to know, is created or constructed through interactions between the child and the environment. Knowledge construction in a particular domain depends on access to experiences out of which that kind of knowledge can be created. Without such access, a "natural" learner cannot come to know.

All environments, no matter how commonplace, are contrived—they *could* be different. Experiences relating to some kinds of knowledge such as number, space, and classification are so redundant, however, that universal acquisition of concepts could occur without adults being aware that they and the physical environment have made a contribution. The same may be said for oral language, but with a difference: a strong social environment would also be required. We need not look far to find children who have few or no books in their homes, no adults who read to them or respond positively to their questions, and no pencils or crayons and paper on which to attempt to write. The current disparities in the occurrence of oral and written language in the population may be due to disparities in the universal availability of environments that support each.

If written language acquisition is similar to oral language acquisition in the way suggested, then we must do more than wait for it to emerge "naturally." We probably need not employ the "formal" instructional programs currently used in many primary grade classrooms. But "informal approaches" to reading instruction cannot be devoid of contact with print in context. Exposure to print experiences—actually, involvement in print experiences—can be incidental, but not accidental. Environments that are robust and reduntant with print experiences must be deliberately contrived.

We must adopt the processes as well as the content of effective parental practices. The practice of reading stories to young children, for example, often distorts and makes ineffective the parental reading situation. Parents read to individual children or to two or three who are in their lap or sitting close; teachers read to groups of children sitting at a distance. Parents allow children to select the book to be read and reread the same book over and over again, both at the same sitting and over a period of weeks or months; teachers often select the book that is to be read and read it once at each sitting and infrequently in the course of a week or month. Parents allow children to turn the pages, pause to look at pictures or to ask questions, and read along if they wish. Teachers, on the other hand, are more likely to set the pace, turn the pages, and discourage reading along during the story episode. Parents keep their children's books accessible over a number of years; teachers often keep books out of children's reach, particularly if the books have been obtained from a library, and they return borrowed books promptly, allowing children little long-term access.

It is not easy to employ the informal methods used by effective parents, and it may be unrealistic to think that they can be adopted completely. We need to study exactly what effective parents do and then think carefully about how essential features of these practices can be adapted to classrooms. In the meantime, we must not assume that parents who say they do not teach their children to read in fact do not. The evidence denies this, although the methods they use differ significantly from those typically used in schools.

Simplifying Complex Situations for Naïve Learners

Formal reading instruction typically involves the teaching of isolated skills in a predetermined sequence. These procedures are based on the notions that reading must be simplified if children are to understand it and that learning is primarily linear, a matter of gradually building up associations until everything comes together.

Arguments against using reductionist simplification strategies are often based on evidence that some children learn to read before receiving such instruction and that these instances demonstrate that no simplification is necessary and may even be a hindrance.

At issue here are basic assumptions about knowledge. The direct teaching of subskills assumes that knowledge exists in external reality and that learning is a matter of getting what is "out there" into children's heads. However, a different assumption about knowledge is that it exists neither in external reality nor within the learner, but rather is constructed through interactions between the two. If knowledge is derived from actions on objects or experiences, then a learner must be placed in a situation where such acting can occur.

Phonemes do not exist as perceptible units of separate sounds. They "cannot be segmented physically because the acoustic properties of formants of any letter in a syllable are spread across the entire syllable" (Singer, 1979, p. 111). Our knowledge of distinct sounds does not exist as such in objective reality but is constructed somehow from interactions with speech and print. The problem with much subskill instruction as practiced is that it makes an erroneous assumption about the nature of this knowledge. "Sounds" are regarded as "out there" and objective, something children can "hear." When teachers talk about the "sounds" that certain letters make, they may know what they mean, but many children don't.

One reason why children who learn to read with holistic methods before they enter school usually become such good readers may be because they have access to experiences that are complex enough that essential knowledge about the reading process can be derived. But we should not jump too quickly to the assumption that no simplification of the reading situation has been provided. The simplification, however, is not reductionist. A discussion of learning in other areas will serve as an introduction to a discussion of the kind of simplification that may occur.

A complicated form box frustrates children one or one-and-one-half years old. We provide simple form boxes at first (fewer holes and pieces). We give children one-piece puzzles at first, too, not ten-piece puzzles. If we misjudge a young child's ability to interact with such materials, however, or if for some reason the child selects a toy too complex, we usually comment on the baby's behavior in sentences such as "He likes to open the lid and put all of the shapes in and then dump them out again," or "Wooden objects are great for teething," or "Look, he likes to put his fingers through the holes in the lid and then pull it up to see them sticking through the other side." In short, we change our expectations and behavior in relation to the baby and the objects, and the baby copes with the physical objects by doing much more with them than was intended by their designers. And baby, or even an older child in a similar situation, does not become frustrated with being unable to perform the intended task "correctly" because no one demands that it be performed in a certain "fluent" way. In short, we commonly accommodate or "simplify" situations for children by allowing them to *add* behaviors that are not an essential part of the task for those more experienced.

In addition, parents often add something to the situation to keep it within the child's realm of experience and ability. We add training wheels to bicycles and thickness to the diameters of pencils and the pages of infant picture books. Perhaps most important, we add social interaction that provides redundancy. This may be especially true of the language we use with very young children (Snow, 1978; Moerk, 1974): "What's this? Yes, that's your nose. What's this? Yes, that's your mouth. What are these? Uh-huh, those are your eyes. Where are *my* eyes? Yes, those are my eyes. Where's my nose?" These additions simplify situations, but they do not destroy the essential nature of language, puzzles, bicycles, form boxes, or whatever. They allow children to construct essential knowledge—knowledge perhaps unattainable unless children can act on the "whole ball of wax."

These informal observations and speculations suggest that we might start children on the course of understanding written language by providing "real" reading experiences, but with supports not needed by the mature reader. If we consider storybooks, for example, redundancy is added in a number of ways: rhyme and repetition of phrases make learning the story line easy, pictures support the text and serve as clues to what a page says, and the adult's social behavior of reading the story again and again gives the child a way of knowing what the print says without having had to decipher it. Storybooks seem to fit perfectly the criteria for simplification suggested earlier: (1) reductions in complexity, such as little text, few pages, and uncomplicated plots, do not result in distortion of the essential characteristics of written language; and (2) other simplifications are additions or redundancies, both physical and social. In addition, the situation can be simplified by other additions that consist of information provided by interactions with the adult: "We must start at the front, not the back, of the book"; "move your finger; you're covering the words and I can't see to read them"; "wait a minute; I haven't finished reading that page yet"; "yes, Max does have a wolf suit on just like it says right here"; "you have to point to each word as you say a word, not to each letter, like this." Finally, the child's knowledge of the story, obtained from having heard it read, provides an important means for discovering mysteries of print—it becomes a monitoring device as was discussed earlier.

Many aspects of reading may be understood only when approached in this manner, for they are complicated rules, not surface structure information. But we will probably not be served well by thinking in dichotomies that suggest that we must simplify situations by cutting them apart or that we must keep them totally complex. Experiences of the sort described above might be called *simplified complexities*. We need to create and use these in beginning reading instruction.

Written Language Learning Is a Developmental Process of Developing Rules or Generalizations

> The roots of literacy are growing strongly long before schools begin instruction.
>
> Children learn that print represents meaning. They learn general and specific meanings of specific print sequences in situational contexts: stop signs, cereal boxes, toothpaste cartons. At the same time, children develop some awareness of the form of print: directionality, letter names, key features. They distinguish print from pictures. They can handle books and know the basic function of books, letters, newspapers.
>
> Literacy development in school needs to be built on this base. It must be seen as an extension of natural development [Goodman, 1979, p. 661].

Literacy development in schools is often not based on "natural" development because the reading behaviors children present upon entrance are not recognized as the precursors of skilled performance in reading and writing. Traditional diagnostic tools often require all-or-none responses: accurate naming of letters *or* inaccurate naming, letters written in correct orientation *or* errors in orientation, and so on. Most standardized tests are based on reductionist principles that assume precursors of final knowledge to be recognizable, perfect pieces of final knowledge. Errors indicate deficiencies—the absence of specific pieces of knowledge. An *F* faces to the right, not to the left.

A different view assumes precursors to be qualitatively different from, but nevertheless related to, the final forms of knowledge. The qualitative differences are due to the use of different generalizations or rules to organize and manipulate the surface structures of various aspects of language. Errors in this view do not indicate the absence of knowledge but rather the presence of different knowledge.

With respect to letter orientation, for example, we can assume that in the beginning many reversals are due to application of a generalization children bring with them from experience with the three-dimensional world: orientation is irrelevant to naming objects; therefore, letters may face any direction, and indeed they do in children's early writing. Somewhat later, children realize that orientation of two-dimensional symbols is meaningful. They then seek rules for orientation by observing letters themselves. If almost all of the left-right asymmetrical letters face right (B,D,E,L, and so on), then all left-right asymmetrical letters must face right, even the J, which, of course is an exception (Watt and Jacobs, 1975).

This behavior is similar to a child's assumptions about inflections in oral language: if the past tense of most verbs is formed by adding *ed*, then the past tense of all verbs must be formed in this way, the child reasons. The result is the creation of words such as *teached, runned, swinged,* and so on. When such errors are assumed to be failures to make discriminations rather than to be applications of different rules, teachers assume children cannot *see* orientation, that they are unable to perceive it. Training in seeing is often provided, and children are told to look carefully at their writing. But when teachers assume instead that children can see orientation, but have not mastered general rules and their exceptions—that the problem is one of *knowing*, not perceiving—training in visual discrimination is not provided. Indeed, the problem isn't seen as a problem in need of training at all. It is assumed that these errors will be corrected as children use print more and more just as errors in oral language are corrected. Instructional activities provided are thus less specific and trivial, and more meaningful and comprehensive.

Errors due to application of different underlying rules by children can also be seen in their early spellings (invented spellings). Children's early categories of sounds are not identical to the categories used by adults. For example, they typically spell words containing *tr* with the letters *ch* because the *t* preceeding an *r* is affricated just as *ch* is. If this phonetic feature, rather than place of articulation, is used as the basis for categorizing sounds, then *tr* will be considered more closely related to *ch* than to *t* as in *toy* or *top.* In other words, our categories of phonemes—the distinct sounds we recognize in standard spelling—are not the same as the young child's. Specific developmental stages have been documented for phonological development and its impact on how children spell words which they do not know by sight (Henderson, 1980; Read, 1975).

In addition, young children generally assume that spelling is phonetic. They have yet to understand that phonetic relations are often violated in standard spelling in order to preserve lexical relationships or similar meanings in words as in nation and nationality, medicine and medical, muscle and muscular (Chomsky,

1980). English orthography is based on phonetic and lexical considerations. Young children, however, are "super-phoneticians." "What they discern in the phonetic sequence of spoken words is quite free of higher level 'orthographic overlay,' and so they proceed to construct each word by setting out each named letter to its sound" (Henderson, 1980, p. 140).

It is probably a mistake to view children's early spellings as evidence that they know nothing about spelling and to seek to remedy this perceived problem by presenting word lists whose spellings are to be learned one-by-one. The problem is of a different order, one of underlying rules and generalizations, one most easily corrected by continued exposure to written words and the need to create them. It seems inefficient to provide instruction focusing on learning to spell single words when rules relating to many words can be abstracted from broader experiences which would contribute as well to many other literacy skills and keep children meaningfully engaged in, rather than bored with or afraid of, literacy development.

Summary

The research reviewed here holds much promise for informing us about what is involved in learning to read. Of particular interest are the studies indicating that preschool children who grow up in socially mediated literate environments develop literacy skills very early and in ways that approximate oral language development. But we need to know more about exactly what these children know and how they develop such knowledge if we are to develop early childhood programs that lead to the same results.

In the meantime, we can attempt to approximate in classrooms both the social and physical environments that appear to foster literacy development in young children. We need to abandon ideas and practices that assume early literacy development to be simply a matter of teaching children a few basic skills such as alphabet recognition or letter-sound associations. Much more is involved. Limiting children's reading experiences to contacts with bits and pieces of print isolated from meaningful contexts may actually prevent them from developing broader and more complex insights that are the key to understanding what written language is all about. We may have become masters at making reading hard in classrooms; we need to learn to make it easier. This will require that we provide experiences with real, whole print that we have often assumed in the past to be too complex for young children to understand. We must also learn how to simplify these complexities in ways that don't distort them.

Preparation of this chapter was supported in part by grant number 6007–902–351 from the U.S. Office of Education to the Boston University Preelementary Reading Improvement Collaborative.

References

BERTHOUD-PAPANDROPOULOU, I. An experimental study of children's ideas about language. In A. Sinclair, R. J. Jarvella, and W. J. Levelt (eds.), *The Child's Conception of Language*. New York: Springer-Verlag, 1978.

BISSEX, F. GNYS at Work: *A Child Learns to Write and Read*. Cambridge, Mass.: Harvard University Press, 1980.

BOND, G. L., and DYKSTRA, R. The cooperative research program in first-grade reading instruction. *Reading Research Quarterly*, 1967, 2.

CALFEE, R. C., CHAPMAN, R., and VENEZKY, R. How a child needs to think to learn to read. In L. W. Gregg (ed.), *Cognition and Learning in Memory*. New York: Wiley, 1972.

CHALL, J. *Learning to Read: The Great Debate*. New York: McGraw-Hill, 1967.

CHOMSKY, N. Reading, writing, and phonology. In M. Wolf, M. McQuillan, and E. Radwin (eds.), *Thought and Language/Language and Reading. Harvard Educational Review Reprint Series*, 1980.

CLAY, M. *What Did I Write?* Auckland, New Zealand: Heinemann Educational Books, 1975.

DeHIRSCH, K., JANSKY, J. J., and LANGFORD, W. D. *Predicting Reading Failure: A Preliminary Study*. New York: Harper and Row, 1966.

DOAKE, D. Preschool book handling knowledge. Paper presented at the Annual Meeting of the International Reading Association, May 1979, Atlanta, Georgia.

DOWNING, J. Children's concepts of language in learning to read. *Educational Research*, 1970, *12*, 106–112.

DURKIN, D. *Children Who Read Early*. New York: Teachers College Press, 1966.

DURRELL, D. Success in first grade reading. *Boston University Journal of Education*, 1958, *3*, 2–47.

EHRI, L. C., and WILCE, L. S. Does orthography influence a reader's matalinguistic awareness of syllabic and phonemic segments in words? Paper presented at the International Reading Association/University of Victoria International Reading Research Seminar on Linguistic Awareness and Learning to Read, June 1979, Victoria, British Columbia.

FARR, R., and ROSER, N. *Teaching a Child to Read*. New York: Harcourt Brace, 1979.

FORESTER, A. What teachers can learn from "natural readers." *The Reading Teacher*, 1977, *31*, 160–166.

FOX, B., and ROUTH, D. K. Analyzing spoken language into words, syllables, and phonemes: A developmental study. *Journal of Psycholinguistic Research*, 1975, *4*, 331–342.

FRAIBERG, S. Intervention in infancy: A program for blind infants. In B. Z. Friedlander, G. M. Starritt, and G. E. Kirk (eds.), *Exceptional Infant*, Vol. 1. New York: Brunner/Mazel, Inc., 1975.

GIBSON, E., and LEVIN, H. *The Psychology of Reading*. Cambridge, Mass.: M.I.T. Press, 1975.

GLEITMAN, L. R. Metalinguistics is not kid's stuff. Paper presented at the International Reading Association/University of Victoria International Reading Research Seminar on Linguistic Awareness and Learning to Read, June 1979, Victoria, British Columbia.

GLEITMAN, L. R., and ROZIN, P. The structure and acquisition of reading I: Relations between orthographies and the structure of language. In A. S. Reber and D. L. Scarborough (eds.), *Toward a Psychology of Reading*. Hillsdale, N.J.: Lawrence Erlbaum Associates, 1977.

GOLINKOFF, R. M. Critique: Phonemic awareness skills and reading achievement. In F. Murray and J. Pikulski (eds.), *The Acquisition of Reading*. Baltimore, Md.: University Park Press, 1978.

GOODMAN, K. S. The know-more and the know-nothing movements in reading: A personal response. *Language Arts*, 1979, 59, 657–663.

GOODMAN, K. S., and GOODMAN, Y. Learning about psycholinguistic processes by analyzing oral reading. *Harvard Educational Review*, 1977, 47, 317–333.

GUTHRIE, J. Research reviews: Teaching methods. *The Reading Teacher*, 1981, 34, 492–494.

GUTHRIE, J. T., and TYLER, S. J. Cognition and instruction of poor readers. *Journal of Reading Behavior*, 1978, 10, 57–78.

HARSTE, J. E., and CAREY, R. F. Comprehension as setting. *Monograph in language and reading studies*, 1979, Number 3, 4–22.

HENDERSON, E. H. Word knowledge and reading disability. In E. H. Henderson and J. W. Beers (eds.), *Developmental and cognitive aspects of learning to spell*. Newark, Del.: International Reading Association, 1980.

HIEBERT, E. H. Preschool children's understanding of written language. *Child Development*, 1978, 49, 1231–1234.

HIEBERT, E. H. Developmental patterns and interrelationships of preschool children's print awareness. *Reading Research Quarterly*, 1981, 16, 236–259.

HILDRETH, G. Developmental sequences in name writing. *Child Development*, 1936, 7, 291–303.

HUEY, E. B. *The Psychology and Pedagogy of Reading*. New York: Macmillan, 1908.

JENKINS, J., BAUSELL, R., and JENKINS, T. Comparison of letter name and letter sound training as transfer variables. *American Educational Research Journal*, 1972, 9, 75–86.

KRIPPNER, S. The boy who read at eighteen months. *Exceptional Children*, 1963, 30, 105–109.

LAVINE, L. Differentiation of letterlike forms in prereading children. *Developmental Psychology*, 1977, 13, 89–94.

LEGRUN, A. Wie und was "schreiben" Kindergarten-Zöglinge? *Zeitschrift für Pädagogische Psychologie*, 1932, 33, 322–331.

LIBERMAN, I. Y., SHANKWEILER, D., FISCHER, F. W., and Carter, B. Explicit syllable and phoneme segmentation in the young child. *Journal of Experimental Child Psychology*, 1974, 18, 201–212.

Mason, J. M. When do children begin to read: An explanation of four year old children's letter and word reading competencies. *Reading Research Quarterly*, 1980, 15, 203–227.

MELTZER, N. S., and HERSE, R. The boundaries of written words as seen by first graders. *Journal of Reading Behavior*, 1969, 1, 3–14.

MENYUK, P. Relations between acquisition of phonology and reading. In J. T. Guthrie (ed.), *Aspects of Reading Acquisition*. Baltimore, Md.: Johns Hopkins University Press, 1976.

MOERK, E. Changes in verbal child-mother interactions with increasing language skills in the child. *Journal of Psycholinguistics Research*, 1974, *3*, 101–116.

MORRIS, D. Beginning readers' concepts of word. In E. H. Henderson and J. W. Beers (eds.), *Developmental and Cognitive Aspects of Learning to spell*. Newark, Del.: International Reading Association, 1980.

PAPANDROPOULOU, I., and SINCLAIR, H. What is a word? Experimental study of children's ideas on grammar. *Human Development*, 1974, *17*, 241–258.

PFLAUM, S. W., WALBERG, H. J., KAREGIANES, M. L., and RASHNER, S. P. Reading instruction: A quantitative analysis. *Educational Researcher*, 1980, *9*, 12–18.

PIAGET, J. *The origins of intelligence in children* (M. Cook, trans.). New York: W. W. Norton and Company, 1954.

PICK, A., UNZE, M. G., BROWNELL, C. A., DROZDAL, J. G., and HOPMANN, M. R. Young children's knowledge of word structure. *Child Development*, 1978, *49*, 669–680.

PLESSAS, G. P., and OAKES, C. R. Prereading experiences of selected early readers. *The Reading Teacher*, 1964, *17*, 241–245.

READ, C. *Children's Categorization of Speech Sounds in English*. Urbana, Ill.: National Council of Teachers of English, 1975.

REID, J. Learning to think about reading. *Educational Research*, 1966, *9*, 56–62.

ROSSMAN, F. P. Preschoolers' knowledge of the symbolic function of written language in storybooks. Unpublished doctoral dissertation, Boston University, 1980.

SAMUELS, S. J. Letter-name versus letter-sound knowledge in learning to read. *The Reading Teacher*, 1971a, *24*, 604–608.

SAMUELS, S. J. The effect of letter-name knowledge on learning to read. *American Educational Research Journal*, 1971b, *1*, 65–74.

SAMUELS, S. J. Hierarchical subskills in the reading acquisition process. In J. T. Guthrie (ed.), *Aspects of Reading Acquisition*. Baltimore, Md.: Johns Hopkins University Press, 1976.

SAVIN, H. B. What the child knows about speech when he starts to learn to read. In J. Kavanagh and I. Mattingly (eds.), *Language by Ear and by Eye*. Cambridge, Mass.: M.I.T. Press, 1972.

SAVIN, H. B., and BEVER, T. G. The nonperceptual reality of the phoneme. *Journal of Verbal Learning and Verbal Behavior*, 1970, *9*, 295–302.

SCHICKEDANZ, J. What do preschoolers know about reading? Paper presented at the Annual Meeting of the International Reading Association, May 1979, Atlanta, Georgia.

SCHICKEDANZ, J. Hey. This book's not working right! *Young Children*, 1981, *37*, 18–27.

SINGER, H. Learning to read and learning from text: A multidimensional process. Paper presented at the International Reading Association/University of Victoria International Reading Research Seminar on Linguistic Awareness and Learning to Read, June 1979, Victoria, British Columbia.

SMITH, F. *Understanding Reading: A Psycholinguistic Analysis of Reading and Learning to Read*. New York: Holt, Rinehart and Winston, 1971.

SMITH, F. Learning to read by reading: A brief case study. *Language Arts*, 1974, *53*, 297–299.

SMITH, F. Making sense of reading—And of reading instruction. *Harvard Educational Review*, 1977, *47*, 386–395.

Snow, C. E. The development of conversation between mothers and babies. *Journal of Child Language*, 1978.

Snow, C. E., and Ferguson, C. A. *Talking to children*. Cambridge, Mass.: Harvard University Press, 1977.

Sutton, M. H. First grade children who learned to read in kindergarten. *The Reading Teacher*, 1964, *19*, 192–196.

Templeton, S. What is a word? In E. H. Henderson and J. W. Beers (eds.), *Developmental and Cognitive Aspects of Learning to Spell*. Newark, Del.: International Reading Association, 1980.

Watt, W. C., and Jacobs, D. The child's conception of the alphabet. *Claremont Reading Conference*, 1975, 131–137.

Witty, P., and Coomer, A. A case study of gifted twin boys. *Exceptional Children*, 1955, *22*, 104–108, 124–125.

CHAPTER 12

Cognitive Learning in Early Childhood Education: Mathematics, Science, and Social Studies

Gary G. Price

THIS CHAPTER REVIEWS research concerning mathematics, science, and social studies education in early childhood. The review is limited primarily to reports of empirical research and discussions of theories subjected to empirical tests. For the nonspecialists in these areas of research, I have tried to provide a context that will enable persons to make sense of the research and gain a feel for the orientations and questions attracting researchers' attention.

Mathematics Education

Research into the mathematics education of young children has been especially active. Useful supplements to this review are those by Carpenter (1980), Hiebert (1981), Johnson and Wilson (1976), and Payne (1975), and a book about the psychology of mathematics by Resnick and Ford (1981). For practical recommendations based on research, see materials by Ginsburg (1977), Kamii and DeVries (1976), Wang and Resnick (1978), and Zaslavsky (1979). For a survey of kindergarten mathematics curricula, see the article by Kurtz (1978).

Recent History in Mathematics Education

During the last decade there have been three prevalent types of research concerns in mathematics education. Research concerned with Piagetian theory (Inhelder & Piaget, 1964; Piaget, 1952, 1968); and its place in mathematics education has been predominant. A second type of research is primarily descriptive. It suspends the Piagetian quest for an integrative theory and is concerned with describing mathematical and educational phenomena other than those with which Piaget was concerned. A third type of research—broadly described as information-processing psychology (which uses computers and computer programs as metaphors for describing human thinking and its development)—retains the Piagetian quest for an integrative theory, but seeks to account for a different, potentially larger set of phenomena.

Piagetian Theory

Mathematics education, probably more than any other content area, has shown an affinity to Piagetian theory. One reason is that Piagetian theory addresses aspects of mathematics learning with which mathematics educators have been concerned, such as the inventing and constructing that children do when they make sense of mathematics (Ginsburg, 1976, 1977; Lesh, 1977; Smock, 1976). In contrast, learning theories give little or no attention to the processes by which children make sense of mathematics for themselves, as Brownell (1948) noted in Thorndike's (1924) learning theory and as Beilin (1976) noted in Gagne's (1977).[1] Piagetians also speak a common language with mathematicians when they seek to characterize young children's thought in terms of formal logico-mathematical structure. Manipulative materials, whose pedagogical value was recognized in this country before Piagetian theory became widely known (for example, Cuisenaire & Gattengo, 1954; Kieren, 1969; Minor, 1937), are given a psychological rationale by Piagetian theory. In addition, the Piagetian conception of stage-wise cognitive growth offers a psychological rationale for postponing certain kinds of learning, thus giving new theoretical clothing to the concept of readiness.

Piagetian research in mathematics education can be divided roughly into studies of the theory's application and tests of the theory.

STUDIES OF THE THEORY'S APPLICATIONS

Applications of Piagetian theory to mathematics education fall into two general types. In the first, Piagetian theory's landmarks of cognitive development are used as educational objectives. In effect, educators try to accelerate children's progress through Piaget's stages of development. This presupposes that stage-related concepts are more valuable to educe in children than are alternative objectives (a presupposition better argued on philosophical and political grounds than on psychological ones). It also presupposes that progress through stages of development can be hastened by the efforts of educators. Piaget did not support such uses of his theory; he referred to accelerative efforts as "the American question." Among the many efforts to accelerate math-related development were those by

---

[1] On the other hand, Brainerd (1977) has reviewed failures of Piagetian theory to account for phenomena readily explainable by learning theories.

Beilin (1965), Gruen (1965), Sigel, Roeper, and Hooper (1966), Johnson (1977), and Becher (1978). Many efforts have indeed induced children to perform criterion tasks precociously, but benefits to mathematics learning in general have not been demonstrated. To be sure, precocity on Piagetian tasks is positively correlated with mathematics achievement (Bearison, 1975; Cathcart, 1971; Dimitrovsky & Almy, 1975; Kaufman & Kaufman, 1972). Furthermore, that correlation is not readily attributable to general intelligence (for instance, DeVries & Kohlberg, 1977; Stephens, McLaughlin, Miller & Glass, 1972), although one can find eloquent arguments to the contrary (Humphreys, 1980; Humphreys & Parsons, 1979). At any rate, it would be inappropriate to conclude that the ability to perform Piatgetian tasks is essential for learning basic mathematical concepts and skills (Ginsburg, 1975).

In its second general type of educational application, Piagetian theory is used to build a technology of instruction in which Piagetian assessments of children guide decisions about their readiness for an activity. In terms of formal, logical structure, many concepts and operations in early mathematics do presuppose Piagetian concepts. Accordingly, Piagetian assessments have been advocated as guides in the timing of mathematical instruction (Smock, 1973; Steffe, 1976). But young children sometimes learn and do things for which they lack logical prerequisites, as illustrated in a study of first grade children by Steffe, Spikes, and Hirstein (1976). Nonconservers learned some number skills that logically presuppose conservation of quanity; however, they did not transfer those skills to new situations (as did most conservers). Neither benefit nor harm from incomplete learning like this has been demonstrated, so discussions of its value rest on philosophical positions about curriculum priorities and economical positions about the allocation of teachers' efforts.

TESTS OF PIAGETIAN THEORY

Some of the research has been concerned more with testing Piagetian theory than with educational applications per se. These tests have been concerned for the most part with the sequences in which various Piagetian phenomena occur. For instance, according to Piagetian theory, number conservation and length conservation should occur before weight conservation and area conservation (Piaget, 1952; Piaget, Inhelder & Szeminska, 1948). Closely related to questions of sequence are questions of whether children who demonstrate understanding of a concept in one context transfer that understanding to other contexts.

Training studies in which researchers examine whether children can learn Piagetian concepts out of sequence have been commonplace (see reviews by Beilin, 1971; Brainerd, 1978). The results of many studies are consistent with Piagetian theory; others appear to contradict it. The findings that contradict Piagetian theory have damaged the theory less than one might expect, because Piagetians have argued that the observations were based on too narrow a spectrum of behavior. So long as Piagetians and non-Piagetians disagree over what would constitute satisfactory criteria for testing Piagetian theory (Brainerd, 1977; Gruen, 1966; Reese & Schack, 1974), there will be no agreement about the theoretical implications of training studies. Consequently, training studies intended to be tests of Piagetian theory are becoming less common in mathematics education research.

One general insight did emerge from these training studies: the difficulty of classical Piagetian tasks can be raised or lowered by making changes on previously overlooked dimensions of those tasks. For instance, in many cases children perform better if the assessment procedure uses simpler language (Brush, Brett & Sprotzer, 1978) and does not require children to respond verbally (S. A. Miller, 1976). Studies of identity conservation by Gelman (1972) and Achenbach and Weisz (1975) provide another instance. By using one set of objects (instead of two) to assess whether children understand that quantities undergoing irrelevant transformation remain unchanged, it was found that children understand that concept much earlier than Piaget claimed.

The implications of such findings for Piagetian theory are disputable. However, there are some clear implications for educational practice. The readiness of a child for an activity depends on the activity's freedom from unnecessary sources of difficulty as well as on the child's general level of cognitive development. It is becoming more and more apparent that the logico-mathematical characteristics of an activity are not the only determinants of its difficulty nor are they necessarily the most fundamental determinants of difficulty (Pascual-Leone, 1976).

Increasing numbers of researcher-theorists have begun to reinterpret many of Piaget's observations, thereby subsuming educationally interesting parts of Piagetian theory under their own psychological theories (Brainerd & Hooper, 1978; Case, 1978; Pascual-Leone, Goodman, Ammon & Subelman, 1978). Attention is also turning to mathematical phenomena other than those identified by Piaget. This shift is a broadening of focus to include other mathematical activities of young children (Gelman & Gallistel, 1978; Ginsburg, 1976; Resnick & Ford, 1981).

Description of New Mathematical and Educational Phenomena

The second type of research seeks to describe the mathematical knowledge and activities of young children. Many of these studies use interviews to probe children's understanding of mathematics and in that sense borrow from Piaget's *méthode clinique* (for example, Erlwanger, 1973). Apart from those methodological similarities, however, the research is to a large extent unfettered by psychological disputes about the general nature of cognitive development. Some of this research, like Gelman's studies of number concepts, has spun off from earlier studies that were sparked by Piagetian theory. Some of it, like Carpenter and Moser's (1979) study of elementary thought problems involving addition and subtraction, derived its substantive focus from primary school curricula. This body of research is not easily summarized; selected parts of it are reviewed below. Research into phenomena not covered here is reviewed by Cohen and Gross (1979).

NUMBER CONCEPTS

The state of knowledge about children's understanding of number was summarized and extended by Gelman and Gallistel (1978). Their research points to counting as a key ingredient in the development of that understanding. They represent the development of counting as a succession of how-to-count principles:

1. Use as many distinct tags as there are objects. This principle would be satisfied by a child who says, "one, eight, nine, three" when counting four items.
2. Use a list of tags that has a stable order (for example, "one, two, three" always uttered in that order).
3. When asked how many objects there are in a set one has counted, answer with the last tag assigned during the counting sequence.

As evidence that children do induce and obey such principles, Gelman and Gallistel note that even children who use idiosyncratic tags for counting are self-consistent. More evidence is provided by the fact that typical counting errors like double-counting, skipping, and erring at the beginning or end of a counting sequence do not violate the principles. Still other principles of counting are the abstraction principle (know what to count and what not to count) and the order-irrelevance principle (that the sequence in which items are enumerated is of no consequence).

Gelman and Gallistel confronted young children with numerical problems both verbally and nonverbally. An important line of development, they concluded, is "an increase in the facility with which information given or requested verbally can access the arithmetic domain" (1978, p. 224). They concluded that routinization of the counting process is a prerequisite to solving addition and subtraction problems.

COUNTING

There is now widespread appreciation for the importance of counting (Hendrickson, 1979). After it becomes a familiar routine, the counting scheme is so readily invoked that children use it to determine set size even with sets so small that direct perceptual apprehension of number (Klahr & Wallace, 1976) would suffice (Gelman & Gallistel, 1978; Silverman & Rose, 1980). Once counting is routinized, children can use it to tackle new situations. Numerals are much easier to learn if the child is practiced at counting (Wang, Resnick & Boozer, 1971). As

Barr (1978) found, kindergarten children catch on to two-digit numeration faster through counting activities (especially counting by tens) than through grouping sets by tens and ones.

ADDITION AND SUBTRACTION

Addition and subtraction have traditionally been introduced through the joining and separating of concrete object sets. That tradition assumes that children find verbal approaches more difficult. There is mounting evidence to the contrary; children tend to approach addition and subtraction via counting, a verbal process (Fuson, 1982; Starkey & Gelman, 1982). Children of different cultures adopt these strategies regardless of alternative algorithms taught by schools (Ginsburg, in press). Young children's ready use of counting was illustrated in a study by Groen and Resnick (1977). Four-and-a-half-year-olds were taught to add by counting separately two groups of objects and then counting the combination of the two. Thereafter, half the sample spontaneously jumped to the more efficient technique of counting on from the larger number. Preschool children are evidently capable of understanding simple addition and subtraction (Brush, 1978). Carpenter and Moser (1979) found that many children can solve word problems involving addition and subtraction before receiving formal instruction in arithmetic. Carpenter and Moser suggest that verbal problems may provide more meaning than do concrete introductions. Instead of being deferred until children become familiar with written mathematical symbolism, verbal problems might fruitfully be used to assess readiness for written symbolization (Hamrick, 1979).

GEOMETRIC AND SPATIAL CONCEPTS

There are clear age differences in the sophistication of children's geometric and spatial concepts (Moyer, 1978). With respect to geometric shapes, some developmental progressions have been found. For a given geometric shape, children can recognize it by touch before they can construct it, and they can construct it before they can draw it (Fuson & Murray, 1978). But in this domain, too, the conventional emphasis on physical operations with concrete materials is being reconsidered (Lesh, 1978). The figurative aspects of materials are now being recognized as important. Displays that use picture sequences and artistic motion cues to illustrate mathematical relationships seem promising (Campbell, 1979; Friedman & Stevenson, 1975).

As with addition and subtraction, verbal processes play an important role in the development of geometric and spatial concepts. In an illustrative study, Grover (1979) found that when four-year-olds were required to formulate verbal hypotheses about three-dimensional block designs they were building, they became better able to reproduce designs from photographs.

Theories of Information Processing

Information processing theories use computers and computer programs as analogies for human thinking and its development. Some analogies emphasize the computer itself, and in that sense the theories are mechanistic. Computer programs, however, can be as dynamic, dialectical, structurally integrated, and organic as the theorist's imagination can invent. In that sense the human-as-a-computer-executing-programs metaphor places no limits on the complexity and dynamism of information-processing theories. To date, however, most information processing theories have emphasized mechanistic features inherent in all things that act on information—humans included (Simon, 1969). Those inherent features include means of taking in information and representing it, means of temporarily accumulating incoming information until a usable chunk has been assembled, means of storing and retrieving information, means of transforming information, and so on. The psychologically useful distinction between short-term memory and long-term memory was inspired by the computer analogy.

SYSTEM LIMITATIONS OF COMPUTERS AND HUMANS

Just as there are limits on the ability of computers to process information, so, too, are there limits with humans. Although the long-term memory of humans seems effectively unlimited, it is a modern-day truism that our short-term memory limits adults to handling without confusion no more than between five and nine chunks of information at one time (G.A. Miller, 1956). This capacity (which is not always fully used) expands gradually through childhood. Age norms for one-chunk increments in this capacity correspond roughly with age norms for the stage-wise development documented by Piaget. That fact led Pascual-Leone (1970) to hypothesize that periodic growth in this capacity by one-chunk increments underlies the qualitative shifts observed by Piaget. Subsequent experiments have shown that this neo-Piagetian model does accurately predict children's performance on certain classical Piagetian tasks (Case, 1972; Pascual-Leone & Smith, 1969).

It is better to think in terms of effective capacity than in terms of capacity per se. As Case, Kurland, and Daneman (1979) found, effective capacity varies according to a person's familiarity with the content involved. Adults performed the digit span task (one measure of processing capacity) on a par with preschool children when they were required to use the number names of an unfamiliar language. This effect of familiarity is commonly attributed to the automaticity with which persons can bring facts and procedures to bear on a problem. The transition from *faltering unfamiliarity* to *effortless routinization* may be more important than the transition from slow and effortless routinization to fast and effortless routinization. Kurland (1981) gave first grade children massive practice at counting, which modestly raised their speed of counting. This speeding up of an already routinized operation did not improve children's performance on an ancillary, attention-demanding span task (remembering how many dots were in each of several sets counted). Fuller discussion of automaticity in connection with mathematics instruction is given by Resnick and Ford (1981, pp. 30–35). Effective capacity is also affected by the efficiency with which information is represented, as illustrated by Hatano and Osawa's (1981) finding that some expert abacus operators with otherwise average abilities could repeat as many as fifteen to sixteen digits by representing strings of numbers on a mental abacus.

This notion of effective capacity (affected conjointly by maturation and knowledge) has potential applications, which have been elaborated elsewhere (Case, 1978; Pascual-Leone, Goodman, Ammon & Subelman, 1978). Case (1982) shows how the notion can be used to structure and sequence the content of elementary arithmetic to make learning easier for young children. Of particular noteworthiness is the lucidity with which these neo-Piagetians (for example, Ammon, 1981) have explained the educational tradeoff between *easy learning,* which assures mastery of content by more children, and *capacity-demanding learning,* which keeps effective capacity stretched to its maturational potential. Another potential application is the refinement of a technology for assessing readiness. Effective capacity in a given content domain provides a good prediction of whether a child will get full benefit from a lesson involving that content. But it is important to regard effective capacity as specific to content domains, since there is mounting evidence that it is not a general trait (Hiebert, 1979; Romberg & Collis, 1980).

COGNITIVE STRUCTURES AND PROCESSES

The notion of a maturationally constrained capacity suggests neuropsychological structures akin to computer circuitry. The concept of effective capacity softens the mechanistic character of that person-computer analogy and moves closer to a person-program analogy, which is more common in information-processing research. Person-program analogies have dealt mainly with cognitive structures (such as schemas, knowledge states, and procedural lists) and processes. The processes that have been studied may be grouped into two broad categories: (1) processes by which cognitive structures are used by children as they perform mathematical tasks; and (2) processes by which those cognitive structures change. Most models of cognitive structures and processes have dealt with a particular type of task (counting, addition, and solving word problems), although there have been attempts to build general models of cognitive development (Klahr & Wallace, 1976; Osherson, 1974).

There are basic differences between the information-processing approach and the Piagetian approach. The information-processing approach analyzes mathematical activities in terms of their information processing requirements, whereas the Piagetian approach analyzes them in terms of their logical and mathematical properties. Even complicated mathematical activities are treated in information-processing theories as concatenations of elementary processes, whereas Piagetian theory treats them as more organic. Information processing theories typically assume that elementary processes are done serially (in a one-at-a-time sequence), whereas Piagetian theory suggests that processes occur simultaneously. By assuming that component processes occur serially, researchers are able to estimate the time taken up by each process through a research method known as chronometrics (Estes, 1978). The assumption of serial processing has disputable validity (Anderson, 1977). Despite this, chronometric methods have provided valuable insights into the mathematical thinking of young children (Groen & Resnick, 1977). Chronometrics is distinctive to information-processing research, but it is not the only means of data collection. The analysis of protocols and of children's errors—both techniques used by Piaget—are also used.

Greeno (1978) has argued that information-processing research elucidates three types of theoretical models, all of which affect educational practice. The first is a model of (to be) acquired knowledge, which describes desirable educational outcomes in terms of the cognitive structures and processes that children learn to use. Relatively speaking, it is a description of what young experts know and do. He cites the previously mentioned knowledge of how children use various counting procedures to add and subtract as an example. Another example is the knowledge accumulating about how children solve word problems (Carpenter & Moser, 1979; Riley, Greeno & Heller, 1982).

The second is a model of initial knowledge, which is a description of children's cognitive states at the beginning of instruction. A model to represent children's knowledge of counting (Gelman, Greeno & Riley, 1978) is one example. A model of procedural misunderstandings that lead elementary school children to make computational errors is another and has proven useful for diagnostic teaching (Brown & Burton, 1978). Other current efforts seek to shed light on specifically what it is that makes preschool children able to solve certain word problems with concrete props but unable to do so without them.

The third is a model of learning, which bridges the gap between initial knowledge and to-be-acquired knowledge. The task of building models like this has scarcely begun. The bridge would specify the sequence(s) of cognitive changes followed by children who make a successful transition to expertise in the curriculum. An example of research addressed to this task is Lawler's (1980) case study, in which he studied changes in his young daughter's understanding of mathematical concepts as she used a computer. Lawler used an information-processing framework to characterize these changes. The bridge between initial knowledge and to-be-acquired knowledge would also specify the common dead ends and pitfalls that can slow the transition to expertise. Although Greeno's third type of theoretical model is at this date closer to a promissory note than a product of research, it deserves comment. It bespeaks an emerging Zeitgeist in which traditional distinctions between learning and development are relaxed. Heretofore, learning theories have tended to emphasize the goal states toward which children are helped, and they have tended to treat the initial state of the child as having little consequence. Conversely, developmental theories have tended to emphasize the initial state of children and to give scant attention to the goal states. The current view, which Greeno has articulated, is that both must be considered explicitly. Moreover, the current view holds that even an intimate understanding of both the initial state and the goal state still leaves more to be learned about the processes of transition that educators can help children to make.

Summary

It should be apparent to the reader that research in young children's mathematical thinking is a field in theoretical ferment. In many cases, the phenomena with which the theories are concerned are drawn from a "basic skills" curriculum. Romberg (1982) has cautioned, however, that much of this research fails to question the value in a modern world of the mathematics curriculum with which it is concerned. It thus runs the risk of leading to a set of powerful instructional techniques that teach obsolete skills. With that warning acknowledged, an enriched view of children and the mathematics they learn seems to be emerging.

Science Education

Of the three content areas included in this chapter, it is ironic that science education in early childhood appears to have had the fewest persons subjecting it to "scientific" (empirical) examination. That comes as no surprise when one recalls that science was not even a subject in the primary grades until recent years. In addition, perhaps by historical accident, questions germane to science education in early childhood seem to have attracted fewer researchers than mathematics and social studies education from related disciplines such as psychology. This review is confined to general themes of the field and is consequently short. A more detailed review was done by Dietz and Sunal (1976), and a specialized but useful review is included in a book by Kamii and DeVries (1978). A collection of research and reviews edited by Barufaldi (in press) is forthcoming.

Recent History in Science Education

There have been many curriculum development projects in science education over the last twenty years (Sabar, 1979). Welch (1979) reports that more than 500 different curriculum improvement projects were listed in 1977 with the ERIC Clearinghouse on Science and Mathematics. Most such curricula for early childhood are part of a series that covers the years from kindergarten to grade twelve. Dietz and Sunal (1976) and Spodek (1978) describe several of the better known curricula for young children. Many of the curricula were developed with federal funds, and, like most federally budgeted efforts, were evaluated (Welch, 1976).

Piagetian Theory in Science Education

Many of the questions that science education researchers have asked were inspired by Piagetian theory, as was the case in mathematics education research. Piagetian research in science education has taken the same themes: studies of the theory's applications and tests of the theory. The tests of the theory (Gates & Jay, 1978; Za'Rour, 1977) draw on literature already reviewed and will not be repeated. In science education, too, Piagetian theory has been used as a source of educational objectives by those who seek to accelerate Piagetian development (for example, Henry, 1978). The more common application of the theory, however, has been to use it as a way of characterizing children's readiness or lack thereof for particular types of science learning (Herron, 1978). In other words, logical operations such as seriation, correspondence, and reversibility have been regarded as developmental prerequisites of certain science concepts.

A contrary view has been energetically put forth by Novak (1977). Novak advocates Ausubel's (1968, 1970) theory of meaningful learning. According to that theory, advance organizers from the teacher help to link new knowledge to existing knowledge (Barnes & Clawson, 1975; Lawton & Wanska, 1977). In many circumstances, use of advance organizers would be at odds with the popular "discovery-oriented" approach (West & Fensham, 1974). Ausubel's notion of meaningful learning is consistent with accumulating evidence of the influence that prior knowledge has on cognitive processes (Borkowski, in press; Chi, 1978).

Description of New Phenomena

Descriptive studies of young children's science concepts are beginning to appear. These studies are methodologically similar to Piagetian studies, but the phenomena studied are dictated more by the structure of a science discipline than by Piagetian theory. One example is a study by Albert (1978), who described a developmental progression in the concepts children have of heat. Another study of this type described the strategies that children employ when asked to place varying numbers of objects into order according to length and weight (Smith & Padilla, 1977). Another study described the activities of preschool children using a pendulum toy (O'Sullivan, 1980). All of these studies concern activities and materials designed to educe particular science concepts. Like Carpenter and Moser's (1979) study of elementary thought problems involving addition and subtraction, these studies derive their substantive focus from the primary school curriculum. If research in science education follows the pattern of research in mathematics education, more studies of this kind can be expected. It is too early at this time, however, to conclude that a trend has been established.

Summary

In science education research concerning older students, there has been a trend to reassert the importance of subject matter knowledge and to describe the way in which different persons represent scientific knowledge (Shavelson, 1974; Stewart, 1979). It is hard to assess whether research with young children will follow this route, too.

There seems to be a lack of unanimity among researchers about what constitutes a research-worthy core of topics that are distinctively concerned with science education in early childhood. Preprimary teachers often associate science education with activities believed to foster logic necessary for scientific thinking and with the kinds of physical knowledge highlighted by Piaget. But there is no similar consensus among researchers about the purposes and achievable goals of science education in early childhood. The efforts of different researchers are topically scattered rather than focused on a particular topic.

In the primary grades, science education is still a newcomer which is often justified for its value as an adjunct to other parts of the school curriculum rather than on its own merits. This linkage of science education to other parts of the curriculum is healthy from a pedagogical point of view, but it seems unbalanced. One can find research showing that science education activities help reading (Barufaldi, 1977) and listening skills (Barufaldi & Swift, 1980), but one cannot find research exploring whether reading and listening activities help scientific development.

Research into science education might acquire more of a shared focus if researchers identified their efforts with one of the three types of models in Greeno's (1978) framework. That research approach might also clarify the unique purposes and value of science education in early childhood. Greeno's framework (described more elaborately in connection with mathematics education) distinguishes: (1) models of initial knowledge; (2) models of to-be-acquired knowledge; and (3) models of the processes involved in moving from initial knowledge to to-be-acquired knowledge. An integrated research program would pursue a selected aspect of science knowledge through all three types of models.

Social Studies

The review of research in social studies for early childhood begins with a brief look at its history. Following that, research on different aspects of social studies education will be presented. Other reviews that give attention to social studies for young children are those by Cartledge and Milburn (1978) and Jantz (1976). Research-based recommendations for classroom practice are also available (Moore, 1977; Shelton, Slaby & Robinson, 1975).

Recent History in Social Studies Education

A problem in reviewing research in social studies education is the lack of agreement among scholars on the definition and priorities of social studies. These differences in expert opinion are summarized briefly here; more detailed summaries are available elsewhere (Barr, Barth & Shermis, 1977). As elaborated by Barr, Barth, and Shermis (1977), there are three sometimes-contending views of social studies. First, it is seen as citizenship transmission (also, cultural transmission), a set of educational processes by which certain values and sanctioned types of behavior are instilled in children. Second, it is seen as age-appropriate exposure to the lore and methods of the social sciences. Third, it is seen as exposure to reflective inquiry, in which children learn skills of making reasoned decisions and giving attention to the sociopolitical context and consequences of these decisions. Educational practice typically does some of each. According to Spodek's (1974) review of past practices in kindergartens, there have historically been diverse priorities in early childhood education. Today's social studies in early childhood education tend to emphasize the development of social skills and socially desirable behavior, which can be construed as a mixture of cultural transmission and reflective inquiry. Research does not always reflect the diverse concerns of practice, however, because research is seldom done on those outcomes of social studies education that are slow to be manifest or are otherwise hard to measure.

Research in early childhood social studies is typically concerned with a particular desired outcome in children and conditions that are favorable to that outcome. It is rare to find research that begins with extant social studies curricula and then evaluates the various ways in which each curriculum affects children. This review emphasizes social behavior and social thinking, and it does not cover the related literature on self-esteem or emotional health.

Nonaggression

Nonaggressive behavior is a fundamental social requirement. In most reviews of the topic, both aggression and nonaggression in preschool children are seen as parts of a learned constellation of behavior (for example, Achenbach, 1977; Patterson & Cobb, 1971). Means by which parents, television, and preschools contribute to such learning have been studied. Three patterns of parental response to aggressive behavior are associated with aggression in young boys: belated recognition of aggressive behavioral sequences and responding with inconsequential scolding; disinclination to stop aggressive behavior even though it is noticed; role specialization in which one parent is a harsh disciplinarian and the other is a permissive comforter (Patterson, Cobb & Ray, 1973). Since the pioneering work of Bandura, Ross, and Ross (1961), it has been recognized that children can acquire aggressive behavior by imitating an aggressive model. There has been an accumulating research literature concerning the effects of television violence on aggression of preschool children (Slaby & Quarforth, in press). Reinforcement processes in preschools can provoke aggressive behavior (Patterson, Littman & Bricker, 1967) and tamer forms of antisocial behavior, such as disregard for the expressed wishes of peers (Furman & Masters, 1980b).

Previously, research into techniques by which aggression can be reduced emphasized the use of contingent reinforcement to modify behavior (for instance, Brown & Elliott, 1965). Such approaches ignore the thought processes of the child. Recently, more attention has been given to the thought processes that underlie aggressive behavior. Zahavi and Asher (1978), for instance, found that aggressive behavior in some preschool children was enduringly reduced simply by having teachers analyze for them the relative costs and benefits of aggressive and prosocial behavior. The shift toward an emphasis on children's thoughts has been hastened by findings that aggression can be reduced by building competence in social thinking (Camp, Blom, Herbert & Van Doorninck, 1977; Meichenbaum & Goodman, 1971; Shure & Spivack, 1980). Research into the building of competent social thinking will be discussed later.

Prosocial Behavior

There is some evidence that young children's prosocial behavior—helping others without anticipation of reward—is related to their level of moral judgment (Dreman, 1976; Eisenberg-Berg & Hand, 1979). For that reason, there is an ongoing interest in means of fostering growth in moral judgment—a topic mentioned again later in this chapter. Research into conditions that foster prosocial behavior has been reviewed extensively (Bryan, 1977; Mussen & Eisenberg-Berg, 1977; Rushton, 1976; Staub, 1975), and this book contains a chapter on the topic. Most of the earlier research examined the influence of adults. Apparently, exposure to prosocial adult models can have an enduring effect on the prosocial behavior of young children (Rice & Grusec, 1975). Children seem more likely to follow a prosocial example if the model is a person with some immediate control over the child (Bryan, 1975) or is one who has been consistently friendly and helpful (Yarrow, Scott & Waxler, 1973). Children also seem to be influenced by the cognitive content of adults' injunctions to behave prosocially. In a recent study of mothers and children, the emotional intensity of injunctions appeared important (Zahn-Waxler, Radke Yarrow & King, 1979). Use of induction to explain the situation of other persons appears effective, though the supporting research has focused on conscience rather than on prosocial behavior (Aronfreed, 1976).

Recently, there has been more research into the effects of interaction between children. Preschool and kindergarten children are not passive recipients of a given child's actions, but react in ways that bring new knowledge, pleasure, and displeasure to that child. As Furman and Masters (1980a) found, positive affect usually ensues in children who have behaved positively toward others and negative affect in those who have behaved negatively. Research into the influence of peers on social development in general was reviewed by Hartup (1976) and Asher (1978). This emerging field of research promises to yield educationally useful perspectives on peer influences.

Sociableness

Social isolation in school is a lasting problem for some children (Gronlund, 1959). Besides the loneliness that usually accompanies social isolation, its long-range correlates include dropping out of school, delinquency, and mental health problems (Cox & Gunn, 1980). Consequently, development of sociableness—especially the prevention of isolate behavior—is a concern of early childhood educators. There are, of course, normal personality differences in sociableness; the preference that some young children have for playing with objects rather than people is positively related to some nonsocial competencies and is usually not symptomatic of a social problem (Jennings, 1975).

In this society, unattractive children are at greater risk of becoming isolates than attractive children. Preschool and primary children associate behavioral stereotypes with physical attractiveness, and when judging unfamiliar peers as potential friends, they prefer attractive ones and dislike unattractive ones (Dion, 1973). Fortunately, stereotyping of this kind is lessened by familiarity (Styczynski & Langlois, 1977). Unfortunately, there is some evidence of a self-fulfilling prophecy. Unattractive children tend to conform progressively over the course of early childhood with negative behavioral stereotypes of them (Langlois & Downs, 1979; Synder, Tanke & Berscheid, 1977). Appearance may be a predisposing factor, but children's popularity among familiar peers can be traced more directly to their behavior (Gottman, Gonso & Rasmussen, 1975). Like aggressive behavior, isolate behavior tends to diminish when children gain social competence. Educators can help to prevent isolation by directly teaching children social skills that help them to make friends—skills like giving attention, talking, giving help, and taking turns (Oden & Asher, 1977). Sociableness can also be increased through social reinforcement techniques (Allen, Hart, Buell, Harris & Wolf, 1964). There is also evidence that assignment to play with a younger partner leads to increased sociableness (Furman, Rahe & Hartup, 1979).

Social Competence

Social competence (behavior and thought processes that result in effective interpersonal relationships) has been actively researched in recent years, as reviewed by Cartledge and Milburn (1978) and Urbain and Kendall (1980). Several working definitions of "effective interpersonal relationships" have been used in this research. In some cases it means nonaggression and in other it means popularity or peer acceptance gauged by sociometric methods. Despite the narrowness of such definitions, efforts to make children more effective in their interpersonal relationships have had encouraging results.

Different ingredients of social competence have been studied. Four types of skills have received most of the attention: (1) situation-specific behavioral repertoires; (2) interpersonal problem solving; (3) role taking; and (4) verbal self-direction and impulse control. Actions that help to build friendships are an example of a situation-specific behavioral repertoire. That research was mentioned in connection with sociableness and will not be repeated here.

INTERPERSONAL PROBLEM SOLVING

Spivack and Shure (1974) and Spivack, Platt, and Shure (1976) sought to describe cognitive skills that are needed to solve interpersonal problems. They found two that are evidently key ingredients of the ability to solve interpersonal problems. The first, alternative thinking, is the fluency with which a child can generate different strategies that might solve an interpersonal problem. Socially competent children can usually generate many strategies for a given problem, whereas less competent children cannot. The second, consequential thinking, is the ability to evaluate strategies in terms of their prospective consequences. The researchers devised an Interpersonal Cognitive Problem-Solving (ICPS) curriculum for four-year-olds (Shure & Spivack, 1971) and five-year-olds (Shure & Spivack, 1978). The curriculum is effective at raising alternative thinking and consequential thinking, and teachers' ratings indicate that socially competent behavior increases (Shure, 1980).

Role Taking

Role taking skill is positively correlated with measures of interpersonal adjustment (Rothenburg, 1970). It is generally believed to be an important component of social competence, although most of the supporting evidence is subject to rival interpretations (Shantz, 1975). Participation in role-taking activities has been found to increase helping behavior (Dreman, 1976; Friedrich & Stein, 1975). A common belief is that role taking fosters cognitive abilities required to understand and appreciate the perspective of another person (Freyburg, 1973; Smilansky, 1968). Shure (1980) has suggested a simpler mechanism, which is that role taking makes young children more attentive to emotional cues of others—an interpretation consistent with findings of Zahn-Waxler, Radke-Yarrow, and King (1979).

Role-taking activities of different kinds have been used successfully to develop sociableness and social competence. Marshall and Hahn (1967) found that children trained to role-play and fantasize showed increased sociableness. Sociodramatic play was found to improve role-taking skills and group problem-solving processes (Rosen, 1974). In a large experiment, Smilansky (1968) found that verbal communication skills and positive affect increased and aggression decreased when preschool and kindergarten teachers interjected sociodramatic play into free-play activity.

Role-taking activities have been used successfully in conjunction with the ICPS techniques of Shure and Spivack. Elardo and Cooper (1977) have developed a curriculum for elementary school called Project AWARE. Although older children seem to benefit from these techniques less rapidly than younger children, Project AWARE appears to increase social competence and prosocial behavior when consistently used throughout the school year (reported in Shure, 1980). J. H. Patterson (1979) combined ICPS alternative thinking experiences with Smilansky's sociodramatic play technique in an experiment and found that six play sessions increased kindergarten children's scores on a measure of alternative thinking.

Verbal Self-direction and Impulse Control

Research by Vygotsky (1962) and Luria (1961) alerted researchers to the role of private speech in the self-regulation and direction of overt behavior, and research on that topic was reviewed by Pressley (1979). Meichenbaum and Goodman (1971) successfully applied that theoretical insight by training young impulsive children to use verbal self-instructions. Socially impulsive and aggressive boys whose verbal development is otherwise normal make less use of private speech (Camp, 1977). This observation suggests that their social competence might be raised by teaching them to make better use of private speech. A program called Think Aloud was developed and tried with first and second grade children (Camp & Bash, 1980). Increases in prosocial behavior, decreases in aggression, and improvement in cognitive test performance were found in all trials of the program, though the superiority over control groups was not always statistically significant.

Summary

To summarize the research into various aspects of social competence, it appears useful to think in terms of specific skills that compose social competence in young children. Both direct and indirect means of developing these skills seem to be effective.

Social Concepts, Attitudes, and Thinking

Social studies curricula for kindergarten and the primary grades are often designed to introduce social science concepts (Jantz, 1976; Serdus & Tank, 1970). Spodek (1974) provided both a rationale and guidelines for teaching social science concepts to young children, but there has been scant empirical research on the topic. There is evidence that first graders, at least, can comprehend certain technical concepts (Larkins & Shaver, 1969; Rogers & Layton, 1966). Preschool children are able to learn some social science concepts, so long as they are not overloaded by too many at once (Schwab & Stern, 1969). These findings are consistent with the view presented earlier that the limiting factor in children's ability to comprehend new content is often the effective capacity of their working memory. In this view, children can comprehend anything either familiar enough or simple enough so that it does not exceed the effective capacity of working memory.

Educators in the United States are often wary of trying to influence attitudes of children. Still, most would agree that certain types of attitudes are desirable in members of this society (racial tolerance, openness to handicapped children). Lately, there have been abundant studies of the attitudes that are fostered in young children through "mainstreaming." This literature was reviewed by Karnes and Lee (1979) and is not repeated here.

Research into the social thinking of young children (social thinking taken here as reflective inquiry) has been confined mainly to moral reasoning. Interest in moral reasoning derives partly from its presumed influence on moral behavior, a topic reviewed by Blasi (1980). Educational efforts to affect moral development were reviewed by Lockwood (1978) and are not reviewed here.

Summary

The most active areas of social studies research have been those dealing with social skills. More particularly, the social skills have been skills of individual children in contexts involving other children. Skills of groups (for instance, teamwork) have not received much attention nor have skills of individual children with adults. Young children's learning of social studies concepts appears to have been researched much less than their learning of mathematical concepts. The reasons for this discrepancy probably lie more in the nature of the disciplines than in the nature of young children.

Conclusion

The Roles of Verbal Processes

Emerging from recent research is a more elaborate view of verbal processes in early childhood education. Vocabulary and communication skills have, of course, been commonplace concerns of early childhood educators for a few decades. Recent research has highlighted other ways in which language figures prominently in early childhood. Apparently, young children can use private speech to guide themselves through strategies, mental checklists, frames, algorithms, procedures for solving and avoiding social problems, and so forth. This has made increasing numbers of educators interested in ways of teaching children to use various verbally guided procedures.

Limitations in Effective Capacity

It has been realized for some years that adults have limited ability to juggle multiple chunks of information at one time. There is a now growing appreciation for the greater extent to which such limitations in effective capacity impinge on the cognition of young children. Effective capacity is considered to be conjointly affected by maturation, familiarity, and the parsimony with which a person mentally represents information.

The emerging theories provide useful and surprisingly novel predictions about the kinds of task demands that are most likely to give young children difficulty. The theories also indicate that some activities are inappropriate for young children because the activities place too great a demand on effective capacity. But the educator need not be resigned simply to wait for maturational bottlenecks to be removed. Activities can be simplified to lower the demands on attentional capacity. Children can be introduced to concepts that bring manageable parsimony to something previously too complex. Educators can work to foster familiarity with elements that, if unfamiliar, could not be assembled by a child into a manageable whole.

To the extent that familiarization enlarges effective capacity and alleviates difficulty, further rethinking of educational folklore is needed. There is a popular assumption that educators' expectations for mastery (by children) come close on the heels of efforts to teach. Educational interventionists and anti-interventionists share the assumption that efforts to teach and expectations for mastery are closely coupled. Interventionists make efforts to teach and typically do expect mastery, whereas anti-interventionists avoid teaching what they perceive as difficult, because they fear that children will be harmed by unreasonable expectations for mastery. The first of these approaches could be characterized as the *teach earlier–expect earlier* approach, and the second could be characterized as the *teach later–expect later* approach. Both approaches prevent children from experiencing a prolonged, pressure-free period of familiarization, which would be possible if efforts to teach and expectations for mastery were uncoupled from each other. Familiarity would be maximized and difficulty minimized by following a *teach earlier–expect later* approach.

Models of Initial and To-Be-Acquired Knowledge

Attempts to describe the initial states at which children begin an education experience and the to-be-acquired states toward which they progress are increasingly common. The educational programs that have improved young children's social competence are distinctive for their success and for the clarity with which they have described the mental processes used by socially competent children. They have also developed clear descriptions of common pitfalls that interfere with social competence.

Models of children's initial states are familiar to early childhood educators in the form of developmental theories. Models of to-be-acquired knowledge are less familiar. A model of to-be-acquired knowledge is a description of mental states and cognitive processes—not simply a description of behavior and not simply a list of facts to be memorized. Such a model is potentially more useful than a description of the behaviorally specified performance one wants a child to be able to do. Such models can help to clarify discussions of researchers and educators, because they require three often disconnected matters to be tied together explicitly: (1) cirriculum priorities (what kinds of expertise are most important to acquire?); (2) cognitive process descriptions (what kinds of thought processes distinguish one who possesses a valued type of expertise from one who does not?); and (3) developmental-instructional psychology (what factors affect children's transition toward the to-be-acquired state?).

In sum, present-day research promises to broaden and solidify the empirical foundations of early childhood education. Most important, it also promises to transcend and integrate some outworn divisions in our thinking.

Several persons gave valuable information and suggestions to the author. Thanks are due to Janice H. Patterson, Thomas P. Carpenter, Fred N. Finley, James Hiebert, James M. Moser, Susan A. Penn, Thomas. A. Romberg, and James H. Stewart.

References

ACHENBACH, T. M. Behavior disorders in preschool children. In H. L. Hom, Jr., and P. A. Robinson (eds.), *Psychological Processes in Early Education.* New York: Academic Press, 1977.

ACHENBACH, T. M., and WEISZ, J. R. A longitudinal study of developmental synchrony between conceptual identity, seriation, and transitivity of color, number, and length. *Child Development,* 1975, *46,* 840–848.

ALBERT, E. Development of the concept of heat in children. *Science Education,* 1978, *62,* 389–399.

ALLEN, K. E., HART, B., BUELL, J. S., HARRIS, F. R., and WOLF, M. M. Effects of social reinforcement on isolate behavior of a nursery school child. *Child Development,* 1964, *35,* 511–518.

AMMON, P. Communication skills and communicative competence: A neo-Piagetian process-structural view. In W. P. Dickson (ed.), *Children's Oral Communication Skills.* New York: Academic Press, 1981.

ANDERSON, J. A. Neural models with cognitive implications. In D. LaBerge and S. J. Samuels (eds.), *Basic Processes in Reading: Perception and Comprehension.* Hillsdale, N. J.: Lawrence Erlbaum Associates, 1977.

ARONFREED, J. Moral development from the standpoint of a general psychological theory. In T. Lickona (ed.), *Moral Development and Behavior: Theory, Research and Social Issues.* New York: Holt, Rinehart & Winston, 1976.

ASHER, S. R. Children's peer relations. In M. E. Lamb (ed.), *Social and Personality Development.* New York: Holt, Rinehart & Winston, 1978.

AUSUBEL, D. P. *Educational Psychology: A Cognitive View.* New York: Holt, Rinehart & Winston, 1968.

AUSUBEL, D. P. *The use of ideational organizers in science teaching* (Occasional Paper Series—Science Paper 3). Columbus: Ohio State University, ERIC/SMEAC Information Reference Center, March 1970 (ED 050 930).

BANDURA, A., ROSS, D., and ROSS, S. A. Transmission of aggression through imitation of aggressive models. *Journal of Abnormal Social Psychology,* 1961, *63,* 575–582.

BARNES, B. R., and CLAWSON, E. U. Do advance organizers facilitate learning? Recommendations for further research based on an analysis of 32 studies. *Review of Educational Research,* 1975, *45,* 637–659.

BARR, D. C. A comparison of three methods of introducing two-digit numeration. *Journal for Research in Mathematics Education,* 1978, *9,* 33–43.

BARR, R. D., BARTH, J. L., and SHERMIS, S. S. *Defining the Social Studies* (Bulletin 51). Arlington, Va.: National Council for the Social Studies, 1977.

BARUFALDI, J. P. Children learning to read should experience science. *The Reading Teacher*, 1977, *30*, 388–393.

BARUFALDI, J. P. Special issue: Science and mathematics education in early childhood education. *School Science and Mathematics*, in press.

BARUFALDI, J. P., and SWIFT, J. The influence of the BSCS elementary school sciences program instruction on first grade students' listening skills. *Journal for Research in Science Teaching*, 1980, *17*, 484–490.

BEARISON, D. J. Induced versus spontaneous attainment of concrete operations and their relationship to school achievement. *Journal of Educational Psychology*, 1975, *67*, 576–580.

BECHER, R. M. The effects of perceptual transformation experiences and numerical operational experiences on numerical correspondence and equivalence. *Journal for Research in Mathematics Education*, 1978, *9*, 69–74.

BEILIN, H. Learning and operational convergence in logical thought development. *Journal of Experimental Child Psychology*, 1965, *2*, 317–339.

BEILIN, H. The training and acquisition of logical operations. In M. F. Rosskipf, L. P. Steffe, and S. Taback (eds.), *Piagetian Cognitive Development Research and Mathematical Education*. Washington, D.C.: National Council of Teachers of Mathematics, 1971.

BEILIN, H. Linguistic, logical and cognitive models for learning mathematical concepts. In A. R. Osborne (ed.), *Models for Learning Mathematics*. Columbus, Ohio: ERIC Center for Science, Mathematics, and Environmental Education, 1976.

BLASI, A. Bridging moral cognition and moral action: A critical review of the literature. *Psychological Bulletin*, 1980, *88*, 1–45.

BORKOWSKI, J. G. Signs of intelligence: Strategy generalization and metacognition. In S. R. Yussen (ed.), *The Growth of Insight during Childhood*. New York: Academic Press, in press.

BRAINERD, C. J. Cognitive development and concept learning: An interpretive review. *Psychological Bulletin*, 1977, *84*, 919–939.

BRAINERD, C. J. Learning research and Piagetian theory. In L. S. Siegel and C. J. Brainerd (eds.), *Alternatives to Piaget: Critical Essays on the Theory*. New York: Academic Press, 1978.

BRAINERD, C. J., and HOOPER, F. H. More on the identity-equivalence sequence: An update and some replies to Miller. *Psychological Bulletin*, 1978, *85*, 70–75.

BROWN, J. S., and BURTON, R. R. Diagnostic models for procedural bugs in basic mathematical skills. *Cognitive Science*, 1978, *2*, 155–192.

BROWN, P., and ELLIOTT, R. Control of aggression in a nursery school class. *Journal of Experimental Child Psychology*, 1965, *2*, 103–107.

BROWNELL, W. A. Learning theory and educational practice. *Journal of Educational Research*, 1948, *41*, 481–497.

BRUSH, L. R. Preschool children's knowledge of addition and subtraction. *Journal for Research in Mathematics Education*, 1978, *9*, 49–59.

BRUSH, L. R., BRETT, L. J., and SPROTZER, E. R. Children's difficulties on quantitative tasks: Are they simply a misunderstanding of relational terms? *Journal for Research in Mathematics Education*, 1978, 9, 149–151.

BRYAN, J. H. Children's cooperation and helping behaviors. In E. M. Hetherington (ed.), *Review of Child Development Research*, Vol. 5. Chicago: University of Chicago Press, 1975.

BRYAN, J. H. Prosocial behavior. In H. L. Hom, Jr., and P. A. Robinson (eds.), *Psychological Processes in Early Education*. New York: Academic Press, 1977.

CAMP, B. W. Verbal mediation in young aggressive boys. *Journal of Abnormal Psychology*, 1977, 86, 145–153.

CAMP, B. W., and BASH, M. A. Developing self-control through training in problem solving: The "Think Aloud" program. In D. P. Rathjen and J. P. Foreyt (eds.), *Social Competence*. Elmsford, N.Y.: Pergamon Press, 1980.

CAMP, B. W., BLOM, G. E., HERBERT, F., and VAN DOORNINCK, W. J. "Think Aloud": A program for developing self control in young aggressive boys. *Journal of Abnormal Child Psychology*, 1977, 5, 157–169.

CAMPBELL, P. F. Artistic motion cues, number of pictures, and first-grade children's interpretation of mathematics textbook pictures. *Journal for Research in Mathematics Education*, 1979, 10, 148–153.

CARPENTER, T. P. Research in cognitive development. In R. J. Shumway (ed.), *Research in Mathematics Education*. Reston, Va.: National Council of Teachers of Mathematics, 1980.

CARPENTER, T. P., and MOSER, J. M. *An investigation of the learning of addition and subtraction* (Theoretical Paper No. 79). Madison: University of Wisconsin, Wisconsin Research and Development Center for Individualized Schooling, 1979 (ERIC Document Reproduction Service No. ED 188 892).

CARTLEDGE, G., and MILBURN, J. F. The case for teaching social skills in the classroom: A review. *Review of Educational Research*, 1978, 48, 133–156.

CASE, R. Validation of a neo-Piagetian capacity construct. *Journal of Experimental Child Psychology*, 1972, 14, 287–302.

CASE, R. A developmentally based theory and technology of instruction. *Review of Educational Research*, 1978, 48, 439–463.

CASE, R. General developmental influences on the acquisition of algorithms in arithmetic. In T. P. Carpenter, J. M. Moser, and T. A. Romberg (eds.), *Addition and Subtraction: A Cognitive Perspective*. Hillsdale, N.J.: Lawrence Erlbaum Associates, 1982.

CASE, R., KURLAND, D. M., and DANEMAN, M. Operational efficiency and the growth of M-space. Paper presented at the biennial meeting of the Society for Research in Child Development, San Francisco, March 1979.

CATHCART, G. W. The relationship between primary students' rationalization of conservation and their mathematical achievement. *Child Development*, 1971, 42, 755–765.

CHI, M. T. H. Knowledge structures and memory development. In R. S. Siegler (ed.), *Children's Thinking: What Develops?* Hillsdale, N.J.: Lawrence Erlbaum Associates, 1978.

CHI, M. T. H., and KLAHR, D. Span and rate of apprehension in children and adults. *Journal of Experimental Child Psychology*, 1975, 19, 434–439.

COHEN, M. A., and GROSS, P. J. *The Developmental Resource: Behavioral Sequences for Assessment and Program Planning*, Vol. 2. New York: Grune & Stratton, 1979.

COX, R. D., and GUNN, W. B. Interpersonal skills in the schools: Assessment and curriculum development. In D. P. Rathjen and J. P. Foreyt (eds.), *Social Competence: Interventions for Children and Adults*. Elmsford, N.Y.: Pergamon Press, 1980.

CUISENAIRE, M. G., and GATTEGNO, C. *Numbers in Color*. Mount Vernon, N.Y.: Cuisenaire Company of America, 1954.

DAVYDOV, V. V. The psychological characteristics of the formation of elementary mathematical operations in children. In T. P. Carpenter, J. M. Moser, and T. A. Romberg (eds.), *Addition and Subtraction: A Cognitive Perspective*. Hillsdale, N.J.: Lawrence Erlbaum Associates, 1982.

DEVRIES, R., and KOHLBERG, L. Relations between Piagetian and psychometric assessments of intelligence. In L. Katz (ed.), *Current Topics in Early Childhood Education*, Vol. 1. Norwood, N.J.: Ablex Publishing Corp., 1977.

DIETZ, M. A., and SUNAL, D. W. Science. In C. Seefeldt (ed.), *Curriculum for the Preschool-Primary Child: A Review of the Research*. Columbus, Ohio: Charles E. Merrill, 1976.

DIMITROVSKY, L., and ALMY, M. Early conservation as a prediction of arithmetic achievement. *The Journal of Psychology*, 1975, *91*, 75–80.

DION, K. Young children's stereotyping of facial attractiveness. *Developmental Psychology*, 1973, 9, 183–188.

DREMAN, S. B. Sharing behavior in Israeli children: Cognitive and social learning factors. *Child Development*, 1976, 47, 186–194.

EISENBERG-BERG, N., and HAND, M. The relationship of preschoolers' reasoning about prosocial moral conflicts to prosocial behavior. *Child Development*, 1979, 50, 356–363.

ELARDO, P. T., and COOPER, M. *Project AWARE: A Handbook for Teachers*. Reading, Mass.: Addison-Wesley, 1977.

ERLWANGER, S. H. Benny's conception of rules and answers in IPI mathematics. *Journal of Children's Mathematical Behavior*, 1973, *1*, 7–26.

ESTES, W. K. The information-processing approach to cognition: A confluence of metaphors and methods. In W. K. Estes (ed.), *Handbook of Learning and Cognitive Processes; Vol. 5: Human Information Processing*. New York: Wiley, 1978.

FREYBURG, J. T. Increasing the imaginative play of urban disadvantaged kindergarten children through systematic training. In J. L. Singer (ed.), *The Child's World of Make-Believe*. New York: Academic Press, 1973.

FRIEDMAN, S. L., and STEVENSON, M. B. Developmental changes in the understanding of implied motion in two-dimensional pictures. *Child Development*, 1975, *46*, 773–778.

FRIEDRICH, L. K., and STEIN, A. H. Prosocial television and young children: The effects of verbal labeling and role playing on learning and behavior. *Child Development*, 1975, *46*, 27–38.

FURMAN, W., and MASTERS, J. C. Affective consequences of social reinforcement, punishment, and neutral behavior. *Developmental Psychology*, 1980a, *16*, 100–104.

FURMAN, W., and MASTERS, J. C. Peer interaction, sociometric status, and resistance to deviation in young children. *Developmental Psychology*, 1980b, *16*, 229–236.

FURMAN, W., RAHE, D. F., and HARTUP, W. W. Rehabilitation of socially withdrawn preschool children through mixed-age and same-age socialization. *Child Development*, 1979, *50*, 915–922.

FUSON, K. C. An analysis of the counting-on solution procedure in addition. In T. P. Carpenter, J. M. Moser, and T. A. Romberg (eds.), *Addition and Subtraction: A Cognitive Perspective*. Hillsdale, N.J.: Lawrence Erlbaum Associates, 1982.

FUSON, K. C., and MURRAY, C. The haptic-visual perception, construction, and drawing of geometric shapes by children aged two to five: A Piagetian extension. In R. Lesh (ed.), *Recent Research Concerning the Development of Spatial and Geometric Concepts*. Columbus, Ohio: ERIC Clearinghouse for Science, Mathematics, and Environmental Education, 1978.

GAGNE, R. M. *The Conditions of Learning* (3rd ed.), New York: Holt, Rinehart & Winston, 1977.

GATES, L., and JAY, B. Children's understanding of "all" and "some." *Science Education*, 1978, *62*, 359–363.

GELMAN, R. Logical capacity of very young children: Number invariance rules. *Child Development*, 1972, *43*, 75–9.

GELMAN, R., and GALLISTEL, C. R. *The Child's Understanding of Number*. Cambridge, Mass.: Harvard University Press, 1978.

GELMAN, R., GREENO, J. G., and RILEY, M. S. Young children's counting and understanding of principles. Paper presented at the meeting of the Psychonomic Society, San Antonio, November 1978.

GINSBURG, H. P. Young children's informal knowledge of mathematics. *Journal of Children's Mathematical Behavior*, 1975, *1*, 63–156.

GINSBURG, H. P. Learning difficulties in children's arithmetic: A clinical cognitive approach. In A. R. Osborne (ed.), *Models for Learning Mathematics*. Columbus, Ohio: ERIC Center for Science, Mathematics, and Environmental Education, 1976.

GINSBURG, H. P. *Children's Arithmetic: The Learning Process*. New York: Van Nostrand Company, 1977.

GINSBURG, H. P. The development of addition in the contexts of culture, social class, and race. In T. P. Carpenter, J. M. Moser, and T. A. Romberg (eds.), *Addition and Subtraction: A Cognitive Perspective*. Hillsdale, N.J.: Lawrence Erlbaum Associates, 1982.

GLASER, R. Components of a psychology of instruction: Toward a science of design. *Review of Educational Research*, 1976, *46*, 1–24.

GOTTMAN, J., GONSO, J., and RASMUSSEN, B. Social interaction, social competence, and friendship in children. *Child Development*, 1975, *46*, 709–718.

GREENO, J. G. A study of problem solving. In R. Graser (ed.), *Advances in Instructional Psychology*, Vol. 1. Hillsdale, N.J.: Lawrence Erlbaum Associates, 1978.

GROEN, G. J., and RESNICK, L. B. Can preschool children invent addition algroithms? *Journal of Educational Psychology*, 1977, *69*, 645–652.

GRONLUND, N. *Sociometry in the Classroom*. New York: Harper, 1959.

GROVER, S. C. Hypothesis formation as a facilitator of conceptual development. *Canadian Journal of Behavioral Science*, 1979, *11*, 53–63.

GRUEN, G. E. Experiences affecting the development of number conservation in children. *Child Development*, 1965, *36*, 963–979.

GRUEN, G. E. Note on conservation: Methodological and definitional considerations. *Child Development*, 1966, *37*, 977–983.

HAMRICK, K. B. Oral language and readiness for the written symbolization of addition and subtraction. *Journal for Research in Mathematics Education*, 1979, *10*, 188–194.

HARTUP, W. W. Peer interaction and the behavioral development of the individual child. In E. Schopler and R. Reichler (eds.), *Psychopathology and Child Development: Research and Development*. New York: Plenum Press, 1976.

HATANO, G., and OSAWA, K. Digit memory of grand experts in abacus-derived mental calculation. Paper presented at the Annual Meeting of the American Psychological Association, Los Angeles, August 1981.

HENDRICKSON, A. D. An inventory of mathematical thinking done by incoming first-grade children. *Journal for Research in Mathematics Education*, 1979, *10*, 7–23.

HENRY, J. A. The transition from pre-operational to concrete-operational thinking: The effect of discrimination and classification activities. *Journal of Research in Science Teaching*, 1978, *15*, 145–152.

HERRON, J. D. Role of learning and development: Critique of Novak's comparison of Ausubel and Piaget. *Science Education*, 1978, *62*, 593–605.

HIEBERT, J. The effect of cognitive development on first-grade children's ability to learn linear measurement concepts. Unpublished doctoral dissertation, University of Wisconsin–Madison, 1979.

HIEBERT, J. Children's thinking. In E. Fennema (ed.), *Research in Mathematics Education: Implications for the 80s*. Alexandria, Va.: The Association for Supervision and Curriculum Development, 1981.

HUMPHREYS, L. G. Methinks they do protest too much. *Intelligence*, 1980, *4*, 179–183.

HUMPHREYS, L. G., and PARSONS, C. Piagetian tasks measure intelligence and intelligence tests assess cognitive development: A reanalysis. *Intelligence*, 1979, *3*, 369–382.

INHELDER, B., and PIAGET, J. *The Early Growth of Logic in the Child* (E. A. Lunzer and D. Papert, trans.). New York: Norton, 1964 (originally published in French, 1959).

JANTZ, R. K. Social studies. In C. Seefeldt (ed.), *Curriculum for the Preschool-Primary Child: A Review of the Research*. Columbus, Ohio: Charles E. Merrill, 1976.

JENNINGS, K. D. People versus object orientation, social behavior and intellectual abilities in preschool children. *Developmental Psychology*, 1975, *11*, 511–519.

JOHNSON, M. L. The effects of instruction on length relations on the qualitative seriation behavior of first- and second-grade children. *Journal for Research in Mathematics Education*, 1977, *8*, 145–147.

JOHNSON, M. L., and WILSON, J. W. Mathematics. In C. Seefeldt (ed.), *Curriculum for the Preschool-Primary Child: A Review of the Research*. Columbus, Ohio: Charles E. Merrill, 1976.

KAMII, C., and DEVRIES, R. *Piaget, Children, and Number*. Washington: National Association for the Education of Young Children, 1976.

KAMII, C., and DEVRIES, R. *Physical Knowledge in Preschool Education: Implications of Piaget's Theory*. Englewood Cliffs, N.J.: Prentice-Hall, 1978.

KARNES, M. B., and LEE, R. C. Mainstreaming in the preschool. In L. G. Katz (ed.), *Current Topics in Early Childhood Education*, Vol. 2. Norwood, N.J.: Ablex Publishing, 1979.

KAUFMAN, A. S., and KAUFMAN, N. L. Tests built from Piaget's and Gesell's tasks as predictors of first-grade achievement. *Child Development*, 1972, *43*, 521–535.

KIEREN, T. E. Activity learning. *Review of Educational Research*, 1969, *39*, 509–522.

KLAHR, D., and WALLACE, J. G. *Cognitive Development: An Information-Processing View*. Hillsdale, N.J.: Lawrence Erlbaum Associates, 1976.

KURLAND, D. M. The effect of massive practice on children's operational efficiency and short term memory span. Unpublished doctoral dissertation, University of Toronto, 1981.

KURTZ, V. R. Kindergarten mathematics: A survey. *Arithmetic Teacher*, 1978, *25*, 51–53.

LANGLOIS, J. H., and DOWNS, A. C. Peer relations as a function of physical attractiveness: The eye of the beholder or behavioral reality? *Child Development*, 1979, *50*, 409–418.

LARKINS, G., and SHAVER, J. P. Economics learning in grade one: The use of assessment studies. *Social Education*, 1969, *33*, 958–963.

LAWLER, R. W. *The progressive construction of mind (One child's learning: Addition)* (LOGO Memo No. 57). Cambridge, Mass.: M.I.T., Artificial Intelligence Laboratory, June, 1980.

LAWTON, J. T., and WANSKA, S. K. Advance organizers as a teaching strategy: A reply to Barnes and Clawson. *Review of Educational Research*, 1977, *47*, 233–244.

LESH, R. Recent cooperative research concerning the acquisition of spatial and geometric concepts. *Journal for Research in Mathematics Education*, 1977, *8*, 317–320.

LESH, R. (ed.), *Recent research concerning the development of spatial and geometric concepts*. Columbus, Ohio: ERIC Clearinghouse for Science, Mathematics, and Environmental Education, 1978.

LOCKWOOD, A. L. The effects of values clarification and moral development curricula on school-age subjects: A critical review of recent research. *Review of Educational Research*, 1978, *48*, 325–364.

LURIA, A. R. *The Role of Speech in the Regulation of Normal and Abnormal Behavior*. New York: Pergamon, 1961.

MARSHALL, H., and HAHN, S. C. Experimental modification of dramatic play. *Journal of Personality and Social Psychology*, 1967, *5*, 119–122.

MEICHENBAUM, D. H., and Goodman, J. Training impulsive children to talk to themselves: A means of developing self control. *Journal of Abnormal Psychology*, 1971, *77*, 115–126.

MILLER, G. A. The magical number seven, plus or minus two: Some limits on our capacity for processing information. *Psychological Review*, 1956, *63*, 81–97.

MILLER, S. A. Nonverbal assessment of Piagetian concepts. *Psychological Bulletin*, 1976, *83*, 405–430.

MILLER, S. A. Identity conservation and equivalence conservation: A critique of Brainerd and Hooper's analysis. *Psychological Bulletin*, 1978, *85*, 58–69.

MINOR, R. *Early Childhood Education: Its Principles and Practices*. New York: Appleton-Century, 1937.

MOORE, S. G. Considerateness and helpfulness in young children. *Young Children*, 1977, *32*, 73–76.

MOYER, J. C. The relationship between the mathematical structure of Euclidean transformations and the spontaneously developed cognitive structures of young children. *Journal for Research in Mathematics Education*, 1978, 9, 83–92.

MUSSEN, P., and EISENBERG-BERG, N. *Roots of Caring, Sharing, and Helping: The Development of Prosocial Behavior in Children.* San Francisco: W. H. Freeman, 1977.

NOVAK, J. D. An alternative to Piagetian psychology for science and mathematics education. *Science Education*, 1977, *71*, 453–477.

ODEN, S. L., and ASHER, S. R. Coaching children in social skills for friendship making. *Child Development*, 1977, *48*, 495–506.

OSHERSON, D. N. *Logical Abilities in Children*, Vol. 1. New York: Wiley, 1974.

O'SULLIVAN, K. A. Development of an observational instrument for recording the behaviors of preschool children interacting with a pendulum toy. Unpublished doctoral dissertation, University of Texas at Austin, 1980.

PASCUAL-LEONE, J. A mathematical model for the transition rule in Piaget's developmental stages. *Acta Psychologica*, 1970, *32*, 301–345.

PASCUAL-LEONE, J. On learning and development, Piagetian style: II. A critical historical analysis of Geneva's research programme. *Canadian Psychological Review*, 1976, *17*, 289–297.

PASCUAL-LEONE, J., GOODMAN, D., AMMON, P., and SUBELMAN, I. Piagetian theory and neo-Piagetian analysis as psychological guides in education. In J. M. Gallagher and J. A. Easley (eds.), *Knowledge and Development: Vol. 2, Piaget and Education.* New York: Plenum Press, 1978.

PASCUAL-LEONE, J., and SMITH, J. The encoding and decoding of symbols by children: A new experimental paradigm and a neo-Piagetian model. *Journal of Experimental Child Psychology*, 1969, 8, 328–355.

PATTERSON, G. R., and COBB, J. A. A dyadic analysis of "aggressive" behaviors. In J. P. Hill (ed.), *Minnesota Symposia on Child Psychology*, Vol. 5. Minneapolis: University of Minnesota Press, 1971.

PATTERSON, G. R., COBB, J. A., and RAY, R. S. A social engineering technology for retraining the families of aggressive boys. In H. E. Adams and I. P. Unikel (eds.), *Issues and Trends in Behavior Therapy.* Springfield, Ill. Charles C. Thomas, 1973.

PATTERSON, G. R., LITTMAN, R. A., and BRICKER, W. Assertive behavior in children: A step toward a theory of aggression. *Monographs of the Society for Research in Child Development*, 1967, *32*, Number 5.

PATTERSON, J. H. Sociodramatic play as a technique for increasing young children's generation of potential strategies for solving interpersonal problems. Unpublished doctoral dissertation, University of Wisconsin–Madison, 1979.

PAYNE, J. N. (ed.), *Mathematics Learning in Early Childhood.* Thirty-Seventh Yearbook. Reston, Va.: National Council of Teachers of Mathematics, 1975.

PIAGET, J. *The Child's Conception of Number.* New York: Norton, 1952.

PIAGET, J. Quantification, conservation, and nativism. *Science*, 1968, *162*, 976–979.

PIAGET, J., INHELDER, B., and SZEMINSKA, A. *The Child's Conception of Geometry* (E. A. Lunzer, trans.). New York: Basic Books, 1960 (originally published, 1948).

PRESSLEY, M. Increasing children's self-control through cognitive interventions. *Review of Educational Research*, 1979, 49, 319–370.

REESE, H. W., and SCHACK, M. L. Comment on Brainerd's criteria for cognitive structures. *Psychological Bulletin*, 1974, 81, 67–69.

RESNICK, L. B., and FORD, W. W. *The Psychology of Mathematics for Instruction*. Hillsdale, N.J.: Lawrence Erlbaum Associates, 1981.

RESNICK, L. B., WANG, M. C., and KAPLAN, J. Task analysis in curriculum design: A hierarchically sequenced introductory mathematics curriculum. *Journal of Applied Behavior Analysis*, 1973, 6, 679–710.

RICE, M. E., and GRUSEC, J. E. Saying and doing: Effects of observer performance. *Journal of Personality and Social Psychology*, 1975, 32, 584–593.

RILEY, M., GREENO, J. G., and HELLER, J. The development of children's problem solving ability in arithmetic. In H. Ginsburg (ed.), *The Development of Mathematical Thinking*. New York: Academic Press, 1982.

ROGERS, V., and LAYTON, D. An exploratory study of primary grade children's ability to conceptualize based upon content drawn from selected social studies topics. *Journal of Educational Research*, 1966, 59, 195–197.

ROMBERG, T. A. An emerging paradigm for research in addition and subtraction skills. In T. P. Carpenter, J. M. Moser, and T. A. Romberg (eds.), *Addition and Subtraction: A Cognitive Perspective*. Hillsdale, N.J.: Lawrence Erlbaum Associates, 1982.

ROMBERG, T. A., and COLLIS, K. F. *The Assessment of Children's M-Space* (Technical Report 540). Madison: University of Wisconsin, Wisconsin Research and Development Center for Individualized Schooling, 1980.

ROSEN, C. E. The effects of sociodramatic play on problem-solving behavior among culturally disadvantaged preschool children. *Child Development*, 1974, 45, 920–927.

ROSENHAN, D. Prosocial behavior of children. In W. W. Hartup (ed.), *The Young Child: Reviews of Research*, Vol. 2. Washington, D.C.: National Association for the Education of Young Children, 1972.

ROTHENBERG, G. Children's social sensitivity and the relationship to interpersonal competence, intrapersonal comfort and intellectual level. *Developmental Psychology*, 1970, 2, 335–350.

RUSHTON, J. P. Socialization and the altruistic behavior of children. *Psychological Bulletin*, 1976, 83, 898–913.

SABAR, N. Science, curriculum and society: Trends in science curriculum. *Science Education*, 1979, 63, 257–269.

SCHWAB, L., and STERN, C. Effects of variety on the learning of a social studies concept by preschool children. *Journal of Experimental Education*, 1969, 38, 81–86.

SERDUS, M., and TANK, M. L. A critical appraisal of twenty-six national social studies projects. *Social Education*, 1970, 34, 383–449.

SHANTZ, C. U. The development of social cognition. In E. M. Hetherington (ed.), *Review of Child Development Research*, Vol. 5. Chicago: University of Chicago Press, 1975.

SHAVELSON, R. Methods for examining representations of a subject matter in a student's memory. *Journal of Research in Science Teaching*, 1974, 11, 231–249.

SHELTON, W., SLABY, R. G., and ROBINSON, H. B. *Social Development in Young Chil-*

dren: A Report for Teachers. Seattle: University of Washington, 1975 (ERIC Document Reproduction Service No. ED 110 166).

SHURE, M. B. Real-life problem solving for parents and children: An approach to social competence. In D. P. Rathjen and J. P. Foreyt (eds.), *Social Competence.* Elmsford, N.Y.: Pergamon Press, 1980.

SHURE, M. B., and SPIVACK, G. *Solving Interpersonal Problems: A Program for Four-Year-Old Nursery School Children: Training Script.* Philadelphia: Department of Mental Health Sciences, Hahnemann Community Mental Health/Mental Retardation Center, 1971.

SHURE, M. B., and SPIVACK, G. *A Mental Health Program for Kindergarten Children: Training Script.* Philadelphia: Department of Mental Health Sciences, Hahnemann Community Mental Health/Mental Retardation Center, 1978.

SHURE, M. B., and SPIVACK, G. Interpersonal problem solving as a mediator of behavioral adjustment in preschool and kindergarten children. *Journal of Applied Developmental Psychology,* 1980, *1,* 29–43.

SIGEL, I., ROEPER, A., and HOOPER, F. A training procedure for acquisition of Piaget's conservation of quantity: A pilot study and its replication. *British Journal of Educational Psychology,* 1966, *36,* 301–311.

SILVERMAN, I. W., and ROSE, A. P. Subitizing and counting skills in 3-year-olds. *Developmental Psychology,* 1980, *16,* 539–540.

SIMON, H. A. *The Sciences of the Artificial.* Cambridge, Mass.: M.I.T. Press, 1969.

SLABY, R. G., and QUARFOTH, G. R. Effects of television on the developing child. In B. W. Camp (ed.), *Advances in Behavioral Pediatrics,* Vol. 1. Greenwich, Conn.: Johnson Associates, Inc., in press.

SMILANSKY, S. *The Effects of Sociodramatic Play on Disadvantaged Preschool Children.* New York: Wiley, 1968.

SMITH, E. L., and PADILLA, M. J. Strategies used by first-grade children in ordering varying numbers of objects by length and weight. *Journal of Research in Science Teaching,* 1977, *14,* 461–466.

SMOCK, C. D. Discovering psychological principles for mathematics instruction. In R. Lesh (ed.), *Cognitive Psychology and the Mathematics Laboratory.* Columbus, Ohio: ERIC Clearinghouse for Science, Mathematics, and Environmental Education, 1973.

SMOCK, C. D. A constructivist model for instruction. In A. R. Osborne (ed.), *Models for Learning Mathematics.* Columbus, Ohio: ERIC Center for Science, Mathematics, and Environmental Education, 1976.

SPIVACK, G., and SHURE, M. B. *Social Adjustment of Young Children: A Cognitive Approach to Solving Real-Life Problems.* San Francisco: Jossey-Bass, 1974.

SPIVACK, G., PLATT, J. J., and SHURE, M. B. *The Problem-Solving Approach to Adjustment: A Guide to Research and Intervention.* San Francisco: Jossey-Bass, 1976.

SPODEK, B. Social studies for young children: Identifying intellectual goals. *Social Education,* 1974, *38,* 40–45.

SPODEK, B. *Teaching in the Early Years* (2nd ed.). Englewood Cliffs, N.J.: Prentice-Hall, 1978.

STARKEY, P., and GELMAN, R. The development of addition and subtraction abilities prior to formal schooling in arithmetic. In T. P. Carpenter, J. M. Moser, and T. A.

Romberg (eds.), *Addition and Subtraction: A Cognitive Perspective.* Hillsdale, N.J.: Lawrence Erlbaum Associates, 1982.

STAUB, E. A. To rear a prosocial child: Reasoning, learning by doing and learning by teaching others. In D. J. DePalma and J. M. Foley (eds.), *Moral Development: Current Theory and Research.* Hillsdale, N.J.: Lawrence Erlbaum Associates, 1975.

STEFFE, L. P. On a model for teaching young children mathematics. In A. R. Osborne (ed.), *Models for Learning Mathematics.* Columbus, Ohio: ERIC Center for Science, Mathematics, and Environmental Education, 1976.

STEFFE, L. P., SPIKES, W. C., and HIRSTEIN, J. J. *Summary of Quantitative Comparisons and Class Inclusion as Readiness Variables for Learning First Grade Arithmetical Content.* Athens: The Georgia Center for the Study of Learning and Teaching Mathematics, 1976.

STEPHENS, B., McLAUGHLIN, J., MILLER, C., and GLASS, G. Factorial structure of selected psycho-educational measures and Piagetian reasoning assessments. *Developmental Psychology,* 1972, *6,* 343–348.

STEWART, J. Content and cognitive structure: Critique of assessment and representation techniques used by science education researchers. *Science Education,* 1979, *63,* 395–405.

STYCZYNSKI, L. E., and LANGLOIS, J. H. The effects of familiarity on behavioral stereotypes associated with physical attractiveness in young children. *Child Development,* 1977, *48,* 1137–1141.

SYNDER, M., TANKE, E. D., and BERSCHEID, E. Social perception and interpersonal behavior: On the self-fulfilling nature of social stereotypes. *Journal of Personality and Social Psychology,* 1977, *35,* 656–666.

THORNDIKE, E. L. *The Psychology of Arithmetic.* New York: Macmillan, 1924.

URBAIN, E. S., and KENDALL, P. C. Review of social-cognitive problem-solving interventions with children. *Psychological Bulletin,* 1980, *88,* 109–143.

VYGOTSKY, L. S. *Thought and Language* (E. Haufmann and G. Vakar, eds. and trans.). Cambridge, Mass.: M.I.T. Press, 1962 (Originally published 1934, 1956).

WANG, M. C., and RESNICK, L. B. *The Primary Education Program,* 12 vols. Johnstown, Pa.: Mafex, 1978.

WANG, M. C., RESNICK, L. B., and BOOZER, R. F. The sequence of development of some early mathematics behaviors. *Child Development,* 1971, *42,* 1767–1778.

WELCH, W. W. Evaluating the impact of national curriculum projects. *Science Education,* 1976, *60,* 475–483.

WELCH, W. W. Twenty years of science curriculum development: A look back. In D. C. Berliner (ed.), *Review of Research in Education,* Vol. 7. Washington, D.C.: American Educational Research Association, 1979.

WEST, L. H. T., and FENSHAM, P. J. Prior knowledge and the learning of science: A review of Ausubel's theory of this process. *Studies in Science Education,* 1974, *1,* 61–81.

YARROW, M. R., SCOTT, P. M., and WAXLER, C. Z. Learning concern for others. *Developmental Psychology,* 1973, *8,* 240–260.

ZAHAVI, S., and ASHER, S. R. The effect of verbal instructions on preschool children's aggressive behavior. *Journal of School Psychology,* 1978, *16,* 146–153.

ZAHN-WAXLER, C., RADKE-YARROW, M., and KING, R. A. Child rearing and children's prosocial initiations toward victims of distress. *Child Development*, 1979, *50*, 319–330.

ZA'ROUR, G. I. Identity versus equivalence in weight conservation. *Science Education*, 1977, *61*, 541–547.

ZASLAVSKY, C. *Preparing Young Children for Math*. New York: Schocken Books, 1979.

CHAPTER 13

The Visual Arts in Early Childhood Education: Development and the Creation of Meaning

Nancy R. Smith

REPRESENTATION AND THE CREATION of meaning through it is a fundamental capacity of humans; through representation experience can be objectified and given form, fantasy imagined, meaning crystallized, and visions of reality shared. The capacity for representation of experience using visual means emerges naturally in the course of development, and visual materials offer a particularly satisfying mode of expression to many young children. As a consequence, the visual arts are a powerful means for helping children to organize experience of both fantasy and reality. Through them children can come to know themselves and their world more fully.

Art activities are beneficial to children because they contribute to children's capacity to make and understand meaning; education in art should be directed toward this end. Thus, this chapter will focus on research as it applies to the creation of meaning and will take up issues in the development of this capacity, including construction of concepts of materials, of visual properties, of the formation of imagery, and of the meaning of images. Research covering these issues over the age span from infancy through the eighth year will be discussed.

Since a number of studies do not fall within this rubric, a *Survey of Other Research* has been included just before the *Conclusion*. Research in art education is comparatively new and suffers from difficulties in examining complex and elusive phenomena; as a consequence, the quality of studies varies widely. Accordingly, the evaluation of individual studies reported in this chapter will be left to the interested reader.

In order to frame the discussion in an historic context we begin with a review of art educational practice over the past century.

Contemporary Art Educational Practice and Its Sources

In the recent past, working with art materials has been thought therapeutic to the emotional health of young children. It has been valued as a release from anxiety and inhibition and as an appropriate outlet for aggressions and fantasies. Similarly, it is understood to supply adults with insight into the emotions of children (Alschuler & Hattwick, 1947; Winnicott, 1971) and it is thought conducive to the development of creative capacities (Lowenfeld, 1949). Interwoven with these goals has been the belief that both the therapeutic and the creative functions of art will occur best without direction from the teacher. Schaffer-Simmern (1947) enjoins the teacher not to interfere with the natural unfolding of artistic activity.

Serious attention to children's art began at the end of the nineteenth century. Numerous descriptive accounts of the developmental changes in drawings were written in biographies of infants by parent-psychologists (for example, Luquet, 1927). These studies established a serious attitude toward children's art work and also set forth a sequence of natural development in drawing that began with scribbles, passed through a phase of schematic work, and achieved more adultlike representations in later childhood.

At the same time that these studies were taking place, there was a shift in education toward a more child-centered pedagogy. In Germany, Froebel (1900) called attention to the natural interests of the child and capitalized specifically on the child's desire to manipulate materials. There were also art educators such as Britisch (1926), who proposed a curriculum based on the organic evolution of artistic forms from simple to complex, and Cizek (1912), who professed to offer children no instruction until asked. Cizek claimed instead to substitute sympathy and understanding, allowing creative expression to come from within the child.

During the same period, John Dewey called attention to the whole child. He theorized that children were organisms developing in and through interaction with the environment, and he held that they needed freedom to exercise their intelligence in the environment. The principle of noninterference also received reinforcement from the work of Freud. His *On the Interpretation of Dreams* had been published in 1900, and as the relation between art and unconscious needs and desires was recognized, art came to be seen as an avenue for therapy.

Another important factor contributing to an emphasis on freer forms of artistic activity was the emergence of the Modern movement in art. Expressionism, Surrealism, and Cubism came into being and were recognized as styles during this period. Indeed, in 1913 the famous Armory Show held in New York, Chicago, and Boston heralded to Americans art as expression, experiment, and individual innovation.

These historical trends—the study of child development; the liberalization of educational practice through the work of Froebel, Cizek, Dewey, and others; the relating of art to unconscious needs by Freud; and the emergence of innovation and expression as explicit values in art—came together in the work of Victor Lowenfeld, an Austrian art educator who came to the United States at the time of

Hitler's rise to power in Germany. Lowenfeld was personally affected by the inflexible dogmatism and disregard for individual differences in German educational practices at the time. He believed that such training had made the eventual acceptance of Nazi totalitarianism possible.

His book, *Creative and Mental Growth,* first published in 1947, proposed freedom for the child, nonintervention by the teacher, respect for the sequence of developmental stages, and mental health-*cum*-creativity as the ultimate goals of art in the schools. Creativity was associated with innovation and was held to be innate, emerging organically with development. The role of the teacher was to keep damaging influences out so that the natural unfolding of creativity would not be stunted or impaired. This book was the single most influential factor in American art education in the twenty years following its publication. Viewed in historical context, it is possible to understand how this point of view came to permeate American educational thought and practice.

It is interesting to note that despite widespread interest there has been comparatively little empirical research on creativity in early childhood art (more general research is offered in Terman, 1925, and Torrance, 1961). In the visual arts most studies have been efforts to determine or describe attributes of creativity (for example, Lewis & Mussen, 1969).

The drawbacks of Lowenfeld's program are evident in the light of contemporary developmental psychology. Current theory holds that development is the result of interactions between genetically prompted structures in the child and stimulation from the environment; consequently, children are believed to need stimulation to progress normally. Lowenfeld acknowledged the need for outside stimulation when he advised teachers to evoke children's memories of real-life experiences as sources of content. At the same time, he called for isolation from adult artistic influences, inveighed against copying, and omitted observational drawing from his program for young children. In so doing he eliminated important experiences and rich sources of artistic stimulation. It seems only reasonable to suppose that children deprived of these sources would lack knowledge and skill; and it is probably not extreme to attribute some portion of the ineptitude felt by many adolescent children to these omissions.

It may be that Lowenfeld believed outside influences would stifle children because he equated children's creative processes with those of adults. However, children's artistic activities differ significantly from those of adults. For children, making art is the creation of order in a relatively limited and disorganized state of knowledge. With few rules and minimal information, children strive to organize and image their thoughts and feelings about the world of experience. Adult artists, working with much more information and many more rules strive to move beyond conventional rules and constraints to imagine new visions of reality. The children's goal is order; the freshness of their work is a sign of their lack of rules as well as their nascent ingenuity in the creation of meaning (Dudek, 1975). Conversely, for artists the goal is freshness of vision and the struggle is to achieve subservience of order to freshness of vision. Lowenfeld seems not to have recognized this crucial difference and to have transposed the adult need for freedom from cultural constraints to freedom from culture for children. Apparently, he was unable to imagine how adult artistic influences might beneficially be provided for children. This may be because he had no general theory of cognitive-affective development in art and could not select content from artistic sources in accordance with an organized view of children's developmental needs and abilities. His own discussion of developmental stages in art is limited to a descriptive account of imagery and reference to emotional needs and benefits. There is little mention of cognitive processes or theory. Furthermore, since he had omitted drawing from observation from his program for young children, the stages he described were based on memory work and offer a restricted picture of children's abilities. His caution is understandable; and, indeed, without a deep understanding of children's artistic processes, teachers may impose on them as he feared. But with the awareness of this problem and more insight into child development, no such negative outcome need occur.

This discussion has called into question some current educational beliefs and practices. Among them are that (1) the role of teachers is to help children make images of the sort described by Lowenfeld but otherwise to refrain from intervention; (2) a major purpose of art in the schools is to provide opportunities for uninhibited expression; and (3) children should not be exposed to adult art forms or work from observation. These beliefs and practices are contrary to the dynamics of child development, and their revision through study of cognitive-affective processes in art is necessary to foster the creation of meaning in art education.

Symbolization and Art Education

The study of meaning creation may fruitfully be approached through the analysis of the processes of symbolization as discussed in developmental psychology. In order to avoid confusion with more current uses of the words symbolization and representation, it will be helpful to clarify the meanings as used here. Symbolization is the more general of the two referring to any and all events in which people use some means to call to mind nonpresent persons, objects, or events. Gestures, words, graphic images, play, and dreams are all vehicles of symbolization. A symbol is more usually thought of as an image that refers to another entity metaphorically—for example, when a lion is used to denote strength. This form is subsumed, together with all other forms of reference, in the term symbolization as it will be used here.

Representation refers to a limited subset of visual symbolizations in which some physical quality of a symbolizing medium is in an isomorphic correspondence with some physical quality of a referent. Thus, in a painting of a tree there is physical correspondence of shapes and colors between tree and painted lines.

There are nonobjective as well as objective forms of symbolic reference. In nonobjective symbols, expressive properties of symbols (Arnheim, 1954; Smith,

1979a; Werner, 1948) are understood to convey meaning without referring to concrete objects. For example, lines can convey qualities such as speed or uprising movement and emotions such as excitement or depression without depicting objects.

The dynamic nature of the process of symbolization is most powerfully etched in the theory of Werner and Kaplan (1963). Their theory proposes that a symbol and the concept of the object to which it refers are created in relation to each other by "form-building processes." It is the activity of these form-building processes that brings experience into realization for children as well as for adults. Symbolization takes place in several modes: gesture, language, play, and the arts. However, the arts are distinguished from other modes of symbolization by three significant characteristics. First, in art, deliberate consideration is given to aesthetic and formal qualities. The way in which a symbol is designed is as important as the object or event to which it refers. Second, in a work of art, conscious attention is given to emotional content both by the artist and by the audience. This is not true in more objective modes of communication. Third, these two attributes are united in a work of art because emotional content is embodied in the formal qualities as well as represented in the imagery (Arnheim, 1954; Langer, 1953). Because of the interplay between thought and feeling in form and content, it is possible in the arts to symbolize the complex blend of objective and expressive qualities in the experience of real life. Through art the inner and outer worlds of experience may be brought into relation. Thus, the arts serve a particular psychological function: to capture and embody meanings that bridge thought and feeling.

Doyle (1976) describes the important role of the medium in the bridging process with admirable clarity.

> The artist, in fact, every thinker needs such a medium, a vehicle for organizing and thinking about experience. And although some psychologists associate thought with logical operations and abstract verbal generalization, the artist, thinking in a medium, thinks differently. He thinks forms, and people talking, and images, and rhythms. When the artist thinks in this way certain so-called logical distinctions disappear—for example, the distinction between intellect and emotion. In life we simultaneously grasp an experience and feel it emotionally; we understand that someone is helping us with no apparent benefit to himself and we feel gratitude. We feel the grayness of the day as rain approaches and feel the melancholy. In a medium, an artist can simultaneously communicate event and feeling [1976, p. 10].

Doyle also refers to the medium as "a kind of reality principle" because its characteristics make specific demands on artists and set up limits against which they must test their dawning conceptualizations. In this respect, materials serve a function similar to that proposed by Erikson (1972) for the rules or limits in play. These, he says, provide the structure for "leeway" in play so that the "free" experimentation that develops mastery can take place. In the visual arts, the physical and visual properties of materials provide structure and anchor the form-building process in the concrete.

Three different components of knowledge are used in forming a symbol: the symbolizer's knowledge of the material, of the referent, and of the possible modes of correspondence between them. What finally appears in the symbol is a selection from the sum total of information the symbol maker has about the referent and about the material. This selection is based on the symbol maker's understanding of how the two may be related as well as factors relating to the symbol maker's personal and immediate intention. Thus, in order to understand any given symbol one must consider all three components of the process; and to understand children's symbolization, it is necessary to study the development of all three components.

Better understanding of the development of the three components of symbolization would enable teachers to design appropriate curricula using a full range of resources. It would also enable them to plan lessons and curricula that engage in the creation of the most substantive sorts of meaning from the point of view of the child.

Review of Research: Components of Symbolization in Children's Art

Understanding the Nature of Materials: Physical and Visual Properties

Several comprehensive studies cover the first years of artistic activity during which children come to understand the nature of materials. Those of Biber (1932), Kellogg (1969), and Smith (1972) are based on collections of spontaneous drawings and paintings. Biber offers a careful analysis of the characteristics of children's drawings in relation to cognitive and affective development; Kellogg provides a classification system of typical configurations; and Smith traces the evolution of visual concepts and includes step-by-step process records of paintings and drawings. There is one full-length case study of an individual child (Eng, 1931); Arnheim (1954) discusses the period theoretically. The account that follows draws on all these sources generally but relies most specifically on Smith.

The influence of a material on the form of the symbol has been a major point for a number of authors (Arnheim, 1954; Olson, 1970; Salomon, 1979; Wolf & Gardner, 1979). These investigators have emphasized the fact that a given material elicits and also limits the content of a symbol; some have discussed the child's gradual acquisition of information about materials, but there has been relatively little recognition that it is necessary for children to learn the nature of materials before they can use them in symbols.

Works of art are made of substances manipulated into patterns of lines, colors, and shapes (whether representational or nonobjective). In order to arrange a material into such patterns, it is necessary to understand its physical properties (weight, plasticity, cohesiveness, and so forth), its visual properties (line, shape, color, texture, and so forth), and the performatory actions of hand and eye that produce such patterns (Olson, 1970).

Perceptual response to visual properties such as shape and color is present very early. By the end of the first year of life, sensory response is much like that of adults. There are, of course, considerable differences between adults' and children's understandings of such stimuli (Bryant, 1974; Vurpillot, 1976). However, the ability to respond to visual configurations, as for example a straight line, does not make it possible to produce controlled versions of them, as children's scribbles and copying problems make clear (Olson & Pagliuso, 1968). Nor can we attribute the disorderly appearance of these early efforts to the child's limited motor skills; the drawings would be more random if they were the product of poor control (Arnheim, 1954; Olson, 1970; Piaget & Inhelder, 1956).

It seems more likely that in the beginning, children lack the necessary concepts of physical and visual properties to give direction to their hands. This interpretation is suggested by the logic of the sequence in which their abilities emerge. As children grow their work demonstrates an orderly progression of visual properties from simple to ever more complex.

In the beginning, with no concepts of the possible visible consequences, children move arm and hand in reflexlike motoric rhythms. These movements produce characteristic forms in the material which, over time, the child begins to recognize and differentiate. Piaget and Inhelder (1956) suggest that the origin of drawing is the rhythmic pattern of the child's movement and the tangle of lines so produced. In these tangles is contained, in an undifferentiated state, the fundamental elements of drawing from which more complex concepts will be developed. Smith (1972) traces the evolution of the concepts of line, shape, and picture space in three- to five-year-olds. Lines begin as traces of rhythmic zigzag movements, as noted by Piaget and Inhelder; thereafter, children master, in order, discontinuity versus continuity, straightness versus curvedness, changes in direction, orientation, and intersection, thus becoming able to control lines on paper.

In the course of this evolution, an early capacity to produce vertical lines was noted. Connolly and Elliott (1972) report a greater proportion of vertical lines in spontaneous easel paintings of children whose mean age is four. However, Gesell and Ames (1946) found that children of eighteen months can copy vertical (and horizontal) lines. Apparently children's motor skills are sufficient for copying verticals at eighteen months, but their conceptual skills are not sufficient for producing them without prompting until later (see also Maccoby, 1968).

Construction of the concept of graphic verticals may depend on body factors and also on the coordination of the orientation of lines within the axes-frame of the paper space (Arnheim, 1954; Berman, 1976; Smith, 1972). A further extension of these vertical and horizontal coordinations may be the child's preference for perpendicular angles (Goodnow, 1977; Ibbotson & Bryant, 1976).

The capacity to produce controlled shapes emerges from the capacity to produce controlled lines. Children of three and four first create rectangular shapes by drawing a set of parallel verticals and then adding a set of parallel horizontals to them. Only later do they draw a continuous pathway around the perimeter of the shape (Gesell & Ames, 1946; Smith, 1972). Spielman (1976) reasons that children's first lines are understood by them as autonomous entities and that, when used to form a shape, they lose their autonomy. Thus, the child requires more time to develop the capacity to draw controlled shapes with a continuous line.

Eventually, children construct a complement of visual concepts of line, space, shape, and color that make it possible for them to create organized designs of considerable complexity (Smith, 1972). It is assumed that the necessary physical concepts of materials are constructed at the same time. The role of motor activity in the construction of both these sets of concepts would be central in the theory of Piaget. Whatever role it does in fact play, it is clear that children teach themselves the performance skills and motor sequences required to create controlled forms of visual graphic elements through manipulative experimentation with materials.

Children come to know the different capacities of materials but they also come to generalize properties of materials that are not medium-specific (Olson, 1970). They are more likely to discover these similarities and differences because their initial movements with each material are very similar (Smith, 1979a). However, because of the different physical and visual properties of each material, similar movements produce different results. Repeated back and forth motions produce patches of color in paint, tangled lines in crayon, and coils or balls in clay. Nevertheless, some similarities emerge; and in time, it is possible for children to produce similar shapes in different media. Thus, manipulation leads to both differentiation and generalization. The same pattern of motor activity leading to differentiation and generalization of properties may be seen in other media. Golomb (1974) writes of development in the use of playdough as well as drawing. Hirsch (1974) traces development of concepts in block-building.

It is essential to the creation of meaning with materials for the child to develop a deep and rich understanding of the physical and visual properties of materials. In order for this to take place, opportunities for experimentation with appropriate materials over sufficient time are necessary. More empirical research is needed to determine clearly the evolution of the capacity to produce basic visual elements and also to combine them in designs.

The development of an understanding of the physical and visual properties of materials occupies the child's first several years of working with materials. Sometime during the third or fourth year after the child is knowledgeable about materials, the innate capacity for symbolization begins to emerge in the use of materials, and another dimension of expression is added to children's work.

The Creation of Visual Symbols: Expressive and Objective Modes of Correspondence

Although the capacity for symbolization is first evidenced during the second year beginning with gestured imitations, it evolves rapidly to include other forms including language and play (Franklin, 1973; Piaget, 1951; Werner & Kaplan, 1963). Nevertheless, the representational shaping of art materials begins considerably later, during the third and fourth years following the development of basic understandings of materials.

Werner and Kaplan hold that the form a symbol takes is the consequence of the maker's conception of the material, the referent, and of the possible correspondences between them. Young children's concepts of possible correspondences derive from objective similarities familiar to adults but also from another less familiar mode of correspondence based on physiognomic perception. Werner (1948) proposed that we have a set of perceptions that respond to expressive characteristics in phenomena (see also Arnheim, 1954; Gombrich, 1963). He called this mode of perception physiognomic and described it as more dependent on physical sensation and emotion than on logic. It is natural to young children, available to adults, and much used by artists. Through it, nonobjective imagery is perceived as expressing emotions and concepts, objective imagery is given emotional force, and composition is used to convey meaning. Through it, we may perceive lines as sad, trees as suffering, and compositions as turbulent.

Some characteristics of children's drawings based on physiognomic perception make them difficult for adults to understand; the objective contours of shapes may be ignored and objects may be rendered in simple circles or lines; spatial relationships are simplified and based on topological concepts; movement is often used as a feature of correspondence. In addition, the images of children offer few correspondences (Smith, 1979b) while those of adults are redundant, offering multiple cues from lines, spaces, color, and spatial arrangements. For example, a child may call a vertical line "a tall building." In this example, verticality and relative length are the only correspondences the child feels are necessary. Thus, children create sparse images using expressive features, such as movement in line for correspondence, and omitting more objective geometric properties of shape and spatial arrangement.

However difficult it may be to decode individual configurations (without verbal assistance from the child), these images in particular deserve serious study, for they embody the foundation of expression in art. In their fusion of form and content, of expressive and objective correspondences, resides the germ of all later creations of meaning and the bridging of thought and feeling through visual means (Smith, 1979b).

Children often begin symbolizing by naming configurations they have already made. In this proto-symbolic activity, the child's choice of referent is prompted by the configuration of the finished drawing. As a consequence, the choice of referents reflects children's interpretations of properties in the material more than it does their need to present a particular theme. There is an interesting consequence of the influence of materials on the choice of referents at this time. Since different materials have different properties (physical and visual), typical referents identified by young children differ from material to material (Smith, 1979a). In paint, frequently named referents are smoke, rain, and fire; those in clay are food in various forms; and those in blocks are buildings and portable objects (tools, dishes, and so on).

Names are often prompted by favorite design configurations. For example, a circle with radiating lines is a common design. It combines a number of visual concepts the child has recently learned, including straight and curved lines, enclosure, spacing at regular intervals along a line (in this case the curved boundary line), orientation of lines, joining of lines at perpendicular angles, and so forth. (This interpretation differs from that of Kellogg, 1969, who attributes the form of the configuration to the influence of the collective unconscious rather than cognitive developmental processes.)

When beginning to symbolize, the child often calls this configuration "a spider" (Biber, 1932; Smith, 1972). Physiognomic perception is involved in this creation of a relationship between the lines and the child's conception of a spider. It involves affect in that spiders are frightening and lines that poke or jut out into space are perceived as dangerous (Werner, 1948). The form of the spider is perceived with global simplicity as a mass in the middle of the many radiating lines.

A common early planned symbol is that of "a man" or "a person," and a common form of it is the so-called tadpole man, that is, a configuration composed simply of a circle with two descending lines. Inside the circle there are usually other circles or lines standing for eyes, nose, and mouth. There is no trunk depicted in the drawing and a number of explanations have been offered for this omission. Arnheim (1954) and Golomb (1974) consider that the circle represents head and body in one shape, standing syncretically for the total figure. Piaget and Inhelder (1969), citing Luquet (1927), hold that the trunk is omitted because of the child's inability to synthesize. Freeman (1977) suggests that the head-legs configuration may be the result of an end-anchoring memory effect. Kellogg (1969) and Smith (1972) refer to the influence of the child's prior knowledge of circular designs on the configuration. Goodnow (1977) studies the influence of the children's rules of sequencing and layout. Werner (1948) attributes the large size of faces in general to emotional perspective, that is, emphasis on features with emotional salience.

The pattern of this group of interpretations is suggestive. One group of observers focuses on the child's conception of the referent (Piaget & Inhelder; Werner; Freeman); another, on the child's conception of the material (Kellogg; Smith); and another, on the mode of correspondence between material and referent (Arnheim; Golomb; Goodnow). The most penetrating explanation will probably be found in an interpretation that takes each of the three components of symbol formation into account.

In general, the rules of relationship between material and referent shift with development from expressive and simplified relationships to ever more differentiated objective and conceptual relationships. The shift to more conceptual relationships is particularly evident in the representation of the three-dimensional world on the two-dimensional surface. Studies record the gradual introduction of occlusion, vertical positioning, and obliques to indicate recession into space in drawing; but specific rules of correspondence are still to be identified (Lewis, 1973–1974; Phillips, Hobbs & Pratt, 1978; Willats, 1977). Salkind (1972) discusses correspondences in color.

The shift from simple to more complex rules of representation is paralleled by the child's growing awareness of modes of correspondence. Korzenik (1977) studied the child's gradual recognition of the necessity for communicative imagery. Children of five blame any lack of understanding on the viewer, while older children recognize themselves as responsible for making the image comprehensible. Elkind (1969) also reports on the development of metasymbolic awareness.

Research is needed to clarify these aspects of correspondence and to examine other areas of correspondence as well. Among these is correspondence in three-dimensional media (see Brown, 1975, for development of figures in clay) and how expressive correspondences continue to be used and elaborated in older children (Carothers & Gardner, 1979).

Concepts of the Referent

It is important to attend to the child's gradually evolving understanding of experiences of objects and events. This constitutes the reservoir of information about referents upon which the child draws in forming a symbol. Here particularly, it is important to attend to the child's evolving understanding of what constitutes an appropriate referent for an image. For example, the child of five to seven may understand the act of representation as the depiction of a generic form rather than of an individual object (Barrett & Light, 1976), and thus choose salient parts for their ability to offer categorical definition. Children's use of simple categorical thought during this age span has been observed in a variety of symbolic modes (Ives, 1979; Rosch, Mervis, Gray, Johnson & Boyes-Braem, 1976). If in their early planned representations children have in mind an illustration of a generic car, house, or tree, that might account in part for some of the simplicity of these configurations. Certainly, it is true that there is a developmental shift from representation of basic types such as a person to representation of more differentiated types such as a little girl. Later, children come to add individual objects to their array of possible referents for images. If this progression is the result of changing definitions of an acceptable referent, then the attitude educators have had toward early so-called stereotypes needs to be revised.

Rand and Wagner (1970), tracking developmental change in children's representations of a motivated act, observe a similar sequence and note that it is the adult finally who sees the general in the specific. A charming example of changes in the definition of the referent is offered by S. Fein (1976). Here, a pictorial record of one child's horse drawings from earliest representations of essential horseness to adolescent considerations of the social context is offered.

Children's development of the concept of space has received a great deal of attention (Laurendeau & Pinard, 1970; Piaget & Inhelder, 1956), and the theme of perspective taking in particular has been much studied. This topic is of interest in relation to children's ability to use the conventions of perspective. The research derives from a particular study carried out by Piaget and Inhelder (1956) in which children, looking at a model of three mountains, were asked to identify viewpoints other than their own. The Piagetian study found that children of six to eight choose their own for all viewpoints, while children of nine to ten distinguish those of others. Piaget and Inhelder suggest that egocentrism declines as the result of internal coordination of all possible viewpoints and that one consequence of this coordination is older children's ability to use the rules of perspective.

However, subsequent studies have challenged the Piagetian account. Some have considered social influences (Fishbein, Lewis & Keiffer, 1972) and some, the rotation of the display rather than the subject (Huttenlocker & Presson, 1973). Many of these report fewer egocentric errors from younger children than did the Piagetian study (Borke, 1975). The question of children's perspective-taking ability and its relation to drawing is unresolved and needs further study.

More generally, we may conclude that conscientious assessment of art forms must take into account the child's changing conceptualization of each of the three components of symbolization. This is as true for researchers as it is for teachers. Recognition that a number of factors impinge on the representational process is growing, and many observers are questioning the practice of interpreting art products as indicators of any one factor (Freeman, 1977; Goodnow, 1977; Smith, 1979b) but the three components of symbolization deserve much more recognition.

Several other factors may need attention as well. These are central processes, emotional status, performatory processes, and the development of the child's capacity to respond to works of art. It is to the consideration of these factors associated with symbolization that I now turn.

Central Processes, Production Processes, and Emotional Status

There may be a central symbolizing function. While the presence and nature of such a function is yet to be determined, the importance of considering such a possibility is underscored by observations of the unlikely ability of the blind to make simple drawings (Kennedy, 1979; Millar, 1975). If those who have no visual experience of objects or images can make rudimentary drawings, it may be that there are general capacities for making symbolic correspondences buried deep in the human mind (Smith, 1979c).

The role of memory has been largely disregarded in the children's art literature. It has been assumed that there is no significant difference in young children's work made from memory or from observation, because children at five, six, and seven seem to ignore the scene in front of them. Goodenough (1926) and Eng (1931) express this conviction and cite a study by Kershensteiner (1905) in which young children, when asked to draw a schoolmate, drew other poses in addition to the one before them. However, several recent studies put this assumption to question. Children drawing from observation have been found to produce more articulate contours, to include more details, and to use occlusion at a younger age

(Freeman & Janikoun, 1972; Willats, 1977). Furthermore, when assisted in the recall of details by dictation, children's representations are more detailed and well integrated (Golomb, 1974). Thus, some simplifications in children's art may reflect difficulties in accessing from memory. The effects of drawing from observation and the role of memory in young children's art require further study.

The processes involved in producing appropriate hand movements also deserve more attention. Olson (1970) has given particular attention to the problem of performance and Rand (1973) has examined task analysis, motor skills, and motor training in drawing. Studies in which figures are assembled from provided parts (thus eliminating performance problems) indicate greater ability to include parts and to relate parts to the whole (Bassett, 1977; Celotta, 1973). Goodnow (1977) has carried out a particularly fruitful series of studies on children's sequencing, economy of means, and rules of layout. Others who have looked at sequencing in drawing are Ames (1945), Freeman (1977), and Smith (1972).

As we have already noted, children's art is often used as a means of personality assessment and diagnosis (Koppitz, 1968; Winnicott, 1971). However, more research on the role of needs and emotions in the formation of symbols by normal children is needed (Drucker, 1979). A better understanding of the interplay of cognitive and affective factors in the forming of children's imagery would offer a more well-balanced, thorough, and comprehensive view of what constitutes normal expression of emotions in art.

This review of factors influencing graphic symbolization has included a wide range of issues including central processing, performatory processing, emotional status, and the three components of symbol formation. The error of attributing any feature of a child's work to a single source will be even more apparent at this juncture. As research continues, one can only hope that more precise means of studying relevant influences and their interactions will be found.

Responding to Works of Art

Interest in children's responses to works of art has been growing for some time. Much of it reports children's art preferences based on criteria such as color and subject matter (Child, 1970; Lark-Horovitz, 1939; Machotka, 1966; Rosensteil, Morison, Silverman & Gardner, 1978). Children's increasing preference for realism is another frequent observation (Hardiman & Zernich, 1977). Developmental stages of aesthetic experience based on experimental data have also been formulated (Parsons, Johnston & Durham, 1978). In yet other studies it is reported that preference for complexity increases with age (French, 1952) as do comprehension of style (Gardner, 1970, 1973–1974) and aesthetic principles (Clark, 1973). Gardner, Winner, and Kircher (1975) asked children questions relating to artistic training, media, display, formal properties, and the sources of works of art. They report the relative inaccuracy of younger children's replies.

A related area of investigation is picture perception. Factors involved in the recognition of images have been studied by a number of investigators (Braine,

1972; Mackworth & Bruner, 1970; Potter, 1966; Spitz & Borland, 1971). Perception of depth cues in flat images has received particular attention (Jahoda & McGurk, 1974; Yonas & Hagen, 1973).

Research on children's responses to art has much helpful information to offer teachers. It is essential in educating children to understand artistic meaning to provide them with access to adult art. For this to succeed developmentally, appropriate lessons and curricula must be designed. Teachers need to know much more about the aesthetic understandings and interests of children and to present much more of the world of fine arts to them.

Additional Research on Children's Art

Comprehensive Reviews

Several authors offer reviews of research in the context of other topics: Gardner (1973) in an analysis of development across the arts; Harris (1963) in a survey of research in drawing and the Draw-A-Man-Test; and Lark-Horovitz, Lewis, and Luca (1973) in a general survey of research in children's art.

Cognition and the Arts

Current research has begun to identify cognitive benefits to children resulting from participation in the arts. Ives and Pond (1980), in reviewing this material, cite studies of improvements in cognitive abilities after children engage in activities including fantasy and dramatic play (G. Fein, 1979; Golomb & Cornelius, 1977; Saltz, Dixon & Johnson, 1977). They also discuss a renewed interest in mental imagery and its functional effect in problem solving.

In addition, Greenfield and others have found parallels between some children's manipulative activities and other cognitive tasks (Greenfield & Schneider, 1977; Roos-Beagles & Greenfield, 1979). These studies point to the intellectual as well as the affective significance of art activities and underscore the need for art in education.

Individual Differences and Learning Styles

Although the interest in learning styles is increasing in general, relatively little research has been done regarding the relation of personal or perceptual styles to art products. Some exceptions are Grossman (1970), Lovano (1970), and Wolf and Gardner (1979). Feinburg (1977) studied sex differences; Wallach & Leggett (1972), individual stylistic consistency.

Disadvantaged and Special Needs Children

There is a glaring and puzzling lack of research in the areas of special needs and disadvantaged children. Among the few studies on special needs children are reports on learning disabled children by Walker (1980) and development of representation in retardates by Golomb and Barr-Grossman (1977); a case study of a very atypical autistic girl by Selfe (1977); and a diagnosis and remediation program proposed by Gair (1975–1976). In the area of the disadvantaged, Eisner (1969) reports on drawing abilities; Castrup, Ain, and Scott (1972) offer an art skills instrument for inner city and suburban preschoolers; Renick (1972) reports on an assessment of reasoning and perception in black and white children; and Mills (1973) offers a study of the effect of an art program on the reading scores of rural children. There is a pressing need for more extensive study of the art of special needs and disadvantaged children.

Cross-Cultural Influences

Here again, there has been little work. Exceptions are Anastasi and Foley (1936), Belo (1955), Dennis (1966), and Wilson and Wilson (1979). For a review, see Anderson (1979). For the Draw-A-Man-Test, see Harris (1963).

Instruments

Human figure drawings have been a frequently used means of assessment since the work of Goodenough (1926). Laosa, Swartz, and Holtzman (1973) question their use as a measure of intelligence.

Teaching Strategies

Rather more attention has been given to evaluation of teaching strategies. Various studies examine the effects on children's art of perceptual and perceptual-motor training (Dorethy, 1973; Salome & Reeves, 1972), enriched environment (Taylor & Trujillo, 1973), verbal focusing and reinforcement (Kratochwill, Rush & Kratochwill, 1979; Seefeldt, 1979), and children's critical comparisons between their own or their own and other children's drawings (Lewis, 1963; Nelson & Flannery, 1967). Another group of studies discuss copying (Pariser, 1979) and instruction versus drawn examples (Rush, Weckesser & Sabers, 1980) in teaching drawing.

Studies reporting on training for increased responses to works of art are Gardner (1970) and Silverman, Winner, Rosensteil, and Gardner (1975).

Conclusion

This chapter has reviewed research in art in relation to educational practice and has proposed a shift of focus based on cognitive-affective development and directed toward increasing the ability of children to create meaning with visual materials. The rationale presented for this shift begins with the understanding that mankind is fundamentally symbol-making; that the invention of symbols is natural and yet a source of great pleasure and satisfaction; that through symbols, experience is clarified and shared. The arts are seen as a very rich form of symbol making because in them it is possible to bridge thought and feeling and thus portray the rich amalgam of ideas and emotions with which we experience life.

A number of consequences for education flow from this view of art. Among them is the belief that children will gain the most benefit from art programs designed to enhance their capacity to create meaning with visual materials and that this may best be approached by structuring curricula around the three components of symbol formation: concepts of the material, of the referent, and of the modes of correspondence between them.

The visual arts are a particularly appropriate means of expression for young children because art materials are concrete, allowing for direct manipulation and immediate feedback. However, to achieve the most from working with them it is important for children to conceptualize as fully as possible their physical, visual, and expressive properties. To plan for this, teachers need to understand the development of these concepts from their origin in motoric activities to their use in objective and nonobjective forms of symbolization. Attention to conceptualization of referents is also required. Teachers need to help children select developmentally appropriate objects and events as subjects and to help them expand their range of responses to these experiences. Direct as well as indirect experiences of objects, events, and works of art are needed in the classroom.

The parallel development of children's objective and expressive modes of correspondence requires particular emphasis. These two modes of symbolization emerge in a fused state, and as they become differentiated, they interact in changing patterns. This interaction is central to the creation of meaning in art and deserves much more attention from researcher and teacher alike. Children's changing concepts of what constitutes an appropriate referent for an image is another important consideration. More accurate knowledge about this, together with more accurate knowledge of how children believe it possible to relate lines, shapes, and colors to such a referent will make it possible for teachers to offer developmentally relevant assistance in the process of forming symbols rather than to avoid this for fear of imposing adult modes of correspondence on children. More research is needed that is sensitive to the complex interplay of forces influencing the forms of imagery. Information from research will make it possible for teachers to be more active in helping children in work with materials and, in addition, it will help them offer adult works of art to children with more assurance and success.

With the creation of meaning as a goal and attention to children's cognitive-affective development as a safeguard, far more comprehensive and substantive art programs are possible. Children can be offered information and experience of the everyday world and of art without harm if these are selected and presented with respect for the children's growing capacities and individual differences. Through more substantive programs, children can be helped to use a broader range of possibilities in the bridging of thought and feeling and of fantasy and reality. Teaching can then be an invitation to full participation in communication and the creation of meaning through art.

I wish to thank Margery B. Franklin for her insightful editorial assistance.

References

ALSCHULER, R., and HATTWICK, L. *Painting and Personality*. Chicago: University of Chicago Press, 1947.

AMES, L. B. Free drawing and completion drawing: A comparative study of preschool children. *The Journal of Genetic Psychology*, 1945, *66*, 161–165.

ANASTASI, A., and FOLEY, J. An analysis of spontaneous drawings by children in different cultures. *Journal of Applied Psychology*, 1936, *20*, 689–726.

ANDERSON, F. E. Approaches to cross-cultural research in art education. *Studies in Art Education*, 1979, *21*, 17–26.

ARNHEIM, R. *Art and Visual Perception*. Berkeley: University of California Press, 1954.

BARRETT, M. D., and LIGHT, P. H. Symbolism and intellectual realism in children's drawings. *British Journal of Educational Psychology*, 1976, *46*, 198–202.

BASSETT, E. Production strategies in the child's drawing of the human figure: Towards an argument for a model of syncretic perception. In G. Butterworth (ed.), *The Child's Representation of the World*. New York: Plenum, 1977,

BELO, J. Balinese children's drawings. In M. Mead and M. Wolfenstein (eds.), *Childhood in Contemporary Cultures*. Chicago: University of Chicago Press, 1955.

BERMAN, P. Young children's use of the frame of reference in construction of the horizontal, vertical, and oblique. *Child Development*, 1976, *47*, 259–263.

BIBER, B. *Children's Drawings*. New York: Bank Street College of Education, 1932.

BORKE, H. Piaget's mountains revisited: Changes in the egocentric landscape. *Developmental Psychology*, 1975, *11*, 240–243.

BRAINE, L. G. A developmental analysis of the effect of stimulus orientation on recognition. *American Journal of Psychology*, 1972, *85*, 157–188.

BRITSCH, G. *Theorie der bildenden Kunst* (A theory of pictorial art). Munich: F. Bruckmann, 1926.

BROWN, E. V. Developmental characteristics of clay figures made by children from age three through age eleven. *Studies in Art Education*, 1975, *16*, 45–53.

BRYANT, P. E. *Perception and Understanding in Young Children*. London: Methuen, 1974.

CAROTHERS, J. T., and GARDNER, H. When children's drawings become art: The emergence of aesthetic production and perception. *Developmental Psychology*, 1979, *15*, 570–580.

CASTRUP, J., AIN, E., and SCOTT, R. Art skills of preschool children. *Studies in Art Education*, 1972, *13*, 62–69.

CELOTTA, B. Knowledge of the human figure as measured by two tasks. *Developmental Psychology*, 1973, *8*, 377–381.

CHILD, I. Aesthetic judgments in children. *Transaction*, 1970, 7, 47–51.

CIZEK, F. Die Organisation und die kunstpaedagogischen Probleme des Jugendkurses. (Organization and problems of the children's art course). Paper delivered at the fourth Internationales Kongress für Kunstunterricht, Zeichnen und angewandte Kunst, Dresden, 1912.

CLARK, G. Analyzing iconic learning in the visual arts. *Studies in Art Education*, 1973, *14*, 35–47.

CONNOLLY, K., and ELLIOTT, J. The evolution and ontogeny of hand function. In M. N. Blurton-Jones (ed.), *Ethological Studies of Child Behavior*. Cambridge: At the University Press, 1972.

DENNIS, W. *Group Values through Children's Drawings*. New York: Wiley, 1966.

DORETHY, R. Motion parallax as a factor in the differential spatial abilities of young children. *Studies in Art Education*, 1973, *14*, 15–27.

DOYLE, C. The creative process: A study in paradox. In C. Winsor (ed.), *The Creative Process*. New York: Bank Street College of Education, 1976.

DRUCKER, J. The affective context and psychodynamics of first symbolization. In N. R. Smith and M. B. Franklin (eds.), *Symbolic Functioning in Childhood*. Hillsdale, N.J.: Lawrence Erlbaum Associates, 1979.

DUDEK, S. Creativity in young children: Attitude or ability. *Journal of Creative Behavior*, 1975, *8*, 282–292.

EISNER, E. The drawings of the disadvantaged: A comparative study. *Studies in Art Education*, 1969, *11*, 5–19.

ELKIND, D. Developmental studies of figurative perception. In L. Lipsitt and H. W. Reese (eds.), *Advances in Child Development and Behavior*, Vol. 9. New York: Academic Press, 1969.

ENG, H. *The Psychology of Children's Drawings*. London: Routledge & Kegan Paul, 1931.

ERIKSON, E. Play and actuality. In M. Piers (ed.), *Play and Development*. New York: W. W. Norton, 1972.

FEIN, G. Play and the acquisition of symbols. In L. Katz (ed.), *Current Topics in Early Childhood Education*. Vol. 2. Norwood, N.J.: Ablex, 1979.

FEIN, S. *Heidi's Horse*. Pleasant Hills, Calif.: Exelrod Press, 1976.

FEINBURG, S. G. Conceptual content and spatial characteristics in boys' and girls' drawings of fighting and helping. *Studies in Art Education*, 1977, *18*, 68–72.

FISHBEIN, H., LEWIS, S., and KEIFFER, K. Children's understanding of spatial relations: Coordination of perspectives. *Developmental Psychology*, 1972, 7, 21–33.

FRANKLIN, M. B. Non-verbal representation in young children: A cognitive perspective. *Young Children*, 1973, *29*, 33–53.

FREEMAN, N. How young children try to plan drawings. In G. Butterworth (ed.), *The Child's Representation of the World*. New York: Plenum Press, 1977.

FREEMAN, N., and JANIKOUN, R. Intellectual realism in children's drawings of a familiar object with distinctive features. *Child Development*, 1972, *43*, 1116–1121.

FRENCH, J. E. Children's preferences for pictures of varied complexity of pictorial pattern. *Elementary School Journal*, 1952, 8, 90–94.

FREUD, S. *On the Interpretation of Dreams*. New York: Avon, 1965 (first edition, 1900).

FROEBEL, F. *Pedagogics of the Kindergarten* (J. Jarvis, trans.). New York: Appleton, 1900.

GAIR, S. An art-based remediation program for children with learning disabilities. *Studies in Art Education*, 1975–1976, *17*, 55–67.

GARDNER, H. Children's sensitivity to painting styles. *Child Development*, 1970, *41*, 813–821.

GARDNER, H. *The Arts and Human Development*. New York: Wiley, 1973.

GARDNER, H. The contribution of color and texture to the detection of painting styles. *Studies in Art Education*, 1973–1974, *15*, 57–62.

GARDNER, H., Winner, E., and KIRCHER, M. Children's conceptions of the arts. *Journal of Aesthetic Education*, 1975, 9, 60–77.

GESELL, A., and AMES, L. B. The development of directionality in drawing. *The Journal of Genetic Psychology*, 1946, *68*, 45–61.

GOLOMB, C. *Young Children's Sculpture and Drawing*. Cambridge, Mass.: Harvard University Press, 1974.

GOLOMB, C., and BARR-GROSSMAN, T. Representational development of the human figure in familial retardates. *Genetic Psychology Monographs*, 1977, 95, 247–266.

GOLOMB, C., and CORNELIUS, C. B. Symbolic play and its cognitive significance. *Developmental Psychology*, 1977, *13*, 246–252.

GOMBRICH, E. H. On physiognomic perception. In E. H. Gombrich, *Meditations on a Hobby Horse*. London: Phaidon, 1963.

GOODENOUGH, F. *Measurement of Intelligence by Drawings*. New York: Harcourt, Brace & World, 1926.

GOODNOW, J. J. *Children Drawing*. Cambridge, Mass.: Harvard University Press, 1977.

GREENFIELD, P. M., and SCHNEIDER, L. Building a tree structure: The development of hierarchical complexity and interrupted strategies in children's construction activity. *Developmental Psychology*, 1977, *13*, 299–313.

GROSSMAN, M. Perceptual style, creativity, and various drawing abilities. *Studies in Art Education*, 1970, *11*, 51–54.

GUANELLA, F. The block building activities of young children. *Archives of Psychology*, 1934, *174*.

HARDIMAN, G. W., and ZERNICH, T. Influence of style and subject matter on the development of children's art preferences. *Studies in Art Education*, 1977, *19*, 29–35.

HARRIS, D. B. *Children's drawings as measures of intellectual maturity*. New York: Harcourt, Brace & World, 1963.

HIRSCH, E. (ed.), *The Block Book*. Washington, D.C.: National Association for the Education of Young Children, 1974.

HUTTENLOCKER, J. and PRESSON, C. Mental rotation and the perspective problem. *Cognitive Psychology*, 1973, *4*, 277–299.

IBBOTSON, A., and BRYANT, P. The perpendicular error and the vertical effect in children's drawing. *Perception*, 1976, *5*, 319–326.

IVES, S. W. Parallels in the development of language and drawing: A search for underlying principles in symbolization. *Presentations on Art Education Research*, 1979, *3*, 25–34.

IVES, W., and POND, J. The arts and cognitive development. *The High School Journal*, 1980, *63*, 335–340.

JAHODA, G., and McGURK, H. Pictorial depth perception: A developmental study. *British Journal of Psychology*, 1974, *65*, 141–149.

KELLOGG, R. *Analyzing Children's Art*. Palo Alto, Calif.: National Press, 1969.

KENNEDY, J. M. Element, configuration and metaphor in depiction. *Presentations on Art Education Research*, 1979, *3*, 45–57.

KERSCHENSTEINER, D. G. *Die Entwicklung der zeichnerischen Begabung*. (The development of drawing talent.) Munich: Gerber, 1905.

KOPPITZ, E. M. *Psychological Evaluation of Children's Human Figure Drawings*. New York: Grune & Stratton, 1968.

KORZENIK, D. Saying it with pictures. In D. Perkins and B. Leondar (eds.), *The Arts and Cognition*. Baltimore, Md.: Johns Hopkins University Press, 1977.

KRATOCHWILL, C., RUSH, J., and KRATOCHWILL, T. The effects of descriptive social reinforcement on creative responses in children's easel painting. *Studies in Art Education*, 1979, *20*, 29–39.

LANGER, S. K. *Feeling and Form*. New York: Charles Scribner's Sons, 1953.

LAOSA, L., SWARTZ, J., and HOLTZMAN, W. Human figure drawings by normal children. *Developmental Psychology*, 1973, *8*, 350–356.

LARK-HOROVITZ, B. On art appreciation of children: III. Textile pattern preference study. *Journal of Educational Research*, 1939, *38*, 7–35.

LARK-HOROVITZ, B., LEWIS, H., and LUCA, M. *Understanding Children's Art for Better Teaching* (2nd ed.). Columbus, Ohio: Charles E. Merrill, 1973.

LAURENDEAU, M., and PINARD, A. *The Development of the Concept of Space in the Child*. New York: International Universities Press, 1970.

LEWIS, H. P. The relationship of picture preference to developmental status in drawing. *Journal of Educational Research*, 1963, *57*, 43–46.

LEWIS, H. P. Spatial relations in children's drawings: A cross-generational comparison. *Studies in Art Education*, 1973–1974, *15*, 49–56.

LEWIS, H. P., and MUSSEN, P. H. The development of an instrument for evaluating children's artistic creativity. *Studies in Art Education*, 1969, *10*, 25–48.

LOVANO, J. The relation of conceptual styles and mode of perception to graphic expression. *Studies in Art Education*, 1970, *11*, 39–51.

LOWENFELD, V. *Creative and Mental Growth*. New York: Macmillan, 1949.

LUQUET, G. H. *Le dessin enfantin*. Paris: Alcan, 1927.

MACCOBY, E. E. What copying requires. *Ontario Journal of Educational Research*, 1968, *10*, 163–170.

MACHOTKA, P. Aesthetic criteria in childhood: Justifications of preference. *Child Development*, 1966, *37*, 877–885.

MACKWORTH, N. H., and BRUNER, J. S. How adults and chidren search and recognize pictures. *Human Development*, 1970, *13*, 149–177.

MILLAR, S. Visual experience or translation rules? Drawing the human figure in blind and sighted children. *Perception*, 1975, *4*, 363–371.

MILLS, J. C. The effect of art instruction upon a reading development test: An experimental study with rural Appalachian children. *Studies in Art Education*, 1973, *14*, 4–8.

NELSON, T. M., and FLANNERY, M. E. Instructions in drawing techniques as a means of utilizing drawing potential of six-and seven-year-olds. *Studies in Art Education*, 1967, *8*, 58–65.

OLSON, D. *Cognitive Development*. New York: Academic Press, 1970.

OLSON, D., and PAGLIUSO, S. From perceiving to performing: An aspect of cognitive growth. *Ontario Journal of Educational Research*, 1968, *10*, (whole issue).

PARISER, D. A. Two methods of teaching drawing skills. *Studies in Art Education*, 1979, *20*, 30–42.

PARSONS, M., Johnston, M., and DURHAM, R. Developmental stages in children's aesthetic responses. *Aesthetic education*, 1978, *12*, 83–104.

PHILLIPS, W. A., HOBBS, S. B., and PRATT, F. R. Intellectual realism in children's drawings of cubes. *Cognition*, 1078, *6*, 15–33.

PIAGET, J. *Play, dreams and Imitation in Childhood*. New York: W. W. Norton, 1951.

PIAGET, J., and INHELDER, B. *The Child's Conception of Space*. London: Routledge & Kegan Paul, 1956 (originally published, 1948).

PIAGET, J., and INHELDER, B. *The Psychology of the Child*. New York: Basic Books, 1969.

POTTER, M. C. On perceptual recognition. In J. Bruner, R. Olver, and P. Greenfield (eds.), *Studies in Cognitive Growth*. New York: Wiley, 1966.

RAND, C. W. Copying in drawing: The importance of adequate visual analysis versus the ability to utilize drawing rules. *Child Development*, 1973, *44*, 47–53.

RAND, G., and WAGNER, S. Graphic representations of a motivated act: An ontogenetic study. *Studies in Art Education*, 1970, *12*, 25–30.

RENICK, P. An assessment of perception and reasoning among negro and white third, fourth, and fifth grade students. *Studies in Art Education*, 1972, *14*, 24–46.

ROOS-BEAGLES, J., and GREENFIELD P. M., Development of structure and strategy in two-dimensional pictures. *Developmental Psychology*, 1979, *15*, 483–494.

ROSCH, E., MERVIS, C. B., GRAY, W., JOHNSON, D., and BOYES-BRAEM, P. Basic objects in natural categories. *Cognitive Psychology*, 1976, *8*, 382–439.

ROSENSTIEL, A., MORISON, P., SILVERMAN, J., and GARDNER, H. Critical judgment: A developmental study. *Journal of Aesthetic Education*, 1978, *12*, 95–107.

RUSH, J., WECKESSER, J., and SABERS, D. A comparison of instructional methods for teaching contour drawing to children. *Studies in Art Education*, 1980, *21*, 6–12.

SALKIND, N. Realistic use of color by children. *Studies in Art Education*, 1972, *13*, 38–42.

SALOME, R. A., and REEVES, D. Two pilot investigations of perceptual training of two- and five-year-old kindergarten children. *Studies in Art Education*, 1972, *13*, 3–10.

SALOMON, G. *Interaction of Media, Cognition, and Learning.* San Francisco, Calif.: Jossey-Bass, 1979.

SALTZ, E., DIXON, D., and JOHNSON, J. Training disadvantaged preschoolers on various fantasy activities: Effects on cognitive functioning and impulse control. *Child Development,* 1977, *48,* 367–380.

SCHAFFER-SIMMERN, H. *The Unfolding of Artistic Activity.* Berkeley: University of California Press, 1947.

SEEFELDT, C. The effects of a program designed to increase young children's perception of texture. *Studies in Art Education,* 1979, *29,* 40–44.

SELFE, L. *Nadia: A case of extraordinary drawing ability in an autistic child.* New York: Harcourt, Brace, Jovanovich, 1977.

SILVERMAN, J., WINNER, E., ROSENSTIEL, A., and GARDNER, H. On training sensitivity to painting styles. *Perception,* 1975, *4,* 373–384.

SMITH, N. R. Developmental origins of graphic symbolization in the paintings of children three to five. Unpublished doctoral dissertation, Harvard University, 1972 (University Microfilms No. 179–9892, 1979).

SMITH, N. R. Developmental origins of structural variation in symbol form. In N. R. Smith and M. B. Franklin (eds.), *Symbolic Functioning in Childhood.* Hillsdale, N.J.: Lawrence Erlbaum Associates, 1979a.

SMITH, N. R. How a picture means. *New Directions for Child Development,* 1979b, *3,* 59–72.

SMITH, N. R. How is it that the blind can draw? *Presentations on Art Education Research,* 1979c, *3,* 65–70.

SPIELMAN, K. Development of the perception and production of line forms. *Child Development,* 1976, *47,* 787–793.

SPITZ, H., and BORLAND, M. Redundancy in line drawings of familiar objects: Effects of age and intelligence. *Cognitive Psychology,* 1971, *2,* 196–205.

TAYLOR, A. P., and TRUJILLO, J. L. The effects of selected stimuli on the art products, concept formation, and aesthetic judgemental decisions of four-year-old children. *Studies in Art Education,* 1973, *14,* 57–66.

TERMAN, L. *Mental and Physical Traits of a Thousand Gifted Children.* Stanford, Calif.: Stanford University Press, 1925.

TORRANCE, E. P. Factors affecting creative thinking in children: An interim research report. *Merrill-Palmer Quarterly,* 1961, *7,* 171–180.

VURPILLOT, E. *The Visual World of the Child.* New York: International Universities Press, 1976.

WALKER, B. The relative effects of painting and gross-motor activities on the intrinsic focus-of-control of hyperactivity in learning disabled elementary school pupils. *Studies in Art Education,* 1980, *21,* 13–21.

WALLACH, M. A., and LEGGETT, M. I. Testing the hypothesis that a person will be consistent: Stylistic consistency versus situational specificity in size of children's drawings. *Journal of Personality,* 1972, *40,* 309–330.

WERNER, H. *Comparative Psychology of Mental Development.* New York: International Universities Press, 1948.

WERNER, H., and KAPLAN, B. *Symbol Formation.* New York: Wiley, 1963.

WILLATS, J. How children learn to represent three-dimensional space in drawings. In G. Butterworth (ed.), *The Child's Representation of the World*. New York: Plenum, 1977.

WILSON, B., and WILSON, M. Figure study, figure action, and framing in drawings by American and Egyptian children. *Studies in Art Education*, 1979, *21*, 36–43.

WINNICOTT, D. W. *Therapeutic Consultations in Child Psychiatry*. New York: Basic Books, 1971.

WOLF, D., and GARDNER, H. Style and sequence in early symbolic play. In N. R. Smith and M. B. Franklin (eds.), *Symbolic functioning in Childhood*. Hillsdale, N.J.: Lawrence Erlbaum Associates, 1979.

YONAS, A., and HAGEN, M. A. Effects of static and kinetic depth information on the perception of size in children and adults. *Journal of Experimental Child Psychology*, 1973, *15*, 254–265.

PART IV

Public Policy and Early Childhood Education

Paths Not Taken: Seminal Models of Early Childhood Education in Jacksonian America

Charles E. Strickland

EVER SINCE THE FIRST colonial woman organized a "dame school," generations of Americans have provided extra-familial education for youngsters before they were considered old enough to enroll in formal schooling. The enterprise of early childhood education today is a far cry from those simpler arrangements, having transformed itself into a profession complete with an organizational basis, trained personnel, and a research enterprise. Moreover, a steadily rising proportion of children under the age of six have experienced care and education outside their homes. Never before in American history has there been such a demand for preprimary education. Despite these remarkable advances, however, the institution of early childhood education remains on the periphery of the educational establishment, and as yet, less than half of American children under five years of age are exposed to preprimary schooling. The statement of such well-known facts leads, then, to two questions: (1) how can we account for the development of early childhood education beyond its dame school beginnings; and (2) why has the institution, despite its impressive growth, failed thus far to become a part of the "normal" experience of all American children?

A clue to answering both questions lies in understanding social transformations during the Jacksonian era, for it was in those years before the Civil War that Americans began taking seriously the matter of early childhood education. This is not to say that Americans possessed, by 1850, all the ideas and institutions that have come to influence the education of small children. The kindergarten, day nursery, and the nursery school lay in the future, while the ideas of Charles Darwin, Sigmund Freud, G. Stanley Hall, John Dewey, Edward L. Thorndike, Maria Montessori, Arnold Gesell, and Jean Piaget were scarcely dreamed of. Nevertheless, antebellum Americans had already enunciated the basic goals of early childhood education, and they had experimented with three radically different approaches to the education of small children, ways that one can call "seminal models."

Only one of these models conforms to what we have since come to recognize as early childhood education; namely, an institution specifically designed for the particular nature and needs of children under the age of six. That this model, originally called the "infant school," did not become a universal institution lay in the fact that it was compelled to compete not only with lingering apathy but also with two other, more conservative approaches to the education of small children. One of these alternative models—and the one favored by many parents at the time—consisted of the simple idea of sending young children to the conventional "common" school, along with their older brothers and sisters. The third model, and the one that rose to such dominance during the Jacksonian era that it threatened to obliterate the other two altogether, was the idea of reforming American families through the process of parent education. Thereafter, "fireside education," as it was then called, described the parameters within which early childhood education would develop during the following century.

Social Transformation in Jacksonian America and the Cult of Childhood

"In the history of the world the doctrine of reform had never such scope as at the present hour," Ralph Waldo Emerson declared in 1840 (Vol. 7, p. 403). Indeed, there seemed to be reform movements everywhere, winning enthusiastic converts to the cause of abolition of slavery, the abolition of war, equal rights for women, reform of prisons, reform of the treatment of the insane, temperance, religious revivalism, vegetarianism, public education, and the founding of utopian communities (Tyler, 1944). There was not, Emerson accurately concluded, a "kingdom, town, statute, rite, calling, man or woman, but is threatened by the new spirit." The toleration, if not the enthusiasm, which Jacksonian Americans displayed toward social reform was astounding and not to be matched by any generation before or since, with the possible exception of the countercultural revolt of the 1960s.

This host of reform movements was spawned by less dramatic but more profound transformations in the social and economic realm that left hardly any sphere of life untouched during the early decades of the nineteenth century. A rising population, the growth of urban centers, the surge of a market economy, and the spectacle of a people seemingly in constant motion generated a mood of optimism and expectancy (Tyler, 1944). It seemed to many that in such a dynamic society as America was becoming, all things were possible, including the eradication of chattel slavery, sexual inequality, war, disease, and poverty. Among the more optimistic, there was even talk of creating in this New World a new man, who would cast off centuries of ignorance and sin and rise to new levels of human perfection (Lewis, 1955). Alexis de Tocqueville, for one, agreed it might be possible for Americans to create a more just society if not a perfect man. That shrewd French observer of the social scene visited America and came away with the impression that he had witnessed in America the wave of the future (Meyers, 1957).

Among the beneficiaries of this ferment of reform were the young, and there arose in the early years of the nineteenth century a veritable cult of childhood (Strickland, 1971). In part, this revolution in sentiment reflected a more gradual transformation in Western culture described by Philippe Ariès (1962) as the "discovery of childhood," but more immediately it was part of a general concern, as expressed by Jacksonian reformers, with the problems of the least powerful and most dependent members of society. Just as reformers felt dismay about the lot of the slave, the mentally ill, and the prisoner, so too did the child become a focus of sentiment. Writers and artists in particular served to direct popular attention to the young, demonstrating that they were worthy of attention and that they possessed a nature distinctive from that of adults. Charles Dickens, the most popular of nineteenth-century novelists, placed children at the center of his fiction, emphasizing their innocence and vulnerability. He marched before his American readers a succession of morally pure, yet doomed young heroes and heroines, who were exploited, betrayed, and, in many instances, destroyed by vicious adults. American writers also took up the theme and made children important if not central figures in their fiction (Stone, 1961). Nathanial Hawthorne blazed the trail with his "Gentle Boy," and with his portrayal of Pearl in *The Scarlet Letter*. Soon, Harriet Beecher Stowe followed with her creation of Little Eva in *Uncle Tom's Cabin*. American painters, too, expressed new interest in portraying children, and by mid-century, artists like William Bartoll and William Mount were reminding their viewers that children are different from adults and engage in activities unique to their stage of development (Humm, 1978).

The surge of interest in the young was matched by an enthusiasm for their education, and for the first time, Americans began to give widespread attention to the instruction of small children. This is not to say that beleaguered parents had not, from time immemorial, resorted to the informal support systems of relatives and neighbors to provide custodial care of their young offspring. Historians know as yet little of these informal arrangements, but there is little reason to doubt that relatives continued to provide extra-familial care of the young in antebellum America. Nor is it true that Jacksonian Americans invented the idea that the deliberate education of small children is important. After all, colonial America had produced moralists who perceived the educational importance of the early childhood years. Puritan clergyman, although taking a dim view of the nature of childhood, entertained no doubts that children were important, and they were fond of lecturing parents on their duties to provide instruction in reading and religion to their sinful offspring, an exhortation which in several New England colonies acquired the force of law (Bailyn, 1960; Cremin, 1970; Morgan, 1966). But although networks of kith and kin provided custodial care and although clergymen might talk of the importance of early childhood education, it appears that before the nineteenth century, relations between old and young tended to be casual affairs. Consequently, the education of most young children probably occurred only as incidental to their custodial care. Generation after generation of clergymen, while exhorting parents to give more thought to the treatment of children, also bitterly complained that parents were paying little attention (Greven, 1973, pp. 9–79). Moreover, those historians who have examined surviving descriptions of colonial family life most closely have found in them little reference to the treatment of small children, let alone to the subject of their education (Frost, 1973; Greven, 1977; Spruill, 1972).

By 1830, there were ample signs that this popular indifference to the deliberate education of small children was giving way to a novel concern, fueled by the sentiments generated by the Cult of Childhood. Educators and clergymen fell to appropriating the Enlightenment foundations that had been laid by the English philosopher John Locke and the practical reforms of the Swiss educator Johann Pestalozzi (Strickland, 1971, pp. 78–80). This body of thought provided Americans with educational and social justification for the importance of the early years, providing substance to the inchoate sentiment generated by the Cult of Childhood. Rejecting the bleak view of childhood promulgated by Puritan clergymen, this body of thought stressed the modifiability of human nature and emphasized the power that proper method placed in the hands of parents and teachers. According to this view, the younger the child, the more plastic his nature, and the greater the power adults could wield in shaping his intellect and character.

This Enlightenment theory was soon joined by another and radically different attitude toward the young child. Drawing inspiration from the work of Wordsworth, Blake, and Coleridge, this Romantic view shared with the Enlightenment theories a recognition of the critical importance of early childhood (Plotz, 1979). It was, after all, the poet Wordsworth who announced that "the child is father to the man." The Romantics rejected, however, the Enlightenment stress on the plasticity of the child's nature. Instead, they advanced the exotic notion that the child is, in effect, a saint (Strickland, 1971). This conclusion was derived not so much from direct observation of children as from a radical dissatisfaction with the society that adults had created. In America, men and women like Bronson Alcott, Emerson, Henry David Thoreau, Elizabeth Peabody, and Margaret Fuller admired the child or, rather, their image of the child, because it exhibited none of the greedy materialism or spineless conformity that characterized its elders. The secret of education was, therefore, to protect the innocent child from corruption and allow its innate divinity to unfold. Condescension toward childhood, so characteristic of Enlightenment thought, now gave way under the Romantic impulse to reverence.

The theoretical differences that divided the American champions of early childhood education were less immediately urgent, however, than a more practical question: who was responsible for putting into effect the early education of children? Granting that the early years were important—and hardly any Jacksonian educator denied it—were parents capable of handling the novel burdens that the idea of early childhood education imposed? The prognosis did not seem hopeful. Writers, poets, educators, and clergymen might take seriously the education of small children, but it was not yet clear that parents would give up their casual ways with the young. Doubts on this score were exacerbated by the worry, expressed by some, that poor families were failing in their duty to provide even custodial care. The emerging market economy was removing production from the household, and many a caretaker was compelled to leave the home in search of employment. In 1830, the inspectors of New York's Auburn Penitentiary reported that two-thirds of the inmates sampled were in prison because of childhood abuse and neglect (Rothman, 1971, p. 65). During the following decades, newly organized orphanages and children's aid societies swept from the streets many children who were not in fact orphans, but whose parents were simply unable to provide for them (Rothman, 1971, p. 207; Langsam, 1964, pp. 17–19). How could such poor parents, unable to meet the most basic physical needs of their children, hope to fulfill the ebullient dreams of those who promulgated the Cult of Childhood?

The First Model: Sending Young Children to the Common School

For many parents the response to the challenge of early childhood education consisted simply of sending their small children to the "common" school, along with their elder siblings, whether out of concern for their educational development or out of a more basic desire for relief from child care (Kaestle and Vinovskis, 1978). The practice was, in a sense, merely an extension of the traditional dame school, although enrollment was now at public expense, and the child's teacher was, in the early decades of the nineteenth century, more likely to be a man than a woman (Fitts, 1979). Sending off the little ones to the district school reflected also a customary indifference to the matter of age distinctions and certainly betrayed no belief that little children have different educational needs than their older brothers and sisters. The traditional character of the response, together with the lure of free custodial care, doubtless accounts for its popularity among parents. As Kaestle and Vinovskis have pointed out (p. 49), children as young as three years of age were entering the schools of Massachusetts by the early decades of the century, and most towns had no rules excluding them. By 1850, a full 15 percent of the enrollment of Massachusetts schools were children under the age of five (p. 62).

As the enrollment of small children grew, there emerged two sources of resistance which, when combined, eventually doomed the practice despite its popularity with parents. One source of resistance came from the school establishment, which was beginning to worry about the cost (Kaestle and Vinovskis, 1978, pp. 49–50). This concern became evident as early as 1818, when the Boston School Committee debated the question of whether to provide schooling for children under the age of six. A subcommittee appointed to investigate the matter found nothing inappropriate in the schooling of small children, which suggests that sensitivity to the special needs of the early years was as yet not widespread. What bothered the subcommittee was the expense involved, and it recommended that instruction of small children should be the sole responsibility of parents. Notwithstanding this recommendation, the committee settled for a compromise, excluding from the Boston schools only children younger than the age of four.

Other communities made no restriction whatsoever, but, as enrollment of the little ones expanded, resistance to the practice spread. School authorities were beginning to worry not only about expense but also about the effect of the practice on discipline, for it seems that the small children created disruptions and inconvenience. As one school committee remarked, "If children under four years of age are sent to school in order to give temporary relief to parents, it should be remembered that no teacher, male or female, is authorized . . . to convert his appropriate vocation into that of a nurse" (Kaestle and Vinovskis, p. 59).

Given the nature of most common school classrooms in mid-nineteenth century America, it is not surprising that teachers would experience difficulty in accommodating children as small as three years of age. The world of the nineteenth-century common school was, as Barbara Finkelstein has pointed out, a world relentlessly dedicated to strict discipline and to the narrow acquisition of reading, writing, and arithmetic.

> It was an atmosphere designed to stamp out differences among individual students, to secure a rigid conformity to rules and regulations as dictated by teachers, to substitute the rule of law for the rule of personal persuasion, to disconnect children from networks of personal communication and engage them, instead in a highly controlled world of books and print [Finkelstein, 1979, p. 119].

To the resistance of common school authorities and teachers was added the concern of educators who adhered to some of the newer Romantic theories about young children. They raised, for the first time, the question of the child's welfare. One objection heard more and more was the danger of "forcing" the educational development of small children. William Woodbridge, editor of the *American Journal of Education*, sounded a warning to parents in 1830. Characteristically romantic, Woodbridge laced his argument with the organic analogy of the child and the plant.

> All the efforts of misjudging teachers and parents who wish to see their children early prodigies only sacrifice the fruit in order to produce an earlier expansion of the flower, and resemble the hot-bed in their influence in "forcing" a plant to maturity, whose feebleness or early decay must be proportional to the unnatural rapidity of its growth, and a consequent want of symmetry in its parts [May and Vinovskis, 1977, p. 84].

Further warning was supplied by Amariah Brigham, who published in 1833 *Remarks on the Influence of Mental Excitement upon Health*, a book which argued that precocious mental development, especially in early life, threatened the child's sanity. Soon, school authorities themselves were taking up the argument that enrollment of young children in the common school was not only expensive and disruptive of discipline but also harmful to the child itself. The secretary of the Massachusetts Board of Education remarked in 1852 that "education in its widest sense commences as soon as one is born. From the time till the school-going age, which with most children does not properly begin till after they are six years old, the freedom and activity natural to childhood may better be accorded to it than denied" (Kaestle & Vinovskis, p. 60). As Kaestle and Vinovskis point out (pp.

62–71), parents were reluctant to heed this outpouring of advice, but school authorities grew increasingly rigid and eventually resorted to the adoption of rules excluding children under the age of five or six years, especially in more urbanized and industrialized communities. It was evident, then, that those concerned about the education of small children would be compelled to locate it outside the conventional classrooms of the public school.

The Second Model: The Infant School

Another approach to early childhood education lay in the creation of an entirely new institution, specifically designed to accommodate the nature and needs of small children. This new institution, called the "infant school," sprang from the work of Robert Owen, an Englishman who represented a bizarre combination of industrialist and social reformer and who reflected in his thinking the influence of Pestalozzi's educational reform as well as the influence of some of the more radical social theories to emerge from the Enlightenment (Harrison, 1969). Expressing disdain for organized religion as well as for a society organized along "individualistic" lines, Owen set out to prove that the emerging industrial order could be humane. Owen established himself first as the successful manager of cotton mills and then used his reputation for industrial management as a springboard to experiment with the creation of an industrial order that would be more productive and more just. With the sometimes reluctant cooperation of his partners, Owen sought to transform a Scottish cotton mill town, New Lanark, into a utopian community (Bestor, 1950, pp. 66–68). He wanted to produce cotton more efficiently, but he wished also to improve the lives of his workers by banning the labor of children under ten, reducing hours, maintaining full employment, and providing low-rent housing, free medical service, and inexpensive schools. New Lanark was to provide the model for a new social order, in Owen's view, and his efforts to ameliorate the condition of the working classes were merely prelude to a larger scheme, which was nothing less than the toal reorganization of society upon the basis of utopian communities.

At the heart of Owen's scheme was the provision of education from the cradle to the grave, and here again, the influence of the Enlightenment reveals itself. Owen, like John Locke, was firmly convinced of the modifiablity of human nature. "The character of man," Owen declared, "is without a single exception always formed for him" (Owen, 1813, p. 77). Given the basic premise, it was only a small step for Owen to the conclusion that society may be totally transformed through the process of education. As he remarked, "any general character, from the best to the worst, from the most ignorant to the most enlightened, may be given to any community, even to the world at large, by the application of the proper means" (Owen, 1813, p. 41). The "proper means" included schools provided by the community. Consequently, in 1816, Owen opened his "Institution Established for the Formation of Character." He specifically included small children from the age of one year, for it was Owen's conviction that education should be broadly defined to include "instruction of all kinds which we receive from our earliest infancy" (Owen, 1813, p. 27). There is evidence that Owen may have been motivated by more than theoretical considerations in including the small children. He was in a unique position to witness the impact of the industrial revolution on the household, and he was aware of the fact that two-thirds of the workers in his mills were women, many of whom would need child care for their small youngsters (Harrison, 1969, p. 154). Nevertheless, it is clear that Owen had in mind more than custodial care for the small children, and his thinking about their education clearly reflected the influence of reformers like Pestalozzi. As Owen recalled,

> The children were trained and educated without punishment or any fear of it, and were while in school by far the happiest human beings I have ever seen. The infants and young children, besides being instructed by sensible signs—the things themselves or models or paintings—and by familiar conversation, were from two years and upwards daily taught dancing and singing [Owen, 1857–58, p. 135].

Owen's ideas attracted the attention of American reformers, who fell to imitating his innovations. Owen's first visit to America, in 1824, sparked a wave of enthusiasm for the idea of founding utopian communities, one result of which was the establishment of the bold but short-lived experiment in New Harmony, Indiana (Bestor, 1950). Less ambitious, but more significant for the history of early childhood education, was the rash of infant school societies that appeared in all the large cities along the Eastern seaboard. The patrons of these new societies were, as May and Vinovskis (1977) point out, composed for the most part of women who were members of the "civic-minded social elite" and who were intrigued by Owen's invention as a device to reach the children of the poor. They were joined by working men's associations and reform-minded journalists, who saw in the infant school a lever for social reform stripped, of course, of Owen's more radical schemes for community reorganization. In lending its encouragement, the Working Men's Committee of Philadelphia remarked in 1830 that "an opinion is entertained by many good and wise persons, and supported to a considerable extent by actual experiment, that proper schools for supplying a judicious infant training, would effectually prevent much of that vicious depravity of character which penal codes and punishments are vainly intended to counteract" (Working Men's Committee, 1830, p. 36). The committee also noted that the infant school would "relieve, in a great measure, many indigent parents, from the care of children, which in many cases occupies as much of their time as would be necessary to earn the children a subsistence" (p. 36). Equally enthusiastic were the editors of *The Boston Recorder and Religious Transcript* who noted:

> Infants, taken from the most unfavorable situations in which they are ever placed, from the abodes of poverty and vice, are capable of learning at least a hundred times as much, a hundred times as well, and of being a hundred times as happy, by the system adopted in infant schools, as by that which prevails in the common schools throughout the country [May and Vinovskis, 1977, p. 62].

So great was the enthusiasm for the new institution that more affluent parents demanded infant schools for their own children, and soon fee-charging schools were established alongside the charitable institutions (May and Vinovskis, 1977, pp. 78–79).

Backed by civic-minded women, working men, and reform journalists, the infant school movement provided a platform for reformers such as Bronson Alcott, who was one of America's first early childhood educators (Strickland, 1969). Not surprisingly, Alcott sprang from the margins of America's educational establishment and consequently owed no debt to traditional educational ideas. Born in 1799, the son of a poor Connecticut farmer, Alcott spent much of his youth engaged in farming and peddling, acquiring more formal learning only through primitive rural schools and by dint of this efforts at self-education. At the age of twenty-three, he found himself a district school teacher, which was in itself not so unusual. What else could a young man with bookish inclinations and no advantages aspire to? But Alcott, though poorly educated, possessed both intelligence and a demonic energy, and he began to think of himself as a Messiah, come to save the world through the reform of education. He also discovered, during his years as a Connecticut schoolmaster, that he had a way with children, especially with the little ones. He banned the rod from his classroom, put backs on the benches, and took to playing games with the children as a form of instuction. He also began reading about the work of European reformers such as Pestalozzi, which encouraged him to believe that he was on the right track. These educational heresies won him no friends in the rural districts, and he was asked to leave, but Boston proved more tolerant of an educational Messiah. In 1828, Alcott accepted an invitation to conduct an infant school in America's intellectual capital, and within two years he had acquired a reputation as a reformer of education for young children.

After serving for a time in the Salem Street Infant School, under the auspices of the local infant school society, he moved on to establish a private infant school and turned attention to publicizing his ideas. Soon, Alcott occupied a strategic position in translating the sentiments of the Cult of Childhood into the organizational form of the infant school. As with Owen, there was nothing modest in Alcott's claims.

> Of the many methods by which the wise and good of the present day are contributing to the best interests of the mind, redeeming it from the slavery of ignorance and vice, to the liberty of intelligence, virtue and happiness, the institutions of Infant Schools, now so generally established among us, are full of much promise and hope [Alcott, 1830, pp. 3–4].

Again like Owen, he recognized the special character of the young. Challenging directly the Puritan distrust of childhood and its activities, Alcott declared that children have a right to enjoy themselves. "Play," he said, "is the appointed dispensation of childhood" (Alcott, 1830, p. 5). He argued that the common school, with its emphasis on external discipline, systematic exercise, and appeals to distrust and fear, cannot serve as the educator of small children. Instead, young children should have conversation, singing, marching, story-telling, pictures, and the study of "objects" such as animals, insects, and wooden blocks. Above all, the infant school should concern itself with the moral character of the young not by preaching sermons but by setting examples of kindness and love and by appealing to the child's "natural" affection. Alcott's philosophy, based on a sanguine view of the nature of childhood, would lead, he hoped, to the radical improvement of mankind.

The movement to establish infant schools spread during the early 1830s among urban communities on the Eastern seaboard, but, just as quickly as they arose, they were snuffed out (May & Vinovskis, 1977). Part of the difficulty lay with the attitude of the public school establishment. Dominated by educational conservatives, common school committees had no more interest in providing financial support for the infant school than they did in admitting young children to regular classrooms. As a consequence, the infant school was placed in a vulnerable financial position, dependent upon fees paid by parents or on charity provided by civic-minded patrons, a dependence that proved fatal during the economic panic of 1837. Still another difficulty encountered by the new institution was its association with ideas that were regarded by the public as radical or heretical. Owen, the father of the infant school, attracted attention by his American visits in the 1820s, and soon it was rumored that his communitarian ideas had led him to advocate the elimination of private property (Bestor, 1950, pp. 77–93). The charge was false, as it turned out, but the rumor considerably damaged Owen's reputation among those who were expected to pay the bills for the infant school. Equally damaging and more accurate was the report that Owen opposed organized religion. In 1829, he engaged in a well-publicized debate with the religious leader Alexander Campbell and shocked Americans with his blunt intention "to prove that the principles of all religions are erroneous, and that their practice is injurious to the human race" (Bestor, 1950, p. 228).

More direct damage to the cause of the infant school was inflicted by Bronson Alcott himself, who was beginning to share Owen's more radical and heretical ideas. After a time spent teaching school in Pennsylvania, Alcott returned to Boston in 1834. He promptly opened the Temple School, which represented an expanded version of the infant school, including now children six years and older (McCuskey, 1940). The school, named for the Masonic Temple in which it was located, revealed that Alcott had subtly shifted his views on the education of young children during his years of absence from Boston. Without surrendering his belief in the importance of infant education, Alcott had fallen more and more under the influence of the Romantic wing of the Cult of Childhood. From a follower of Pestalozzi, Alcott was becoming a disciple of Transcendentalism, a doctrine which advanced the then heretical notion that mankind was potentially divine (Strickland, 1969, pp. 10–11). What this intellectual shift meant in educational practice soon became apparent in Alcott's conduct of the Temple School. Alcott was beginning to believe that he could learn as much from the young child as he could teach him. With the assistance of Elizabeth Peabody, who would later win renown as the leader of the kindergarten movement in America, Alcott initiated a series of conversations with his small pupils about the gospels. In these dialogues, he sought to elicit the wise reflections of the children on the spiritual meaning of the teachings of Jesus, for he was persuaded that the children, being closer then adults to God, were possessed of superior moral insight. He barred no subjects in his discussions with the children, and in a decision that would prove fateful, he even questioned them about matters of childbirth, eliciting from one six-year-old the information that infants are formed out of "the naughtiness of other people" (McCuskey, 1940, p. 101).

For two years, the Temple School flourished, and Alcott enjoyed both financial prosperity and the admiration of Boston's intelligentsia, but unfortunately for the fate of his school, Alcott had arranged for Miss Peabody to make a full record of the conversations for the purposes of publication. With the appearance of *Conversations with Children on the Gospels,* the full extent of Alcott's heresies became known to the public, and Boston journalists greeted with ridicule his belief in the inherent spiritual wisdom of young children. As one irate editor remarked, "These conversations appear to be the first fruits of the new attempt to draw wisdom from babies and sucklings" (Shepard, 1937, p. 193). Miss Peabody had worried in particular about the passages relating to childbirth and attempted in vain to have those sections eliminated before publication. Alcott stuck by his principles, Miss Peabody fled the school in a panic, and enrollments plummeted (McCuskey, 1940, pp. 100–113). When Alcott, the consistent radical, admitted a black pupil to his school, the experiment failed altogether. Thereafter, Alcott was compelled to confine the teaching of children to his own daughters, and he turned his talents to the education of adults and to promoting a variety of reform movements, including the founding of an utopian community (Shepard, 1937, pp. 210ff).

The Third Model: "Fireside Education"

The collapse of the infant school movement and the growing resistance of common-school authorities to the admission of young children left only one strategy available for those dedicated to the education of small children, namely, the reform of the family through parent education. It proved to be the most popular of the three models, a popularity due in part to a revolution in print media, which provided the vehicle for parent education movements. Improvements in printing such as the steam press made possible after 1830 the publications of cheap books, newspapers, and periodicals for mass consumption, vastly expanding readership and providing new opportunities for writers (Douglas, 1977, pp. 81–85). For the first time, large numbers of talented women took up publication: Catharine Beecher, Mrs. Lydia Childs, Mrs. Sarah Hale, Mrs. Almira Phelps, Catharine Sedgwick, and Mrs. Lydia Sigourney. They were joined by clergymen like John and Jacob Abbott, Horace Bushnell, Theodore Dwight, and Heman Humphrey, who found in popular publication a new pulpit from which to combat the secular doctrines of the age. Together, the clergymen and their female allies supplied a multitude of books and articles on domestic topics, including courtship, marriage, religion, home management, and, most important of all, what was then called "fireside education" (Douglas, 1977, p. 84; Kuhn, 1947).

The popularity of the antebellum parent education movement rested, in the final analysis, on the way in which it meshed smoothly with a conservative counterrevolution during the Jacksonian era (Douglas, 1977; Kuhn, 1947). If the social and economic transformations of the early decades of the century had spawned a mood of expectancy, they had generated also a feeling of anxiety. There were those of a more conservative temperament who feared that in moving so quickly toward an unknown future, Americans were leaving behind the solid virtues of an earlier, simpler society (Meyers, 1957). If the new era was opening up vistas of human progress, it also provoked worry about law and order in a nation that seemed ungoverned and ungovernable. Emerson put his finger on the ambivalent mood of Americans when he divided social commentary of the age into the "party of hope" and the "party of memory," between those who looked forward with confidence to the future and those who regarded it with trepidation (Lewis, 1955).

The women and clergymen who promoted the cause of "fireside education" fell, for the most part, into Emerson's party of memory. They shared with such optimistic reformers as Bronson Alcott an enthusiasm for the Cult of Childhood and for the cause of early childhood education, but they worried more about the restless, egalitarian, and secular tendencies of the age. In particular, they were concerned about what they perceived to be a weakening of the church and the family under the onslaught of such enthusiasms as Transcendentalism and feminism. In discussing such matters as religion and family life, these parent educators sometimes talked as if they were bent on reviving the church and the family of the colonial era. But, as we shall see, the fireside educators actually promoted a new way of looking at the family and they envisioned a new role for women. At the heart of this flood of domestic advice lay three themes—the home, the woman, and the child—which the fireside educators bound together inextricably. In the process they erected, beside the Cult of Childhood, a Cult of Domesticity and a Cult of Motherhood.

The centerpiece in this literary vision was the Cult of Domesticity. Never before had the household been made the object of such adoration as the clergymen and the women authors now heaped upon it. It was as if all the utopian impulses of the Jacksonian era were here directed into the private sphere of the nuclear family. It was, in the view of Sarah Hale, a "sacred" institution (Hale, 1830b, p. 217), and indeed, it appeared that the home was now more important than the church in the preservation of religious values. Horace Bushnell argued, in fact, that the future of the Christian religion lay not in the efforts of preachers but in the dedication of parents, who were to bring up a child as a Christian who was never to know himself as anything other than a Christian (Bushnell, 1860). In the process of sanctifying the home, the domestic authors also widened into a yawning chasm the boundary between the nuclear family and the world around it. To use the words of a then popular song, there was literally "no place like home." The home was the repository for what we would today call the "expressive" values of love, warmth, and intimacy, in stark contrast to the cold competitiveness of the market place, a sentiment leading to a melodramatic confrontation between "home, sweet home" and the "cold, cruel world" (Grimstead, 1968, pp. 165, 227–229). In celebrating the home as an emotional refuge, the parent educators were in fact providing ideological reinforcement of the economic changes that were removing economic production from the household, especially among more affluent classes. But if the household was receding in importance as a unit of economic production, it was, in the eyes of the parent educators, becoming ever more important as a moral counterweight to the restless, materialistic tendencies of the larger society.

These extravagant expectations of home life were linked, in the literature of domestic advice, to a new role for American women. If colonial Americans had held up any role for women as pre-eminent, it was that of a "help mate" to her husband, assisting him in the economic survival of the family (Ryan, 1975, pp. 19–82). Because the colonial family was the center of economic production, women were busy with many tasks, and the colonial family looked to the woman as well as to the man to clothe and feed them (Douglas, 1977, pp. 48–51). Conversely, when Puritan clergymen wrote books of advice to parents, they assumed as a matter of course that a man's role of "governor" of his children would equal his role as breadwinner. By contrast, the Jacksonian parent educators assumed as a matter of course that father was only a minor presence in the household and they directed their message to mother (Kuhn, 1947, p. 4), arguing that if women were no longer needed as economic help-mates to their husbands, they had far more important tasks to perform as mothers and cultural arbitrators. For this task women are endowed by nature, the parent educators insisted, with superior moral character and superior intuitive insight. For one thing, women are less interested than men in sexual passion. For another, women are endowed with greater capacity for tenderness and a greater sensitivity to others. For these reasons, Catharine Beecher argued, women should have a superior influence "in matters pertaining to the education of their children, in the selection of a clergyman, in all benevolent enterprises, and in all questions relating to morals and manners" (Beecher, 1841, p. 9). In short, parent educators placed women on that famous moral pedestal from which they have descended only lately. In the process, they lent their weight to the Cult of Motherhood, which took its place beside the Cult of Childhood and the Cult of Domesticity in the Literature of domestic advice.

In ascending this moral pedestal, mothers would have to be on special guard against the twin temptations of fashion and feminism (Kuhn, 1947, p. 5). In their strictures against conspicuous consumption, the parent educators provided inadvertent testimony to the new leisure and affluence that economic growth had afforded, and they feared that women would use their leisure for social climbing. Sarah Hale, for example, complained of "fashionable follies" (Hale, 1830a), while the Reverend Bushnell, too, found that among the most serious impediments to proper nurture are "vain, fashionable" mothers (Bushnell, 1860, p. 73). If idle vanity threatened to deflect women from their moral mission, equally dangerous were the doctrines of sexual equality. With the exception of Lydia Child, the parent educators were opposed to the movement for women's rights. Sarah Hale urged the importance of women's education, not to "usurp the station or encroach on the prerogative of the man, but that each individual may lend her aid to perfect the moral and intellectual character of those within her sphere" (Hale, 1828, p. 2). Catharine Beecher was equally adamant on the subject, arguing that American women enjoyed privileges superior to mere political and economic equality: "In order to secure her the more firmly in all these privileges, it is decided that, in the domestic relation, she take a subordinate station, and that, in civil and political concerns, her interests be intrusted to the other sex, without her taking any part in voting, or in making and administering laws" (Beecher, 1841, p. 4).

Exclusion of women from the worlds of fashion and politics would make it possible for them to come into their true inheritance and to begin to wield "genuine" power in human affairs. In return for the sacrifice of mere political rights, women secured the influence that only a mother could enjoy. In celebrating the significance of motherhood, not even the most enthusiastic supporters of the infant school surpassed the fireside educators in testifying to the critical importance of early childhood education. "How entire and perfect is this dominion over the unformed character of your infant," Lydia Sigourney told mothers in 1838. "Write what you will upon the printless tablet with your wand of love" (Douglas, 1977, p. 75). Catharine Beecher reminded women that in confining themselves to domestic activities they were engaged in building a "glorious temple," which was nothing less than laying the foundations of civilization: "No American woman . . . has any occasion for feeling that hers is a humble or insignificant lot. The value of what an individual accomplishes is to be estimated by the importance of the enterprise achieved, and not by the particular position of the laborer" (Beecher, 1841, pp. 13–16).

The key to woman's identity lay, therefore, in the proper discharge of her responsibilities for the nurture and education of the young child, and she was advised not to share this sacred responsibility with others. The parent educators were united in praising breast-feeding and in condemning the practice of wet nursing, which had been a widespread custom among the affluent in colonial America (Sunley, 1955, p. 153). Mothers were specifically warned that babies would imbibe the servant's moral character along with her nourishment (Kuhn, 1947, p. 134). "Would you wish your child to be like the nurse?," Bushnell pointedly asked (1860, p. 249). As the infant grew older, servants would find other ways to corrupt its health and morals by teaching it lower class habits of speech, granting unwise indulgence to the child's whims, and foisting upon it harmful drugs (Kuhn, 1947, pp. 134–138). If the parent educators are to be believed, the use of alcohol and even opium for fretful children was widespread in Jacksonian America (Sunley, 1955, p. 155). Mothers were also advised to monitor carefully influences emanating from outside the home, including the neighboring children with whom the child played and the books he read (Beecher, 1841, pp. 233–234; Kuhn, 1947, p. 108; Bushnell, 1860, p. 121). So persuaded were the fireside educators of the superiority of mothers as educators that some of them even urged mothers to keep their older children out of school, even after the age of five, in order to prevent exposure to evil examples (Kuhn, 1947, p. 106). In short, mothers were enjoined to erect around their young a screen behind which the subtle and sacred process of mother nurture could do its work. It is not surprising that the fireside educators provided so little endorsement of the extra-familial education of young children.

In advising mothers on their new responsibilities, the parent educators made clear that it was the moral development of the child more than his intellectual development that concerned them. In keeping with the emerging Cult of Childhood, they insisted that small children possessed needs unique to their stage of development, and they were particularly worried about the dangers of "forcing" intellectual precocity. Lydia Sigourney believed that the ambition of parents to have children read at an early age was "evil," because the small child is usually not ready for it (Kuhn, 1947, p. 99). The Reverend Heman Humphrey observed that it is difficult to persuade parents "to let their sprightly little darling alone, till the rain and the sunshine have opened the bud and prepared the way for mental culture," and he bluntly declared it "extremely fallacious" that an infant can be taught to read in its third or fourth year (Kuhn, 1947, p. 100). It is evident that the parent educators shared with the founders of the infant school a conviction that small children possessed needs for balanced development that the traditional common school could not supply. At the same time, the tendency of parent educators to assign a subordinate value to intellectual development reinforced their conviction that mothers are uniquely qualified for the education of young children.

It was, therefore, on the subject of moral education that the domestic authors waxed most eloquent, and here they revealed their ability to employ the latest, most sophisticated theories of child development in the service of what were, in the main, conservative goals. With a few notable exceptions such as John Abbott, who adopted a decidedly somber tone in discussing discipline (Strickland, 1969, pp. 36–37), the parent educators left behind the stern tradition of "will-breaking" advocated by generations of Puritan clergymen, while at the same time declining to endorse the more radical theories of Romantics like Bronson Alcott. The fireside educators adopted instead a moderate position which revealed that they had grasped the significance of John Locke's advice on securing control of children through subtle manipulation (Kuhn, 1947, p. 160; Sunley, 1955, p. 163; Wishy, 1968). For the most part, the authors discouraged parents from the use of corporal punishment, advocating instead the use of "gentle means" and the establishment of a "rule of affection" (Sunley, 1955, p. 153; Kuhn, 1947, p. 160). It was, after all, a view perfectly consistent with their notion that women were the gentler, more sensitive sex. Consequently, mothers were enjoined to establish a bond of affection with their offspring and then to use that bond as a leverage with which to shape the child's character. Since the educators recognized that small children are imitative beings, they urged upon mothers the importance of a good example, but when—as they also recognized—small children sometimes go astray, they advocated the use of isolation and withdrawal of affection as forms of punishment.

Horace Bushnell best exemplified this moderate opinion, and he provided in his *Christian Nurture* a remarkably humane and psychologically sophisticated child-rearing manual.

Conclusion

Insofar as American mothers heeded this flood of advice from the fireside educators, there is little doubt that the movement raised the quality of childcare in America, rescuing many children from that parental indifference which historians have found to be characteristic of family life before the nineteenth century (deMause, 1974, p. 1; Shorter, 1975, p. 170). It was, after all, a step in the right direction to urge parents to stop sating their offspring with drugs to keep them quiet and in other ways to give more careful attention to matters of health and hygiene. Surely it was also a sign of progress to urge parents to abandon corporal punishment in favor of more "gentle measures" in the discipline of children. Only the most cynical, or those who believe that child nurture is something that can be taken for granted, could deny that the parent education movement benefited many of America's young.

The difficulty with the parent education movement was that it exacted an enormous price from both women and from poor children. As many feminist historians have pointed out, the Cult of Domesticity and the Cult of Motherhood rigidly confined both the role and the identity of women, who were expected to find in the ideal of motherly self-sacrifice the female equivalent of self-fulfillment (Jeffrey, 1971; Ryan, 1975; Sklar, 1973). The major difficulty with the model of parent education lay, however, in its neglect of the needs of poor children. The alternative models of early childhood education had given promise, however limited, that the benefits of the Cult of Childhood would be extended to children from all classes of society, either as a matter of charity through the infant school or by expenditure of public funds through the common school. The authors of the parent education literature, on the other hand, did not trouble even to pretend that they were addressing the poor. The fireside educators assumed, as a matter of course, that their readers were, if not rich, at least in comfortable circumstances, and all that they lacked was sufficient knowledge and the correct attitudes. The poor were simply outside the pale of concern, except as a potential threat to the sanctity of the proper household. In point of fact, it is difficult to imagine what a poor working woman would have done with the advice handed her by the fireside educators, except to acquire a sense of guilt for neglecting her duties. The extraordinary demands which the parent education movement placed on families could be met only by parents who possessed considerable formal education and enough money to support a full-time homemaker in providing the steady, alert, knowledgeable and caring attention that the parent educators demanded. What, however, if the man was unable or unwilling to play his role as breadwinner? Nineteenth-century America, even as it worshiped at the Cult of Childhood, the Cult of Motherhood, and the Cult of Domesticity, provided a legion of examples of mothers and children bereft of economic support by men who died, abandoned their families for some frontier lure, turned to alcoholism, or were simply unable to meet the requirements that competitive society imposed for success in the market place (Bremner, 1956; Riis, 1892; Ryan, 1975, pp. 195–249; Spargo, 1906). For such families as these, the usual resort in case of difficulty was to the traditional help of relatives and neighbors, an informal system which has continued to supply the needs of many poor mothers and children until the present day (Stack, 1974; Woolsey, 1977).

After 1860, reformers such as Elizabeth Peabody recognized these difficulties. In the free kindergarten movement, she revived the spirit if not the form of the infant school (Weber, 1969, pp. 24–27). Likewise, civic-minded women such as Mrs. Arthur M. Dodge bent their concern and energies to the founding of day nurseries to provide custodial care to the children of working mothers (Steinfels, 1973). Here at last was recognition that poor parents needed help as much as they needed good advice. There is even evidence, in the period after the Civil War, that the extra-familial education of young children was gaining respectability. The kindergarten was, after all, providing education as well as "mere" custodial care, and when Froebel's institution was ultimately given the blessing of the public school establishment, it appeared that early childhood education might achieve legitimacy (Weber, 1969, pp. 27–35). The appearance of the Nursery School movement, in the 1920s, lent additional credence to the idea that the education of young children outside the home might, in fact, represent a positive good rather than an unfortunate necessity (Weber, 1969, pp. 169–175). Always, however, the champions of extra-familial education were compelled to combat the influence of the parent educators, who had convinced most mothers that the nature and needs of the young child could be fulfilled only within the sacred precincts of the family (Steinfels, 1973, p. 66). So strong was the legacy of Jacksonian America that not until the decades after World War II did most American women begin to decide that they could safely share the education of their little ones with others.

References

ALCOTT, A. B. *Observations on the Principles and Methods of Infant Instruction.* Boston: Carter and Hendee, 1830.

ARIES, P. *Centuries of Childhood: A Social History of Family Life.* New York: Knopf, 1962.

BAILYN, B. *Education in the Forming of American Society: Needs and Opportunities for Study.* Chapel Hill: University of North Carolina Press, 1960.

BEECHER, C. *A Treatise on Domestic Economy for the Use of Young Ladies at Home and at School.* Boston: Marsh, Capel, Lyon, & Webb, 1841.

BESTOR, A. E. *Backwoods Utopias: The Sectarian and Owenite Phases of Communitarian Socialism in America: 1663–1829.* Philadelphia: The University of Pennsylvania Press, 1950.

BREMNER, R. *From the Depths: The Discovery of Poverty in the United States.* New York: New York University Press, 1956.

BUSHNELL, H. *Christian Nurture.* New York: Scribner's Sons, 1860.

CREMIN, L. *American Education: The Colonial Experience, 1607–1783.* New York: Harper and Row, 1970.

DEMAUSE, L. (ed.). *The History of Childhood.* New York: The Psychohistory Press, 1974.

DOUGLAS, A. *The Feminization of American Culture.* New York: Knopf, 1977.

EMERSON, R. W. *Journals and Miscellaneous Notebooks.* Cambridge, Mass.: Belknap Press, 1960.

FINKELSTEIN, B. (ed.). *Regulated Children/Liberated Children: Education in Psychohistorical Perspective.* New York: The Psychohistory Press, 1979.

FITTS, D. Una and the lion: The feminization of district school teaching and its effects on the roles of students and teachers in nineteenth century Massachusetts. In B. Finkelstein (ed.), *Regulated Children/Liberated Children: Education in Psychohistorical Perspective.* New York: The Psychohistory Press, 1979.

FROST, J. W. *The Quaker Family in Colonial America.* New York: St. Martin's Press, 1973.

GREVEN, P. *The Protestant Temperament: Patterns of Child-Rearing, Religious Experience, and the Self in Early America.* New York: Knopf, 1977.

GREVEN, P. (ed.). *Child-Rearing Concepts, 1628–1861: Historical Sources.* Itasca, Ill.: Peacock Publishers, 1973.

GRIMSTEAD, D. *Melodrama Unveiled: American Theatre and Culture, 1800–1850.* Chicago: University of Chicago Press, 1968.

HALE, S. Introduction. *Ladies Magazine*, 1828, *1*, 1–2.

HALE, S. Fashionable Follies. *Ladies Magazine*, 1830a, *3*, 181–187.

HALE, S. Home. *Ladies Magazine*, 1830b, *3*, 217–220.

HARRISON, J. F. C. *Quest for the New Moral World: Robert Owen and the Owenites in Britain and America.* New York: Scribner's Press, 1969.

HUMM, R. O. *Children in America: A Study of Images and Attitudes.* Atlanta, Ga.: The High Museum of Art, 1978.

JEFFREY, K. The family as utopian retreat from the city: The nineteenth-century contribution. In S. TeSelle (ed.), *The Family, Communes, and Utopian Societies.* New York: Harper and Row, 1971.

KAESTLE, C. F., and VINOVSKIS, M. A. From apron strings to ABCs: Parents, children and schooling in nineteenth century Massachusetts. In J. Demos and S. S. Boocock (eds.), *Turning Points: Historical and Sociological Essays on the Family.* Chicago: University of Chicago Press, 1978.

KUHN, A. *The Mother's Role in Childhood Education: New England Concepts, 1830–1860.* New Haven, Conn.: Yale University Press, 1947.

LANGSAM, M. Z. *Children West: A History of the Placing-Out System of the New York Children's Aid Society, 1853–1890.* Madison, Wisc.: The State Historical Society, 1964.

LEWIS, R. W. B. *The American Adam: Innocence, Tragedy and Tradition in the Nineteenth Century.* Chicago: University of Chicago Press, 1955.

MAY, D., and VINOVSKIS, M. A ray of millennial light: Early education and social reform in the infant school movement in Massachusetts, 1826–1840. In T. Harevan (ed.), *Family and Kin in Urban Communities, 1700–1930.* New York: New Viewpoints, 1977.

McCUSKEY, D. *Bronson Alcott, Teacher.* New York: Macmillan, 1940.

MEYERS, M. *The Jacksonian Persuasion: Politics and Belief.* New York: Vintage Books, 1957.

MORGAN, E. *The Puritan Family: Essays on Religion and Domestic Relations in Seventeenth Century New England.* New York: Harper and Row, 1966.

OWEN, R. A new view of society (1813). In J. F. C. Harrison (ed.), *Utopianism and Education: Robert Owen and the Owenites.* New York: Teachers College Press, 1968.

OWEN, R. *Life of Robert Owen* (1857–58). Reprinted, London: Charles Knight, 1971.

PLOTZ, J. The perpetual Messiah: Romanticism, childhood, and the paradoxes of human development. In B. Finkelstein (ed.), *Regulated Children/Liberated Children: Education in Psychohistorical Perspective.* New York: The Psychohistory Press, 1979.

RIIS, J. *The Children of the Poor.* New York: Charles Scribner's Sons, 1892.

ROSS, E. D. *The Kindergarten Crusade: The Establishment of Preschool Education in the United States.* Athens, Ohio: Ohio University Press, 1976.

ROTHMAN, D. *The Discovery of the Asylum: Social Order and Disorder in the New Republic.* Boston: Little, Brown, 1971.

RYAN, M. P. *Womanhood in America: From Colonial Times to the Present.* New York: New Viewpoints, 1975.

SHEPARD, O. *Pedlar's Progress: The Life of Bronson Alcott.* Boston: Little, Brown, 1937.

SHORTER, E. *The Making of the Modern Family.* New York: Basic Books, 1975.

SKLAR, K. K. *Catharine Beecher: A Study in American Domesticity.* New York: Norton, 1973.

SPARGO, J. *The Bitter Cry of the Children.* New York: Macmillan, 1906.

SPRUILL, J. C. *Women's Life and Work in the Southern Colonies.* New York: Norton, 1972.

STACK, C. B. *All our Kin: Strategies for Survival in a Black Community.* New York: Harper & Row, 1974.

STEINFELS, M. O. *Who's Minding the Children: The History and Politics of Day Care in America.* New York: Simon and Schuster, 1973.

STONE, A. E. *The Innocent Eye: Childhood in Mark Twain's Imagination.* New Haven, Conn.: Yale University Press, 1961.

STRICKLAND, C. A Transcendentalist Father: The Child-Rearing Practices of Bronson Alcott. *Perspectives in American History,* 1969, 3, 5–73.

STRICKLAND, C. American attitudes toward children. In *The Encyclopedia of Education.* New York: Macmillan, 1971, 2, 77–92.

SUNLEY, R. Early nineteenth-century American literature on child rearing. In M. Mead and M. Wolfenstein (eds.), *Childhood in Contemporary Cultures.* Chicago: University of Chicago Press, 1955.

TYLER, A. F. *Freedom's Ferment: Phases of American Social History from the Colonial Period to the Outbreak of the Civil War.* New York: Harper and Row, 1944.

WEBER, E. *The Kindergarten: Its Encounter with Educational Thought in America.* New York: Teachers College Press, 1969.

WISHY, B. *The Child and the Republic: The Dawn of Modern American Child Nurture.* Philadelphia: University of Pennsylvania Press, 1968.

WOOLSEY, S. H. Pied Piper politics and the child-care debate. *Daedalus,* 1977, *106,* 127–146.

Working Men's Committee, Philadelphia Report, 1830. Quoted in D. B. Davis, *Antebellum American Culture.* Lexington, Mass.: D. C. Heath, 1979.

CHAPTER 15

Day Care and Early Education

Bettye M. Caldwell
Marjorie Freyer

TWO DECADES AGO, day care was not thought of as part of the legitimate province of either early childhood education or child development. One decade ago, many people in these two related fields were still either ignoring it or hoping it would go away or, even worse, were denouncing it as a modern version of the "institutionalization" which had been proven detrimental to the development of children during the 1950s. Today, no one can ignore it, even though there are still quite a few who wish it would go away. Although it is not likely to go away, it may well diminish in visibility. If that occurs—and our prediction is that it will—it will not be because the importance of the service to children and families is not recognized, but simply because by that time researchers and practitioners will have convinced themselves that day care is conceptually indistinguishable from other early childhood education programs.

Demographic Aspects of Day Care

Anything written about the numbers of children in day care or the percentage of families who use the service is sure to be obsolete by the time it appears in print. Nonetheless, we think it important that the magnitude of the day-care population be kept in mind as research relating to day care is reviewed. In early 1981, approximately 50 percent of America's children under the age of five were in day-care facilities part-time or full-time. The percentage of women in the work force with children under six is hovering at the mid-point and will undoubtedly soon move on into a clear majority. Quantitatively, this means that in 1979 there were slightly more than thirty million children under eighteen whose mothers were in the labor force (up more than four million from 1970). According to Johnson (1980), the labor force participation rate for all women was 50.7. For women with children under eighteen, that rate was 61.6. The figures for women with children under six and three were 45.4 and 40.9 percent, respectively, large numbers of human beings.

In two-parent families, fewer white children (49 percent) have working mothers than do blacks (61 percent). In one-parent families, these percentages are reversed (67 percent for whites and 53 percent for blacks). As is well-known, these figures represent a sharp increase from 1970. What levels they will reach in the 1990s can be extrapolated only tentatively at this time, as the rates will be influenced by the employment picture and actual numbers by population figures. By the end of the present decade, what we often disparagingly call "an alternative child rearing environment"—day care—will be clearly the modal type of early child care.

Although it is impossible to obtain precise figures, it is estimated (Sager, 1974) that 70 percent of the children within the age range needing day care are cared for either in their own homes or family day care. Morgan (1974) conjectures that no more than 5 to 10 percent of the family day-care facilities are licensed, which means that the vast majority of children in day care are still in settings that are out of the public view, often unsupervised, and perhaps of very poor quality. It is of great importance that we try to open *Windows on Day Care*, to borrow a title from an influential book (Keyserling, 1972) and look at what goes on. It is equally important that we bring to the arena of day care the research tools of the social sciences and make conscientious efforts to determine what effects are associated with the experience and what actually takes place in that developmental setting that we call, for lack of a better term, day care.

Scope of This Chapter

We are steadily accruing a respectable data base for day-care practice, and major reviews of research evidence relating to day-care effects are appearing with some regularity (Belsky & Steinberg, 1978; Etaugh, 1980). Materials are cited selectively in this review to highlight issues pertinent to policy in the day-care field. Our discussion will relate primarily to work done in the United States, although America was rather slow to catch up with what other countries were doing in day care for infants and young children (Kamerman, 1980; Robinson, Robinson, Darling & Holm, 1979). With a few major exceptions, the bulk of the research discussed deals with some aspect of infant care.

Organization of the Chapter

We have divided the research presented here into *outcome* and *process* studies. Outcome studies deal with the effects of day care on children, families, or social institutions. Process studies are concerned with what goes on in day care and with program components associated with some specified outcome. Many outcome studies, however, are concerned with certain processes that might be operative in influencing outcomes, and vice versa. We shall also suggest implications of the research for day-care program operation and for helping to shape the directions of growth of the field of early childhood education as a whole.

Multivariate Outcome Studies

In the early 1960s, there was an almost simultaneous development of a number of infant day-care programs in different parts of the country (with the exception of North Carolina, which had two), all designed and implemented by persons who did not know one another at the time, all with certain commonalities, but all with unique features.[1] By the mid-1960s, most of the people developing these programs knew one another, and within another year or two, program descriptions were appearing in print (Caldwell & Richmond, 1964; Chandler, Lourie & Peters, 1968).

All the people in these programs shared a conviction that they provided an opportunity to supply some of the experiences needed by young children from economically underprivileged families and that gains would occur in such children as a consequence of their participation in the programs. In spite of this optimistic hypothesis, the research challenge was to prove that such programs did not harm the children. When one reflects that most of the research generally defined as dealing with early childhood education has been conducted to demonstrate that it is associated with developmental advantages for the children involved, one realizes that from its inception day-care research carried a rather heavy burden.

In an important review of that period, Swift (1964) examined the effects of early experience in "nursery schools" and "day nurseries" (one of the terms then in use for day care) and could cite only two studies that had specifically dealt with the day nursery per se. The large number of studies dealing with teacher–child relationships, curriculum variations, peer relationships, and the physical setting were all done in "nursery schools," and they were rarely if ever checked for generalizability to day care. On the basis of her review, Swift concluded that "more research is needed on the effects of the long hours and the necessarily greater degree of routine and regimentation in the full day program. There is as yet no evidence that these are likely to prove deleterious to the child, if carried out within a professionally adequate program" (Swift, 1964, p. 281).

This, then, was essentially the *applied* research underpinning for infant day care in the 1960s. To several of us, the *theoretical* foundation was secure and

[1] If there is one person in this country who deserves the most credit for helping to establish a research base for the operation of quality day care it is Dr. Charles P. Gershenson, who, as director of the Research Division of the Children's Bureau (now part of the Administration for Children, Youth, and Families) helped to create a number of demonstration day-care programs about the country. As he largely worked behind the scenes, his important contribution to the evolution of knowledge and expertise in this field is not always appreciated. Dr. Gershenson not only helped provide funding for program development in this area, but he also helped ensure a salutary balance between quality program operation and research.

substantial (see Caldwell, 1968). Independently, but with an essentially common goal, researchers in a number of demonstration day-care centers began conducting short-term outcome studies on a small scale to try and determine what effects, good or ill, were associated with early day care.

Small-Scale Outcome Studies

Most of these small-scale early projects had a multidisciplinary focus and were concerned with many different child and family variables. Among other important contributions of these projects has been their stimulation of specific hypotheses to be tested in subsequent research. If for no other reason they deserve at least brief mention here.

THE SYRACUSE PROJECT

Planned as the early intervention arm of a research project concerned with infant development as a function of different patterns of family and social care, the Syracuse Children's Center in Syracuse, New York, began operation in 1964 with twenty-five children under the age of three (Caldwell & Richmond, 1964; Caldwell & Richmond, 1968). During the next year, thirty children older than three were included. Many individual research projects were conducted with the participating children, both by the original investigators and subsequently by other persons in the Syracuse scientific community. Cognitive gains, in the form of day-care–control differences in longitudinal changes in Cattell Infant Intelligence Scale and Stanford-Binet quotients, significantly favored the day-care children (Caldwell, 1971). IQ changes within the experimental sample resulted in a normalization of the distribution of test scores, that is, a reduction in the initial overrepresentation of the children in the 60–90 IQ range (Caldwell & Smith, 1970). Psychiatric evaluation of all the children who were at least three years old (Braun & Caldwell, 1972) by a skilled clinician with no previous contact with any of the children revealed no significant adjustment differences between those who had entered day care prior to age three and those who had enrolled after traditional age for out-of-home experience.[2] In addition to being carefully monitored for evidence of healthy cognitive and socioemotional development, families in the program served as the initial standardization sample for the HOME Inventory (Caldwell, Heider & Kaplan, 1966; Caldwell & Bradley, 1979), which has since served as a major evaluation tool for determining the effects of interven-

[2] In addition to formal research evaluations of the social and emotional status of the children, we arranged with some of the nation's leading clinicians (including Dr. Lois Murphy and the late Dr. David Levy) to spend time with the children individually and in groups, to talk with parents and teachers at will, and form clinical opinions about the children. Dr. Levy wrote one of the shortest clinical reports one might ever expect from a psychiatrist: "There are no blots on the escutcheon."

tion on parents, and the APPROACH technique (Caldwell & Honig, 1971), which will be referred to in the section concerned with process studies.

One study done by the Syracuse group (Caldwell, Wright, Honig & Tannenbaum, 1970) deserves a longer description because it appears to have stimulated the subsequent wave of research dealing with infant day care and maternal attachment. When eighteen of the infant day-care children who had attended the Center for at least one year and twenty-three of the comparison group reached the age of two-and-a-half, they were observed in interaction with their mothers in a three-hour session involving testing, interviewing, and observation of mother–child interaction. The setting was a laboratory totally unfamiliar to all children. At the end of the session, the children were rated on seven scales, with these ratings summed to give an overall rating of attachment to their mothers. The mothers were similarly rated as to their attachment to the children. The results revealed no significant differences between the attachment of the day-care and home-reared children to their mothers, with the only significant difference in the mothers being on a scale of Permissiveness (home mothers higher).

As is often true for longitudinally oriented research, both the original developers of the Syracuse project moved out of the state. Fortunately, Schwarz (Schwarz, Krolick & Strickland, 1973; Schwarz, Strickland & Krolick, 1974) took the responsibility for coordinating two important follow-up studies with the group, and Lay and Meyer (1973) added another. In the first of these, twenty of the Children's Center "graduates" and a group of carefully matched children who were entering group day care for the first time (but almost half of whom had been cared for by sitters or neighbors) were observed for five forty-minute periods on their first day of attendance at a new center and again five weeks later. Ratings of affect, tension, and social interaction revealed a few significant differences, with the early day-care children showing more positive affect upon initial arrival and higher positive social interaction ratings both initially and five weeks later. The authors concluded that their data contradicted "the view that infant day care leads to emotional insecurity" (Schwarz, Krolick & Strickland, 1973, p. 340).

In their second study, the same authors (Schwarz, Strickland & Krolick, 1974) found a slightly different pattern of results. Four months after entry into the new program, children in the early day-care group were rated as showing more verbal and physical aggression, less cooperation with adults, and more movement. Lay and Meyer (1973) also examined the behavior of these children and reported that the early day-care group engaged in more positive social interactions and interacted more with their own group. These investigators also noted that the early day-care children spent relatively more time in the motor area of the new center and less in the cognitive and expressive areas. It is difficult to reconcile the differences in these studies. One explanation may be that the early day-care group "had done it all before" and that the teaching materials in the new center did not engage their attention and motivation as much as they did the other children. However, differences may also have been attributable to factors other than age of entry into day care. For example, the Schwarz, Krolick, and Strickland (1973) report indicates that only twelve of the twenty children in the late group were being cared for at home by their mothers at the time of entry into the new center. Four were being cared for in neighbors' homes (presumably family day care), three were with babysitters, and one child was described as having been in several foster homes. Thus, although group care was presumably new to all the later entering children, day care per se was not. Whatever differences between the groups were noted in the studies (more positive social interactions in two, more aggresssion in one, more apparently aimless wandering in two, and so on) may well be due to factors other than early or late day care per se.

The North Carolina Projects

North Carolina can boast of three historically important projects, two of which have been in the same setting at different times. The first of these was the Frank Porter Graham Child Development Center in Chapel Hill (Robinson, 1968). Although the day-care center established as the nucleus of the Child Development Center ceased operation in the early 1970s, a much broader-based child development research unit emerged from the foundations established largely through the day-care program. The original Chapel Hill project was an omnibus program with a broad multidisciplinary focus which allowed careful studies of the health of infants in day care to be conducted as well as research into cognitive and social responses.

Robinson and Robinson (1971) reported significant differences between approximately twenty-four center children who had entered the program either as young infants or around age two and two groups of control children on a variety of cognitive and language measures. Differences between experimental and control children were evident as early as eighteen months, which suggested to the authors that the period prior to that might be a crucial one for early experience. The greatest impact was in verbal rather than motor areas, and the widest differences between experimentals and controls were found in the most disadvantaged groups.

The second North Carolina project was located in Greensboro and was developed by Keister (1970) to serve primarily middle class children and their families rather than disadvantaged children. Evaluation of performance of the infants and toddlers on a variety of measures revealed essentially no differences between the Center children and a control group of home-reared children, leading Keister to conclude that for middle class children there was no deficit associated with infant day care.

The current Chapel Hill program, called the Abecedarian Project (Ramey & Campbell, 1977) will be discussed under several sections of this chapter and will be mentioned only briefly here. A current component of the Frank Porter Graham Center, this project is notable among such programs for its achievement of truly random assignment of high-risk infants (from high-risk families) to the group care arrangement or the longitudinal study group. Mobility in the project has been low, and the longitudinal data collected on this sample for close to five years at this time will prove invaluable in helping to understand developmental processes of these important early years.

THE BOSTON PROJECT

The final small-scale study (Kagan, Kearsley & Zelazo, 1977) to be cited which offered important outcome data on the effects of early day care is one that began somewhat later than the others but was well conceptualized and dealt with an ethnic group rarely used in child development research in this country: working and middle class Chinese Americans. This project differed from the others in another significant way also, namely, in the form of "a prior prejudice of one of the principal investigators" (p. 137) that infant day care had hidden psychological dangers.

The sample for the study consisted of approximately 100 Chinese and Caucasian children (different numbers available for different assessments) who were repeatedly assessed on a number of psychological variables between 3.5 months of age, at which time most of the day-care sample entered the program, and twenty-nine months of age. The major outcome assessments were at twenty and twenty-nine months. Most of the day-care children attended a day-care center in which the investigators were involved as program consultants. For some of the analyses, sixteen children described as attending "other forms of group care outside the home, either a day care center or custodial care" (p. 116) were also included. Assessment in this project was in the form of performance on a number of discrete cognitive tasks (vocabulary recognition, Bayley Scale, Concept Familiarity Index, Embedded Figures Task, and Memory for Locations) and social and emotional situations (attachment, free play, peer play, separation, play with unfamiliar children).

The most dramatic finding of this study is the extent to which the home-reared and day-care children functioned similarly so long as social class and ethnicity were controlled. The day care sample performed slightly better than the home sample on nonlanguage items of the Bayley, but there were no other cognitive differences of any magnitude or importance between the major groups. In the carefully planned measures of social behavior, there were no differences of any moment as a function of day care versus home rearing. The day-care children related a little more easily to a strange peer, which might certainly be expected. The attachment and separation situations produced remarkably similar responses in day-care children and home controls. However, there were many differences related to ethnic or class differences, leading the authors to conclude that "children from intact and psychologically supporting families who experience surrogate care during infancy and early childhood, resemble home-reared children from their own social and ethnic group to a greater degree than they do children of other ethnic and class backgrounds who are in the same extrafamilial environment" (p. 139).

Comment

Much of the research just cited in these historically important small-scale outcome studies has been flawed in a number of areas. The programs do not represent the day care available to most children. The association of a research team with a day care project is likely to mean that there will be a great deal of intellectual excitement associated with working in the project, that training and standards will be higher, and that many of the characteristics presumed to be associated with quality will prevail. Also, in most of the studies it was not possible to maintain completely blind testing conditions and to guarantee that experimental bias did not influence results (although the Kagan, Kearsley & Zelazo, 1977, study might offer some reassurance that such was not the case).

One of the biggest flaws in the research relates to sample size. Most of these projects cited had to pay for the day care and the research out of the same budget. From personal knowledge we can report that, for the Syracuse project, approximately 75 percent of the total budget went to operate the day care. The largest number of children enrolled at any one time was seventy-five, and these were spread out over five age groups (from six months to five years), two sexes, different social class status backgrounds for families, different ethnic groups. If all the samples from these research-oriented day-care programs could have been combined, a total of no more than 100 children of a given age/race/sex/SES group at any one period of time would probably have been available. Such tiny samples hardly provided a comfortable basis for generalization to the total society about such extremely important social issues.

Most of the program developers were not too explicit in describing the nature of their programs, so the comparisons were largely between some sort of "package"—love, stimulation, parent involvement, good food and medical care, exposure to interesting events—and essentially undescribed home environments. The educational researchers who looked for differentiated outcomes associated with different types of early experience (curriculum research) generally did not evaluate full-day programs. Thus, the first major type of comparative design to appear with any frequency was one which involved an examination of effects associated with group day care and family day care, with the implicit assumption that each of these types carried with it a type of hidden curriculum.

Type of Care and Outcome

In spite of their generally positive nature, results from these early studies did not seem to reassure the many people who feared the consequences of the care of infants in groups. In fact, the word "group" became something of a shibboleth that helped to strengthen a type of day care that had been available for a long time but that had had very little professional scrutiny and even less public awareness. This is what has been called family day care, a term that has been criticized as inaccurately describing the type of service provided. The more awkward term encouraged by many—day-care family homes—much more accurately describes the nature of the service; however, most people resist using the longer terminology. In many respects, it is as inaccurate to refer to the care provided children in homes or apartments of women who may care for usually up to six children as being within a "family" as it is to imply that children who are in group day care are attending an "institution." The nature of the social roles may bear no more resemblance to family social roles than is the case in a group setting. Nonetheless, because we are accustomed to thinking of the family as the only appropriate place for young children, many have assumed that what has come to be called "family day care" would somehow be better for young children than group day care.

A number of research studies have been conducted to examine the outcomes associated with participation in types of group care. Early in the 1970s, Saunders and Keister (1972) reported that children attending day-care centers performed better on the Bayley Scale than infants in family day care. Fiene (n.d.) conducted a study which observed the language behavior of three groups of sixteen three-year-old children. One-third attended day-care centers; one-third were enrolled in family day care, and the remaining sixteen were at home with their parents. The children were observed in different types of play areas (dramatic play, art, blocks, cognitive games). The total number of spontaneous verbalizations made by the children during the observations were recorded and classified as simple or complex. The largest number and the highest rate of both simple and complex verbalizing occurred in the family day-care homes, with the next highest level being in the home group. The study does not make clear whether the children in their own homes had other children with whom they could converse during the observation period, a contingency that could obviously reduce the frequency of verbalization of children in the home setting.

In a Swedish study, Cochran (1977) observed sixty children whom he described as "home-based" (thirty-four of these were in their own homes and twenty-six were with a day mother) and sixty children enrolled in twelve centers in Gothenburg. Cochran's major finding was not unlike that of the Kagan, Kearsley, and Zelazo (1977) study; that is, many experiences were common to children in both types (really three types) of settings. The children who were in their own homes and in day homes interacted slightly more often in cognitive-verbal situations. They also functioned in ways that elicited more limit-setting behavior by the adults. There were no stable differences as a function of group status on an infant scale or in responses to separation.

In a somewhat similar experiment, Winett, Fuchs, Moffat, and Nerviano (1977) looked at thirty-five children who were in a full-time day-care center, fifteen children who remained at home all day with a babysitter, a mixed group of thirty-one children who spent half a day in a group setting and the other half day at home with a sitter, forty-three children cared for in their own homes. On a variety of measures of cognitive and language functioning and ratings of parent–child interactions, the groups were found to be more similar than different. The group participating in mixed care (part sitter, part center) tended to score higher than the other groups on measures of mental ability. However, this particular group was significantly higher than all other groups on socioeconomic status, which means that differences in the children were probably related more to SES than to the type of care arrangements. The study illustrates the difficulty of adequately controlling for social and demographic variables in such research, as choice of type of day care is clearly related to these variables. One interesting finding in this study was that maternal warmth was rated higher for those mothers who worked full-time and whose children were cared for full-time outside the home than for the group who cared for their children at home exclusively.

One other study which compared group and family day care has been reported by Howes and Rubenstein (1978). These investigators observed forty toddlers, aged nineteen months, from similar backgrounds, half of whom were enrolled in eight community-based day-care centers and half of whom were being cared for in sixteen different family day-care homes. Each child was observed for a total of two hours by means of a time-sampling procedure. In addition, caregivers were interviewed regarding training and other aspects of job functioning. In this study, the investigators concluded that the two types of day-care settings created different types of child-rearing environments. In the family day-care homes there were fewer children, and the groups were more heterogenous. The caregivers were more isolated from other adults and carried out various types of housework along with child-care activities. In contrast, the centers featured a more exclusively child-oriented arrangement of the physical environment and the daily schedule. Using factor analysis, the authors identified five discrete factors in the behavior directed by the children to the adults: positive social skills, dependent behaviors, high affect with imitation, negative affect, and violating adult standards. Toddlers in family day care were rated significantly higher in the area of positive social skills (which included spontaneous, responsive, and contingent talk). Similarly, four factors of caregiver behavior were isolated: skillful care, restrictive and negative behavior, negative responsiveness to toddler demands, and positive responsiveness to sharing and child vocalization. Again, there was significant difference in only one factor score, with adults in family day care scoring higher on the restrictive and negative factor (reprimands, negative responses to positive behavior, and ignoring positive bids for attention). The authors compared the incidence of social speech to adults in both of their day care samples to that found for home-reared children in a companion study (Rubenstein & Howes, 1979) and noted that the incidence was lower for both day care groups (30 percent of observation time for home, 20 percent for family day care, and 12 percent for center-care toddlers).

The authors of the study suggested that the statistically significant differences they found were not very meaningful in part because incidence rates were low for both groups. They concluded that, inspite of setting differences, there were virtually no significant differences between the facilitative behavior emitted by the adults and the responsive behavior of the children in the areas of affect and dependence and that group day-care and family day-care environments can promote social competency in toddlers. As has been true in virtually all of these studies, the investigators also indicated that within-group variation may be far more important than differentiation according to some designated category.

One final study concerned with type of care (Rubenstein, Pedersen & Yarrow, 1977) dealt with the early effects of what is actually the most common type of day care: informal arrangements made with family members or acquaintances. So frequently do people fail to realize that such children are indeed in day care that they are occasionally included in research studies as home-reared controls (see Schwarz, Strickland & Krolick, 1974)! The sample for this study consisted of sixty-five black five- to six-month-old infants from low-income families, thirty-eight of whom were being cared for primarily by their mothers and twenty-seven of whom were cared for by other caregivers (fifteen relatives) in either the child's or the caregiver's home. Behavior of the adults and the children was sampled during two three-hour home visits made when the children were awake.

Of the eleven measures of caregiving behavior, five showed significant differences in favor of the mothers which indicated that the infants being cared for by their own mothers were in a more stimulating and affectively pleasant milieu. The sixteen measures on the infants, however, revealed essentially no differences between the two groups (focused exploration being the only exception). The authors concluded that their data "highlight the relative invulnerability of infants to daily separation from mother in their first six months of life despite less positive affect and less varied stimulation from substitute caregivers" (Schwarz, Strickland & Krolick, 1974, p. 530). No information was given as to whether there were differences between caregiving practices as a function of licensing status and training.

Large-Scale Multivariate Outcome Research

In the late 1960s and early 1970s, a new philosophy of research design and funding allowed a few studies to break out of the traditional mold of the isolated small-sample project. Cooperative funding from multiple sources, consortia of investigators, and large-scale federal funding for a few studies occasionally became available. Within the framework of outcome studies, one result of this new philosophy was the New York City Infant Day Care Study, a research project begun in 1970 and not completed until 1978.

THE NEW YORK CITY INFANT DAY CARE STUDY (NYCIDCS)

Directed by Golden and Rosenbluth (1978) and administered by the Medical Health Research Association of New York City, the NYCIDCS set a precedent as being the first large-scale study of "typical" public and private day-care programs rather than of the academically oriented, research-based model day-care centers. It was an omnibus study concerned as much with the health and nutrition of young children and with total family functioning as it was with the psychological responses of the children to the day-care experience. The sample consisted of approximately 400 children and their families participating in a total of thirty-one licensed community-sponsored day-care programs. Of this total, eleven were group infant care programs (defined as center-based care with eight to ten children of approximately the same age with several caregivers per room), and twenty were family day care programs (licensed homes or apartments with fewer than six children of different ages with one caregiver).

Using a unique design, the investigators managed simultaneously to examine for major day-care/no day-care effects and to compare cross-sectional outcomes associated with different types of infant day care—all without having an entirely home-reared control group. They achieved this by assessing the development of the children attending the two types of day care longitudinally at approximately six, twelve, eighteen, and thirty-six months of age. For the thirty-six month assessment, they brought in a new group of children who had just entered day care at that time and who had not had a regular pattern of extra-home care during the first thirty-six months. Thus, by controlling for age of entry, they actually had what was in effect a no-day-care sample at different evaluation points, although all the children were actually drawn from day-care programs. This type of design, combining longitudinal and cross-sectional measures, represents an ingenious way of overcoming problems associated with proper selection of controls for day-care research.

The three main areas in which program outcomes were studied were (1) physical health and nutrition; (2) psychological development, including cognitive, language, social, and emotional functioning; and (3) family impact.

Health and Nutrition.   The health care of the children in both groups was roughly comparable to that of children from similar socioeconomic backgrounds. The staff in the group day-care centers seemed to have more knowledge of children's medical problems, kept better records, and were more concerned with follow-up of medical problems uncovered in the study than family day-care workers. The children in group care continued to receive appropriate immunization, while the number of those in family day care who continued to be immunized according to preferred medical schedules dropped drastically as the children got older.

In the area of nutrition, significant differences were found in the nutritional value of the food served in the two different kinds of programs. Children in family day care tended to receive more "junk food" (potato chips, soft drinks, luncheon meats, sweets), whereas those in group day care received more nutritional foods at meals and snacks. Similar differences existed in environmental safety hazards, with more noted in the family day-care homes. However, no differences were observed in the safety practices of the caregivers in the two settings.

Psychological Development.   Data collection in this area was exhaustive and complex, and only the highlights can be presented here. At all the major evaluation time points, the children were assessed both by formal tests and by naturalistic observation in the areas of language competence, cognitive style, social competence with adults, social competence with peers, and adequacy of emotional functioning. In most of these areas at most evaluation points, there were no significant differences between the groups. However, differences in social skills tended to favor children who were in family rather than group day care. In terms of functioning on intelligence tests, the reverse pattern was found. By age three, the children in group day care obtained significantly higher scores than the family day-care children on the Stanford-Binet. No difference had been noted at eighteen months of age, and at twelve months the children in family day care had scored slightly higher in terms of cognitive-language functioning. At thirty-six months, the children who had been in group infant day care had an average overall rating on the Stanford-Binet, whereas those who had been in family day care and who came into group day care at age three scored in the low average range. Although the differences were not great, they were statistically significant. The investigators were somewhat surprised to note a decline in the scores of the children in family day care, as an eductional aide visited each family day-care home twice a week to suggest activities that would stimulate the intellectual development of children. The difference in the Standord-Binet test scores at thirty-six months was essentially the only statistically significant difference obtained at that point in time.

Family Development.   No measurable impact of the day care, either short-term or long-term, on these families could be identified. Contrary to popular expectation, having children enrolled in licensed day care seemed to have no effect on a family's welfare status. Approximately 70 percent of the families were on welfare at both the beginning and the end of the study. The authors do not indicate whether this is the same 70 percent, so it is conceivable that there could have been individual family change or movement with regard to the welfare variable.

On the basis of their finding of no major differences associated with type of care during the first two years, the investigators suggested that family day care be considered the method of choice for this age group because of its lower cost. After age two, however, center care should be preferred, as the group appears to add a level of intellectual stimulation missing in the smaller setting. They felt that this kind of transfer would be easier if, operationally, group and family day-care programs were integrated into a single service pattern.

Circumscribed Outcome Studies

In this section, research relating to three dependent variables is summarized: cognitive functioning, socioemotional behavior (specifically, attachment), and health of children. By far the largest number of such studies deals with the question of whether day care affects the attachment of infants to their mothers.

Attachment

The first study to appear in this area is the one from the Syracuse project (Caldwell et al., 1970) which reported essentially no differences between toddlers in day care and in home-rearing settings. A few years later, a study by Blehar (1974) appeared which not only challenged the findings but also gave the field a methodology with which to examine this issue more objectively. She used the Strange Situation Test of Ainsworth and Wittig (1969). Briefly, this involves placing a child and his or her mother in a laboratory room containing two adult chairs and a few children's toys. Observers record the child's physical distance from the mother, positive and negative affective responses, amount of exploratory manipulation, and proximity-seeking or avoidance. These behaviors are observed in seven three-minute episodes in which the child is with her or his mother and/or stranger or is alone. The procedure elicits quite a negative emotional reaction in some children, and most investigators terminate either an individual episode or the entire procedure if a child cries for as long as a minute.

In her study, Blehar (1974) observed forty children ranging in ages from two to four and divided into younger (thirty months) and older (forty months) groups, all of whom were from intact, middle class families. Half of the children in each group had attended private day-care centers for five months at the time of the study, and the other half were cared for by their mothers at home. Using the Strange Situation procedure, Blehar reported deviant attachment patterns for both the younger and older day care groups. The thirty-month day-care group was described as showing "anxious-avoidant" attachment and the forty-month group showed "anxious-ambivalent" attachment. There were no significant differences in the behavior of either group toward the stranger nor were there differences between the mothers in the two groups on a scale of maternal sensitivity and warmth and on HOME Inventory scores.

An early challenge to the Blehar study came from Moskowitz, Schwarz, and Corsini (1977), who applied the Strange Situation procedure with two groups of twelve children, all approximately forty-two months old, half of whom had been in day care for approximately six months and half of whom were being cared for at home. These investigators were conscious of several possible flaws in the Blehar study, including the fact that the observers were aware of the care status of the children and of the hypothesis of the study that day care would impair attachment. Accordingly, their observers were naïve both as to group membership of the individual mother–child pairs and the purpose of the study. Their findings showed that the behavior of children in both groups was quite similar. The day care children showed less distress than the home children toward the end of the procedure, but their behavior toward their mothers was not distinguishably different from that of the home-reared children. Although this study had certain design improvements over the original Blehar study, there were significant differences between the samples (middle class intact families and mostly first-born children in Blehar; only half of the families intact in the second study and less than half of the children first-born) that might have accounted for some of the differences in results. Thus, it is encouraging that other replications have occurred.

Another partial replication of the Blehar study was done by Portnoy and Simmons (1978) using thirty-five white middle class children forty-one to forty-five months old from intact families. In addition to a no-day-care and group day-care group, this study had a third group that had been in family day care since around one year of age and had transferred into group care around three years of age. Using the Strange Situation Test, these investigators found no significant differences as a function of group status. On the basis of their data, they questioned the assumption that age of entry into day care "differentially affects the mother/child attachment relationship" (p. 241).

The final quasi-replication of Blehar to be reported is that of Roopnarine and Lamb (1978) who used the same methodology but who used the procedure immediately before admission to day care and again three months later for both a day-care and a home-reared group. The sample of twenty-three (twelve day care) children was similar to the Blehar sample in most social characteristics. They found several significant differences between the groups at the time of the first assessment. Children about to be enrolled in day care showed less exploratory manipulation, more proximity-seeking and search behavior, and more of both positive and negative emotional behavior. At the time of the second procedure, the only two between-group differences were that the non-day-care group cried more and sought contact more than the day-care group. Furthermore, there were several significant within-group differences for the day care group measured longitudinally, while the non-day-care group's performance was highly consistent in the two measurement situations. In speculating on the meaning of the initially higher levels of anxiety in the children who were soon to begin day care, the researchers rejected the conclusion that these children had anxious and insecure attachments to their mothers and inferred instead "that they probably represent temporary (rather than permanent) anxiety on the part of children whose parents are preparing them for the entry into group care the next week" (p. 93).

An important contribution to the worth of these studies in terms of their ecological relevance has been made by Blanchard and Main (1979), who observed responses during reunion after separation in twenty-one toddlers in day care in two different settings: the natural day care environment and the laboratory. Each child was observed three times as the mother came to pick up the child at the end of the day and also for one hour during the regular day. Within six weeks of the observations in the center, each child/mother pair participated in the Strange Situation Test. The data showed that hours per week in day care and age were unrelated to avoidance reactions under either condition. However, avoidance was negatively related to length of time in day care in both the naturalistic and laboratory situations. Similarly, avoidance in the laboratory was significantly correlated with avoidance in the center reunion episodes. Finally, however, the authors reported that mean scores for avoidance in the lab situation were quite comparable to those established for non-day-care children in other experiments. The longer the infants were in day care, the better their social adjustment and the less likely they were to show resistance or avoidance upon reunion with their mothers. Similar findings were reported by Ragozin (1980), who found essentially no differences in behavior toward their mothers in day-care and home-reared toddlers in the Strange Situation Test, although the home-reared group was more attentive to the stranger. In the naturalistic setting in day care, attachment patterns were consonant with what would be predicted for children of a comparable age group, leading the author to conclude that children participating in quality day care demonstrate normal attachment patterns.

Working with slightly older children, Cornelius and Denney (1975) looked at dependency (defined in terms of proximity- and attention-seeking) as a function of day-care attendance. Day-care and non-day-care subjects were rated on these measures when they were alone with their mothers, with their mothers and another adult, and with their mothers and another child. Although they found no differences between day-care and non-day-care children, they did find an interaction between day care and sex. That is, home-care girls sought more proximity than home-care boys, whereas there were no differences between boys and girls in the day-care sample. The authors felt that these findings suggested that children in day care might be less sex-typed than children who do not have this experience.

One of the most interesting studies relating to attachment is that of Farran and Ramey (1977) who paid attention to a component of the attachment situation generally totally neglected, namely, the behavior and status of the adults. These investigators modified the Strange Situation procedure and designed a slightly different mild stress situation. In a square room they placed chairs in three corners and a number of toys right in the middle. Twenty-three black children, ranging in age from nine to thirty-one months, who had been enrolled in the North Carolina Abecedarian Project since early infancy were the subjects. The mother sat in one chair, the center teacher with whom the child had presumably the "best" relationship sat opposite her, and a stranger sat in the third chair. Toward the end of the observation period, an assistant brought in a cookie in a jar that the child could not open without help. During the fourteen-minute observation period, the children spent significantly more time near their mothers than near their "favorite" caregiver, and none asked the caregiver for help in opening the cookie jar. To the investigators, this clear preference for the mother was somewhat surprising, as many of these children lived in extended family situations and several of them went to a home other than the mother's when leaving the center. Yet, their "attachment" appeared to be much stronger to their mothers than to their center caregiver. In the most fascinating part of the study, Farran and Ramey examined the relationships between their measure of attachment and certain maternal variables. They found that the percentage of time the children spent in the maternal quadrant of the room correlated $-.55$ with maternal IQ and $-.67$ with the Maternal Involvement subscale of the HOME Inventory. Thus, those children whose mothers might be described as less competent and less involved with them appeared, on this measure, to be the most strongly attached. This study opens up a whole new area for study in the area of attachment and day care. It may be that we have concentrated so exclusively on the reaction of the children that we have ignored other variables which might be more important or which at least might account for more of the generally unexplained variance in the different studies.

Upon reading this study, we took a new look at the old Caldwell et al. (1970) study, remembering a part of the report that has been overshadowed by the evidence relating to day care and attachment. In that study, we examined strength of attachment and the child's developmental level (we did not have data on maternal IQs) and found that the better developed children tended to have stronger attachments to their mothers. We also pooled our day-care and non-day-care samples and looked at the association between strength of attachment and scores on the HOME test (this was an earlier version than the one used by Farran and Ramey). In that analysis, we found a strong positive association between HOME scores and strength of child's attachment and a similarly strong association between HOME scores and the rating of strength of attachment of the mother for the child. This finding pertains to the pooled day-care and non-day-care samples, whereas in Farran and Ramey all the children were in day care. Nonetheless, it appears unlikely that the relationship would be completely reversed in the day-care-only example. These data, collected a decade apart, suggest an important new direction of research effort concerned with the relationship between attachment, day care, and the total environment milieu in which the child is developing.

Cognitive Development

As so many of the multivariable studies already discussed dealt with cognitive functioning, only three will be mentioned here. The first two of these are reports by Ramey and Campbell (1977, 1979) on the intellectual development of the day-care and longitudinal children in their sample. Children considered at risk for mental retardation were randomly assigned to either a longitudinal or day-care group and assessed repeatedly on a number of psychological functions. Children in both groups had a mean Bayley quotient of around 104 at six months. Between six and eighteen months, the day-care group remained stable, while the longitudinal group declined to a mean quotient of 86. At twenty-four and thirty-six months, the longitudinal controls continued to drop, scoring 83 and 81 at those times. The mean quotient for the experimental day-care sample continued to hover around 100 (94 at twenty-four months, 96 at thirty-six months). In the lastest follow-up, which occurred at forty-two months, the experimental children were still superior to the controls on the McCarthy Scale of Children's Abilities. The differences were significant in the verbal, perceptual-performance, quantitative, and memory scales, but there was no significant difference in the motor area.

The other study to be mentioned is the Milwaukee Project of Heber, Garber, Harrington, and Hoffman (1972). This study was not discussed in the initial section because it did not purport to be concerned with multiple variables but was clearly designed to try to prevent culturally determined mental retardation and because it could not be described as part of the day-care movement. In fact, in the reports on this project, the authors tend to refer to the intervention as either education or rehabilitation. However, as the care of the children was provided by project staff seven hours a day for five days every week, it would have to be classified as day care.

The ramdomly assigned experimentals and controls in this study consisted of forty newborns whose mothers were black and undereducated and who had a measured IQ of 75 or less. When the experimental children were three months of age, they were assigned to a carefully trained teacher and attended a special center for seven hours a day five days a week. There was one teacher per child during the first year, after which time the children were placed in small groups of three. The mothers were not involved in these special educational activities, as additional rehabilitation activities were carried out with them in the area of job skills, grooming, academic review, and some training in growth and development. The results of the intensive day-care experience were spectacular. At age five, the experimental group scored an average IQ of 124, whereas the controls had predictably dropped to 94.

Health

Without the advances in control of communicable diseases that have been made within the past twenty years, questions about whether group care would harm children psychologically might be purely academic. Thus, the research done in this area, although somewhat limited, has been critical for the development of the field of day care.

The most important study to date remains that of Loda, Glezen, and Clyde (1972), part of the original Chapel Hill Project. Recognizing that advances in immunizations and sanitary practices and the availability of antibiotics do not necessarily ensure that respiratory illnesses will not multiply if social contact is increased, these investigators studied thirty-nine children from one month to five years of age over a forty-month period. The observed rate of respiratory illness of 8.4 per year in the day-care sample was similar to the incidence in children of similar backgrounds in home care. The illness rate of children under twelve months was slightly but not significantly higher than the controls. Even in the very young children, the illness rate did not differ from the general population if one looked only at home controls with more than one sibling. The types of viruses found as well as incidence rates were similar to those reported for the whole community, with comparable variations in terms of seasonal incidence and age.

Although the New York City Infant Day Care Study (Golden et al., 1978) did not include data on incidence of different types of illness, presence of health problems in the longitudinal sample was described as comparable to that of children from similar backgrounds. Maintenance of immunization schedules and follow-up on health problems was reported as more adequate in group than in family day care.

Chang and associates (Chang, Zukerman & Wallace, 1978; Chang, 1979; and Chang, Showalter, Pastcan & Kosanovic, 1980) have conducted a series of studies examining health care practices in group and family day care and in infant care centers. In the first study, Chang et al. (1978) used an interview questionnaire in fifty-two licensed centers in the Berkeley, California, area. About two-thirds of the centers had someone designated as health coordinator (variously trained), and about the same proportion displayed written emergency guidelines. More health services were offered by centers with federal and/or state financial support. Almost all the centers had some procedures worked out for referral for acute medical problems and emergency first aid. Only one-fifth of the centers admitted mildly ill children. In the family day-care study (Chang, 1979) which had responses from seventy licensed homes, concern about health issues was much less apparent. Almost all the family day-care homes had on file the name of a physician or clinic, but only a small percentage had immunization records and information about present or pass illnesses. Only half the homes had written emergency procedures, and fewer still had written health guidelines. Closer liaison between family day-care mothers and other community health care personnel was strongly advised.

The final study was concerned with thirteen Santa Clara County, California, infant care centers. In general, the administrators of the infant programs met all the standards specified for health care, but not all had written policies that were communicated to parents. Eleven of the thirteen centers had a designated staff person to serve as health coordinator, but only six of these had received formal health training. Staff in the centers indicated the need for sensory, language, dental, and developmental screening of infants and help in ensuring annual physical examinations. Recording of information indicative of health status took place in only a few of the centers. Most of the centers admitted handicapped children but excluded acutely ill children.

The question of whether to admit children who are ill continues to be debated, with most day-care administrators excluding such children. This appears to be common practice inspite of data from the Chapel Hill study (Loda et al., 1972) as evidence that there is no need to exclude or send home ill children, provided staff are able to care for them and a separate area is available.

Process Research

This section examines research that has tried to look closely at what goes on in day care and to tease out components of the day-care experience which might help to account for observed patterns of behavior.

Large-Scale Studies

THE NATIONAL DAY CARE STUDY (NDCS)

This study was funded by the Administration for Children, Youth, and Families and was conducted by a private research group, Abt Associates (with evaluations of the children conducted by personnel from the Stanford Research Institute). To date, reports of the methodology and of results of the main studies have been published (Ruopp, Travers, Glantz & Coelen, 1979), but considerable information is yet to be analyzed and assimilated. The study was commissioned as a means of obtaining information relating to federally proposed standards for day care. The original Federal Interagency Day Care Requirements (FIDCR) proposed certain standards such as adult/child ratios and required levels of training of caregivers which some considered too stringent and others too lenient. These standards are closely related to the question of how much day care will cost. Regardless of individual persuasion about whether FIDCR standards were too stringent or too lenient, most people agreed that relatively little information was available as a basis for policy decisions. The NDCS was commissioned to help obtain such information—i.e., to examine day care on a large scale to determine whether certain program characteristics made a difference in program quality.

The design of the study did not call for a non-day-care group, which is why we did not classify NDCS as an outcome study. The question raised was not whether day care was good for children, but rather what kinds of day care would best meet the needs of the children who were served. Considered in this context, this study represents an example par excellence of what we mean by process research, namely, establishing relationships between day care as it exists in the community and the development of the participating children.

The study dealt with a total of sixty-four centers in Atlanta, Detroit, and Seattle. In these centers, some 1,800 children were observed and tested, 1,100 parents interviewed, and caregivers in 129 classrooms were observed and interviewed. Program and cost data were collected in all the centers.

The major variables examined in the study were staff/child ratio, group size, and staff education and training, all of which are relevant to national social policy about day care. Assessment instruments were observational techniques focused on either the adult or the child and standardized tests of the children. Results were aggregated to either classroom or center level for analysis.

Major Findings. Differences in the federally regulated characteristics (staff/child ratio, group size, and caregiver qualifications) did result in differences in the quality of care received and in the cost of care. The highest quality of care was observed when the classroom had the following combination of characteristics: a high staff/child ratio, a low ceiling on group size, and staff qualifications of child-related education and training. In the classrooms where there were higher ratios, the lead teachers were able to spend more time on center-related activities and less time on commanding and correcting children. A ratio of 1:7 was found to be the best for preschoolers aged three to five.

The most important predictor of quality and an important correlate to the staff/child ratio is the group size. By itself the staff/child ratio is not enough. The NDCS recommended that the group size be limited to twice the maximum number of children allowed per adult by the staff/child ratio requirement. If the ratio is 1:7, the group size should be limited to fourteen. Although the mathematical ratio remains 1:7 in a group of four caregivers and twenty-eight children, the *human* ratio is 1:28. Each caregiver must know the names and needs of twenty-eight children. Smaller groups of children and caregivers were associated with more desirable classroom behavior and higher test score gains. The children were more cooperative, and there was more verbal initiative and reflective/innovative behavior. Conflicts, aggression, aimless wandering, and apathy were observed less frequently. The smaller group also allowed the lead teacher to engage in more social interaction with the children.

In regard to staff qualifications, the study found that child-related training and experience was more important than the number of years of formal education. Lead teachers with child-related training spent more time in social interaction with the children. The children in turn were more cooperative and more persistent in their work and less frequently uninvolved in tasks or activities. The children also made greater gains on the Preschool Inventory in centers where the proportion of teachers having child-related education/training was higher.

Costs.   The single most powerful predictor of day care is the staff/child ratio. Caregiver qualifications and variations in group size only marginally affected the cost of day care per child. Therefore, the NDCS recommended that the staff/child ratio requirement for preschoolers be no more stringent than 1:7.

Children under Three.   The NDCS included a small substudy on infant day care for children under three years of age. As in the case of the preschoolers, group size and staff/child ratio were both important. Classroom behavior and the frequency and quality of adult interaction were more strongly associated with group size for the infants than for the preschoolers. The staff recommended an adult/child ratio of 1:4, a group size no greater than eight for children under two and no greater than twelve for children ages two to three, and specialized child-related education or training.

During the four years it took to bring this study to its completion, experts in day care and child development, psychologists, economists, and a special minority task force regularly reviewed the study, scrutinizing its design, analyses, and findings to insure the objectivity and technical integrity. Such efforts, together with the technical quality control maintained by the research organizations that conducted the study, helped to ensure that the obtained information would be objective, reliable, and applicable to policy questions.

NEW YORK CITY INFANT DAY CARE STUDY

Some of the data from the New York City Infant Day Care Study are also relevant to a process analysis. Golden et al. (1978) evaluated the group and family day-care programs in the areas of physical environment (stimulation and freedom of restrictiveness, caregiver/child ratio, social interaction, and cognitive and language interaction provided by caregivers). Although they found differences in such environmental patterns as a function of type of day care, they found few associated child behavior differences. Group day-care programs offered more stimulating physical environments and had more play materials and space, but these were unrelated to the children's development at age three. Family day-care environments offered more social interaction and individual attention, had more favorable staff/child ratios, and provided more positive social-emotional stimulation during mealtime. Only the variables of interaction and individual attention related to psychological development at age three.

We have tended to be very laudatory about these large-scale cooperative research efforts. Thus, it might be appropriate to put such praise into perspective by offering the reminder that the variables chosen for study did not appear out of thin air. Rather they have come from important, painstakingly conducted small-scale research such as that by Prescott, Kritchevsky, and Jones (1972) which paved the way for the bigger studies by helping to identify the relevant variables. Without these early and important smaller efforts, the larger, more definitive studies would not have been possible.

Characteristics and Qualities of Providers

There are certain aspects of caregivers which have led to recommendations for staffing patterns without the benefit of a solid research base. A few isolated research studies were found which dealt with some of these characteristics.

Cummings (1980) conducted a study concerned with whether stability in caregiving (defined in terms of length of continuous employment and regularity of attendance) would be associated with the type of relationship established with the children. Using a laboratory situation somewhat similar to the Strange Situation Test, he observed the behavior of thirty day-care toddlers when their mothers were paired with either a stable or nonstable caregiver or a stranger. Results showed that the mother was preferred over either caregiver, and both caregivers were preferred over the stranger; however, there was no preference for the stable as opposed to the nonstable caregiver.

In the second part of his study, Cummings observed the day-care children in their centers on two different days, on one of which the child was handed over by the mother to a stable caregiver and on another to a nonstable employee. Of the thirty children used in this analysis, fourteen responded in similar fashion to the stable and nonstable caregivers. However, positive affect was more likely to be shown when the transfer was to a stable caregiver. Although the children had cried in forty of the laboratory separations, they cried in only seven of the "real" separations; separation in the laboratory obviously connoted something quite different to most of the day-care children.

A common recommendation for program operators is that infants and toddlers have "special" caregivers assigned to them who will provide most of their needed physical care and with whom they can develop a more intense relationship. The importance of such a staff assignment was investigated by Wilcox, Staff, and Romaine (1980). Twenty infants were cared for in one section of an infant center, with one caregiver assigned the care of four infants. In another section of the same center, five caregivers took care of twenty infants. Thus, the adult/child ratio was identical in the two groups, but the expected pattern of service differed. Effects of these individual or multiple assignments were assessed by means of observations of the children in their daily activities, in separations and reunions with their mothers, and developmental tests. There were few significant differences in the infant behaviors noted in the two groups, leading the authors to conclude that exclusive caregiving dyads are not necessary in infant care.

In recent years, more attention has also been given to characteristics of family day-care providers. As part of a large-scale training program for family day-care providers, Wattenberg (1977) obtained information from over 900 licensed and unlicensed providers in Minnesota (estimating that 90 percent of the total pool of providers were unlicensed). On the basis of the responses to questionnaires and training opportunities, she concluded that a traditional and a modernized type of providers can be identified. Traditional providers revel in the role of the feminine woman, do not drive cars, are intuitive about what children need, confident of their abilities, resist formal training as deprecatory of their natural skills, and perceive themselves as "super-moms." The more modern family day-care mothers are career-oriented and are interested in the professionalization of family day-care, are committed to training, and are eager for certificates and other visible proof of their qualifications. Wattenberg suggested that, since women in the first group are willing to accept help from their peers rather than from professionals, women in this second category may form a cadre of people who could provide needed training for the more traditionally oriented providers.

Parent Involvement

Parent involvement is a key point in the philosophy of day care. Scores of articles offer excellent suggestions about how to achieve or increase it. However, there is little information about the effects of different kinds and degrees of parent participation on either child-oriented outcomes or actual operating processes. The studies which have tended to show greater cognitive gains for young children in programs which involve the parents (for example, Levenstein, 1970; Radin, 1972) were conducted with children who were being cared for at home rather than in day care.

Shapiro (1977) studied fifteen municipally run day-care centers in New York City. She interviewed the director and two classroom teachers, observed for $3\frac{1}{2}$ hours in each teacher's classroom, and classified the centers as high, moderate, or low in parental influence and the programs as child-centered, moderately child-centered, or adult-centered. Results indicated that the number of parents on the board or the degree to which parents dominated the board was not a good indication of parental influence as indicated by the director. Sometimes, boards comprised solely of parents left all major decisions to the director or staff, and vice versa. Parent influence was felt to be higher in the administrative than in the curriculum area.

A surprising finding of Shapiro's study related to parental influence and degree to which the program was child-centered. With the exception of two centers serving college campuses, the highest degree of child-centeredness was found in centers with the least amount of parental involvement. Shapiro concluded that in centers where parents shape policy, the programs will be more adult-centered, and she implied that there were certain dangers associated with too much parental impact.

Powell (1978) also arrived at some pessimistic conclusions about the policy framework for parent involvement in a study done with some 212 parents and eighty-nine caregivers employed in day-care centers in the Detroit area. He examined the communication frequency and diversity, the communication systems used, the attitudes toward different types of communications, and preferences as to type of communications held by both parents and caregivers. The parent sample contained about equal numbers of blacks and whites and about half the parents represented single-parent families. Powell found that most caregiver-parent communications occurred at transfer points, when the parent left or picked up a child. The traditionally advocated parent conferences were rare, and home visits by center staff simply did not occur. Powell concluded that the social worlds of the home and day care may be fragmented and discontinuous, with little connection between them. There was little evidence from his study of clear efforts to coordinate socialization experiences for children in the two settings, and many of the actual communications were shallow and perhaps insignificant. He proposed that the concept of "parent involvement" which is so consistently advocated in day care needs more specificity.

Possibilities for this sort of fragmentation of socialization have been recognized by Falender and Mehrabian (1979), who have stressed the need for a better theoretical underpinning of day-care experiences. They suggest that some of the apparently contradictory empirical findings (for instance, Blehar versus other attachment studies) may be due to the failure to evaluate both home and day-care environments in terms of their potential to arouse certain kinds of perceptual and emotional states and the likelihood of concordance or discordance between them. With more sophisticated analyses of the different environments, one can only hope that a better understanding will emerge of the potential for more meaningful involvement of parents in day-care policies and programs.

Program Descriptions

The last type of process research are careful descriptions of what actually takes place in day care settings. Two examples of this type of research will be cited.

The first comes from Caldwell and associates (Caldwell, 1968; Honig, Caldwell, and Tannenbaum, 1970) and uses the APPROACH technique developed by Caldwell and Honig (1971). Approach breaks the ongoing flow of behavior down into a grammatical behavioral statement coded numerically to represent a subject (for example, specific child or adult), a predicate (attending, using objects, crying), and possibly an adverb (with verbalization, ineptly, intensely). Figure 15–1, taken from Honig, Caldwell, and Tannenbaum (1970), demonstrates the type of information relating to the behavior of children in groups that can be obtained with the technique.

Figure 15–1 graphically shows the behaviors emitted by five children, each chosen at random from five classrooms in the Syracuse Children's Center, during the morning structured teaching time. One can see clear age and developmental trends (reductions in general bodily activities and manual activities, increase in information exchange, in requesting or directing someone to do something) between the ages of one and five. In the right-hand field of Figure 15–1 is a description of what the adults in their environment did as they interacted with these five children. They spent less time just looking at or checking on the children as the children got older (attending) and more time giving them information. Also, as the age of the sample children increased from one to five, the frequency of commands and requests increased from toddler to four-year-old and decreased again, as the child turned five.

Such observation techniques allow one either to look at the full range of be-

Figure 15–1. Classroom behaviors of five children (left) chosen at random from different classrooms in an educational day-care program; and (right) teacher behaviors emitted in the five groups at the same time that the children were observed.

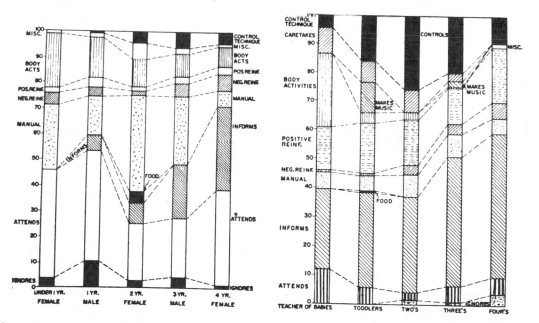

Source: Honig, Caldwell, and Tannenbaum (1970). Copyright © by The Society for Research in Child Development, Inc. Used by permission.

havior or to concentrate primarily on selected areas of action. Honig, Caldwell, and Tannenbaum (1970) isolated information-processing behaviors in thirty-two children, eight each aged one, two, three, and four, attending the Syracuse Center. On the left side of Figure 15–2 it can be seen that the amount of information exchange with adults in such a day-care center decreases with age, as does the act of saying something to no one in particular (coded in APPROACH language as "to self"), while information exchange with another child increases from less than 5 percent to over one-third of the total exchanges. The right side of Figure 15–2 shows the source of informational inputs for day-care children in the different age groups. Input from adults remains by far the most common pattern, but note that adult input addressed to the child alone decreases from 65 percent to 35 percent. If direct adult input to an individual child is a key type of interaction which can help a child continue to achieve normal developmental progress (as some of the family day-care and home care data might suggest), then such a decline in individually directed information exchange may well be quite significant. These represent but a few examples of the richness of information that can be gained from intraprogram process research.

Figure 15-2.   Types of information exchange (left) emitted by day-care children in four different age groups; and (right) recipients of information exchange responses emitted by the children.

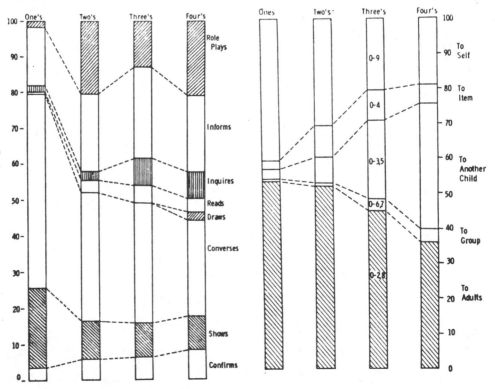

The final process study to be cited is by Rubenstein and Howes (1979), who used naturalistic observation to delineate just what it is in the day care and/or home experience that is associated with different patterns of child behavior. The sample for the study consisted of fifteen healthy, middle class white infants attending one of five day-care centers and fifteen carefully matched home-reared toddlers. Data consisted of five hours of time-sampled observation per infant, using categories covering four areas: caregiver–infant interaction, infant–peer interaction, infant–toy interaction, and infant affect.

No single generalization can be offered as to which type of environment was more stimulating or responsive, as both similarities and differences could be identified. Furthermore, observed differences appeared to reflect initiation of responses by the children as much as stimulation from the adults. Frequencies of verbal input and adult responsiveness were similar in the two settings, as was availability of stimulating toys, but the frequency of responsive speech in the infants was higher in the homes, an oft-reported finding. Both settings were similar in provision of cognitive input and in responding positively to talking, smiling, or crying from the infant. Differences were found, however, in affect, in restrictiveness, in the staging of play opportunities, and in elaboration or labeling on objects being used in play, in all of which day-care staff provided more positive input. The greater number of negative affective interchanges between caregivers and infants at home led the authors to suggest that caregiving may be a more pleasurable experience for both infants and adults in a small group setting. As one type of evidence for this, they offered the fact that for the home sample, maternal reprimands occurred less frequently when peers visited. Frequency of interactive play was higher in day care than at home, and the child's overall level of play was higher in day care. The facilitative effect of peer interaction was clear in both settings.

Program Implications of Research

On the basis of the comparative wealth of data we now have about both outcomes and processes in day care, it seems that there are at least a few research-based inferences that can be drawn for program operation.

1. *Keep programs small.* The day-care research data consistently point to the advisability of caring for young children in relatively small groups. Many teachers of the young have long felt that there is something almost toxic about having too many children together in large groups, no matter how many adults might be available to supervise them. There is a sort of contagion effect, difficult to buttress with data until recently, but common knowledge among teachers. Data from the National Day Care Study clearly support this wisdom, as does some of the information coming out of the family day-care studies. It may well be that the truly unique feature of family day care is size rather than presumed role of caregivers and children

2. *Attachment of children to their own parents is not impaired by early day care.* The bulk of research in the past ten years is overwhelmingly supportive of

this position. The separation followed by daily reunion with parents which is part of day care is in no way comparable to the kind of extended group-care arrangement in which children experience prolonged separation from their parents or perhaps do not have identifiable parents at all. These are obviously qualitatively different kinds of group experiences, and we are now ready to try to understand the dynamics of the process. Recent findings relating to the contribution of maternal characteristics to attachment add an exciting new dimension to the subject.

3. *Staff turnover may be less debilitating than had been feared.* Research indicates that children in day care interact positively with several people in the setting. Many people had worried that rapid staff turnover might impair the development of day-care children, as caregiver turnover has been offered as one explanation of the poor development of children in institutions. In the day-care setting, family stability, coupled with the pleasure of peer support may override any lack of stability in caregivers.

4. *Health of infants in groups can apparently be maintained.* The data obtained in the few programs which have taken the trouble to look at this variable have been encouraging indeed. However, this is an area in which a great deal more research is needed.

5. *There is a need to re-evaluate the role of prohibitions and control in daily programs.* A few studies have suggested that infants in family day care show a slight superiority over group day-care infants in language development around one year (which may or may not hold up over time). Naturalistic studies have shown that children in their own homes and in family day care are exposed to more prohibitions and corrections and restraints than children in group day care. Trainers of teachers and caregivers in the area of early child development have for years encouraged adults to give children more freedom to explore and have urged them to avoid direct commands and reprimands. If these early differences in types of environmental input, associated at least contemporaneously with important behaviors in the children, are found to predict subsequent behavior, the potential value of setting limits on children may need to be re-examined.

6. *Research offers little curriculum guidance.* To date most of the research has dealt with the effects of some day care versus no day care, or family day care as opposed to group day care. We hope that in the future we will be able to compare different kinds of daily programs and curricula.

7. *Parent involvement takes many forms and remains elusive and difficult to attain for many day care programs.* We discussed relatively few studies dealing with parent involvement. Such data as could be found suggest that parent involvement takes many forms in day care and that our objectives of getting the parents directly involved may not be necessary in order to achieve parent support.

Research Implications of Program Realities

Researchers in the field of child development and early education have learned a great deal from attempts to conduct quality research on day-care issues. The main thing we have learned is that it is not an easy field in which to do research. Parents and day-care operator do not wait breathlessly for our findings to be published as a means of providing guidance for program activities. The use of day care has increased at breakneck speed over the last ten years, and the persons seeking the service and offering the service have occasionally not even seemed to care about whether day care might impair attachment or might enrich or impair cognitive development. Day care as a service has moved forward as an inexorable social reality, and those who do research in this area must adapt to that reality. There are a few clear research implications of these program realities.

1. *Clean-cut experimental-control designs are not feasible.* There is hardly a study cited in this chapter which the investigator would describe as representing exemplary research methodology. A continued naïve search for a difference between day-care and home-reared children which is presumably due entirely to the day care is doomed to failure because the groups may already differ on significant variables which themselves have determined group membership. Important control variables such as social class, education, and income level appear to determine the type of day care service likely to be used and even the age at which enrollment will occur. It is literally impossible to compare various patterns of day-care services in terms of their effects on children when previously existing differences have determined the use of these different patterns. In most research there is some kind of confounding of these other variables; wealthier families are more likely to use in-home care; welfare families may have access only to Title XX programs, and so on. Actually, even the designation of the rearing environment as "home" or "day care" may be roughly comparable to an example of superstitious conditioning—that is, we assume that what we can see is the relevant variable whereas we may be overlooking an obscured aspect of the variable that is psychologically more meaningful.

2. *Day-care research exemplifies the need for ecological relevance.* This point, of course, has been made more frequently and more eloquently by Bronfenbrenner (1979) than by anyone else, and day-care research is an excellent area in which to validate the principle. For example, the large number of studies dealing with attachment reviewed in this chapter have by and large used some adaptation of a highly contrived laboratory test designed for infants originally and then applied to older children. The fact that the reported intensity of the disturbance noted in the laboratory contradicts what day-care workers observe repeatedly after children have had a week or so to become adapted to the new situation has until recently been of little concern to researchers. Such things must concern us all if our work is to have ecological validity.

3. *Research in the future needs to be more process-oriented.* The unattainability of rigorous experimental-control group designs supports the continued and increased importance of heavier concentration on descriptions of what actually takes place in early child-care environments rather than on transitory differences associated with possibly arbitrary and artificial categories. Important beginnings have been made in this area, and it is to be hoped that there will be major increases in this type of research.

4. *We need a theoretical underpinning for research on day care.* This has been a field in which empiricism has been rampant. We have seized upon the ex-

istence of different types of child-care environments and have sought to determine the impact of these environments without giving much thought to ways in which these variations of early childhood environments can relate to other major theoretical issues in child development research. One totally neglected area relates to concordance or discordance between the home environment and day-care environment. We still have a poor theoretical understanding of why the day-care environment, which often occupies a major portion of a young child's waking hours, has as little impact as it does. Better theory can lead to research more likely to provide answers to important questions.

Implications for Early Childhood Education

There are a few implications of both program and research findings for the broader field of early childhood education.

1. *Is day care a separate field?* Day care began as a field that was quite distinct from early education, but gradually the two fields have merged in certain respects. Some have not been happy to see this new affiliation; others have questioned why it took so long to occur. Essentially, we need to ask questions that relate to whether length of day in and of itself identifies a particular set of events as a differentiated experience in the lives of children. Is the time dimension of such importance that day care must remain a separate and distinct early childhood service?

2. *What can early childhood education learn from day care?* Much early educational research has been oriented toward demonstrating the value of such programs in the lives of children. Day care, on the other hand, has been conceptualized as a potentially damaging service. These two different stances for research have led to totally different research orientations and have occasionally resulted in an apparent tendency to ignore findings coming from the other closely related field. For example, we could not find a single study that raised questions about the effects of attachment on young children participating in a part-time early childhood education program. And yet, if this is such an important theoretical and practical issue for the development of children, can we afford to ignore it as a potential hazard associated with any kind of early childhood education? Conversely, there is virtually no curriculum research in day care. A smoother articulation of the concepts from both fields can only be beneficial to both.

3. *If the two fields merge, what will be the distinctive role of early childhood education as currently defined?* We are on the threshold of seeing day care as the modal early childhood environment rather than as a nontraditional alternative. As more women enter the work force, and as it possibly becomes socially unacceptable for them not to do so, what will be the role for the traditional half-day preschool? Likewise, as public schools become more aware of their obligation to perform relevant service for families by lengthening or adjusting the school day to accommodate work schedules, will there be less interest in the availability of part-

day or part-week programs? Many traditional (part-day) early childhood programs have already become clearly class-oriented, as only families with a certain pattern of social and economic background can use them.

In the years ahead, early childhood education will need to answer these questions in order to ensure its own survival.

Summary

During the past two decades, major changes which have helped to integrate the previously separate fields of day care and early education have occurred. Gone is much of the defensiveness on the part of the people who have struggled to obtain funding for day care, to give the field respectability, and to make certain that a firm research base existed as a guide for program development. Weakening is the tendency to act as though day care were a unitary function, not an accumulation of diverse experiences which may differentially affect different children or the same child at different times. Hopefully weaker still is the tendency many people have had to encourage stereotypes about different patterns of day-care service—e.g., to assume that "family day care" is better because it has the word "family" in it and that "group day care" is bad because it has the word "group" in it. And hopefully getting stronger is the willingness to do some of the same kind of painstaking observational research in the day-care setting that has provided such rich insights into patterns of social functioning within families in recent years. In general, the outlook for public support of early education and day care as valuable services to children and families and recognition of the importance of these settings for the conduct of ecologically relevant research are good.

References

AINSWORTH, M. D. S., and WITTIG, B. A. Attachment and exploratory behavior of one-year-olds in a strange situation. In B. M. Foss (ed.), *Determinants of Infant Behavior* Vol. 4. London: Methuen, 1969.

BELSKY, J., and STEINBERG, L. D. The effects of day care: A critical review. *Child Development*, 1978, *49*, 929–949.

BLANCHARD, M., and MAIN, M. Avoidance of the attachment figure and social-emotional adjustment in day-care infants. *Developmental Psychology*, 1979, *15*, 445–446.

BLEHAR, M. C. Anxious attachment and defensive reactions associated with day care. *Child Development*, 1974, 45, 683–692.

BRAUN, S. J., and CALDWELL, B. M. Emotional adjustment of children in day care who enrolled prior to or after the age of three. *Early Child Development and Care*, 1972, 2, 13–21.

BRONFENBRENNER, U. *The Ecology of Human Development*. Cambridge, Mass.: Harvard University Press, 1979.

CALDWELL, B. M. The fourth dimension of early childhood education. In R. D. Hess and R. M. Baer (eds.), *Early Education*. Chicago: Aldine Publishing Co., 1968.

CALDWELL, B. M. Impact of interest in early cognitive stimulation. In H. Rie (ed.), *Perspectives in Psychopathology*. Chicago: Aldine-Atherton, 1971.

CALDWELL, B. M. What does research teach us about day care: For children under three. *Children Today*, 1972, *1*, 6–11.

CALDWELL, B. M., and BRADLEY, R. Home observation for measurement of the environment. Little Rock: University of Arkansas, 1979.

CALDWELL, B., HEIDER, J., and KAPLAN, B. The Inventory of Home Stimulation. Paper presented at the Annual Meeting of the American Psychological Association, 1966.

CALDWELL, B. M., and HONIG, A. S. *APPROACH* (A procedure for patterning responses of adults and children). Washington, D.C.: Journal Supplement Abstract Service, 1971.

CALDWELL, B. M., and RICHMOND, J. B. Programmed day care for the very young child: A preliminary report. *Journal of Marriage and Family*, 1964, *26*, 481–488.

CALDWELL, B. M., and RICHMOND, J. B. The children's center: A microcosmic health, education, and welfare unit. In L. Dittman (ed.), *Early Child Care: The New Perspectives*. New York: Atherton Press, 1968.

CALDWELL, B. M., and SMITH, L. E. Day care for the very young: Prime opportunity for primary prevention. *American Journal of Public Health*, 1970, *60*, 690–697.

CALDWELL, B. M., WRIGHT, C. M., HONIG, A. S., and TANNENBAUM, J. Infant day care and attachment. *American Journal of Orthopsychiatry*, 1970, *60*, 690–697.

CHANDLER, C. A., LOURIE, R. S., and PETERS, A. D. *Early Child Care: The New Perspective*. New York: Atherton Press, 1968.

CHANG, A. Health services in licensed family day care homes. *American Journal of Public Health*, 1979, *69*, 603–604.

CHANG, A., SHOWALTER, S., PASTCAN, R., and KOSANOVIC, B. Health services in infant day care centers. *Child Care Quarterly*, 1980, *9*, 51–58.

CHANG, A., ZUKERMAN, S., and WALLACE, H. M. Health services needs of children in day care centers. *American Journal of Public Health*, 1978, *68*, 373–377.

COCHRAN, M. M. A comparison of group day and family childrearing patterns in Sweden. *Child Development*, 1977, *48*, 702–707.

CORNELIUS, S. W., and DENNEY, N. W. Dependency in day-care and home-care children. *Developmental Psychology*, 1975, *11*, 575–582.

CUMMINGS, E. M. Caregiver stability and day care. *Developmental Psychology*, 1980, *16*, 31–37.

ETAUGH, C. Effects of nonmaternal care on children: Research evidence and popular views. *American Psychologist*, 1980, *35*, 309–319.

FALENDER, C. A., and MEHRABIAN, A. The effects of day care on young children: An environmental psychology approach. *Journal of Psychology*, 1979, *101*, 241–255.

FARRAN, D. C., and RAMEY, C. T. Infant day care and attachment behaviors toward mothers and teachers. *Child Development*, 1977, *48*, 1112–1116.

FIENE, R. J. The differential structural characteristics of sentences formed by preschool children in family and group day care centers. Unpublished manuscript, State University of New York at Stony Brook, n.d.

GOLDEN, M., and ROSENBLUTH, L. *The New York City Infant Day Care Study*. New York: Medical and Health Research Association of New York City, Inc., 1978.

HEBER, R., GARBER, H., HARRINGTON, S., and HOFFMAN, C. *Rehabilitation of Families at Risk for Mental Retardation*. Madison, Wisc.: Rehabilitation Research and Training Center in Mental Retardation, University of Wisconsin, 1972.

HONIG, A., CALDWELL, B. M., and TANNENBAUM, J. Patterns of information processing used by and with young children in a nursery school setting. *Child Development*, 1970, *41*, 1045–1065.

HOWES, C., and RUBENSTEIN, J. *Toddler social development in two day care settings*. Paper presented at the Annual Meeting of the Western Psychological Association, April 1978.

JOHNSON, B. Marital and family characteristics of the labor force, March 1979. *Monthly Labor Review*, April 1980, *103*, 48–52.

KAGAN, J., KEARSLEY, R. B., and ZELAZO, P. R. The effects of infant day care on psychological development. *Evaluation Quarterly*, 1977, *1*, 109–142.

KAMERMAN, S. B. Child care and family benefits: Policies of six industrialized countries. *Monthly Labor Review*, November 1980, *103*, 23–28.

KEISTER, M. E. A demonstration project: Group care of infants and toddlers. Final report submitted to the Children's Bureau, Office of Child Development, U.S. Dept. of Health, Education, and Welfare, June 1970.

KEYSERLING, M. D. *Windows on Day Care*. New York: National Council of Jewish Women, 1972.

LAY, M., and MEYER, W. Teacher/child behaviors in an open environment day care program. Mimeographed. Syracuse University Children's Center, 1973.

LEVENSTEIN, P. Cognitive growth in preschoolers through verbal interaction with mothers. *American Journal of Orthopsychiatry*, 1970, *40*, 426–432.

LODA, F. A., GLEZEN, W. P., and CLYDE, W. A., JR. Respiratory disease in group day care. *Pediatrics*, 1972, *49*, 428–437.

MORGAN, G. G. This home needs a license. *Day Care and Early Education*, 1974, *2*, 8–13.

MOSKOWITZ, D. S., SCHWARTZ, J. C., and CORSINI, D. A. Initiating day care at three years of age: Effects on attachment. *Child Development*, 1977, *48*, 1271–1276.

NORTH, A. F., JR. *Health services: A guide for project directors and health personnel.* Office of Child Development, Stock Number 1791–0162. Washington, D.C.: U.S. Government Printing Office, 1972.

PORTNOY, F., and SIMMONS, C. Day care and attachment. *Child Development*, 1978, *49*, 239–242.

POWELL, D. R. The interpersonal relationship between parents and caregivers in a day care setting. *American Journal of Orthopsychiatry*, 1978, *48*, 680–689.

PRESCOTT, E., KRITCHEVSKY, S., and JONES, E. The day care environmental inventory. Part 1 of Final Report: *Assessment of Child-Rearing Environments: An Ecological Approach*. Pasadena, Calif.: Pacific Oaks College, 1972.

RADIN, N. Three degrees of maternal involvement in a preschool program: Impact on mothers and children. *Child Development*, 1972, *43*, 1355–1364.

RAMEY, C., and CAMPBELL, F. The prevention of developmental retardation in high-risk children. In P. Mittler (ed.), *Research to Practice in Mental Retardation. Vol. 1: Care and Intervention*. Baltimore, Md.: University Park Press, 1977.

RAMEY, C. T., and CAMPBELL, F. A. Early childhood education for psychosocially disadvantaged children: Effects on psychological processes. *American Journal of Mental Deficiency*, 1979, *83*, 645–648.

ROBINSON, H. B. The Frank Porter Graham child development center. In L. Dittman (ed.), *Early Child Care: The New Perspectives*. New York: Atherton Press, 1968.

ROBINSON, H. B., and ROBINSON, N. M. Longitudinal development of very young children in a comprehensive day care program: The first two years. *Child Development*, 1971, *42*, 1673–1683.

ROBINSON, N. M., ROBINSON, H. B., DARLING, M. J., and HOLM, G. *A World of Children: Daycare and Preschool Institutions*. Monterey, Calif.: Brooks/Cole, 1979.

ROGOZIN, A. S. Attachment behavior of day-care children: Naturalistic and laboratory observations. *Child Development*, 1980, *51*, 409–415.

ROOPNARINE, J., and LAMB, M. The effects of day care on attachment and exploratory behavior in a strange situation. *Merrill-Palmer Quarterly*, 1978, *24*, 85–95.

RUBENSTEIN, J. L., and HOWES, C. Caregiving and infant behavior in day care and in homes. *Developmental Psychology*, 1979, *15*, 1–24.

RUBENSTEIN, J. L., PEDERSEN, F. A., and YARROW, L. J. What happens when mother is away: A comparison of mothers and substitute caregivers. *Developmental Psychology*, 1977, *13*, 529–530.

RUOPP, R., TRAVERS, J., GLANTZ, F., and COELEN, C. *Children at the center: Final report of the national day care study*, Vol. 1. Cambridge, Mass.: Abt Associates, Inc., 1979.

SAGER, L. How a licensing worker sees it. *Day Care and Early Education*, November 1974, *2*, 9–10, 40–41.

SAUNDERS, M., and KEISTER, M. E. Family day care: Some observations. Unpublished manuscript, University of North Carolina at Greensboro, 1972.

SCHWARZ, J. C., KROLICK, G., and STRICKLAND, R. G. Effects of early day care experience on adjustment to a new environment. *American Journal of Orthopsychiatry*, 1973, *43*, 340–346.

SCHWARZ, J. C., STRICKLAND, R. G., and KROLICK, G. Infant day care: Behavioral effects at preschool age. *Developmental Psychology*, 1974, *10*, 502–506.

SHAPIRO, S. Parent involvement in day care: Its impact on staff and classroom environments. *Child Welfare*, 1977, *56*, 749–760.

SWIFT, J. W. Effects of early group experience: The nursery school and day nursery. In M. L. Hoffman and L. W. Hoffman (eds.), *Review of Child Development Research*, Vol. 1. New York: Russell Sage Foundation, 1964.

WATTENBERG, E. Characteristics of family day care providers: Implications for training. *Child Welfare*, 1977, *56*, 211–229.

WILCOX, B., STAFF, P., and ROMAINE, M. F. A comparison of individual with multiple assignment of caregivers to infants in day care. *Merrill-Palmer Quarterly*, 1980, *26*, 53–62.

WINETT, R. A., FUCHS, S. L., MOFFATT, S. A., and NERVIANO, V. J. A cross-sectional study of children and their families in different child care environments: Some data and conclusions. *Journal of Community Psychology*, 1977, *5*, 149–159.

CHAPTER 16

Regulating Early Childhood Programs in the Eighties

Gwen Morgan

ALL SOCIETIES FIND it necessary to regulate. Regulation in the United States goes beyond basic protections; it attempts to assure justice and equity. Faced with some social evil, the American public's response is to support laws to regulate. The tendency to correct social ills through regulation has not lessened in today's society. However, the American resistance to authority continues to create a basic ambivalence among the public toward effective regulation. A fickle public that pushes for regulatory reform is likely to be hostile toward the attempts of the regulators to protect the public.

A mood of resistance to overregulation characterizes the general public at present. Deregulation is a popular slogan. The public is not so sure it wants all the protection it is offered by the regulators. At the same time, there is strong support for regulation against known dangers, and recognition of the value of such protection when harm is averted. Government may deregulate airline routes and fares, but there is no suggestion of deregulating the qualifications of airline pilots nor the safety of airplane design, maintenance of equipment, and air traffic control.

The debate over how to regulate day care has grown steadily more emotional during the past fifteen years. Some day-care operators have feared that enforcement of federal requirements would force day-care fees to a level at which the nonsubsidized family would be priced out of the market. Others have feared that any change in the requirements would open the door to exploitation of poor children by commercial interests. The debate has been confused by the fact that two different regulatory strategies were simultaneously being pursued. Efforts to improve state licensing and improve federal fiscal regulation have been working at cross-purposes, undermining one another.

There is no evidence that children need less protection now than in the past. On the contrary, the need for protection through licensing continues. For example, there appears to be an increase in reported cases of sexual abuse in unlicensed child care. With the dramatic growth in numbers of children whose mothers work, there is a great need for effective regulation of the growth of new day-care centers and of family day-care homes. The child development field as a whole needs to gain a greater understanding of the issues in regulation and a greater consensus about effective strategies for the 1980s.

This chapter will present some basic assumptions about regulation which should underlie thinking about the topic, some background history of both licensing and funding requirements, some recommendations for the future, and some questions for future research.

Basic Assumptions

The following general principles are a set of givens, from a legal-political perspective. Few of the following statements are accepted and thoroughly understood by all. The basis of these statements lies in law rather than in social science research and practice.

1. *Licensing requirements are different in nature and in purpose from funding requirements* and cannot appropriately be compared with funding requirements.

2. *Licensing requirements are lawlike statements adopted by state agencies* under mandates from state legislatures. Every state has day-care licensing laws that form the basis for these requirements. There is no federal licensing law and no federal day-care licensing.

3. *Licensing requirements apply to all children in day care* as defined in a particular state; funding requirements apply only to subsidized children or to children in subsidized programs.

4. *Licensing requirements in the future will be enforced.* Not to enforce the requirements or to enforce them arbitrarily exposes the staff and the state to the possibility of liability suits. The history of standards and some ambiguity between professional use of the word and legal use of the word have caused confusion.

5. *Licensing requirements are policy statements, not program specifications.* They do not, and probably should not, dictate exactly how to run a program. Funding regulations are closer to program specifications.

6. Because they are policy statements, not program descriptors, *licensing requirements do not have to be precisely met but no program may provide less than the requirements.* Program operators may and do go beyond requirements to higher levels of quality. The requirements define "minimum acceptable" quality but do not define maximums. Funding requirements, on the other hand, are more likely to set levels for exact compliance. The funding agency usually will accept no lower quality and will pay for no higher quality than that specified. There is no validity to the concept of overcompliance in licensing.

7. *Licensing requirements have to do with children's rights, not children's needs.* A need is not a right until it is enforceable in a court of law. Requirements spell out what a state has adopted, under its democratic processes, as a code of rights that children have when they are in child day care.

8. *Licensing is basic consumer protection.* Providers are liable, under tort law, for any abridgment of children's rights. Parents are responsible for representing their children.

9. *Funding requirements are also consumer protection,* but in a less basic sense. They spell out what the funding agency expects in exchange for the public dollar.

10. *Safeguarding children through licensing establishes a basic floor of protection* below which no child-care provider may provide care. This floor protects children's health and safety, including basic psychological as well as physical needs.

11. *Providers have constitutional rights to due process,* and have a vested interest in their licenses which licensing staff cannot unfairly take from them.

12. *One regulatory method alone is not enough.* Licensing is only one of several avenues to assure the quality of care children receive. Funding requirements at the state or federal level are another avenue. These two are only part of a range of regulatory and nonregulatory actions that can be adopted to promote different levels of quality.

13. *Requirements, whether for licensing or for funding, are established by a democratic process* of consensus building, not by experts alone. No set of requirements can be implemented without public acceptance and the agreement of the regulated. The role of the expert, and of research data, is to persuade and enlighten that process.

14. Requirements, whether for licensing or for funding, must be written in such a way as to be implementable. *They must be feasible, measurable, clear, and understandable to a reasonable person.* They must do greater good than harm. If the requirements are written in general language, there have to be clear guidelines behind them. These, too, will need consensus and the consent of the governed.

15. If the licensing method used includes the expectation of prelicensing inspection, then *the state agency responsible for licensing must have adequate staff to do the inspections.* Similarly, if funding requirements are to be enforced, some staff must be available to inspect.

16. *Licensing rests on the police powers of government,* which simply means that the people can act together for the common good. *Funding requirements rest on the law of contracts.* The legal principle of paren patriae which permits the government to intervene in the family to protect the child is not an appropriate basis for regulation of day care, since parents are taking responsibility for the care of their children and there is no presumption of any reason to intervene into the family.

17. *A license is a permission to operate and is used to regulate the private sector*, not the public sector. The same level of quality should be expected of publicly operated programs, but the administrative method is not the same as licensing.

When considering a set of legally imposed requirements, we should not ask, "What should the standards be?" but "What elements of day care do we want the government to regulate?" For some elements, such as curriculum, it may well be that quality would be impeded by the imposition of uniform requirements.

It is a mistake to try to put all our eggs of quality into the one basket of licensing. If we want to be effective in bringing knowledge to bear on policy, the appropriate question is "What is the most feasible and appropriate mix of regulatory and nonregulatory actions that is most likely to eliminate harmful quality and stimulate high-quality child care?"

Standards

The word standard is so broad and encompasses so many different meanings that one can no longer use it without some kind of qualifying adjective, such as goal standards, licensing standards, professional standards, funding standards, or the like.

To avoid confusion, it is probably better not to use the term standards at all in a regulatory context. One could imagine three levels of regulated quality, from a floor of licensing to a ceiling of voluntary accreditation. The word standards in its goal sense might be used to describe the top tier, and the clearer words requirement or regulation might be used for the other levels of quality definition.

The field of day-care licensing has begun to develop a common conceptual framework (Class, 1973). A "floor of service" is represented by the line drawn by the states in establishing their licensing requirements. Also at the base line are the regulatory codes of other systems: the state statutes protecting people from fire and from unsafe buildings and those protecting people from the spread of disease and health hazards. This base level is the minimum, meaning "at least"; it does not mean "low."

Other methods of regulation establish different requirements which may be above the base level. High quality standards for model programs represent a "ceiling" of quality to which we may aspire, a ceiling which may be raised over time as our knowledge grows.

There are ways of approaching the question of quality which are not regulatory. Table 16–2 presents the major means of regulation between the floor and the ceiling and includes a list of nonregulatory means to achieve quality (Education Commission of the States, 1975). Publicly operated programs are not licensed; they are regulated in another way. State licensing agencies cannot grant

TABLE 16–1.   Methods of Regulating Quality

Type of regulation	To whom applied	By whom implemented
Accreditation or credentialing	All who voluntarily seek it	Peer group, local 4-C or state agency
Fiscal regulation	All using funds from the agency writing the regulation	Funding agency
Licensing	All	State or local licensing agency

TABLE 16–2. Levels of Quality

Nonregulatory means	Regulatory method	Types of standard
TRAINING		
CONSULTATION		
EVALUATION		
PARENT EDUCATION		
COMMUNITY EDUCATION		
NEWSLETTERS		
INFORMATION AND RESOURCE		☐ GOAL STANDARDS
. . . . CEILING		
	○ Accreditation or Recommended Programs	☐ Standards for model programs
All of above	○ Credentialing	☐ Regulations for qualifications required of staff
All of above	○ Fiscal regulation: Certification for funding Rate-setting should reflect cost of meeting	☐ Funding specifications
All of above	○ Approval	☐ Administrative regulations for public programs
All of above	○ Licensing ○ Safety ○ Sanitation	☐ Basic preventive requirements
, ... FLOOR OF QUALITY		
	○ Operating a program below an acceptable standard or without a license is a civil wrong.	
	○ child abuse and neglect by a day-care operator is a crime.	

or deny public agencies permission to operate. This reflects a legal difference in appropriate regulatory methods developed to achieve the same or better level of quality that is expected of the private sector.

The Process of Standard Formulation

In formulating goal standards which represent the best thinking of a particular field, the process is to assemble some of the leading specialists to work out agreement on their recommendations. For requirements which are to be enforced, whether licensing standards or funding standards, the process becomes more complex, and a variety of different interests become involved.

Two major principles apply: (1) procedural due process; and (2) interest representation. Most states have delegated the formulation of licensing to an administrative agency responsible for reviewing and writing new requirements and for assuring that interest representation and consensus building results in a draft that receives public hearings and amendment before being promulgated. A similar process should be used for funding requirements since these standards also have the effect of rate setting.

Due process, relating to ever widening interpretations of the Fifth and Fourteenth Amendments to the United States Constitution and to Administrative Procedures Acts at federal and state levels, refers to the concept that government must deal fairly and in a nonarbitrary way with citizens affected by its actions. The techniques center on giving notice, allowing an opportunity to be heard, giving access to information, rights to appeal, and generally checking undue discretion of the regulatory agency. Since the 1940s, there has been growing citizen access to the standard formulation process.

The concept of interest representation is related to procedural due process. The administrative agency formulating the standards needs to include in its deliberations those with an interest in the outcome (Jambor, 1964). Some states establish advisory committees with broad representation for this purpose. States recently updating their licensing standards have usually established a task force or committee representing a broad range of interests. If all groups are represented in the discussions, it is more likely that they will support the resulting standards. An excluded group is much freer to oppose the standards during public hearings. The process generally takes at least a year and should be repeated about every five years (Class, 1968).

The difficulty such a group may have in reaching consensus is not described in the literature. Orientation of the participants to the basic regulatory principles has not received much attention in print. A group representing diverse interests, democratic as it is, will not automatically succeed if its members do not share a common set of assumptions. Such a group needs basic information about regulatory principles, type of standards they are establishing, the value of regulation to children and their families and to providers of service. It needs to know how types of regulation differ from one another and how licensing and funding requirements differ from goal standards. It needs to be aware of past experience with the existing requirements, of comparative data on the degree to which these requirements have been met, and what requirements other states may have adopted. How are the requirements to be enforced? What is the overall timetable and process through which the group will seek consensus and participate in hearings and revisions until new requirements are promulgated? Finally, the group needs to understand the importance of consensus among the group and among the public for later implementation.

Legal Defense of a Standard as Reasonable

Every standard to be enforced, whether a licensing standard or a funding standard, needs to be defensible in rational terms. When a license is revoked in court, the licensee may attack the standard as unreasonable and unfounded. Courts are not totally predictable and could agree with a licensee who made a good case that the standard itself is capricious. Although this is less of an issue for funding than for licensing standards, the Congress itself asked for a rational basis of the standards in its mandate for a report on their appropriateness in 1978.

Standards can be defended on four different bases: expert opinion, scientific data, common practice, and a consensus among interests represented.

Expertise is no longer the solid base it once was (Melli, 1971). Courts tend to distrust experts when there is not a body of scientific knowledge on which to agree. In a field such as child care, where experts can be found on two sides of almost any issue, policy makers cannot rely on experts.

It might be thought that the most convincing evidence of the need for a standard are hard, measured data. However, there are limitations to a scientific back-up to standards. Many people question whether social science research offers tools fine-tuned enough to measure important intangible effects. If research fails to find a measurable effect, it could mean either that there is no effect or that we do not know how to measure it. Researchers often disagree with one another's findings if they do not support some cherished value.

Scientific data alone do not produce a standard. Standards are value statements, with the scientific data providing evidence of the desired effect. Desired goals may change over time, becoming more or less ambitious and based on value paradigms (Rein, 1973).

Nevertheless, a wealth of data exists to support particular requirements. It should be possible in the future to document the scientific basis for particular requirements with increasing persuasiveness. Several states, such as Nebraska, have assembled information justifying each requirement. State regulatory agencies will be seeking to compile research findings in relation to requirements. The federal government made a start on such an effort in response to a congressional mandate to study the appropriateness of the Federal Interagency Day Care Requirements.

A third argument to support particular requirements is common practice. It could be difficult to produce scientific data to support a requirement of 35 rather than 30 square feet of floor space per child in a center. Yet, because most states have adopted 35 square feet, this has become the standard, and building codes are now written in the expectation that this practice will continue.

Unfortunately, there are few requirements which most states commonly use. The federal government has been engaged in a national study of all the state requirements and laws and is expected to disseminate this information and develop model materials on licensing sometime in 1982. If such information becomes continually available, practice would probably become less diverse across states.

In the absence of acceptable expert testimony, hard scientific data, or common practice, a requirement could be defended as the final agreement of a process which has involved many different interests. As the states perfect their processes of standard formulation, they build strong legal defense against challenge to the requirements, reducing the likelihood that such challenges would be made. The process itself, if it involves many interests and the general public, helps to support its own outcome.

This process of consensus building is not easy at the state level, but it is even more difficult at the national level. The long discussion on federal funding requirements has had great difficulty reaching consensus. Funding requirements define compliance levels more exactly than licensing requirements. It is difficult to create consensus around federal funding requirements for several reasons. (1) Programs in those states that have achieved a higher level of quality are likely to lose some funding if standards are reduced. On the other hand, programs in states that have not achieved such a high level fear the state would not pay more money if standards were raised. Most providers will be in disagreement for one of these two opposite reasons. (2) Defining one precise point that is acceptable to the many states and all their citizens and providers is nearly impossible, given the varied past practice and the variability of state licensing. (3) Because the country is so large, more people need to have a voice in the democratic process than is feasible.

History of Day-Care Standards in the United States

The United States has used the idiom "child care standards" without reference to enforcement for over 100 years. Historical factors have led to a great confusion in state licensing offices and at the federal level over what standards are and how they are to be enforced (Class, 1981).

In 1863, Massachusetts created by statute the State Board of Charities, a lay group of prominent citizens appointed by the Governor to give advice to superintendents of services, to publish an annual report of their visitations, and to suggest "standards." In the years following, other states passed statutes creating similar boards. In the 1880s, these citizens began meeting at the national level in a National Conference of Charities and Corrections each year. Much of the material from their meetings includes discussion of standards.

The field of child welfare in the years that followed was concerned with social change. Standards were used to contrast the conditions of life for children with what they should be. By highlighting the contrast, they could attract more volunteers, more philanthropic gifts, more church involvement, and more grants-in-aid from the states.

Change was certainly needed. Foundlings in institutions were not surviving. According to an early observer, "in 1868, at the great Foundlings' Hospital on Wards Island, near New York, 1,527 children were received in 11 months, and all died within the first year but 80 . . . and . . . these have small chance for life" (quoted in Langer, 1972). At the state Almshouse in Tewksbury, Massachusetts, "153 motherless infants only were admitted in 5 years ending 1873, all died but 15" (Lord, 1978, p. 171).

Scandals over the abuse of children in these institutions during the nineteenth century brought public support for stronger government controls. The first licensing law regulating care of children by private individuals was passed in 1885 in Pennsylvania; other states followed suit. The early laws were weak and poorly enforced. In the few states where they existed, there was no change from the approach of the Boards of Charities. Standards and exposés were used to build the needed public support.

In 1874, Etta Angel Wheeler, a New York City social worker, found a little girl wandering naked through the streets, driven from home after being beaten and slashed by a drunken foster mother. Miss Wheeler went for help to the Society for the Prevention of Cruelty to Animals. The Society agreed to give protection to "the child being an animal." This incident helped to organize the need for a Society for the Prevention of Cruelty to Children.

During this period, citizens from the Boards of Charities, representing public concern, visited programs and inspected them, advising operators of program improvements toward which they should be working. They therefore had great concern to discuss and agree on standards. Standards at this time were ideals derived from introspective thought; the word monitoring was used but without any implication of control.

This emphasis on the investigation of human conditions grew larger until the muckraking period. Journalists such as Lincoln Steffens and novelists such as Theodore Dreiser aroused widespread interest among the general public in changing these conditions, resulting in a great increase in regulatory administration as a characteristically American type of social action.

On other fronts of social progress, government regulation moved at once in a more scientific direction. In 1907, the Food and Drug Administration was created. As more and more issues were identified in American life, more and more regulatory law emerged.

Life in "the good old days" presented many hazards and evils for children (Bettman, 1974). These conditions, which the child welfare field generally addressed, are substantially different today in large part because of government regulation. In 1900, Florence Kelley of the National Consumers' League and a fighter against child labor, proposed a United States Commission for Children to investigate and make available facts about the lives of children (Bradbury, 1962). In 1909, the first White House Conference on the Care of Dependent Children called together such prominent figures as Jane Addams, Theodore Dreiser, Lillian Wald and Booker T. Washington (York, 1970). Among their recommendations was state inspection of child-caring institutions.

This conference gave the major impetus to a bill, passed in 1912, that created the United States Children's Bureau. Its functions were to investigate and report: "The said Bureau (shall) . . . investigate and report upon all matters pertaining to the welfare of children and child life among all classes of our people"; its object was "the betterment of the conditions of children."

President Theodore Roosevelt had favored the creation of such a federal agency and supported eleven bills which were introduced in the House and Senate until final passage in 1912. In 1909, he sent a message to Congress urging favorable action on the pending bills. The emphasis was on fact gathering and on observations of objective conditions. The facts were to be used to educate public sentiment for action and change under federal leadership. The federal government was to provide leadership in the "best methods" of dealing with children so that each community would not have to invent its own wheel. Facts were to be accompanied by standards as guidance material (Bradbury, 1962).

Although Roosevelt does not mention "standards" in his support of the bill and although the statute itself does not emphasize standards, the dual approach of facts and guidance material in the form of standards is evident. A later chief of the Children's Bureau describes its work this way: "From its earliest days and throughout its life, the Bureau has, with the help of outstanding authorities, developed standards of care in many fields. It has put the technical knowledge and skills of its specialists at the service of public and voluntary agencies working for children" (Oettinger, 1964, pp. 4–5).

In the period following the creation of the Children's Bureau, more and more states passed licensing laws. The child welfare field, responding to the prevalence of government regulation in other fields of social reform, pushed for licensing to regulate children's services. Day care and foster care were usually combined in these early laws. They used the term "licensing standard" rather than "requirement" and did not view licensing as a sharp break from their fifty years of discussion of ideals. Between 1910 and the early 1960s, most states passed and improved their licensing laws. But until the 1960s, there was no systematic attempt to enforce standards, which were regulatory rhetoric (Class, 1981). There were a number of reasons for this.

1. Most services were under philanthropic auspices, benevolent in nature. Not wanting to add to the cost of charitable endeavors, regulatory agencies did not take an adversary stance to licensees.

2. Many services were under religious auspices. An argument of separation of church and state was widely used to resist licensure. In some states, day care under religious auspices is still exempt from licensing today, and in others, where it is not exempted, it is expected that enforcement will be lenient.

3. There was public subsidy to private child-care operations. Licensing agencies did not have to enforce their standards, because the subsidizing agency, usually the same agency, could threaten to withdraw the money.

4. Between 1925 and 1930, professional social workers controlled licensing in the state agencies. Social work at that time was characterized by a "passive approach"; one did not offer help unless asked. Molding their licensing tasks to fit their professional training, the agency staff saw themselves as helpers, not regulators, and their training led them to be hostile to the use of legal authority.

5. During the Great Depression, with cutbacks in public subsidy and evaporation of Community Chest funds, standards were hard to enforce. At the beginning of World War II, there was little or no day-care regulation, even in states that had licensing laws. Strong licensing would have inhibited the massive expansion of day care which was seen as in the national interest at that time.

One pioneer in licensing describes the wartime period.

By now nursery schools were spreading rapidly across the country, whether good, bad or indifferent. As women went into war industries, young children with latch keys around their necks were roaming the streets or being exploited by caretakers of every description. The Division of Day Care and Foster

Homes, comprised of a multi-professional staff of consultants, put *far-sighted, high, mandatory standards* into effect for over 20,000 children under six years of age [Goldsmith, 1975, p. 64; emphasis added].

Emphasis was not on the immediate enforcement of the standards; licensing was seen as a help to operators so that some day the goal of meeting the standards would be achieved. From a legal point of view, this is a strange interpretation of "mandatory," but in the light of historic development it was a major advance over the nineteenth century.

The Child Welfare League of America was established around 1930, oriented to the child welfare field, setting standards for a range of child welfare services, including day care. The League is an organization whose members are agencies, primarily multiservice agencies receiving United Way and other charitable funds and delivering a range of child welfare services. League members see their day-care programs, if they have them, as models of quality in their communities.

The League described its standards as goal standards. A 1955 internal study of the League's function and program reaffirmed the continued development of standards as objectives or goals, based on tested knowledge and approved practice in the various fields of service. The introduction to the publication of the League's day-care standards emphasizes that "these standards are intended to be goals for continuous improvement of services to children. They are not the criteria for accreditation for League membership, although they will be used as the basis for establishing membership requirements. They represent practices considered to be most desirable" (Child Welfare League of America, 1969, p. ix).

The League's standards stimulated improvement of services as they brought about dissatisfaction with existing practices, a view similar to the traditional view of standards around the turn of the century. However, the League's standards were also to be used "in establishing state and local licensing requirements" and to "help to explain and justify expenditures, budget requests to federate fund-raising bodies, and appropriation requests to legislatures," a shift toward a regulatory use, but without a shift away from goal type of standards.

By the time of the publication of the League standards, the entrance of the federal government as a provider of day care had introduced new uncertainties. The introduction to a description of the work of the committee developing the standards mentions:

> Ensuing developments, resulting mostly from Federal legislation, made it difficult to define the scope of the CWLA Standards for Day Care Service. . . . The need for continuing revision of these standards is recognized. The Standards, as in the first edition, are intended to be a model of the best way to provide a day care service. They are conceived as goals to be attained; they are to be distinguished from minimum requirements for licensing, approval, or accreditation for membership in the Child Welfare League of America [Child Welfare League of America, 1969, p. x].

It was not assumed that League members could meet standards.

As long as standards were not enforced, it was possible for national organizations to be ambiguous and to evade unresolved issues and unexamined assumptions within and among the advocate groups. In 1974, with the writing of standards into law in Title XX of the Social Security Amendments, it became necessary to be clear on issues which previously could be glossed over. At present, however, owing to historical factors and lack of clarity over what standards are, the picture is almost hopelessly muddled.

Licensing Today

In 1962, the Social Security Amendments made federal money available for day care, but only if licensed by the state. Most of the states which had not licensed earlier did so under this federal leadership. The Department of Health, Education and Welfare, which had assisted states in developing new legislation, did not follow up at that time in training licensing staffs in regulatory concepts. Licensing workers in the newer offices, following the model of earlier state licensing, tried to tailor their professional training, usually in social work or early childhood education, to their new quasi-legal responsibilities. The result was often poor and sometimes arbitrary enforcement, an emphasis on consultation not connected with requirements, and a lack of understanding of the rights of licensees.

Without training, sometimes with weak laws, and almost always without administrative support for negative action, licensing staffs felt helpless to move against existing centers, usually "grandfathered" in when new laws passed. Their concern for children was very real, and they did what they could to raise quality. They also screened out new potential licensees not capable of running good centers, substituting gatekeeping for enforcement. Thus, existing poor centers continued, but licensing barred new programs from starting. Some licensing offices used a degree of discretion which bordered on discrimination in their efforts to assure quality care for children.

A further problem was the lack of training in the distinctions between home finding (in foster child care), child placement, and day-care regulation. The addition of federal funding requirements often resulted in a very muddled operation.

Toward the end of the 1960s, a changed public opinion created two serious problems for licensing offices. First, there was serious concern for children who needed day care and did not have it. There was a determination to close the gap and bring day care to those children in inadequate arrangements. Whereas in the early 1960s the licensing staffs had been seen as protectors of children who were in day care, now a new ambivalence arose out of concern for the children not in day care. For new groups trying to get day care started, standards meant costs. And if the group was in any way different from the majority culture, there was the suspicion that licensing was being used unfairly. Child advocates pushed for high licensing standards, but they were hostile to law enforcement.

Second, the licensing process itself had become cumbersome and intolerably time-consuming. According to the Abt studies of exemplary day-care programs and the survey of state licensing done by Conserco, it took an average of one man-year to get a license. This problem was incorrectly diagnosed as resulting from the standards. In reality, the problem was a statutory one, arising out of the dysfunctional lack of fit between the statutory mandates of four major regulatory systems of which licensing is only one (Morgan, 1974). Not understanding this, many people including federal officials concerned to get more day care under way, began to assume that federal funding would bypass the cumbersome state processes. It is unlikely that Congress would or could have superseded state and local laws protecting children, but the failure to distinguish between federal funding standards and state licensing contributed to the growing confusion.

During the period between 1965 and 1975, most states improved their licensing systems. The last state, Florida, finally passed a licensing law in 1974, making the licensing of centers national. New codes for infant, family, and day care were adopted along with systematic processes for regulation review and revision. States have since also begun to develop effective enforcement procedures and have successfully moved against out-of-compliance programs.

Some of this new vigor came from a federal stimulus (Guides for Day Care Licensing, 1972), some from the new awareness on the part of state attorneys general that the state is potentially liable, and some from increased training and the exchange of information between states. Activity among the states in regulating staff–child ratios is an indication of this upsurge in regulatory activity. Between 1965 and 1975, forty-four states either issued ratio requirements for the first time or changed their requirements (Johnson & Associates, 1980).

The National Day Care Study found that many centers in the United States have more staff than required under state licensing or federal funding requirements, when measured overall, suggesting that there are probably some natural standards that feel right to most operators, regardless of requirements (Coelen, 1979).

Despite strong citizen interest in staff–child ratios, practice varied more in measuring this element in day care than in any other aspect of regulation. These varied measurement practices make any comparison meaningless unless the basis for the number is also discussed. The National Day Care Study found that a tightly measured ratio can be a more rigorous requirement even at a higher official ratio number than a lower ratio measured more leniently. Uniform measurement policy is a more important potential reform than a uniform number with continued variation in measurement policy (Ruopp, 1980).

The National Day Care Study investigated the effects of ratios and caregiver professionalism on children, and found positive effects of both these regulatable characteristics. The study found, however, that the single most important element of quality is the overall size of the group of children and adults that are assigned to be together. Somewhere between 14 and 18 children appeared to be the range of group sizes that might most effectively be regulated to achieve quality. Not all states have regulated group size in the past, but the data are persuasive to include this element in future revisions of state licensing requirements.

The Evolution of Standards for Day Care

There has been substantial evolution from the nineteenth century to today in the use of the word "standards." Initially, there was widespread use of the concept of standards as ideals arrived at through introspection. We now try to base standards on some objective observation of children's needs. We have moved from the idea of standards as nonenforceable goals that highlight investigative activities, to legal guarantees subject to legal challenge. We have come to understand that more careful distinctions must be made among different types of standards established for different purposes. In day care particularly, we have moved from protective to preventive standards.

We have lost some of our innocent faith in an ever rising standard. The 1940 White House Conference on Children, for example, took for granted a continually rising "standard of living," despite temporary depressions and rude shocks in individual fortunes. This optimistic, open-ended improvement has characterized American thinking throughout history. The 1940 Conference pointed to improved dietary habits, health, and material goods such as electric refrigerators, washing machines, vacuum cleaners, and irons. From today's perspective, we are less sure about what constitutes improvement. We have come up against limited resources, we have faced dangers to our environment and unforeseen health hazards in food and other products caused by our technology; we are also aware of inequities, worldwide in standards of living. The assumptions that standards of all kinds will and should continue to be raised is not quite so easy to accept any more.

The legal profession has moved in the direction of spelling out the rights of the regulated and the procedures for the behavior of the regulatory agencies with ever increasing precision. The present legal meaning of standards is different from the way the term may be used by professionals in the field of early childhood.

The Special Problem of Family Day-Care Regulation

Although state legislatures have included family day care in statutes regulating day-care services, it has not been possible to inspect and license all the homes by traditional means. Unlike centers, where thirty or one hundred children per visit are protected, family day care scatters the care of one to eight children in each of many locations, averaging fewer than four.

A method of regulation that cannot regulate all the units defined as regulatable provides no hope of equal protection for all children. The states have been discussing different models of solving this problem. In some states, the effort to implement licensing has encountered fierce provider and parent resistance. Some states are considering deregulating family day care, regulating only subsidized homes, or finding a more feasible form of regulation.

Twelve states have in place a method of regulation called registration, which is still experimental. Texas and Michigan have done extensive research on the effectiveness of this method (Texas Department of Human Resources, 1980). They found it is less effective at collecting paper requirements, such as medical records, than licensing, because registered homes may operate while collecting the paper. They found a massive increase in coverage. Texas's regulated homes increased by 248 percent between January 1975 and July 1978. Serious noncompliance, that is, homes placing children at real risk, was not found, even though there has been an increase in complaints of child abuse in unregistered homes. The method appears to be accomplishing its purposes.

Registration is controversial. It is not well understood and its difference from traditional licensing adds to the present confusion. In states that have licensed in the past, the licensed providers tend to support the continuation of licensing, feeling that it gives them greater status than registration would. Center operators tend to want homes to be licensed. In both cases, providers appear to be seeking a competitive edge and maintenance of their own provider system as well as the protection of children. If the mythical approaches of the past are not viable in a climate of potential state liability, some states will prefer to regulate only subsidized homes. State administrators sometimes may prefer to deregulate rather than register, since registration requires them to make a genuine effort to reach all the homes caring for children to offer state regulatory protection, a large undertaking.

Regulation as Public Policy

At present, regulatory policy is fragmented and lacks the public commitment needed for vigorous implementation. In part, this is due to the current climate of opinion favoring deregulation, in part, to the lack of a clear overall regulatory strategy.

Advocates at the federal level launched a push for effective federal requirements for federal funding for child care without a clear strategy to reach consensus among the different perspectives and without a clear idea how this strategy would dovetail with other regulatory actions. The resulting controversy has weakened not only the federal strategy but also the public commitment to licensing.

State licensing offices are having difficulty in sustaining their efforts to protect all children in private day care. Challenges have come from several directions. Fundamentalist church groups have sought exemptions for church-run child care and have succeeded in several states, as happened recently in Virginia. Montessori groups have sought special exemptions or treatment. Family day-care providers, resistant to federal requirements which they believe were designed with centers not homes in mind, also sometimes resist traditional approaches to licensing. The confusion between licensing and federal requirements has undermined the efforts to develop new and more effective approaches. Further, the field itself has changed. With more qualified administrators and staff in day care, there may be more role conflict as licensors attempt to impose the "program and activities" requirements.

A further problem arises as states reorganize to improve their Title XX purchase of service management systems. The distinction between fiscal monitoring and licensing of all services is likely to be lost as states face the need to control the quality and quantity of public expenditures. For day care, however, which is primarily paid for by parents rather than by government, some important basic protections for all children are likely to be traded off as a result of the lack of clarity in improving the regulatory systems.

If the gains of the 1970s are to be preserved and an effective regulatory system maintained, it is important that advocates and experts have a coherent overall strategy and an understanding of both the issues and the policy-making process.

Climate of Deregulation

There is general agreement at present that some types of regulation should be abolished and that others should be reformed. The rhetoric of deregulation is obscuring the fact that there is a concurrent trend toward greater regulation in the interest of accountability of public funds. It is important to distinguish what types of regulation are on their way out and why if effective future regulatory reform is to be accomplished.

Much research has been done on regulation and on its politics, with recent work beginning to link up with what is known about political processes (Wilson, 1980). Most of the analysis has focused on the large federal regulatory agencies.

Public regulation can be categorized by types. Frohnmayer (1980) proposes three categories of regulation: control of prices and entry, public interest control of the environment for social goals, and the regulation of government by government. The first is the control of prices and the conditions of entry in various industries. These attempts to remedy perceived deficiencies in the market, such as "natural monopolies" by the telephone companies, are public responses to serious economic instabilities in particular industries. This category of regulatory activity also includes occupational licensing, which is concerned with professional quality control or with the desire to limit competition and control the market, or with a mixture of both motives. This type of regulation is now being seriously questioned by scholars, who challenge whether such regulation is really in the public interest and whether the regulatory agency is inevitably "captured" by the industry regulated and is acting to protect the interests of the regulated (Stigler, 1971).

A second category of governmental regulation includes the social regulatory agencies such as the Environmental Protection Agency, Consumer Product Safety Commission, Equal Employment Opportunity Commission. Such agencies are seldom popular with the industries they regulate. They are developed as a result of a view that the social and physical environment must take precedence over the pursuit of economic gain when the public interest is affected. These regulatory actions have undeniably positive benefits, but critics have claimed that they have not taken into account economic costs, clashing demands of different social goals, or the wishes of the public. It is probable that both this support and this desire to limit regulation will continue into the future, with new types of regulation added as the public seeks to correct newly perceived threats and social evils. Regulation will undoubtedly be challenged more and more to prove its necessity by rational scientific evidence. Cost and effects analyses will become routine. Whether regulation is supported or abolished will depend on the public perception of the effectiveness of the protection it offers and on the importance of the dangers it averts or the injustice it corrects.

The third category of regulation is the regulation of government by government and the increasing efforts of one level of government to establish goals, priorities, and procedures for other governments, particularly state and local governments. This type of regulation is adopted with relative speed and may impose large unanticipated costs. The increasing costs of government have stimulated taxpayers' revolts, and local governments are not compliant about mandates placed upon them without additional funds for relief of the local tax burden (for example, special education mandates). Block grants are a response to these complaints against governmental red tape and control.

There are different types of regulatory action. Broad generalizations and analyses cannot refer to all these types of regulation with validity. Behind most of the criticism has been a theory that the regulators are inevitably captured by the regulated (Stigler, 1971). The theory may not fit the social protection type of regulation at all. Certainly, there is evidence that capture has happened in the regulation of prices and entry in the large industries regulated by federal commissions. Even here, however, it is not entirely clear that the capture is complete, and there is evidence of some vigorous action in the public interest that does not entirely fit with the statement that regulation is acquired by the industry and is designed and operated primarily for its benefit. Some of the recent deregulatory actions of the Congress in the airline and trucking fields resulted from leadership by the regulatory agencies.

A part of the capture theory includes the belief that a regulatory agency has a life cycle (Bernstein, 1955). A regulatory agency begins its life with a youthful organizational outlook centered on its mission to protect the public. In its organizational adolescence, it encounters many checks and balances as the regulated industry learns to use the political processes. The agency as it matures learns to adapt to these realities and to be friendly with the regulated, with whom it has much in common. In its organizational old age, it becomes a maintainer of the status quo and, at worst, the captive of the regulated industry.

Recent writers find evidence indicating that the situation is considerably more complex and that the theory applies more to the first of the three types of regulators than the others described above. For example, it was thought that the regulatory agencies would be, in their senility, staffed by bland nonentities influenced into passivity by the hopelessness of their organizational setting. But when an agency is perceived as offering a step toward a vigorous future career, its staff may be highly motivated to pursue its regulatory mission with skill and visibility. Wilson (1980) analyzes the staff of regulatory agencies in a more complex way as being either careerists who will value their own integrity and effectiveness above maintaining the organizational interests of the agency, professionals who value the good opinion of their fellow professionals more highly than the organizational interests of the agency, and politicians who are more likely to place higher value on agency interests.

Older theories of regulatory life cycle and capture have now reached the public consciousness and the Congress. At the same time, there is evidence that inventive regulatory reforms have already been instituted to avoid the anticipated danger of agency senility or capture. Newer theorists, observing these successful efforts, suggest a new metaphor to replace the idea of inevitable capture, the concept of "recycling."

> Recycling implies a deliberate provision for invigorating and redefining the goals of the regulatory agencies, as contrasted with (1) the pessimistic metaphysical pathos of the "life cycle" metaphor that despairs of change in the absence of a jarring crisis in the regulated activity, or overwhelming evidence of senility in the regulatory agency, and (2) excessive optimism of those who would have the regulatory agencies operating at an unremittingly feverish pitch [Moore, 1972, p. 29].

In applying these ideas to the field of early childhood, an effective strategy for the future would ally itself with regulatory reform. A new rhetoric and devices for self-renewal need to be built into the regulatory system to be recommended during the 1980s. Clues may be found in the regulatory theory suggesting that strategies for reform might succeed if the field adopts the following ideas.

1. *Avoid the appearance of control of entry or protection of pricing.* It is important that the regulators not be viewed as inhibiting the growth of a needed service out of an alliance with the present service providers. This means a willingness to encourage new types of services, such as family day-care and group day-care homes and taking steps to create some kind of system of the separate regulatory actions of zoning, sanitation, fire and building safety, day-care licensing, and contract management. Somewhere in government there should be a technical assistance office to act as troubleshooter and facilitate new providers as they go through all these regulatory processes; the processes themselves may be consolidated in the case of home-based types of care.

2. *Stress the public interest*, and the protection of children and families, rather than the interests of the early childhood professionals. Day-care licensing fits into the category of consumer protection regulatory action and is an example of the social protection type of regulation which retains public support. Steps to increase the role of parents as advocates for their rights and their children's rights will greatly improve the regulatory processes' vigor as well as its image. It is important to lay heavier emphasis on consumer interests than on provider interests, even though it is obvious that they cannot be separated.

3. *Reduce discretion and the arbitrary use of authority by the regulators.* In the past, some poorly trained regulators acting under vaguely worded regulations made decisions that were overly narrow or culturally biased, as in the case of the licensor who told a Chinese day-care center that they could not serve Chinese food

to Chinese children because it was not nutritious. We have a responsibility to be sure there are not more mistakes like that in the regulatory field. This means clear and explicit wording and training for uniform interpretation of all requirements, with alternative ways of meeting the requirements spelled out. Because such reform leads to wordiness, it may be that the 1980s will see a return to a few clear, well-expressed requirements which are well understood and supported by the public, with detailed interpretative guidelines available to licensors and licensees.

There must also be deadlines for responsiveness by the regulators to those seeking to meet the requirements and get licensed.

4. *Train the regulators well*, not only in child development, so that they can enforce requirements, but also in regulatory concepts and understanding the rights of licensees.

5. *Avoid any regulation that cannot be justified as necessary*, since it will weaken the case for regulation overall.

6. *Develop clear and rational scientific evidence* of the positive effect of the regulation on children, making use of recent research findings wherever possible. Change regulations if new evidence suggests appropriate change.

7. *Avoid mythical regulation.* If there is to be a set of requirements applied, there must be a feasible system of implementation. In family day-care licensing, for example, if there is not sufficient staff for a prelicensing inspection, a system of registration could be considered. If the state is regulating only funded homes, shift to a system of fiscal regulation rather than licensing. If the state does not have enough staff to license centers, do not add other responsibilities. Analyze work loads and be sure the state can meet its obligations for regulation, or else reduce the obligations.

8. *Avoid the ridiculous.* The one risk a regulatory agency cannot afford is ridicule. Professionals should be sufficiently tuned in to the public perspectives to know when a requirement would be viewed as silly. An example would be applying standards to care by grandparents.

9. *Urge excellence of appointments* for the head of licensing offices, trying to create a climate in which the regulatory head is a visible official bringing credit to the government by vigorous action in the public interest.

10. *Cut down on paper work and red tape*, both in fiscal regulation and in licensing. Energy spent in designing simple forms saves countless dollars in time spent filling out forms. Give the regulatory agency an image of red-tape cutting, rather than red-tape creating.

11. *Find ways for more visible preventive enforcement.* Reward licensure with publicity, give special recognition for higher or swift compliance, letters of praise or fee rebates for rapid compliance, post notices of noncompliance, and, possibly, publicize suspension and revocations with the reasons.

12. *Know the cost effects of any change* in regulations and consider carefully the benefits of a change. If the benefits are important and necessary, seek ways of reducing the initial cost impact, such as subsidy or a revolving loan fund, and structure the initial compliance process to minimize polarization over the costs and benefits.

When considering costs and benefits, pay attention to the distribution of benefits and costs as well as the magnitude. If a fiscal requirement, for example, benefits subsidized children but has an adverse effect on the costs of nonsubsidized children, that consideration is relevant and should be directly considered. All regulation should be justified with careful backup and written documentation of the magnitude and distribution of both benefits and costs.

13. *Support for regulation* if it is necessary, important, and well done, *should be a responsibility of any early childhood professional* as a part of the ethic of the field. Teaching of regulatory principles and the policy-making process should be included in all professional development in the early childhood field.

14. *Give thought to devices for regulatory self-renewal.* Revising requirements every five years is important; states have already adopted this practice. It might be useful for states to keep track of which particular requirements have most potential for disagreement among staff over interpretation, which ones are most troublesome to meet, and the like. A requirements log and an annual state-of-the-art report on requirements, including new relevant research findings, might be helpful to the director as an internal procedure.

15. *A broader range of sanctions* would give the agency more options for vigorous enforcement. If the only sanction is closing down an operation, the effect is to inhibit enforcement except in extreme cases. Between total annihilation and a slap on the hand is an area for negotiated agreements between regulator and regulated. States should permit fines, publication of the names of out-of-compliance services, parent meetings, powers of search and injunction for the suppression of illegal activities, and reduction of reimbursement rates as other tools for implementation. Above all, the development of improved complaint procedures and the stimulation of parent interest in monitoring quality will invigorate the regulatory processes. Parents should regard the licensing system as a rights mechanism, much as they use civil rights, fair housing, or other processes for assuring rights.

16. *Lawsuits* against the state have already had the effect of causing decision makers to take the responsibilities of regulation more seriously and to commit more resources to the support of the licensing operation. Public opinion as well as recent court decisions appear to indicate that the liability of the state is being increasingly broadened rather than restricted (Illinois Economic and Fiscal Commission, 1974). Awareness of this trend may serve to vitalize the regulatory agencies.

Issues for Future Research Investigation

There continues to be a need for additional knowledge and reporting of experience in the field of regulation. Data are needed for decision making in two general aspects: (1) administration of the regulatory program; and (2) quality of the service programs.

The issues in administration are being addressed in state-level reports, often in connection with efforts to reorganize for more effective government. Questions frequently raised include: What is a realistic and cost-effective work load for licensing staff and for registration of family day-care homes? How should the facilitating role be built into the government so that there is no conflict of interest with the regulating role? Which agency should do the licensing? How should government be organized for the most effective performance of the related functions of licensing of private sector programs, approval of public sector programs, evaluation and monitoring of contracted services? Should regulatory functions be specialized or generic? How can the regulatory actions of the major bureaucratic systems—health, safety, and licensing—be organized so that they do not become systemic barriers to services? How much should the state attempt to control local zoning policy for centers and homes providing day care? What wording should local zoning ordinances include for day care? What is the appropriate balance between centralized regulatory organization, with the advantages of uniform interpretation of uniform policy for all children in day care, and decentralized administration needed to provide for strong citizen participation and support at the local level?

The issues for quality of services as affected by regulation will require continued research in the field of child development and the development of more summaries of research findings to assist the regulatory agencies. It is clear that during the 1980s large numbers of children will have working mothers. Research is no longer needed on questions of whether children are affected by day care, but on questions of what are the characteristics of day care programs likely to result in positive effects compared to those that could result in negative effects, particularly if these characteristics could be required or eliminated through regulation.

It would be useful if research efforts could focus on those characteristics already regulated to see whether supporting evidence can be produced to justify the continuation of particular regulations or to suggest changes in them. New characteristics, not now regulated, such as continuity of care or new roles for parents, could be added to the aspects of day care that are regulated if there are important effects on children and families that justify a requirement and if measureable specific requirements can be worked out.

Research can also be helpful in working out techniques for measurement. Regulation through licensing is limited to measurable requirements. Thus, licensing requirements often appear top-heavy in areas of physical space and have less to say about the important intangibles. It is not possible to go into court and take away a provider's license because she did not demonstrate "warmth" or did not provide "adequate privacy" for children. Yet, it is possible that the 1980s will bring advances in measurement of these less tangible aspects of day care, and it is likely that aspects of day care that were thought unmeasurable could be measured.

It is unlikely that the federal government will impose uniform practice on state licensing requirements in the near future. The difficulty in reaching consensus even on federal funding requirements and the time-consuming futile struggle to adopt an enforceable set of funding requirements is an indication that the policy-making processes have not been well understood in the field of early childhood. Yet, there is a need for more uniformity of practice across the states in funding and in licensing practices. It is likely that there will be evolution toward more consistency as citizens have access to more information. Leadership is needed from the federal government and the research community.

Guidance material accessible to the citizens is needed when state requirements are under revision, spelling out what we know of good practice, with documented rationales based on scientific data. In addition, citizens need data on the changing requirements and statutory improvements in all the states.

There are also actions other than regulatory ones that can be perfected in the next decade. Simpler and less threatening techniques for formative evaluation and more consumer interest through information and resource programs could affect quality, and research findings on their effects would be useful.

Regulation is an important public issue, but it is one of the more limited avenues to high levels of quality. A set of goal standards that is not regulatory is needed to inspire the field. Knowledge, skills, and human commitment are the ingredients of high quality; the law is a blunt instrument for these sensitive purposes. Yet, the field of early childhood should not be so arrogant as to believe that children can be protected from exploitation without regulation. Professionals must be committed to every avenue to quality and they must be sophisticated in distinguishing among them.

References

American Institutes for Research. Project Connections. Phase I, Results: A national profile of child care information and referral services, Cambridge, Mass., 1979.

The appropriateness of the federal interagency day care requirements: A report of findings and recommendations. Washington, D.C.: Department of Health, Education, and Welfare, 1978.

BERNSTEIN, M. H. *Regulating Business by Independent Commission*. Princeton, N.J.: Princeton University Press, 1955.

BETTMAN, O. L. *The Good Old Days, They Were Terrible!* New York: Random House, 1974.

BRADBURY, D. *Five Decades of Action for Children*. Washington, D.C.: U.S. Children's Bureau, 1962.

CHILD WELFARE LEAGUE OF AMERICA. *Standards for Day Care Service*. New York: Child Welfare League of America, 1969.

CLASS, N. E. *Child Care Licensing of Facilities by State Welfare Departments*. Washington, D.C.: U.S. Children's Bureau, 1968.

CLASS, N. E. Safeguarding day care through regulating programs: The need for a multiple approach. Paper presented at the Annual Meeting of the National Association for the Education of Young Children, Seattle, Wash., 1969.

CLASS, N. E. Child care licensing and interstate child placements: An essay on public planning. In J. C. Hall, D. M. Hamperian, J. M. Pettibone, and J. L. White (eds.),

Major Issues in Juvenile Justice Information and Training: Reading in Public Policy. Columbus, Ohio: Academy for Contemporary Problems, 1981.

CLASS N. E. Licensing standards revisited. Paper presented at Tufts University Summer Institute in Day Care Licensing, Medford, Mass., June 1975.

COELEN, C. *Day Care Centers in the United States.* Cambridge, Mass.: Abt Associates, 1980.

EDUCATION COMMISSION OF THE STATES. *State Services in Child Development.* Denver, Colo.: E.C.S., 1975.

FRANK, E. P. Who's minding the children? *Good Housekeeping,* February 1979, 111ff.

FROHNMAYER, D. B. Regulatory reform: A slogan in search of substance. *American Bar Association Journal,* 1980, *66,* 871–876.

GOLDSMITH, C. The beginning of things. *BAEYC Reports, 17,* 2, December/January 1975.

Guides for Day Care Licensing. Washington, D.C.: U.S. Department of Health, Education, and Welfare, 1972.

ILLINOIS ECONOMIC AND FISCAL COMMISSION. *Day Care Licencing and Regulation: A Program Evaluation.* Springfield, Ill.: 1974.

JAMBOR, H. A. Theory and practice in agency participation in the formulation of child care licensing standards. *Child Welfare,* 1964, *63,* 521–528.

JOHNSON, L. and ASSOCIATES, *Comparative Licensing Study,* Washington, D.C.: Lawrence Johnson and Associates, 1980.

LANGER, W. L. Checks on population growth: 1750–1850. *Scientific American,* 1972, *226,* 92–99.

LORD, H. W. Dependent and delinquent children, with reference to girls. *Proceedings of the Fifth Annual Conference of Charities.* Boston: A. Williams & Co., 1978.

Michigan Department of Social Services. Demonstration project for the registration of family day care homes. Interim Report, February 12, 1976.

MELLI, M. Legal issues in enforcement of health and welfare. In I. Winograd (ed.), *Delivery of Services in a Regulated Society.* Milwaukee, Wisc.: University of Wisconsin, 1971.

MILLETT, R., MAYER, R. T., IRWIN, N., and PORTER, B. *Family Day Care in the United States: Site Case Studies.* Final Report of the National Day Care Home Study, Volume 6. Cambridge, Mass.: Abt Associates, 1980.

MOORE, J. E. Recycling the regulatory agencies. *Public Administration Review,* 1972, *32,* 291–298.

MORGAN, G. It's time to change the rules on regulations. *Day Care and Early Education,* 1974, *2,* 15–20.

OETTINGER, K. B. *It's Your Children's Bureau.* Washington, D.C.: U.S. Children's Bureau, 1964.

PRESCOTT, E., and DAVID, T. The effects of the physical environment on day care. Concept paper for USDHEW, *ASPE Study of the Appropriateness of the FIDCR,* 1976.

REIN, M. Values, knowledge, and social policy. In S. H. White (ed.), *Federal Programs for Young Children: Review and Recommendations,* Vol. III. Cambridge, Mass.: Huron Institute, 1973.

RUOPP, R., TRAVERS, J., GLANTZ, F., and COELEN, C. *Children at the Center,* Cambridge, Mass.: Abt Associates, 1979.

STIGLER, G. J. The theory of economic regulation. *Bell Journal of Economics and Management Science*, 1971, 2, 3.

TEXAS DEPARTMENT OF HUMAN RESOURCES. *The National Conference on the Registration of Family Day Homes.* San Antonio, Texas, 1977.

TEXAS DEPARTMENT OF HUMAN RESOURCES, LICENSING BRANCH. *Registration: Evaluation of a Regulatory Concept,* 1980.

White House Conference on Children in a Democracy, *Final Report,* 1940.

WILSON, J. W. *The Politics of Regulation.* New York: Basic Books, 1980.

YORK, M. N. A history of the White House Conference on Children and Youth, mimeo, 1970.

CHAPTER 17

The Preparation and Certification of Early Childhood Personnel

Bernard Spodek
Olivia N. Saracho

ANY DISCOURSE about the preparation and certification of early childhood personnel is fraught with pitfalls. The area is a confused one with a lack of agreement about what types of personnel should be staffing early childhood programs, what qualifications they should have, as well as how and where they should be prepared. There is even a lack of agreement as to the nomenclature to be used to describe the personnel. With such basic issues in conflict there is no agreement as to the preparation persons in the field ought to have or the minimum qualifications that should be established. This chapter will attempt to identify knowledge of practices that exist in the field and of policy issues that are in conflict, suggesting a research agenda that could inform future decisions.

Early Childhood Personnel

The education of young children takes place in a number of institutions designed to serve a number of different purposes. The period of early childhood is generally conceived as the period of the child's life until about eight years of age. From about six through eight, the child is enrolled in primary grade classes and is thus served by the elementary school. During the child's fifth year, it is the kindergarten, most often a part of the elementary school, that provides early childhood educational services. Since American public education does not generally extend below kindergarten level, the majority of children ages three to five are served by nonpublic nursery schools and day-care centers. The nursery school is primarily an educational institution which enrolls children for half-day sessions and often follows the academic calendar established by public schools. Day-care centers are designed to provide a safe and healthy environment for children during extended periods daily, often because parents work or attend **399** school and thus cannot care for them directly. Day-care centers generally include educational programs. Head Start and other special programs supported by public funds exist for children below the entry age for the public schools. The conceptions of education underlying such programs are generally broader than that of a kindergarten or nursery school, however, and are designed to prevent future difficulties and to counteract any deficiencies in the child or in his background. Head Start provides health and social services as well as education in a comprehensive child development program. Programs for handicapped children may be developmental or may be narrowly focused on the child's deficiencies.

Children below the age of two-and-a-half or three years are often served by day-care homes or infant-toddler centers. The centers may be separate institutions, but day-care homes represent an informal arrangement whereby a person may enroll a small group of children for care within a home setting. This service is a close approximation to informal babysitting arrangements.

Thus, a range of services within a number of different institutions, both formal and informal, constitute early childhood education. Different services need to be provided by persons with different competencies. These competencies vary in levels of sophistication as well as in kind. A teacher in a primary school must do different things than a teacher in a nursery school. A person responsible for providing care for an infant must do things that are different from what a person providing care for an eight-year-old does. Caring for a group of children in an institutional setting is different from caring for a single child in a home.

The conventions of the field of early childhood education identify all those who work with young children as "teachers." For example, Katz (1980) distinguishes the roles of mother from that of "day care, pre-school and primary school teacher" (p. 49). Similarly, Hess and Croft (1972) identify a range of programs for children ages one through six, including day-care centers, home day care, compensatory programs, kindergartens, laboratory/demonstration schools, nursery schools, parent cooperatives and playschools as providing employment opportunities for teachers of young children. The lack of distinction in practice, and the lack of clarity regarding the kind of preparation appropriate for each form of practice, may increase the confusion about the appropriate preparation and minimum qualifications for early childhood practitioners. In the diverse field of early childhood education, the kinds of practices in which these persons are engaged may not actually be interchangeable.

Distinguishing Roles

One distinction among practitioners that has been identified over the past half-century is the distinction between teacher and caregiver. As far back as the twenty-eighth yearbook of the National Society for the Study of Education, *Preschool and Parental Education* (Whipple, 1929), the day nursery, as day-care centers were called then, was seen as serving a relief function, providing aid to families rather than being primarily concerned with the needs of children. The nursery school, in contrast, was seen as serving primarily an educational function for young children. Following on this distinction, both the authors of the yearbook and Ethel Beer (1938), writing a decade later, considered the nursery school teacher to be too narrowly prepared to have the background necessary to serve the many needs of children within a day nursery facility. Thus, a distinction between early childhood practitioners was made on the basis of function: teachers serve primarily an educational function while caregivers (day-care personnel) serve primarily a caregiving/nurturing function. However, this distinction is not a particularly clear one, for the line between education and nurture in the early years is not a distinct one.

Another distinction that can be made is between personnel with different levels of preparation and responsibility. Spodek (1972) distinguished between professional roles and auxiliary roles in early childhood education. Teachers and supervisors were considered to be professionals, while teacher aides, assistants, and volunteers were characterized as auxiliaries. Some distinction by level of preparation and responsibility is helpful in understanding this area, although the distinction suggested above may not be particularly useful. One serious challenge is whether any early childhood educational personnel can be considered professionals.

Drawing on a variety of authoritative sources, Howsam, Corrigan, Denemark, and Nash (1976) characterize teaching as a semiprofession since, according to their analysis, teachers fall short of meeting the criteria of professionals. A profession, according to Howsam et al. (1976), is a way of providing essential services to individuals and the society; is concerned with an identified area of need or function; possesses a body of knowledge, behaviors, and skills not possessed by nonprofessionals; is involved in decision making in the service of the client; is based on one or more undergirding disciplines; is organized into one or more professional associations which is granted autonomy in control of the work and conditions of the professions; has agreed upon performance standards for admission; requires a protracted period of preparation and induction; has a high level of public trust and confidence; is characterized by a strong service motivation and a commitment to competence by its practitioners; is accountable to the profession and the client; and has relative freedom from on-the-job supervision.

As a semiprofession, Howsam et al. (1976) suggest that teaching manifests the following characteristics: lower occupational status; a shorter training period; a lack of societal acceptance of the nature of the service; a less specialized and less highly developed body of knowledge and skills; less emphasis on theoretical and conceptual bases of practice; a tendency to identify more with the employment institution and less with the profession; be subject to greater administrative and supervisory control; have less autonomy in decision making; provide management of organizations by persons who have themselves served as semiprofessionals; a preponderance of women; an absence of the right of privileged communication; and little or no involvement in life and death matters. While Howsam and his collegues did not identify the sex of practitioners as a criteria of a profession, their characterization of teaching as a semiprofession reflects the fact that female-dominated fields have lower status in our society.

If, as in the above analysis, teachers might be considered semiprofessionals, many practitioners in the early childhood field might be characterized by an even lesser degree of professionalism. Early childhood education has a lower level of societal acceptance than do other levels of education. Occupational status, as measured by income, for example, is lower for child-care workers than for public school teachers and less preparation is required for admission to the field. Katz (1980) identifies rationality and spontaneity as two of the dimensions on which mothers and teachers differ. These two dimensions may also differentiate professionals from nonprofessionals. It may well be that caregivers are more like mothers (nonprofessionals) along these dimensions than like primary teachers (semiprofessionals). Thus, if we accept this analysis, many early childhood practitioners might not even be considered semiprofessionals.

The issue of the degree of professionalism in the field might be illustrated by the discussion that raged in the 1970s within the National Association for the Education of Young Children regarding the adoption of a code of ethics for the organization. Since it was felt that service to children should be based upon ethical considerations, a number of members of that association, the largest association related to early childhood education in the United States, suggested that it adopt a code of ethics that should be adhered to by all of its members. Arguments were presented in favor of and against the adoption of such a code, in terms of both the nature of the code itself and the appropriateness of its adoption. A decision was finally made against the adoption of a code of ethics, not because having such a code in the field would be bad, but because requiring such a code of the association's members would be inappropriate. The association viewed itself as a membership services association rather than a professional association, concerned with including a wide range of potential members, both practitioners and non-practitioners. Thus, such a code could not be enforced. Since such a code would be exclusionary, one characteristic of a professional association, a statement of common commitment was adopted in its place (Spodek, 1977).

The Preparation of Early Childhood Personnel

Both the issues of level of professionalism and the kinds of services provided intrude on questions of where and how practitioners will be prepared. Kindergarten and primary teachers are generally prepared in four-year colleges and universities within departments of education. These practitioners are expected to complete programs that lead to a bachelor's degree and to certification as teachers. Day-care workers are often prepared within a child development tradition rather than an education tradition. Although many of these practitioners are graduates of programs in four-year colleges, they may also be graduates of vocationally oriented programs at two-year or community colleges or secondary schools.

Sometimes, day-care practitioners have no formal preparation at all. Nursery school teachers may either be prepared within an education tradition or within a day-care/child development tradition. They may or may not be subject to certification requirements in the states in which they practice. Different requirements exist in different states for practitioners in public schools, and these have an impact on preparation as much as any conception that exists within the field.

Early childhood personnel are prepared in a number of programs affiliated with different kinds of departments in a variety of institutions. There is no authoritative source of information on the preparation of early childhood personnel, in relation to either the programs that are designed to serve practitioners or the institutions that sponsor such preparation. A *Directory of Educational Programs for Adults Who Work with Children* (Rothenberg, 1979), although not comprehensive, lists over 800 postsecondary institutions preparing early childhood personnel in fifty states, the District of Columbia, Guam, and Puerto Rico. Four hundred and forty of these institutions offer programs leading to a bachelor's or master's degree, 761 offer programs leading to an associate degree, and some offer programs at both levels. In addition, many offer nondegree courses, some of which lead to some form of certification or provide preparation for the Child Development Associate Credential. The programs listed are housed in a variety of departments, including education, early childhood education, child development, child care, and human development and family life, to list a few of the more popular affiliations.

In Illinois, a survey was done to develop a resource directory of early childhood and child-care programs at secondary and postsecondary levels (Hutchinson, Hall and Orlofsky, n.d.). Respondents to the survey included programs in ninety high schools and area vocational centers, forty two-year colleges, and twenty-four four-year/graduate schools. Programs in high schools and two-year colleges were primarily identified as child-care or child development programs, while those in four-year/graduate colleges were primarily identified as early childhood education programs. The distinction in program labels may reflect the availability of an early childhood education teaching certificate for which university and college level programs may be preparing students.

The Illinois survey might be reflective of the situation in other states as well. In Illinois in 1979, 5,390 students were enrolled in high school/vocational centers programs, 3,775 students were enrolled in two-year college programs, and 1,754 students were enrolled in four-year programs of early childhood education. Thus, those early childhood programs at the highest levels of academic preparation had the smallest enrollments. However, the two-year colleges had the lowest percentage of students completing their programs—61 percent compared to 83 percent at the high school level and 87 percent at the four-year college level. Only 30 percent of the high school program graduates were reported as having found positions in the field as compared with 61% of the two-year college graduates and 68 percent of the four-year college graduates. As far as continuing preparation is concerned, 41 percent of the four-year college graduates were reported as continuing, as compared with 27 percent of the high school graduates and 21 percent of the two-year college graduates.

It is difficult to interpret such information without further inquiry into the nature of the programs and the nature of the clients of these programs, including their backgrounds and their purposes for taking training in the area. It is possible that many of the high school students enrolled in this training area do not see it as an area of continued vocational interest. It may be that for them a child development and day-care program serves as much as preparation for family life as for a vocation. This could account for the small number that seek employment in the field. Those programs requiring the greatest length of preparation, and hence the greatest commitment on the part of their participants, had the greatest proportion of their graduates entering the field. These graduates also seek additional preparation more often than do graduates of the other programs. It may very well be that a pattern of stratification exists in the field. Early childhood personnel who are graduates of four-year programs seek increased preparation to a much greater extent than do graduates of other programs, thus providing a group of practitioners that are more highly qualified to begin with and are continually seeking to improve their qualifications while another stratum enters the field less qualified and remains close to their entry qualifications. If this is the case, clearly delineated levels of professionalism could be identified between practitioners in the field. Rather than the "career ladder," with persons entering at lower levels and advancing through a combination of experience and continued preparation, we may actually see increased distinctions between strata in the field, with those persons entering with the highest levels of preparation more likely to continue their education and advancing, and those entering at lower levels being less likely to continue their education and thus be limited in advancement.

Programs to Prepare Teachers

No studies exist on the nature of early childhood teacher education programs, although descriptions of individual programs can be found. Some inferences can be made using elementary teacher education programs as their basis. Differences that do exist could be related to the younger age level of the students to be served, which might lead to increased child development content as well as some differences in methods courses and practicum sites for early childhood students. Similar inferences could not be made about programs at the two-year college or high school level since no basis for inference is available.

The National Survey on the Preservice Preparation of Teachers (NSPPT) has been reported in the *State of Teacher Education, 1977* (Lewin & Associates, 1977). The demographic information included would be useful in determining where teacher education students come from. The report suggests that students are predominantly female (72.5 percent) and are drawn primarily from small towns and rural areas. A large proportion of the graduates are over twenty-four years of age. Eleven percent of the group are from ethnic minorities. Although the teacher education students are drawn from all segments of the population, teachers somewhat more often come from families where parents are professionals or managers. About 4 percent of the group have fathers who were teachers.

No comparable data have been collected about those who enter the field of early childhood education, but the National Day Care Study (Roup, Travers & Goodrich, 1980) does provide a profile of caregivers. Interestingly, 20 percent of the head teachers and 13.5 percent of the teachers surveyed had degrees or certificates in elementary education, 5.7 percent of the head teachers and 4.3 percent of the teachers were qualified to teach secondary education, and 17.1 percent of the head teachers and 20.7 percent of the teachers were degreed or certified in preschool education. Caregivers were overwhelmingly female (93.7 percent), and about two-thirds of them were between eighteen and thirty-five years of age. Of the classroom staff, 66 percent were white, 28 percent black, and 7 percent members of other minority groups. As far as educational attainment is concerned, 31.4 percent of the head teachers and 29.3 percent of the teachers held bachelors degrees, 11.4 percent of the head teachers and 8.2 percent of the teachers held advanced degrees, while 20.0 percent of the head teachers and 12.5 percent of the teachers held associate degrees. Interestingly, 8.6 percent of the head teachers and 15.9 percent of the teachers held no degree at all including a high school diploma. The educational attainment of directors was somewhat higher while that of assistant teachers and aides was lower.

Thus, in comparison to teachers in general, day care teachers and head teachers include a considerably greater proportion of women and members of minority groups. Since elementary and secondary teachers are graduates of four-year degree programs, the educational attainment of day-care teachers would be lower than teachers in general.

Although the initial choice of teacher education is through self-selection, college programs do have criteria for admission. The information considered most significant includes grade point average, personal interview, secondary school grades, standardized test scores, and secondary school class rank. Thus, academic achievement is the predominant criterion for admission to teacher education programs. The use of this criterion is reflected in the fact that teacher education students are above the mean of the general college population in mathematics and verbal abilities as measured by College Entrance Examination Board tests given at the senior level, suggesting that teacher education programs may be somewhat more selective than college programs in general.

Programs of teacher education usually consist of a general education or liberal arts and science component, a professional studies component, and a clinical experiences component. The NSPPT survey compared data compiled in 1976 with similar data collected in 1961 and 1973. In general, there seemed to be very slight increases in the amount of general education and professional studies required of teacher education students. A more substantial increase can be found in the requirement for clinical experiences. In total, 41 percent of the elementary education student's four-year program is done in the area of teacher education, with field experiences included throughout the four years, moving from unsupervised contacts with children, through observations, co-participation with teachers, and actual teaching and internships. Actual teaching represented the greatest part of the field experience component.

Certification, Credentialing, and Accreditation

Admission to the teaching profession, at least within the public schools, is controlled by a state certificate or state credential in the United States. Certification is a "legal admittance to the profession." Its major purpose is to provide evidence that one possesses the minimum competencies needed for successful teaching. A teaching certificate attests that professionals have a "safe level" of beginning teaching skills to initiate a prospective teaching career (Howsam, Corrigan, Denemark & Nash, 1976).

Certification is a process that protects both the practitioner and the client. Through certification, the public is "safeguarded against the charlatan and the quack" and is provided with a guarantee of the quality of service. In addition, the practitioner is protected against competition from the unqualified (Haberman & Stinnett, 1973).

Certification is generally based upon completion of a recognized program of teacher preparation, graduation from a bachelor's degree program, and the recommendation of the preparing institution that the individual is qualified as a beginning practitioner. States require that public schools hire only certified and, thus, qualified teachers for their program.

In the most recent survey of early childhood certification requirements available, all of the states replying to the survey, with the exception of Mississippi, certified kindergarten teachers. The agency responsible for this certificate was the state's department of education or its equivalent. Twenty-three of the reporting states certified prekindergarten teachers and only seven certified day-care personnel. The responsibility for determining qualifications for day-care personnel falls on departments of health, welfare, or social services in four of these states (Education Commission of the States, 1975). The state legislature generally consults with the state department of education (or state department of public instruction) before establishing qualifications which professional personnel must meet to become certified. Standards and qualifications vary in each state, but a general agreement exists on the following:

1. Authority for the teachers' certification is centralized in the state department of education.
2. Certificates are issued based on subject fields or specified grade levels.
3. Certificates usually have to be renewed periodically.
4. A baccalaureate degree is required to attain a teaching certificate.
5. Certain courses in education and a specific number of semester hours in a subject matter or teaching field are required (Hughes & Schultz, 1976).

Acknowledging state and national standards, colleges and universities are the source of preparation for professionals. Most of the instruction occurs at the university. The teaching certificate or credential has a baccalaureate degree as a prerequisite. The teacher candidates attend and pass the courses which are prescribed in their educational plan, student-teach under professional supervision, and provide evidence that they have acquired the minimum competencies to be certified by the state. What are considered minimum teaching competencies may vary in differing circumstances.

The completion of an approved program of teacher education may no longer be considered as the sole basis for receiving a state teacher's certificate. A number of states, including Florida, New York, Georgia, South Carolina, Alabama, Mississippi, Arkansas, and Louisiana, are developing or implementing some form of teacher competency test. These tests may assess basic skills or knowledge of subject matter specialization. They may take the form of classroom observation as well as written tests. The assessment of competencies is seen by these states as a requirement for certification in addition to graduation from a teacher education program. This trend may be spreading in the next several years.

Regulation

Qualifications for those working in nursery schools and day-care centers are generally found in the standards established to license those centers. Two types of standards currently exist: licensing standards which are established by the states, and fiscal regulations such as the Federal Interagency Day Care Regulations (FIDCR) established by the U.S. Department of Health, Education, and Welfare (now Health and Human Services) for centers receiving federal support. The distinction between licensing standards and fiscal regulations is discussed in Chapter 16. The personnel standards established by these agencies are generally lower than teacher certification standards.

In 1980, a new set of FIDCR regulations were approved supplanting those in force since 1968. Funds necessary to enforce these regulations have not been appropriated as of this writing. The 1968 regulations established vague qualifications for caregivers, stating that "educational activities must be under the supervision and direction of a staff member trained or experienced in child growth and development," "the person providing direct care for children in the facility must have training or demonstrated ability in working with children" (Department of Health, Education, and Welfare, 1976, p. 9–10). The nature and extent of the training, the kind or amount of experience, and the criteria for demonstrating ability are nowhere spelled out.

No entry-level qualifications are included in the 1980 FIDCR regulations. Caregivers without previous experience or training are required to have an on-site orientation on how to care for children in groups before assuming any caregiving responsibilities. In addition, caregivers without nationally recognized child development credentials are required to participate regularly in specialized training related to child care. A plan for such training is to be established and implemented by state day-care agencies (Department of Health, Education, and Welfare, 1980).

In establishing a model day-care licensing act for states to use, the Department of Health, Education, and Welfare (n.d.) suggests the following personnel regulation: "Each caregiver must have the skill and competency necessary to contribute to the child's physical, intellectual, personal and social development" (p. 23). The qualifications suggested include:

1. Bachelor's or Associate of Arts degree with at least twelve semester hours in child development, child health, or directly related fields; *or*
2. high school diploma or its equivalent, plus at least three years of satisfactory experience in a related educational, early childhood, or day-care program; *or*
3. certification as a child development associate or similar status where a local, state, or federal certification program exists (n.d., p. 23).

The standards suggested for establishment here are considerably lower than those established for teacher certification in every state. Whereas teacher certification is considered to be a state function, there is a suggestion here for the establishment of federal certification for day-care personnel.

The extent to which these recommendations show up in state licensing standards might be illustrated by reference to the day-care licensing standards of the state of Illinois (Office of Child Development, n.d.). In these regulations, day-care personnel are identified as child development directors, child development associates, and child development assistants. The child development director, the person with the highest status in a center and thus reflecting the highest personnel standards in a center, is required to have the equivalent of two years of postsecondary work with eighteen hours in child-related courses, of which six in early childhood development. Child development associates and assistants are expected to have less in the way of preparation, and equivalences are established that allow practitioners to have even less in the way of academic preparation. It should be noted that in many states, nursery schools are licensed as day-care centers and thus the qualifications for child caregivers or child development specialists would apply to nursery school teachers. Those standards that have been established recently are an improvement over lower standards that were in effect in years past or the absence of standards that has existed in some states.

The reason for the absence of certification standards for caregivers and nursery school teachers similar to those for kindergarten and primary school teachers is probably more economic than academic. Raising the requirements for entry into the field would undoubtedly increase the pressure for higher pay for practitioners, and day-care practitioners are the lowest paid child welfare workers.

Credentialing

The Child Development Associate Consortium (CDAC) was established as a credentialing agency without the responsibility for training. Its purpose has been to upgrade the qualifications of those who care for young children. Although funded by the Department of Health and Human Services, CDAC is a private nonprofit organization whose board consists of representatives of the public and of organizations consisting of over a half-million persons concerned with the education and development of young children.

The CDAC has developed a system to assess the qualifications of caregivers and to grant credentials to competent individuals. The credential is a national one. It is not a professional license to practice nor is it necessarily recognized by state certification or licensing agencies. The credential derives its authority from the requirement that practitioners in Head Start programs have it. In addition, some states have used the credential as a means of documenting staff qualifications in day-care centers.

To qualify for the credential, the child development associate (CDA) must demonstrate competence in each of six areas:

1. establish and maintain a safe and healthy learning environment;
2. advance physical and intellectual competence;
3. build positive self-concept and individual strength;
4. promote positive functioning of children and adults in a group;
5. bring about optimal coordination of home and center child-rearing practices and expectations;
6. carry out supplementary responsibilities related to children's programs (Ward et al., 1976).

The original CDA credentialing system was designed around a competency-based assessment system. At present, some formal or informal training is required of those being assessed for credentialing. An assessment team, consisting of the candidate, a trainer/adviser, a parent-community representative, and a CDAC representative judge the candidate. For the assessment, the individual collects materials into a portfolio that best reflect the work he/she actually does with children, parents, and staff members. The adviser observes the candidate and reports on his/her ability in working with children, parents, and other staff members. The parent-community representative collects opinions of the candidate's work from other parents and also observes the candidate at work. The consortium representative also observes the candidate at work and interviews the candidate about his/her work (Maynard, 1978). At an assessment meeting, the team then judges the materials collected and the observations of the candidate's performance and determines whether or not the candidate should be awarded the credential. The credential is presently granted for a period of three years. To date, over 6,000 candidates have been credentialed by CDAC (Klein, 1980).

Accreditation

Just as the certification and credentialing of personnel provide protection for clients and society at large by requiring that practitioners meet minimum requirements, so also does the accreditation of institutions that prepare practitioners protect both the practitioner-to-be and the client and society at large by establishing standards for programs that prepare practitioners. As a result of accreditation, the public can have confidence that the graduate of a program has been provided with an appropriate experience with adequate resources supporting it that should be expected to lead to competent practice. The student entering the program can also feel confident that the accredited institution will live up to its promise in providing what is necessary to enhance preparation for practice, including adequate facilities, competent instructional staff, and appropriate program design.

Unlike the licensing of programs for children, accreditation of institutions of higher education is a voluntary process under the supervision of a voluntary organization rather than government agencies. Accreditation is defined as "approval of an educational institution, usually by an association of educators who have voluntarily banded together to enforce reasonable standards. . . . Accreditation seeks to protect the integrity of the program of education offerred" (Haberman & Stinnett, 1973, p. 171). The total programs of institutions of secondary and postsecondary education are accredited by regional agencies, such as the North Central Association of Colleges and Secondary Schools. In addition, some professional associations establish accreditation for programs within a university that prepare practitioners for their profession. Thus, within a multipurpose institution, it is possible to find programs accredited by many different associations.

In the area of teacher education, the accreditation agency is the National Council for the Accreditation of Teacher Education (NCATE). NCATE was originally established in 1954, although efforts at accrediting teacher education programs go back further. It was the result of the joint efforts of the Council of Chief State School Officers, the National Commission on Teacher Education and Professional Standards of the National Education Association (NEA), the National Association of State Directors of Teacher Education and Certification, and the American Association of Colleges for Teacher Education (AACTE). The history of the accreditation movement in teacher education has been characterized by concerns for power and influence. Members of the teaching profession—practitioners organized within the NEA and the American Federation of Teachers (AFT) and teacher educators as represented by the AACTE—have felt that they should have the greatest voice in determining the basis for accrediting programs of teacher education. Before 1974, there was greater involvement by teacher educators than by practitioners. Since 1974, a significant minority of the board of NCATE and of all accreditation visiting teams have been composed of representatives of practicing teachers, as this group has been able to increase its input into the accreditation process (Bush & Enemark, 1975).

The process of NCATE accreditation requires that a program of teacher education must demonstrate that it has met established standards. The most recent set of standards went into effect in 1979 and covers such areas as the governance of the basic program, the teacher education curriculum, the faculty, students, institutional resources and facilities, and evaluation, program review, and planning. A self-report is written by the institution to be accredited and a visitation team evaluates both the report and the institution itself. This visitation team is representative of the educational community at large and includes teacher educators, educational administrators, classroom teachers, and students in teacher education programs. Members of visitation teams are instructed in the evaluation process.

Although accreditation is a national means of establishing quality control in teacher education, the voluntary nature of the process limits its effectiveness since not all programs of teacher education are accredited. Clark and Guba (1976) report that 72 percent of all four-year institutions (a total of 1,367) have one or more state-approved programs of teacher education. Only 39 percent of these institutions (540) are NCATE accredited. Thus, less than half of those institutions of higher education that prepare teachers have been accredited. Some of these institutions have chosen not to be accredited in order to avoid the investment in faculty time and effort needed for the accreditation process, but others no doubt would not be able to demonstrate adherence to standards.

It is possible that in the coming years the proportion of accredited teacher-preparing institutions will increase. Several states now require institutions that prepare teachers for certification to be accredited by NCATE. In addition, some states accept graduates of out-of-state teacher education institutions only if those institutions are NCATE accredited. In recent years, a number of teachers' contracts with local school systems have stipulated that new teachers hired by the district be graduates of NCATE-approved teacher education programs, in addition to being certified. Each of these moves increases the importance of the accrediting process by making graduation from an accredited institution a requirement for employment. Even though the accreditation of teacher education may continue to remain voluntary, colleges may be obliged to seek accreditation to secure the employability of their graduates.

The accreditation of institutions that prepare teachers has been seen as an important vehicle for maintaining the quality of teacher education programs, but its application to early childhood education is unclear. The National Association for the Education of Young Children has only recently become involved in the NCATE accreditation process. Programs that prepare early childhood teachers may exist in institutions subject to NCATE accreditation. However, many of the persons employed in preschool centers are not graduates of teacher education programs in four-year colleges but are prepared in child development programs or in two-year colleges which are not subject to NCATE accreditation. Still others are prepared in high school programs or have no formal preparation at all. There is at present no system of accreditation that oversees the quality of programs preparing early childhood practitioners outside the framework of teacher education.

Research on Teaching and Teacher Education

It is often thought that knowledge of teaching could provide a rational basis for decisions about the preparation of teachers and about requirements for admission to the field. Thus, research on teaching and on teacher effectiveness should be useful in addressing issues of content, if not issues of method in teacher education, as well as issues about prerequisite knowledge and skills for teachers.

There is a long tradition of research on teaching, much of which has been designed to identify attributes of teacher behavior that are significant and that can be instilled in teachers or teachers-to-be. Rosenshine and Furst (1973), for example, assert that there are at least ten category systems found in *Mirrors for Behavior* (Simon & Boyer, 1967, 1970) that were designed with this purpose in mind. To what extent teacher education strategies can be prescribed as a result of research on teaching, however, is open to question.

Research on Teaching

There seem to be two general approaches that have been taken in studying teaching. One of these might be considered a constructivist approach. Assumptions that underlie constructivist conceptions of research include the following: (1) the subjects under study are knowing beings; (2) the control of their behavior rests within them; (3) their teaching and learning behavior has been constructed by them purposively; (4) human beings develop knowledge by organizing complexity rapidly; (5) they attend to meanings rather than to the surface elements of complex communications; and (6) they take on and reconstruct elaborate roles (Magoon, 1977). Examples of constructivist studies of teaching include Bussis, Chittenden, and Amarel (1977), Jackson (1968), Lortie (1975), and Smith and Geoffrey (1968). Halliwell (1981), Hutchins (1981), N. R. King (1976), and R. King (1978) have developed constructivist studies of teachers at the early childhood level. Although the first three of these studies focus on the kindergarten curriculum, they illuminate the role of the kindergarten teacher because the teacher is conceived as critical in developing curriculum in these studies. These studies are designed to portray a complex teaching–learning situation, often embedded in an even more complex institutional setting. The meanings that the actors give to the situation are portrayed and explored. Although these studies provide rich descriptions of practice, they seldom prescribe practice and often do not address the issue of what constitutes effective practice.

Another approach to research on teaching has concerned itself with teacher effectiveness. Typically, studies in this area have attempted to identify those elements of teacher performance or teacher characteristics that are related to valued student outcomes. Some of these studies have been experimental in nature, and researchers have manipulated particular teacher variables in controlled situations. Other studies have looked for relationships between student outcomes and teacher behavior as they have occurred in natural situations. Studies of teacher effectiveness have typically been done at the elementary and secondary school level. Teacher effectiveness is most often assessed by measuring pupil gains on standardized achievement tests. Thus, the valued outcomes of education assumed in these studies are increases in academic achievement as reflected in these test scores. Few teacher effectiveness studies have been done below grade one. This is partly because of problems of instrumentation in regard to child outcomes in the early childhood period. As Goodwin and Driscoll (1980) have suggested, there are greater problems of measurement encountered in evaluating young children. These problems relate to the reliability, validity, and usability of the instruments available. In addition, it has been difficult to specify clearly the expected outcomes of many early childhood programs defined in measurable terms. Goals in the affective, social, and psychomotor domains have been especially difficult to assess.

Reviews of studies of teacher effectiveness have been done by Cruikshank (1976), Kohut (1980), Rosenshine and Furst (1973), and Rosenshine (1976). Rosenshine (1976), in summarizing recent teacher effectiveness studies, concluded that factual questioning of children was functional for low-ability children. There seemed to be no identifiable optimum type or sequence of questions that is useful for all types of children. He also concluded that tutoring does increase student outcomes, although the most effective procedures for tutoring have not been identified. There seemed to be conflicting evidence as to whether there are effective specific or generic teaching skills in relation to teaching academic skills. With low socioeconomic students, Rosenshine suggests that direct instruction, narrow questioning, positive feedback by teacher, and supervised study in groups are all related to positive student achievement. Although providing praise has been shown to have a consistent positive correlation with pupil achievement, there were no consistent results for teacher management or control statements. The results of some studies also show a positive relation to pupil achievement.

Rosenshine (1979) characterizes the successful teacher as "one who structures and selects activities, whose students are academically engaged for many minutes each day, who tends to ask questions that have specific answers in a controlled-practice format, who places students in groups where they are supervised by the teacher and who does all this in a controlled but convivial classroom" (p. 47). Thus, the model for teaching to obtain gains in reading and mathematics is characterized as a "behavior-analytic, detail-specific, teacher-directed, larger-group and narrow-questioning approach" (p. 50).

Peterson (1979) views the picture of direct instruction as undimensional, focusing only on measured outcomes in reading and math achievement. She presents a review of research that suggests that more open approaches appear to be better for increasing students' creativity, independence, curiosity, and positive attitudes toward school. In addition, different students tend to respond differently to alternative teaching approaches, suggesting that competent teachers might use a mix of direct and open approaches in their classrooms.

Soar and Soar (1976) raise some interesting issues in relation to the correlation studies of student achievement and teacher performance. They found a curvilinear relationship or inverted U effect in their studies. The greatest amount of student gain seemed to be related to a moderate amount of particular teacher behaviors. Thus, moderate teacher structuring increased student learning more than no or high levels of structuring. The kinds of learning outcomes studied as well as the socioeconomic status of the learner were important variables in the study.

On the basis of the research that exists to date it is safe to say that, at least at the primary level, there is a relationship between some of the things that teachers do and some of the things that children learn. This relationship, however, is complicated by a number of factors that impinge on it, including the nature of the learner and the nature of what is to be learned. What may be an effective teaching strategy for one group of children in one setting may be less effective with other children in other settings. One may recall that the compensatory education programs of the 1960s were developed because it was felt that those educational strategies that seemed to work for middle class children did not work equally well for children of low socioeconomic backgrounds. In addition, teacher characteristics or behaviors that might enhance learning in regard to one set of outcomes might not be equally enhancing in regard to other sets of outcomes. Most of the studies on teacher effectiveness have been done in relation to outcomes in academic areas such as reading or mathematics. What may make a difference in these areas might not make a similar difference in outcomes related to children's problem solving, creative performance, or the enhancement of a positive self-concept, which are also valued outcomes of early childhood programs.

One of the major goals of the Head Start program has been the development of social competence in children. This goal has not been adequately evaluated, and this is at least partially due to the absence of instruments that reliably assess social competence. The Program Effects Measurement Project has been funded by the Administration for Children, Youth, and Families to select or prepare instruments to assess the impact of Head Start and similar programs on young children (Mediax Associates, 1978). One can only hope that the instruments that result from this project will enable researchers to better evaluate the broad range of outcomes related to various program elements, including teacher characteristics, as a result of having a greater range of assessment instruments than is now available.

The studies of teacher effectiveness reviewed above have been done with children in grades one or beyond, but there is little that we know about what constitutes effective teaching at the kindergarten or prekindergarten level. Gordon and Jester (1973), after reviewing techniques of observing teaching in early childhood, concluded that there was a need for more studies of teaching in early childhood education, especially in day-care and nursery school settings. They also felt the need for more time-sampling studies and studies that focused on the level of interaction in classrooms. In addition, they felt there should be more comprehensive studies and a greater use of common instrumentation to allow for replication of findings.

Meyer (1977) and Oyemade and Chargois (1977) were commissioned to review the state of the art in relation to staffing characteristics and child outcomes in day care. These reviews were commissioned along with others to provide a basis for establishing the new Federal Interagency Day Care Regulations. In both reviews, one finds little research that can inform the field and provide a rational basis for establishing regulations in this area. The void identified by Gordon and Jester (1973) had not yet been filled. The National Day Care Study (Roup, Travers & Goodrich, 1980) did find a relationship between the qualifications of caregivers and their behaviors. Caregivers who had specialized in child-related fields (for example, developmental psychology or early childhood education) engaged in more social interactions with children and spent less time interacting with other caregivers. They also seemed to engage in less management behavior. There were, however, no systematic effects of these behaviors on any of the observable child variables in the study. Children associated with caregivers who had specialized in child-related fields did show higher gains on the Preschool Inventory and there was a weak positive relationship to gains on the Peabody Picture Vocabulary Test as well. A simple correlation between social interacting with children and years of education of caregivers was found, but this effect was confounded with the variables of caregivers' race and children's SES. The variable "years of education," however, did not distinguish among the different contents of those educational years. Education that is specifically designed to prepare early childhood practitioners is quite different from general education. "Years of education" is not a very good index of level of preparation. Thus, there is some evidence to support a relationship between staffing characteristics related to preparation and teacher performance and child outcomes at the preschool level.

Research on Teacher Education

Just as teaching has been a topic of research in the field of education, so has teacher education. Notable reviews of research in the area have been presented by Peck and Tucker (1973) and by Turner (1975). Although, as in research on teaching, very little of this research has been directly related to the preparation of early childhood personnel, it is possible to extrapolate to that area.

Peck and Tucker (1973), in their review of studies on teacher education, identified six major themes: (1) a systems approach to teacher education improves its effectiveness; (2) teacher educators should serve as role models to improve the chances of their pupils adopting desired styles of teaching behavior; (3) direct involvement in field-based experiences, sensitivity laboratories, and simulation is more likely to produce desired teaching behaviors; (4) it is possible to induce self-initiated, self-directed effective patterns of learning; (5) traditional ways of teacher training have both intended and unintended effects; and (6) the common use of pupil-gain measures as the criterion for teacher education effectiveness.

Turner (1975) organized the research in relation to the selection, training, placement, and work success aspects of teacher education, including studies that illuminated each area and those that showed relationships between the areas. He identified studies, for example, that showed that the ratings of admissions selection committees correlated with later administrators' judgments of teacher success, while scores on entrance examinations and on achievement tests as well as grade point averages did not. Although studies of training procedure generally deal with their power to affect immediate behavior, Turner found few studies that examined the relationship of these procedures to criteria of teacher success. Interestingly, Turner suggests that the placement of beginning teachers has a substantial impact on their continued development as well as a moderating impact on those characteristics that were viewed as salient to teacher success.

On the whole, studies of teacher education have been successful in identifying some of the characteristics of training that can modify the short-term behavior of teachers and that might affect their pupils immediately. The studies are less successful in identifying what elements of a program have a long-range impact on teacher success. There is also a suggestion that the personal characteristics of a teacher, which can be identified by selection committees as well as training, have an impact on success. This might add support to the work of scholars like Almy (1975) who focus on the importance of certain personal characteristics in the early childhood educator.

Teacher education is seldom provided in discrete experiences but rather in entire programs, with preservice preparation containing more than teacher preparation experiences. Atkin and Raths (1974) identified a number of different approaches to teacher education in the United States. They found institutions that supported multiple approaches, each based on a different conception of teaching and teacher education, as characterized by practices at the University of Massachusetts, as well as cooperative training arrangements between educational work sites and teacher preparing institutions, as characterized by the work at Northeastern University. Individual institutions also fostered particular models of teacher education. Performance-based or competency-based teacher education was identified as being developed in institutions such as the University of Houston, while humanistic programs of teacher education were identified in a few institutions such as the University of Florida. These newer approaches were juxtaposed with traditional approaches to teacher education. Traditional teacher education was viewed as lacking in distinctiveness and clarity, as having a degree of program segmentation and a separation of methods instruction into curriculum areas. These traditional programs are often found in larger, more prestigious institutions that tend to have strong programs of liberal education associated with them.

Although it might be interesting to identify the various approaches to teacher education available, it is often difficult to characterize a program by the label it is given. One of the more popular innovations in teacher education in the 1970s was performance-based or competency-based teacher education. Elam (1971) has identified the essential characteristics of this approach to teacher education. The competencies to be demonstrated are derived from explicit conceptions of the teacher role. The assessment criteria are based upon specific competencies and the assessment is based on performance and strives to be objective. The students' progress is determined by demonstrated competencies and the instructional program facilitates the development and evaluation of these specified competencies. Some of the implied characteristics are that the program should be individualized and guided by feedback, that it should emphasize completion requirements and hold students accountable for performance.

There is no "Underwriters Laboratory" in education as in home appliances that tests programs and determines their degree of purity or adherence to a model. Program developers often attempt to gain a broad base of support for their innovations. One way of insuring a range of support is to describe the attributes of a model vaguely. Then, a wide range of programs can be described as fitting that model since each will view the essential characteristics of the model from a particular perspective. Another way of gaining support is to modify the model to conform to the curent values of the field and to respond to criticism of innovative practice and theory. Many program developments have gone this route, including performance-based or competency-based teacher education. When this happens, the label ascribed to a program may not accurately communicate the substance of the program, and relying on labels to understand programs becomes a dangerous practice.

Lickona (1976) described a "person centered approach to CBTE" that was developed at the State University of New York at Cortland. One of the characteristics of this program involved students in decisions about what and how they learned, and competencies were defined broadly in terms of personal growth. There were collegial student–staff relations with teachers teaching each other, and students were helped to derive ideas for teaching from their personal experience. Comparing these characteristics with the ones identified by Elam for competency-based teacher education, one might characterize it more as a humanistic program than a competency program.

A humanistic approach to teacher education has probably been best articulated by Combs (1974) who views teacher education as a problem in "personal becoming, of helping a student discover how best to use himself/herself as a professional educator" (p. 58). Learning, according to Combs, must be personal and experiential and proceeds best when the learner has a need to know. Field experiences provide the student with a chance to confront problems and to discover what one needs to know. Teacher educators are viewed as educational generalists who are facilitators in human relationships and growth processes rather than specialists in content and method.

Perhaps more studies are needed that describe the actual experiences provided to students in a teacher education program as well as the meanings the students derive from those experiences. Templin (1979) studied the program in a small, charismatic, early childhood teacher education institution concerned with self-reflection in teachers. The program was characterized as a personalized program of teacher education reflecting a child-centered ideology. Templin found that students went through a series of stages in the program and that each stage was characterized by a particular set of dilemmas. There seemed to be a confounding of personal self-reflection with professional self-reflection in the program. The image of the institution was reflected in the way students interpreted their experiences.

Innovations in Teacher Education

Even though the amount of research on teacher education has increased in the past several years, it has not had a great impact on practice. Howey, Yarger, and Joyce (1978) argue that there has been little major conceptual and operational change in initial teacher education in the recent past nor is there much of an empirical base on which program development can be built. Yet, according to the NSPPT study (Lewin & Associates, n.d.), innovative practices have been encouraged during the past decade in at least three area: increased use of clinical settings for training, increased use of instructional technology, and the establishment of performance-based or competency-based teacher education (CBTE) programs.

Clinical Settings

As discussed earlier, the NSPPT study, *The State of Teacher Education, 1977,* shows that there has been an increase in the requirement of clinical experiences in teacher education programs and of the earlier introduction of clinical experiences within programs. The study also shows that although there was initial interest in simulation and micro-teaching, their use has decreased, and sensitivity training has had little impact on teacher education. However, observation systems that use interaction analysis or that are based on Bloom's *Taxonomy of Educational Objectives* (1956) have had widespread use (Lewin & Associates, n.d.).

Competency-Based Teacher Education

During the 1970s, there was a great deal of interest in performance-based or competency-based programs to prepare people to become teachers. Suggested methods of certifying teachers are based upon this concept. The Child Development Associate Credential was originally proposed as a competency-based credentialing system. However, there has been widespread criticism as well as support for CBTE. Among the criticisms that Taylor (1978) cites is that the research base of CBTE is specious and that the term "competence" has its origins in the discourse of politics rather than of research. Taylor also wonders whether it is possible to assemble discrete teaching skills into whole teaching acts and whether CBTE is a threat to such values as freedom, uniqueness, creativity, productivity, responsibility, wholeness, and interdependence.

Some educators feel that the competency-based movement has peaked without having had a major impact on teacher education. Hermanowicz (1978) attributes this failure to "simpleminded advocates who hopped on the bandwagon" and to insufficient research into program development and refinement. He also cites the fact that generic teaching skills, which should have been the basis for such programs, did not seem to exist. Too often, the objectives of newly developed CBTE programs were abstracted from existing programs, and there was an overemphasis on technical training and an underemphasis on the underlying theoretical and conceptual knowledge. The use of primitive assessment strategies and the simplistic specification of teaching competencies also hurt the movement. Howey, Yarger, and Joyce (1978) suggest that competency-based teacher education is to be found more in rhetoric than in practice. Many institutions developed competency statements for their programs, but few faculties engaged in further developments including the modification of program elements and delivery systems. Howey and colleagues attribute the lack of progress in CBTE to a lack of resources for coordinated approaches to program development.

Limits to Innovation

Although individual teacher educators have been engaged in developing, implementing and testing discrete innovations in teacher education, major innovations at the program level seem to be lacking. This may in part result from the lack of resources for coordinated approaches, but it is also due at least in part to the many interests that are tied up in teacher education. The impact of these interests on the decision-making process has been satirized by Spodek (1974). Programs of teacher education are shaped by state policies as much as by the organized teaching profession. State teacher certification requirements need to be met by programs before they receive program approval. Established criteria for content and resources need to be met before institutions are accredited. Thus, both certification and accreditation serve a conservative purpose even though they are not designed to limit innovations.

Teacher education programs are embedded within larger programs of colleges and universities and are required to conform to the pressures within those institutions. The majority of the offerings in any program that prepares teachers is not provided by the teacher education faculty but rather by faculty from other units in the institution. Program innovations have to be approved not only by the teacher education faculty but also by general university administration and often by the faculty at large. The commitment of the noneducation faculty to teacher education may indeed place severe limits on what can be offered by an institution.

Even the ethic of academic freedom can limit innovation in teacher education. If each faculty member has the right to espouse particular intellectual ideas and ideals in his teaching, it is questionable to what extent he can or should be required to adhere to a particular orientation of a general program. From a practical point of view, the faculty member who does not favor a program innovation will give less than his full efforts toward its success and may, in fact, practice a subtle form of sabotage. Added to this is the fact that the control of field experiences, increasingly considered an important element of teacher preparation, is not in the hands of the teacher-preparing institution. The field experience may be supervised in part by someone from the teacher education institution, but these supervisors have little impact on the experience (Morris, 1974).

Finally and unfortunately, the limited resources given to the preparation of teachers place severe limits on the amount of innovation that can be expected. Programs preparing teachers in general have been financially supported in institutions of higher education to a lesser degree than have programs that prepare other professionals such as physicians, lawyers, or engineers. These professions have greater status and their practitioners receive greater remuneration. When day-care practitioners earn even less than public school teachers and are viewed as having lower status, there is a hesitancy to expect too much from them in the way of effort or achievement in their preparation programs.

A Look Ahead

There are a number of traditional roles in early childhood practice which have been implicitly defined by common agreement, but these agreements are no longer certain. Should a practitioner in a day-care center be considered a teacher or do we need titles that reflect role differentiation in the field? Should the preparation of practitioners in day-care centers and in educational institutions be identical or comparable? Traditionally, the terms caregiver and day-care worker have been reserved for those who work in formal or informal caregiving institutions and are primarily concerned with nurturance rather than education. Even though the two roles overlap, a distinction may need to be drawn between them.

Recently, a new role, that of *early childhood educator*, has been introduced to the field (Almy, 1975). This role, while not fully defined, would include the function of teacher but would go beyond it. The idea, although attractive, has not yet been adopted in the field. Another type of practitioner, the *child development associate* suggests that there is a practice of child development that is found within the field of early childhood education. As noted earlier, the concept of child development specialist has been picked up by licensing agencies such as those in Illinois as well as by the CDAC. Yet, nowhere in the literature can there be found an exposition of what a child development practitioner does, what such a practitioner's qualifications might be, and how this practitioner might be different from other forms of early childhood practitioners labeled more traditionally.

Perhaps a commission could look at the practice and come up with a set of standard labels and definitions of practice that could be adopted by the field of early childhood education. If such a commission were to be assembled, it would need to be composed of persons of reasonably high status in the field. The results of their deliberations would certainly not be free from controversy.

Along with definitions, we need good descriptions of current practice. The exercise of listing competencies for early childhood practitioners which was done to some extent in the 1970s has proved to be of limited value. The general areas of competencies that was arrived at by the CDA Consortium (Ward et al., 1976) are so vague that they are not descriptive of practice. What we need are rich descriptions of how teachers and other practitioners function in a classroom and how they interpret the educational world around them. There is a beginning to this kind of collection of descriptions of practice in the work of N. R. King (1976), R. King (1978), Halliwell (1981), and Hutchins (1981) referred to earlier. But this is just the beginning of a range of descriptive studies of practice that are needed not just in the kindergarten but in the primary grades and in nursery schools and day-care centers as well.

A number of studies have attempted to relate child outcomes to teacher characteristics. At present, these studies have been confined primarily to the elementary grades. The National Day Care Study (Roup, Travers & Goodrich, 1980), cited earlier, contains within it an attempt, however primitive, to look at comparable relationships at the preprimary level. One of the problems we have with such studies is determining which teacher characteristics are worthy of assessing. To some extent, this is a value issue. Another, and possibly more important, problem is the identification of child outcomes. Existing studies generally focus on academic outcomes, particularly in reading and mathematics, as measured by standardized achievement tests. Neither the outcomes nor the measures used would be appropriate for education at the preschool level. As stated earlier, there is currently an attempt to develop instruments to measure social competence, a valued outcome of early childhood education. The development of this and similar instruments would be helpful in moving this line of inquiry along.

In addition to the above, we need to learn more about the selection and preparation of early childhood practitioners. We do not now have adequate knowledge of the people and institutions who prepare early childhood practitioners, the nature of that preparation, and the kinds of existing standards and safeguards. Surveys of training and certification practices would help provide a baseline from which policy recommendations could be developed. Surveys of the demographic characteristics of practitioners would also be helpful. Do early childhood practitioners look like teachers at other levels in socioeconomic, ethnic, sex, academic achievement, and other characteristics? Are there differences among the different kinds of practitioners on these characteristics? Such information could inform policy relating to entry and retention in the field.

In the area of teacher education, Spodek (1974) views practice as combining empirical knowledge of the field with an acceptable value framework and suggests the following propositions as guides to early childhood teacher education:

1. Teacher education at all levels, but especially at the early childhood level, needs to be taken seriously.
2. All teaching, at all levels, requires an act of faith.
3. An empirical data base is needed to improve teacher education.
4. Feedback is as important for teacher educators as it is for classroom teachers.
5. Teacher education programs should elicit student satisfactions, but student satisfactions alone do not justify any teacher education activity.
6. Every teacher education goal can be achieved through a variety of sets of activities and, conversely, any set of teacher education activities can lead to a variety of goals.

7. Teacher educators, much like early childhood educators, must be concerned with the "problem of the match" in designing learning activities for their students.
8. At best, all we can provide are the necessary, but not sufficient, conditions for teacher development (pp. 93–95).

Finally, it would help to have studies that would allow state and other agencies to establish standards for practitioners. Early childhood teacher certification does not apply to all types of practitioners in the field nor would it be appropriate for all practitioners. The child development associate credential has been established as another type of certification. Some standards are embedded in day-care licensing regulations as well as in formal certification regulations. We need to know what impact methods of certification or credentialing and standards for credentialing have on practice.

Early childhood education is alive and developing. Practice has continually changed as the field has been asked to address the many social concerns relating to young children. There is a belief in the field that early childhood programs are only as good as the adults who implement them. If that is the case, the more we know about the nature of practitioners and what constitutes effective preparation for practice, the more we can improve the education of young children.

References

ALMY, M. *The Early Childhood Educator at Work*. New York: McGraw-Hill, 1975.

ATKIN, J. M., and RATHS, J. C. *Changing patterns of teacher education in the United States*. A report for the Organization for Economic Cooperation and Development. February, 1974.

BEER, E. S. *The Day Nursery*. New York: Dutton, 1938.

BLOOM, B. S. (ed.). *Taxonomy of Educational Objectives*. New York: David McKay Co., 1956.

BUSH, R. N., and ENEMARK, M. Control and responsibility in teacher education. In K. Ryan (ed.), *Teacher Education*, 74th yearbook of the National Society for the Study of Education. Chicago: University of Chicago Press, 1975.

BUSSIS, A. M., CHITTENDEN, E. A., and AMAREL, M. *Beyond Surface Curriculum*. Boulder, Colo.: Westview Press, 1976.

CLARK, D. L., and GUBA, E. G. An institutional self-report on knowledge production and utilization in schools, colleges and departments of education. In *Research on Institutions of Teacher Education*. Bloomington, Ind., 1976.

COMBS, A. W. *The Professional Education of Teachers*, 2nd ed. Boston: Allyn and Bacon, 1974.

CRUIKSHANK, D. R. A synthesis of selected recent research on teacher effects. *Journal of Teacher Education*, 1976, 27, 57–60.

EDUCATION COMMISSION OF THE STATES. *Early Childhood Programs: A State Survey, 1974–75.* Denver, Colo.: The Commission, April 1975.

DEPARTMENT OF HEALTH, EDUCATION, AND WELFARE. *Federal Interagency Day Care Requirements.* Washington, D.C.: Office of Human Development, 1976.

DEPARTMENT OF HEALTH, EDUCATION, AND WELFARE. HEW day care regulations. *Federal Register,* 1980, 45, 17870–17885.

DEPARTMENT OF HEALTH, EDUCATION, AND WELFARE. *Guides for Day Care Licensing.* Washington, D.C.: Office of Child Development, n.d.

ELAM, S. *Performance-Based Teacher Education: What is the State of the Art?* Washington, D.C.: American Association of Colleges for Teacher Education, 1971.

GOODWIN, W. L., and DRISCOLL, L. A. *Handbook for Measurement and Evaluation in Early Childhood Education.* San Francisco: Jossey-Bass, 1980.

GORDON, I. J., and JESTER, R. E. Techniques of observing teaching in early childhood and outcomes of particular procedures. In R. M. W. Travers (ed.), *Second Handbook of Research on Teaching.* Chicago: Rand McNally, 1973.

HABERMAN, M., and STINNETT, T. M. *Teacher Education and the Profession of Teaching.* Berkeley, Calif.: McCutcheon, 1973.

HALLIWELL, G. Kindergarten teachers and curriculum construct systems. Paper presented at the Annual Meeting of the American Educational Research Association, Los Angeles, April 1981.

HERMANOWICZ, H. J. Teacher education: A retrospective look at the future. *Journal of Teacher Education,* 1978, 29, 10–14.

HESS, R. D., and CROFT, D. J. *Teachers of Young Children,* 2nd ed. Boston: Houghton-Mifflin, 1972.

HOWEY, K., YARGER, S., and JOYCE, B. Reflections on preservice preparation: Impressions from the National Survey. *Journal of Teacher Education,* 1978, 29, 38–40.

HOWSAM, R. B., CORRIGAN, D. C., DENEMARK, G. W., and NASH, R. J. *Educating a Profession.* Washington, D.C.: American Association of Colleges for Teacher Education, 1976.

HUGHES, J. M., and SCHULTZ, F. M. *Education in America,* 4th ed. New York: Harper & Row, 1976.

HUTCHINS, E. A preschool screening program in a kindergarten. Paper presented at the Annual Meeting of the American Educational Research Association, Los Angeles, April 1981.

HUTCHINSON, B., HALL, A., and ORLOFSKY, T. *Resource Directory, Secondary and Post-Secondary Early Childhood/Child Care Programs, State of Illinois: 1978–1979.* Springfield: Illinois Office of Education, n.d.

JACKSON, P. *Life in Classrooms.* New York: Holt, Rinehart & Winston, 1968.

KATZ, L. G. Mothering and teaching: Some significant distinctions. In L. G. Katz (ed.), *Current Topics in Early Childhood Education,* Vol. 3. Norwood, N.J.: Ablex, 1980.

KING, N. R. The hidden curriculum and the socialization of kindergarten children. Unpublished doctoral dissertation, University of Wisconsin, Madison, 1976.

KING, R. *All Things Bright and Beautiful?* New York: Wiley, 1978.

KLEIN, J. W. The CDA program and the competency standards. *Conference Proceedings of the Child Development Associate Day.* July 1980.

KOHUT, S., JR. Research and the teacher: Teacher effectiveness in early childhood education. In D. G. Range and J. R. Layton (eds.), *Aspects of Early Childhood Education: Theory to Research to Practice.* New York: Academic Press, 1980.

LEWIN and ASSOCIATES. *The State of Teacher Education, 1977.* Washington, D.C.: U.S. Department of Health, Education, and Welfare, 1977.

LICKONA, T. Project Change: A person-centered approach to CBTE. *Journal of Teacher Education,* 1976, 27, 122–128.

LORTIE, D. C. *Schoolteacher: A Sociological Study.* Chicago: University of Chicago Press, 1975.

MAGOON, A. J. Constructivist approaches in educational research. *Review of Educational Research,* 1977, 47, 651–693.

MAYNARD, J. B. The CDA assessment handbook (draft). Washington, D.C.: Child Development Associate Consortium, September, 1978.

MEDIAX ASSOCIATES. Focus on program outcomes. *Newsletter, Issue I,* Westport, Conn.: Mediax Associates, June 1978.

MEYER, W. J. Staffing characteristics and child outcomes. Paper prepared for the U.S. Department of Health, Education, and Welfare, January 1977.

MORRIS, J. R. The effects of university supervision on the performance and adjustment of student teachers. *Journal of Educational Research,* 1974, 67, 358–362.

Office of Child Development. *Licensing Standards: Day and Night Care Centers.* Springfield: Illinois Department of Children and Family Services, n.d.

OYEMADE, U. J., and CHARGOIS, M. The relationship of staffing characteristics to child outcomes in day care. Paper prepared for the U.S. Department of Health, Education, and Welfare, 1977.

PECK, R. F., and TUCKER, J. A. Research on teacher education. In R. M. W. Travers (ed.), *Second Handbook of Research on Teaching.* Chicago: Rand McNally, 1973.

PETERSON, P. L. Direct instruction reconsidered. In P. L. Peterson and H. J. Walberg (eds.), *Research on Teaching: Concepts, Findings and Implications.* Berkeley, Calif.: McCutcheon, 1979.

Resolutions Committee. *A Report on Teacher Competency Testing.* Springfield: Illinois Association of School Boards, 1980.

ROSENSHINE, B. Recent research on teaching behaviors and student achievement. *Journal of Teacher Education,* 1976, 27, 61–64.

ROSENSHINE, B. Content, time and direct instruction. In P. L. Peterson and H. J. Walberg (eds.), *Research on Teaching: Concepts, Findings and Implications.* Berkeley, Calif.: McCutcheon, 1979.

ROSENSHINE, B., and FURST, N. The use of direct observation to study teaching. In R. M. W. Travers (ed.), *Second Handbook of Research on Teaching.* Chicago: Rand McNally, 1973.

ROTHENBERG, D. *Directory of Educational Programs for Adults Who Work with Children.* Washington, D.C.: National Association for the Education of Young Children, 1979.

ROUP, R., TRAVERS, J., and Goodrich, N. M. *Final Report of the National Day Care Study.* Cambridge, Mass.: Abt Associates, 1980.

SIMON, A., and BOYER, E. G. *Mirrors for Behavior: An Anthology of Classroom Observation Instruments*, Vols. 1–6. Philadelphia: Research for Better Schools, 1967.

SIMON, A., and BOYER, E. G. *Mirrors for Behavior: An Anthology of Classroom Observation Instruments*, Vols. 7–14. Philadelphia: Research for Better Schools, 1970.

SMITH, L. M., and GEOFFREY, W. *The Complexities of the Urban Classroom*. New York: Holt, Rinehart & Winston, 1968.

SOAR, R. S., and SOAR, R. M. Attempts to identify measures of teacher effectiveness from four studies. *Journal of Teacher Education*, 1976, 27, 261–267.

SPODEK, B. Staff requirements in early childhood education. In I. J. Gordon (ed.), *Early Childhood Education*, 71st yearbook of the National Society for the Study of Education. Chicago: University of Chicago Press, 1972.

SPODEK, B. (ed.). *Teacher Education*. Washington, D.C.: National Association for the Education of Young Children, 1974.

SPODEK, B. From the president. *Young Children*, 1977, 32, 23.

TAYLOR, W. *Research and Reform in Teacher Education*. Windsor, England: NFER Publishing Co., 1978.

TEMPLIN, P. Self-evaluation in teacher education. Unpublished doctoral dissertation, University of Illinois, 1979.

TURNER, R. L. An overview of research in teacher education. In K. Ryan (ed.), *Teacher Education*, 74th yearbook of the National Society for the Study of Education. Chicago: University of Chicago Press, 1975.

WARD, E. H., and associates. The Child Development Associate Consortium's assessment system. *Young Children*, 1976, 31, 244–254.

WHIPPLE, G. M. (ed.). *Preschool and Parental Education*. 28th yearbook of the National Society for the Study of Education. Bloomington, Ill.: Public Schools Publication, 1929.

CHAPTER 18

Parent Involvement in Early Childhood Education

Alice Sterling Honig

ABOUT TWO DECADES AGO, research findings began to confirm the dimensions of the learning risks for children from poor families. Heber, Denver, and Conry (1968) documented cumulative decrements in developmental scores of children raised in environments characterized by poverty and low parental education. When maternal IQ was under 80, children's IQs at successive ages revealed a progressive drop from 95 on infant tests to about 80 by age four and about 65 by age 14. Heber (1978) observed that "the mentally retarded mother residing in the slum creates a special environment for her offspring which is distinctly different from that created by her next-door neighbor of normal intelligence" (p. 45). Ramey and Campbell (1982) report scores for children of mothers with a tenth-grade education level and mean IQ of 82. At six, twelve, and eighteen months, the Infant Bayley MDI scores were respectively 102.2, 105.5, and 89.1. Subsequent Stanford-Binet scores at twenty-four and thirty-six months were 80.6 and 84.2, respectively.

Such findings, in conjunction with the civil rights movement for equality of opportunity of all citizens and in concert with a new conceptualization of the plasticity of early intelligence and its receptivity to environmental nourishment, galvanized energetic public efforts in the decade of the 1960s on behalf of young children. A variety of experimental programs to prevent or to stem intellectual declines among the young who live in poverty environments were funded. Their goals were to enhance children's learning opportunities and chances for school success.

Many of the new early childhood education programs proposed and carried out exciting, creative curricula for enriching the learning careers of preschoolers but little attention was given to the influence of what has been called "the hidden curriculum of the home" (Strodtbeck, 1965) or to the possible lack of congruence between the efforts of school and home. Once in school, scores of experimental children declined somewhat. Scores of control youngsters, without previous school experience, began to rise as they, too, now encountered learning opportunities. This pattern of "washout of effect" was found for programs that had been well-staffed and well-run and had adhered to very different theories of child learning. Thus, the pattern was found for Schaefer's home tutorial program for infants (Schaefer & Aaronson, 1977), Caldwell's and Richmond's (1968) enriched day-care program with high cognitive-language component, and Bereiter and Englemann's (1966) group program that emphasized rote drill methods. Follow-up assessments revealed slow erosion of gains after the programs ended (Honig, Lally & Horsburgh, 1982).

So persistent was the pattern of failure to maintain IQ and language gains when parental involvement was minimal that child development experts began to rethink their initial premises that early education, by focusing on the child alone, could compensate for grinding poverty of environment, and that a teacher singlehandedly could sustain learning skills of disadvantaged young children without the support and meaningful efforts of those other, far more salient, teachers back at home—the parents. Schaefer, whose tutors worked one-on-one with toddlers at home until the children were three years old, saw the children's IQ gains erode within three years after the program had ended. Schaefer became convinced that efforts must focus on family-oriented rather than child-centered programs. Schaefer has become an eloquent advocate of family-based programs that can:

- increase the level of consciousness of parents;
- make them aware of their importance in their children's lives;
- help them obtain the information they need;
- provide the help they need to be more effective with their children; and
- make them aware of community resources they can use in educating their children.

Honig (1979) has suggested that a Parent's "Bill of Rights" should include rights to:

- knowledge about child development—both emotional and cognitive;
- observation skills for more effective parenting;
- alternative strategies for problem prevention and discipline;
- knowledge about how to use a home for learning experiences for children;
- language tools and story-reading skills;
- awareness of being the most important early teachers of their children.

Parental Process Variables

During the time that preschool programs proliferated, evidence from other research sharpened awareness of the functions of family milieu, socialization patterns, and socioeconomic conditions that could either support or fail to optimize the growth and educational environment provided for the young.

Process variables refer to intellectual expectations and facilitations of parents and are contrasted with demographic status variables, such as parental education or income. Quality of maternal language, amount of reading and conversation, cultural level of home discussions, and opportunity for the child to learn new words had multiple correlations of .76 and .80 respectively with child intelligence and child achievement. Bradley and Caldwell (1976) have also reported impressive correlations of later child IQ and language scores with maternal involvement assessed when the child was two years old. Appropriate play materials and emotional and verbal responsivity of mother correlated significantly with the child's Stanford-Binet IQ scores at fifty-four months. In summarizing such correlational studies, Schaefer (1972) concluded that "children's test scores were much more related to degree of parent interest than to variations in the quality of schools" (p. 234).

Investigations into parent–child exchanges pointed up differences in the abilities of parents to teach their children effectively. Maternal teaching styles varied widely from limited, reactive teaching (with heavy use of control and demands) to effective parental use of suggestions, instructions, modeling, and pointing out critical perceptual cues. Bing (1963) emphasized that a democratic home atmosphere as well as maternal acceleration of intellectual achievement was significantly associated with high achievement of children by the fifth grade.

Research across Socioeconomic Class

Meticulous research by Hess and Shipman (1965) demonstrated differences in maternal teaching strategies of black mothers from different socioeconomic groups. The mothers were asked to teach their four-year-olds how to sort blocks by different attributes and how to create geometric designs with an Etch-A-Sketch toy. The children's task success and IQ could be predicted from maternal teaching behaviors. Low-social-class mothers offered "predetermined solutions and few alternatives for consideration and choices" (p. 869). A decade later, Bee and colleagues (1975) were even more specific in pointing up the social class differences in teaching strategies which support or impede problem-solving success. The middle class mother tended to allow her child to work at his own pace. She offered many general structuring suggestions on how to search for a solution to the problem. She confirmed the child's correct actions so that he could acquire general methods to use in future problem-solving solutions. In contrast, the lower-class mother as a rule did not encourage the child to attend to the basic features of the problem. Her suggestions were highly specific, did not emphasize strategies, and seldom required a reply from the child. By nonverbal intrusions into the child's attempts, she often deprived the child of the opportunity to solve the problem on his own.

Research within Social Class

Research within social class as well as across social class confirmed the crucial nature of family variables in relation to learning progress of children. Resnick

(1973) found that the amount of conversation in the home, particularly talk directed toward the child, related significantly to the child's performance on tests. Yet, all families in his project were low-income. Wolf (1964) and Davè (1963) also related family process variables to child achievement.

The Relation between Affect and Cognitive Competence

Another important research area helped to focus parent involvement efforts more broadly on the total development of the child. Parents are not only the first and most consistently available teachers of their young children, but they also provide the emotional base of security and the motivational roots that nourish exploratory curiosity.

An infant well attached to a nurturant parent who is sensitive to infant cues and signals and who offers baby floor freedom to explore living space tends to be developmentally advanced (Ainsworth, 1979).

Sroufe (1979) has reported that securely attached babies, when tested in toddlerhood, proved to be more persistent problem solvers. They had fewer temper tantrums and did not give up as readily as poorly attached tots. Moreover, they tended to use the parent as a resource to help them solve problems more often than poorly attached children. Thus, if parent involvers were to focus only on cognitive aspects of parental teaching, important emotional aspects that support learning might be neglected. The attachment literature suggests that loving attachment between tutor and child in the family situation sets the occasion for success in attending to learning problems and in consolidating learning experiences in order to solve problems.

Positive Parenting Practices

Even under adverse socioeconomic circumstances, many families manage to rear children as competent, well-adjusted learners. Such families give clues for ways in which parent involvement programs can work to support such efforts. Swan and Stavros (1973) interviewed parents of low-income black five- and six-year-old children who were effective classroom learners. These children got along well with peers and teachers. They exhibited sustained, self-motivated learning styles. Parents described these children in a very positive and competent light. The parents fostered independence and encouraged the children to help in the home. They read to their children and talked about a wide range of topics.

Positive parenting dimensions were also pinpointed by Carew, Chan, and Halfar (1976). Their naturalistic home observations revealed what family variables (such as daily reading to infants and toddlers, restricting television, and arranging learning experiences) correlated with preschooler competence across social class. Honig (1979, pp. 19–20) provides a summary of positive parenting practices that enhance child competence.

Family Involvement as the Magic Key to Early Education Success

Suddenly, parent involvement became the indispensible ingredient for engendering optimal learning habits in children and for sustaining the accomplishments of enrichment programs. Some experts concluded that for teachers "to work with children alone is to invite failure and frustration" (Biber, 1970, p. 1). Others agreed with Chilman (1974) that basic income maintenance for poor people "must undergird any program that seeks to deal effectively with poverty and disadvantaged parents and children" (p. 459). Chilman urged the need for individual counseling, supportive services, and participation in the school.

The new thrust to involve parents resulted in federally mandated guidelines for adding a parent involvement component to already existing preschool programs such as Head Start. Whenever an agency provides day care for forty or more children, the Federal Interagency Guidelines state that there must be a Policy Advisory Committee, the composition of which must include not less than 50 percent parents or parent representatives.

Varieties of Parent Involvement Models

It is difficult to capture the richness of national efforts. Gordon's (1971) analysis of specific programs suggests a way of listing conditions, variables, and parameters of a program in a column on the left side of a sheet. Program names are listed horizontally at the top of the page. An X can indicate the presence of that particular variable for a program. Such an array permits ready visual comparison of the qualities, comprehensiveness, and unique aspects of different programs. Table 18–1 presents a sample of the kind of molecular analysis this method permits. Only three programs have been "diagnosed" in this example. Certainly, more variables can be added, and presence or absence noted, depending on the interests of the program analyst.

This presentation will not be a detailed description but will follow a more descriptive taxonomy developed by Honig (1979) and will refer to exemplary programs under each model. Some programs have such a broad focus that they will undoubtedly fit under more than one rubric.

Programs directed to special populations where aspects of several models are incorporated into services will be described separately and outcome data when available will be summarized.

Home Visitation Model

The theory behind home visitation emphasizes the continuing impact that a parent can have as a support for and facilitator of the child's learning long after other program supports are terminated. Gordon (1971) pioneered the develop-

TABLE 18–1. Parent Involvement Program Variables: Presence or Absence

	FDRP	CFRP	Levenstein Mother–Child Home Program
Length of program service			
about one year			X
two years			X
preschool years	X	X	
beyond preschool years		X	
Bilingual staff			
Theoretical rationale for curriculum	X		X
(for example, Piaget, Erikson)			
Special services for parents:			
toy lending or giving	X		X
crisis or hot line			
Retreat house for family weekends			
Parent group meetings	X		
home visits with focus on parent	X	X	X
nutrition service	X	X	
medical services	X	X	
liaisons with community agencies	X	X	
family trips: to zoo, etcetera	X		
Provision of formula, diapers, and so on, to families			
Frequency of family contact			
daily			
weekly	X		X
several times per year			
as needed		X	
Use of paraprofessional family worker	X		X
Frequency of staff training			
several times per week	X		
weekly			X
several times per year		X	
Ages of children in families served			
infants–toddlers	X	X	X
preschoolers	X	X	
school age children		X	
Special population served			
ethnic groups	X	X	X
teen mothers	X	X	
fathers		X	
abusing parents		X	
handicapped children		X	
low-income families	X	X	X
Educational group program for children			
parents assist in the classroom	X		
Goals specified			
for parents	X	X	X
for children	X	X	X
for staff	X	X	X

(cont.)

TABLE 18.1 *Cont.*

	FDRP	CFRP	LEVENSTEIN MOTHER–CHILD HOME PROGRAM
Language and/or cognitive assessments			
for children	X	X	X
for families	X		
Socioemotional assessments			
for children	X		X
for parents	X		
Demographic data available	X	X	X
Use of audio-visuals, such as TV programs			
Follow-up assessments after program ends	X		X
Liaison provided between families and public schools	X		
Parent advisory board	X	X	
Control groups			
randomized assignment			X
matched controls	X	X	
no controls			
Replications			X

ment of the home visitation model, and there are now well over 200 such programs in operation. Gordon envisaged that by using trained paraprofessionals, costs could be curtailed and greater empathy and close rapport could be established between the worker and the low-income parents served. Such rapport would enhance the probability that the home visitor would be accepted as a model by the parents. In this project, the primary focus was on teaching the mother learning games during a weekly home visit. The games were based on Piagetian sensory-motor competencies, and a copy of a new game was left in the home weekly, so that the mother could try out the learning activities whenever she found time. Activities were ordered by area of competence, such as object-permanence games, and were graded by level of difficulty (Lally & Gordon, 1977).

Significantly higher general quotients for trained infants were found on the Griffith's Mental Development Scale for 127 trained versus eighty-four control infants. Trained infants also scored significantly higher on personal social skills; hand-eye coordination, and hearing and speech skills. Testing was done between one and two years of age.

Lally (1969) has documented both the positive strengths and the pitfalls encountered. Some of the problems encountered in training were:

1. difficulty in getting abstract ideas communicated both from training staff to parent educators and from parent educators to mothers;
2. missionary zeal at project commencement which turns to boredom or disillusionment as parents show reluctance to become involved with infants or as infants fail to show rapid intellectual growth;

3. rigid use of the training materials without regard to whether an activity was far above or far below the level of the child's present functioning;
4. reluctance to accept responsibilities for filling out weekly home visit forms and engage in other research data collection and record-keeping efforts;
5. difficulty in accepting freedom to program own time and still be responsible for making all home visits;
6. lack of patience with some families who did not cooperate;
7. resentment that professionals would never understand all the hardships and difficulties that can happen in the field;
8. a desire to work directly with the infants rather than with the mothers.

These problems do not negate the valuable contribution to family involvement that the paraprofessionals made. Their insights into family difficulty and their ability to help some parents feel at ease with and accepting toward the project were often remarkable. Staff problems were dealt with in a variety of ways. Project goals and requirements were re-emphasized. Role playing and role switching were used as techniques to increase empathy among paraprofessionals, parents, and professionals.

Gordon's projects established the viability and vigor of the home visitation model and its unique effectiveness when family difficulty with transportation or family reluctance to venture out into "institutional" settings may effectively close out a family from receiving needed service.

SERVICE DELIVERY

Home visitation has since become a widespread method of delivery of support for families with the goal of enhancing early development through work with the parent. Home visits may also serve as an adjunct to group services provided primarily for children, as in Head Start programs in many communities.

Honig (1979) has summarized the process of home delivery in such programs:

> Through demonstration and practice, the visitors teach mothers at home how to provide facilitating sensorimotor experiences and language games for their infants. Particularly emphasized are ways in which parents can use daily interactions and caregiving situations with infants to create learning occasions and opportunities. Exercises and games appropriate to the level of development of the baby are taught each week; sample fact sheets describing the purpose of each new game and ways to carry out the game are left with mothers. The home visitor focuses on the parent as the important person to work with rather than the baby [Honig, 1979, p. 16].

EDUCATIONAL EMPHASIS

Educational programs for parents are often delivered as the integral component for a demonstration research project. The Ypsilanti-Carnegie Infant Education

Project (Lambie, Bond & Weikart, 1974) demonstrated that a Piagetian-based curriculum could be implemented in the home for low-income parents and their infants in order to enhance the mother's ability to optimize her infant's cognitive development.

The goal of Levenstein's Verbal Interaction Project (1977) was to prevent educational disadvantage by aiding the two-year-old's early cognitive growth within the family. The mother-child home program was designed to strengthen parents in their conviction and know-how to be verbally active teachers of their own toddlers. Levenstein has stressed the importance of training and supervision in the success of her home visitors who are called toy demonstrators. Her program is very cost-effective ($400 per child first year; $550 in eleven replications) and securely places responsibility for the learning process with parents not project personnel (Levenstein, 1972).

The toy demonstrator's role requires development of a warm relationship with the mother and child, demonstration of verbal stimulation techniques, and the development of maximum mother participation. The toy demonstrator visits each pair twice a week for a half-hour home session. On the first visit each week she brings either a toy or a book which she uses as Verbal Interaction Stimulus Material (VISM). She introduces the VISM to the child, encouraging it to talk by asking questions, listening to answers, and replying. At the same time, she draws the mother into the session by modeling verbal stimulation techniques, which the mother then imitates. She also encourages the mother to read and play with the child between home sessions. During the year, eleven toys and twelve books are brought to the home to stimulate the mother–child verbal interaction.

The model program was run with professionals, and a mean IQ gain of about 17 points was found. The second year, trained paraprofessionals, recipients of the program themselves, were toy demonstrators. Mean IQ gain was 11 points. Replications show that "satisfactory IQ scores were retained by program graduates at least into first grade" (Madden, Levenstein & Levenstein, 1976, p. 1024). At the end of a two-year program for replication, the treated children had a Stanford-Binet score of 104.8 and the control children scored 100.9. These replication results do not suggest as much of the promise as the model program, possibly because many more of the original families had fathers present in the home and were not on welfare.

HOME VISITATION: A VARIED AGENDA

When the home visitation model is used in connection with a research and demonstration project, the process generally includes assessment of family needs, planning, implementation—including role modeling by home visitors for parents on how to teach activities (which may be jointly planned by the worker and parents), and follow-up procedures.

Sometimes, a home visit includes several aspects. There may be a brief period of prescribed activities aimed at the target child in the family at the same time that the parent is taught a given lesson to be carried out with the child. There may be a period of group activities for other children in the home. Often, there is a period in which the home visitor discusses some of the family's needs as expressed by parents. Child development information, including nutrition and health information, is given. Other information relative to family needs may be supplied, such as how to contact the nearest family planning clinic or how to find low-cost legal services.

Forrester (1972) describes such a home visitation project, the DARCEE program at George Peabody College. In weekly visits, mothers were provided with the coping skills and assurance they needed to handle the job of being their preschool child's teacher at the end of a year of program participation.

EDUCATIONAL PROGRAMS: PITFALLS

Sometimes, unless certain crucial fundamentals, such as establishing friendly, trusting relations are accomplished, the cognitive aspects of program may prove undeliverable. In Adkins's (1971) program in Hawaii, home visitors were to deliver specific language or mathematics curricular lessons for parents to boost the learning of their children who were enrolled in preschool projects emphasizing such areas. Many mothers simply were not at home time and again, despite carefully made appointments. The parents assigned to one home visitor, however, were home and available. That worker had made sure that she always took time to listen to family problems and to develop a helpful and friendly relationship with the mothers she served. There is little sense in assessing the "impact" of a program when most home visits cannot be made. Only as they feel that they are cared about will many families begin to give back the active learning and participation desired.

Weikart (1969) has pointed out that the home teacher is in a position of low power in the home and must adjust to the pre-eminent position of the parent in her or his own home. Certainly, not all classroom teachers will qualify as home teachers under these conditions.

CLINICAL AND MENTAL HEALTH EMPHASIS

Some home visitation projects are more concerned with provision of emotional support and the building of self-confidence in families than they are with educational curricula. Van Doorninck (1980) reports on a project in which there was an attempt at a parametric variation of the *intensity* of supportive parent involvement efforts. Pregnant mothers were assigned randomly to one of three treatment groups: (1) routine services of the local health department clinics; (2) home visits weekly through the baby's first birthday by trained visitors; and (3) home visits plus invitations to parent group meetings held every two weeks during the same time period. The purpose of the home visitor was "to provide support to parents, especially mothers, so as to help them cope with their own lives and enhance their abilities to care for their children" (p. 59).

No significant treatment effects were found for measures such as maternal attachment, maternal perception of self-confidence as a mother, use of community helping services, or mother's educational efforts for herself. The project staff reported that about one-third of the full-treatment group seemed to have little or no overall benefit. They speculated that lack of hard data might be due to the overall excellent level of existing community health services for mothers. The project continued only during the first postnatal year and on the average no more than two home visits of 60 minutes each were made per month. Few mothers attended parent group meetings more than a few times.

Certainly, sensory-motor tests of infant development rarely reflect rearing milieu differences before one year, the time at which this program was terminated. The lack of any specific educational goals may also be implied in the lack of "hard" effects found. Some families need long-term efforts of support before family involvement with project goals becomes visible. Sometimes, the effects of parent support may not show up on maternal measures during the program. Child abuse rates or school difficulties may ensue several years after such supports are withdrawn. Parent involvement may take long commitment to some families.

A clinical model which presents no outcome data but is characterized by an interesting theoretical rubric is the UCLA Maternal Behavior Progression Program (Bromwich, 1976). The initial emphasis is on enhancing the quality of mother–infant interaction. This goal requires constant assessment of the mother's feelings toward and skills with the baby. The six levels of Maternal Behavior Progression which the staff or team assists a mother to achieve are: (1) mother enjoys infant; (2) mother is a sensitive observer of her infant; (3) mother engages in a quality and quantity of interaction with her infant that is mutually satisfying and provides opportunity for the development of attachment and the beginning of a system of communication; (4) mother demonstrates an awareness of materials, activities, and experiences suitable for the infant's current stage of development; (5) mother initiates new play activities based on those modeled for her; and (6) mother independently generates a wide range of developmentally appropriate experiences, interesting to the infant and adaptive to changing needs. Bromwich objects to parent intervention models that teach a mother how to play with baby. She feels that optimization of parenting can best be approached by enhancing the mother–infant relationship and quality of interaction at the basic level first and then building maternal confidence level by level. Thus, Bromwich combines clinical plus educational components in a progressive model that evolves as the parent shows signs of being ready for different aspects of this home visitation model.

The emphasis on observation skills is fundamental to a parent program. They ensure project sensitivity to present level of parents' understanding and parents' involvement.

The Clinical Model with Abusive Parents

Many programs are designed to help child-abusing families with home visitation. Child abuse is epidemic at about 2,000 cases per day in the United States. Some projects use two home visitors—one to support the parents and be a parent friend and advocate and another to work on child development activities.

Fraiberg (1980) used a kitchen therapy intervention model to reach abusive mothers of infants. A skilled, highly trained therapist continues weekly with home visits to build a trusting, caring relation with the neglecting and/or abusing parent. Only as the therapist reaches deeply into the earlier childhood experiences of the young mother do changes occur. As the young mother begins to feel not just talk about her past rage, pain, and grief, she also begins to feel with and for her baby. She may suddenly hear that her baby has been crying for twenty minutes in the living room; and she may run and pick up and comfort the infant.

The home visitation model has proved successful in clinical programs that deal with cases of disturbed parenting and failure-to-thrive babies. A succinct synopsis of a variety of such clinical infant programs, their research goals, and the assessment instruments they are currently using, has been published by the National Center for Clinical Infant Programs (1979).

Home Visits and the Handicapped Child

Many state education departments have worked hard to help teachers of handicapped children look at parents as a source of stimulation for the children. The most common approach is to have the parent educator come into the home and work with both mothers and their handicapped children. At the University of Wisconsin, counseling as well as practical guidance is provided for parents of blind infants. The home visitor focuses on helping a parent establish a personal relationship with her blind infant and showing the parent how to interest her child in such activities as discovering, grasping objects, and crawling. At the Shield of David program in the Bronx, New York, a home visitor worked with the parent of a retarded two-and-a-half-year old on (1) selecting a more varied diet; (2) suggesting exercises to use with her child on the playground; (3) toilet training; (4) how to associate articles of clothing with specific body parts; and (5) how to make contact with other children (IMC Reports, 1973).

Frost (1975) has commented that members of the family with a child at risk for developmental delay reinforce one another in caregiving attitudes and practices. To be successful, the parents must recognize and accept the child's problems. Helping the mother to learn positive caregiving practices may be less important for what it does for the handicapped child than what it does for the parent. Home-centered training for handicapped or retarded children does not divorce the child from his strongest emotional ties and his most diverse models—the family members. Nor is there any problem of "transfer of training" from an institutional setting to the home. Frost reports that "researchers are still unsure about persisting effects of long-term intervention. Short-term effects are positive and significant" (p. 304).

The Wisconsin Portage Project (Shearer and Shearer, 1972) provides parents with activities for multihandicapped preschoolers. Most of the families served live in rural areas so that the home visitation model is more feasible and useful. Parents are taught how to write a behavioral prescription and how to keep daily frequency records of behaviors being learned. They are taught what to teach, what to reinforce, and how to shape behaviors through the technique of initially providing and then "fading out" reinforcements. Each child is assigned individual weekly goals which can be achieved within the week regardless of severity of handicap. The parent is left with written materials and encouraged to carry out each acitivity several times daily and record what happens.

Possible Ethical Problems in Home Visitations

Levenstein (1979) has analyzed the ethical problems of the home-based intervention model. Because home visitors are generally so strongly and lovingly committed to their work, it may be difficult for a family to think of a reason to resist participation. Also, the degree to which confidentiality about family matters as well as minimal intrusiveness into family privacy can be managed may be problematic. Skill mismatch may occur when family lifestyles or problems require more knowledge and ability than a home visitor can provide. The right to worker acknowledgment of a need for further help or professional adjunct services may be a healthy item for a home-based program to keep in mind.

Home Visitation with Linkages to Other Program Provisions

The most comprehensive home visitation model, Home Start, was launched as an alternative to provision of Head Start services through group child care. The objectives of the Home Start program are to strengthen parents' capacity for facilitating the development of their children and for direct involvement in their children's education. Home Start workers provide supports not only for early childhood education but also for good nutrition, use of social services, budgeting, use of medical and dental facilities, creation of social networks for families, obtaining scraps and materials so parents can create toys and learning activities, and ways that household activities can be turned into learning games. With Home Start, direct and optimal benefits can accrue to all children in the family, not just to the target child of preschool age. Home Start children score comparably with Head Start youngsters, and program costs are about the same (Collins, 1980).

Two of the three federally funded Parent Child Development Centers in the United States have also used home teaching as an active aid to program for children. In the New Orleans PCDC, parents are provided with a spiral-bound notebook entitled "In the Beginning: A Parent Guide of Activities and Experiences from Birth to Six Months" (Rabinowitz, Weiner & Jackson, 1973). Simple activities, puzzles in text, easy "tests," and observation activities all help the parent to become a more effective child rearer and teacher.

The Houston, Texas, PCDC uses home visitation for the first year of the program in order to build basic trust with the Mexican-American families served. Mothers are offered lessons in English, car-driving, and domestic skills as well as child development. After a year, the children are brought into group care. The home visitation component has served to create a secure base of mutually shared goals in a trusting atmosphere for branching out to other forms of family enrichment for children. Parents in the second year of the program participated daily in classroom activities with their children.

In the Birmingham, Alabama, PCDC (Lasater et al., 1975), mother–child pairs attend the center together. After fifteen months on a part-time basis, the mother becomes eligible for Model Mother (teaching mother) status, which means a regular 40-hour work week in the preschool program. Outcomes for the children are significantly positive. Stanford-Binet scores for program boys and girls at four years of age are 99.5 and 104.2, compared with randomly assigned control group boys and girls who score at 85.5 and 90.2, respectively.

Parents Participate as Aides and Teachers in Group Care Settings

The reasons for the movement toward parent involvement are often based on the experiences of dedicated professionals trying to work exclusively with children. Poulton and Poulton (1979) found in a poor Yorkshire, England, community, for example, that after the first eighteen months, "a more important factor in early education than curricular design and approaches was the degree of understanding and preparation of parents as educators of their children" (p. 74). More and more sophisticated ways were found to involve mothers and fathers in the education of their children. These children did better on the English PPVT after one year of such parent involvement.

Unless the parents could be shown their educative role with their children, the Poultons found that there was little chance of maintaining any momentum gained through the children's early childhood education experiences. Introductory family visits were very important in establishing trust in a future partnership. Soon parents made arrangements to spend an afternoon once or twice a week at the preschool.

FOLLOW THROUGH

Under the auspices of Dr. Ira Gordon, one of the twenty-one planned variation Follow Through models mandates participation of parents in their children's elementary school classrooms (Datta, 1973).

Mothers as Models for Other Mothers

The Sumner Mobile Preschool Program in Syracuse, New York, is a program in which mothers serve as teachers in their own home with the supervision of a trained teacher. The local teacher chauffeurs a few children from the neighborhood surrounding the local elementary school to the home of a neighborhood mother. Gradually, as toys, activities, concepts of numbers and counting, and taking turns, for example, are modeled by the supervisor, the home mother comes to take over more and more responsibility for teaching activities with the group of preschoolers who attend in her home for a half-day.

Gordon and Guinagh's (1969) Back Yard Center program had a similar concept. Mothers in whose homes preschool activities occurred for a small group of children were employed as helpers to the backyard center directors. These directors themselves were paraprofessionals who had served earlier as teachers in Gordon's home visitation program.

Stimulus-Response Theory and Parent Training

Juniper Garden Preschool in Kansas City, Missouri, was a token-reinforcement preschool for culturally deprived four-year-olds. With the premise that, in the long run, more child progress could be achieved if parents of the children were involved, the staff began to provide lessons for mothers on how to teach their preschoolers. The thirty mothers chosen were characterized as from "upwardly mobile poverty families." Each mother was rewarded with dinnerware each week for coming to preschool with her child. Every day, each mother at first retired to a booth with materials to teach her child. Initial findings were that "the mothers were poor teachers. They used almost no praise or approval, and they showed little grasp of the technique of attacking a complex problem by starting with its simplest form" (Risley, 1970, p. 145).

Changes in the program were then introduced. The mothers were given instructions on how to start with the simplest tasks. They were to praise a child for each correct response, such as naming an object pictured. Mothers were then paired with children other than their own. Threats to children subsequently decreased. Teachers kept records of when a mother praised. They flashed a red light, mounted where the mother could see it. Mothers were asked to press a foot pedal whenever a child answered a question correctly. After a mother had learned how to praise another child, she again was allowed to work with her own child. Mothers also worked as classroom teachers. In unstructured situations in the classroom, mothers found some difficulty in putting principles of positive reinforcement into practice. Staff continued work with the principle that mothers were to reinforce with attention only that behavior that they wanted the children to continue. From the beginning to the end of the program, the children's PPVT IQs rose from a mean of 69 to 87.

Parent Group Meetings

One of the best known methods of involving parents in the education of their children is to invite them to parent group meetings, usually at a school which the child attends.

Programs which involve parents of preschoolers in groups have sometimes opted for cognitive emphasis, for example, on teaching mothers how to improve children's language skills. Other parent groups have focused on:

- increasing parental self-awareness
- knowledge of ways to motivate children
- expression of parental needs
- home management skills
- making and learning to use inexpensive home learning materials
- increasing self-esteem in the family
- helping parents acquire job skills.

Toy Lending and Demonstrating

One of the most widely used models for helping parents use toys to teach their children was created by Nimnicht et al. (1971) at the Far West Parent/Child Toy Library Program. Parents are involved in eight two-hour sessions, usually meeting once a week. Child development topics are discussed and a new toy is introduced at each meeting. The toy as a means to boost children's problem-solving skills is demonstrated, discussed, and illustrated in films. Parents at the group meeting role-play with each other the many ways they could use a toy to promote thinking and problem solving. They use these ideas later at home with the toy to help the child make discoveries and increase his skills.

Stevens (1973) has reported that an eleven-week program of small group parent meetings which included toy/book demonstrations and lending produced significant IQ gains for children of project participants. He suggests that the parent consultants would have been even more effective had they provided feedback to a parent during his or her interaction with a child in the home.

Language Development

"Teach Your Child to Talk" (Pushaw, 1969) is a parent group meeting plan to help parents encourage language development from infancy onward through the preschool years. Parent workshops are carefully programmed with slides, cassette-illustrated vocalization examples, and a manual for workshop leaders.

Programs that involve parents in their child's school learning may be particularly crucial for culturally different or non-English-speaking children. A variety of commercial programs exists to establish such linkages between home and school experiences. One such is Amanecer (A Multicultural Action Network for Early Childhood Education) developed in San Antonio, Texas. Based on the theories of Piaget, Montessori, and Maslow, the model was developed as part of the Head Start strategy for Spanish-speaking children. Teachers are helped to initiate parent contacts, plan parent learning activities, organize parent projects, and create a culturally sensitive learning environment. The goal is to increase the process by which parents become valuable resources in planning and implementing the curriculum for young children.

PARENT GROUP MEETINGS IN COMBINATION WITH SCHOOL EXPERIENCES

Parent workshops or group metings are often inaugurated as supportive services to ensure at-home continuity of teaching with the learnings of the child in an educational setting. Karnes and colleagues (1969) provided a mothers' group meeting along with an enriched preschool for the children. However, no significant added effect of the parent group was found beyond score enhancement found for preschool alone. In contrast, Gray (1971) has reported encouraging results for mother participation plus child preschool experience. IQs of children whose mothers were in the parent group remained relatively stable after two years; IQs of children with preschool only decreased further during that same time span.

Boger and colleagues (1974) arranged for groups of mothers to meet in twelve weekly two-hour sessions with their children's teacher in a developmental or structured language workshop or in a placebo group workshop. The mothers who participated in the specific language interaction groups increased their own language skills. Their children also increased in language skills and had a more positive perception of their mother's view of them compared to placebo treatment group children. This program has been replicated with rural as well as urban parents.

"Education for Parenthood" recently has served as a parenting program curriculum for many Head Start project parenting groups. The program provides three learning modules: working with children; seeing development; and family and society. Parents gain insight not only into children's development but also into themselves as learners. Keeping a journal and learning to observe children are program techniques that help sensitize parents to their children.

CULTURAL DIVERSITY

Lane (1975), the director of the NICE (Nurseries in Cross-Cultural Education) program in California, was an early believer in the importance of parent participation in the classroom. Lane further advanced the NICE program goal of helping parents to be more effective teachers of their own and others' children by creating training classes taught by the director and staff members of NICE. The classes met for two hours once a week for fifteen consecutive weeks. Each participant parent was required to spend one day per week at the nursery school trying out ideas discussed in the class. Each parent was required to learn to observe and record the behavior of a child and read the report in class. In addition, parents shared their backgrounds, their dreams for their children, feelings about their own childhood, and problems they had with their children and with each other. The parents drew much closer together, although they came from quite different backgrounds.

What were the outcomes? Mothers were judged by the staff to be competent enough to operate the school classes one day per week with the assistance of graduate students. Staff used this time for meetings. Several parents developed a degree of competency that qualified them as teacher aides. Parents became involved in assessing the program of the public schools to get to know the types of class programs their preschoolers would soon be entering. Parents developed considerable confidence in their own resources.

PUBLIC SCHOOL AND PARENTS

Public school systems, too, often use parents as supports for children's learning. The Benton Harbor Area schools in Michigan have formed a home-school-community partnership, in a Title I project called Project Help. This model provides for a group of teachers to design together with parents a series of activities that will work to support children's school learning in their community. Activities are written recipe-style on a single piece of paper. They are short, easy activities that use kitchen items or living room furniture, for example. These lessons build on school learnings.

There are special advantages to the model when parents participate creatively in planning for experiences in the schools in which their children are already enrolled. As parents learn early education skills, they must examine their goals and values concerning children in order to develop curriculum, select facilities and equipment, and even hire teachers (Charnley & Myre, 1977). Also, "the opportunity to meet and share experiences with other mothers in similar situations provides parents with social contact, emotional support, intellectual stimulation, . . . and a sense of fulfillment and self-esteem to counteract the physical and psychological isolation frequently experienced by mothers" (p. 19).

Parents in Job Training

In Heber's program (1978) in Milwaukee, the parent involvement component consisted of carefully supervised on-the-job training experiences in laundry and dietician aide work. Parent group meetings helped to build self-confidence as these mothers of low IQ and low income struggled with each others' help as well as with training to increase job and communication skills. The remarkable child IQ gains after five years in the program, however, cannot be attributed only to the parental program since the child development component was all-embracing from infancy onward and was most carefully programmed to meet the children's needs in all curricular areas.

HANDICAPPED CHILDREN AND PARENT GROUPS

Parent education groups are often active in programs for handicapped children (Levitt & Cohen, 1979). Methods of encouraging parents to attend meetings include providing transportation, paying for babysitters, writing or calling parents in advance of meeting, and arranging small groups for those who seem uncomfortable at larger meetings. Other group techniques include showing parents videotapes of their interactions with their children and encouraging a parent-child album (Riley, 1977).

The Portland Center for Hearing and Speech taught parents of language-delayed children in weekly sessions. Parents observed their children's language enrichment program. The meetings had two purposes: (1) to discuss information about home management of communications problems; and (2) to provide emotional support for parents. The children's progress during their eight-week summer session typically revealed an average of about six to nine months gain in general language functioning and in receptive vocabulary. What parts the parents' efforts played and what part the individualized curriculum played in such gains is not discernible, nor is it known how long these gains lasted. What is clear is that parents rated their own knowledge of factors affecting special problems higher after their group experience (Weybright et al., 1979).

Some programs for handicapped children use a wide variety of parent involvement techniques. The Delayed Development Project in Stockton, California (Jew, 1974), for example, provides home visitation for children under eighteen months. From that age on, babies are bused into a program with individual therapy and small group activities. Parents spend one morning a week in school with their tots. "Dad's Day" classes are held on Saturdays. Evening group meetings with a psychologist allow parents to support each other as they discuss their fears, hopes, anxieties, and problems.

Bricker and Bricker (1971), in their program for integration of Down's Syndrome and normal preschoolers have consistently involved parents in care-giving activities toward behavioral goals. Bassin & Drovetta (1976) report that parent-to-parent contact is particularly helpful when trained parents help those who are newly facing the problems that ensue with the birth of a handicapped child. Their St. Louis, Missouri, program trains parents to help each other with jargon-free explanations about disabilities, helpful hints on home training, and assistance in locating community resources.

Teenage Parenting: The Problems and the Programs

In 1979, 29 percent of births to white teenagers and 83 percent of births to black teenagers occurred outside of marriage (*New York Times*, October 26, 1981). One of five babies born in the United States today is born to a teenage girl. At Johns Hopkins University, Dr. Hardy and her associates found that among children sixteen years or under who were below grade level in school, 75 percent had teenage mothers. Among children who had started major fires, 70 percent had young mothers (Westoff, 1977).

There are about 700 programs around the country that try to help pregnant teenagers and their babies. "Education for Parenthood" was originally designed as a multimedia program to help teenagers learn about children and how to care for them.

Badger (1972) brought groups of low-income teenage mothers into group meetings in a hospital setting during evenings when the teenagers were not at jobs or continuing their schooling. Her program offered a wide variety of information and skills at levels that these very young mothers can understand. Demonstrations of infant competencies, talks on good nutrition and infant care, encouragement of affectionate mother–infant contact were among the activities. Young mothers were challenged when they exhibited attitudes of withdrawal and hopelessness. Honig (1980) noted that Badger's own enthusiasm for positive parenting practices was a major ingredient in encouraging some of these young mothers to become involved with their babies.

Many programs for teen parents not only focus on parenting and child development skills, but they also encourage continuation toward a high school diploma by offering special educational programs housed in a building where infant care is also provided. Innovative and flexible programming is needed to deal with the national "epidemic" of teen parenting (Honig, 1978; Phipps-Yonas, 1980).

Omnibus Models

The Family Development Research Program and Children's Center in Syracuse, New York, has tried to actualize an "omnibus model" (Lally & Honig, 1977a,b). Paraprofessional home visitors, indigenous to the low-income community, brought nutritional, child development, and child care information to pregnant mothers. After the infant's birth, the family was taught special games to encourage visual alerting, hand-eye coordinations, and vocalizations. Mothers were encouraged to improve their own and their babies' diets. At six months, infants entered the Children's Center, a developmental day-care program. Families continued to be visited by the Child Development Trainers (CDTs), and parents continued to receive child development information and skills until the child reached school age. Language, sensory-motor, and later preoperational games and tasks as well as child-management ideas and techniques were presented. CDTs lent toys and books. They provided information and references to community resources to help with legal aid, health care, housing, food stamps, and other problems. They provided loyal friendships to mothers often beset with severe emotional, sexual, social, and financial crises.

CDTs served as liaison persons between the parent and the center. Complaint department, information clearing house about center activities, escort service for parents visiting the center, participant in parent group monthly discussion meetings, active worker at weekly parent workshops, bearer of special family news a teacher may need to know—all these roles filled by the CDT as her repertoire of family-facilitating skills expanded. CDTs held parent group meetings in homes for those parents who were interested in group discussion about special topics. Topics which parents requested included effective parent participation in the public school after the child entered the school, sexuality and early childhood, and working mothers and young children.

The FDRP gave particular attention to the importance of selection, preservice, and in-service training of the home visitors. The paraprofessionals initially underwent eight weeks of training in nutrition, health, interviewing techniques, and games and activities to facilitate early cognitive development (Honig & Lally, 1981).

At forty-eight months, FDRP children were significantly ahead of low-education matched control groups on all seven ITPA language subtests used. By seventy-two months, however, these differences were no longer found. Stanford-Binet mean scores for program children at forty-eight months and seventy-two months were 100 and 109 respectively, compared to 101 and 105 for low-education controls and 136 and 138 for high-education contrast group children. Thus, program children were functioning well in early elementary school grades but they lagged markedly in IQ scores compared to children from intact, college-educated families.

The Child and Family Resource Program (CFRP)

One of the most comprehensive program efforts to involve families of preschoolers in enhancing living and learning conditions for their children is the Child and Family Resource Program (CFRP), a national Head Start demonstration program, which was initially funded in June 1973. CFRP uses Head Start as a base for developing a community-wide service delivery network (O'Keefe, 1978).

A key feature of CFRP programs is flexibility and thoroughness in meeting family and child needs. This individualization and tailoring of programs to fit each family is a strength that augurs well for the success of CFRP programs. Another feature of CFRP programs is the attempt to involve resources in each community to serve the diagnostic and remediation needs of family members. A third is the provision of continuity of services from the prenatal period through early elementary school years. The fourth objective of CFRP is to enhance and build upon the strengths of the individual family as a child-rearing system with distinct values, culture, and aspirations.

A Potpourri of Models

A variety of innovative programs for parents has arisen as parents needs are articulated ever more clearly. Locales and program personnel may be nontraditional (Honig, 1980). Pediatricians' offices serve as a meeting place for parents as does the storefront "Parent Place" and outpatient waiting rooms of hospital pediatric services. Hot lines provide instant telephone information and comfort to parents who need help in coping with early child rearing and educating. Libraries institute toy and book lending programs. Grass-roots self-help parenting-education groups are being started in many communities by mothers who find they need to learn with each other and share their problems and adventures in child rearing. Programs that dovetail home visits and parenting activities with television programs for children have proved cost-effective and are widely accepted (Alford, 1972). The Look-At-Me television series highlights discipline, family relationships, child emotions, and how parents can nurture child curiosity and learning. TV guides to stimulate family discussion are available from Prime Time School Television in Chicago. Many publications and audio-visual media are now available as self-help guides for parents.

Some materials are designed primarily to help parents develop positive communication systems and loving relationships with children. Examples are books by Bessell and Kelly (1978) and Ginott (1965).

Other packages can be used in parent groups with a leader. Gordon's "Parent Effectiveness Training" is the most famous of these programs. Parents are taught how to use "no lose" problem solving techniques, appropriate "I" and "You" messages, and "Active Listening" to help increase positive family communication. Interviews with parents who have undergone PET reveal ways in which the program helped families (1976).

The Systematic Parent Effectiveness Training Program (STEP) teaches parents how to analyze the goals of children's misbehaviors and positive behaviors and to respond in ways to increase the latter (Dinkmeyer & McKay, 1976). Both of these programs deal more with parents of school-age children.

Some self-help materials are designed for specific parenting groups, such as Spanish-speaking parents or low-literacy parents. New Reader's Press in Syracuse, New York, has parenting materials and activities designed for readers with less than a fifth-grade education.

Interpersonal Cognitive Problem Solving (ICPS)

Shure and Spivack (1978) have taken a problem-solving approach to training low-income parents and teachers of inner-city children to teach the children to generate solutions to interpersonal problems and to foresee consequences of their own behaviors in such a way that the children can make better adjustments: "To date, the most powerful ICPS mediator in young children appears to be the ability to conceptualize multiple solutions to interpersonal problems and, secondarily, the ability to anticipate the consequences of acts" (pp. 7–8).

These findings continued to hold up in comparison to control children one year later. The authors report that those mothers who consistently applied problem-solving techniques when real-life problems arose had children who most improved in ICPS thinking skills and subsequent behavioral adjustment. The kinds of dialogues and scripts that are taught, of course, require that parents acquire new thinking skills of their own. "Training parents to think through solutions to interpersonal problems and to anticipate the consequences of acts helps them appreciate the very thinking process they in turn learn to transmit to their children" (p. 38).

Conclusions

Research findings from parent involvement programs lead to some considerations that should be weighed when launching, conducting, or evaluating parent programs.

1. Some parents in the program may do well with a one-year postnatal support service; others require long-term postnatal suport services, even through the early grades of elementary school.

2. Some parents may feel uncomfortable about direct, immediate participation in certain models. After trust-building, a program can move into the second stage, such as parent participation in the classroom or parent group meetings.

3. Having parents present in classrooms without systematically helping them to notice how children learn and how to use positive reinforcing methods is "pseudo-parent involvement" (to paraphrase Piaget on imitation). Such participation may not make any educational difference for children. Research findings that ineffective parenting styles are associated with parental lack of awareness of child cues and lack of sensitivity to the meaning of child behaviors and interactions lend urgency to this need for parent training. Training for parent involvement in early childhood education must be *preventive.*

4. Parents may be an excellent source of help to other parents in a program. Parents with handicapped newborns may best accept help, advice, and information from other parents who have been through similar experiences.

5. Professionals may be best equipped to provide some parenting education services and interventions. Fraiberg's work with disturbed and abusing/neglectful mothers required therapeutic skills of a highly trained nature.

6. Trained paraprofessionals may be the most fitting choice for work with some groups of parents, such as those whose children are at risk for cultural-educational retardation. Paraprofessionals may bring sensitivities to families living in poverty and be familiar and comfortable with minority cultural mores in a way that some professionals could not.

7. Flexibility is important if parent involvement efforts are to match the needs of families served. Programs should try to match family needs with services just as parent workers try to help match the level of learning games they play to the developmental skills that the child already has acquired.

8. A program may need to mix modalities of involvement. Home-based intervention plus parent group meetings plus parent participation in classroom plus

clinical therapy sessions have been used in intensive efforts to ameliorate and stabilize the family situation with abusive parents.

9. Parent involvement programs that focus only on cognitive development games may not develop sufficient rapport with families so that home visits can be made regularly. On the other hand, home visitors who serve only as a sympathetic ear for all the troubles of a family may not find that the family is increasing its awareness of or skills in the parent education role with young children. When teen mothers of at-risk infants found positive psychological and physical security while participating in the nursery where their children received developmental care, this extra support ensured more significant advantages to the infants and to the mothers (Field et al., 1980).

10. Fathers may need special parent involvement efforts. Tuck (1969) found that male workers with special training could best involve fathers living in a low-income urban housing project in learning and play interactions with their preschoolers.

11. Retraining or team-centered efforts may well be necessary or indispensible when a child-care program adds a parenting component. Asking teachers who are trained for work with children to become expert parenting persons requires a project commitment to aid teachers in developing communication skills and sensitivity to different family styles.

12. Total reliance on volunteers to provide parenting training may jeopardize program goals. Volunteers may not provide the stability and continuity of effort over time so often required to build trust with families served.

13. New educational needs arise as children grow and a program continues. New developmental problems may become a concern to parents. Parent involvement staff will need ongoing information and behavioral guidelines to handle maturing and changing behaviors and any problems that arise.

14. Strong support systems are imperative to prevent burn-out in parent involvers working with families with multiple problems. Parent involvers need a project supervisor to whom they can express their concerns, ask for counsel, and turn to for outside resources when a particular family's needs warrant such aid.

15. Disturbances in the ecological system in which a family lives may vitiate parent involvement efforts focused exclusively on change in early education practices. Coordination of parent involvement programs with social and community agencies that work toward improving job, housing, and other socioeconomic opportunities can profoundly affect the conditions in which a family's child-rearing efforts occur.

16. Charismatic leaders may be more responsible for significant program gains than a particular model, strategy, or theory that informs delivery services. Styles of communication, caring for families, and sharing developmental knowledge may be as important as particular lesson plans, activities, or theories endorsed.

17. The focus of a parent involver's job may need to be widened if project successes are to accrue. Galvanizing parents to become their child's special early

teacher and educational advocate for the future may also require offering help in some management skills, problem-solving strategies, job training, medical and other community service referrals, self-advocacy courses for parents, and so on. Attaining educational objectives becomes more probable if ancillary services are available for parents, too.

18. Assessment of parent involvement efforts requires the wisdom of Solomon. Program effects may be gained through vertical diffusion, with younger siblings.

Child change may be slow. Radin (1972) and colleagues found that the effects of an intensive effort at parent involvement showed up one year later.

Projects should measure target-child change and impact on the trained parent. Intangible changes in the child's surroundings may also positively affect the learning environment. Achievement scores may be significantly higher for experimental children even when IQ gains "wash out."

Assessments that focus on psychometric measures only may overlook significant changes in unobtrusive measures or demographic variables. The number of repeat pregnancies with involved young parents may drop in comparison to untrained parents. Parents may take part more in neighborhood and community groups (Datta, 1973).

Lazar and Darlington (1978) found two highly stable demographic differences for early education programs both with and without parent involvement components: (1) fewer children were retained in grade; and (2) fewer children were placed in special education classes. Children of trained mothers may achieve a high school equivalency diploma more easily than controls (Lally & Honig, 1977b).

Assessments that lump all parents in the program together in contrast to untrained parents may underestimate program effects. For the purpose of learning clinically more about the variables that might predict parent involvement success, it might be useful to break assessment findings into two kinds: (1) those that compare trained and untrained parents; and (2) those that compare trained parents who changed with those who did not and contrast both these groups with control parents.

19. What degree of involvement defines a parenting program? Shall programs that provide eight weeks of two-hour group training be compared with programs with educational as well as health and nutrition components serving families from prenatal through early school years? Comparing effects of programs that differ significantly on parameters of input, length of service, target child's ages, and so on, may be premature. We are not yet sophisticated enough in parent involvement efforts to reject any model outright. We must continue to use the child development and child-rearing literature heuristically as a base for increasing the skillfulness and creativity of our efforts to help parents achieve learning partnerships with their children's teachers.

20. Where flexible parent involvement efforts have resulted in a large number of programmatic offerings for parents, the number of subjects per research cell may be too small to draw anything but tentative hypotheses about

causal effects. Parent involvement programs need to tailor their efforts to meet family needs, but they also need to begin to coordinate their research programs, assessment measures, and programmatic variables such as length of program and intensity of involvement efforts so that data can be pooled from several projects. Cell sizes might then be large enough to permit more secure analyses of outcome effects. Particularly when multiple efforts to reach parents are used, developing a network for data sharing among programs may be a matter that requires far more dialogue and coordination among projects than has yet been obtained.

Education for parenthood until fairly recently was something learned in the bosom of the family. Helping parents with chores, having other family members such as aunts and uncles to lend a helping hand with children, gathering with relatives for special occasions—these were the settings and opportunities for "lessons" in how to share, care, nurture, become competent, and learn responsibility.

The number of family adults who are directly involved in raising a young child has decreased alarmingly with mobility, maternal work, and single parenting. A concerted coalition of cooperating neighbors, agencies, and schools may be required to energize and actualize positive parent participation in early childhood education. Commitment to such an effort should be a high political priority on behalf of our greatest national resource—our young children.

References

ADKINS, D. C. Home activities for preschool children: A manual of games and activities for use by parents with their children at home, to foster certain preschool goals. Honolulu: Hawaii Center for Research in Early Childhood Education, September 1971.

AINSWORTH, M. D. S. Infant–mother attachment. *American Psychologist*, 1979, 34, 932–937.

ALFORD, R. D. (ed.). *Home-Oriented Preschool Education: Curriculum Planning Guide.* Charleston, W. Va.: Appalachia Educational Laboratory, 1972.

BADGER, E. D. A mother's training program: A sequel article. *Children Today*, 1972, 1, 7–11.

BASSIN, J., and DROVETTA, D. Parent outreach. *The Exceptional Parent*, 1976, 6, 6–9.

BEE, H. L., VAN EGEREN, L. F., STREISSGUTH, A. P., NYMAN, B. A., and LECKIE, M. S. Social class differences in maternal teaching strategies and speech patterns. In U. Bronfenbrenner and M. P. Mahoney (eds.), *Influences on Human Development.* Hinsdale, Ill.: Dryden Press, 1975.

BEREITER, C., and ENGLEMANN, S. *Teaching Disadvantaged Children in the Preschool.* Englewood Cliffs, N.J.: Prentice-Hall, 1966.

BESSELL, H. and KELLY, T. P. *The Parent Book: The Holistic Program for Raising the Emotionally Mature Child.* San Diego: Psych/Graph Publishers, 1978.

BIBER, B. Goals and methods in a preschool program for disadvantaged children. Unpublished manuscript, Bank Street College of Education, New York, 1970.

BING, F. Effects of childrearing practices on development of differential cognitive abilities. *Child Development*, 1963, *34*, 631–648.

BOGER, R. B., KUIPERS, J., WILSON, N., and ANDREWS, M. *Parents Are Teachers Too.* East Lansing, Mich.: Institute for Family and Child Study, Michigan State University, 1974.

BRADLEY, R. H., and CALDWELL, B. M. The relationship of infants' home environments to mental test performance at 54 months: A follow-up study. *Child Development*, 1976, *47*, 1172–1174.

BRICKER, D., and BRICKER, W. Toddler research and intervention project report: Year II. *IMRD Behavior Science Monograph 21*, Institute on Mental Retardation and Intellectual Development. Nashville, Tenn.: George Peabody College, 1972.

BROMWICH, R. M. Focus on maternal behavior in infant intervention. *American Journal of Orthopsychiatry*, 1976, *46*, 439–446.

CALDWELL, B. M., and RICHMOND, J. The Children's Center in Syracuse, New York. In L. L. Dittman (ed.), *Early Child Care: The New Perspectives*. New York: Atherton Press, 1968.

CAREW, J. V., CHAN, I., and HALFAR, C. *Observing Intelligence in Young Children.* Englewood Cliffs, N.J.: Prentice-Hall, 1976.

CHARNLEY, L., and MYRE, G. Parent-infant education. *Children Today*, 1977, *5*, 18–21.

CHILMAN, C. S. Child development and social policy. In B. M. Caldwell and H. Ricciuti (eds.), *Review of Child Development Research*, Vol. 3. Chicago: University of Chicago Press, 1974.

COLLINS, R. C. Home Start and its implications for family policy. *Children Today*, 1980, *9*, 12–16.

COMPTROLLER GENERAL. Early childhood and family development programs improve the quality of life for low-income families. Report to the Congress of the United States. February 6, 1979. HRD-79-40.

DATTA, L. E. Parent involvement in early childhood education: A perspective from the United States. Paper presented at the Organization for Economic Cooperation and Development, Centre for Educational Research and Innovation, Conference on Early Childhood Education, Paris, France, October 1973.

DAVÈ, R.H. The identification and measurement of environment process variables that are related to educational achievement. Unpublished doctoral dissertation, University of Chicago, 1963.

DINKMEYER, D. and McKAY, G. D. *Systematic Training for Effective Parenting: Parent's Handbook*. Circle Pines, Minnesota: American Guidance Service, 1976.

FORRESTER, B. J. Parents as educational change agents for infants: Competencies not credentials. Paper presented at the Annual Meeting of the Council on Exceptional Children, Washington, D.C., March 1972.

FIELD, T., WIDMAYER, S. M., STRINGER, S., and IGNATOFF, E. Teenage, lower-class black mothers and their preterm infants: An intervention and developmental follow-up. *Child Development*, 1980, *51*, 426–436.

FRAIBERG, S. (ed.). *Clinical Studies in Infant Mental Health: The First Year of Life.* New York: Basic Books, 1980.

FROST, J. L. At risk! *Childhood Education*, 1975, *51*, 298–304.

GINOTT, H. G. *Between parent and child: New solutions to old problems.* New York: Macmillan, 1965.

GORDON, I. J. Early child stimulation through parent education. Final report. Project No. PHS-R-306, Children's Bureau, Social and Rehabilitation Service, United States Department of Health, Education and Welfare, 1971.

GORDON, I. J., and GUINAGH, B. J. A home learning center approach to early stimulation. Gainesville, Florida: College of Education, Institute for Development of Human Resources, 1969.

GORDON, T. *P. E. T. in Action.* New York: Bantam Books, 1976.

GRAY, S. Home visiting programs for parents of young children. DARCEE Papers and Reports, 1971, 5 (No. 4), George Peabody College for Teachers, Nashville, Tennessee.

HEBER, F. R. Sociocultural mental retardation: A longitudinal study. In D. Forgays (ed.), *Primary Intervention of Psychopathology, Vol 2. Environmental Influences.* Hanover, N.H.: University Press of New England, 1978.

HEBER, F. R., DENVER, R. B., and CONRY, J. The influence of environmental and genetic variables on intellectual development. In H. J. Prehm, L. A. Hammerlynch, and J. E. Crosson (eds.), *Behavioral Research in Mental Retardation.* Eugene: University of Oregon, 1968.

HESS, R. D., and SHIPMAN, V. C. Early experience and the socialization of cognitive modes in children. *Child Development,* 1965, 34, 869–889.

HONIG, A. S. What we need to know to help the teenage parent. *The Family Coordinator,* 1978, 27, 113–119.

HONIG, A. S. *Parent involvement in early childhood education,* 2nd ed. Washington, D.C.: National Association for the Education of Young Children, 1979.

HONIG, A. S. Working with parents of preschool children. In R. Abidin (ed.), *Parent Education and Intervention Handbook.* Springfield, Ill.: Charles C. Thomas, 1980.

HONIG, A. S., and LALLY, J. R. *Infant Caregiving: A Design for Training.* Syracuse, N.Y.: Syracuse University Press, 1981.

HONIG, A. S., LALLY, J. R., and HORSBURGH, D. H. Personal-social adjustment of school children after five years in a family enrichment program. *Child Care Quarterly,* 1982, 11, in press.

IMC Reports to Parents, 1973, 2 (No. 2), Albany, New York.

JEW, W. Helping handicapped infants and their families: The delayed development project. *Children Today,* 1974, 3, 7–10.

KARNES, M. B., HODGINS, A. S., TESKA, J. A., and KIRK, S. A. *Investigations of classroom and at-home interventions, Final report.* Washington, D.C.: Bureau of Research, Office of Health, Education, and Welfare, May 1969.

LALLY, J. R. Selecting and training paraprofessionals for work with infants, toddlers, and their families. In I. Gordon (ed.), *Early Child Stimulation through Parent Education, Final report.* Gainesville, Florida: College of Education, Institute for Development of Human Resources, 1969.

LALLY, J. R., and GORDON, I. J. *Learning Games for Infants and Toddlers.* Syracuse, N.Y.: New Readers Press, 1977.

LALLY, J. R., and HONIG, A. S. *Final Report: Family Development Research Program.* Syracuse, N.Y.: Children's Center, 1977a.

LALLY, J. R., and HONIG, A. S. The family development research program: A program for prenatal, infant and early childhood enrichment. In M. C. Day and R. D. Parker (eds.), *The Preschool in Action: Exploring Early Childhood Programs*, 2nd ed. Boston: Allyn and Bacon, 1977b.

LAMBIE, D. Z., BOND, J. T., and WEIKART, D. P. *Home teaching with mothers and infants.* Ypsilanti, Mich.: High/Scope Educational Research Foundation, 1974.

LANE, M. B. *Education for Parenting.* Washington, D.C.: National Association for the Education of Young Children, 1975.

LASATER, T. M., BRIGGS, J., MALONE, P., GILLIAM, C. F., and WEISBURG, P. The Birmingham model for parent education. Paper presented at the biennial meeting of the Society for Research in Child Development, April 1975.

LAZAR, I., and DARLINGTON, R. B. (eds.). *Lasting Effects After Preschool.* Final report, H. E. W. Grant 900-1311 to the Education Commission of the States, 1978.

LEVENSTEIN, P. But does it work in homes away from home? *Theory into Practice*, 1972, *11*, 157–162.

LEVENSTEIN, P. The mother–child home program. In M. C. Day and R. K. Parker (eds.), *The Preschool in Action: Exploring Early Childhood Programs*, 2nd ed. Boston: Allyn & Bacon, 1977.

LEVENSTEIN, P. Ethical considerations in home-based programs. Paper presented at the Second National Symposium on Home-Based Care for Children and Families, University of Iowa, April 1979.

LEVITT, E., and COHEN, S. Educating parents of children with special needs: Approaches and issues. In L. Baruth and M. Burrgraf (eds.), *Counseling Parents of Exceptional Children.* Guilford, Conn.: Special Learning Corporation, 1979.

MADDEN, J., LEVENSTEIN, P., and LEVENSTEIN, S. Longitudinal IQ outcomes of the mother-child home program. *Child Development*, 1976, 47, 1015–1025.

NATIONAL CENTER FOR CLINICAL INPUT PROGRAMS. Clinical infant intervention research programs: Selected overview and discussion. Washington, D.C.: HEW Publication No. 79–748, 1979.

NIMNICHT, G. P., BROWN, E., ADDISON, B., and JOHNSON, S. *Parent Guide: How to Play Learning Games with a Preschool Child.* Morristown, N.J.: General Learning Corporation, 1971.

O'KEEFE, R. A. *The Child and Family Resource Program: An Overview.* Washington, D.C.: U.S. Department of H.E.W., Administration for Children, Youth and Families, 1978.

PHIPPS-YONAS, S. Teenage pregnancy and motherhood: A review of the literature. *American Journal of Orthopsychiatry*, 1980, 50, 403–431.

POULTON, L., and POULTON, G. Neighborhood support for young families. *Early Child Development and Care*, 1979, 6, 73–82.

PUSHAW, D. (ed.). *Teach Your Child to Talk: A Parent Handbook.* Cincinnati, Ohio: CDBCO Standard Publishing Company, 1969.

RABINOWITZ, M., WEINER, G., and JACKSON, C. R. *In the Beginning: A Parent Guide of Activities and Experiences for Infants from Birth to Six Months*, Book 1. New Orleans, Louisiana: Parent Child Development Center, 1973.

RADIN, N. Three degrees of parent involvement in a preschool program: Impact on mothers and children. *Child Development*, 1972, *43*, 1355–1364.

RAMEY, C. T., and CAMPBELL, F. A. Educational intervention at risk for mild retardation: A longitudinal analysis. In P. Mittler (ed.), *Proceedings of the International Associa-*

tion for the Scientific Study of Mental Deficiency. Baltimore, Md.: University Park Press, 1982.

RESNICK, M. The relationship between language ability and intellectual and behavioral functioning on environmentally disadvantaged two and three year olds. Unpublished doctoral dissertation, University of Florida, 1973.

RILEY, M. T. *Project Laton: A parent involvement concept for training Head Start parents as to the concerns of handicapped children.* Lubbock: The Texas Tech Press, 1977.

RISLEY, T. Learning and lollipops. In P. Cramer (ed.), *Readings in Developmental Psychology Today.* Del Mar, Calif.: CRM Books, 1970.

SROUFE, L. A. The coherence of individual development: Early care, attachment, and subsequent developmental issues. *American Psychologist*, 1979, *34*, 834–841.

SCHAEFER, E. S. Professional paradigms in programs for parents and children. Urbana, Ill.: ERIC Clearinghouse on Early Childhood Education, 1977 (ED 147-033).

SCHAEFER, E. S., and AARONSON, M. Infant education research project: Implementation and implications of a home tutorial program. In M. C. Day and R. K. Parker (eds.), *The Preschool in Action: Exploring Early Childhood Programs*, 2nd ed. Boston: Allyn and Bacon, 1977.

SHEARER, M. S., and SHEARER, D. E. The portage project: A model for early childhood education. *Exceptional Children*, 1972, *39*, 210–217.

SHURE, M. B., and SPIVACK, G. *Problem-Solving Techniques in Childrearing.* San Francisco: Jossey-Bass, 1978.

STEVENS, J. H., JR. Current directions in the study of parental facilitation of children's cognitive development. *Educational Horizons*, 1973, *50*, 62–66.

STRODTBECK, F. L. The hidden curriculum in the middle-class home. In J. D. Krumboltz (ed.), *Learning and the Educational Process.* Chicago: Rand McNally, 1965.

SWAN, R. W., and STAVROS, H. Child-rearing practices associated with the development of cognitive skills of children in low socio-economic areas. *Early Child Development and Care*, 1973, *3*, 23–38.

TUCK, S. A model for working with black fathers. Paper presented at the Annual Meeting of the American Orthopsychiatric Association, San Francisco, Calif., 1969.

VAN DOORNINCK, W. J. Parent-infant support through lay health visitors. Final Report to Maternal and Child Health Service, National Institute of Health, Department of Health, Education, and Welfare Research Grant No. MC-R-08398-03-0, March 1980.

WEIKART, D. P. Preschool pays for itself. *Keys to Early Childhood Education*, 1980, *1*, 1–2.

WESTOFF, L. A. Kids with kids. In J. S. McKee (ed.), *Readings in Early Childhood Education 77/78.* Guilford, Conn.: Dushkin Publishing Group, 1977.

WEYBRIGHT, G., GEIST, T., GOLDMAN, C., PRICHARD, S., ROSENTHAL, J., and TOVEY, S. An intensive speech and language intervention program for preschool children. *The Directive Teacher*, 1979, *2*, 28–30.

WOLF, R. M. The identification and measurement of environmental process variables related to intelligence. Unpublished doctoral dissertation, University of Chicago, April 1964.

CHAPTER 19

Mainstreaming Young Handicapped Children: A Public Policy and Ecological Systems Analysis

Michael J. Guralnick

IN LITTLE MORE THAN A DECADE, remarkable progress has been achieved in our understanding of early education for handicapped children. Spurred by the pioneering work of Kirk (1958), Gray and Klaus (1965), and Skeels (Skeels, 1966; Skeels & Dye, 1939), supported by investigators from numerous fields, and nurtured by a seemingly indomitable enthusiasm and optimism regarding the potential for change through early intervention, a period of intense activity ensued. Combined with the federal government's willingness to support large-scale social action programs affecting education and child development and the formation of highly visible special-interest groups, a substrate was created for the emergence of an extraordinarily diverse, conceptually rich, and extensive number of early intervention programs and theoretical approaches.

When one asks what the reality of developing and testing projects for more than a decade has meant to understanding the value of early education for handicapped children, it is perhaps safe to state that, despite the fact that some of our original notions that may best be categorized as magical thinking have been dispelled, the optimism and enthusiasm of most workers in the field have not diminished. Certainly, the need exists for continued and more rigorous documentation of the effectiveness of early education for handicapped children. This is a particularly pressing issue as demonstrated by the evaluations of environmental intervention programs for children at risk for psychosocial retardation. Extensive reviews of these programs have revealed a general pattern of immediate success followed by a gradual decline of these initial gains over time when programs were terminated (Bronfenbrenner, 1975; Clarke & Clarke, 1976; Haskins, Finkelstein & Stedman, 1978; Horowitz & Paden, 1973; Tjossem, 1976). Taken together, early, intense, and prolonged programs, especially those extensively involving parents, produced the best results; yet, gains remained modest. More recently, however, reports of favorable long-term effects from these early environmental intervention programs have been published (Lazar et al., 1977).

Additional strategies, ultimately directed toward the strengthening of the family–child bond through developmental programs for all concerned but initially requiring a radical and costly intervention, have been attempted. Both the Milwaukee Project (Heber & Garber, 1975) and the Carolina Abecedarian Project (Ramey & Campbell, 1977; Ramey et al., 1976) show great promise in being able to prevent the usual decline in tested intellectual ability and in not impairing family or peer relationships. Given the methodological sophistication of the Abecedarian Project, long-term follow-up data should be very instructive.

For children with clear biological impairments and generally more severe developmental problems, fewer systematic evaluation efforts have been conducted. However, focusing on the federal-level initiative that established a vast network of diverse model demonstration programs (DeWeerd & Cole, 1976), a third-party evaluation did suggest that these early intervention projects for handicapped children with varying disabilities were effective, particularly in the personal-social behavior areas (Stock et al., 1976). Moreover, a number of projects serving children with Down's syndrome have been successful (Hanson & Schwarz, 1978; Hayden & Dimitriev, 1975).

These experiences with early intervention programs have been most helpful in bringing a number of critical issues into focus. We are quite certain that, irrespective of program model or population being served, particular organizational characteristics are associated with successful outcomes. Programs that have clear goals and philosophical perspectives, include considerable planning and feedback, supervision, and monitoring, and maintain an active training component have common prerequisites for success (Guralnick, 1975; Karnes, 1973, 1977; McDaniels, 1977; Weikart, 1972). However, even with many important programmatic dimensions now identified, evaluating the effectiveness of early intervention programs is only at a preliminary stage.

At a more theoretical level, these intense efforts by members of the early childhood community have served also to clarify some fundamental approaches to our understanding of the development of handicapped children. It appears that many of these projects have produced findings most compatible with the acceptance of a "transactional" model of development (Kearsley, 1979; Sameroff, 1979; Sameroff & Chandler, 1975; Sarason & Doris, 1979). In this view, biological impairment is no longer accepted as a static impediment to developmental progress. Rather, development is perceived as proceeding through reciprocal and multiple pathways with environmental events exacerbating, minimizing, and even occasionally overcoming initial biologically based deficiencies. Similarly, there now appears to be a willingness to examine more openly the validity of the concept of the continuity of human development. This concept has significant implications for children with handicaps, including expectations of the caretaking and professional community and the general design of curricula and intervention strategies.

An important implication of the transactional or other interactive models is that a radical alteration of the educational environment of a handicapped child may create new interaction patterns that could significantly affect the course of development. One such potentially dramatic change for handicapped children which occurred quite recently is the setting in which educational and therapeutic services are provided. More and more, such services are being provided in classroom settings containing nonhandicapped children. The impact of mainstreaming or integrating handicapped and nonhandicapped children is a core issue in the early education of handicapped children. Modifying the context of educational service delivery both limits and expands the available experiences for all participants. An examination of this process is critical as it affects virtually all basic educational and developmental variables. This chapter is an effort to come to an understanding of the process of mainstreaming young handicapped children and its broad implications.

Background Issues

In the following two sections, a number of relevant background issues will be discussed in an effort to place the topic of mainstreaming young handicapped children in its proper perspective and context.

Public Policy, Developmental/Educational Programs, and Developmental Principles and Research

The relationship among public policy, developmental/educational programs, and developmental principles and research provides an important framework for understanding the varied aspects of mainstreaming as concept and practice. The importance of understanding these relationships is underscored by the fact that only a limited degree of synchrony exists among these elements as they affect young children, with the research-related element probably being most discrepant. The reasons for this asynhcrony are diverse and complex, and it is not my purpose here to trace the historical antecedents that may have led to this state of affairs. However, it is apparent that many public policy actions, particularly in matters of social significance that relate to educational or applied developmental issues, must move forward despite the absence of policy relevant research. Unfortunately, such research has not been available very often when needed to guide policy development nor, if available, has it been sufficiently definitive to assist in the decision making itself. Despite the fact that some discrepancies are inevitable and occasionally even desirable, it is anticipated that the design of strategies that reduce the extent of this asynchrony will result ultimately in more effective decision making at all levels. As will be seen, one purpose of this chapter will be to develop a model designed to help clarify public policy issues in relation to research and evaluation that are concerned with mainstreaming young handicapped children.

The existence of problems related to the asynchrony of this relationship has not gone unrecognized by early childhood researchers, and it appears to be an especially perplexing issue when handicapped individuals are involved (Etzioni &

Richardson, 1975). From a child development perspective, Bronfenbrenner (1974) has perhaps been most outspoken in this regard. He points out that a straightforward unidirectional conceptualization of the relationship, in which policy makers try to use the scientific data and principles of child development in policy development and evaluation, has simply not been very fruitful. In part, this reflects concerns about the lack of ecological and transcontextual validity of many research designs in this area (Bronfenbrenner, 1977; McCall, 1977; Weisz, 1978). Quite apart from these problems, Bronfenbrenner contends that the entire process and relationship between scientific research and social policy needs to be re-evaluated, as revealed in his statement that "science needs social policy—needs it not to guide our organizational activities, but to provide us with two elements essential for any scientific endeavor—vitality and validity" (1974, p. 1).

In essence, the unidirectional conceptualization is rejected in favor of an interactionist position between developmental research and public policy. From my perspective, it is perhaps most useful to consider three mutually interacting dimensions (see Figure 19-1): (1) fundamental developmental principles and research; (2) their application to applied developmental/educational programs; and (3) public policy. As seen in Figure 19-2 (p. 460), each of these dimensions is conceptualized as maintaining its own independent domain and methodology (unshaded area), yet each is influenced by the other two. Where overlap among all three domains and methodologies occurs in relation to a common problem (stippled area), our knowledge of the issues and quality of our decision making are likely to be maximized. It is anticipated that recognition of interactions among these dimensions will lead to increasing areas of overlap.

Figure 19-1. Diagram illustrating the mutual influences among developmental principles and research, applied developmental/educational problems, and public policy.

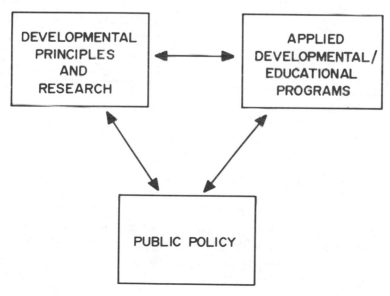

Figure 19-2. An illustration of the convergence among the three dimensions necessary to provide comprehensive solutions to common problems.

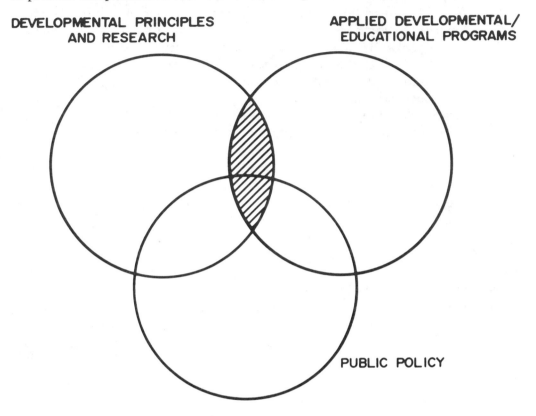

Recent discussions in the literature on clarifying the persistent problem of translating scientific information for use in decision making at the public policy level or in establishing principles with greater validity (McCall, 1977; Weisz, 1978) have been very helpful. Additional progress has occurred as a result of the emergence of an area referred to as applied developmental psychology (Wertlieb, 1979; Zigler, 1980) that promises to be a major link among the key dimensions. Furthermore, direct encouragement of these interactions by consumers of this research (for example, Wald, 1976) are also likely to increase policy-valuable investigations.

Despite these changes, the difficulties in conducting applied research that is timely and can have a definitive impact on the development of public policy are still considerable. Moreover, once a particular policy has been formulated, researchers face a somewhat different set of policy-relevant questions. In particular, they must now attempt to translate policy statements into a systemmatic research and evaluation program that typically has only a limited empirical basis and, perhaps most significantly, is inextricably linked to underlying and dynamic value systems. This research and evaluation task is unquestionably a complex one, but, if properly carried out, it can play a major role in the clarification and subsequent revision of a given policy. The influences of relevant information following, for example, the passage of laws such as Public Law (P.L.) 94–142, The Education for All Handicapped Children Act (1975, 1977), should not be underestimated. Regulations can be modified, guidlines for implementation change frequently, and statements regarding the law are issued regularly in an effort to clarify difficult points or to resolve unanticipated problems. All in all, significant opportunities can affect a given policy statement or legislative act following its formulation.

Issues Related to Mainstreaming Young Handicapped Children

It is precisely with public policy matters that contain fluid concepts, with limited experience in applying the concepts, and that reflect an underlying value structure and philosophy that extends well beyond the confines of the specific policy statement in which it is embodied, that investigators find the greatest difficulties in first identifying and then answering the fundamental questions that should be addressed. This is certainly the case for issues related to mainstreaming, as it appears to be one of the most controversial and perhaps least understood educational policy decisions.

The clearest expression of public policy on this issue is the legislative mandate for educating handicapped and nonhandicapped children in the same setting as stated in P. L. 94–142's (1975, 1977) least restrictive placement principle. This principle is perhaps best thought of as a component of the law's emphasis on meeting children's educational/developmental needs on an individualized basis (see Hobbs, 1975). Viewed in this way, integrated placements constitute one such educational strategy and, as will be seen, can exist in numerous forms or arrangements.[1]

Specifically, the law states that each public agency is responsible for insuring:

(1) That to the maximum extent appropriate, handicapped children, including children in public or private institutions or other care facilities, are educated with children who are not handicapped, and

(2) that special classes, separate schooling or other removal of handicapped

---

[1] A program can be a typical preschool for normally developing children that now includes handicapped children. The proportion of handicapped children in a mainstreamed setting is usually less than one-third of the total number. This discussion also applies, however, to a service model that was previously limited to handicapped children but now includes nonhandicapped children. Although not presented in detail, it is expected that the discussions in this chapter are also applicable, with modifications, to a wide range of alternatives in which handicapped and nonhandicapped children are integrated. This includes both temporal and spatial variations, such as when integrated activities are planned for only certain portions of the day (for example, during free play). Accordingly, each arrangement might require some adjustments with respect to principles and methods outlined here, but the basic concepts should remain intact.

> children from the regular educational environment occurs only when the nature or severity of the handicap is such that education in regular classes with the use of supplementary aids and services cannot be achieved satisfactorily [P.L. 94–142, 1977, p. 42497].

When someone asks what guidlines can be derived to help us judge the ultimate effectiveness of this principle or, more generally, how the concept of mainstreaming is to be understood, it is immediately apparent that considerable interpretation and resolution of ambiguous statements will be required. For example, how are we to interpret the terms "to the maximum extent appropriate" and "achieved satisfactorily"? The flexible nature of the mainstreaming concept is made even more apparent when it is recognized that the term mainstreaming itself does not appear in the legislation at all.

This degree of ambiguity for a vital concept is of great concern since, as Zigler and Trickett (1978) point out, proper outcome evaluation of social programs requires clarity and explicitness of a program's goals and objectives. This lack of clarity is of even greater concern to investigators who seek to understand policy-related concepts such as mainstreaming by extending beyond conventional outcome evaluation and attempting to analyze and integrate the evaluation process within a comprehensive research program. This more comprehensive effort draws upon a wide range of applied developmental research and provides linkages to the fundamental child development literature.

As indicated, such a program of research and evaluation in relation to mainstreaming has the potential not only to affect subsequent policy and implementation at various levels but also to achieve a more complete understanding of the general concept. As Sarason and Doris (1979) point out, "Given our observations about how the law is being implemented, the silence of the law about mainstreaming, as well as its emphasis on due process and least restrictive alternative, suggests that the law's evasiveness about mainstreaming is setting the stage for future court battles about mainstreaming as a value and practice" (p. 370). If these authors are correct, forthcoming decisions could benefit substantially from a clarification of the mainstreaming concept and the results of an associated systematic research and evaluation program.

Accordingly, the remainder of this chapter consists of an attempt to provide a framework or model to assist policy makers, program planners, researchers, developmentalists, and early childhood educators to clarify, organize, analyze, evaluate, and plan future efforts to assess the value and implications of mainstreaming in relation to public policy. Since the mainstreaming concept is subject to such diverse interpretations of intent and is extremely sensitive to the value system in which it is embedded, the construction of such a model and a corresponding review of the literature will be heuristic in nature. In developing the model, I will make an effort to identify essential questions and issues, establish objective criteria, describe assessment approaches, review and integrate relevant literature, and, I hope, accurately portray our current level of knowledge. Finally, it should be noted that this discussion is limited to mainstreaming occuring at the preschool level. The administrative and legal issues, concepts, and developmental/educational goals for preschool-age children are, of course, substantially different from those at the school-age level (Cohen, Semmes & Guralnick, 1979). Consequently, although many of the principles described in sections of this chapter are relevant to the general concept of mainstreaming, the specific interpretations and research plans are designed for the younger population.

A Model for Evaluating the Effectiveness of Mainstreamed Programs in Educational Settings

The Concepts of Feasibility and Efficacy

As a first step in the construction of a comprehensive model for mainstreaming, a framework will be developed that is closely tied to specific legislation and classroom settings. In the most common circumstance in which handicapped children are first enrolled in a typical preschool or nursery, an immediate issue is the feasibility of this educational arrangement. In order to judge if a mainstreamed program is feasible, the following question must be asked: Can the educational/developmental needs of *all* children continue to be met in the mainstreamed context and in relation to the intent of mainstreaming without radically departing from the fundamental assumptions and structure of that program's model? Certain adaptations are necessary, of course, to accommodate children at a variety of developmental levels and/or those who manifest a range of developmental problems. However, if the program's primary theoretical and programmatic approach can be maintained while meeting the basic educational/developmental needs of all children as well as satisfying certain mainstreaming goals to be discussed below, mainstreaming can be considered feasible.

The requirement for ensuring that a program's primary focus be retained while accommodating handicapped children should not suggest either that experimentation with new service delivery models is being discouraged or that only limited and minimal changes within a particular program are necessary. On the contrary, extensive modifications are often essential in terms of staffing patterns and restructuring elements of the classroom environment. A variety of creative early education/intervention models, many directed to specific disability groups, are currently being explored and are testing the elasticity of the integration concept. Nevertheless, it is important to respect the validity of established and presumably effective models and approaches to early childhood education and to insure that mainstreaming produces a modification, but not a distortion, of these programs.

With respect to goals specific to the mainstreaming concept, it is necessary to examine the underlying philosophy and value system upon which they were based (Abeson & Zettel, 1977; Jones et al., 1978). The view adopted here is that, in its most fundamental sense, the intent of P.L. 94–142's least restrictive principle was to create circumstances in which mutual understanding, tolerance for diversity, and ultimately the recognition of the value of diversity by both handicapped and nonhandicapped children would flourish. Indeed, we can even consider that the least restrictive concept implicitly reaffirms the principle of the continuity of human development. Furthermore, policy makers were apparently concerned about the adverse effects of labeling and separation of children and, although not wishing to eliminate segregated education entirely (in fact, a continuum of alternatives was encouraged), there was an intent to eliminate the problems associated with that educational approach. Clearly, for mainstreamed programs in any form to be considered feasible, evidence relating to these humanistic and social goals must be obtained.

The efficacy question as applied to mainstreaming young handicapped children is used in a limited sense in this chapter. Specifically, it encompasses but goes beyond feasibility and asks whether a mainstreamed program provides clear *benefits* to children in comparison to segregated programs. There are a number of educational and developmental principles (see Guralnick, 1976, 1978b) that would suggest that well-designed mainstreamed environments could be more effective in this regard. In addition, recent developmental research pointing to the independent contributions of young children to the social and communicative development of their peers (Guralnick, 1981a, 1981c; Hartup, 1976, 1978; Mueller, 1979; Mueller & Brenner, 1977; Rubenstein & Howes, 1976, 1979) also suggests that mainstreamed programs may prove to be more effective than segregated ones. Nevertheless, it is important to note that although the efficacy concept is of considerable significance, an evaluation of the effectiveness of mainstreaming in relation to public policy is linked only to feasibility. It is certainly *not* essential to establish that mainstreamed programs are more effective than conventional ones to satisfy the intent of the least restrictive principle.

Evaluation Criteria and Outcome
Measures for Effectiveness

The next step in developing the research and evaluation model is to identify a comprehensive and integrated set of specific evaluation criteria and measurement strategies. As with any complex concept, these evaluation criteria and measures can take many forms, each representing an important dimension of the problem. Although numerous systems are possible, four categories for evaluation and associated outcome measures have been selected: (1) product measures—focusing on developmental outcomes; (2) process measures—emphasizing classroom-related factors; (3) social integration and attitude measures; and (4) measures reflecting the developmental potential of interactions occurring between handicapped and nonhandicapped children.

The first two classes of measures are related to meeting children's educational/developmental needs; the remaining two are unique to the mainstreaming process (see right hand portion of Figure 19–3). It should also be noted that these

Figure 19-3.   Description of key variables related to the feasibility of mainstreamed classrooms.

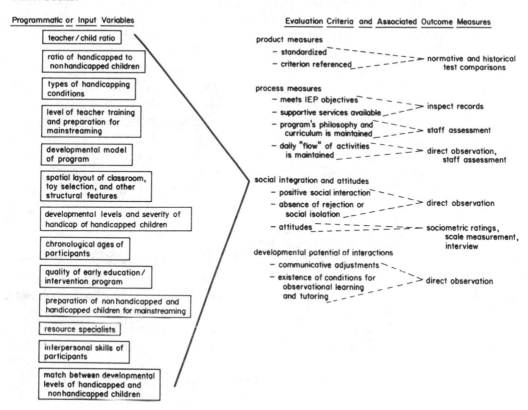

four categories have been selected for descriptive and organizational purposes only. Although presented separately, they should not be seen as independent dimensions since clear interrelationships exist both within and between categories. Moreover, although Figure 19–3 specifies feasibility, virtually all of the concepts apply to efficacy as well.

At the product level, standardized tests or criterion-referenced instruments can be used to assess cognitive and social growth as well as other areas of development, such as a child's self-concept. It is important to note here that adequate assessment requires that measures of social competence be included and be considered as vital as measures of intellectual development (Zigler & Trickett, 1978, 1979).

Judgments of effectiveness, either feasibility or efficacy, require some form of comparative analysis. Unfortunately, irrespective of the assessment area, product level comparative evaluation strategies in this area will not be able to utilize conventional procedures. This results from the fact that in attempting to directly compare mainstreamed and nonmainstreamed programs, it is difficult to achieve not only the initial equivalence of subjects across programs but also to obtain comparability of program related factors. In fact, educational programs differ along so many dimensions, especially those related to program quality, that even with elaborate sampling procedures and stratification it is virtually impossible to eliminate alternative and competing explanations of outcomes. These methodological problems plague effectiveness studies in special education in general (Kaufman & Alberto, 1976) as well as those related to mainstreaming at all educational levels (Corman & Gottlieb, 1978; Guralnick, 1981d).

Accordingly, strategies for product-level analyses of effectiveness are forced to rely on approaches that require numerous assumptions to be made and will typically permit only estimates for comparing differences in development as they occur over time. These include internally generated expectations of development based on previous experiences with children in segregated programs, projections of development estimated from an individual child's developmental history, predictions from normative information, and direct comparisons between programs serving similar but not matched groups of children.[2] Clearly, the careful application of some form of quasi-experimental design will be needed in most instances (Campbell & Stanley, 1963).

Despite these problems, a creative application and combination of approaches are capable of generating information that is sufficient to provide convincing support for arguments related to effectiveness. One example is the study by Ispa and Matz (1978), who employed information based on children's histories of development in combination with expectancies derived from normative data. This is a particularly common strategy for assessing the effectiveness of a newly established mainstreamed program. Administering the McCarthy Scales of Children's Abilities (MSCA) to assess cognitive growth in children in two mainstreamed classrooms, these investigators obtained significant pre–post increases in MSCA scores across all children, with the average child's developmental growth being accelerated considerably. Further analyses indicated that, despite the lower average performance of the handicapped children in their sample, their rate of increased development was virtually identical to that of their nonhandicapped classmates. This rate of growth was far in excess of that which would be expected on the basis of the developmental histories of these handicapped children.

At a process, day-to-day level, criteria for effectiveness should include aspects of what is perhaps best characterized as the face validity of the program. More explicitly, we would ask: Do activities flow as they had prior to the involvement of handicapped children; are teachers able to interact with all children as needed; are the individualized educational plans (IEPs) sensible; are the appropriate services provided; do teachers and administrators perceive the program's theoretical approach as remaining intact; and are all children acquiring educational objectives at an acceptable rate? Relevant measures at the process level using strategies such as inspection of records and objective and subjective staff assessments are another essential component for judging the effectiveness of a program.

---

[2] Although it is beyond the scope of this chapter to discuss this point further, selection of segregated programs for comparison should be carefully carried out since they too vary widely in quality and other relevant characteristics.

An evaluation of activities that relate directly to the integration of handicapped and nonhandicapped children and their developmental implications should include a criterion focusing on the extent to which actual social integration occurs. The inclusion of this measure clearly reflects an important intent of mainstreaming and, although this issue will require clarification, it is likely that most observers would concur that social integration should be evident to some extent. At a minimum, social isolation and rejection of handicapped children by their classmates should not be detected to any substantial degree nor should there be evidence of interference with their typical social patterns. Evaluating the extent of social integration in relation to effectiveness is a difficult issue and will be discussed in more detail in a later section.

Similarly, measurements of the attitudes of all concerned toward handicapped children, including teacher and child satisfaction with the preschool experience and affective and cognitive aspects of relationships with handicapped children, are important to obtain. The use of interviews, rating scales, and sociometric techniques could be employed toward this end. It is recognized that assessments of children's attitudes are of questionable stability and interact with the stages of cognitive development of the participants. However, it is essential that efforts to assess these characteristics continue, and we should be encouraged by the recent progress that has been made in developing reliable measures of sociometric choice for preschool children (Asher et al., 1979).

The final category, and one not often considered, consists of evaluation criteria and measures related to the potential developmental value of interactions to the participants when interactions occur. That is, based on our knowledge of the events and conditions that foster development in young children, we should ask if the interactions in mainstreamed environments have the potential for contributing to each child's growth. For example, are reciprocal social and communicative interactions occurring among children at different developmental levels or are children failing to adjust to the differences in cognitive and language levels that exist between normally developing and handicapped classmates? From a somewhat different perspective, we can ask if conditions exist in which observations of more advanced behavior by the handicapped children can occur and if the program is organized to permit the use of advanced peers as adjuncts in educational and therapeutic activities (Guralnick, 1976, 1977, 1978b).[3]

Guidelines for Determining Effectiveness

At some point, a decision as to the feasibility or efficacy of a specific mainstreamed classroom program must occur. Such a decision should be guided by relevant

---

[3] Peers as agents of change is included here but can be considered as an entirely independent domain. Mainstreaming does permit, if properly carried out, the use of tutorial techniques not available in homogeneously grouped segregated classes of handicapped children.

qualitative and quantitative criteria outlined above, although establishing absolute cut-off points does not seem advisable at this time. Rather, this decision should reflect a careful, relative, and balanced analysis of each of the four major categories of proposed effectiveness measures and their criteria as well as considerations of the quality and extent of the information at hand. As noted earlier, judgments of effectiveness will be based in part on the apparent validity of the assumptions of group comparability or estimates of development. If this approach seems somewhat cavalier, it is important to recognize that although precision would be welcome, a more realistic goal is to seek approximations that are sufficiently reliable to permit a judgment by informed observers as to the effectiveness of a mainstreamed program.

With respect to product and process measures for assessing educational and developmental progress, the existence of substantial differences in outcomes between comparable children in mainstreamed and segregated programs or between expected and actual development of children enrolled in mainstreamed programs can be used as a standard for evaluating effectiveness. As noted, data based on normative standards, comparisons of similar children in mainstreamed and segregated settings, and expectations based on the past history of results of a program for individual children should suffice for a product analysis. In addition, inspecting records to assess the quality of each child's IEP, determining the availability of supportive services as described in that IEP, and obtaining estimates of daily child progress can be easily accomplished and evaluated in terms of readily developed criteria for determining if substantial differences exist. Similarly, the essential structure and flow of a program must be maintained; instruments to measure this should not be difficult to construct.

Despite the admittedly subjective nature of the decision-making aspect of this process, new quantitative techniques related to product measures have been developed that bear directly on this issue. Although still in experimental phases, these techniques are useful both in quantifying what is meant by substantial differences and in addressing the problem of comparing groups that are not strictly comparable along all critical dimensions other than that of the intervention. In this case, the mainstreamed program would be considered as the intervention. Essentially, in this approach the possibility of statistically adjusting for differences when samples are not strictly controlled through random assignment (for example, by using analysis of covariance procedures) is rejected as unalterably biased. In its place, the development of standards of comparison based upon estimates of performance that would have occurred in the absence of the intervention are recommended (Bryk & Weisberg, 1977; Weisberg, 1979). Perhaps most promising in this regard is the value-added analysis proposed by Bryk and Weisberg (1976), which, although requiring important historical information and assumptions regarding growth in the absence of intervention, is capable of testing effectiveness by employing various growth estimates as standards. Other empirical approaches, such as the Bayesian analyses suggested by Rubin (1978), have direct applications to the problem of effectiveness as well. A strength inherent in these statistical models is their insistence on making assumptions explicit and in establishing a range of estimates to be used for comparison. Such explicitness permits a level of professional consensus not normally found in feasibility or efficacy studies.

The importance of evaluating the effectiveness of a particular program in comparison to other *similar* programs should be underscored. Despite the fact that there are a number of product measures that transcend individual program models, theoretical frameworks and goals of early education/intervention programs are so diverse, focus on so many different priorities, and are so specific in including children with only certain types of handicaps as to render universal comparisons difficult if not impossible to obtain. This point further emphasizes the fact that overall judgments of effectiveness, particularly at the product and process levels, must await cumulative outcomes from numerous programs with multiple evaluation approaches (see Light & Smith, 1970). However, at the individual program level, programs should be encouraged, within their framework, to develop their own criteria for detecting substantial differences for product and process measures (for example, Bryk, Meisels & Markowitz, 1979).[4]

Guidelines for evaluating the effectiveness of social integration are even more elusive. A strong developmental framework is lacking for interpreting the frequency of positive social interactions with different companions and their possible developmental consequences (Goldman, 1976; Hartup, 1978). Even the quantitative evaluation of "how much" social integration constitutes an effective mainstreamed program is subject to considerable interpretation and value judgments. Certainly, we cannot expect to achieve complete social integration, since social separation occurs along many dimensions, including chronological age, sex, physical characteristics, and socioeconomic status (Feitelson, Weintraub & Michaeli, 1972; Goldman, 1976; Langlois & Downs, 1979). In fact, there are many positive reasons why social separation should exist to some extent (Guralnick, 1981a).

Compounding these problems in interpretation is the fact that virtually no information is available to permit investigators to gauge how socially interactive handicapped children are in segregated programs. Although current research may yet provide us with the necessary baseline information (Field, 1980; Guralnick & Weinhouse, in preparation), the peer relations of handicapped children remain a little understood area of development (Guralnick, 1981a). Furthermore, qualitative assessments in areas such as friendship formation among children pose important questions but generate even greater degrees of complexity.

Accordingly, we should await a reasonable consensus from the early childhood community on these issues while continuing to gather data and developing our conceptual models of peer-related social development. Until this

---

[4] There is no doubt that programs vary in terms of their effectiveness and that a common metric could be of value. The importance of variations in program quality is considered as a programmatic variable and is discussed in that context.

occurs, it seems reasonable to propose that mainstreaming is effective under this criterion if two conditions are met. First, observations indicate no evidence to suggest that handicapped children are being almost totally rejected by their non-handicapped classmates. Second, no substantial reductions or other deviations in the frequency and quality of positive, sustained social interactions with classmates, handicapped or not, occur.

Direct observations of social interactions should be supported by data from sociometric ratings and attitudinal assessments obtained across time in main-streamed settings. Although it is premature to state specific effectiveness standards, feasible programs at minimum must ensure that attitudes toward handicapped children remain similar to those prior to contact in mainstreamed programs. If there are indications that more positive attitudes are developing as a result of this contact, as many proponents of mainstreaming suggest will occur, then a possible case for efficacy can be established.

We are on firmer ground with respect to assessing the developmental potential of those social/communicative interactions when they do occur among handicapped and nonhandicapped children, since considerable developmental data are available. For example, research centering on communicative interactions among normally developing children at different chronological ages has demonstrated that even four-year-olds adjust the syntactic complexity, semantic features, functional use, and discourse characteristics of their speech in accordance with the cognitive and linguistic abilities of younger listeners (Gelman & Shatz, 1977; Masur, 1978; Sachs & Devin, 1976; Shatz & Gelman, 1973). In fact, Shatz and Gelman (1973) point out that "the nature of the adjustments suggests that young speaker and very young listener interact to produce a linguistic environment favorable to the process of language acquisition" (p. 34). Clearly, similar adjustments by nonhandicapped classmates when communicating with handicapped children at different developmental levels would be essential in order for effective communication to occur or to have the potential for creating a linguistic environment that can foster language acquisition. Other frameworks must be constructed to guide an assessment of interactions for children with sensory, motor, or behavioral problems.

Opportunities should also be available for observational learning. At minimum, considerable physical proximity should be apparent between handicapped and nonhandicapped children in order to encourage such learning. Assessing the proximity of children to one another during play activities, particularly during parallel play, could be easily accomplished along with measures of immediate and delayed imitation. Similarly, classroom activities and structure should be conducive to procedures that directly use nonhandicapped children as agents of change for handicapped children (Guralnick, 1976, 1978c; Strain, 1977). This can be considered conceptually similar to cross-age tutoring programs for nonhandicapped children. Mainstreamed programs present this unique and important opportunity for handicapped children, and evidence for the systematic use of nonhandicapped peers should be available. This can include groups composed explicitly for therapeutic or educational purposes or specific one-to-one tutoring programs (see V. L. Allen, 1976).

Programmatic or Input Variables

Whether or not minimal criteria for the four major evaluation categories are reached by an individual program depends upon important characteristics associated with that program, such as the administrative structure, staffing pattern, access to related services, and the nature and characteristics of the children participating. A listing of these programmatic factors can be found on the left-hand side of Figure 19–3. This list is not intended to be exhaustive (see Blacher-Dixon & Turnbull, 1979, for an extensive description of potential influences) but is designed to illustrate the wide range of factors that are likely to affect measures related to the effectiveness of mainstreamed programs. (For an expanded discussion of these programmatic factors, see Guralnick, 1981b.) Some of these programmatic variables are fundamental to any early education program, such as the quality of the program's organizational structure, accountability systems, inservice activities, or the consistency between the model's theoretical position and practical application (see Guralnick, 1975; Karnes, 1977; McDaniels, 1977; Weikart, 1972). However, most of the variables have been selected for characteristics unique to mainstreaming. The essential point here is that these programmatic factors will moderate the effectiveness of a mainstreamed program and do so in an interactive and compensatory fashion. For example, extensive differences between the developmental levels of children in a mainstreamed classroom would likely require greater access to resource specialists, more extensive teacher preparation for mainstreaming, and probably a higher teacher/child ratio in order for the program to be considered feasible. Similarly, for those early education/intervention programs adopting the normal developmental model (see Anastasiow, 1978), the programmatic variable profile necessary to achieve feasibility if severely handicapped children were to be included would differ vastly from a program that included only speech-impaired youngsters, for example. This profile, in turn, would differ for behaviorally based programs. Certainly, not all of these factors equally affect evaluation criteria for effectiveness, and there are likely to be limits to the compensatory abilities of these factors.

This relationship between programmatic or input variables and the evaluation criteria for effectiveness highlights an important direction for future research. Although it is generally agreed that the level of these programmatic factors will limit the effectiveness of mainstreamed programs, especially in relation to the area of social interactions (Guralnick, 1981b), virtually no research has been conducted in the context of mainstreamed programs. Nevertheless, these programmatic factors can function in practice as a guide to program design when mainstreaming is being considered. If the levels of these variables are identified and recorded, they can form what Bell and Hertz (1976) describe as "marker variables;" a strategy useful in defining significant parameters for relatively new areas of investigation.

An Ecological Systems Approach

Up to this point, the concepts of feasibility and efficacy have been discussed primarily within the boundaries typically associated with P. L. 94–142, that is, the classroom. Although the social forces that guided the development of P. L. 94–142 and the authors who ultimately cast it into legislation certainly intended that its impact transcend classroom interactions, the processes and procedures of the law quite properly center on classroom events. However, for a complete understanding and comprehensive assessment of the impact of mainstreaming to occur, it must be viewed in a much broader context. Major social/educational programs affect and are affected by numerous factors, including formal and informal systems established at every level of our society, institutional patterns, and overarching cultural values. To capture this more comprehensive perspective, a model that is capable of recognizing and organizing our knowledge of these complex factors, that reflects the interrelationships that exist at many levels, and that is compatible with the concepts of feasibility and efficacy previously described would be of great use.

Bronfenbrenner (1977) has proposed an ecological model of human development that appears to meet these criteria. Of most interest here is his multilevel conception of the environment and the nature of the interrelationships postulated to occur among the structures composing that environment and the developing individuals. In essence, four ecological levels are identified, each consisting of interrelations among its elements and containing properties specific to its own level. Although Bronfenbrenner's paper and his extensive discussion in a later publication (1979) should be consulted directly to appreciate the richness and significance of his approach to human development research, his organization of the ecological environment will be expanded in this chapter to incorporate the concepts of feasibility and efficacy as applied to mainstreaming. Figure 19–4 anticipates this discussion by depicting a matrix that joins these two major components. As will be seen, this matrix is designed not only to function as a means of organizing our present knowledge but also to function as a heuristic device. Toward these ends, the following sections will consist of a description of the ecological levels, a discussion of the types of questions addressed at each level in relation to feasibility and efficacy, and finally, a review of the available evidence for each cell of the matrix.

The *microsystem* is the first of the four ecological levels and consists of *"the complex of relations between the developing person and the environment in an immediate setting containing that person (e.g., home, school, workplace, etc.)"* (Bronfenbrenner, 1977, p. 514; emphasis in original). Given this definition, it can be seen that the mainstreaming issues discussed up to this point have focused exclusively on the microsystem. Figure 19–3 reflected this fact as it described only child–environment interactions in the classroom setting. As we have seen, ques-

Figure 19-4. Matrix joining the outcome focus of mainstreamed programs with ecological levels.

ECOLOGICAL LEVELS

	Microsystem	Mesosystem	Exosystem	Macrosystem
Feasibility				
Efficacy				

(left vertical label: OUTCOME FOCUS)

tions relating to this cell are concerned with the existence of reasonable levels of cognitive and social development for all children, determining the extent of social integration and associated attitudes that develop, examining the nature and type of adjustments that occur among children at different developmental levels, evaluating the potential of these interactions for facilitating development, and assessing the opportunities that are available for observational learning and tutoring. It is also possible to consider analyses of subsystems within a setting and to ask many of the same questions as they apply to one or more of these subsystems. For example, the extent of social integration can be analyzed as it occurs during indoor free play as well as during gross motor activities. These types of subsystem comparisons, within a given setting, are important issues related to effectiveness and are particularly useful in providing program planners with empirical information that may assist in decision making with respect to the form and extent of mainstreaming (Guralnick, 1980a).

Since the microsystem involves an analysis of the relationship between the immediate setting and the developing child, effectiveness questions here are limited to the relatively short-term impact of different environments. Although the possibility exists that the effects of mainstreaming may not manifest themselves until well beyond the preschool years (Brown, 1978; Lazar et al., 1977), evaluating the immediate impact of different environments is nevertheless of great interest, particularly if negative effects are uncovered.

The second ecological system, the *mesosystem*, *"comprises the interrelations among major settings containing the developing person"* (Bronfenbrenner, 1977, p. 515; emphasis in original). From this perspective, questions of most interest involve the relationship between the home and classroom as well as between the effects of classroom experiences and later development. For example, it is important to determine if parents are as satisfied with mainstreamed programs as they had been with the segregated arrangement or if significant changes in satisfaction occur as a result of this new educational strategy. Similarly, assessments of possible changes in general parental attitudes toward their handicapped child and to specific parent–child relations are essential areas for investigation.

Since a mesosystem analysis also encompasses assessments of the effects of a mainstreamed preschool experience on later school performance or on specific behavioral or social characteristics, important questions are how the system affects long-term developmental patterns and whether these patterns differ substantially from those that existed before mainstreaming. The inclusion of measures of social and interpersonal competence as well as academic and intellectual performance (see Zigler & Trickett, 1978) should be underscored again not only as important variables related to feasibility but also because many proponents of mainstreamed programs are hopeful that efficacy studies will reveal gains in the social domain on the part of the handicapped child that exceed those that would have occurred through participation in segregated programs.

Complex formal and informal networks that affect the person being focused upon constitute the level of the *exosystem*, defined as "*an extension of the mesosystem embracing other specific social structures, both formal and informal, that do not themselves contain the developing person but impinge upon or encompass the immediate settings in which that person is found, and thereby influence, delimit, or even determine what goes on there*" (Bronfenbrenner, 1977, p. 515; emphasis in original). An analysis at this ecological level raises a number of important questions in relation to mainstreaming. For example, it is essential to determine mainstreaming's impact on the public or private nursery school system. The inclusion of handicapped children in typical preschool settings will likely generate new pressures, such as those resulting from increased needs to deliver health care and modifications required in transportation systems. The social networks and support systems within the neighborhood are likely to be affected, and assessments of the consequences of mainstreaming on these domains have important developmental and social policy implications. It is also probable that our institutions of higher education will be affected, with collaboration between special and general education becoming more common. As a result, we may see a broadening of a curriculum for training personnel in this area that encompasses the entire spectrum of child-family-community interactions (Hirshoren & Umansky, 1977; Kaiser, 1980).

The feasibility and efficacy questions related to the exosystem are more difficult to address objectively since outcome criteria for assessing the impact of social/educational programs on complex systems are not well established. Even though it might be useful at this level simply to adopt an uncritical empirical orientation, we would like assurance that our major institutions and informal and formal networks are accommodating effectively to mainstreaming in the same manner that individual classrooms may be accommodating to the presence of handicapped children. Whether parents and their handicapped children participate satisfactorily in neighborhood activities and whether generic agencies of all types are able to provide reasonable services are questions that deserve our attention. Should segments of the exosystem not be able to expand and adjust to these pressures without radical change, severe limitations to the effectiveness of mainstreaming will result. Finally, from an efficacy perspective, it would be interesting to determine if the introduction of handicapped children into the young child service community can have the impact of modifying and enlarging that system's conceptualization of child growth and development.

The clearest expression of the embeddedness of these ecological levels within one another can be found in Bronfenbrenner's concept of the *macrosystem:* "A *macrosystem refers to the overarching institutional patterns of the culture or subculture, such as the economic, social, educational, legal, and political systems, of which micro-, meso-, and exo-systems are concrete manifestations*" (1977, p. 515; emphasis in original). The fundamental commitment of society to handicapped children, including their right to education in the mainstream of our culture, is being tested, particularly in these times of economic stress. Similarly, it is possible that, for many members of society, fundamental concepts of human ontogeny in relation to atypical modes of development are being challenged. It is in this world of assumptions and habit patterns that often take on qualities of reflexive behaviors that we may be able to evaluate most validly the strength of the commitment to mainstreaming as well as to examine critically the underlying ideologies we all hold.

Since it is most apparent that the concepts of feasibility and efficacy must be integrated within a dynamic value system at the level of the macrosystem, evaluating shifting societal attitudes with respect to diversity and deviance, prompted by social legislation, is most critical. As in other types of related social legislation and judicial decision-making, such as that concerned with racial integration, contact with handicapped children in a particular context with specified resources can create a wide range of effects, many of which may be diametrically opposite to those intended by the legislation itself. In any event, mainstreaming may emerge as a true "transforming experiment" (Bronfenbrenner, 1977, p. 528), and our instruments should be prepared to assess its impact at all ecological levels.

Evaluation of Research Findings

The following section will provide a brief review of the evidence for effectiveness at each of the four ecological levels. In selecting materials for this review, isolated individual case studies and general programmatic descriptions of projects claiming effectiveness have been omitted. Included, however, are a number of systematic case study investigations, studies providing evidence of objective measures consistent with their own theoretical framework, and reports considered as having a substantive empirical base. Data have been drawn from studies reflecting a wide range of educational arrangements. Although not reviewed here, the growing number of published impressionistic and anecdotal reports does suggest, with certain exceptions (for example, Simon & Gillman, 1979), that with proper support, teachers and administrators generally perceive mainstreaming as a highly positive educational strategy (Guralnick, 1978a; Turnbull & Blacher-Dixon, 1981). One must hope that these programs will take a more objective approach in the future compatible with the criteria for effectiveness outlined in this chapter.

Evidence for Feasibility and Efficacy at the Microsystem Level

PRODUCT MEASURES

As expected, most of the research relating to the effectiveness of mainstreamed programs for preschool children that used product measures has been conducted at the level of the microsystem. In an early study, Bricker and Bricker (1972) described an intervention project composed of twelve handicapped and thirteen nonhandicapped toddlers. Using Bayley Developmental Quotients, these investigators found substantial developmental gains for both groups during the year, clearly suggesting the project's feasibility. In a more comprehensive study, Ispa and Matz (1978) evaluated the developmental progress of twenty-eight preschool-age children enrolled in two mainstreamed classrooms. Pre- and posttests on the McCarthy Scales of Children's Abilities revealed that considerable progress was achieved over the school year; in fact, for all children an average gain of over two months in mental age for each month of actual preschool experience was obtained. Further analysis indicated that scores for both handicapped and nonhandicapped children increased at about the same rate despite initial differences in the distribution of their scores.

Similar findings were obtained in two large-scale community program evaluations. Galloway and Chandler (1978) analyzed developmental changes in fifty developmentally delayed children enrolled in community-based integrated programs, using the Alpern-Boll Developmental Profile as the measure of change. Assessments of child growth were obtained across an average of approximately a six-month period. The results revealed that substantial gains occurred for mildly delayed children (approximately six months gained in each developmental area throughout the six months enrolled in the program) and for those children considered moderately delayed (gains ranged from two to five months per six-month period). However, children considered severely/profoundly handicapped did not show any developmental progress.

In an equally extensive study but one that was designed to compare children's progress in segregated and integrated settings, Cooke, Ruskus, Peck, and Apolloni (1979) employed a battery of assessments related to social and cognitive development to evaluate growth in these settings across a one-year period. These evaluations revealed that nonhandicapped children in integrated settings fared as well or slightly better than nonhandicapped children enrolled in segregated programs (private preschools, parent co-op, and small rural school, none containing handicapped children). Handicapped children, most of whom were mildly delayed but who were all enrolled in integrated programs, showed marked developmental progress, well beyond that expected from their past histories of development.

Follow-up analyses with different comparisons obtained over a three-year period (Cooke, Ruskus, Apolloni & Peck, 1981), although indicating small variations in outcomes as a function of the type of measure employed, still provided strong support for the feasibility of mainstreaming. Since these comparisons were made across intact groups, they were likely to be nonequivalent along certain dimensions. Accordingly, it should be noted once again that the persuasiveness of the feasibility argument in such studies rests both with projections of expected development and the probable similarity of the groups along characteristics that could affect the outcome measures.

Direct assessments of social and play behaviors of children also constitute important dimensions of effectiveness. For example, Novak, Olley, and Kearney (1980) found that the social behaviors of handicapped children enrolled in an integrated setting, in contrast to those enrolled in a segregated setting, more closely resembled those of nonhandicapped children. This is a particularly intriguing finding, but the observations were of children enrolled in pre-existing programs. In an effort to avoid this problem of nonequivalent groups, Guralnick (1981e) employed a within-subjects design. In this approach, the availability of a child's playmates (and their corresponding developmental characteristics) was systematically manipulated, but since all children participated in the different experimental conditions, the usual confoundings related to teacher behavior, toy availability, and subject selection and assignment were of no concern. This design was limited to an assessment of relatively immediate short-term effects, and care must be taken to rule out possible carryover effects from condition to condition.

In this investigation, the social participation, constructiveness of play, and communicative interactions of four- to six-year-old delayed and nonhandicapped children were obtained when these children interacted in playgroups homogeneous with respect to developmental level and in heterogeneous playgroups. Selected teacher behaviors, such as prompting and positive and negative interactions, were also recorded. Analyzing data separately for children classified as mildly, moderately, and severely delayed and nonhandicapped, the group composition variable (the developmental level of the children in the play setting was systematically varied) produced a significant effect only for the constructiveness of play measure. Additional analyses of the data revealed that this effect was due to a reduction in the inappropriate play of severely delayed children while they interacted in a heterogeneous playgroups (including children from all developmental levels). Although this latter finding has a bearing on the efficacy issue, the most important outcomes relate to the feasibility of mainstreamed programs. Specifically, no detrimental effects as a function of group composition were obtained for any developmental-level group of children for any social or play measure nor were teacher interactions adversely affected.

PROCESS MEASURES

Only limited information is available on issues related to the process measures of mainstreaming (see also section on Head Start below). Nevertheless, teachers generally tend to maintain a positive attitude toward mainstreaming (see review by K. E. Allen, 1980) which may suggest that they are able to maintain their primary educational approach to development and obtain necessary supportive services. Direct observations of teachers distributing their interactions among children with diverse characteristics and their ability to meet instructional objectives further supports the feasibility of mainstreaming at the process level. Teachers do modify the frequency and quality of their exchanges when interacting with handicapped children, but this does not appear to affect the typical flow of activities (Fink & Sandall, 1978; Guralnick, 1981e; Ispa, 1981; Ispa & Matz, 1978).

Social Integration

The extent to which handicapped preschool children are socially integrated with nonhandicapped children has received a considerable degree of attention. Early work by Ray (1974) revealed that handicapped and nonhandicapped toddlers interacted to only a very limited degree with one another. More recent investigations, however, have indicated that the extent of social integration varies most closely with the severity of a child's handicap. For example, in the previously described Ispa and Matz (1978) study, a large number of social behavior categories such as "asks for help," "complies," "takes," and "gives/shows" were assessed. These investigators then compared the expected frequency of interactions for each behavior category (based on the availability of handicapped and nonhandicapped children) to the observed frequency as a measure of the extent of social integration. With minor exceptions, this analysis revealed that integration from the perspectives of both groups was virtually complete. It is important to note that despite the diversity of types of handicap manifested by children in this study, their handcaps were generally mild in contrast to Ray's (1974) group. This is perhaps most apparent when it is noted that the level of social participation for Ispa and Matz's children as measured by the Parten (1932) scale did not differ between the handicapped and nonhandicapped groups. Moreover, the handicapped group's average chronological age was higher by approximately one year than their nonhandicapped classmates.

Further evidence for the interpretation that the extent of social integration varies with the severity of a child's handicap was obtained in a recent study by Guralnick (1980b). Also using a criterion of availability, the social/communicative interactions of severely, moderately, mildly, and nonhandicapped children were assessed in two time segments over a one-year period. The results supported previous findings in that nonhandicapped and mildly handicapped children (developmentally delayed children in this case) were completely socially integrated with one another. Moderately and severely delayed children, on the other hand, received only limited social/communicative interactions (14 percent) from the developmentally advanced children.

The consistency of results related to social integration and severity of handicap is remarkable in view of the diverse nature of the outcome measures employed. The studies reviewed above as well as others (Arnold & Tremblay, 1979; Cavallaro & Porter, 1980; Ispa, 1981; Peterson & Haralick, 1977; Porter et al., 1978; White, 1980) have included measures such as vocalizations, proximal and distal gazing, mutual object play, gestures, location in group, and seating choices. In addition, the findings generally seem to hold across types of handicap (for example, primary sensory or motor disability), but this conclusion must remain tentative since only a small number of studies focusing on children with other than primary cognitive (developmental) delays have been conducted.

A consistent but different pattern has also been obtained when social integration from the perspective of the handicapped child is considered. Specifically, handicapped children appear to direct their social interactions equally to both handicapped and nonhandicapped groups. This is true for mildly and moderately handicapped children (for instance, Ispa, 1981) and for children with profound hearing impairments (Arnold & Tremblay, 1979). Severely developmentally delayed children also do not reveal a preference, but this likely reflects an absence of an ability or desire to discriminate among playmates (Guralnick, 1980b).

Despite the fact that social separation exists as a function of severity of handicap, other related findings are relevant to the issue of feasibility. First, negative comments addressed to handicapped children appear to be very rare, and there is little evidence of actual rejection in other forms as well. Second, opportunities for observational learning by the handicapped children seem extensive. For example, in the Guralnick (1980b) study, approximately 30 percent of the parallel play interactions involved both developmentally advanced and less advanced children. In contrast to measures of active involvement such as associative play, more passive measures such as looking evaluated across the social integration studies noted above indicated less social separation (Guralnick, 1981d).

ATTITUDES

Research related to the effects of mainstreaming on teacher and child attitudes has been almost totally neglected. Admittedly, assessing these attitudes in young children is extremely difficult from a methodological perspective, but dimensions of sociometric choice (for instance, Asher et al., 1979) are certainly potentially useful. Even programs designed to foster children's attitude change in mainstreamed programs are only at a preliminary stage (Cohen, 1977).

Positive teacher attitudes, of course, are crucial to the success of any mainstreamed program (Klein, 1975). The effects of their absence is perhaps most clearly seen in a report by Simon and Gillman (1979) involving visually impaired children. Fortunately, a number of surveys do suggest that initially positive attitudes seem characteristic of most preschool teachers (see review by K. E. Allen, 1980). Well-designed preschool classrooms with adequate support personnel can also promote positive teacher attitudes (Clark, 1976).

DEVELOPMENTAL POTENTIAL

Communicative Adjustments.   As discussed earlier, the occurrence of communicative adjustments by nonhandicapped children when addressing children at different developmental levels or types of handicap is vital for effective communication and for establishing the potential of such interactions to facilitate social/communicative development. The nature of these communicative interactions for children at different developmental levels was the focus of a series of studies conducted by Guralnick and Paul-Brown (1977, 1980, in preparation). In the first study, a wide variety of linguistic parameters derived from the speech of nonhandicapped children as addressed to delayed and other nonhandicapped children was examined. Assessing communicative interactions in both instructional and free-play contexts, these investigators found that, in general, the nonhandicapped children's speech was less frequent, less complex, and less diverse when addressed to the developmentally less advanced children. Additional analyses of the data suggested that the language environment of children at different developmental levels as provided by nonhandicapped children was sufficiently adjusted to ensure effective communication yet press for the development of more advanced language.

Further work replicated these findings for structural parameters (productivity and syntactic complexity measures) and also assessed adjustments of selected functional and discourse characteristics of the speech of nonhandicapped children (Guralnick & Paul-Brown, 1980). Functional measures included an analysis of the way an utterance was used—for example, as behavior request or in seeking information. Also assessed were such discourse features as the use of repetitions, turn taking, and the amount of nonverbal assistance that was provided. The evidence from this analysis supports the proposition that nonhandicapped children adjust their communicative interactions so that messages can be understood and responded to. These adjustments to handicapped children also seemed consistent with the communicative goals of the speaker, the demands of the situation, and the perceived roles of the participants.

In the most recent study of this series (Guralnick & Paul-Brown, in preparation), communicative episodes in a tutorial situation were examined under circumstances in which nonhandicapped children did not obtain initial compliance from delayed children to their behavior requests. Analyses of these episodes focused on the adaptiveness of the strategies employed by nonhandicapped children to seek a resolution to this lack of compliance. Sequential analysis techniques for individual child–child exchanges were applied to evaluate the resolution patterns that emerged as a function of the developmental level of the listener. Once again, based on a variety of criteria that included a content analysis of specific adaptive strategies and resolution outcome patterns, these results supported earlier work in that the communicative interactions of nonhandicapped children appeared to be adjusted appropriately in accordance with the developmental levels of their listeners.

Taken together, results based on structural, functional, and discourse pat-

terns of adjustment of nonhandicapped children's speech as addressed to handicapped children at different developmental levels have converged to suggest the
occurrence of appropriate communicative adjustments. Of course, these studies
establish only that the communicative environment is potentially supportive of
the communicative development of handicapped children. To establish that the
mainstreamed environment actually benefits handicapped children to a greater
extent than segregated environments requires a series of experimental investigations with designs substantially different from those discussed here. Nevertheless,
these findings for developmentally delayed children are compatible with the
growing developmental literature concerned with communicative adjustments
that young children make to even younger normally developing children (Gelman
& Shatz, 1977; Guralnick, 1981c; James, 1978; Masur, 1978; Sachs & Devin,
1976; Shatz & Gelman, 1973). The potential value of a communicative environment with adjustments in this manner has been previously established in the
parent–child data (for example, Broen, 1972; Snow, 1972; Snow & Ferguson,
1977). Accordingly, it would certainly not be surprising if future work found that,
in comparison to segregated environments, adaptive communication in
mainstreamed settings contributes substantially to the development of the communicative competence of handicapped children.

Despite the consistency of these findings, it is not clear how "finely tuned"
these interactions of the nonhandicapped children are to the level of the listener
(see Mahoney, 1975; Mahoney & Seely, 1976). Additional sequential designs applied to interactive data obtained from free play and other multiperson settings
are essential to corroborate findings that are based primarily on situations that
were instructional in purpose. The effectiveness of interactions with children with
sensory, orthopedic, communicative, or emotional disabilities has not been
systematically studied. The limited data that are available suggest that nonhandicapped children do not appropriately adjust their social/communicative interactions to hearing-impaired children (Arnold & Tremblay, 1979; Vandell &
George, 1981).

Of special interest, but from a different perspective, are possible adjustments
made by the handicapped children themselves when communicating with children at different developmental levels. Recent work by Fey, Leonard, and Wilcox
(1981) suggests that language-impaired children do in fact modify their speech as
a function of listener, pointing toward certain therapeutic applications (see
Guralnick, 1981c). This form of "code-switching" (Gleason, 1973) for all children
may be an important developmental skill, and mainstreamed programs provide
extensive opportunities for its development and refinement.

Imitation. As indicated in the earlier section on social integration,
naturalistic observations of children in mainstreamed settings during parallel play
suggested that certain conditions would enable observational learning by handicapped children. The potential for observation and consequent imitation of more
advanced behavior by handicapped children in mainstreamed settings is considered to be an important element of effectiveness (Bricker, 1978; Guralnick,

1976, 1978b; Hartup, 1978; Nordquist, 1978). Unfortunately, we know very little about the extent to which imitation occurs in natural classroom settings among handicapped and nonhandicapped children. An exception is Devoney, Guralnick, and Rubin's (1974) anecdotal report of the existence of deferred imitation by handicapped children of nonhandicapped children's advanced play activities (see also Feitelson, Weintraub & Michaeli, 1972).

Despite the absence of data from naturalistic settings, the general developmental literature does suggest that more competent models are imitated more frequently, and it is likely that the effectiveness of modeling among children at different developmental levels will be subject to the same influences (Akamatsu & Thelen, 1974; Bandura, 1971; Strichart, 1974). In support of this conjecture, Peterson, Peterson, and Scriven (1977) have provided evidence from a laboratory study that handicapped preschool children prefer to imitate nonhandicapped peers. The benefits of imitation, then, appear to be strongly rooted in developmental principles, but we have not yet identified if or how this process operates in typical mainstreamed settings. It is quite likely that in order to maximize the potential developmental value of observational learning in mainstreamed settings, particularly where discrepancies in developmental levels among children are substantial, planned, structured, and guided interactions will be needed (Cooke, Apolloni & Cooke, 1977; Guralnick, 1976).

Peers as Agents of Change.   This leads to the final proposed criterion for effectiveness: the planned, systematic use of advanced peers as agents of change. The availability of peers as agents of change or as tutors in a variety of ways is an often overlooked benefit that is unique to mainstreamed settings, especially since the potential value of peers serving in this capacity has a considerable theoretical and empirical base. For example, summarizing earlier work in this area and anticipating the extensive use of this strategy within the past decade, Hartup (1970) noted that "direct reinforcement from peers is a potent form of social influence during childhood. The effects of social influence are evident in very early childhood. In addition, very young children can serve effectively as the confederates of teachers and experimenters in bringing about behavior change through this medium" (p. 429). Similarly, V. L. Allen (1976) has discussed the significance of tutoring in relation to the socialization process. It appears that both the tutor and the student can gain from such an enterprise. Finally, the use of peers as agents of change in therapeutic interventions, especially in social-emotional areas, may be the most effective strategy for obtaining generalizable and durable outcomes (Guralnick, 1978b).

It is beyond the scope of this chapter to review the extensive literature in this area, especially since a number of selective reviews are available (Furman, 1980; McGee, Kauffmann & Nussen, 1977; Strain, 1981). However, in order to clarify the potential value of peers as agents of change in mainstreamed programs, it is important to identify the structural dimensions that define such peer–peer interactions and relate them to the outcomes and limitations of this strategy. Essentially, two independent procedural dimensions can be identified: (1) the extent and specificity of the training of the peers who will serve as the agents of change; and (2) the degree of participation of adults during the intervention itself (see Guralnick, 1978c). For example, some researchers, such as Wahler (1967), extensively trained peers through role-playing and other techniques to modify a variety of behaviors of their peers, including play, speech, and passive and aggressive behaviors. Adult intervention beyond this training did not occur. Others, such as Nordquist and Bradley (1973), enlisted the services of a nonhandicapped child to play cooperatively with a handicapped classmate. This technique relied primarily on the teachers to reinforce the handicapped child for the cooperative play that was induced by the "confederate" peer. In the study by Devoney et al. (1974), no training was provided to nonhandicapped children but teachers structured interventions and activities in an effort to improve the level of play of handicapped children during the times in which the children were integrated. Certain parallels for these procedural dimensions can be found for the tutoring situation, but adult intervention beyond training is not likely to occur in that context.

Finally, some investigators have ingeniously capitalized on the natural qualities of children, such as the occurrence of certain behavioral characteristics associated with particular ages, or have selected children for specific abilities. In this strategy, neither peer training nor adult intervention is provided, yet this approach can achieve rather remarkable results under certain conditions (see Furman, Rahe & Hartup, 1979). It should be noted that, apart from the fact that studies in this latter category tend to focus on specific behavioral dimensions, this strategy is conceptually equivalent to the benefits to handicapped children that program planners anticipate will occur in typical, well-designed, mainstreamed programs. That is, through proper teacher training, selection of materials, matching of children, general instructions and encouragement, arrangements of physical space, and so on, it is hoped that the interactions that develop will mutually and significantly benefit all participants.

The apparent effectiveness of these techniques, including the use of vicarious processes (O'Connor, 1969), has created an important new therapeutic strategy for teachers and clinicians. However, it is essential to recognize that the vast majority of studies have involved children with relatively mild or focal social, cognitive, or interpersonal difficulties. In fact, as discussed below, recent extensions of these approaches directed to children with less circumscribed and more severe deficits have not met with nearly the same level of success.

In an initial study with mildly and moderately developmentally delayed preschool children, Guralnick (1976) demonstrated that the combined techniques of modeling, prompting, and selective reinforcement by normally developing peers could improve their levels of social participation. In this study, peers were extensively trained but adults were not involved during the intervention. Interactions took place in a playroom containing two nonhandicapped children and one handicapped child, but no measurements were obtained in the actual classroom. Similarly, Strain, Shores, and Timm (1977) successfully trained normally developing peer "confederates" to improve the social interactions of behaviorally disordered, moderately delayed preschool children in a playroom setting. Following up on earlier work, Strain (1977) assessed generalization of any changes occurring in the playroom to classroom interactions. The results indicated that playroom interactions increased for all three handicapped children in the study and did generalize to the classroom for two of the children. Even so, generalization was not complete, reaching a level of interaction of only one-half of that obtained in the playroom. Moreover, the durability of these changes over time was not investigated.

These studies, centering on children with more severe deficits are few in number and have not yet demonstrated clinically useful levels of generalization. As indicated, a child's initial level of social responsiveness and the severity of behavioral problems appear to be the primary predictors of success. Other studies using highly structured procedures, such as the series described by Apolloni and Cooke (1978) on imitative responding, support these general patterns. The work with children with more severe deficits stands in contrast to the successful studies obtained with children manifesting relatively mild problems (for instance, Furman, Rahe & Hartup, 1979).

A report by Guralnick (1978c) containing descriptions of eleven clinical applications of the use of peers as agents of change underscores the major problems associated with this strategy for handicapped preschool children with relatively severe developmental problems and points toward some potential solutions. In this study, two clinical training strategies were developed for use in an integrated classroom. The first was designed to encourage the formation of appropriate attitudes and to instruct normal peers in educational techniques to enable them to promote the social development of their handicapped classmates. No unusual adult intervention was scheduled. Training took place in a playroom setting but the assessment of this procedure's impact focused on generalization to free play in the classroom. If this strategy was unsuccessful, a second clinical training approach was implemented which consisted of the direct involvement of adults and nonhandicapped peers in the free-play setting itself. The techniques for this were similar to those described by Baer and Wolf (1970) and consisted of combined peer and adult interventions. For the most part, a particular handicapped child was matched with specific nonhandicapped children based on teacher-assessed compatibility and other criteria. This procedure also included instances in which "naturally occurring groups" of nonhandicapped children were trained to work with a designated handicapped child.

The results of these clinical efforts unfortunately supported earlier concerns regarding the clinical significance of this strategy for this group of children (see Kazdin, 1977). First, despite extensive efforts with both approaches, virtually no changes were obtained for the five children classified as moderately or severely handicapped. Improved social interactions were noted in the playroom but they did not generalize to the classroom at any point. Even for the six children classified as mildly handicapped, success was modest at best. The first stategy rarely had an impact and even the second (a highly intensive, high-cost effort) produced limited generalization to peers beyond those participating directly in the therapeutic program. Accordingly, even the positive changes that occurred were highly dependent on the specific therapeutic agents who participated.

It must be concluded at this time that despite the apparent face validity and developmental and clinical principles suggesting that normally developing preschool children are potentially valuable adjuncts in educational or therapeutic programs for handicapped children, the available empirical information indicates that the effectiveness of this strategy remains to be verified.[5] As discussed by Guralnick (1978c), there appear to be numerous reasons why only limited success has been achieved with the more severely handicapped populations. Of particular note is the issue regarding the need to bring the training content of social/communicative development more within a developmental framework. In addition, it appears that significant change will occur for this group only under circumstances that include substantial adult involvement during intervention as well as during peer training.

Head Start

The Economic Opportunity Act of 1972 mandated that 10 percent of the children enrolled in Head Start programs be handicapped. As such, mainstreamed classrooms are the legally mandated context within which services to handicapped children in Head Start are to be provided. In view of this, the effectiveness of this program will be reviewed separately.

During the first year of implementation of this mandate (1973–1974), Ensher, Blatt, and Winshell (1977) conducted a national evaluation and found relatively modest accomplishments toward the goal of providing effective services to handicapped children in Head Start. Although only limited satisfaction with regard to mainstreaming was obtained, Ensher et al. did note that "clinical observations suggested that seriously handicapped children were often victims of an emotional distancing, or psychological separateness, even when physical proximity with other children was maintained" (1977, p. 206). As these authors pointed out, given that this was the first year of implementation, this finding can be attributed partly to the lack of specialized teacher training and supportive services.

A second evaluation has recently been completed focusing on the 1976–1977 program year, and it provides data more closely related to feasibility issues as defined in this chapter (*Evaluation of the process of mainstreaming handicapped children in Project Head Start, Phase I,* 1978). This evaluation consisted of data obtained from a stratified sample of handicapped children enrolled in fifty-nine Head Start programs. One section of the report focused directly on the extent of social integration of the handicapped children. Based on direct classroom observations, the following analyses were reported: "More than 66 percent of the 269 children observed were judged be fully integrated into Head Start classroom activities. Children diagnosed as mentally retarded or emotionally disturbed were

---

[5] Research using advanced peers as agents of change to teach specific language forms in structured settings appears promising but is highly limited in scope and not reviewed in detail in this chapter. The interested reader should consult the following sources: Goosen, 1977; Guralnick, 1976; 1981c; Nordquist, 1978; and Rauer, Cooke, and Apolloni, 1978.

less likely to be fully socially integrated than children with other handicaps. Fifty-seven percent of those children with severe or profound disabilities were judged to be socially integrated, whereas this was so for 81 percent of those children with mild handicaps" (p. 3.25). The report further indicated that nearly 85 percent of the handicapped children were engaged in group activities that included non-handicapped peers; only 5 percent of the observations of handicapped children in social situations were found to consist solely of handicapped children.

Without question, this evaluation provides the most optimistic statement of social integration in the context of mainstreamed settings, particularly for children considered severely or profoundly handicapped. However, the existence of certain discrepancies with other work in this area and the fact that the categories used for rating the degree of social integration were very general and not subject to standard reliability procedures suggest that a cautious interpretation of these results is in order. Finally, the report addressed other aspects of effectiveness at the process level, including an assessment of written IEPs, their comprehensiveness, the design of individualized activities, as well as whether the physical facilities were able to meet the needs of handicapped children. Although many programs were found to be effective, extensive inadequacies were also noted. We can anticipate that programs other than Head Start will engage in similar process assessments in the future.

With regard to the efficacy of services to handicapped children enrolled in Head Start, a recent effort by the Administration for Children, Youth, and Families (*Evaluation of the process of mainstreaming handicapped children into Head Start, Phase II*, 1978) provides additional but still limited information. Comparisons were obtained among a total of 833 children divided into three groups: handicapped children enrolled in Head Start, handicapped children enrolled in non-Head Start preschools, and an unserved population of handicapped children. Unfortunately, due to external pre-existing differences among the groups and other confounds and biases, conclusions with respect to efficacy must be viewed with extreme caution. At best, this report suggested that parents of children in both Head Start and non-Head Start programs supported mainstreaming as part of the overall service program for their child and this positive attitude was maintained throughout the year (a mesosystem analysis). Moreover, children classified as speech-impaired appeared to fare best in comparison to unserved children but, even with problems encountered in interpretation, it is distressing to learn that the "developmental gains for Head Start and non-Head Start children identified as physically handicapped, mentally retarded, or health impaired were generally not significantly greater than those of non-served children" (1978, p. XVI).

Summary of Effectiveness at the Microsystem Level

Taken together, what overall assessments of feasibility at the level of the microsystem can be made? Perhaps the most obvious fact is that research and evaluation efforts are highly limited in number and scope and often lack a necessary level of methodological sophistication. Also clear is that despite some recent efforts statements regarding the efficacy of mainstreaming must await additional research. Nevertheless, from the limited data available, the product and process measures do tend to support the feasibility of mainstreaming, particularly for children with relatively mild handicaps. Even for children with more severe handicaps, creative educational arrangements appear to provide an effective integrated program. Similarly, for developmentally delayed children at least, the social and communicative environment in mainstreamed programs seems appropriately adaptive and supportive from the perspective of the handicapped child, and conditions do appear to exist that can foster observational learning. On the negative side, a number of significant reservations remain with regard to the extent of social integration of the more severely handicapped children as well as regarding the potential clinical value of advanced peers as agents of change. In fact, these issues will not be fully resolved until a more complete understanding of the peer relations of handicapped children is obtained. Finally, research on attitudes, seen as essential elements underlying many of the goals and outcomes of mainstreaming, has rarely been attempted.

Many of these conclusions are based on programs that are experimental in nature. It is not known if these results apply to the universe of community-based mainstreamed programs since programmatic factors often were not well documented. In addition, virtually all of the data have been based on analyses of intact groups of children in pre-established programs. No systematic research has attempted to match children along a variety of developmental characteristics—a crucial programmatic factor. Future work correlating this and other programmatic variables with effectiveness criteria should be very helpful in assessing the representativeness and replicability of the programmatic efforts to date. Finally, a glaring omission in the existing research is the absence of investigations designed to examine the effects of individual child characteristics in different contexts, which is related to research on programmatic characteristics. Future studies must probe beyond currently employed classification variables of chronological age, type, and severity of handicap. In fact, teachers and administrators will benefit most directly from research conducted at this level of specificity.

Evidence for Effectiveness at the Mesosystem, Exosystem, and Macrosystem Levels

The virtual absence of research related to the effectiveness of mainstreamed programs at the levels of the meso-, exo-, and macrosystems is most striking. At the level of the mesosystem, the absence of longitudinal studies can be understood in view of the relatively brief period in which systematic work focusing on mainstreaming issues has been conducted. Research with hearing-impaired populations is a notable exception to this (Kennedy & Bruininks, 1974; Kennedy et al., 1976; Northcott, 1978; Rister, 1975); it has generally supported the feasibility of mainstreamed programs for this group of children. Unfortunately, attitudinal issues associated with both handicapped and nonhandicapped children have not been addressed systematically at this level of analysis. The lack of research on parental attitudes and behaviors, as well as the impact of mainstreaming on the home setting in general, severely restricts our understanding of the overall effects of this process.

The importance of conducting investigations related to parents has been discussed by Turnbull and Blacher-Dixon (1980) who point out that parent satisfaction with mainstreaming can vary widely. Their analysis suggested that although satisfaction is a function of many factors, the parents' stage of adjustment in the process of coping with a handicapped child appears most vital. These authors further point out that even the act of considering enrollment of their handicapped child in a mainstreamed preschool may create a number of dilemmas for parents. For example, though they may believe that a mainstreamed environment is potentially the most beneficial one, enrollment of their child in a mainstreamed setting produces a situation in which parents face daily reminders of discrepancies between their child and normally developing children, the potentially stigmatizing effects of having a handicapped child, a lack of common interests with parents of nonhandicapped children, the possible limitations of support services suited to their needs, and problems encountered in assisting their child to adjust socially to a classroom containing mostly normal children (p. 34).

In addition to the lack of information regarding effectiveness at the mesosystem level, there have been no systematic attempts to link effectiveness at this level with its corresponding programmatic factors. Programmatic factors associated with the microsystem have been discussed previously. For the mesosystem, however, it is certain that the administrative structure and the quality of educational experiences in the primary grades will be major influences. That is, these variables will determine to a substantial degree whether children previously and perhaps successfully mainstreamed during the preschool years will continue to progress. Similarly, parent satisfaction will depend, in part, upon the generic service system's ability to meet their needs as well as the support provided by various informal networks. As can be seen, programmatic factors at each ecological level include characteristics unique to their own level as well as factors from other levels.

Conceptualizing systematic approaches to understand problems at the levels of the macro- and exosystems is a very complex undertaking. The process of social change created by mainstreaming as well as other movements consistent with the "normalization" principle (Wolfensberger, 1972) may well have significant effects on formal and informal social systems and institutions and on future legislation concerning the rights and privileges of handicapped children in general. Whether these systems can make the necessary adjustments is a critical but as yet unanswered question. Some progress can already be detected in our institutions of higher education with the development of programs combining both early childhood and special education, but we have no empirical information concerning their impact. Future research may determine if early childhood educators trained in combination programs are able to promote the development of all children as effectively (or perhaps even more so) as those trained in conventional programs. Similarly, overarching attitudes at the exosystem level in the future may be revealed directly through attitude assessment as well as indirectly through our setting of priorities, the nature of forthcoming legislation, and the allocation of funds.

Finally, it is worthwhile to emphasize the embeddedness and mutuality that exist among the ecological systems. Although the following hypothetical situation is certainly idealized and a clear oversimplification of a possible process, let us suppose that irrefutable evidence has been gathered to indicate that, with only a moderate increase in resources, mainstreaming is indeed both a feasible and a more effective environment for promoting the development of handicapped children. In addition, observations indicate the absence of adverse effects for any participant. Given this situation, we would expect that an effective dissemination strategy (an extremely difficult task; see Gallagher, 1979) at the level of the mesosystem would favorably influence the attitudes of all concerned toward the acceptance of mainstreaming. In particular, a resolution of parental dilemmas in the direction of support for mainstreaming may be facilitated. If this were to occur, it is further anticipated that these changes would ultimately affect the outcome of a longitudinal analysis. Furthermore, it is possible that our informal and formal social systems would be more willing to accommodate to handicapped children if this evidence were properly and effectively presented. Values and moral stances, the fundamental and final arbiters of policy and decision making, are difficult to modify, but they are modifiable.

Summary and Conclusions

This chapter has attempted to establish a comprehensive framework to analyze existing knowledge and to guide a systematic research and evaluation program in order to improve our understanding of the issues and effects of mainstreaming young handicapped children. To accomplish this, a series of goals and objectives relating to mainstreaming were derived from various sources, including the least restrictive placement principle as stated in P. L. 94–142, the apparent intent of the legislation, and related perceptions of the overall concept of mainstreaming. After having established these organizing propositions, the concepts of feasibility and efficacy were introduced and, in conjunction with various evaluation criteria, incorporated into a comprehensive ecological systems model. The available evidence for feasibility and efficacy were then reviewed within the structure of this model.

If the overall framework for the analyses and associated propositions can be accepted, this process has revealed a number of important points. Specifically, the initial emphasis on outcomes at the microsystem level has generated work of only limited scope and quality to date. Most persuasive is the cumulative evidence that has consistently supported the feasibility of mainstreaming. Of course, the qualifying conditions and parameters for that statement in relation to children, settings, resources, and outcomes remains a primary task for future investigations. With regard to the efficacy of mainstreamed preschool programs, however, it is not possible to draw even tentative conclusions.

The absence of systematic efforts linking programmatic or input factors and evaluation criteria at the microsystem level is a major barrier to a more comprehensive understanding of mainstreaming. Systematic studies of obviously critical variables, such as the severity of the child's handicap, ratio of handicapped to nonhandicapped children in the setting, the extent of teacher and child preparation, and teacher/child ratios, are not in evidence. Of equal importance is the type of integrated educational setting. A program may be feasible for one arrangement (a reverse mainstreamed program) but be totally inadequate for another (severely handicapped children enrolled in a regular nursery school). Similarly, without knowledge of the boundary conditions for feasibility carried out at the level of individual child characteristics, the development of truly individualized child programs will not be possible. Moreover, as has been suggested earlier, the interpretation of mesosystem-level effects depends heavily upon outcomes at the microsystem level.

Certainly, the fact that investigators have not attended to assessing the effects of mainstreaming much beyond the level of the microsystem is of great concern. This lack of information regarding, for example, relevant attitudes held by both handicapped and nonhandicapped children and their families or the long-term impact of mainstreaming are significant gaps in our knowledge. In fact, it is fair to state that only preliminary information is available concerning the relationship between the mainstreamed setting and any other setting.

Consequently, a more informed judgment as to whether mainstreaming is feasible or perhaps provides a more effective environment than segregated programs must await the results of a systematic and extensive series of studies. The acquisition of cumulative knowledge can be the only realistic path to complete understanding of this process. It is anticipated that this task will become more manageable as evaluation criteria and underlying goals become more fully articulated and lend themselves to more objective analyses. A plan to accomplish this has been a major focus of this chapter.

A corresponding effort has been made here to analyze objectively the available research and evaluation studies. Even at the level of the microsystem, an investigator's ability to carry out and interpret research objectively and to develop a dispassionate review or analysis in an area of major social significance is extremely difficult to accomplish. Despite an awareness of potential sources of bias, an inextricable relationship exists between one's values and every step in the process of evaluation (Messick, 1975). Accordingly, the extent to which the conclusions of this chapter can be accepted with confidence rely upon the reader's acceptance of both the external framework that has been put forth, including the interrelationships among the goals, intents, and objectives, and on the interpretations of the outcomes of specific investigations. To extend this notion to the extreme, it may be possible to argue forcefully and cogently that mainstreaming is feasible or not feasible on the basis of the same data. The arguments in support of one or the other position may require only relatively minor and subtle shifts in our value system which would, in turn, lead to numerous other modifications within a given framework. This extreme position may be a distortion of reality, but it does point to the rather fragile nature of the research and evaluation enterprise, particularly when it involves areas that touch some of our basic concepts, values, and ideologies (Katz, 1975; Sarason & Doris, 1979).

Finally, progress in this area should be accelerated by a recognition of the points of contact between developmental research and principles, applied developmental/educational programs, and public policy. As has been pointed out, a reciprocal relationship exists among these three areas, each modulating and influencing the direction and outcomes of the others. Perhaps most apparent in the context of mainstreaming is the need for a greater integration of developmental principles and research. Although we are beginning to recognize the implications of peer influences on development and the importance of constructing curricula and intervention strategies derived from accepted developmental principles, this knowledge has not been extensively applied as a guide to the design of mainstreamed educational environments. In fact, our understanding of mainstreamed programs could benefit from knowledge in the areas of sibling relationships, friendship development, the relationship between cognitive development and the perception of differences, the development of social cognition, and empathy development. Future research and educational programs concerned with mainstreaming issues must recognize the interdependence of knowledge across all domains.

References

ABESON, A., and ZETTEL, J. The end of the quiet revolution: The Education for All Handicapped Children Act of 1975. *Exceptional Children*, 1977, *44*, 114–128.

AKAMATSU, T., and THELEN, M. A review of the literature on observer characteristics and imitation. *Developmental Psychology*, 1974, *10*, 38–47.

ALLEN, K. E. Mainstreaming: What have we learned? *Young Children*, 1980, *35*, 54–63.

ALLEN, V. L. (ed.). *Children as Teachers: Theories and Research on Tutoring*. New York: Academic Press, 1976.

ANASTASIOW, N. J. Strategies and models for early childhood intervention programs in integrated settings. In M. J. Guralnick (ed.), *Early Intervention and the Integration of Handicapped and Nonhandicapped Children*. Baltimore, Md.: University Park Press, 1978.

APPOLLONI, T., and COOKE, T. P. Integrated programming at the infant, toddler, and preschool levels. In M. J. Guralnick (ed.), *Early Intervention and the Integration of Handicapped and Nonhandicapped Children*. Baltimore, Md.: University Park Press, 1978.

ARNOLD, W., and TREMBLAY, A. Interaction of deaf and hearing preschool children. *Journal of Communication Disorders*, 1979, *12*, 245–251.

ASHER, S. R., SINGLETON, L. C., TINSLEY, B. R., and HYMEL, S. A reliable sociometric measure for preschool children. *Developmental Psychology*, 1979, *15*, 443–444.

BAER, D. M., and WOLF, M. M. The entry into natural communities of reinforcement. In R. Ulrich, T. Stachnik, and N. Mabry (eds.), *Control of Human Behavior*, Vol. 2. Glenview, Ill.: Scott, Foresman, 1970.

BANDURA, A. Analyses of modeling processes. In A. Bandura (ed.), *Psychological Modeling*. Chicago: Aldine-Atherton, 1971.

BELL, R. Q., and HERTZ, T. W. Toward more comparability and generalizability of developmental research. *Child Development*, 1976, 47, 6–13.

BLACHER-DIXON, J., and TURNBULL, A. P. Preschool mainstreaming: Definitions, rationale, and implementation. *Education Unlimited*, 1979, 1, 16–21.

BRICKER, D. A rationale for the integration of handicapped and nonhandicapped preschool children. In M. J. Guralnick (ed.), *Early Intervention and the Integration of Handicapped and Nonhandicapped Children*. Baltimore, Md.: University Park Press, 1978.

BRICKER, D., and BRICKER, W. Toddler research and intervention project report: Year II. IMRID Behavioral Science Monograph 21, Institute on Mental Retardation and Intellectual Development. Nashville, Tenn.: George Peabody College, 1972.

BROEN, P. A. The verbal environment of the language-learning child. American Speech and Hearing Association Monograph, 1972, 17.

BRONFENBRENNER, U. Developmental research, public policy, and the ecology of childhood. *Child Development*, 1974, 45, 1–5.

BRONFENBRENNER, U. Is early intervention effective? In B. Z. Friedlander, G. M. Sterritt, and G. E. Kirk (eds.), *Exceptional Infant*, Vol. 2. New York: Bruner/Mazel, 1975.

BRONFENBRENNER, U. Toward an experimental ecology of human development. *American Psychologist*, 1977, 32, 513–531.

BRONFENBRENNER, U. *The Ecology of Human Development: Experiments by Nature and Design*. Cambridge, Mass.: Harvard University Press, 1979.

BROWN, B. (ed.). *Found: Long-Term Gains from Early Intervention*. Boulder, Colo.: Westview Press, 1978.

BRYK, A. S., MEISELS, S. J., and MARKOWITZ, M. T. Assessing the effectiveness of open classrooms on children with special needs. In S. J. Meisels (ed.), *Special Education and Development*. Baltimore, Md.: University Park Press, 1979.

BRYK, A. S., and WEISBERG, H. I. Value-added analysis: A dynamic approach to the estimation of treatment effects. *Journal of Educational Statistics*, 1976, 1, 127–155.

BRYK, A. S., and WEISBERG, H. I. Use of nonequivalent control group design when subjects are growing. *Psychological Bulletin*, 1977, 84, 950–962.

CAMPBELL, D. T., and STANLEY, J. C. *Experimental and Quasi-Experimental Designs for Research*. Chicago: Rand McNally, 1963.

CAVALLARO, S. A., and PORTER, R. H. Peer preferences of at-risk and normally developing children in preschool mainstream classrooms. *American Journal of Mental Deficiency*, 1980, 84, 357–366.

CLARK, E. A. Teacher attitudes toward integration of children with handicaps. *Education and Training of the Mentally Retarded*, 1976, 11, 333–335.

CLARKE, A. M., and CLARKE, A. D. B., *Early Experience: Myth and Evidence*. New York: Free Press, 1976.

COHEN, S. Fostering positive attitudes toward the handicapped: A new curriculum. *Children Today*, November-December 1977, pp. 7–12.

COHEN, S., SEMMES, M., and GURALNICK, M. J. Public Law 94–142 and the education of preschool handicapped children. *Exceptional Children*, 1979, 45, 279–285.

COOKE, T. P., APOLLONI, T., and COOKE, S. A. Normal preschool children as behavioral models for retarded peers. *Exceptional Children*, 1977, 43, 531–532.

COOKE, T. P., RUSKUS, J. A., APOLLONI, T., and PECK, C. A. Handicapped preschool children in the mainstream: Background, outcomes, and clinical suggestions. *Topics in Early Childhood Special Education*, 1981, 1, 73–83.

COOKE, T. P., RUSKUS, J. A., PECK, C. A., and APOLLONI, T. *A Comparative Evaluation of the Outcomes of Integrated and Segregated Preschool Arrangements. Comparing Change Scores: Can the Nonhandicapped Child Keep Up?* Santa Rosa, Calif.: Human Services Associates, 1979.

CORMAN, L., and GOTTLIEB, J. Mainstreaming mentally retarded children: A review of research. In N. Ellis (ed.), *International Review of Research in Mental Retardation*, Vol. 9. New York: Academic Press, 1978.

DEVONEY, C., GURALNICK, M. J., and RUBIN, H. Integrating handicapped and nonhandicapped preschool children: Effects on social play. *Childhood Education*, 1974, 50, 360–364.

DEWEERD, J., and COLE, A. Handicapped children's early education program. *Exceptional Children*, 1976, 43, 155–157.

ENSHER, G. L., BLATT, B., and WINSCHEL, J. F. Head Start for the handicapped: Congressional mandate audit. *Exceptional Children*, 1977, 43, 202–210.

ETZIONI, A., and RICHARDSON, S. A. Guided societal change and mental retardation. In M. J. Begab and S. A. Richardson (eds.), *The Mentally Retarded and Society: A Social Science Perspective.* Baltimore, Md.: University Park Press, 1975.

Evaluation of the Process of Mainstreaming Handicapped Children into Project Head Start, Phase I, Final Report. Silver Spring, Md.: Applied Management Sciences, 1978.

Evaluation of the Process of Mainstreaming Handicapped Children into Project Head Start, Phase II, Final Report. Silver Spring, Md.: Applied Management Sciences, 1978.

FEITELSON, D., WEINTRAUB, S., and MICHAELI, O. Social interaction in heterogeneous preschools. *Child Development*, 1972, 43, 1249–1259.

FEY, M. E., LEONARD, L. B., and WILCOX, K. A. Speech style modifications of language-impaired children. *Journal of Speech and Hearing Disorders*, 1981, 46, 91–96.

FIELD, T. M. Self, teacher, toy, and peer-directed behaviors of handicapped preschool children. In T. M. Field, S. Goldberg, D. Stern, and A. M. Sostek (eds.), *High-Risk Infants and Children: Adult and Peer Relations.* New York: Academic Press, 1980.

FINK, W. T., and SANDALL, S. R. One-to-one vs. group academic instruction with handicapped and nonhandicapped preschool children. *Mental Retardation*, 1978, 16, 236–240.

FURMAN, W. Promoting social development: Developmental implications for treatment. In B. B. Lahey and A. E. Kazdin (eds.), *Advances in Clinical Child Psychology*, Vol. 3. New York: Plenum Press, 1980.

FURMAN, W., RAHE, D. F., and HARTUP, W. W. Rehabilitation of socially withdrawn preschool children through mixed-age and same-age socialization. *Child Development*, 1979, 50, 915–922.

GALLAGHER, J. J. Rights of the next generation of children. *Exceptional Children*, 1979, *46*, 98–105.

GALLOWAY, C., and CHANDLER, P. The marriage of special and generic early education services. In M. J. Guralnick (ed.), *Early Intervention and the Integration of Handicapped and Nonhandicapped Children*. Baltimore, Md.: University Park Press, 1978.

GELMAN, R., and SHATZ, M. Appropriate speech adjustments: The operation of conversational constraints on talk to two-year-olds. In M. Lewis and L. A. Rosenblum (eds.), *Interaction, Conversation, and the Development of Language*. New York: Wiley, 1977.

GLEASON, J. B. Code switching in children's language. In T. E. Moore (ed.), *Cognitive Development and the Acquisition of Language*. New York: Academic Press, 1973.

GOLDMAN, J. A. The social participation of preschool children in same-age vs. mixed-age groupings. Unpublished doctoral dissertation, University of Wisconsin, 1976.

GOOSEN, J. The effects of a normal peer model on verbal production of descriptive adjectives by handicapped children. Unpublished master's thesis, University of Kansas, 1977.

GRAY, S. W., and KLAUS, R. A. An experimental preschool program for culturally deprived children. *Child Development*, 1965, *36*, 887–898.

GURALNICK, M. J. Early classroom-based intervention and the role of organizational structure. *Exceptional Children*, 1975, *42*, 25–31.

GURALNICK, M. J. The value of integrating handicapped and nonhandicapped preschool children. *American Journal of Orthopsychiatry*, 1976, *46*, 236–245.

GURALNICK, M. J. Early childhood intervention: Nonhandicapped peers as educational and therapeutic resources. In P. Mittler (ed.), *Research to Practice in Mental Retardation: Care and Intervention*, Vol. 1. Baltimore, Md.: University Park Press, 1977.

GURALNICK, M. J. Integrated preschools as educational and therapeutic environments: Concepts, design, and analysis. In M. J. Guralnick (ed.), *Early Intervention and the Integration of Handicapped and Nonhandicapped Children*. Baltimore, Md.: University Park Press, 1978a.

GURALNICK, M. J. (ed.). *Early Intervention and the Education of Handicapped and Nonhandicapped Children*. Baltimore, Md.: University Park Press, 1978b.

GURALNICK, M. J. Promoting social interactions among children at different developmental levels: Processes and problems. Paper presented at the Annual Meeting of the Council for Exceptional Children, Kansas City, April 1978c.

GURALNICK, M. J. Mainstreaming young handicapped children: Organizing our knowledge base. Paper presented at the Annual Meeting of the Council for Exceptional Children, Philadelphia, April 1980a.

GURALNICK, M. J. Social interactions among preschool children. *Exceptional Children*, 1980b, *46*, 248–253.

GURALNICK, M. J. The development and role of child–child social interactions. In N. Anastasiow (ed.), *New Directions for Exceptional Children: Socioemotional Development*. San Francisco: Jossey-Bass, 1981a.

GURALNICK, M. J. Programmatic factors associated with mainstreaming young handicapped children. *Exceptional Education Quarterly*, 1981b, *1*(4), 71–91.

GURALNICK, M. J. Peer influences on the development of communicative competence. In

P. Strain (ed.), *Utilization of Classroom Peers as Behavior Change Agents*. New York: Plenum Press, 1981c.

GURALNICK, M. J. The efficacy of integrating handicapped children in early education settings: Research implications. *Topics in Early Childhood Special Education*, 1981d, *1*, 57–71.

GURALNICK, M. J. The social behavior of preschool children at different developmental levels: Effects of group composition. *Journal of Experimental Child Psychology*, 1981e, *31*, 115–130.

GURALNICK, M. J., and PAUL-BROWN, D. The nature of verbal interactions among handicapped and nonhandicapped preschool children. *Child Development*, 1977, *48*, 254–260.

GURALNICK, M. J., and PAUL-BROWN, D. Functional and discourse analyses of nonhandicapped preschool children's speech to handicapped children. *American Journal of Mental Deficiency*, 1980, *84*, 444–454.

GURALNICK, M. J., and PAUL-BROWN, D. Sequential analyses of communicative episodes among children at different developmental levels, in preparation.

GURALNICK, M. J., and WEINHOUSE, E. M. *Peer Related Social Interactions among Handicapped children: Their Development and Characteristics*, in preparation.

HANSON, M. J., and SCHWARZ, R. H. Results of a longitudinal intervention program for Down's syndrome infants and their families. *Education and Training of the Mentally Retarded*, 1978, *13*, 403–407.

HARTUP, W. W. Peer interaction and social organization. In P. H. Mussen (ed.), *Carmichael's Manual of Child Psychology*, Vol. 2. New York: Wiley, 1970.

HARTUP, W. W. Peer interaction and the behavioral development of the individual child. In E. Schopler & R. J. Reichler (eds.), *Psychopathology and Child Development: Research and Treatment*. New York: Plenum Press, 1976.

HARTUP, W. W. Peer interaction and the process of socialization. In M. J. Guralnick (ed.), *Early Intervention and the Integration of Handicapped and Nonhandicapped Children*. Baltimore, Md.: University Park Press, 1978.

HASKINS, R., FINKELSTEIN, N. W., and STEDMAN, D. J. Infant stimulation programs and their effects. *Pediatric Annals*, 1978, *7*, 123–144.

HAYDEN, A. H., and DIMITRIEV, V. The multidisciplinary preschool program for Down's syndrome children at the University of Washington Model Preschool Center. In B. Z. Friedlander, G. M. Sterritt, and G. E. Kirk (eds.), *Exceptional Infant*, Vol. 3. New York: Bruner/Mazel, 1975.

HEBER, R., and GARBER, H. The Milwaukee Project: A study of the use of family intervention to prevent cultural-familial mental retardation. In B. Z. Friedlander, G. M. Sterritt, and G. E. Kirk (eds.), *Exceptional Infant*, Vol. 3. New York: Bruner/Mazel, 1975.

HIRSHOREN, A., and UMANSKY, W. Certification for teachers of preschool handicapped children. *Exceptional Children*, 1977, *44*, 191–193.

HOBBS, N. A. *The Futures of Children*. San Francisco: Jossey-Bass, 1975.

HOROWITZ, F. D., and PADEN, L. Y. The effectiveness of environmental intervention programs. In B. M. Caldwell and H. C. Ricciuti (eds.), *Review of Child Development Research*, Vol. 3. Chicago: University of Chicago Press, 1973.

Ispa, J. Social interactions among teachers, handicapped children, and nonhandicapped children in a mainstreamed preschool. *Journal of Applied Developmental Psychology*, 1981, *1*, 231–250.

Ispa, J., and Matz, R. D. Integrating handicapped preschool children within a cognitively oriented program. In M. J. Guralnick (ed.), *Early Intervention and the Integration of Handicapped and Nonhandicapped Children*. Baltimore, Md.: University Park Press, 1978.

James, S. L. Effect of listener age and situation on the politeness of children's directives. *Journal of Psycholinguistic Research*, 1978, 7, 307–317.

Jones, R. L., Gottlieb, J., Guskin, S., and Yoshida, R. K. Evaluating mainstreaming programs: Models, caveats, considerations, and guidelines. *Exceptional Children*, 1978, *44*, 588–601.

Kaiser, C. E. Preparation of preschool teachers for mainstreaming: Current realities and future directions. Paper presented at the Annual Meeting of the American Educational Research Association, Boston, April 1980.

Karnes, M. B. Evaluation and implications of research with young handicapped and low-income children. In J. C. Stanley (ed.), *Compensatory Education for Children Ages Two to Eight: Recent Studies of Educational Intervention*. Baltimore, Md.: Johns Hopkins University Press, 1973.

Karnes, M. B. Exemplary early education programs for handicapped children: Characteristics in common. *Educational Horizons*, 1977, *56*, 47–54.

Katz, L. G. Early childhood programs and ideological disputes. *The Educational Forum*, 1975, *3*, 267–271.

Kaufman, M. E., and Alberto, P. A. Research on efficacy of special education for the mentally retarded. In N. R. Ellis (ed.), *International Review of Research in Mental Retardation*, Vol. 8. New York: Academic Press, 1976.

Kazdin, A. E. Assessing the clinical or applied importance of behavior change through social validation. *Behavior Modification*, 1977, *1*, 427–452.

Kearsley, R. B. Iatrogenic retardation: A syndrome of learned incompetence. In R. B. Kearsley and I. E. Sigel (eds.), *Infants at Risk: Assessment of Cognitive Functioning*. Hillsdale, N.J.: Lawrence Erlbaum Associates, 1979.

Kennedy, P., and Bruininks, R. Social status of hearing impaired children in regular classrooms. *Exceptional Children*, 1974, *40*, 336–342.

Kennedy, P., Northcott, W., McCauley, R., and Williams, S. M. Longitudinal sociometric and cross-sectional data on mainstreaming hearing impaired children: Implications for preschool mainstreaming. *Volta Review*, 1976, 78, 71–81.

Kirk, S. A. *Early Education of the Mentally Retarded*. Urbana: University of Illinois Press, 1958.

Klein, J. W. Mainstreaming the preschooler. *Young Children*, 1975, *30*, 317–326.

Langlois, J. H., and Downs, C. A. Peer relations as a function of physical attractiveness: The eye of the beholder or behavioral reality? *Child Development*, 1979, *50*, 409–418.

Lazar, I., Hubbell, V. R., Murray, H., Rushe, M., and Royce, J. The persistence of preschool effects. U.S. Dept. of Health, Education, and Welfare publication No. OHDS 78–30130. Washington, D.C.: U.S. Government Printing Office, 1977.

LIGHT, R., and SMITH, P. Choosing a future: Strategies for designing and evaluating new programs. *Harvard Educational Review*, 1970, *40*, 1–28.

McCALL, R. B. Challenges to a science of developmental psychology. *Child Development*, 1977, *48*, 334–344.

McDANIELS, G. Successful programs for young handicapped children. *Educational Horizons*, 1977, *56*, 26–33.

McGEE, C. S., KAUFFMANN, J. M., and NUSSEN, J. L. Children as therapeutic change agents: Reinforcement intervention paradigms. *Review of Educational Research*, 1977, *47*, 451–477.

MAHONEY, G. J. An ethological approach to delayed language acquisition. *American Journal of Mental Deficiency*, 1975, *80*, 139–148.

MAHONEY, G. J., and SEELY, P. B. The role of the social agent in language acquisition: Implications for language intervention. In N. R. Ellis (ed.), *International Review of Research in Mental Retardation*, Vol. 8. New York: Academic Press, 1976.

MASUR, E. F. Preschool boys' speech modifications: The effect of listeners' linguistic levels and conversational responsiveness. *Child Development*, 1978, *49*, 924–927.

MESSICK, S. The standard problem: Meaning and values in measurement and evaluation. *American Psychologist*, 1975, *30*, 955–966.

MUELLER, E. (Toddlers + toys) = (An autonomous social system). In M. Lewis and L. A. Rosenblum (eds.), *The Child and Its Family*. New York: Plenum Press, 1979.

MUELLER, E., and BRENNER, J. The growth of social interaction in a toddler playgroup: The role of peer experience. *Child Development*, 1977, *48*, 854–861.

NORDQUIST, V. M. A behavioral approach to the analysis of peer interactions. In M. J. Guralnick (ed.), *Early Intervention and the Integration of Handicapped and Nonhandicapped Children*. Baltimore, Md.: University Park Press, 1978.

NORDQUIST, V. M., and BRADLEY, B. Speech acquisition in a nonverbal isolate child. *Journal of Experimental Child Psychology*, 1973, *15*, 149–160.

NORTHCOTT, W. H. Integrating the preprimary hearing-impaired child: An examination of the process, product, and rationale. In M. J. Guralnick (ed.), *Early Intervention and the Integration of Handicapped and Nonhandicapped Children*. Baltimore, Md.: University Park Press, 1978.

NOVAK, M. A., OLLEY J. G., and KEARNEY, D. S. Social skills of children with special needs in integrated and separate preschools. In T. M. Field, S. Goldberg, and A. M. Sostek (eds.), *High-Risk Infants and Children: Adult and Peer Interactions*. New York: Academic Press, 1980.

O'CONNOR, R. D. Modification of social withdrawal through symbolic modeling. *Journal of Applied Behavior Analysis*, 1969, *2*, 15–22.

PARTEN, M. B. Social participation among preschool children. *Journal of Abnormal Social Psychology*, 1932, *27*, 243–269.

PETERSON, N. L., and HARALICK, J. G. Integration of handicapped and nonhandicapped preschoolers: An analysis of play behavior and social interaction. *Education and Training of the Mentally Retarded*, 1977, *12*, 235–245.

PETERSON, C., PETERSON, J., and SCRIVEN, G. Peer imitation by nonhandicapped and handicapped preschoolers. *Exceptional Children*, 1977, *43*, 223–224.

PORTER, R. H., RAMSEY, B., TREMBLAY, A., IANCOBO, M., and CRAWLEY, S. Social interactions in heterogeneous groups of retarded and normally developing children: An observational study. In G. P. Sackett (ed.), *Observing Behavior*, Vol. 1. Baltimore, Md.: University Park Press, 1978.

PUBLIC LAW (P. L.) 94–142, The Education for all Handicapped Children Act, 1975: 20 U.S.C. 1401 et. seq.: *Federal Register* 42(163): 42474–42518, August 23, 1977.

RAMEY, C. T., and CAMPBELL, F. A. Prevention of developmental retardation in high-risk children. In P. Mittler (ed.), *Research to Practice in Mental Retardation*, Vol. 1. Baltimore, Md.: University Park Press, 1977.

RAMEY, C. T., COLLIER, A. M., SPARLING, J. J., LODA, F. A., CAMPBELL, F. A., INGRAM, D. L., and FINKELSTEIN, N. W. The Carolina Abecedarian Project: A longitudinal and multidisciplinary approach to the prevention of developmental retardation. In T. D. Tjossem (ed.), *Intervention Strategies for High-Risk Infants and Young Children*. Baltimore, Md.: University Park Press, 1976.

RAUER, S. A., COOKE, T. P., and Apolloni, T. Developing nonretarded toddlers as verbal models for retarded classmates. *Child Study Journal*, 1978, 8, 1–8.

RAY, J. S. Ethological studies of behavior in delayed and non-delayed toddlers. Paper presented at the Annual Meeting of the American Association on Mental Deficiency, Toronto, 1974.

RISTER, A. Deaf children in mainstream education. *Volta Review*, 1975, 77, 279–291.

RUBENSTEIN, J. L., and HOWES, C. The effects of peers on toddler interaction with mother and toys. *Child Development*, 1976, 47, 597–605.

RUBENSTEIN, J. L., and HOWES, C. Caregiving and infant behavior in day care and in homes. *Developmental Psychology*, 1979, 15, 1–21.

RUBIN, D. B. Bayesian inference for causal effects: The role of randomization. *The Annals of Statistics*, 1978, 6, 34–58.

SACHS, J., and DEVIN, J. Young children's use of age-appropriate speech styles. *Journal of Child Language*, 1976, 3, 81–98.

SAMEROFF, A. J. The etiology of cognitive competence: A systems perspective. In R. B. Kearsley and I. E. Sigel (eds.), *Infants at Risk: Assessment of Cognitive Functioning*. Hillsdale, N.J.: Lawrence Erlbaum Associates, 1979.

SAMEROFF, A. J., and CHANDLER, M. J. Reproductive risk and the continuum of caretaking casualty. In F. D. Horowitz, M. Hetherington, S. Scarr-Salapatek, and G. Siegel (eds.), *Review of Child Development Research*, Vol. 4. Chicago: University of Chicago Press, 1975.

SARASON, S. B., and DORIS, J. *Educational Handicap, Public Policy, and Social History: A Broadened Perspective on Mental Retardation*. New York: Free Press, 1979.

SHATZ, M., and GELMAN, R. The development of communication skills: Modifications in the speech of young children as a function of listener. *Monographs of the Society for Research in Child Development*, 1973, 38, No. 5.

SIMON, E. P., and GILLMAN, A. E. Mainstreaming visually handicapped preschoolers. *Exceptional Children*, 1979, 45, 463–464.

SKEELS, H. M. Adult status of children with contrasting early life experiences: A follow-up study. *Monographs of the Society for Research in Child Development*, 1966, 31, No. 3.

SKEELS, H. M., and DYE, H. E. A study of the effects of differential stimulation on mentally retarded children. *Proceedings of the American Association on Mental Deficiency*, 1939, *44*, 114–136.

SNOW, C. E. Mothers' speech to children learning language. *Child Development*, 1972, *43*, 549–565.

SNOW, C. E., and FERGUSON, C. A. (eds.), *Talking to Children: Language Input and Acquisition*. Cambridge: At the University Press, 1977.

STOCK, J. R., WNEK, L. L., NEWBORG, J. A., SCHENCK, E. A., GABEL, J. R., SPURGEIO, M. S., and RAY, H. W. Evaluation of handicapped children's early education programs (HCEEP). Washington, D.C.: USOE, Bureau of Education for the Handicapped. Final report from Battelle Institute, Columbus, Ohio. May 14, 1976.

STRAIN, P. S. An experimental analysis of peer social initiations on the behavior of withdrawn preschool children: Some training and generalization effects. *Journal of Abnormal Child Psychology*, 1977, *5*, 445–455.

STRAIN, P. S. Peer-mediated treatment of exceptional children's social withdrawal. *Exceptional Education Quarterly*, 1981, *1*, 93–105.

STRAIN, P. S., SHORES, R. E., and TIMM, M. A. Effects of peer social initiations on the behavior of withdrawn preschool children. *Journal of Applied Behavior Analysis*, 1977, *10*, 289–298.

STRICHART, S. Effects of competence and nurturance on imitation of nonretarded peers by retarded adolescents. *American Journal of Mental Deficiency*, 1974, *78*, 665–673.

TJOSSEM, T. D. (ed.), *Intervention Strategies for High Risk Infants and Young Children*. Baltimore, Md.: University Park Press, 1976.

TURNBULL, A. P., and BLACHER-DIXON, J. Preschool mainstreaming: Impact on parents. In J. Gallagher (ed.), *New Directions for Exceptional Children: The Ecology of Exceptional Children*. San Francisco: Jossey-Bass, 1980.

TURNBULL, A. P., and BLACHER-DIXON, J. Preschool mainstreaming: An empirical and conceptual review. In P. Strain and M. M. Kerr (eds.), *Mainstreaming of Children in Schools: Research and Programmatic Issues*. New York: Academic Press, 1981.

VANDELL, D. L., and GEORGE, L. B. Social interaction in hearing and deaf preschoolers: Successes and failures in initiations. *Child Development*, 1981, *52*, 627–635.

WAHLER, R. G. Child–child interactions in free-field settings: Some experimental analyses. *Journal of Experimental Child Psychology*, 1967, *5*, 278–293.

WALD, M. S. Legal policies affecting children: A lawyer's request for aid. *Child Development*, 1976, *47*, 1–5.

WEIKART, D. P. Relationship of curriculum, teaching, and learning in preschool education. In J. C. Stanley (ed.), *Preschool Programs for the Disadvantaged: Five Experimental Approaches to Early Childhood Education*. Baltimore, Md.: Johns Hopkins University Press, 1972.

WEISBERG, H. A. Statistical adjustments and uncontrolled studies. *Psychological Bulletin*, 1979, *86*, 1149–1164.

WEISZ, J. R. Transcontextual validity in developmental research. *Child Development*, 1978, *49*, 1–12.

WERTLIEB, D. Applied developmental psychology: New directions. *APA Monitor*, 1979, *10*, 10–24.

WHITE, B. N. Mainstreaming in grade school and preschool: How the child with special needs interacts with peers. In T. M. Field, S. Goldberg, D. Stern, and A. M. Sostek (eds.), *High-Risk Infants and Children: Adult and Peer Interactions.* New York: Academic Press, 1980.

WOLFENSBERGER, W. *The Principle of Normalization in Human Services.* Toronto: National Institute on Mental Retardation, 1972.

ZIGLER, E. Welcoming a new journal. *Journal of Applied Development Psychology,* 1980, *1*, 1–6.

ZIGLER, E., and Trickett, P. K. IQ, social competence, and evaluation of early childhood intervention programs. *American Psychologist,* 1978, *33*, 789–798.

ZIGLER, E., and TRICKETT, P. K. The role of national social policy in promoting social competence in children. In M. W. Kent and J. E. Rolf (eds.), *Primary Prevention of Psychopathology: Social Competence in Children,* Vol. 3. Hanover, N.H.: University Press of New England, 1979.

CHAPTER 20

The Sociocultural Context of Evaluation

Luis M. Laosa

MY PURPOSE in this chapter is to examine certain implications of sociocultural diversity and pluralism for educational evaluation. Although the examples and illustrations are drawn primarily from early childhood education, the general principles apply equally well not only to other levels of education but also to other types of services. My reason for selecting program evaluation as the chapter's organizing theme is fourfold. First, with the increasing scarcity of fiscal resources, evaluative information is likely to gain in importance as a means of deciding among alternative ways of allocating the available resources. Second, evaluation theory and practice have failed to deal adequately with the challenges presented by sociocultural diversity and pluralism, a point I wish to illuminate. Third, the evaluative context provides a useful framework for bringing into sharp relief the issues regarding diversity and pluralism that I seek to analyze. And fourth, a discussion within the context of program evaluation, probably more so than within any other context, is likely to stimulate constructive debate regarding program and policy decisions. Program evaluation, in the view of many (for example, Alkin, 1972), is the process of ascertaining the decision areas of concern, selecting appropriate information, and collecting and analyzing information in order to report summary data useful to decision makers in selecting among alternatives.

Some Perspectives on the Future of Evaluation

What can we say about the future of evaluation? On the one hand, the availability of public funds for social action programs will no doubt continue to diminish drastically in the wake of the current taxpayers' revolt and the proposed cuts in federal expenditures. As a result, policy makers more than ever before will face difficult decisions as to which programs to curtail or eliminate. Although many factors—mostly political—enter into these decisions, evaluation data, because of their ostensible objectivity, are likely to acquire increasing value for making these decisions and for justifying them. In short, we are likely to see a growing concern with whether those programs that do receive support succeed or fail (Zigler & Trickett, 1978), and this desire for "proof" of program impact is likely to be defined as *program evaluation.*

Other events likely to have an influence on future developments in evaluation and measurement include the social upheavals of the past fifteen years. The most lasting outcome of these social changes may well be the acceptance of the individual's right to decide, even if the decision departs sharply from conventional norms. Such readiness among contemporary Americans to accept differences is having sweeping import for theory and practice in education (Turnbull, 1977). No longer will professional educators alone determine educational goals and objectives, and therefore the curriculum. Many other sources of influence—parents, citizens' groups, and students themselves—now claim a growing voice in determining the nature of education. It is clear that education will pursue an expanding array of roles (McNeil & Laosa, 1975). The field of evaluation and measurement must achieve rapid progress if it is to meet the evolving needs created by such change.

An illustration of the impact of social change on the theory and procedures of evaluation is afforded by the emerging research stimulated by the emphasis upon improving educational opportunities for ethnic and socioeconomic minorities. Efforts to appraise the educational progress of minority individuals are producing new ideas and new means of educational and psychological evaluation that extend beyond the field of minority education (Laosa, 1977a; Oakland & Laosa, 1977). Much of this new scientific knowledge still awaits application in the field of evaluation.

The Process of Evaluation

Program evaluation is much easier to describe in the ideal that it is to do. In early childhood education the problems are made even more complicated by the vagaries of measurement with very young children and by the occurrence of rapid changes during the early years (Messick & Barrows, 1972). In other respects, the key issues in the evaluation of early childhood programs are generally the same as those arising in the evaluation of programs at any educational level. Program evaluation consists of five basic stages: (1) finding out the goals of the program; (2) translating the goals into measurable indicators of goal achievement; (3) collecting data on the indicators for those who have been exposed to the program; (4) collecting similar data on an equivalent group that has not been exposed to the program; and (5) comparing these two groups in terms of goal criteria (Weiss, 1972). In addition, some evaluators advocate the assessment of unintended effects. Once these steps have been followed and the data have been analyzed, it becomes possible with a given level of confidence to accept or reject the hypothesis that the program is succeeding and to specify its measured impact on the students. This is much easier said than done, particularly when the program serves a socioculturally diverse population.

To demonstrate that program evaluation can attain a ponderous level of complexity, we need but focus on the first stage of the evaluation process. The identification of program goals in terms specific enough to measure is often the most difficult task of the evaluator. Occasionally, program goals will be straightforward and relatively easy to operationalize, such as those in some of the educational games used in the Ecuador Nonformal Education Project (Laosa, 1976), for example. More often, program goals are many and diffuse. Indeed, program objectives tend to be stated either in broad terms such as "social competence," "school readiness," or "perceptual, cognitive, and language development" without any further conceptualization of what to teach, or in a myriad of minute terms such as "colors," "numbers to ten," "prepositions such as 'over' and 'under'," "shapes," and "letters" (Kamii, 1971). The evaluator faces an even more complex and challenging problem when the program operates in a socioculturally diverse context. In such a context, there might not be a consensus regarding the goals of the program. Such absence of agreement over program goals exists in early childhood education partly because the field, relatively new, grows out of various social forces and intellectual orientations that have not coalesced. Another cause lies in early childhood education's efforts to regain certain of the grass-roots qualities, the direct community involvement, and the ensuing local control by parents already lost—through standardization, formalization, and centralization—in elementary, secondary, and higher education. These attempts to reach out create of necessity a dialectic involving not only diverse disciplinary orientations but also various sociocultural perspectives.

The analysis of Head Start that follows is intended to illustrate some of the problems inherent in this type of situation. A brief account of certain events surrounding Head Start's emergence will help provide a sociohistorical context for the ensuing analysis.

Head Start: A National Experiment

Public education was designed, in theory, to provide an equal opportunity for all children to learn and develop—in other words, a chance for upward mobility and achievement regardless of the advantages or disadvantages provided by family circumstances. That public education had for many failed to accomplish this social objective became, by the late 1950s, acutely noticeable. By then, it had become clear that, amid advancing prosperity and growing affluence, the United States was facing a serious social crisis of poverty and ethnic conflict and isolation. This crisis was further complicated by the special conditions of the history of this country, which produced social isolation and economic disadvantage for many members of certain ethnic minorities. Under those conditions, there were diverse cultures embedded within a larger social system. Members of some of these cultures felt ignored, unknown, unappreciated, and sometimes even oppressed by the dominant groups who controlled important extrafamilial institutions. Salient among these institutions was public education, which to many appeared unable or unwilling to fit itself to the special needs of poor and ethnic minority children.

Partly as a result of concern over this situation, an increasing number of psychologists and educators began, during the early 1960s, to study the effects of early experience on human development. Much of this research suggested that preschool compensatory education might be an important step toward disrupting the cycle of poverty experienced by large numbers of Americans. Consequently, in 1964 Head Start was launched (Cooke, 1972; see also Horowitz & Paden, 1973; White, 1973; Zigler & Valentine, 1979).

The Goal of Head Start

What is the goal of Head Start? Head Start seeks to bring about greater "social competence" in children of low-income families. In this sense, social competence refers to "the child's everyday effectiveness in dealing with both present environment and later responsibilities in school and life. Social competence takes into account the interrelatedness of cognitive and intellectual development, physical and mental health, nutritional needs, and other factors that enable a developmental approach to helping children achieve social competence" (U.S. Department of Health, Education, and Welfare, 1975, p. 1). Underlying this goal is the premise that all children share certain needs and that children of low-income families, in particular, can benefit from a comprehensive developmental program to meet those needs. To the accomplishment of this goal, Head Start objectives and performance standards seek: (1) the improvement of the child's health and physical abilities, including appropriate steps to correct present physical and mental problems, and to enhance every child's access to an adequate diet; the improvement of the family's attitude toward future health care and physical abilities; (2) the encouragement of self-confidence, spontaneity, curiosity, and self-discipline, which will assist in the development of the child's social and emotional health; (3) the enhancement of the child's mental processes and skills, with particular attention to conceptual and communications skills; (4) the establishment of patterns and expectations of success for the child, which will create a climate of confidence for present and future learning efforts and overall development; (5) an increase in the ability of the child and the family to relate to each other and to others; (6) the enhancement of the sense of dignity and self-worth within the child and his family (U.S. Department of Health, Education, and Welfare, 1975).

Looking back on the history of Head Start, White (1973) abstracted three parallel conceptions of its goal. Some proponents of Head Start conceived of it as a nucleus of community action. Others saw it as a long sought mechanism for coordinating services to children. A third group contended, on the basis of technical arguments, that education in the preschool years might have unsuspected potency for increasing the child's intelligence. While these conceptions existed simultaneously, the focus tended to shift from the first to the third.

The original objectives of the legislation authorizing Head Start (see White, 1973) were directed toward funding community action programs for low-income individuals and families. The education of the low-income child was not singled out as a focus. Rather, the original objectives of the Child Development Centers sponsored by Head Start were comprehensive, including medical, psychological, nutritional, educational, and social-work intervention with community and parent decision making and involvement. Such programs could include employment, health, vocational rehabilitation, housing, job training, home management, and educational assistance.

The most recently published official document on the purpose of Head Start (U.S. Department of Health, Education, and Welfare, 1975) still reflects a strong allegiance to a comprehensive, interdisciplinary set of objectives. But it is significant that one of the original objectives of Head Start is no longer listed as part of the official goal of the program. Specifically, "fostering constructive opportunities for society to work together with the poor in solving their problems," one of the original objectives, does not appear in the most recent official document on the purpose of Head Start (see U.S. Department of Health, Education, and Welfare, 1975; White, 1973). Does this reflect a movement toward a more narrow emphasis on the formal education and physical health of the child and away from the objective of changing extrafamilial institutions to make them more responsive to the needs of diverse families? Whether or not it does, it is a fact that evaluations of Head Start have focused largely on children's IQ and academic achievement but have tended to neglect assessing the programs' impact on extrafamilial institutions (see review by Mann, Harrell & Hurt, 1978). I shall return to this point.

The guidelines for Head Start do not set forth an agreed-upon curriculum. Rather, each program is to provide a set of preschool experiences that is determined on the local level. Hence, each grantee or delegate agency (the public or private nonprofit agency that has been granted federal assistance to carry on a Head Start program) must develop its own plan for attaining the general goal and objectives encompassed by the term "social competence." Each program (grantee, delegate agency, or Head Start center) has almost complete autonomy to decide its own orientation and emphases within the guidelines and services specified by the policy promulgated by the central federal office (U.S. Department of Health, Education, and Welfare, 1975). This approach has important implications for understanding the programs and for evaluating their impact on children's development. Specifically, on a national basis, Head Start is not *a* program, that is, the broad goal and objectives set forth in the guidelines do not constitute a program in the sense of a uniform set of experiences, since there are so many local program configurations that address the general goal. This emphasis on local initiative no doubt results in varied perceptions and interpretations of the goal and objectives of Head Start and in varied emphases in their implementation. Indeed, evidence of such diversity can be seen in the results of a recent national survey (Royster et al., 1978).

Other sources of diversity no doubt affect the interpretation and operationalization of Head Start's goal and objectives. I refer here to sociocultural diversity present within the Head Start population. Evidence of this diversity can be adduced from the results of the same survey conducted by Royster and his co-workers (Royster & Larson, 1978). The data show that centers are about equally distributed in the four quadrants of the country. Hence, regional differences contribute to the diversity within the Head Start population. In addition, the survey reveals considerable ethnic diversity. Slightly over half of the children in Head Start are non-Hispanic black, about one-quarter are non-Hispanic white, 15 percent are Hispanic, and 10 percent are of other ethnic groups. The data also show differences in the schooling level of parents. Specifically, 46 percent of the mothers of Head Start children had not completed high school, 44 percent received high school diplomas, and 10 percent had some schooling beyond high school. Still another source of sociocultural diversity in Head Start is that contributed by the staff. The distribution of staff ethnic types in the survey data indicates an equal number of blacks and whites.[1,2]

Another study (Mediax Associates, 1978) provides more direct evidence of heterogeneity in the perception of Head Start's goal and objectives. The study consisted of a series of two-day input workshops designed to find out from parents of Head Start pupils, Head Start faculty and staff, and elementary school teachers what knowledge, skills, attitudes, and habits they expected children to develop as a result of experiences in Head Start. Seven such workshops were conducted in different regions of the nation. Table 20–1 shows these regions and the distribution of participants by ethnic group. The participants were selected to represent the ethnic and residential (urban, rural, migrant) make-up of the regions. In each region, they were organized into small groups separately by ethnic background and residential area. Each group was assigned a trained facilitator of ethnic and language background similar to that of the group members. (This manner of grouping was used to obtain as much as possible a comfortable, secure conversational context among participants. Pilot testing of other manners of grouping revealed that mixing of roles, ethnic backgrounds, and areas of residence created tension and limited open expression as a result of differences in experiences, values, knowledge, and concerns. For example, many parents could be observed to defer to teachers and appeared uncomfortable with the use of professional terminology.)

At the end of two days of discussion, each group produced a list of responses to twenty-six discussion topics. I will discuss here the results of the eleven topics that dealt with cognitive and perceptual development. These topics were stated as follows (Mediax Associates, 1978, p. 2 & appendix C):

> Describe those things you want a child to be able to do that prove he or she (a) can solve problems and reason well; (b) is good with numbers and has

---

[1] It is unfortunate that the Royster et al. (1978) national survey excluded centers enrolling primarily Hispanic children, thus making it impossible to obtain such information for this ethnic group.

[2] Ironically, when one examines staff-to-child ethnic composition, one finds that, relative to the distribution of minority children, there is a lower proportion of minority staff members than of non-minority staff members. In this regard, Head Start does not differ from many other programs designed to serve low-income and ethnic minorities.

TABLE 20–1. Input Workshops with Head Start Parents and Teachers

Meeting Places	Head Start Regions Represented	Distribution of Participants by Ethnic Group					
		Black	Hispanic	American Indian	Asian	Other	Total
Atlanta	IV	26	0	0	0	25	71
Chicago	V	19	13	0	0	24	56
Dallas	VI, VIII[a], XI	32	35	19	0	22	108
Kansas City	VII	12	0	0	0	5	17
New York City	I, II, III	38	11	0	7	26	82
San Francisco	VIII[a], IX, X	7	14	0	5	35	61
All		134	73	19	12	137	395

Source: Mediax Associates, 1978.

[a] Participants from this region were present at meetings in two cities.

arithmetic skills; (c) has reading readiness skills; (d) is able to use senses (hearing, seeing, feeling, smelling, tasting); (e) knows rules and customs of society; (f) has school readiness skills; (g) understands things about nature; (h) understands about the things in the world that humanity has created.

Two additional topics were:

We are living in a society of many nationalities and races: (a) Is there anything you want your children to learn or be able to do to help them get along with other races and nationalities? (b) Is there knowledge or skill particular to their own race or ethnic group that you want them to have?

Finally, participants were asked to "list any other skills, knowledge, attitudes, or habits not covered in the above you would like your children to have." In each case, they were asked to describe "what children would be able to do that proves attainment."

Although the recorded responses have not been thoroughly cross-tabulated as of this writing, the raw data sheets have been made available (see Mediax Associates, undated). In scanning these data, one can see considerable variability in the perceptions of the Head Start goal and objectives. Not only can one detect differences among the five ethnic groups, but even within groups there is variability. Moreover, one can see differences in perceptions between Head Start teachers and parents. The data provide confirmatory evidence for the view that there is a great deal of diversity in how the goal and objectives of Head Start are perceived and interpreted.

Evaluations of Head Start

Given (1) the sociocultural diversity in the Head Start population and the accompanying heterogeneity in its members' needs and characteristics and (2) the emphasis on local initiative, a hallmark of Head Start, and the resultant diversity in the interpretation of the programs' goals and objectives, one must ask: have the evaluations of Head Start appropriately reflected such diversity and pluralism in their designs, that is, in the choices of information-gathering techniques? To answer this question, I have reviewed five national studies generally considered to be among the major evaluations of Head Start. Table 20–2 (p. 510) presents, for each study, the techniques used to gather data on Head Start's impact on children's cognitive development. As can be seen, standardized IQ tests were used in almost all the evaluations. In addition, standardized measures of school-related achievement were used in several evaluations.

Do the choices of information-gathering techniques in these evaluations do justice to Head Start's diverse and pluralistic nature? A clue to an answer can be found in the most frequently heard criticism of standardized IQ tests. The principal allegation against such tests is that they measure largely (non-Hispanic) white, middle-class values and attitudes and hence are biased against members of certain cultural and socioeconomic minorities. To the extent that this criticism is valid for a given measurement instrument, a "cultural deficit" approach is implied in the evaluator's choice of that instrument (Laosa, 1980). Specifically, the evaluator who uses such a test is making judgments about program success on the basis of *whether the served children come to resemble the cultural norms* implicit in what the test measures.

Many evaluators who used standardized IQ tests recognize that they are leaving to chance the "match" between the course content and the examination content. They justify their practice by arguing that since such tests predict school success, preschools must raise the child's IQ in order to attain the instructional objective of "readiness for school." But this argument raises additional problems. For example, it brings to mind another criticism of standardized assessment, specifically, the allegation that such form of assessment rigidly shapes school curricula and restricts educational change. In this regard, one should not forget that many conceive of Head Start as an effort to modify extrafamilial institutions (such as schools) in order to make them more responsive to the needs of Head Start-eligible children and families. How many evaluations have assessed the impact of Head Start from the perspective of this conception? Not many, indeed.

From another side, the issue can be further probed by restating the question as follows: does the choice of information-gathering techniques in these national evaluations reflect the diverse criteria of program success that can result from local initiative? Local initiative in the interpretive formulation of program goal and objectives is, insofar as it may occur within the latitudes provided by the guidelines, a principal characteristic of Head Start. We have seen that this characteristic can result in diverse formulations of program goal and objectives. To answer the question, it appears unlikely, on the face of it, that instrument selection in these evaluations has done adequate justice to the diverse nature of Head Start.

Granted, the kind of pluralistic approach to program assessment that my analysis thus far suggests would be required will present to the field of evaluation a multitude of difficult, nay, portentous challenges. But regardless of the seemingly Sisyphean nature of the challenges, they should not remain unmet. Why? Because program evaluations are part of the process of formulating public policy, and therefore, great care must be exercised to conduct them within the assumptions of pluralistic ideology or, if one prefers, within the concepts of democracy and equal participation. To apply this to our example, consider that Head Start's multiple constituencies include eligible children, their families, the sociocultural groups to which they belong, teachers, program administrators, the federal agency responsible for the program, and the general public. Consider also that these constituencies have a common need for evaluative information to answer the question, "Is the program effective in meeting certain specified objectives?" Evaluation, then, should be directed toward judging the worth of the program by examining its effectiveness in the attainment of the program's goal and objectives as formulated by each of the varied sectors and subgroups of its diverse constituencies.

TABLE 20–2. Techniques Used to Assess Cognitive Development in Five Major Evaluations of Head Start

EVALUATION	TECHNIQUES	TECHNIQUE DESCRIPTIONS
System Development Corporation (1972a)	Stanford Binet Intelligence Test	An IQ test.
System Development Corporation (1972b)	Stanford Binet Intelligence Test	An IQ test.
	Wechsler Preschool and Primary Scale of Intelligence: Animal House subtest	A measure of ability to learn.
	Caldwell Preschool Inventory	A measure of achievement in areas considered essential for success in school.
Walker, Bane, & Bryk (1973)	Stanford Binet Intelligence Test	An IQ test.
	Wide Range Achievement Test	An achievement test of skills in reading, spelling, and arithmetic.
	Caldwell Preschool Inventory	A measure of achievement in areas considered essential for success in school
	ETS Enumeration Test	A test of three components of enumeration: counting, pointing, and matching.
	NYU Booklet 3-D	An achievement test of relational premath, prescience, and linguistic concepts.
	NYU Booklet 4-A	An achievement test of knowledge of numbers, letters, and shapes.
	Relevant Redundant Cue Concept Acquisition Test	A measure of concept acquisition, learning ability, and attention.

Granville, Love, & Morris (1977)	Wechsler Preschool and Primary Scale of Intelligence: Block Design Subtest	A proxy measure of IQ. Also regarded specifically as a measure of problem-solving ability, flexibility in response style, and visual-motor organization and execution.
	McCarthy Scales of Children's Abilities:	
	Verbal Memory Test	A measure of skill in short-term retention of verbal information.
	Verbal Fluency Test	A measure of ability to recall information by conceptual categories.
	Draw-A-Child Test	A measure of visual-motor coordination and conceptual development.
Royster, Larson, Ferb, Fosburg, Nauta, Nelson, & Takata (1978)	Wide Range Achievement Test	An achievement test of skills in reading, spelling, and arithmetic.

511

The Identification of Program Objectives

A principal aspect of evaluation involves measuring student performance relative to important program objectives in order to identify strengths and weaknesses of the program. As we have seen, program objectives can be diverse, can be interpreted in various ways, and are seldom clear-cut. Therefore, a major challenge for the evaluator is their identification. How can program objectives be identified? They can be identified by two very different approaches: the independent approach and the collective viewpoints approach. The independent approach is the more common. It depends largely upon the rational insights of the policy maker, who typically proceeds alone or with the input of only a few professionals or organized interest groups. The major advantage of this approach is its relatively uncomplicated nature. The major disadvantage is that it does not allow for a systematic appraisal of the objectives felt to be important by other relevant groups.

In contrast, the collective viewpoints approach can be used to determine systematically what various groups consider to be the objectives of the program (Hoepfner et al., 1972; McNeil & Laosa, 1975). In this way, the policy maker has more information before making decisions about which objectives should be assessed, and these decisions become directly accountable to the various groups surveyed. The inclusion of a broad array of relevant groups provides a more balanced approach, tends to reduce criticism of outcomes, and offers an opportunity for policy makers, staff, and community to share their concerns with one another. It also provides a base for involvement of people when further collective decision making is required. Moreover, it lets the policy makers know the perceptions that people representing a broad array of relevant constituencies have about the objectives of the program. The use of such information can also help in the selection of certain objectives over others, given the usually limited time and budget available for evaluation. Where the program constituency is diverse, the collective viewpoints approach is thus the more justifiable one, as it yields a broader base of information and provides a pluralistic basis for the selection of objectives on which to focus the evaluative process.

Some Measurement Considerations

The discussion thus far brings us to consider the *population validity* of the measures used to assess program impact. Specifically, do the results yielded by a given assessment technique have the same meaning when administered to persons of different sociocultural backgrounds? How can we tell whether or not an assessment procedure measures the same psychological construct when administered to persons of different sociocultures? If it does not, the results of the evaluation are likely to be erroneous. If an assessment procedure does not measure the same thing for different persons, or even if it is impossible to tell, the evaluator is in trouble.

One reason the problem exists is that, to use Frederiksen's words, "performance is influenced by many factors other than the amount of the construct that exists in the subject" (1977, p. 15). For example, some children do poorly on perceptual tests because they are impulsive. Some may excel on certain reasoning tests because they possess specific verbal knowledge. Thus, the problem exists even when the sample is socioculturally homogeneous. It becomes greatly magnified, however, when there is sociocultural diversity. Indeed, the threats to population validity can become particularly real when we deal with a sample of individuals of different cultural experiences or sociolinguistic characteristics.

Let us focus on four threats to population validity: familiarity effects, communication problems, role-relation effects, and situational effects.

Familiarity Effects

When interpreting the performance of individuals in order to assess their relative ability to perform some cognitive task, one wants to be sure of two things: that a cognitive act is involved in the task demands and that any interindividual differences that are found are not the result of differential familiarity with the task material (Glick, 1975). Thus, when evaluating a program, one wants to be sure that the variance observed in the performance indeed reflects the impact of the program on the cognitive construct one is trying to measure and is not merely the effect of such peripheral factors as differential familiarity with the types of materials or procedures one is using to assess the construct.

The term familiarity can mean a number of different things, however, and different bases of familiarity should be distinguished. These include the mode of representation of the materials (for instance, two-dimensional versus three-dimensional), the familiarity of the objects and dimensions (a dimension may be considered to be familiar when it is used to label a distinction), and the familiarity of the application of a dimension to a domain (some collections are typically analyzed in terms of certain dimensions, although the same dimension may not be appropriate when applied to a different domain). Glick (1975) has summarized the basic problem: to be able to study a cognitive operation one must be sure that the task demands the use of the operation and that the solution of the task reflects that operation and none other.

Communication Problems

The most obvious problems of communication in assessment situations occur when different languages are involved. Many of these problems have been given attention elsewhere and will not be repeated here (see, for example, DeAvila, 1973; Sechrest, Fay & Zaidi, 1972). Instead, I will focus on a rather subtle and frequently neglected communication problem, namely, the problem of achieving genuine semantic equivalence of assessment instruments (Holtzman, 1968; Laosa, 1973a, 1973b, 1977a). Even with the best of cultural adaptations and/or translations of instruments, the semantic value of particular words and phrases may still differ appreciably between sociocultures, leading to different sets and interpretations of meaning. This point is well illustrated in a series of studies by Peck and Díaz-Guerrero (Díaz-Guerrero, 1975) dealing with the usage and subtle meaning of such Spanish and English words as "love" and "respect" as they are used in communities ranging from central Mexico to the southwestern United States. The traditional Mexican connotation of the word "respect" includes strong overtones of obedience, expectation of protection, and concern not to invade the respected one's rights—overall, a connotation of duty and deference to authority. By contrast, the modal Anglo-American concept of respect emphasizes admiration without any feelings of subordination, a kind of democratic give-and-take while being considerate of the other person's feelings and ideas. Obviously, such differences in meaning could easily lead to misinterpretations of such data as responses to interviews, tests, and questionnaires and even behavioral observations.

Role-Relation Effects

Even under the best of conditions, the evaluator's role relation to the subject may be inextricably embedded in the culture, so that it becomes confounded with the major variables in the evaluation design (Holtzman, 1968). Indeed, an individual's performance in an assessment situation may be inextricably embedded in his or her role relationship to the evaluator. There appear to be cultural and possibly other sources of individual differences in these role relationships (Holtzman, 1965, 1968). Evidence of this can be found in the results of a large-scale study of Mexican and American children (Holtzman, et al., 1975; Laosa, Lara-Tapia & Swartz, 1974). It was found that, when facing standardized testing situations, the average Mexican child appeared cautious and seemed to look for ways to please the examiner. The average Anglo-American child, on the other hand, seemed to approach the testing situation as a challenge to be mastered, an opportunity to show how much he or she could do. Such cultural differences in role relations and in approaches to evaluative tasks may conceivably affect performance and, if ignored, lead to misinterpretation of assessment data.

Situational Effects

Performance on tasks typically used to assess competence can be subject also to the influence of situational or contextual effects. Such tasks are usually taken out of their natural contexts and presented in a specified set of conditions (Sigel, 1974). It is typically assumed (1) that the task (for example, the test items) represents a sample of items from a universe of tasks; and (2) that the respondent's behavior in the assessment situation represents a sample of the individual's proficiency. But how is one to interpret behavior that occurs in response to a situation that has been taken out of its natural context? Does it represent the individual's reponse to a similar task in its natural context?

A context or situation is not defined solely or even necessarily by the physical setting (e.g., living room, sidewalk) or by person combinations (e.g., child and mother, child and sibling) (Erickson & Schultz, 1977); rather, it includes what people are doing and when and where they are doing it. Compelling evidence of the effects of the context on performance comes from the work of Labov (1970). Cole and Bruner (1971) have described a relevant facet of his work:

> One example of Labov's approach is to conduct a rather standard interview of the type often used for assessment of language competence. The situation is designed to be minimally threatening; the interviewer is a neighborhood figure, and black. Yet, the black eight-year-old interviewee's behavior is monosyllabic. He is a candidate for the diagnosis of linguistically and cultur-ally deprived.
>
> But this diagnosis is very much situation dependent. For, at a later time, this same interviewer goes to the boy's apartment, brings one of the boy's friends with him, lies down on the floor, and produces some potato chips. He then begins talking about clearly taboo subjects in dialect. Under these cir-cumstances the mute interviewee becomes an excited (competent) participant in the general conversation [1971, p. 86].

It is important, therefore, to distinguish between *proficiency* and *performance*. Performance is what a person actually does in a particular situation. Proficiency is what the person would do under conditions that are optimally conducive to eliciting what he or she is capable of doing.

Social Competence

The primary goal of many early childhood education programs is to bring about a greater degree of social competence in children. What is meant by the term social competence? Most views of children's development of social competence have dealt with sociocultural diversity either by ignoring it or by invoking the concept of deficit or social pathology. Typically, social competence has been defined as a unitary set of standards or norms. Almost without exception, these norms have tended to represent the characteristics of a few groups. Persons are judged to be socially competent if their characteristics match this set of norms. In contrast, per-sons are considered to be deficient or pathological if they deviate from these norms. This certainly has been true in the United States where, because of this reliance on a unitary set of standards representing the values of a few groups, the prevalent orientation toward defining social competence has been aggressively ethnocentric.

We must vigorously scrutinize our theories for such tacit outlooks that force us to unreflectively take our own socioculture's values as objective reality and as the context for judging unfamiliar objects or events. Likewise, we must examine our theories for the presence of a more complex form of ethnocentrism, which acknowledges the existence of multiple sociocultural points of view but automatically dismisses them as incorrect, inferior, or immoral (LeVine & Campbell, 1972).

An alternative to such absolutist outlooks is what I have termed the *developmental, socioculturally relativistic paradigm* (Laosa, 1979). When considered from the perspective provided by this paradigm, a person is judged to be socially competent or incompetent only in the context of specific roles and value judgments. An example will serve to illustrate the general principle underlying the developmental, socioculturally relativistic paradigm and to reveal some of its implications for the topic at hand.

The example is based on a study of Chicano and Anglo-American children (Kagan & Madsen, 1971). The study results showed that the Chicano children were more cooperative than their Anglo-American counterparts. In contrast to the Chicano children, the Anglo-American children often appeared highly competitive. This finding is readily interpretable when one considers that cooperation is a culturally rooted value among many Chicanos. As such, many Chicanos view cooperation as a component characteristic of social competence. Further consider, however, that in many school situations culturally insensitive teachers are likely to view as undesirable certain manifestations of this cooperative orientation (for example, they may interpret it as "cheating"). Thus, a Chicano child, who in the context of family and neighborhood is regarded as socially competent by virtue of being cooperative, may in the context of the classroom be judged deviant (socially incompetent) as a result of exhibiting the same type of cooperative behavior. Such inconsistencies, incompatibilities, and lack of articulated continuity between the family experience and the school experience can be bewildering and psychologically deleterious for the child (Cárdenas & Cárdenas, 1973; Laosa, 1974, 1977b). An adequate conceptualization of the development of social competence must allow, then, for an inclusive and integrated account of sociocultural relativity.

Evaluation, Public Policy, and Scientific Inquiry

Many omens portend that the field of evaluation and measurement will burst forth during the next several years with a significance and magnitude at least comparable to that during and after World War I. In contrast to the emphasis at that time (see Laosa, 1977a), the new emphasis will probably be on program evaluation (Wertheimer et al., 1978). That is, the development of new assessment techniques is likely to be seen in large part as a contribution to program evaluation. Moreover, evaluation studies probably will not be circumscribed to such concerns, typical of the past, as assessing the effectiveness of specified teaching methods on student achievement. Rather, evaluation efforts are likely to include studies to determine the strengths and weaknesses of broad aspects of social systems. If program evaluators are to meet the intellectual demands and rise to the technical challenges of their roles as shapers of public policy, the field must raise its current level of sophistication.

The field of evaluation and measurement, instead of primarily helping institutions to compare and choose among individuals, will probably be used increasingly as a tool for gathering information to serve the dual purpose of (1) aiding policy makers in making policy decisions and (2) evaluating the impact of public policies. Already, students in many of the traditional disciplines are being trained to play broader roles than before in the public policy arena. So much so, in fact, that we must guard against the temptation to substitute applied pursuits for basic inquiry. Basic inquiry is needed to generate the fundamental knowledge without which real progress in the applied fields is impossible. The field of evaluation owes many of its developments to the progress of behavioral and social scientists as they have required and created more and more sophisticated methodologies to carry out their inquiry into basic problems. One of the challenges we face is the closing of the gap between the present store of knowledge derived from research on the one hand, and the application and use of this knowledge to the design and conduct of evaluations, on the other. Applied work in program evaluation must be open to the new developments contributed by social and behavioral research. Conversely, the work of evaluators has great potential for stimulating progress not only in the burgeoning field of evaluation and in public policies, but also in the basic academic disciplines. Indeed, the pursuit of the evaluator should not be merely a role-playing one—as Koch (1978) lamented that it may have been thus far—but rather an intellectually responsible commitment to discover differentiated and meaningful, perhaps illuminating, knowledge about the human condition.

The research for this chapter was supported in part by the United States Administration for Children, Youth, and Families (Contract #105-77-1006 with Mediax Associates).

References

ALKIN, M. C. Evaluation theory development. In C. H. Weiss (ed.), *Evaluating Action Programs: Readings in Social Action and Education.* Boston: Allyn and Bacon, 1972.

CÁRDENAS, B., and CÁRDENAS, J. A. Chicano, bright-eyed, bilingual, brown, and beautiful. *Today's Education*, 1973, *62*, 49–51.

COLE, M., and BRUNER, J. S. Cultural differences and inferences about psychological processes. *American Psychologist*, 1971, *26*, 867–876.

COOKE, R. Improving the opportunities and achievements of the children of the poor. (Recommendations for a Head Start Program, by panel of experts chaired by R. Cooke, February 19, 1965.) Washington, D.C.: U.S. Department of Health, Education, and Welfare, Office of Child Development, 1972.

DEAVILA, E.A. I.Q. and the minority child. *Journal of the Association of Mexican American Educators*, 1973, *1*, 34–38.

DÍAZ-GUERRERO, R. *Psychology of the Mexican: Culture and Personality.* Austin: University of Texas Press, 1975.

ERICKSON, F., and SCHULTZ, J. When is a context? Some issues and methods in the analysis of social competence. *The Quarterly Newsletter of the Institute for Comparative Human Development*, Vol. 1, No. 2. New York: The Rockefeller University Press, 1977.

FREDERIKSEN, N. How to tell if a test measures the same thing in different cultures. In Y. H. Poortinga (ed.), *Basic Problems in Cross-Cultural Psychology*. Amsterdam: Swets and Zeitlinger, 1977.

GLICK, J. Cognitive development in cross-cultural perspective. In F. D. Horowitz (ed.), *Review of Child Development Research*, Vol. 4. Chicago: University of Chicago Press, 1975.

GRANVILLE, A. C., LOVE, J. M., and MORRIS, M. A process evaluation of Project Developmental Continuity. Interim report VII (Vol. 3): Assessment of program impact through the Head Start year. Ypsilanti, Mich.: High/Scope Educational Research Foundation, August 1977.

HOEPFNER, R., BRADLEY, P. A., KLEIN, S. P., and ALKIN, M. C. *CSE/Elementary School Evaluation Kit: Needs Assessment*. Boston: Allyn and Bacon, 1972.

HOLTZMAN, W. H. Cross-cultural research on personality development. *Human Development*, 1965, 8, 65–86.

HOLTZMAN, W. H. Cross-cultural studies in psychology. *International Journal of Psychology*, 1968, 3, 83–91.

HOLTZMAN, W. H., DÍAZ-GUERRERO, R., and SWARTZ, J. D., in collaboration with Lara-Tapia, L., Laosa, L. M., Morales, M. L., Lagunes, I. R., and Witzke, D. B. *Personality Development in Two Cultures: A Cross-Cultural Longitudinal Study of School Children in Mexico and the United States*. Austin: University of Texas Press, 1975.

HOROWITZ, F. D., and PADEN, L. Y. The effectiveness of environmental intervention programs. In B. M. Caldwell and H. N. Ricciuti (eds.), *Review of Child Development Research*, Vol. 3. Chicago: University of Chicago Press, 1973.

KAGAN, S., and MADSEN, W. C. Cooperation and competition of Mexican, Mexican-American, and Anglo-American children of two ages under four instructional sets. *Developmental Psychology*, 1971, 5, 32–39.

KAMII, C. K. Evaluation of learning in preschool education: Socioemotional, perceptual-motor, cognitive development. In B. S. Bloom, J. T. Hastings, and G. F. Madaus (eds.), *Handbook on Formative and Summative Evaluation of Student Learning*. New York: McGraw-Hill, 1971.

KOCH, S. In Wertheimer et al., 1978.

LABOV, W. The logic of nonstandard English. In F. Williams (ed.), *Language and Poverty*. Chicago: Markham Press, 1970.

LAOSA, L. M. Cross-cultural and subcultural research in psychology and education. *Interamerican Journal of Psychology*, 1973a, 7, 241–248.

LAOSA, L. M. Reform in educational and psychological assessment: Cultural and linguistic issues. *Journal of the Association of Mexican American Educators*, 1973b, 1, 19–24.

LAOSA, L. M. Child care and the culturally different child. *Child Care Quarterly*, 1974, 3, 214–224.

LAOSA, L. M. Developing arithmetic skills among rural villagers in Ecuador through non-formal education: A field experiment. *Journal of Educational Psychology*, 1976, 68, 670–679.

Laosa, L. M. Nonbiased assessment of children's abilities: Historical antecedents and current issues. In T. Oakland (ed.), *Psychological and Educational Assessment of Minority Children*. New York: Brunner/Mazel, 1977a.

Laosa, L. M. Socialization, education, and continuity: The importance of the sociocultural context. *Young Children*, 1977b, *32*, 21–27.

Laosa, L. M. Social competence in childhood: Toward a developmental, socioculturally relativistic paradigm. In M. Whalen Kent and J. E. Rolf (eds.), *Primary Prevention of Psychopathology*, Vol. 3: *Social Competence in Children*. Hanover, N. H.: University Press of New England, 1979.

Laosa, L. M. Parent education, cultural pluralism, and public policy: The uncertain connection. Paper presented at the Conference on Parent Education and Public Policy, Chapel Hill, N.C., March 1980.

Laosa, L. M., Lara-Tapia, L., and Swartz, J. D. Pathognomic verbalizations, anxiety, and hostility in normal Mexican and United States Anglo-American children's fantasies: A longitudinal study. *Journal of Consulting and Clinical Psychology*, 1974, *42*, 73–78.

LeVine, R. A., and Campbell, D. T. *Ethnocentrism: Theories of Conflict, Ethnic Attitudes, and Group Behavior*. New York: Wiley, 1972.

McNeil, J., and Laosa, L. M. Needs assessment and cultural pluralism in schools. *Educational Technology*, 1975, *15*, 25–28.

Mann, A. J., Harrell, A. V., and Hurt, M. A review of Head Start research since 1969. In B. Brown (ed.), *Found: Long-Term Gains from Early Intervention*. Boulder, Colo.: Westview Press, 1978.

Mediax Associates. Report of attainments identified in input workshops as part of the Project to Develop Head Start Profiles of Program Effects on Children. Part I: Group data. Westport, Conn.: Mediax Associates, not dated.

Mediax Associates. Report on the process of input workshops. Westport, Conn.: Mediax Associates, May 27, 1978.

Messick, S., and Barrows, T. S. Strategies for research and evaluation in early childhood education. In I. J. Gordon (ed.), *Early Childhood Education: The Seventy-First Yearbook of the National Society for the Study of Education*. Chicago: University of Chicago Press, 1972.

Oakland, T., and Laosa, L. M. Professional, legislative, and judicial influences on psychoeducational assessment practices in schools. In T. Oakland (ed.), *Psychological and Educational Assessment of Minority Children*. New York: Brunner/Mazel, 1977.

Royster, E. C., and Larson, J. C. *Executive Summary of a National Survey of Head Start Graduates and Their Peers*. Cambridge, Mass.: Abt Associates, 1978.

Royster, E. C., Larson, J. C., Ferb, T., Fosburg, S., Nauta, M., Nelson, B., and Takata, G. *A National Survey of Head Start Graduates and Their Peers*. Cambridge, Mass.: Abt Associates, 1978.

Sechrest, L., Fay, T. L., and Zaidi, S. M. H. Problems of translation in cross-cultural research. *Journal of Cross-Cultural Psychology*, 1972, *3*, 41–56.

Sigel, I. E. When do we know what a child knows? *Human Development*, 1974, *17*, 201–217.

System Development Corporation. Effects of different Head Start program approaches on children of different characteristics: Report on analysis of data from 1966–67 and

1967–68 national evaluations. Santa Monica, Calif.: System Development Corporation, 1972a.

System Development Corporation. The effects of the Head Start classroom experience on some aspects of child development: A summary report of national evaluations 1966–1969. Santa Monica, Calif.: System Development Corporation, 1972b.

TURNBULL, W. W. The President's report: Power to the person. *Educational Testing Service 1976 Annual Report.* Princeton, N.J.: Educational Testing Service, 1977.

U.S. Department of Health, Education, and Welfare; Office of Human Development Services; Administration for Children, Youth, and Families; Children's Bureau. *Head Start Program Performance Standards,* 1975 (OCD Notice N-30-364-4).

WALKER, D. R., BANE, M. J., and BRYK, T. *The Quality of the Head Start Planned Variation Data,* Vols. 1 and 2. Cambridge, Mass.: Huron Institute, 1973.

WEISS, C. H. Evaluating educational and social action programs: A "treeful of owls." In C. H. Weiss (ed.), *Evaluating Action Programs: Readings in Social Action and Education.* Boston: Allyn and Bacon, 1972.

WERTHEIMER, M., BARCLAY, A. G., COOK, S. W., KIESLER, C. A., KOCH, S., RIEGEL, K. F., RORER, L. G., SENDERS, V. L., SMITH, M. B., and SPERLING, S. E. Psychology and the future. *American Psychologist,* 1978, *33,* 631–647.

WHITE, S. H. *Federal Programs for Young Children: Review and Recommendations,* Vols. 1–3. Washington, D.C.: U.S. Government Printing Office, 1973.

ZIGLER, E., and TRICKETT, P. K. IQ, social competence, and evaluation of early childhood intervention programs. *American Psychologist,* 1978, *33,* 789–798.

ZIGLER, E., and VALENTINE, J. (eds.). *Project Head Start: A Legacy of the War on Poverty.* New York: Free Press, 1979.

PART V

Research Methods in Early Childhood Education

CHAPTER 21

Measuring Young Children

William L. Goodwin
Laura D. Goodwin

MEASUREMENT IS the process of determining, through observation or testing, an individual's traits or behaviors, a program's characteristics, or the properties of some other entity, and then assigning a number, rating, or score to that determination. It involves numbers, scales, constructs, validity, and reliability. Thorndike (1918) proposed that anything that exists, exists in some amount and therefore can be measured. Since then (and to some extent even earlier), formal and informal measurements have become central features of American education, although their influence has waxed and waned. Thousands of individual traits and behaviors relevant to education, such as readiness, achievement, IQ, motivation, language, creativity, field dependence, conceptual tempo, listening skills, attentiveness, self-concept, attitudes, interests, values, coordination, stamina, health, and nutrition, have been measured. There are measures unique to programs, as in the case of effectiveness, environmental setting, climate, and side-effects. This definition of measurement includes many measuring devices other than paper-and-pencil tests (an orientation later made explicit), such as observation systems. Curiously, given the close affiliation between observation and measurement, "observing" has captured the hearts of most early childhood educators, in sharp contrast to the connotations often accorded "testing" and "measuring."

The organizational framework of this chapter owes much to earlier schemes used by W. B. Webb (1970) and Evans (1974). Basic questions about measuring young children are asked—why, how, and what—and answered. The related questions of when, where, and by whom are so specific to certain programs or settings that no general attempt is made to answer them. However, with regard to the when of measurement, two items are noteworthy. First, "when" now literally extends to before birth, with medical personnel making numerous assessments of the fetus or even of the mother's medical history before conception. Second, the concepts of formative and summative evaluation, applied to student learning, **523** furnish some principles of interest, as noted briefly in the "how" section. The central questions of why, how, and what, describe well the current status of measurement in early childhood education. The concluding section of the chapter examines sourcebooks of relevant measures.

Why Measure Young Children?

Responses to the "why" question vary with the occupation of the answerer. Researchers, seeking to determine what is, view measurement of young children as a critical step in the process. Evaluators, operating under any of the seven different conceptual mantles identified by Glass and Ellet (1980), similarly consider measurement as an important adjunct process. Developers, striving to improve a program or product, use measures frequently. Governmental and private funding agencies, wanting to commit their shrinking dollars wisely, see measurement as central in determining "what works." Teachers, desiring to foster children's development and learning, most often welcome only those measures that provide directives on how better to meet such responsibilities to their young charges. Teachers we have spoken to invariably wanted measures to yield information with prompt practical applications (see also Somach, 1978).

Mehrens and Lehmann (1978) identified four somewhat overlapping decision categories in education and psychology that are influenced by measurement. Measurement relevant to *guidance* decisions encompasses instruments related to making educational and vocational choices or to better understanding oneself or one's problems. Decisions involving *administration* concern selection, classification, and placement. Decisions surrounding *instruction* revolve about providing students with feedback on their learning efforts and teachers or others with guides to the effectiveness of past activities or to the appropriateness of proposed student experiences. Decisions within a *research* context cross the three categories already cited; research could be conducted on any of the many ramifications of reaching guidance, administrative, or instructional decisions. In early childhood education over the past fifteen or twenty years, the last three decision categories have predominated.

Considerable measurement activity has occurred in early childhood education settings over the past two decades. Interpreting such activity as a strong endorsement of measurement by educators would be unwarranted. Although most researchers, evaluators, developers, and funding agencies see measurement and testing as central to their own work, many early childhood educators do not. However, personnel in the field (especially teachers) may be less opposed to measurement itself than to the instruments now in wide use. Whatever the source of measurement's negative connotations, we remain optimistic that early childhood educators will increasingly view it as valuable.

Many issues surround the use of measurement and evaluation in early childhood education (Goodwin & Driscoll, 1980). Three are particularly germane to the "why" question under discussion: the fairness of tests for certain children, the "net worth" of testing in society, and the influence of measurement on early childhood educators.

Issue One: Are Measures Used with Young Children Fair?

This issue often is presented in terms of *test bias*. If a test's outcomes contain systematic errors due to factors unrelated to what it is supposed to be measuring, then the test is biased. Many contend that both IQ and achievement tests are unfair to ethnic minorities (Mercer, 1973, 1974; Oakland, 1977; and Samuda, 1975). This issues is addressed in Chapter 20.

Issue Two: What Is the Net Worth of Testing to American Society?

This issue emerged in the 1970s and has focused on education where test industry products are so prominent in influencing instruction and, especially, in reaching administrative decisions involving classification, placement, and selection. Does testing serve the public interest; does it have a positive influence on American education?

The Representative Assembly of the National Education Association endorsed a national moratorium on standardized testing—intelligence, achievement, and aptitude tests—pending a critical review and appraisal of existing testing programs (National Education Association, 1972). A Task Force on Testing was established and subsequently issued a report (National Education Association, 1977) that allowed that some measurement was necessary in education and that some measures exhibited satisfactory validity and reliability and, therefore, had utility. In general, however, the report issued wide-ranging criticisms of tests (especially intelligence tests), selected special-use tests (such as the National Teacher Examination), and even item and test types (lamenting overemphasis on recall-type cognitive items and tests and underemphasis on items and tests that measured higher-level mental processes and affective skills and attitudes).

Related pronouncements were issued by other organizations (National School Boards Association, 1977; Oakland & Laosa, 1977). Such initiatives were buttressed by criticisms of tests from individuals (Hein, 1975; Houts, 1977; Perrone, 1977; and Quinto & McKenna, 1977) as well as from new groups formed to scrutinize the relationship between testing and society, such as the National Consortium on Testing within the Huron Institute, Cambridge, Massachusetts. Such activities and concerns led to so-called "truth-in-testing" legislation in some states.

This second issue is likely to be obvious and tenacious in the 1980s. We do not perceive any important threat to measurement's use when it is clearly linked to instruction, especially in terms of screening, diagnosing, planning subsequent activities, and providing feedback on content mastered. However, measurement related to administrative decisions—placement, selection, classification—and to research purposes conceivably could be profoundly affected by the prevailing societal position on the issue. Lerner's (1981) analysis of ten opinion surveys of public attitudes toward standardized testing found neither pervasive nor profound dissatisfaction with such tests, so possibly much of the recent criticism of tests does not reflect the prevailing public view.

Issue Three: Is Measurement Influential with Early Childhood Educators?

To the extent that measurement is not influential, one might question its usefulness. In education as a whole, it is clear that many aspects of measurement are not uniformly well received (Stetz & Beck, 1981).

Among early childhood educators, instructional planning is viewed by many as the only justification for testing young children. LaCrosse (1970) implies that such teachers' reliance on intuition and their uncomplicated view of causality results in little need for measurement data. Most early childhood education programs do not use systematic evaluation strategies (Goodlad, Klein & Novotney, 1973; Goodwin, 1974).

Although measurement is not enthusiastically endorsed by early childhood educators now, it can become more influential if certain events occur. First, improvement in existing measures, following leads repeatedly provided by Buros (1977, 1978), would help greatly. A second and related event would be the increased availability of high-quality measures covering a wide range of developmental characteristics and competence areas—not only tests but also rating scales, observation procedures, records, and performance indicators (Anderson & Messick, 1974). Many early childhood educators seem less opposed to measurement per se than to the specific instruments now available. A third event would be an increased sophistication on the part of educators as to appropriate roles for measurement. Most early childhood educators realize that accurate assessment can help facilitate children's learning. Systematic measurement and evaluation to facilitate learning and development provide the early childhood educator and the children served with important advantages (Hendrick, 1975).

Measurement can do much to help adults assist children to learn effectively and develop fully. Professionals who rely only on their intuition for making important decisions and judgments involving young children are, in our opinion, denying themselves an important means for improving such deliberations.

The logic of measurement, therefore, implies that most teachers and others are subject to biases and other unknown influences when attempting to intuitively measure the quality of behavior or performance. Measurement proponents urge the use of more objective means, such as "neutral" observers or the actual recording of events using videotape or the like, in order to increase the accuracy and generalizability of the measurements made. The logic of measurement does not seek to displace the human interpreter and judge, but rather to provide the human judge with solid data relatively uncontaminated by various biases [Goodwin & Klausmeier, 1975, p. 495].

How Should Young Children Be Measured?

Despite the important advantages of the systematic use of measurement and evaluation, many early childhood education programs, perhaps the majority of them, approach measurement and evaluation casually. However, some general principles of measurement can be offered, extending ideas from Brophy, Good, and Nedler (1975) and Hendrick (1975):

1. use multiple measures that correspond closely to the major objectives of the program—cognitive, affective, and psychomotor;
2. use measures with a suitable range of difficulty levels and include measures of higher-order skills;
3. create an informal relaxed situation to ensure that children are comfortable and not anxious during assessment;
4. introduce and present tasks to children in a standard way; standard procedures are needed to increase the meaning and comparability of the data obtained;
5. record and store the measurement data and products in an easily retrievable, well organized, and readily comprehendable form;
6. schedule measurement sessions on a timely, reasonable basis; seek a balance between the extremes of once-a-year assessment (typically too little) and "continuous" evaluation (usually unfeasible) by assessing at those times when data can affect instructional planning and decision making;
7. beware the "getting-better-and-better" syndrome; when assessing the child several times during the year, a bias may exist toward viewing the child's performance or behavior as improved with each assessment when, in reality, this is not always the case;
8. manage data obtained on children professionally, confidentially, and for the announced purpose of the assessment;
9. report candidly to parents on their child's progress, following interpretation guidelines for any measures used and providing actual descriptions of skills performed and work samples when available; open communication between the parent and educator serves the child well in both home and school.

Other ideas on how to measure young children can be gained from the *Handbook on Formative and Summative Evaluation of Student Learning* (Bloom, Hastings & Madaus, 1971) and *Evaluation to Improve Learning* (Bloom, Madaus

& Hastings, 1981). These authors noted Scriven's (1967) concepts of formative and summative evaluation, the former involving frequent judgments directed toward the improvement of an ongoing activity or a developing product, the latter encompassing judgments made of the overall worth of an activity or product, normally at an end or critical decision point. Adapting these concepts to student learning, they viewed formative evaluation as providing data necessary to facilitate student progress toward established instructional objectives (that is, to improve learning), whereas summative evaluation measures and interprets the degree of attainment of more general objectives at the end of a course or after a substantial portion of it. Secondary purposes of summative evaluation are to report to parents and administrators and to grade students. The work by Bloom and his associates illustrates important aspects of "how" to measure young children and also provides insights into "when" and "what" to measure.

Standards for Educational and Psychological Tests

When constructing or selecting a measuring instrument, it is vital to ensure that it will actually measure what it is intended to measure, yield accurate scores, and be relatively straightforward to administer, score, and interpret. These characteristics refer, respectively, to the instrument's validity, reliability, and usability. The *Standards for Educational and Psychological Tests* (American Psychological Association, 1974) describes fully the validity, reliability, and usability of measures and provides important leads as to how young children, or anyone, should be measured. The 1974 *Standards* revised an earlier (1966) document and presented recommendations and psychometric requirements for measure respectability; Lerner (1978) noted the increasing reliance on the *Standards* exhibited by the U.S. Supreme Court when it sought authoritative, objective answers to technical measurement questions arising in judicial proceedings. Only a brief overview of the validity and reliability recommendations is given here; readers seeking a full discussion should examine Anastasi (1976), F. G. Brown (1980), Hopkins and Stanley (1981), Mehrens and Lehmann (1978), Thorndike and Hagen (1977), or recent measurement texts.

Validity

The validity of a measure is the degree to which it fulfills its intended purpose. A measure may be valid for a given purpose but not for others; the question of validity always pertains to specific uses. The central question is not, "Is this measure valid?," but rather "Is this measure valid for this particular purpose?" Three types of validity have been identified in the *Standards*—content, criterion related, and construct—and generally correspond to types of inference that can be made from test scores. *Content validity* is the extent to which test items or tasks represent the content or processes of a given curricular universe or domain. Content validity makes it possible to infer how well a student would do on the larger set of items or tasks that the test purportedly represents. Typically associated with achievement tests, either standardized or teacher-made, content validity is ascertained primarily through logical analysis of a test by subject-matter experts and potential users. *Criterion-related validity* indicates the correspondence between test scores and present or future performance as measured in another way (the criterion). The inference permitted is about the student's present or future probable standing on some other relevant test or task. Two types of criterion-related validity are identified: concurrent validity occurs when the intent is to substitute the measure for another, already available measure of the same behavior, trait, or ability; predictive validity applies when the intent is to use the measure to predict future performance (such as using a readiness test given in kindergarten to predict reading performance at the end of first grade). Criterion-related validity typically is reported in the form of correlation coefficients. *Construct validity* conveys how well a test measures a theoretical, psychological construct of interest. It provides the basis for inferences about the student's relative standing on a theoretical construct presumed to be the major determinant of that test performance. The three types of validity require different types of evidence; nevertheless, thorough validation of a measure often involves information of all three types.

RELIABILITY

The reliability of a measure speaks to the accuracy or consistency of the scores it yields. A measure must correlate reasonably well with itself to be reliable; if it does not, it cannot correlate well with any external criterion. Evidence on reliability, as compared to validity evidence, is relatively easy to obtain. Reliability is secondary in importance to validity; reliability is a necessary, but not sufficient, condition for validity. Four types of operational reliability coefficient are described in the *Standards*. The *coefficient of stability* (or test–retest reliability coefficient) expresses the consistency of scores over time. It is obtained by administering the same measure twice to a single group of students and correlating the two sets of scores. In general, the longer the time interval between testings, the lower the stability reliability will be. The *coefficient of equivalence* (or equivalent-forms or alternate-forms reliability coefficient) estimates the equivalence between two forms of the same test. It is determined by giving two forms of a test at about the same time to a single group of students and correlating the two sets of resultant scores. The *coefficient of stability and equivalence* results when two forms of the same test are administered at different times to a single group of students and the resulting sets of scores are correlated. Often, the construction of alternate forms of a test is not feasible because of the time and cost involved. Under such conditions, several procedures exist to estimate the reliability of a single-form measure administered only once. These procedures, known as *coefficients of internal consistency*, convey the extent of consistency of content within the single-test form.

Better known procedures include the split-half technique, the Kuder and Richardson indexes of homogeneity (KR_{20} and KR_{21}), Cronbach's Alpha, and Hoyt's analysis of variance technique. One additional form of reliability, apart from the four operational types, is of special relevance here given the importance of observation in early childhood education. Termed *interobserver reliability*, it measures the extent of agreement between different observers in their independent recordings of the same events or behaviors.

Usability

In selecting measuring instruments for use with young children (or others), major weight must be given to validity and reliability. Then, a number of practical considerations can be addressed under the general heading of usability—the degree to which a test can be used. Included are matters of cost, technical quality data, administration, scoring, interpretation, format, and sources of irrelevant difficulty.

The *cost* of a measuring instrument should not be a major factor influencing its selection and use. In the abstract, most persons experience no difficulty with such a statement. In the reality of the scant resources supporting many early childhood education programs, however, the same statement can evoke deep consternation. In large-scale testing programs involving many children, even small per-test costs can quickly add up. Some savings occur if tests are packaged as reusable booklets with separate answer sheets. However, young children have been found to be confused by the use of separate answer sheets (Cashen & Ramseyer, 1969). Practicing with separate answer sheets might permit their appropriate use by young children. Additional costs are inherent in other usability considerations yet to be examined—such as the cost of training administrators and scoring tests—whether in actual expenditures of money or commitments of time.

Technical quality data include specific information on the validity and reliability of a measure as well as the nature of groups used in determining them. They are crucial and should be fully and clearly reported in the test manual. Amazingly, given the easy availability of the *Standards*, many test manuals fail to provide adequate technical quality data; manuals of measures for young children often exhibit this deficiency. If only partial data are provided in the manual, the potential user is uncertain as to the full psychometric quality of the instrument; if no data appear, one must wonder whether such data even exist.

Administration features—stimulus standardization, administrator training, group size, and time—directly affect a test's usability. The standardization of the stimulus situation is important; the manual should provide enough detail to permit each child measured to receive an equivalent stimulus. The training required to learn proper administration procedures is likewise significant. Measures display convenience and practicality if they require little special training and if they can be given by teachers and aides. Individually administered intelligence tests, many personality tests, and some observational measures are less convenient due to the extensive examiner or observer training required. Size of test group also influences usability. Too large a test group can impair performance, especially with young children who have had little previous experience with tests. Simply testing smaller groups initially seems to be a good solution, although smaller groups mean more groups to test and, thus, an increase in total testing time. Regrettably, many manuals of tests for young children are silent on proper group size.

Testing time required is a very important usability feature with young children. Some test tasks may not hold a child's attention for a sufficient time period. Possibly very young children have not masterd test etiquette (Ambron, 1978). Consequently, test reliability may be difficult to achieve. Theoretically, reliability can be improved by adding comparable items to an existing measure, if the new, longer test does not cause examinees to become bored or inattentive. If they are so affected (and the very young are likely to be), reliability will not necessarily increase and new sources of error, such as guessing and neighborpoking, may appear. To respect both technical and practical considerations when testing the very young, a test could be designed for administration in several short sessions with a few hours or a day intervening between sessions. Evans (1974) identified a serious time-related problem, the "overtesting" of children in some early intervention programs with extensive formal testing. Related concerns prompted Mediax Associates in recommending the development of Head Start measures, to propose limiting the total time any given child was tested to two 30-minute periods (Taub et al., 1980).

Scoring provisions, such as objectivity of scoring affect a test's usability. On objective tests, the same score results regardless who marks the test. Objective test developers often supply detailed scoring instructions and keys or masks that permit rapid and accurate scoring. Commercial tests publishers provide more and more scoring services (often computerized) for their standardized objective tests. Such services, while costly, allow a marked saving of teacher or aide time and normally result in accurate scoring; however, the turn-around time in getting results back can reduce a test's usefulness. Subjective tests exhibit special scoring difficulties. Less reliable scoring is the rule even with the considerable training of scorers that sometimes is involved.

Test interpretation also influences usability. The time and training required are important; for many measures, skillful interpretation is far more demanding and complicated than satisfactory administration and scoring practices. Interpretation is also affected by the types of score and how they are reported. Transformed scores of several types—standard scores, percentile ranks, and age- or grade-equivalents—should be provided in the manual. Interpretability of norm-referenced tests (discussed below) is greatly influenced by the samples used, which should be described in detail. Norm tables aid interpretation if broken down by sex, age, geographic region, ethnicity, socioeconomic status, and other demographic variables.

Test format should be viewed from several perspectives. Appropriateness for the intended examinees is critical. Obvious features are the adequacy of instructions (their clarity, vocabulary level, and brevity), the number and quality of practice items available, the clarity and visual appeal of the actual items, the organization of the content, and the type of response demanded. Instructions need to be clear and complete; they typically are read aloud to young children. Gelman (1978) pointed out that instructions given by adults are easily misunderstood or perceived differently by the young child. She noted Blank's (1975) observation that preschoolers, in an experimental setting and after being instructed or questioned, are disinclined to state the obvious (whereas adults know that it is permissible to state the obvious in an experimental setting). Thus, sufficient practice items (or even a full practice test) are needed to increase the probability that directions are understood. On paper-and-pencil tests, each page should feature distinct pictures and large, clear print. Ample space between items, or even a single item per page, helps reduce examinee confusion. Items normally should be ordered by increasing difficulty to keep children from becoming discouraged early in the test. Finally, the type of response required can have important consequences. If oral responses are required, a child's command of English becomes a key determinant of response quality, regardless of what is actually being measured. More subtle, the difficulty of items in a paper-and-pencil format may be different for some children than the same items in a slightly varied response format, such as paper-and-crayon or even sand-and-stick. "In her studies of Honduran children, Bernbaum (1974) has shown that unschooled children do not display an age-graded sequence when faced with paper-and-pencil tasks, but do show such a sequence when allowed to trace the same figures with a stick in the sand" (Laboratory of Comparative Human Cognition, 1979, p. 828).

Sources of irrelevant difficulty, a final usability characteristic, refer to test characteristics unrelated to the behaviors, traits, or abilities being measured that nonetheless affect the difficulty level of the test for some examinees. Such sources reduce test accuracy, as examinees of equal ability can earn different scores merely due to irrelevant difficulties. Sources of irrelevant difficulty often spring from insufficient attention to test usability considerations already noted, such as test content, test format, testing conditions, and test-wiseness (Messick & Anderson, 1970). Content can create irrelevant difficulty if items favor one racial group over another or one sex over another due to reasons unconnected to what is being measured. Irrelevant difficulty resulting from test format may occur if children have to read the directions for a test of listening skills; other sources of irrelevant difficulty are implied in the format discussion above. Testing conditions causing some children to feel uncomfortable could likewise create irrelevant difficulty problems. If children vary in their familiarity with test taking, this could bias scores in favor of the more experienced. Most of these sources of irrelevant difficulty can be reduced by careful test selection initially and by using test practice materials or even instructing the children in test-taking strategies.

Usability considerations have substantial significance. Still, their importance relative to validity and reliability must be kept in perspective. Unjustifiable weighting of physical attractiveness, cost, required administration time, scoring ease, or other usability features occurs too frequently in test selection. Wise test consumers concentrate first on the validity of measures under consideration and then their reliability. Once the pool of measures has been narrowed to those displaying high validity and reliability, their comparative usability can be examined.

Types of Measure

Another way to answer the question "How should young children be measured?" is to survey the various types of measure available. The selection of a particular type of measure hinges on the purpose of the measurement, while the specific instrument used will be chosen on the basis of its documented validity, reliability, and usability. Thousands of measures have been developed for use with children, many published commercially, while many others (sometimes termed fugitive instruments) are located in schools, universities, and project offices.

Measures can be categorized according to several schemes. One common system is to divide them by the types of ability or characteristic they assess—cognitive, affective, or psychomotor—a procedure we follow in the "what" of measurement section. Other differentiation schemes are scope, purpose, obtrusiveness, and format. Here, we discuss basic types of standardized tests, teacher-made measures, interviews and questionnaires, and unobtrusive measures. Observational techniques, integral to much of early childhood education (Irwin & Bushnell, 1980), are reviewed in Chapter 22 (see also Goodwin & Driscoll, 1980). Comprehensive summaries of the strengths and limitations of most measurement techniques can be found elsewhere (for example, Worthen & Sanders, 1973, pp. 280–289). First, though, we distinguish between norm-referenced and criterion-referenced tests, given the increasing interest in their differential merits.

Norm-Referenced and Criterion-Referenced Tests

Different interpretations result from norm-referenced and criterion-referenced measures. With norm-referenced measures, often standardized, interpretation occurs by comparing an examinee's performance to that of other examinees, that is, showing how a student performs compared with external norm groups. With criterion-referenced measures, more often nonstandardized, interpretation occurs by comparing an examinee's performance against pre-established levels of mastery, indicating whether or not a student can do a certain thing. Special considerations accompany the determination of both norms and the criterion used for referencing test performance.

Norms are numerical descriptions of the test performance of a defined group of students; they are not standards or goals to be reached. Norm groups often consist of the sample of students used for the national standardization of a measure; however, they can also be locally developed and can consist of the performance of students, say, in the Head Start centers served by one grantee agency. Descriptive norm tables are prepared to convert a student's earned raw score into one or more derived scores, such as age-equivalent, grade-equivalent, percentile-equivalent, or standard scores; thus, the meaning of a child's score is derived by comparing it with those of other children on the same measure. The utility of norms depends heavily on whether the norm group is truly representative of a definable group with which it makes sense to compare others' performance. The intent during norm-referenced measure development is to maximize the variability of student performance so resultant norms will allow specific differentiation among students taking the test subsequently in terms of skills or knowledge. Examples of norm-referenced tests are WPPSI and WISC–R, the intelligence scales for children by Wechsler (1967, 1974), the Cooperative Preschool Inventory (1970), and Animal Crackers (Adkins & Ballif, 1973).

Criterion-referenced measures de-emphasize distinctions between individuals' performances by typically categorizing students into only two groups—those who have achieved the criterion (or mastered the material) and those who have not. "Passing" connotes meeting or passing a minimum criterion, an absolute level of competence or standard. Examples of criterion-referenced measures for young children include the Basic Concept Inventory (Engelmann, 1967), the Learning Aptitude Profile (Sandford, 1974), and, in part, the Denver Developmental Screening Test (Frankenburg et al., 1975). Criterion-referenced measures presume that certain abilities and skills are essential for early academic progress; their assessment permits designing remedial instructional programs for children too often below criterion. Perhaps the most controversial and difficult aspect of criterion-referenced testing is the establishment of standards or criteria, often a process with arbitrary features (see Glass, 1978a, b; Hopkins & Stanley, 1981).

Criterion-referenced achievement tests are becoming more and more available, while some achievement tests exhibit features of both referencing systems. Norm-referenced tests continue to be used, virtually exclusively, in the measurement of intelligence, aptitude, and many personality variables. The choice between criterion-referenced and norm-referenced measures depends primarily on the decision to be made or the information required. Thus, if a measure is needed to select a few gifted young children for a special program, a norm-referenced test would be preferred. However, to determine the extent to which children have mastered prespecified behavioral objectives in a high-structure instructional program, a criterion-referenced test would be favored.

STANDARDIZED TESTS

Measures used in education typically are developed to yield systematic procedures for describing behaviors in numerical or categorical form. Standardized tests extend this effort by prescribing exact administration and scoring procedures, using standard apparatus or format, trying out items empirically, and deriving tables of norms (Cronbach, 1970; Hopkins & Stanley, 1981). Most standardized tests are published commercially, intended for widespread use, and developed over a period of several years. Major distinctions between standardized and teacher-made tests (subsequently discussed) involve the purpose and use of each. Thorndike and Hagen (1977) detailed how standardized and teacher-made measures differed with regard to the types of decision made with resultant test data.

In developing standardized tests, the representativeness of the norming samples is crucial, and more important than the size of the sample. Regrettably, even well-developed norms often are presented only for the total sample and are not broken down and tabulated for large definable subgroups such as differentiation by sex, age, socioeconomic status, region of the country, and race.

Several major types of standardized tests can be identified. *Intelligence tests* are intended to measure an individual's general mental capacity, normally use several types of items in the process, and typically provide a single IQ score (although separate subtest scores, such as verbal, performance, or quantitative scores, frequently are also available). Formal intelligence testing, though less than a century old, has had a volatile history largely due to the nature-versus-nurture dispute (that is, how much of one's intelligence is inherited and how much is a result of environmental factors and experiences) and the related issue of culture bias in tests. The question of exactly what intelligence tests measure has been answered in many ways (White et al., 1973). Some find the term *aptitude* or *scholastic aptitude* more acceptable than the term *intelligence,* as the latter tends to connote innate ability to them (Mehrens & Lehmann, 1978).

Aptitude tests measure specific factors believed to be relevant to later achievement, learning, or performance in a given area. For instance, the Differential Aptitude Tests (Bennett, Seashore & Wesman, 1974) measure high school students' aptitude in eight areas: verbal reasoning, numerical ability, abstract reasoning, clerical speed and accuracy, mechanical reasoning, space relations, spelling, and language usage. Specific aptitude tests for young children are not much in evidence; still, testing for general scholastic aptitude (or intelligence) occurs frequently. Readiness tests might be considered aptitude tests, in one sense, as they assess if children are likely to perform satisfactorily in a later school setting.

Achievement tests measure a child's present level of knowledge, skills, or performance, whereas aptitude tests measure likely ability to learn new tasks. Achievement tests are past- or present-oriented and pertain to completed, formal instruction; aptitude tests are future-oriented (as they purport to predict future performance) and reflect the cumulative effect of learning experiences. Thus, on a continuum from global to specific, the content of intelligence tests would ordinarily lie at the global end, aptitude tests in the middle, and achievement tests at the specific end (as they depend on specific school objectives and experiences). Although it is generally accepted that both genetic and environmental conditions influence intelligence test performance (but it is quite controversial as to how much each contributes), the environment is typically considered more influential on achievement test performance. The representativeness and adequacy of the norming sample is critical to standardized achievement tests' usefulness; an additional concern is the correspondence between a given achievement test's content and local curriculum emphases. Achievement tests currently tend to reflect the "structured" rather than the "open" curricula (White et al., 1973), and their common uses include the evaluation of preschool and Title I, ESEA, programs.

Diagnostic tests differ from achievement tests in purpose and in the specificity of the information yielded. Designed to pinpoint a student's strengths and weaknesses in a particular academic subject, they focus on those elements assumed by subject-matter experts to underlie the learning of a given subject, say, arithmetic or reading. Whereas achievement tests survey general knowledge of a subject area's content and processes by using one or two items on each of several aspects of the area, diagnostic tests concentrate on just a few aspects of content and operations, using many items for each to detail a child's deficiencies. An achievement test typically results in an overall score used for grouping or program evaluation, whereas a diagnostic test produces scores used to design remedial instruction for a particular child. The greater specificity of diagnostic tests normally connotes their lengthy scoring and interpretation processes; given these time requirements, they are usually given only to those children displaying learning problems. Norms are important for diagnostic instruments and should report on a cross-section of children representing the full range of abilities and skills in the specific subject area.

Personality and attitude measures, often standardized, assess affective characteristics rather than cognitive ability (the principal focus of the standardized measures already examined); they supplement subjective assessments of children's noncognitive behaviors.

Personality commonly refers to a wide array of characteristics and traits and to interactions among them. Not all personality measures are standardized tests; observational techniques and sociometric measures frequently assess personality variables. Standardized personality instruments typically are structured self-report inventories (such as problem checklists, adjustment inventories, and needs surveys). Their clear stimuli are intended to be interpreted in much the same way by all respondents and are accompanied by objective scoring and norms. Although administration and scoring of such instruments is relatively straightforward, their interpretation often requires special training. Projective tests, a special case, have standard but ambiguous stimuli (such as sketches, photos, or inkblots), allowing respondents to reveal their personalities while interpreting them. Their relatively unstructured administration, scoring, and interpretation require extensive examiner training. Projective tests are vulnerable to many criticisms involving validity and reliability. However, relative to typical self-report measures, they are richer in that examinees reveal much more than they would by simply answering a standard set of questions, less susceptible to faking, less vulnerable to response sets (tendencies to respond in a given direction regardless of the question asked), and more useful with young children in that some tests de-emphasize verbal abilities and can be presented as games (for instance, finger painting and doll play). Early childhood educators should seek expert help in interpreting personality test results (particularly of projective measures) before making decisions that affect children.

Attitudes are defined as "learned, emotionally cast predispositions to react in a consistent manner, favorable or unfavorable, toward certain objects, people, ideas, or situations. A person's attitudes are normally inferred from his behavior and generally cannot be measured as directly as skills or knowledge of facts or concepts" (Goodwin & Klausmeier, 1975, p. 303). Although one aspect of the global construct of personality, attitudes are less stable than personality. Young children particularly display this instability as they daily learn and modify attitudes. Standardized attitude measures are paper-and-pencil and self-report inventories for the most part (similar in structure to personality inventories and checklists) and thus are subject to faking and response sets. Still, they are easy to administer and score, requiring no special training. Available commercially are measures of attitudes toward school, study and work habits, and self; unfortunately, the technical quality of many of them is lacking. However, carefully developed attitude measures can enhance a teacher's understanding of students, especially if local norms are also assembled.

TEACHER-MADE TESTS

Of great importance are measures of students' daily progress in attaining skills, knowledge, or attitudes specific to a given curriculum. Teachers often construct their own measures to make such assessments and to serve functions such as diagnosis. Their own tests provide an objective check against the informal, subjective assessments that they make continually. Three common devices used to monitor students' individual progress in the cognitive domain are achievement tests, checklists and rating scales, and work samples. Teacher-initiated assessment in the affective domain more often takes the form of observation or unobtrusive measures.

Teacher-made *achievement tests* measure students' level of current knowledge and sample course content. They differ from standardized tests in three ways: they have a narrower focus as they assess specific classroom objectives; they tend to exhibit lower reliability and validity as they are quickly and inexpensively developed; and they rarely have national norms. Such differences are not properly viewed as limitations. The narrower focus can serve diagnostic functions. The minimal development expenditures can still result in sufficiently reliable and valid measures with a close match to actual instructional objectives. The lack of national norms need not imply "reference-less" measures; teachers can develop local norms or, more likely, construct criterion-referenced tests with intuitively established essential levels of mastery. With careful administration, good testing conditions (reduced anxiety, no time pressure, and quiet) and objective scoring procedures (prepared-in-advance detailed keys, "blind" scoring when the teacher does not know which student wrote the answers or when a second person scores), data from teacher-made tests increase in value. To measure achievement, the teacher may opt for individual oral tests rather than paper-and-pencil ones. Regardless of the format, frequent short test periods are preferred over infrequent long ones to assure the student's attention and alertness and to reduce the effects of guessing, fatigue, and response sets. Specifics on test construction are found in Hopkins and Stanley (1981) and Thorndike and Hagen (1977).

Teacher-constructed *checklists* and *rating scales* are easily developed and versatile, for they can assess almost any student behavior. No administration routine is needed—the teacher simply fills out the measures at appropriate times. They provide a convenient way to record the performance of very young children or others unable to respond on paper-and-pencil tests. Criterion-referenced checklists and rating scales often can be designed to match local instructional objectives. First, important behaviors (specific to objectives) are listed. Then the typical checklist format provides places for the teacher or observer to check "yes" or "no," according to whether the student displays the behavior. A rating scale format, on the other hand, permits more varied measurement of behavior by including estimates of frequency ("seldom," "about half the time," or "usually") or ability ("poor," "satisfactory," "good," or "exceptional"). Behaviors in any domain can be checked or rated—counting to ten (cognitive), expressing affection for peers (affective), or balancing on one foot (psychomotor). Detailed construction steps are available (Hendrick, 1975).

Students' products or *work samples* constitute a popular assessment procedure in preschool and kindergarten. Progress is determined by comparing the child's present performance with earlier efforts on the same or similar task. Evidence of a child's improving motor skills, mastery of basic concepts, or attention to detail can be collected. A sample, rather than all products, should be collected. Work samples can extend beyond written or drawn products—cameras and tape recorders can capture progress made in construction, playing, speaking, or even physical growth. In establishing a collection of work samples, the teacher should collect samples at about equal time intervals, date them, and file them for easy access. Systematically maintained work sample files help assess progress and facilitate reporting to parents.

INTERVIEWS AND QUESTIONNAIRES

Typically used to collect interest, attitudinal, and personality information, interviews and questionnaires less often deal with cognitive assessment. Here, we focus on locally developed instruments rather than commercially available standardized ones.

Distinctions are made between structured and unstructured interviews. The former have fixed questions and set sequencing, with little opportunity for interviewer deviation. Unstructured interview schedules are less systematic in wording, questions, sequence, and directions for the interviewer; in the extreme, they require no pre-established elements at all. The specific, closed questions of the structured interview contrast sharply with the general, open-ended questions of the unstructured interview. Although the latter may have advantages (helping the respondent feel comfortable and generating additional comments of interest), they are difficult to tabulate and score, especially if several interviewers are used.

Interviews with young children permit sensitivity to each child's idiosyncratic mode of expression. Further, they can yield otherwise unattainable information. For example, imagine that children's attitudes toward television are of interest, but that the children are too young to answer written questions and do not view television at school, and that observing them during home viewing is not feasible. In such a case, a researcher or teacher could interview them to secure attitudinal data. Kerlinger (1973) examined interview techniques as well as schedule construction and sample questions, while Rich (1968) commented on interviewing children.

The use of *questionnaires* is widespread. Typically used for self-report, they also can be closed or open in structure. The closed questionnaire consists of numerous questions each followed by a standard set of response options. With a Likert scale, the respondent has five choices—"strongly agree," "agree," "no opinion" or "undecided," "disagree," and "strongly disagree." The respondent marks the response that best reflects his or her reaction to the question just read. The Likert scale itself is inappropriate for young children, but variations of it ("yes" and "no," or a series of faces, smiling, neutral, or frowning) are used. Open-ended questionnaires elicit a variety of responses—short answers, longer statements, or pictures ("Draw a picture of how you feel today"). However, the more open the questionnaire format, the more difficult objective scoring and consistent interpretation become.

As self-report devices, both interviews and questionnaires are susceptible to problems such as "faking" and giving "socially desirable" responses rather than views actually held. Nevertheless, if carefully constructed and used, they do assess children's reactions to instructional materials and methods more objectively and reliably than unsystematic procedures (such as simply recording one's impressions of children's likes or dislikes, or asking just a few children questions during casual conversation). Interviews and questionnaires can also assess parental attitudes toward their children's educational experiences.

UNOBTRUSIVE MEASURES

Procedures for collecting data about persons or events without actually having subjects take an objective test, tell about themselves, or perform in a specified way are called unobtrusive measures (Webb et al., 1966, 1981). Such data are collected from records, physical traces of activities, and nonreactive recordings (mechanical or human) or observations of naturally occurring events; the process of measuring does not intrude upon or change the person or event being measured.

Schools and other settings for young children offer opportunities to use unobtrusive measures. The relative wear and tear of different pieces of playground equipment reveals preferences and play habits. The frequency with which various books are checked out of the library can assist a teacher to determine her students' favored types of book, while dirty and dog-eared pages signal favorite passages. Unobtrusive observation of children's social interactions with peers over time could help identify the social leaders or "stars" and the loners or "isolates." Changes in the types of toy brought to school or displayed at "show and tell" might reveal a shift from war-oriented toys to space-oriented toys. The type and amount of food brought for lunch—and that discarded after lunch—speak to children's food preferences and eating habits (Rathje, 1979). Children's activity level could be measured, at least in part, by plotting the rate at which children wear out their shoes.

Unobtrusive measures avoid many threats to validity associated with self-report procedures since subjects do not provide direct answers and are not aware they are being measured. Reactivity (changes in behavior by subjects knowing they are being tested or studied) is prevented. Social desirability is also avoided. For instance, when a teacher asks children what type of book they like (in typical self-report fashion), they may reply what they think she wants to hear rather than their true choice; an unobtrusive measure of book preference circumvents this problem. Some response sets are also avoided, like the tendency to acquiesce (agreeing more often to positively phrased statements than disagreeing with the same statements when negatively stated).

The cleverness and simplicity of unobtrusive measures, however, can lead to a false sense of security in their use. Relying on a single unobtrusive measure—and excluding more conventional measures from use—is short-sighted and may lead to inaccurate measurement. Unobtrusive measures should supplement more typical measures as added evidence that either confirms or makes suspect data from other sources. The use of several unobtrusive measures, matched appropriately with more traditional measures, can improve most measurement or research efforts. Our hesitancy to endorse unobtrusive measures for exclusive use rests on both their subtle complexity and their unknown psychometric quality (in terms of validity and reliability). Used in perspective, unobtrusive measures can make important contributions to measurement and research in early childhood education (for example, Webb et al., 1966, 1981).

What about Young Children Should Be Measured?

Measures are reviewed in three separate domains—cognitive, affective, and psychomotor—a common though not totally defensible practice. Human behavior does not divide itself tidily into three domains; rather, interaction among the domains is substantial. Although arbitrary, the three-domain classification scheme is helpful for organizational purposes and permits three generalizations (White et al., 1973). First, the psychometric respectability of the domains' measures is ordered from cognitive to psychomotor to affective; cognitive measures generally display the strongest validity and reliability, affective measures, the weakest. Second, the psychometric respectability of most measures in all domains increases with the age of the child measured; the younger the child, the more difficult the measurement. Third, the availability of measures for young children is ordered from cognitive to affective to psychomotor, although the actual usage pattern varies markedly with the particular measurement purposes being stressed. A preschool that emphasized social skills might principally use affective measures, while an academically oriented one might focus on cognitive measures. The generalizations position the three domains in rough perspective (although a bevy of qualifications could be added). The following material refines the nature of each domain and denotes current measurement emphases in each in terms of early childhood education.

Cognitive Measures

Cognition is the intellectual process by which knowledge is gained; principal cognitive processes are perceiving, thinking, knowing, learning, and intellectualizing. In his cognitive domain taxonomy, B. S. Bloom (1956) identified two major categories: (1) knowledge; and (2) intellectual abilities and skills. The second category was further differentiated into comprehension, application, analysis, synthesis, and evaluation. Several types of measure are included in this domain—intelligence, instruction-related (readiness and achievement), and creativity tests. Under cognitive measures, we also discuss developmental surveys (which commonly also survey affective and psychomotor behaviors) and language tests.

INTELLIGENCE TESTS

Intelligence has been defined variously (Bouchard, 1968), and IQ tests designed to measure it vary substantially (Scarr-Salapatek, 1975). Young children have been subjected to considerable intelligence testing.

Several points about intelligence and IQ tests for young children (paraphrased from Goodwin & Driscoll, 1980) are significant:

1. Intelligence is societally defined; its meaning changes within a given culture.
2. Elements making up intelligent behavior varies with age (McCall, Hogarty & Hurlburt, 1972); with preschoolers, defining intelligence is complicated through the lack of a pool of common experiences on which to base test items (Anastasi, 1976).
3. IQ test scores received after formal school entrance demonstrate relative stability as intellectual development is cumulative; this stability is more pronounced for groups than for individuals (Honzik, 1973; McCall, Applebaum & Hogarty, 1973; Moriarty, 1966).

4. IQ tests have numerous limitations (Sattler, 1974), such as their questionable fairness for certain children.
5. IQ test scores describe, but do not explain, an individual's performance.
6. An IQ test score is simply a score on a test and, as such, is far from synonymous with intelligence (Glick, 1968).

Sensitivity to these points should help prevent the abuses associated with IQ tests, such as labeling children and making unwarranted interpretations.

The leading individually administered IQ tests for young children are the Stanford-Binet Intelligence Scale or Binet (Terman & Merrill, 1960, 1973), the Wechsler Intelligence Scale for Children-Revised or WISC–R (Wechsler, 1974), and the Wechsler Preschool and Primary Scale of Intelligence or WPPSI (Wechsler, 1967). Other illustrative intelligence tests for preschoolers include the Goodenough-Harris Drawing Test (Harris, 1963), the McCarthy Scales of Children's Abilities (McCarthy, 1972), the Peabody Picture Vocabulary Test (Dunn, 1965), and the Quick Test (Ammons & Ammons, 1962). For school-age children, several group-administered IQ measures exist. For infants, established intelligence tests are the Gesell Developmental Schedules (Gesell & Amatruda, 1947), the Cattell Infant Intelligence Scale (Cattell, 1960), and the Bayley Scales of Infant Development (Bayley, 1969), also called the California Infant Scales. The Brazelton Neonatal Behavioral Assessment Scale (Brazelton, 1973), a recent entrant in the field, is administered to infants three days to four weeks of age. Measuring infant intelligence, birth to age two years, is a difficult task due to difficulties in working with so young a subject, and most such measures are poor predictors of later IQ scores (Darby & May, 1979; Stott & Ball, 1965; Thomas, 1970; and Yang & Bell, 1975).

Piaget-based scales of intellectual development are in evidence. For infants, there are the Einstein Scales of Sensorimotor Development (Corman & Escalona, 1969; Escalona & Corman, 1969), the Piagetian Infant Scales (Honig & Lally, 1970), and the Ordinal Scales of Psychological Development (Uzgiris & Hunt, 1975). For preschool and school-age children, measures available include the Laurendeau and Pinard (1970) scales, the Concept Assessment Kit—Conservation (Goldschmid & Bentler, 1968), and the Cartoon Conservation Scales (De Avila & Havassy, 1975). Although such tests show significant positive correlations with more traditional intelligence measures, they also appear to be assessing different aspects of mental functioning (De Avila & Havassy, 1975; Wachs, 1975).

Gelman's views (1979) are appropriately noted here. "We should study preschoolers in their own right and give up treating them as foils against which to describe the accomplishments of middle childhood. We have made some progress in recent years, but there is still plenty of room for those who are willing to take on the mind of the young child" (Gelman, 1979, p. 904). We agree that shifting the focus to what preschoolers can do rather than what they cannot do represents a healthy reorientation. If operationalized, it should have important implications for cognitive measures of intellectual functioning.

INSTRUCTION-RELATED TESTS

This category of cognitive measures, intended to span readiness and achievement tests, was difficult to form due to the misleading titles and vague purposes of some tests. For instance, standardized achievement tests are usually thought to be content-specific, designed to measure set instructional activities. Yet, in large part, there is no prescribed early childhood education curriculum. Readiness is not always well defined, either—a child may be ready for one type of kindergarten but not for another, or ready for work in language but not in arithmetic. Further complications lie in the overlap between items on different types of test. For example, some achievement tests state that they are not readiness measures, yet contain items much like existing readiness tests. The category of instruction-related tests skirts this definitional jungle by including measures that have in common some relationship to learning and instruction (more so than intellegence tests).

Standardized achievement tests designed for the early grades, available from most educational test publishers, fall in this category. Examples include the Comprehensive Tests of Basic Skills (1974) and the Stanford Early School Achievement Test (Madden & Gardner, 1969, 1971). Readiness measures, such as the Metropolitan Readiness Tests (1976), are much in evidence in kindergarten and early first grade. Instruction-related measures designed for preschoolers include the Basic Concept Inventory (Engelmann, 1967), Circus (1979), the Cooperative Preschool Inventory (1970), and the Tests of Basic Experiences 2 (Moss, 1978).

Someday, the instruction-related measure category might add cognitive-style instruments, measuring risk taking or cautiousness, attentiveness, field independence or dependence, reflection–impulsivity, and the like (Banta, 1970; Goldstein & Blackman, 1977; and Kogan, 1976). Currently, measures of such constructs are typically used in research contexts or available only in research editions; yet, in time, they may have important educational applications.

CREATIVITY TESTS

Since mid-century, research on creativity in this country has been substantial. A historical review of it and of educational programs designed to foster creativity reveals the roller coaster ride that such programs have been on (often due to world events and pressures). Attempts at measure development have shared this ride and also have been hampered by the varying definitions proposed for creativity (Carroll & Laming, 1974; Dellas & Gaier, 1970; Getzels & Dillon, 1973; Treffinger & Poggio, 1972; and Wallach, 1970).

We are witnessing a reaffirmation of the school's responsibilities to gifted, talented, and creative children (variously defined), spawning new programs for identified students and needs for appropriate measuring instruments. For good or ill, such programs (and attempts to measure creativity or the potential for subsequent creative performance) have extended to very young children. Many early childhood educators espouse creative behavior in children such as independence, inventiveness, original thinking, and artistic individuality, yet resist attempts to measure such behavior. We view attempts to measure creativity as neither restrictive nor counterproductive.

The number of standardized creativity tests for very young children is limited. The Torrance Tests of Creative Thinking (Torrance, 1966) represent the most comprehensive battery available for kindergarten and primary grade children. Consisting of separate verbal and figural tests, each with subtests, the Torrance purports to measure children's creative thinking potential. Four scores are generated (but not from all subtests): fluency (the number of responses); flexibility (the number of categories of responses); originality; and elaboration (the extent to which detail is added). In the Make-a-Tree measure in Circus (1979), the child constructs two trees within one week, resulting in three scores: appropriateness, unusualness, and difference (how different the child's two trees are, one from the other). Another attempt to assess young children's creativity is the S.O.I. Learning Abilities Test based on Guilford's (1967) Structure of Intellect model. At kindergarten and grade one, a special edition of the test (Meeker et al., 1975) assesses children's divergent production of figural units (or DFU) much like the Repeated Figures subtest of Torrance's Figural Test. For children in grades two and above, the principal edition of the test (Meeker and Meeker, 1979) measures DFU and also divergent production of both semantic units (DMU) and symbolic relations (DSR). None of the tests have demonstrated sufficient validity and reliability to warrant decisions concerning individual children based on their results. Still, systematic development of measures like these tests might one day permit the use of such measures to help understand children and nurture their development.

DEVELOPMENTAL SURVEYS

Developmental surveys assess affective, cognitive and psychomotor characteristics and have been used extensively as screening instruments for handicapped children. The common rationale for screening young children is that early identification of developmental disabilities or of children at risk permits implementation of corrective programs to reverse or ameliorate such conditions (Meier, 1975).

The Education for All Handicapped Children Act required the placing of handicapped children in the "least restrictive environment" possible. Despite the seemingly simple legislative mandate (Public Law 94–142), its execution has been complex and troublesome for several reasons (Goodwin & Driscoll, 1980):

1. The legislation failed to specify how the screening was to be conducted; resulting procedures vary markedly.
2. Screening and diagnosis have often not been kept distinct. When the screening and diagnosis processes are collapsed into a single phase, in-

struments used are not appropriate for both processes and confusion can easily ensue.

3. Screening and diagnosis are at times conducted without a definitive purpose. Such ambiguity can lead to dysfunctional labeling of children.

4. The requirement for well-trained personnel for screening and (particularly) diagnosis too frequently has not been met.

5. Definitional problems have beset the screening and diagnosis phases (Hobbs, 1975). Cruickshank (1967) described how the same "learning disabled" child would be classified differently as he or she moved from state to state.

6. The array of screening and diagnostic tests available is extensive, but unfortunately this quantity generally is not matched by evidence of quality (Coles, 1978; Keogh & Becker, 1973; Shepard & Smith, 1981).

Four developmental surveys often used for screening are the Comprehensive Identification Process (Zehrbach, 1975a,b), the Denver Developmental Screening Test (Frankenburg et al., 1975), the Developmental Indicators for the Assessment of Learning (Mardell & Goldenberg, 1975), and the Learning Accomplishment Profile (Sanford, 1974). The importance of the decisions being made about children (based on how they perform on developmental surveys or other screening and diagnostic instruments) and the care with which they should be made cannot be underestimated. The good intentions of legislation may not always, or even frequently, result in better situations for children in schools (Zigler & Muenchow, 1979).

LANGUAGE TESTS

Effective communication skills are important elements for performing well in school and in later life, and language research is currently being conducted on a broad front (Appleton, Clifton & Goldberg, 1975; L. Bloom, 1975; Glucksberg, Krauss & Higgins, 1975). Most early childhood education programs recognize the central importance of language. The breadth of language concerns in most preschools is reflected well in Cazden's (1971) review of appropriate objectives for early language development.

Language elements appear in many of the cognitive measures already mentioned. Intelligence tests, such as the Binet and Wechsler Verbal scales, have heavy verbal emphasis. Instruction-related measures commonly include language subtests, as in the Metropolitan Readiness Tests and the Comprehensive Tests of Basic Skills. The four developmental and handicapped screening surveys listed in the previous section all contain language-related components. Also available are a number of language measures that are clinically oriented; possibly the best known at present is the Illinois Test of Psycholinguistic Abilities (Kirk, McCarthy & Kirk, 1968), although it has received considerable negative criticism (Coles, 1978; Lumsden, 1978; Waugh, 1975; and Weiderholdt, 1978).

A new wave of language instruments with direct educational applications may be in the offing. In simple terms, language can be conceptualized as either receptive (typically reading or listening) or productive (typically speaking or writing), with vocabulary an important influence throughout. Educational measures developed will need to address all these functions (although reading and writing for very young children are more appropriately thought of as prereading and prewriting). Measures possibly representing early indications of such a wave include certain measures in Circus (1979), Developmental Sentence Analysis (Lee, 1974), the Productive Language Assessment Tasks (High/Scope Educational Research Foundation, 1976), and the Preschool Language Assessment Instrument (Blank, Rose & Berlin, 1978a,b). Such measures generally are either individually administered or elaborately scored or both, and therefore are time-consuming. Nonetheless, the abilities they assess appear critical to success in both educational and later-life settings.

Affective Measures

The affective domain covers the social, emotional, and feeling aspects of behavior, including emotions, intuitions, preferences, interests, attitudes, values, morals, and philosophies of life. The *Taxonomy of Educational Objectives in the Affective Domain* (Krathwohl, Bloom & Masia, 1964) orders such behavior on a continuum of increasing internalization: receiving, responding, valuing, organizing, and characterizing; it also relates interests, appreciations, attitudes, values, and personal adjustments to the continuum. The taxonomy has helped to guide the development of affective objectives and measures.

Many early childhood educators believe that affective outcomes— children's self-concepts, social skills, attitudes, and the like—equal or even exceed cognitive outcomes in importance (Hartup, 1968; and Zigler, 1970). More early childhood programs than ever have established affective goals (Evans, 1974), and many, like the Bank Street model (Maccoby & Zellner, 1970), place primary emphasis on affective development outcomes. In an evaluation of the California State Preschool Program (Hoepfner & Fink, 1975), 98 percent of the preschool agencies involved ranked self-concept development (clearly an affective outcome) as either first or second in program importance. Thus, there is a marked need for effective affective measures in early childhood education.

Unfortunately, measuring affect in young children is difficult. Ball (1971) noted problems in measuring young children's attitudes: their mercurial attitudes; their limited test-taking skills; their eagerness to please adults administering tests (giving the edge to socially desirable responses); and their proneness to a response set, such as answering "yes" regardless of the question asked. Walker (1973) remarked on young children's short attention span in test-taking situations. White et al. (1973) noted that researchers do not understand the basic issues of noncognitive processes in human development sufficiently to make convincing moves toward index or test development. Some problems can be alleviated by careful test development, but the instability of children's answers and the limited theoretical base for measure development are formidable.

Affective assessment techniques used in education typically are nonprojective: self-report inventories, rating scales and checklists, and observational procedures. Self-report inventories are often designed so that young children (1) select the picture or word with which they identify; (2) reveal their perceptions of how others see them; or (3) specify their preferred activities or interests. Rating scales and checklists provide information about children from someone familiar with them, frequently their parents or teachers.

The technical psychometric data provided for affective measures for young children leave one less than impressed, especially the lack of meaningful information on validity. Some developers claim content validity based on their test construction procedures, but very few provide data on criterion-related or construct validity. One major problem is the lack of meaningful construct-level definitions for variables addressed by the instruments (Walker, 1973). Reliability estimates are frequently provided, and affective measures for young children fare somewhat better than validity. Still, the estimates too frequently (1) are based on small, select samples of children; (2) result in only low to moderate coefficients; and (3) represent internal consistency when interrater or stability coefficients would have been more appropriate. Another weakness of many such measures is inadequate standardization norms.

Representative *personality* measures for young children include Animal Crackers: A Test of Motivation to Achieve (Adkins & Ballif, 1973), the California Test of Personality (Thorpe, Clark & Tiegs, 1953), the Child Behavior Rating Scale (Cassel, 1962), the Preschool and Primary Nowicki-Strickland Internal-External Control Scale (Nowicki & Duke, 1974), and the Primary Academic Sentiment Scale (Thompson, 1968). Illustrative *self-concept* instruments are the Children's Self-Social Constructs Test (Henderson, Long & Ziller, n.d.), the Preschool Self-Concept Picture Test (Woolner, 1966, 1968), and the Self-Concept and Motivation Inventory (Milchus, Farrah & Reitz, 1968), also called What Face Would You Wear? Instruments for children's *attitudes and preferences* include the It Scale for Children (Brown, 1956), the Preschool Racial Attitude Measure II and Color Meaning Test II (Williams, Best & Associates, 1975), and the Sex Stereotype Measure II and Sex Attitude Measure (Williams, Best & Associates, 1976). Circus (1979) also contains two subtests of children's attitudes and preferences toward school-related activities. Illustrative instruments of *social skills and competencies* are the Bristol Social Adjustment Guides (Stott, 1972), the California Preschool Social Competency Scale (Levine, Elzey & Lewis, 1969), the Minnesota Sociometric Status Test (Moore, 1973), and the Vineland Social Maturity Scale (Doll, 1965). After surveying affective measures for young children, Walker concluded that "the most reliable and valid measures available at the present time are the observational, nonverbal techniques" (1973, p. 38).

Psychomotor Measures

The third domain of measures relevant to the "what" question is the psychomotor area. Unlike the cognitive and affective domains, there is less use by educators of a single taxonomic scheme, although several exist. Harrow (1972) defined psychomotor behavior as observable human motion and postulated a six-level taxonomy: (1) reflex movements; (2) basic fundamental movements; (3) perceptual abilities; (4) physical abilities; (5) skilled movements; and (6) nondiscursive communication. Singer (1972) established four overlapping schemes for classifying psychomotor behaviors: (1) by task, based on empirical performance assessment results; (2) by process, based on information; (3) by the type of performance required of the individual; and (4) by complexity from simple perception to automatic performance.

In early childhood, movement takes on important meaning. Young children's everyday activities often are dominated by movement (Ellis, 1973; Herron & Sutton-Smith, 1971). Between birth and age eight, the changes in basic motor control and in motor reponses and skills are phenomenal, and psychomotor and health objectives are frequently in evidence in early childhood education settings. Despite this prominence, the psychomotor domain plays the role of the poor stepsister in terms of the availability of education-related measures as well as of the low frequency with which such measures are used in federally sponsored research on children and adolescents (Heyneman & Mintz, 1977). With the increasing number of books focusing on movement education for preschoolers (Cratty, 1973a; Flinchum, 1975; and Sinclair, 1973), possibly more attention will be given to psychomotor measure development. Mediax Associates, monitoring the development of a battery of measures to be used in national evaluations of Head Start, has placed heavy emphasis on the "domain of health and physical development," encompassing medical, dental, nutritional, fine-motor development, and gross-motor development (Taub et al., 1980).

Categorization of psychomotor behaviors is typically done using one of three schemes. One way is simply to list motor activities or tasks. Espenschade and Eckert (1967) constructed such a list from infancy to old age; Sinclair (1973) published a list specific to ages two to six years. A second scheme is to differentiate behaviors as either gross (those involving large muscle groups) or fine motor (those employing smaller or manipulative muscles). Cratty (1973b) correctly observed that such a distinction is misleadingly simple and suggested adding an intermediate point. Nevertheless, the distinction has been useful in specifying preschool psychomotor objectives and designing measures; most of the developmental surveys noted before contain fine and gross motor sections. The relative absence of handwriting measures is puzzling, given the relevance of this fine-motor behavior to education; we found almost no measures for preschoolers and only three for somewhat older children (L. P. Ayres, 1940; Levine, Fineman & Donlon, 1973; and Zaner-Bloser, 1979). The third classifying scheme is in terms of typical performance measures, such as rate of response, latency of response, amount of response, errors, reminiscence, trials, and retention (Drowatzky, 1975).

Illustrative psychomotor measures in early childhood education include the Developmental Test of Visual-Motor Integration (Beery, 1967; Beery & Buktenica, 1967), the Frostig Movement Skills Test Battery (Orpet, 1972), the Marianne Frostig Developmental Test of Visual Perception (Frostig, 1966; Frostig et al., 1964), the Purdue Perceptual-Motor Survey (Roach & Kephart, 1966), the Southern California Sensory Integration Tests (A. J. Ayres, 1980), and the Test of Motor Impairment (Stott, Moyes & Henderson, 1972), one of several adaptations of the Oseretsky Tests of Motor Proficiency, first published in Russia in 1923.

Psychomotor performance is expressed fairly readily in explicit instructional (or behavioral) objectives (Goodwin & Klausmeier, 1975; Harrow, 1972) because such behaviors are commonly observable and criteria for evaluating their adequacy are relatively easy to state specifically. Early childhood educators could establish relevant psychomotor tests for their own use; over time, local norms could also be determined. Psychomotor performance also can be measured through observational means; mechanical recording via movies and videotape is widespread (Flinchum, 1975).

Sourcebooks of Measures for Early Childhood Education

Sourcebooks of measures in early childhood education differ in several ways: the domain(s) addressed, whether the measures included are available commercially or not, the age range of the measures surveyed, where the measures can be obtained, the amount and type of descriptive and evaluative information included, references describing the psychometric quality of the measures, and so forth. The sourcebooks can be used to identify promising measures for a particular purpose, but careful examination of the actual instruments is a critical second step in instrument selection.

Below are listed a number of sourcebooks and a short description of each.

American Alliance for Health, Physical Education, and Recreation (1973), *Annotated Bibliography on Perceptual Motor Development:* describes over thirty tests, primarily psychomotor, the majority being screening instruments for auditory and visual impairments.

American Alliance for Health, Physical Education, and Recreation (n.d.), *Testing for Impaired, Disabled, and Handicapped Individuals:* Presents over sixty instruments, both commercial and fugitive, in four areas (physical fitness tests; motor ability, perceptual-motor development, and psychomotor tests; developmental profiles; and locally developed assessment devices).

Beatty (1969), *Improving Educational Assessment and An Inventory of Measures of Affective Behavior:* describes 133 published and unpublished measures, categorized as follows: attitude scales, creativity, interaction, miscellaneous, motivation, personality, readiness, and self-concept; only a modest number of the measures are applicable to the two-to-eight-year age range.

Bonjean, Hill, and McLemore (1967), *Sociological Measurements: An Inventory of Scales and Indices:* contains an extensive bibliography of published works that reference

2,080 sociological scales and indexes; the references, primarily from sociology journals, are categorized into seventy-eight conceptual classes.

Boyer, Simon, and Karafin (1973), *Measures of Maturation: An Anthology of Early Childhood Observation Instruments:* presents seventy-three observation systems for recording behaviors of infants and young children, along with detailed instructions for use and background information.

Buros (1938 through 1978), *Mental Measurements Yearbooks* and *Tests in Print:* consists of extensive information about published tests. This and previous editions provide facts, critical reviews, and bibliographies pertaining to all tests published in English-speaking countries; the *Tests in Print* volumes serve as master indexes.

Cattell and Warburton (1967), *Objective Personality and Motivation Tests:* includes a compendium of over 600 objective tests of personality, with information on age range, derived factors, underlying theory, sample items, and administration procedures; a substantial number of the measures are appropriate for children ages six and older.

Chun, Cobb, and French (1975), *Measures for Psychological Assessment:* Provides a comprehensive bibliography of mental health measures, as well as measures of individual traits and moods, attitudes, interpersonal relationships, and group characteristics; all measures can be located in measurement-related journals in psychology and sociology fron 1960 to 1970.

Coller (1971), *The Assessment of "Self-Concept" in Early Childhood Education:* reviews the self-concept literature, discusses fifty assessment instruments for measuring self-concept in young children, and offers suggestions to enhance future measurement efforts in this area.

Comrey, Backer, and Glaser (1973), *A Sourcebook for Mental Health Measures:* describes over 1,000 mental health measures, classified primarily by topic or construct (for example, educational adjustment, personality), including details on development procedures, measurement technique, age range, and validity and reliability evidence.

Doucette and Freedman (1980), *Progress Tests for the Developmentally Disabled: An Evaluation:* reviews forty-seven measures of adaptive function (for instance, self-care) and of environmental settings (school, home) that may influence personal development. Information on content, administration, and interpretation procedures; research and development efforts; and usefulness for certain types of client is included.

Educational Testing Service (variable dates), *Head Start Test Collection:* consists of annotated bibliographies describing measures of attitudes toward school, language development, infant development, social skills, school readiness, self-concept, and tests for Spanish-speaking children.

Frankenburg and Camp (1975), *Pediatric Screening Tests:* describes and reviews many screening tests commonly used with very young children.

Goolsby and Darby (1969), *Bibliography of Instrumentation Methodology and Procedures for Measurement in Early Childhood Learning:* contains an unannotated bibliography of references pertinent to the measurement of young children's achievement, creativity, mental ability, personality, readiness, social maturity, and visual perception.

Hoepfner, Stern, and Nummedal (1971), *CSE/ECRC Preschool/Kindergarten Test Evaluations:* describes and critiques published tests for young children in four domains (affective, intellectual, psychomotor, and subject achievement).

Hoepfner et al. (1972), *Tests of Higher-Order Cognitive, Affective, and Interpersonal Skills:* lists and reviews 2,600 published and unpublished scales and subscales in three general areas (higher-order cognitive, affective, and interpersonal skills); only a portion are appropriate for use at primary and preprimary levels.

Hoepfner et al. (1976), *CSE Elementary School Test Evaluations:* includes critical evaluations of measures for elementary school children in fourteen areas (affective and personality traits, arts and crafts, career education, cognitive and intellectual skills, foreign language, language arts, mathematics, music, perceptual and motor skills, physical education and health education, reading, religion and ethics, science, and social studies).

Johnson and Bommarito (1971), *Tests and Measurements in Child Development: Handbook I;* and Johnson (1976) *Tests and Measurements in Child Development: Handbook II:* contain descriptions of over 1,200 unpublished measures, located in education, psychology, and psychiatry professional journals; classified according to content area (cognition, personality and emotional characteristics, perceptions of environment, self-concept, motor skills, physical attributes, attitudes and interests, and social behavior), each measure is succinctly described and critiqued.

Lake, Miles, and Earle (1973), *Measuring Human Behavior:* focuses on measures of individual and group social functioning, with information provided on conceptual schemes, development, and related research; only a few were developed specifically for use with young children; others could be adapted for use.

Locks, Pletcher, and Reynolds (1978), *Assessment Instuments for Limited-English-Speaking Students:* evaluates commonly used measures for their suitability of use with children (kindergarten through grade six) whose first language is not English; the measures cover a wide range of subject areas.

Mardell and Goldenberg (1972), *Learning Disabilities/Early Childhood Research Project:* surveys ninety screening measures for children ages two-and-a-half to five-and-a-half years in terms of suitability for identifying children with potential learning disabilities; the effort resulted in the Developmental Indicators for the Assessment of Learning (DIAL).

Robinson and Shaver (1973), *Measures of Social Psychological Attitudes:* reproduces and critiques measures of such constructs as self-esteem, locus of control, life satisfaction, alienation and anomie, values, and general attitudes toward people. The nature of some of the constructs covered precludes the use of the measures with very young children.

Shaw and Wright (1967), *Scales for the Measurement of Attitudes:* presents over 175 measures of attitudes toward such social referents as international issues, social practices, social issues and problems, abstract concepts (for example, education), political systems, ethnic and national groups, significant others, and social institutions; several relate to family and school life.

Silverman, Noa, and Russell (1976), *Oral Language Tests for Bilingual Students:* reviews twenty-five language tests' validity, examinee appropriateness, technical excellence, and administrative usability.

Stangler, Huber, and Routh (1980), *Screening Growth and Development of Preschool Children: A Guide to Test Selection:* presents a guide to the selection and use of screening tests in five categories (physical growth; general development, including neuromotor, psychosocial, and self-help skills; hearing; speech and language; and vision).

Stott and Ball (1965), *Infant and Preschool Mental Tests: Review and Evaluation:* describes most of the commercially available measures of intelligence for infants and young children and compares in detail five especially popular measures (Cattell Infant

Scale, California First-Year Mental Scale, Gesell Developmental Schedule, Merrill-Palmer Scale, and Stanford-Binet Scale).

Straus (1969), *Family Measurement Techniques:* reviews 319 instruments intended to measure properties of the family or behaviors of family members. A substantial number of the measures deal with child–parent or child–family interactions, the adjustment of the child to family life, and related topics.

Thomas (1970), *Psychological Assessment Instruments for Use with Human Infants:* reviews in depth nine intelligence tests: Cattell Infant Intelligence Scale, Gesell Developmental Schedule, Griffiths Mental Development Scale, Burnet and Lezine Scale, Bayley's Scales, Northwestern Intelligence Tests, Graham's Behavior Tests for Newborns, Prechtl's Neurological Examination, and Flint's Infant Security Scale.

Walker (1973), *Socioemotional Measures for Preschool and Kindergarten Children:* describes 143 measures of attitudes, general personality and emotional adjustment, interests or preferences, personality or behavior traits, self-concept, and social skills or competency; both published and unpublished measures are included.

Wylie (1974), *The Self-Concept:* describes and critiques a few frequently used self-concept measures (Coopersmith Self-Esteem Inventory and Piers-Harris Children's Self-Concept Scale). This volume is of particular interest to researchers or instrument developers in the area of self-concept.

References

ADKINS, D. C., and BALLIF, B. L. *Animal Crackers: A Test of Motivation to Achieve: Examiner's Manual.* Monterey, Calif.: CTB/McGraw-Hill, 1973.

AMBRON, S. R. Review of Circus. In O. K. Buros (ed.), *The Eighth Mental Measurements Yearbook*, Vol. 1. Highland Park, N.J.: Gryphon Press, 1978.

AMERICAN ALLIANCE FOR HEALTH, PHYSICAL EDUCATION, and RECREATION. *Annotated Bibliography on Perceptual-Motor Development.* Washington, D.C.: American Alliance for Health, Physical Education, and Recreation, 1973.

AMERICAN ALLIANCE FOR HEALTH, PHYSICAL EDUCATION, and RECREATION, *Testing for Impaired, Disabled, and Handicapped Individuals.* Washington, D.C.: American Alliance for Health, Physical Education, and Recreation, n.d.

AMERICAN PSYCHOLOGICAL ASSOCIATION. *Standards for Educational and Psychological Tests.* Washington, D.C.: American Psychological Association, 1974.

AMMONS, R. B., and AMMONS, C. H. The Quick Test (QT): Provisional manual. *Psychological Reports*, 1962, *11*, 111–161.

ANASTASI, A. *Psychological Testing*, 4th ed. New York: Macmillan, 1976.

ANDERSON, S. B., and MESSICK, S. Social competency in young children. *Developmental Psychology*, 1974, *10*, 282–293.

APPLETON, T., CLIFTON, R., and GOLDBERG, S. The development of behavioral competence in infancy. In F. D. Howowitz (ed.), *Review of Child Development Research*, vol. 4. Chicago: University of Chicago Press, 1975.

AYRES, A. J. *Southern California Sensory Integration Tests: Manual*, revised ed. Los Angeles: Western Psychological Services, 1980.

AYRES, L. P. *Ayres Measuring Scale for Handwriting.* Iowa City: Bureau of Educational Research and Service. University of Iowa, 1940.

BALL, S. *Assessing the Attitudes of Young Children Toward School.* Princeton, N.J.: Educational Testing Service, 1971.

BANTA, T. J. Tests for the evaluation of early childhood education: The Cincinnati Autonomy Test Battery (CATB). In J. Hellmuth (ed.), *Cognitive Studies*, Vol. 1. New York: Brunner/Mazel, 1970.

BAYLEY, N. *Bayley Scales of Infant Development.* New York: Psychological Corporation, 1969.

BEATTY, W. H. *Improving Educational Assessment and An Inventory of Measures of Affective Behavior.* Washington, D.C.: Association for Supervision and Curriculum Development, 1969.

BEERY, K. E. *Developmental Test of Visual-Motor Integration: Administration and Scoring Manual.* Chicago: Follett, 1967.

BEERY, K. E., and BUKTENICA, N. A. *Developmental Test of Visual-Motor Integration: Student Test Booklet.* Chicago: Follett, 1967.

BENNETT, G. K., SEASHORE, H. G., and WESMAN, A. G. *Manual for the Differential Aptitude Tests, Forms S and T*, 5th ed. New York: Psychological Corporation, 1974.

BERNBAUM, M. Accuracy in children's coping: The role of different stroke sequences and school experience. Unpublished doctoral dissertation, George Washington University, 1974.

BLANK, M. Eliciting verbalization from young children in experimental tasks: A methodological note. *Child Development*, 1975, *46*, 254–257.

Blank, M., Rose, S. A., and BERLIN, L. J. *Preschool Language Assessment Instrument: The Language of Learning in Practice.* New York: Grune & Stratton, 1978a.

BLANK, M., ROSE, S. A., and BERLIN, L. J. *The Language of Learning: The Preschool Years.* New York: Grune & Stratton, 1978b.

BLOOM, B. S. (ed.). *Taxonomy of Educational Objectives. Handbook I: Cognitive Domain.* New York: McKay, 1956.

BLOOM, B. S., HASTINGS, J. T., and MADAUS. G. F. (eds.). *Handbook on Formative and Summative Evaluation of Student Learning.* New York: McGraw-Hill, 1971.

BLOOM, B. S., MADAUS, G. F., and HASTINGS, J. T. *Evaluation to Improve Learning.* New York: McGraw-Hill, 1981.

BLOOM, L. Language Development. In F. D. Horowitz (ed.). *Review of Child Development Research*, Vol. 4. Chicago: University of Chicago Press, 1975.

BONJEAN, C. M., HILL, R. J., and McLEMORE, S. D. *Sociological Measurement: An Inventory of Scales and Indices.* San Francisco: Chandler, 1967.

BOUCHARD, T. J., JR. Current conceptions of intelligence and their implications for assessment. In P. McReynolds (ed.), *Advances in Psychological Assessment*, Vol. 1. Palo Alto, Calif.: Science and Behavior Books, 1968.

BOYER, E. G., SIMON, A., and KARAFIN, G. R. (eds.). *Measures of Maturation: An Anthology of Early Childhood Observation Instruments.* Philadelphia: Research for Better Schools, 1973.

BRAZELTON, T. B. *Neonatal Behavioral Assessment Scale.* Philadelphia: Lippincott, 1973.

BROPHY, J. E., GOOD, T. L., and NEDLER, S. E. *Teaching in the Preschool.* New York: Harper & Row, 1975.

BROWN, D. G. Sex-Role Preference in Young Children. *Psychological Monographs*, 1956, *70* (14, Whole No. 421).

BROWN, F. G. *Guidelines for Test Use: A Commentary on the Standards for Educational and Psychological Tests*. Washington, D.C.: National Council on Measurement in Education, 1980.

BUROS, O. K. (ed.). *Tests in Print: A Comprehensive Bibliography of Tests for Use in Education, Psychology, and Industry* (I and II). Highland Park, N.J.: Gryphon Press: I, 1961; II, 1974.

BUROS, O. K. Fifty years in testing: Some reminiscences, criticisms, and suggestions. *Educational Researcher*, 1977, *6*, 9–15.

BUROS, O. K. (ed.). *The Eighth Mental Measurements Yearbook*. Highland Park, N.J.: Gryphon Press, 1978.

CARROLL, J. L., and LAMING, L. R. Giftedness and creativity: Recent attempts at definition: A literature review. *Gifted Child Quarterly*, 1974, *18*, 85–96.

CASHEN, V. M., and RAMSEYER, G. C. The use of separate answer sheets by primary age children. *Journal of Educational Measurement*, 1969, *6*, 155–157.

CASSEL, R. N. *The Child Behavior Rating Scale Manual*. Los Angeles: Western Psychological Services, 1962.

CATTELL, P. *The Measurement of Intelligence of Infants and Young Children*, revised ed. New York: Psychological Corporation, 1960.

CATTELL, R. B. *Handbook for the Individual or Group Culture Fair (or Free) Intelligence Test, Scale 1*, Champaign, Ill.: Institute for Personality and Ability Testing, 1962.

CATTELL, R. B., and WARBURTON, F. *Objective Personality and Motivation Tests*. Urbana: University of Illinois Press, 1967.

CAZDEN, C. B. Evaluation of learning in preschool education: Early language development. In B. S. Bloom, J. T. Hastings, and G. F. Madaus (eds.), *Handbook on Formative and Summative Evaluation of Student Learning*. New York: McGraw-Hill, 1971.

CHUN, K., COBB, S., and FRENCH, J. R. P., JR. *Measures for Psychological Assessment: A Guide to 3,000 Original Sources and Their Applications*. Ann Arbor: Survey Research Center of the Institute for Social Research, University of Michigan, 1975.

Circus Manual and Technical Report. Menlo Park, Calif.: Addison-Wesley, 1979.

COLES, G. S. The learning disabilities test battery: Empirical and social issues. *Harvard Educational Review*, 1978, *48*, 313–340.

COLLER, A. R. *The Assessment of "Self-Concept" in Early Childhood Education*. Urbana, Ill.: ERIC Clearinghouse on Early Childhood Education, 1971. (Also available in ERIC, ED 050822.)

Comprehensive Tests of Basic Skills, Expanded ed. Technical Bulletin No. 1. Monterey, Calif.: CTB/McGraw-Hill, 1974.

COMREY, A. L., BACKER, T. E., and GLASER, E. M. *A Sourcebook for Mental Health Measures*. Los Angeles: Human Interaction Research Institute, 1973.

Cooperative Preschool Inventory Handbook, Revised ed. Reading, Mass.: Addison-Wesley, 1970.

CORMAN, H. H., and ESCALONA, S. K. Stages of Sensorimotor Development: A Replication Study. *Merrill-Palmer Quarterly*, 1969, *15*, 351–361.

CRATTY, B. J. *Intelligence in Action: Physical Activities for Enhancing Intellectual Abilities.* Englewood Cliffs, N.J.: Prentice-Hall, 1973a.

CRATTY, B. J. *Teaching Motor Skills.* Englewood Cliffs, N.J.: Prentice-Hall, 1973b.

CRONBACH, L. J. *Essentials of Psychological Testing,* 3rd ed. New York: Harper & Row, 1970.

CRUICKSHANK, W. M. *The Brain-Injured Child in Home, School, and Community.* Syracuse, N.Y.: Syracuse University Press, 1967.

DARBY, B. L., and MAY, M. J. (eds.). *Infant Assessment: Issues and Applications.* Seattle, Wash.: Western States Technical Assistance Resource, 1979.

DE AVILA, E. A. and HAVASSY, B. E. Piagetian alternative to IQ: Mexican American study. In N. Hobbs, M. H. Matheny, L. Odum, W. Molleil, D. A. Bartlett, and J. R. Black (eds.), *Issues in the Classification of Children: A Sourcebook on Categories, Labels, and Their Consequences,* Vol. 2. San Francisco: Jossey-Bass, 1975.

DELLAS, M., and GAIER, E. L. Identification of creativity: The individual. *Psychological Bulletin,* 1970, 73, 55–73.

DOLL, E. A. *Vineland Social Maturity Scale: Condensed Manual of Directions.* Circle Pines, Minn.: American Guidance Service, 1965.

DOUCETTE, J., and FREEDMAN, R. *Progress Tests for the Developmentally Disabled: An Evaluation.* Cambridge, Mass.: Abt Associates, 1980.

DROWATZKY, J. N. *Motor Learning: Principles and Practices.* Minneapolis, Minn.: Burgess, 1975.

DUNN, L. M. *Peabody Picture Vocabulary Test: Manual.* Circle Pines, Minn.: American Guidance Service, 1965.

Educational Testing Service. *Head Start Test Collection.* Princeton, N.J.: Educational Testing Service, variable dates.

ELLIS, M. J. *Why People Play.* Englewood Cliffs, N.J.: Prentice-Hall, 1973.

ENGELMANN, S. *The Basic Concept Inventory: Teacher's Manual,* field research ed. Chicago: Follett, 1967.

ESCALONA, S. K., and CORMAN, H. H. *Albert Einstein Scales of Sensorimotor Development.* New York: Department of Psychiatry, Albert Einstein College of Medicine, 1969.

ESPENSCHADE, A. S., and ECKERT, H. M. *Motor Development.* Columbus, Ohio: Merrill, 1967.

EVANS, E. D. Measurement practices in early childhood education. In R. W. Colvin and E. M. Zaffiro (eds.), *Preschool Education: A Handbook for the Training of Early Childhood Educators.* New York: Springer-Verlag, 1974.

FLINCHUM, B. M. *Motor Development in Early Childhood: A Guide for Movement Education with Ages 2 to 6.* Saint Louis, Mo.: Mosby, 1975.

FRANKENBURG, W. K., and CAMP, B. W. (EDS.). *Pediatric Screening Tests.* Springfield, Ill.: Thomas, 1975.

FRANKENBURG, W. K., DODDS, J. B., FANDAL, A. W., KAZUK, E., and COHRS, M. *Denver Developmental Screening Test: Revised Reference Manual.* Denver, Colo.: LADOCA Foundation, 1975.

FROSTIG, M. *Marianne Frostig Developmental Test of Visual Perception: Administration and Scoring Manual,* 3rd ed. Palo Alto, Calif.: Consulting Psychologists Press, 1966.

FROSTIG, M., MASLOW, P., LEFEVER, D. W., and WHITTLESEY, J. R. B. *Marianne Frostig Developmental Test of Visual Perception, Third Edition: 1963 Standardization.* Palo Alto, Calif.: Consulting Psychologists Press. 1964.

GELMAN, R. Cognitive development. In M. R. Rosenzweig and L. W. Porter (eds.), *Annual Review of Psychology*, Vol. 29. Palo Alto, Calif.: Annual Reviews, 1978.

GELMAN, R. Preschool thought. *American Psychologist*, 1979, *34*, 900–905.

GESELL, A., and AMATRUDA, C. S. *Developmental Diagnosis*, 2nd ed. New York: Hoeber, 1947.

GETZELS, J. W., and DILLON, J. T. The nature of giftedness and the education of the gifted. In R. M. W. Travers (ed.), *Second Handbook of Research on Teaching.* Skokie, Ill.: Rand McNally, 1973.

GLASS, G. V. Standards and criteria. Occasional Paper No. 10. Kalamazoo: Evaluation Center, College of Education, Western Michigan University, 1977. (Also published in the *Journal of Educational Measurement*, 1978a, *15*, 237–261.)

GLASS, G. V. Postscript to "Standards and Criteria." Paper presented at the Winter Conference on Measurement and Methodology of the Center for the Study of Evaluation, University of California, Los Angeles, January 1978b.

GLASS, G. V., and ELLETT, F. S., JR., Evaluation research. In M. R. Rosenzweig and L. W. Porter (eds.), *Annual Review of Psychology*, 1980, *31*, 211–228.

GLICK, J. Some problems in the evaluation of preschool intervention programs. In R. D. Hess and R. M. Bear (eds.), *Early Education: Current Theory, Research, and Action.* Chicago: Aldine, 1968.

GLUCKSBERG, S., KRAUSS, R., and HIGGINS, E. T. The development of referential communication skills. In F. D. Horowitz (ed.), *Review of Child Development Research*, Vol. 4. Chicago: University of Chicago Press, 1975.

GOLDSCHMID, M. L., and BENTLER, P. M. *Manual: Concept Assessment Kit—Conservation.* San Diego, Calif.: Educational and Industrial Testing Service, 1968.

GOLDSTEIN, K. M., and BLACKMAN, S. Assessment of cognitive style. In P. McReynolds (ed.), *Advances in Psychological Assessment*, Vol. 4. San Francisco: Jossey-Bass, 1977.

GOODLAD, J. I., KLEIN, M. F., and NOVOTNEY, J. M. *Early Schooling in the United States.* New York: McGraw-Hill, 1973.

GOODWIN, W. L. Evaluation in early childhood education. In R. W. Colvin and E. M. Zaffiro (eds.), *Preschool Education: A Handbook for the Training of Early Childhood Educators.* New York: Springer-Verlag, 1974.

GOODWIN, W. L., and DRISCOLL, L. A. *Handbook for Measurement and Evaluation in Early Childhood Education.* San Francisco: Jossey-Bass, 1980.

GOODWIN, W. L., and KLAUSMEIER, H. J. *Facilitating Student Learning: An Introduction to Educational Psychology.* New York: Harper & Row, 1975.

GOOLSBY, T., JR., and DARBY, B. *A Bibliography of Instrumentation Methodology and Procedures for Measurement in Early Childhood Learning.* Athens: Research and Development Center in Educational Stimulation, University of Georgia, 1969. (Also available in ERIC, ED 046978.)

GUILFORD, J. P. *The Nature of Human Intelligence.* New York: McGraw-Hill, 1967.

HARRIS, D. B. *Children's Drawings as Measures of Intellectual Maturity.* New York: Harcourt Brace Jovanovich, 1963.

HARROW, A. J. *A Taxonomy of the Psychomotor Domain: A Guide for Developing Behavioral Objectives.* New York: McKay, 1972.

HARTUP, W. W. Early education and childhood socialization. *Journal of Research and Development in Education,* 1968, *1,* 16–29.

HEIN, G. E. *An Open Education Perspective on Evaluation.* Grand Forks: North Dakota Study Group on Evaluation, University of North Dakota, 1975.

HENDERSON, E. H., LONG, B. H., and ZILLER, R. C. *Manual for the Self-Social Symbols Tasks and the Children's Self-Social Constructs Tests.* Charlottesville: Virginia Research Associates, n.d.

HENDRICK, J. *The Whole Child: New Trends in Early Education.* St. Louis: Mosby, 1975.

HERRON, R. E., and SUTTON-SMITH, B. (eds.). *Child's Play.* New York: Wiley, 1971.

HEYNEMAN, S. P., and MINTZ, P. C. The frequency and quality of measures utilized in federally sponsored research on children and adolescents. *American Educational Research Journal,* 1977, *14,* 99–113.

HIGH/SCOPE EDUCATIONAL RESEARCH FOUNDATION. Research report: The productive language assessment tasks. *Bulletin of the High/Scope Foundation,* 1976, Winter (No. 3), 1–8.

HOBBS, N. *The Futures of Children: Recommendations of the Project on Classification of Exceptional Children.* San Francisco: Jossey-Bass, 1975.

HOEPFNER, R., and FINK, A. *Evaluation Study of the California State Preschool Program.* Los Angeles: Center for the Study of Evaluation, Graduate School of Education. University of California at Los Angeles, 1975.

HOEPFNER, R., STERN, C., and NUMMEDAL, S. G. *CSE–ECRC Preschool/Kindergarten Test Evaluations.* Los Angeles: Center for the Study of Evaluation and Early Childhood Research Center, Graduate School of Education, University of California at Los Angeles, 1971.

HOEPFNER, R., HEMENWAY, J., DE MUTH, J., TENOPY, M. L., GRANVILLE, A. C., PETROSKO, J. M., KRAKOWER, J., SILBERSTEIN, R., AND NADEAU, M. *CSE-RBS Test Evaluations: Tests of Higher-Order Cognitive, Affective, and Interpersonal Skills.* Los Angeles: Center for the Study of Evaluation, Graduate School of Education, University of California at Los Angeles, 1972.

HOEPFNER, R., BASTONE, M., OGILVIE, V. N., HUNTER, R., SPARTA, S., GROTHE, C. R., SHANI, E., HUFARO, L., GOLDSTEIN, E., WILLIAMS, R. S., and SMITH, K. O. *CSE Elementary School Test Evaluations.* Los Angeles: Center for the Study of Evaluation, Graduate School of Education, University of California at Los Angeles, 1976.

HONIG, A. S., and LALLY, J. R. *Piagetian Infant Scales.* Syracuse, N.Y.: Syracuse University Children's Center, 1970.

HONZIK, M. P. The development of intelligence. In B. B. Wolman (ed.), *Handbook of General Psychology.* Englewood Cliffs, N.J.: Prentice-Hall, 1973.

HOPKINS, K. D., and STANLEY, J. C. *Educational and Psychological Measurement and Evaluation,* 5th ed. Englewood Cliffs, N.J.: Prentice-Hall, 1981.

HOUTS, P. L. Introduction: Standardized testing in America. In P. L. Houts (ed.), *The Myth of Measurability.* New York: Hart, 1977.

IRWIN, D. M., and BUSHNELL, M. M. *Observational Strategies for Child Study.* New York: Holt, Rinehart & Winston, 1980.

JOHNSON, O. G. *Tests and Measurements in Child Development: Handbook II.* Vols. 1 and 2. San Francisco: Jossey-Bass, 1976.

JOHNSON, O. G., and BOMMARITO, J. W. *Tests and Measurements in Child Development: Handbook I.* San Francisco: Jossey-Bass, 1971.

KEOGH, B. K., and BECKER, L. D. Early Detection of Learning Problems: Questions, Cautions, and Guidelines. *Exceptional Children*, 1973, *40*, 5–11.

KERLINGER, F. N. *Foundations of Behavioral Research*, 2nd ed. New York: Holt, Rinehart & Winston, 1973.

KIRK, S. A., MCCARTHY, J. J., and KIRK, W. D. *Illinois Test of Psycholinguistic Abilities*, Revised ed. Urbana: University of Illinois Press, 1968.

KOGAN, N. *Cognitive Styles in Infancy and Early Childhood Education*. Hillsdale, N.J.: Lawrence Erlbaum Associates, 1976.

KRATHWOHL, D. R., BLOOM, B. S., and MASIA. B. B. *Taxonomy of Educational Objectives: The Classification of Educational Goals. Handbook II: Affective Domain.* New York: McKay, 1964.

LABORATORY OF COMPARATIVE HUMAN COGNITION. Cross-cultural psychology's challenges to our ideas of children and development. *American Psychologist*, 1979, *34*, 827–833.

LACROSSE, E. R., JR. Psychologist and teacher: Cooperation or conflict? *Young Children*, 1970, *25*, 223–229.

LAKE, D., MILES, M., and EARLE, R., JR. (eds.). *Measuring Human Behavior.* New York: Teachers College Press, 1973.

LAURENDEAU, M., and PINARD, A. *The Development of the Concept of Space in the Child.* New York: International Universities Press, 1970.

LEE, L. L. *Developmental Sentence Analysis: A Grammatical Assessment Procedure for Speech and Language Clinicians.* Evanston, Ill.: Northwestern University Press, 1974.

LERNER, B. The Supreme Court and the APA, AERA, NCME test standards: Past references and future possibilities. *American Psychologist, 1978, 33,* 915–919.

LERNER, B. Representative democracy, "men of zeal," and testing legislation. *American Psychologist,* 1981, *36,* 270–275.

LEVINE, E. L., FINEMAN, C. A., and DONLON, G. McG. *Prescriptive Profile Procedure for Children with Learning Disabilities.* Miami, Fla.: Dade County Public Schools, 1973. (Also available in ERIC, ED 074673.)

LEVINE, S., ELZEY, F. F., and LEWIS, M. *California Preschool Social Competency Scale Manual.* Palo Alto, Calif.: Consulting Psychologists Press, 1969.

LOCKS, N. A., PLETCHER, B. A., and REYNOLDS, D. F. *Language Assessment Instruments for Limited-English-Speaking Students: A Needs Analysis.* Washington, D.C.: National Institute of Education, 1978.

LUMSDEN, J. Review of the Illinois test of psycholinguistic abilities, revised edition. In O. K. Buros (ed.), *The Eighth Mental Measurements Yearbook*, Vol. 1. Highland Park, N.J.: Gryphon Press, 1978.

MCCALL, R. B., APPLEBAUM, M. I., and HOGARTY, P. S. Developmental changes in mental performance. *Monographs of the Society for Research in Child Development*, 1973, *38*, (3, Serial No. 150).

McCall, R. B., Hogarty, P. S., and Hurlburt, N. Transitions in infant sensorimotor development and the prediction of childhood IQ. *American Psychologist*, 1972, 27, 728–748.

McCarthy, D. *Manual for the McCarthy Scales of Children's Abilities*. New York: Psychological Corporation, 1972.

Maccoby, E. E., and Zellner, M. *Experiments in Primary Education: Aspects of Project Follow Through*. New York: Harcourt Brace Jovanovich, 1970.

Madden, R., and Gardner, E. F. *Stanford Early School Achievement Test: Directions for Administering*. Levels I and II. New York: Harcourt Brace Jovanovich, 1969 (Level I), 1971 (Level II).

Mardell, C. D., and Goldenberg, D. S. *Learning Disabilities/Early Childhood Research Project*. Springfield: Illinois State Office of the Superintendent of Public Instruction, 1972. (Also available in ERIC, ED 082408.)

Mardell, C. D., and Goldenberg, D. S. *DIAL—Developmental Indicators for the Assessment of Learning: Manual*. Highland Park, Ill.: DIAL, Inc., 1975.

Meeker, M., Mestyaiiek, L., Shadduck, R., and Meeker, R. *S.O.I. Learning Abilities Test: Diagnostic for Reading and Arithmetic*. Special Edition, K-1. El Segundo, Calif.: S.O.I. Institute, 1975.

Meeker, M., and Meeker, R. *S.O.I. Learning Abilities Test: Examiner's Manual*, revised ed. El Segundo, Calif.: S.O.I. Institute, 1979.

Mehrens, W. A., and Lehmann, I. J. *Measurement and Evaluation in Education and Psychology*, 2nd ed. New York: Holt, Rinehart & Winston, 1978.

Meier, J. H. Screening, assessment, and intervention for young children at developmental risk. In N. Hobbs (ed.), *Issues in the Classification of Children: A Sourcebook on Categories, Labels, and Their Consequences*, Vol. 2. San Francisco: Jossey-Bass, 1975.

Mercer, J. R. *Labeling the Mentally Retarded*. Berkeley: University of California Press, 1973.

Mercer, J. R. A policy statement on assessment procedures and the rights of children. *Harvard Educational Review*, 1974, 44, 125–141.

Messick, S., and Anderson, S. Educational testing, individual development, and social responsibility. *The Counseling Psychologist*, 1970, 2, 80–88.

Metropolitan Readiness Tests, Teacher's Manuals, Part II: Interpretation and Use of Test Results. Levels I and II. New York: Harcourt Brace Jovanovich, 1976.

Milchus, N. J., Farrah, G. A., and Reitz, W. *The Self-Concept and Motivation Inventory: What Face Would You Wear? SCAMIN Manual of Interpretation*. Dearborn Heights, Mich.: Person-O-Metrics, 1968.

Moore, S. G. A sociometric status test for young children: Manual of instructions. Unpublished paper. Minneapolis: Institute of Child Development, University of Minnesota, 1973.

Moriarty, A. E. *Constancy and IQ Change: A Clinical View of Relationships between Tested Intelligence and Personality*. Springfield, Ill.: Thomas, 1966.

Moss, M. H. *Tests of Basic Experiences 2: Examiner's Manual*. Levels K and L. Monterey, Calif.: CTB/McGraw-Hill, 1978.

National Education Association. Moratorium on standardized testing. *Today's Education, NEA Journal, 1972, 61,* 41.

NATIONAL EDUCATION ASSOCIATION. *Standardized Testing Issues: Teachers' Perspectives.* Washington, D.C.: National Education Association, 1977.

NATIONAL SCHOOL BOARDS ASSOCIATION. *Standardized Achivement Testing.* Washington, D.C.: National School Boards Association, 1977.

NOWICKI, S., JR., and DUKE, M. P. A preschool and primary internal-external control scale. *Developmental Psychology,* 1974, *10,* 874–880.

OAKLAND, T. (ed.). *Psychological and Educational Assessment of Minority Children.* New York: Brunner/Mazel, 1977.

OAKLAND, T., and LAOSA, L. M. Professional, legislative, and judicial influences on psychoeducational assessment practices in schools. In T. Oakland (ed.), *Psychological and Educational Assessment of Minority Children.* New York: Brunner/Mazel, 1977.

ORPET, R. E. *Examiners Manual: Frostig Movement Test Battery.* Palo Alto, Calif.: Consulting Psychologists Press, 1972.

PERRONE, V. On standardized testing and evaluation. In P. L. Houts (ed.), *The Myth of Measurability.* New York: Hart, 1977.

QUINTO, F., and McKENNA, B. *Alternatives to Standardized Testing.* Washington, D.C.: National Education Association, 1977.

RATHJE, W. L. Trace measures. In L. Sechrest (ed.), *Unobtrusive Measurement Today.* New Directions for Methodology of Behavioral Science, No. 1. San Francisco: Jossey-Bass, 1979.

RICH, J. *Interviewing Children and Adolescents.* New York: St. Martin's Press, 1968.

ROACH, E. G., and KEPHART, N. C. *The Purdue Perceptual-Motor Survey.* Columbus, Ohio: Merrill, 1966.

ROBINSON, J. P., and SHAVER, P. R. *Measures of Social Psychological Attitudes,* revised ed. Ann Arbor: Institute for Social Research, University of Michigan, 1973.

SAMUDA, R. J. *Psychological Testing of American Minorities.* New York: Harper & Row, 1975.

SANFORD, A. R. *A Manual for Use of the Learning Accomplishment Profile.* Winston-Salem, N.C.: Kaplan School Supply, 1974.

SATTLER, J. M. *Assessment of Children's Intelligence.* Philadelphia: Saunders, 1974.

SCARR-SALAPATEK, S. Genetics and the development of intelligence. In F. D. Horowitz (ed.), *Review of Child Developmental Research,* Vol. 4. Chicago: University of Chicago Press, 1975.

SCRIVEN, M. The methodology of evaluation. In R. E. Stake (ed.), *Perspectives on Curriculum Evaluation.* AERA Monograph Series on Curriculum Evaluation No. 1. Skokie, Ill.: Rand McNally, 1967.

SHAW, M. E., and WRIGHT, J. M. *Scales for the Measurement of Attitudes.* New York: McGraw-Hill, 1967.

SHEPARD, L., and SMITH, M. L. *Evaluation of the Identification of Perceptual-Communicative Disorders in Colorado.* Boulder: Laboratory of Educational Research, University of Colorado, 1981.

SILVERMAN, R., NOA, J. K., and RUSSELL, R. H. *Oral Language Tests for Bilingual Stu-*

dents: An Evaluation of Language Dominance and Proficiency Instruments. Portland, Ore.: Northwest Regional Educational Laboratory, 1976.

SINCLAIR, C. B. *Movement of the Young Child: Ages Two to Six.* Columbus, Ohio: Merrill, 1973.

SINGER, R. N. (ed.). *Readings in Motor Learning.* Philadelphia: Lea and Febiger, 1972.

SOMACH, B. The diagnostic teacher. *Early Years,* 1978, *8,* 58–60.

STANGLER, S. R., HUBER, C. J., and ROUTH, D. K. *Screening Growth and Development of Preschool Children: A Guide to Test Selection.* New York: McGraw-Hill, 1980.

STETZ, F. P., and BECK, M. D. Attitudes toward standardized tests: Students, teachers, and measurement specialists. *NCME Measurement in Education,* 1981, *12,* 1–10.

STOTT, D. H. *Bristol Social Adjustment Guides Manual.* San Diego, Calif.: Educational and Industrial Testing Service, 1972.

STOTT, D. H., MOYES, F. A., and HENDERSON, F. A. *Test of Motor Impairment.* Guelph, Ontario, Canada: Brook Educational Publishers, 1972.

STOTT, L. H., and BALL, R. S. Infant and preschool mental tests: Review and evaluation. *Monographs of the Society for Research in Child Development,* 1965, *30* (3, Serial No. 101).

STRAUS, M. *Family Measurement Techniques: Abstracts of Published Instruments, 1935–1965.* Minneapolis: University of Minnesota Press, 1969.

TAUB, H. P., LOVE, J., WILKERSON, D. A., WASHINGTON, E. D., and WOLF, J. M. *Accept My Profile: Perspectives for Head Start Profiles of Program Effects on Children.* Westport, Conn.: Mediax Associates, 1980.

TERMAN, L. M., and MERRILL, M. A. *Measuring Intelligence.* Boston: Houghton Mifflin, 1960.

TERMAN, L. M., and MERRILL, M. A. *Stanford-Binet Intelligence Scale: 1972 Norms Edition.* Boston: Houghton Mifflin, 1973.

THOMAS, H. Psychological assessment instruments for use with human infants. *Merrill-Palmer Quarterly,* 1970, *16,* 179–223.

THOMPSON, G. R. *Primary Academic Sentiment Scale: Examiner's Manual.* Skokie, Ill.: Priority Innovations, 1968.

THORNDIKE, E. L. The nature, purposes, and general methods of measurements of educational products. In G. M. Whipple (ed.), *The Measurement of Educational Products,* 17th Yearbook, Part 2. National Society for the Study of Education. Chicago: University of Chicago Press, 1918.

THORNDIKE, R. L., and HAGEN, E. P. *Measurement and Evaluation in Psychology and Education,* 4th ed. New York: Wiley, 1977.

THORPE, L. P., CLARK, W. W., and TIEGS, E. W. *California Test of Personality Manual.* Monterey, Calif.: CTB/McGraw-Hill, 1953.

TORRANCE, E. P. *Torrance Tests of Creative Thinking: Norms-Technical Manual,* research ed. Lexington, Mass.: Personnel Press, 1966.

TREFFINGER, D. J., and POGGIO, J. P. Needed research on the measurement of creativity. *Journal of Creative Behavior,* 1972, *6,* 253–267.

UZGIRIS, I. C., and HUNT, J. McV. *Assessment in Infancy: Ordinal Scales of Psychological Development.* Urbana: University of Illinois Press, 1975.

WACHS, T. D. Relation of infants' performance on Piaget scales between twelve and twenty-four months and their Stanford-Binet performance at thirty-one months. *Child Development*, 1975, *46*, 929–935.

WALKER, D. K. *Socioemotional Measures for Preschool and Kindergarten Children.* San Francisco: Jossey-Bass, 1973.

WALLACH, M. A. Creativity. In P. H. Mussen (ed.), *Carmichael's Manual of Child Psychology*, Vol. 1., 3rd ed. New York: Wiley, 1970.

WAUGH, R. P. The ITPA: Ballast or bonanza for the school psychologist. *Journal of School Psychology*, 1975, *13*, 201–208.

WEBB, E. J., CAMPBELL, D. T., SCHWARTZ, R. D., SECHRIST, L., and GROVE, J. B. *Unobsures: Nonreactive Research in the Social Sciences.* Skokie, Ill.: Rand McNally, 1966.

WEBB, E. J., CAMPBELL, D. T., SCHWARTZ, R. D., SECHRIST, L., and GROVE, J. B. *Unobtrusive Measures: Nonreactive Research in the Social Sciences*, revised ed. Boston, Mass.: Houghton-Mifflin, 1981.

WEBB, W. B. Measurement of learning in extensive training programs. In P. H. DuBois and C. D. Mayo (eds.), *Research Strategies for Evaluating Training.* Skokie, Ill.: Rand McNally, 1970.

WECHSLER, D. *Wechsler Preschool and Primary Scale of Intelligence: Manual.* New York: Psychological Corporation, 1967.

WECHSLER, D. *Wechsler Intelligence Scale for Children—Revised: Manual.* New York: Psychological Corporation, 1974.

WEIDERHOLT, J. L. Review of the Illinois Test of Psycholinguistic Abilities, revised edition. In O. K. Buros (ed.), *The Eighth Mental Measurements Yearbook.* Vol. 1. Highland Park, N.J.: Gryphon Press, 1978.

WHITE, S. H., DAY, M. C., FREEMAN, P. K., HANTMAN, S. A., and MESSENGER, K. P. *Federal Programs for Young Children: Review and Recommendations.* Vols. 1–4. Washington, D.C.: Department of Health, Education, and Welfare, 1973.

WILLIAMS, J. E., BEST, D. L., and ASSOCIATES. *Preschool Racial Attitude Measure II and Color Meaning Test II. General Information and Manuals of Direction.* Winston-Salem, N.C.: Department of Psychology, Wake Forest University, 1975.

WILLIAMS, J. E., BEST, D. L., and ASSOCIATES. *Sex Stereotype Measure II and Sex Attitude Measure: General Information and Manual of Directions.* Winston-Salem, N.C.: Department of Psychology, Wake Forest University, 1976.

WOOLNER, R. B. *Preschool Self-Concept Picture Test.* Memphis, Tenn.: Department of Curriculum and Instruction, Memphis State University, 1966, 1968.

WORTHEN, B. R., and SANDERS, J. R. *Educational Evaluation: Theory and Practice.* Columbus, Ohio: Charles A. Jones, 1973.

WYLIE, R. *The Self-Concept, Volume One: A Review of Methodological Considerations and Measuring Instruments*, revised ed. Lincoln: University of Nebraska Press, 1974.

YANG, R. K., and BELL, R. Q. Assessment of Infants. In P. McReynolds (ed.), *Advances in Psychological Assessment*, Vol. 3. San Francisco: Jossey-Bass, 1975.

ZANER-BLOSER. *Evaluation Scales for Handwriting.* Columbus, Ohio: Zaner-Bloser Handwriting, 1979.

ZEHRBACH, R. R. *Comprehensive Identification Process: Interviewer's Manual.* Bensenville, Ill.: Scholastic Testing Service, 1975a.

ZEHRBACH, R. R. *Comprehensive Identification Process: Screening Administrator's Manual.* Bensenville, Ill.: Scholastic Testing Service, 1975b.

ZIGLER, E. F. Raising the quality of children's lives. *Children,* 1970, *17,* 166–170.

ZIGLER, E., and MUENCHOW, S. Mainstreaming: The proof is in the implementation. *American Psychologist,* 1979, *34,* 993–996.

CHAPTER 22

Observational Research Methods for Early Childhood Education

Celia Genishi

RECENT RESEARCH METHODS in several disciplines have become more and more eclectic. Experimentalists in education expand their methodologies to include naturalistic observation (Smith, 1978; Venezky & Winfield, 1980), and psychologists and sociologists analyze both naturalistic and laboratory settings (Bronfenbrenner, 1979; Carew & Lightfoot, 1979; Sackett, Ruppenthal & Gluck, 1978). Observational studies of educational settings have traditionally been based on the use of predetermined category systems (Amidon & Flanders, 1967), and analyses of data were primarily quantitative. Currently, the use of methods related to ethnography, which are primarily qualitative, is increasing (Green & Wallat, 1981; Ogbu, 1978; Tikunoff, Berliner & Rist, 1975).

The purpose of this chapter is to present examples from this expanded range of methods for use in early childhood education, including specimen description and other decades-old methods associated with child study, as well as participant observation, a set of methods only recently applied to the study of classrooms. The methods discussed here have been used primarily for the study of children at least two years old in out-of-home educational settings: day-care centers, nursery schools, and primary grade classrooms. The phenomena most often observed have been children's behavior and development, teachers' behavior in classrooms, and interactions between teachers and children.

Observational methods are systematic ways of doing research that depend on direct observation of a phenomenon. Human judgments and perceptual abilities to see, hear, notice, and record are of primary importance in the collection and analysis of data. The method may consist of handwriting an account of one child's behavior in a nursery school or it may be the application of a coding system to a videotaped first-grade lesson. Observation here is contrasted with experimentation or manipulation of what is studied. The events observed occur spontaneously in the setting under study. Formal interviews and tests administered by a researcher are, therefore, excluded as observational methods.

The study of reading acquisition illustrates a contrast between observation and experimentation. A researcher could enter a classroom and observe the process of children's learning to read as it occurs during reading lessons. McDermott (1977) and Piestrup (1973), for example, have analyzed different aspects of beginning reading by viewing the lessons as social contexts that influence how and what children learn. In contrast, a researcher could study how children read and perceive features of printed words in experimental contexts that are carefully controlled. Among others, Gibson (1971) and Juel (1980) have analyzed how children respond to print in analytic contexts, abstracted from classroom activity. Both the experimentalist and the observational researcher learn about the acquisition of reading, but their methods clearly differ.

This chapter is a review of methods rather than a review of findings. Detailed "how-to" techniques are not included, but references to individual methods are cited. There are many available publications that address the interests of practitioners who use observation to improve their teaching of young children (Almy & Genishi, 1979; Boehm & Weinberg, 1977; Cohen & Stern, 1978; Irwin & Bushnell, 1980; Stallings, 1977). The focus here is on research rather than practice.

The chapter is divided into the following sections: reasons for observation, approaches to observation, quantitative approaches, qualitative approaches, and issues related to observation. Advantages and disadvantages of quantitative methods are presented as each method is described. Advantages and disadvantages of qualitative approaches are presented in the final section on issues.

Reasons for Observation

In general, observational researchers think that the best way to answer their research questions is to observe a phenomenon under the conditions that interest them. Researchers from different traditions hold different beliefs about the reasons for using observational methods. Some view observation as a first step, one that lays a foundation for future experimentation. They may regard observational studies as "hypothesis-generating" rather than "hypothesis testing." If one were building a research program based on that view, observation might lead to the isolation of a small number of variables to be tested later under controlled conditions. For other researchers, naturalistic observation is the primary means for understanding a phenomenon. The way to learn about regularities is to see what happens over a period of months, and sometimes years, in the lives of those studied. Questions such as "What is the nature of caregiver–child interaction in the second year of life?" or "What are the child-rearing practices in this community?" are answered largely through extended observation.

Thus, reasons for observing may be related to the state of knowledge and the nature of the research question. Researchers may want to observe an unknown phenomenon before studying it experimentally, or they may be investigating a question that can be answered only through observation. A third reason to use observation in early childhood education is the nature of the phenomenon studied. Researchers who want to learn about the young child have fewer methods available to them than researchers who study adults. Very young children's abilities to understand instructions, respond verbally, or attend to what are to them uninteresting tasks are not yet developed. Consequently, they make poor subjects for methods requiring those skills, such as interviews or experiments. Wright (1960) points out, on the other hand, that because they seem less self-conscious while observed than adults, children make good subjects for observation.

A fourth reason for observing is related to ethics. We cannot experiment with certain aspects of development and learning. For example, we cannot deprive one group of children of experiences with peers to see how deprivation would affect language development. In the classroom we cannot generally ask teachers and administrators to delay mathematics instruction until grade two to suit our experimental interests. An alternative method is to observe how children seem to develop language and mathematical ability in and out of the classroom. A further incentive to observe has been the Family Educational Rights and Privacy Act of 1974, which ensures informed consent of research subjects. The act has led to more limited access to schools and institutions for some experimental researchers whose objectives cannot be revealed to subjects and, therefore, to greater use of observational methods.

Approaches to Observation

Observation has long been used in early childhood education to learn about children in their educational settings. In educational research in general, however, observational methods have until recently been treated as a minor residual category that few employed. Most researchers used questionnaires, interviews, or experiments. A review of recent research in education, however, reveals a growing number of observational studies. The increasing interest in classroom interaction has led to the publication of a seventeen-volume anthology of observational instruments (Simon & Boyer, 1967–1970) and of the *Journal of Classroom Interaction*, devoted to research on student and teacher behavior in the classroom.

At the same time that category systems for observation proliferated, educators and other social scientists began to broaden their methodologies to include other approaches to observation. The precise meaning of observation now depends largely upon the questions the researcher asks, and the nature of the questions will be influenced by the approach or tradition followed.

A distinction that is commonly made in discussions of research traditions is quantitative versus qualitative (see Erickson, 1977, and Rist, 1977, for such discussions). Quantitative studies are dependent on numerical or statistical treatments of data; qualitative studies are not. Like most dichotomies, however, this one is simplistic since qualitative studies may contain some numerical data and some researchers combine methods from both traditions in a single study (Carew & Lightfoot, 1979, and Wilkinson & Calculator, 1982).

Another important distinction can be made between preset and open-ended approaches. Quantitative studies are usually based on preset categories of analysis or on hypotheses to be tested statistically. Stallings's Classroom Observation Instrument (1975), is an example of an observational system with preset categories for classroom research. Qualitative researchers, on the other hand, often avoid establishing categories prior to data collection so that they will be open to patterns that emerge as data are collected. What is significant, then, is not the presence or absence of quantification, but the investigator's attitude and assumptions about the process of research. The quantitative researcher has determined before data collection what and how to observe; the qualitative researcher is likely to observe the situation before choosing aspects on which to focus.

Researchers, for example, could take a quantitative approach to play and apply established categories, such as functional, constructive, and dramatic, to their observations. Rubin, Watson, and Jambor (1978) used such categories to compare the free-play behaviors of preschool versus kindergarten children. Statistical tests were performed, and significant differences were found between the two age groups. A qualitative researcher might, instead, begin with a general interest in sociodramatic play and take extensive notes while observing children in a day-care center before formulating specific questions. Schwartzman (1976) used this approach to study play as a form of communication among preschoolers. In her analysis, she neither used statistical tests nor attempted to make generalizations about groups.

There are a variety of terms that refer to the quantitative versus qualitative distinction. Eisner (1981), for example, writes of scientific versus artistic dimensions. The term normative (Wilson, 1970) has also been applied to quantitative studies since in doing them researchers tend to seek general norms or rules for behavior that will help to predict future behavior. Qualitative studies, on the other hand, are more likely to lead not to prediction but to an understanding of unique events and may, therefore, be called interpretive. One of the researcher's goals is to understand subjects' interpretations or views of their experiences. In a clear and thorough review, Magoon (1977) presents much recent research in the interpretive tradition, which he terms constructivist. The influence of this tradition on educational research is also the topic of a special issue of the *Anthropology and Education Quarterly* (Tikunoff & Ward, 1977).

Geertz (1979) points out that the dichotomous terms that capture various aspects of quantitative/qualitative distinctions are matters of degree and not absolute. Figure 22–1 (p. 568) shows that the terms may be represented as the ends of a continuum and that the methods to be presented in the remainder of this chapter fall, somewhat arbitrarily, between those extremes.

Figure 22-1.   Relationships among Research Approaches and Methods

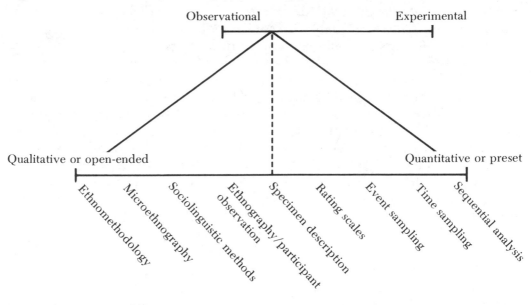

NOTE: In this chapter observational approaches are contrasted with experimental approaches, and qualitative observational methods are contrasted with quantitative methods. Each contrast is shown on a continuum to indicate the lack of a rigid distinction between the extremes. The dotted line between qualitative and quantitative also reflects the artificiality of the dichotomy.

Quantitative Approaches

Wright (1960) has described the four basic methods—time sampling, event sampling, rating scales, and specimen description—in his classic chapter on observational child study. They are tied neither to the observation of children nor to use in educational settings, but researchers have used them to study children in homes, preschools, centers, and primary grade classrooms for decades. The methods are also applicable in laboratory settings, but the focus here is on studies in which researcher manipulation of the setting or subjects is minimal and in which recording of data happens soon after observing. Advantages and disadvantages of each method are presented.

Time Sampling

In both child development and education, time sampling is a widely used observational method. The researcher focuses on selected behaviors as they occur within uniform time intervals. These intervals are usually short, often ranging from a few seconds to less than five minutes. Generally, categories that describe the target behaviors are established before observation. Subjects are often children in groups, and categories may be applied either to the group as a whole or, more commonly, to individual children observed in rotation within the specified time.

Time sampling methods are based on category systems that are either mutually exclusive or concurrent (Bakeman, 1978). The observer codes one of a set of mutually exclusive categories once per time interval. For example, a child may be engaged in social play and can, therefore, not be simultaneously engaged in solitary play. Categories are devised so that only one is applicable at a given time.

Flanders Interaction Analysis Categories (Amidon & Flanders, 1967) have been one of the most frequently used systems for recording teacher and student verbal behavior. Observers using Flanders's system characterize teacher and student talk by selecting from among ten mutually exclusive categories once every three seconds. Categories include praising or encouraging, asking questions, lecturing, and silence or confusion. Guidelines are provided so that coders can select only one category per interval. There are numerous systems similar to Flanders's, many of which are included in *Mirrors for Behavior* (Simon & Boyer, 1967–1970). A more recent example of a mutually exclusive category system was used to measure academic learning time in second and fifth grade classrooms (Filby & Marliave, 1977, cited in Denham & Lieberman, 1980).

Miller and Dyer (1975) used, among other methods, a concurrent time sampling system in their study of four preschool programs. They observed in classrooms to verify that the four programs differed from each other along specified dimensions. Both children's and teacher's behaviors were observed. There were six categories of teaching techniques: role playing, exemplification, manipulation, verbal instruction, requests, and feedback. Within a fifteen-second observation period, any or all of the six techniques could be recorded if they occurred. Manipulation might occur simultaneously with verbal instruction, for example. The frequency of use of the various techniques was the focus of the observations, and each category could conceivably have occurred once per fifteen-second interval.

Time sampling has several advantages. It allows the researcher to focus on specifically defined behaviors within limited time spans. It can lead to the collection of representative samples, reliably coded, because one or more coders can easily make many observations. To advocates of time sampling, the method is objective because they believe that well-trained coders are able to make standardized observations with little bias. Detractors of the method point out that time sampling is limited to behaviors that occur often. Events that occur only once every thirty minutes, for example, are an inappropriate focus for this method. In addition, some time sampling methods yield only frequencies of behaviors without giving a sense of their context or of how the behaviors are related to each other. Only discrete segments of interactions are captured. Critics of classroom interaction analysis systems point out that such systems do not allow the researcher to study the content of what is said in classrooms. The systems tell us about the structure of interaction but not about the content or significance for teacher and children.

Event Sampling

Researchers who use event sampling focus on specified integral events as their units of analysis, and the recording of these units is not time-based. One who uses time sampling is also sampling events (social play, teacher lecture), and the observer can code predetermined categories using either method. Event sampling, however, can allow for analysis of antecedents and consequences of the phenomenon of interest.

These phenomena can be of any kind: crying, running behavior, displays of kindness, teachers' use of humor, or incidence of children's questions. The observer waits for the events to occur and describes it when it happens. The description may be in narrative form or it may be encapsulated in a checklist. An argument, for example, may be summarized by listing the names of the participants, the topic of the argument, whether or not the argument was resolved, and how long it lasted. If category systems are used to code events, they may resemble systems that are time-based, and they can be either mutually exclusive or concurrent.

Many researchers have used event sampling in educational settings. One of the numerous questions that Carew and Lightfoot (1979) asked in their study of four first grade classrooms was, "Did the teacher treat boys differently from girls when asking questions?" The event sampled was teacher's questioning, and a record was kept of whether a boy or girl responded during specified activities, such as "show and tell" or math group. McGrew (1972) analyzed the effect of changes in amount of space on frequency of running behavior in a nursery school. Another event of interest was hitting behavior. Stallings (1975) used a variety of observational instruments in her study of 136 first grade and 137 third grade Follow Through classrooms. Observers employed event sampling when they measured the frequency of occurrence of specific activities by means of a classroom check list. It included 202 categories, such as teacher without children, teacher with one child, teacher with large group, and two children with any adult.

A major advantage of event sampling over time sampling is that it can be used to study rarely occurring phenomena. For example, a child's spontaneous verbalization of a concept that he or she understands is a rare event; yet, it is of interest to educators and psychologists. Event sampling allows us to study naturally occurring units of behavior rather than discrete components. The behavior can be studied in context and relationships sought. In educational studies, teachers may act on findings to improve practice. Children's attempts to teach each other, for example, may occur only during social studies time or when a certain number of children are assembled in a given area.

A disadvantage of event-based data, as Wright (1960) points out, is the possible lack of measurement stability. If events are recorded whenever they occur, it is possible that the phenomenon is somewhat different the first time it is observed than the third time it occurs, particularly if the situation differs. In rarely occurring events in children's lives, the phenomenon does not remain stable because children change over time. Proponents of event sampling assert that the events are defined by the situation at the time of data collection; not by features of the individual being observed.

Sequential Analysis

Time sampling and event sampling are two basic methods for categorizing what we observe. They yield durations and/or frequencies of discrete events. A researcher interested in relating one discrete behavior to another or in seeing whether a behavior is contingent on a previous one may use a related, more sophisticated method, sequential analysis (Gottman & Bakeman, 1979). To analyze sequences of behavior, the observer may begin by using an electronic event recorder, for example, a Datamyte (Bakeman & Brown, 1980, p. 439), which allows the observer to record rapidly and later analyze the data by computer. Although these techniques have not been applied to the study of educational questions, analysis of behavior sequences seems especially useful for the study of caregiver–child interactions. Sequential analysis is only one of several technical methods being developed, primarily by psychologists, and the reader interested in them can refer to Cairns (1979) and Lamb, Suomi, and Stephenson (1979).

Rating Scales

Rating scales yield judgments about what Kerlinger (1973) calls remembered behavior or perceived behavior. In the study of child development, rating scales have been used almost exclusively to see how an individual child compares with a norm or to construct a profile of a child's personality traits. In educational research, scales have often been used to make judgments about teachers and their performance in the classroom (Rosenshine, 1970; Ryans, 1960). Less often, the method has been applied to physical features of educational settings. For example, an item might read, Child-made materials are on display:

        (1) Frequently——
        (2) Sometimes——
        (3) Rarely ——
        (4) Never——

There are clear weaknesses associated with this method (Kerlinger, 1973). Items appear easy to formulate so that the method is often used with little thought or planning. Observers may find the items irrelevant to the subject being rated, or their memories may fail them. More often, the observer tends to rate a subject in a single direction and exhibits a halo effect. If a teacher likes a child, he or she may rate him/her favorably on every item, or if a child is difficult, most items will be rated unfavorably. In addition, observers may have a response set and tend to respond to all items in the same way. Regardless of the individual being rated, the observer may rate consistently too low, too high, or only in the middle of the rating scale.

Researchers use rating scales often as a supplement to behavioral observations because of these advantages: they are generally easy to use and require less time to complete than other methods; they can be used in a wide range of situations; and the number of subjects' characteristics included in one instrument can be large.

Specimen Description

Specimen description could be classified as either a quantitative or a qualitative approach and provides a bridge between the two approaches. The observer's purpose is to record "everything" in sequence and unselectively. Because "everything" is the focus, this method may be difficult if the observer records in longhand. There are now electronic devices, such as audio- and videotape recorders, that allow full recording of events for later analysis. When the use of such equipment is not permitted or not feasible, the observer's shorthand is still the best method. One should be cautious to describe objectively in behavioral terms what occurs and to bracket or otherwise note interpretations and impressions about behavior.

The following is an example of a specimen record I recorded by hand in a preschool classroom. One child, Rory, is the focus of this description:

April 14: Rory (4 yr.), Terry (5 yr.), Spencer (4 yr.), Josh (4 yr.) in one area of the room. Teacher, Ms. Cramer, also present.

8:48 A.M.: Rory working with clay, pounding to flatten ball. (Tallish, looks older than four, disheveled, not enough sleep?) RORY: "Frisbee!" Ms. Cramer: "Rory, would you please sit down?" RORY: "It's kind of heavy. I'm taking a roller [rolling pin]." TERRY: "Me too."

8:50 A.M.: Rory stands up, tosses clay on table so it makes loud thud. Ms. CRAMER: "Where do we play frisbee, Rory?" RORY: "Outside." (pause) "I'm putting all the trash in here." Makes marks in clay with popsicle stick. Says, "I'm cutting a yellow piece of cake for me." Clay is yellow. Cuts round of clay in two. (Looks anxious to keep pieces for self.)

8:52 A.M.: Gives piece to Spencer, but takes it back in few seconds. Has all clay again. Leaves table. Walks over to join Josh with Bristle Blocks. Stays for several seconds. (Skittish sort.) Makes plane quickly with blocks (X-Wing Fighter?). Walks with plane over to rug area. Puts plane down. Sits next to toy castle on floor. Makes siren noises. Teacher straightening materials for kids (on my account?). Rory sitting Indian style, hums, looking closely at castle.

8:54 A.M.: Rory: "Where's the knight in this picture(?)?"

Specimen records are raw or unanalyzed data that are analyzed qualitatively or quantitatively. A qualitative analysis might yield generalizations in narrative form about the play behavior of four-year-olds in day care, or it may provide a normative "portrait" of the typical three-year-old. (Guidelines to qualitative analysis are included in later sections on Participant Observation and Child Language Studies.) Excerpts from the records themselves could be presented as evidence in either the body or the appendix of a report. For rich examples of specimen records of one- to three-year-olds at home and in day care, see Carew (1980).

The quantitative researcher might establish analytic categories to be coded in the specimen records before observation, for example, initiating interaction, social play, aggression, or on-task behavior, and may then quantify the results. Two common techniques are the use of duration scores and frequency scores. A duration score is figured when the specimen records are divided into equal time intervals. Each unit of time is coded as initiating interaction, social play, and so forth. Then the number of units coded for each category is multiplied by the unit of time, such as thirty seconds or one minute. The result, like that of time-sampling, indicates how long children were engaged in any of the designated activities. Frequency scores tell how many times children or teachers exhibited specific behaviors during the period of observation. As with event sampling, the number of times a child argued, had contact with the teacher, engaged in a nonverbal activity, and so on, can be calculated.

The specimen record can also be divided into other units with natural beginning and end points, for example, all child–child interactions or teacher-initiated conversations. Researchers may then examine those units for specified behaviors, such as asks question, attends to peer, or bids for caregiver attention.

Electronic equipment, especially videotape recorders, have made specimen description less common in educational research. Investigators who have no access to such equipment, who find it easy to write quickly in narrative form, and who prefer to work with full descriptions of behavior in context find the method useful. It is least useful for the investigation of questions that can be answered without regard to the context in which the target phenomenon occurred. Observational methods suited to the study of context are presented next.

Qualitative Approaches

Most educational researchers have until recently viewed qualitative approaches as a single vague method. The terms anthropological, sociological, ethnographic, and participant observation have sometimes been used interchangeably. This is unfortunate because the terms seem also to substitute for nonstatistical or casually done.

The terms are related but distinct. Anthropologists and sociologists may use ethnographic methods. Some anthropologists and many sociologists, however, rely primarily on statistical techniques when they do research, and ethnography is also used by linguists and researchers in a variety of disciplines. Participant observation is one of several methods used by the ethnographer; unstructured interviewing is another. Finally, casualness is not a characteristic of qualitative research. When done well, it involves all the rigor and thoughtfulness of complex quantitative studies.

Ethnography

Ethnography is an approach to research traditionally associated with cultural anthropologists and encompasses a variety of methods, one of which is observation. The term literally refers to a written account or representation (-graphy) of a people or cultural group (ethno-). According to Ogbu (1981), an ethnographic description of a school system would include "ecological settings, language and communication, social organization (including age grading, voluntary association, social stratification, etc.), economy . . . , political organization . . . , belief system, folklore, education and socialization, change, and so on" (p. 5).

An ethnographer's goal is to discover the structural or organizational features as well as the values, beliefs, and attitudes of a group. Members of the group are called informants rather than subjects. Hymes (1978) adds to this definition and states that ethnographies are systematic, comprehensive, and topic-oriented. Like other research products, they represent a discovery of knowledge. Like other research approaches, ethnography may be used by investigators in a variety of disciplines. Because the approach was developed for the study of entire cultures, however, it may be inaccurate to say that educational researchers who study schools are ethnographers.

The success of the ethnographer's work seems to depend on certain personal qualities. Ethnographers themselves (Berreman, 1968; Ogbu, 1981) have written about characteristics essential to their research. For example, they need a well-developed sense of perspective or the ability to see quickly, amid the social context they are studying, what is important and what is not in the lives of their informants. They should have empathy since an essential goal is to understand the group under study by experiencing to the extent possible what group members experience; they should be flexible about research goals and procedures; in certain situations, they should learn foreign languages or new dialects; they should be able to have reciprocal relations with their informants. The ethnographer maintains these reciprocal relations with different subgroups of informants and must deal with them in a way that will ensure access to information without alienating any subgroup. In any group or culture, there are conflicting parties, whether they are political factions, antagonistic family members, or children in a classroom who prefer to talk when the teacher wants silence. The ethnographer strives to present the views of all parties. Those who can do this kind of presentation are those who can continually take an objective stance.

Ogbu (1974; 1978) studied neighborhoods of Stockton, California. One of his questions was, "Why do a disproportionate number of minority group children fail in schools?" Rather than focus on psychological characteristics of individual teachers and children, Ogbu sought social and cultural reasons. His goal was to describe the nature of social systems outside and inside the school that might explain low achievement among blacks, Chicanos, and Filipinos.

Observations of group members' behavior on the street, with school authorities, and in the classroom formed the core of data for analysis. After doing an intensive study of the black community, Ogbu came to the following conclusions for one aspect of his research:

1. lack of trust and conflict between blacks and the schools had developed over many decades;
2. students, especially the older ones, were disillusioned about the effects of schooling and believed that doing well in school did not lead to the rewards of employment and high earnings;
3. the "survival strategies" required in the community outside the school were different from and often in conflict with the demands of schools;
4. the experience of blacks in the educational system itself, not only in the classroom but with respect to administrative policy, was different than for majority group members.

The conclusions were derived from many months of observation and participation in Stockton's black neighborhood. Events, documents, interviews, and conversation were also sources of data about the relationships among social customs and school achievement.

Other less recent ethnographic studies of schooling are those of Eddy (1967), Leacock (1969), Rosenfeld (1971), Singleton (1967), and Wolcott (1967). All of these investigators depended upon participant observation to gather their data.

Participant Observation

The ethnographer's primary means for gathering data is participant observation. This requires the researcher to live among the people being studied for an extended period of time. Ogbu (1981) believes that a year is the minimum for the researcher to gain rapport with informants. Data are based on repeated observations and participation in daily activities. Because participation is as important as observation, this method differs considerably from quantitative methods, which are often considered to be valid only if the observer does not enter into the activities of the subjects.

A description of the participant observer's procedures from "pre-field work" to data analysis is available in Bodan and Taylor (1975) and Lofland (1971). A brief summary based on Bogdan and Taylor, both sociologists, is presented here to familiarize the reader with the procedures and to illustrate basic differences between quantitative and qualitative perspectives.

A fundamental difference between the perspectives lies in the formulation of the research question(s). Quantitative researchers generally start with clearly stated, narrowly focused questions, coding categories, or hypotheses. Participant observers have general questions in mind. If they were studying early childhood education, they might ask, "How do young children's experiences at school differ from their experiences outside of school?" or "How do young children and their teachers establish unstated rules for social interaction?" Questions are general because the observer believes specific hypotheses impose preconceptions, which may hinder seeing "what is there." Some participant observers may begin data collection even before formulating general questions because they think that initial immersion in the setting guards against asking erroneous questions. Whereas quantitative researchers may do most of their conceptualization in the planning or design stage, the participant observer may wait until he or she is in the field where experiences and insights influence the specific design of the study.

Selection of the research site may happen before or after formulation of the questions. Depending on the nature of these questions, the site may be a rural village, an urban neighborhood, or an institution. Gaining entry is, of course, crucial. The participant observer attempts to establish rapport with the informants and to be honest about research purposes without affecting the behavior of informants. A nonthreatening presentation with a minimum of jargon is essential.

Data Collection

Establishing rapport requires respecting the routines of informants, and getting to know the routines takes time. The observer does not rush to gather data but instead waits until informants feel comfortable enough to converse and respond to questions freely. The procedures require developing relationships, giving as well as getting confidences from informants, and participating in everyday routines. The participant observer retains an analytic viewpoint while participating.

The observer records what has happened and what has been said in as detailed and accurate a way as possible. What is recorded is everything the observer can remember, sometimes with the aid of tape recorders or cameras. Techniques to help reconstruct events and experiences include leaving the setting as soon as the researcher has observed as much as he or she can remember, not talking to anyone until field notes are recorded, and drawing a diagram of the physical layout of the setting in order to trace his/her movements through it. Electronic equipment helps when it does not inhibit informants. Observers ordinarily do not take notes in the presence of informants. (Classrooms may be exceptional settings since teachers and children may be relatively unaffected by someone's writing.) At all times, the observer is careful to distinguish personal interpretations, observations, or feelings from descriptions of behavior. The researcher keeps a specimen record in which personal reactions are bracketed or otherwise marked. The reader may see some similarities between the participant observer and the classroom teacher, participating in ongoing events and, despite personal reactions, trying to remain objective in order to treat all children fairly. Some teachers keep anecdotal records or journals to improve their teaching or increase their ability to evaluate children objectively.

Data Analysis

Another major difference between quantitative approaches and participant observation is that in the latter, data analysis occurs simultaneously with data collection. The researcher does not wait until the completion of the field work to make interpretations or to collect additional data to support or refute patterns already seen. Unlike quantitative researchers, participant observers view the research process as a dialectic between their hypotheses, which have a changing character, and the data. New data may lead to revised hypotheses. By the end of data collection, the researcher may have developed a series of hypotheses about the "meaning" of the data. The meaning is initially arrived at by searching for "themes," important topics that underlie the main activities of the informants' lives. A researcher in classrooms might, for example, view "handling conflicts among students" or "children's questions" as significant themes.

Field notes can be duplicated and the duplicate cut up into sections to be filed in a separate folder or envelope labeled according to topic. More duplicates can be made if one section or paragraph refers to more than one topic. After studying the various sets of field notes, the researcher establishes classification schemes or categories. These categories may resemble categories that quantitative researchers have determined before data collection. For example, children in a day-care center may be called independent, sociable, or group leaders, depending on the kinds of interaction the observer has recorded. Conversations among teachers may be categorized by topic, for example, curriculum matters, discipline, nonschool topics, or procedural concerns. Participant observers are likely to use what quantitative researchers call concurrent categories; one or more categories can be assigned to a single event or description.

Interviewing

Because interviewing is not a method for observing spontaneously occuring events, it is not included here as an observational method. However, it is often used in conjunction with observation. Like specimen description, interviewing can be either a quantitative or a qualitative method. Quantitative researchers who use structured interviews often do so in the context of an extensive survey. Their respondents answer the same preset, carefully designed questions (see *Interviewer's Manual*, 1969, for guidelines to construct such interviews). Researchers who use qualitative methods, particularly participant observers and ethnographers, depend on unstructured interviews to learn about informants' viewpoints or experiences (see Bogdan & Taylor, 1975, and Lofland, 1971, for introductions to this kind of interviewing). In addition, there are educational researchers who have interviewed teachers intensively to understand their views of curriculum and of children's learning (Bagley, 1982; Bussis, Chittenden & Amarel, 1976; Carew & Lightfoot, 1979), or as an adjunct to other methods. Marshall, Weinstein, Middlestadt, and Brattesani (1980), for example, interviewed elementary school children concerning their beliefs about student achievement and "smartness." This was one of a variety of methods used. Finally, Piaget's clinical method (Piaget, 1965) is a special form of interviewing intended to reveal the nature of children's thought. Interviewers employing this method are also observers as they watch what children do.

Microethnography

Ethnographers, participant observers, and classroom researchers share an interest in patterns of child rearing and the nature of the educational system. Traditional ethnographers (for example, Whiting, 1963) observed patterns of behavior between caregivers and children because these reveal cultural beliefs and values. For several reasons, however, ethnographies based on extended periods of participant observation are uncommon in educational research. One reason is that educational researchers have traditionally been trained to use quantitative methods, so that many are unable or unwilling to do the kind of field work Ogbu describes. Another reason relates to the concerns of educators—and those who have funded their research—who ultimately wish to improve classroom practice. The traditional ethnographer seeks to understand the group or culture. Distinctions between effective or ineffective schools or teachers are not necessarily sought. There is a growing number of researchers that are not ethnographers by Ogbu's definition but that employ participant observation and also address educational concerns, such as McPherson (1972), a teacher who observed her own classroom, Sharp and Green (1975), and Smith and Keith (1971). The term microethnography has been used to refer to studies that focus on classrooms not on entire communities.

An interest in microethnography in early childhood education began in the 1960s. Researchers from a variety of fields (Baratz & Baratz, 1970; Bereiter & Engelmann, 1966; Hess & Shipman, 1968; Jensen, 1969; Labov, 1970) participated in a debate over cultural deficits versus differences. That debate led investigators, including some anthropologists, to describe what they believed were discriminatory practices in classrooms in order to improve the educational experiences of poor and minority children (for instance, Cazden, John & Hymes, 1972). As a consequence of some of these researchers' studies, the methods of microethnographers have become more and more accepted as a means for documenting what happens in schools.

Rist (1970) did a three-year study of children in a ghetto school during their kindergarten, first, and second grade years. Like some microethnographies, Rist's study is more accurately called observational because it is not based on participant observation. Handwritten notes, the main source of data, were taken twice weekly for 1 1/2-hour observation periods, and no mechanical devices were used. Rist's conclusions highlighted the importance of teacher expectations, which were based on child characteristics other than academic performance. Based on his observations and data from interviews and demographic reports, Rist concluded that the inequities in society at large are reflected in individual classrooms and that teacher expectations, not poor teaching techniques, are primarily responsible for unequal treatment of ghetto children in classrooms.

Mehan (1979) has been a consistent and clear proponent of microethnography, which for him is grounded in the sociological perspective of ethnomethodology (Garfinkel, 1967; Mehan and Wood, 1975). Ethnomethodology refers to the study of the people's or group's naturally occurring methods or rules for interacting. Investigators using this approach have taken everyday interactions as subjects of study. For example, Ryave and Schenkein (1974) analyze the rules people follow while walking down a sidewalk, and Schegloff and Sacks (1973) analyze the organization of conversations by focusing on how speakers close conversations. Looking at educational settings, researchers have investigated interactions between teachers and children and children and their peers. Because Mehan and others have focused on the analysis of classroom language to describe interactions, their approach has also been called sociolinguistic. Sociolinguists study the structure of language as it relates to features of the social contexts in which language is used.

Mehan has termed his own methods for observation constitutive ethnography to distinguish it from other studies of classroom interaction. His book, *Learning Lessons*, is an exemplar of the method and includes a discussion of the differences between constitutive ethnography, field studies (traditional ethnography), and quantitative classroom interaction studies. Mehan defines constitutive ethnography as having the following methodological characteristics:

1. Retrievability of data. Neither field studies in which investigators take handwritten notes nor classroom interaction studies that are based on time sampling leave the researcher with a permanent record of the social interactions to be analyzed. Videotape enables the reanalysis and reinterpretation of data so that the researcher or other interested parties can consider alternative interpretations of the interactions.

2. Comprehensive treatment of data. Many qualitative reports of research include a few exemplary instances to support conclusions. It is not known whether unreported events would have supported or refuted the researcher's findings. In constitutive ethnography, all data are analyzed and must be accounted for by the researcher's interpretations or explanations. In Mehan's study, the data consisted of nine videotaped lessons and transcripts of those lessons.

3. Convergence between researchers' and informants' perspectives. The informants' view of an interaction should resemble the researchers'. For

Mehan, the behavior or actions of informants support the psychological reality of the phenomena the researchers have studied.

4. Interactional level of analysis. The goal of constitutive analysis is to arrive at a small set of "recursive coding rules" that apply to all interactions. The behavior of the participants is the source of rules, not the participants' intentions or the researcher's guesses about the participants' motives or predispositions.

These four characteristics may be compared to essential features of observation as other researchers, both quantitative and qualitative, see them. Videotapes clearly provide retrievable behavior samples. Without using the term reliability, Mehan seems to suggest that repeated observations by the researcher and others lead to more accurate and consistent (reliable) analyses. Mehan deviates in spirit from both the quantitative researcher who views reliability as a critical feature and the qualitative researcher who checks his/her interpretations against their informants'.

Mehan's second point about comprehensive treatment of data contrasts with techniques such as time sampling or event sampling. Both of these methods leave many phenomena unobserved. The participant observer also misses phenomena, at least at the level at which Mehan's analysis takes place, because he or she has a broad focus and does not attempt a minute-by-minute analysis of interactions. By studying nine lessons from an academic year, Mehan may do far less than a comprehensive analysis, but his analysis of the limited body of data is extensive.

The third and fourth characteristics of constitutive ethnography are superficially shared with behavioral psychologists' studies. The actions or behaviors of informants lead the researcher to his/her conclusions, and observer influences are kept to a minimum. From some qualitative researchers' viewpoint, a weakness of Mehan's method is that despite an emphasis on convergence of the researcher's and informant's perspectives, only the researchers analyze the behavior. The informants' perspective is supposedly captured in their behavior on videotape, so that their interpretations are not solicited.

Another difficulty, related to Mehan's fourth point, is that complete avoidance of informants' intentions is impossible. Mehan uses the language of informants on videotape as the primary source of data for analysis and develops a set of categories that describe the organization of lessons. The basic unit of analysis is a three-part sequence: teacher initiation—child response—teacher evaluation. Categorizing linguistic data into such units requires some attribution of the speaker's intention, even if it is minimal.

Other researchers whose theoretical framework is similar to Mehan's have studied both verbal and nonverbal interactions in early childhood classrooms. Like Mehan, they are concerned with the social organization of classrooms because they believe that academic and intellectual development are inseparable from the social contexts in which learning occurs. The research of Bremme and Erickson (1977), McDermott (1977), and Shultz and Florio (1979) provide examples of studies of nonverbal interactions, based on highly refined analyses of videotape. McDermott, for example, analyzed "positionings," or body orientations, of participants in order to identify the focus of activities. He concluded that both teacher and children unconsciously know what a specific positioning signifies (for example, as children sit attentively and look at books they are in the position for reading). Videotapes are viewed innumerable times; movements are frozen so that researchers can analyze the intricate components of interaction.

Child Language Studies

Studies of children's spontaneous language represent a particular kind of observational research. In the pioneering studies of language acquisition (Brown, 1973; Cazden, 1968; Ervin & Miller, 1964), investigators were primarily interested in children's development of syntax. By induction, researchers arrived at possible rules by which children combined words. Because spontaneous language in a naturalistic setting—generally, the home—was believed to be the most valid source of data, early studies of language development resemble parental diary studies. The studies of Brown and his collaborators were based on audiotaped recordings, however, not on the recollection of parents. Investigators observed children as they spoke but based their analyses primarily on recordings of thousands of utterances.

Within the last ten years, there has been a shift from the analysis of syntax (form) to the analysis of language in context (form as it relates to function) and a parallel increase in the number of studies of language in the unique setting of classrooms, language used by children who have already acquired many of the forms of language. Some of the authors of these studies, like Mehan, have been interested primarily in what language can reveal about children's social competence and the social organization of classrooms. Others have looked at lessons in first grade classrooms to analyze teaching strategies or to identify points of linguistic conflict or mismatch between teacher and children (Gumperz & Herasimchuk, 1972; Piestrup, 1973).

Still other researchers have investigated children's interactions with each other. For example, Corsaro (1979) investigated a single use of language in the carefully described social contexts of a nursery school. His data, like Mehan's, were videotaped, but, unlike Mehan, Corsaro occasionally checked the convergence between researcher's and informants' viewpoints by asking children for their interpretations of events. Corsaro analyzed children's "access rituals," how they entered into interactions. His methodology was based on grounded theory (Glaser & Strauss, 1967), a sociological perspective on participant observation. Corsaro's procedures are relevant to many studies of language in social contexts (see also Corsaro, 1981). The following is an overview of his method and a summary of the process for categorizing the linguistic data.

> Data collection moved through a series of phases during the year long naturalistic study. The first phase involved unobtrusive monitoring of activities in the school from a concealed observation area, and was followed three weeks later by two months of participant observation. At that time video

equipment was introduced into the setting and for the next five months I videotaped peer interaction at least twice a week and continued participant observation on other days . . . . Overall I collected 27 hours of videotaped data which contained 146 interactive episodes [1979, p. 4].

I selected for analysis all the field notes involving access (to an interaction) and/or withdrawal and 20 of the 146 videotaped episodes. The analysis process involved taking each sequence (datum) involving access or withdrawal behavior from its original source (field notes or from transcripts of videotaped episodes) and recording them verbatim on note cards. The cards were then sorted into groups (piles) based upon initial (intuitive) recognition of similarity. After the sorting process was complete I composed analytic memos which specified what each datum in a group had in common with the others. This phase of analysis (memo writing) often led to some changes in original sorting in that some data were shifted and some groups combined. The memos were the basis of the definitions of the properties of the episode access strategy, access response, episode withdrawal strategy, and withdrawal response categories [1979, pp. 5–6].

The procedures Corsaro describes are similar to those of many qualitative researchers. The researcher develops categories after observing and recording the phenomenon of interest, whether it is children's use of language to enter interactions or teacher's organization of social studies lessons. Once categories were established and applied, Corsaro quantified the data, and he is, therefore, an example of an essentially qualitative researcher who employs some quantitative techniques. He computed frequencies and percentages for each category of access strategy and response, as well as the number of successful entries into interaction. These figures were analyzed according to age group (three-year-olds versus four-year-olds) and developmental patterns.

Many others have used methods comparable to Corsaro's to understand how children use language in early childhood settings. Some of these investigators have studied specific aspects of oral language: Cazden et al. (1979) and Cooper, Marquis, and Ayers-Lopez (1982) looked at children who teach each other. Genishi (1981) studied how bilingual children in a kindergarten and day-care center alternate between Spanish and English.

Recently, children's encounters with written language have become a focus for qualitative observational research. For example, Bussis, Chittenden, and Amarel (1978) engaged in collaborative research, with primary grade teachers as participant observers, to investigate the processes of early reading and writing. Florio et al. (1982) used a variety of methods, including participant observation, to discover the functions of writing in a second/third grade classroom. Sources of information were children, teachers, and the investigators. Dyson (1981) also used participant observation to examine how children use speech to make sense of written language. In her study, data collection took place daily over a three-month period in a kindergarten classroom, and five children were chosen as case studies. Dyson set up a writing center in which children were asked simply to write, according to their own definition of writing. She observed and interacted with the children to gain insight into their perceptions of writing and their reasoning about particular writing behaviors. Data consisted of audiotaped recordings of the children's talk at the center, written products, the investigator's notes, and interviews with the children and their parents. Findings included both analyses of children's talk while writing and hypotheses regarding each child's knowledge of the relationship between talk and writing.

Issues Related to Observation

Observational researchers, regardless of their orientation, risk being subjected to what Bakeman (1978) and others call the "tyranny of data." Bakeman points out, "A large observation project can generate as much data as a small town bank, and both must pay attention to the efficient entry, editing, storage, retrieval, and manipulation of data" (p. 75). The terminology is that of a quantitative researcher, but the problems are also common to qualitative researchers in classrooms. The increasing use of videotape recorders and computers makes data collection and analysis easier in some respects, but electronic aids may seduce researchers into gathering more data than they can analyze. Realistic planning and experience with the methods and equipment are essential to avoid being overwhelmed. Perhaps the observer's tendency to collect too many data is a reason for the lesser use of observation by social scientists.

Reliability

Realistic planning cannot resolve an issue on which observational researchers disagree: reliability, the accuracy of a measure or measuring instrument. A major point of difference between qualitative and quantitative researchers is their judgment of the observer's ability to be reliable. A participant observer takes extensive notes to form a core of data. He or she is unconcerned with reliability figures or standardized techniques for collecting data. Quantitative researchers, who seek to make predictions about future behavior, believe that the participant observer has the disadvantage of irremediably subjective methods.

Kerlinger (1973) suggests that "the major problem of behavioral observation is the observer himself" (p. 538). The observer must first notice a behavior, process it, and then make an inference about a psychological construct, such as "teacher warmth," based on what was observed. The observer's inference may be wrong because of lack of attention, unavoidable distraction or interference, observer bias, and so on. One observer may have a bias against highly structured curricula and, therefore, infer that a teacher using such a curriculum is "punitive" while others have noted that he is "nonpunitive." Yarrow and Waxler (1979) agree that observers can be undependable: "Though exceedingly practiced, the human observer, by many criteria, is a poor scientific instrument: nonstandard, not readily calibrated, and often inconsistent or unreliable" (p. 37).

Reliable measures or methods are dependable and consistent. Those who quantify their data take great care to check reliability between observers, between observations by the same observer, between measures, and between observer and an established criterion. The most common methods for establishing reliability in quantitative observational research are a coefficient of reliability and, more commonly in studies of children, the percentage of agreement. It is argued that a percentage of agreement is only that, a statement about whether observers agree with each other. Hollenbeck (1978) summarizes the view that to measure true reliability or accuracy among observers, we need to compare agreement figures with an established standard. The literature on the issue of reliability grows more technical and complex as our means for collecting and analyzing data become more technical. The reader may refer to Kerlinger (1973, ch. 26) for an overview; to Medley and Mitzel (1963) for a classic and technical presentation of the use of analysis of variance to determine reliability in classroom studies; and to Hollenbeck (1978) and Yarrow and Waxler (1979) for recent discussions from psychologists' viewpoints.

Yarrow and Waxler (1979) also note that although the human observer has failings, "counterbalancing these failings are the human capabilities of extraordinary sensitivity, flexibility and precision. The challenge is to discover how to conduct disciplined observing while making full use of the discriminations of which the human observer is capable" (p. 37). In contrast, qualitative observers tend to assume that they are capable of "disciplined observing," because only the human observer can detect the subtle meanings of behaviors.

Clearly, the quantitative and qualitative researcher are observing different phenomena for different purposes. The former researcher may code whether a child is engaged in one of twenty selected behaviors while the latter may ask how teachers view conflicts among children. Consequently, the quantitative researcher is concerned that all observers see an event in generally the same way, whereas the qualitative researcher seeks out as many perceptions and interpretations as possible, so that together they will yield a complete description of events and informants' views. Some researchers may have a colleague or assistant read their field notes as a check on their objectivity. That person may interpret events differently or detect patterns the field worker has missed. Ultimately, however, the qualitative researcher is less concerned with accurate measurement than with comprehensive description and interpretation of meaning. With all varieties of research, some observers present more objective data and more comprehensive analyses than others. Quantitative researchers have the advantage of formalized techniques to augment objectivity and reliability; but as with all varieties of research, the integrity of the investigator is a primary safeguard against unreliable or distorted data collection, analysis, and interpretation.

Validity

Closely related to reliability is the concept of validity. Findings are valid if we have measured or recorded what we say we have measured or recorded, if we have observed a segment of reality faithfully and without distortion. An advantage of the methods described in this chapter is that they are ecologically valid. That is, the researcher generally observes a naturalistic, not a laboratory or experimental, setting. Classroom processes are observed in classrooms; day-care practices are observed in centers. Observers claim the advantage of seeing unconstrained and "real" behavior.

Within the unconstrained setting, however, quantitative and qualitative researchers diverge in their ways of analyzing reality. Observers using quantitative methods believe these are valid because the researcher intrudes as little as possible while using preset instruments to code behavior. Qualitative researchers, on the other hand, often intrude and participate in the setting. Because they try to understand the experiences of their informants, they believe their methods bring them closer to reality and are, therefore, valid.

From the quantitative perspective, the obtrusiveness of the observer is a threat to validity. Researchers note that after an initial curiosity, children often ignore observers, but some subjects or informants never feel comfortable being observed, and their discomfort would change their behavior. Yarrow and Waxler (1979) sensibly suggest that researchers address the effects of observing in the report of each study.

The only way to eliminate that disadvantage is to have a truly unobtrusive observer whose research function and purposes are unknown to subjects. McPherson (1972) studied her own classroom in this way, and Webb, Campbell, Schwartz, and Sechrest (1966) present a variety of studies done surreptitiously. The difficulty with unobtrusiveness is ethical; a strict interpretation of current requirements for subjects' informed consent would prohibit such methods.

Many observational researchers believe that a single innovation, the videotape camera, makes valid observation of reality more attainable than does the unobtrusive human observer. Because researchers can observe behaviors by stopping the movement of videotape, they can do microanalyses of interaction. However, the fidelity of videotaped records and the techniques that break behavior into minute bits are open to question. A camera lens may have a broad focus, but it cannot "see" everything. A typical videotaped recording of classroom activity shows the backs of some children while others are in full frontal view and others are partly obstructed. The use of more than one camera alleviates this problem, but many cameras and technicians may be disruptive and, therefore, distorting reality. There is an additional element of distortion; the spirit or tone of an interaction may not be captured on videotape. Nuances that determine whether interactions are strained or relaxed may be lost or exaggerated when analysis is based only on the videotape or when an interaction is so segmented that its global sense is missed.

These disadvantages are tolerable because videotapes are more reliable than our memories. Before deciding to videotape a setting of interest, however, two things must be considered: first, the effect of electronic equipment on the setting and participants; and, second, whether the research question is best answered with videotaped data. Those who have had extensive experience with the medium recommend live coding (the observer codes or records in the setting of interest) before using videotape (Sackett, Ruppenthal & Gluck, 1978). The scope of some research questions may not warrant the detailed level of analysis videotape allows.

After educational researchers have used either live or electronic means to observe the settings in their studies, they may be asked how valid their findings are for educational settings in general. The issue of generalizability often arises in comparisons between qualitative and quantitative methods. In-depth qualitative studies of one classroom or of six children within one center may be said to have high internal validity. Results from a comprehensive analysis may be generalizable only to the setting or individuals under study. This is a major disadvantage when researchers wish to affect practice based on their research. Those who must consider the financial cost of research may judge qualitative studies to be too expensive and time-consuming because of their lack of external validity, the extent to which findings are applicable beyond the population studied. When policy makers take research into account, findings based on the study of large numbers of classrooms and children are likely to be more persuasive than studies of small numbers. Usually, results of quantitative research are by design generalizable to groups other than those studied, and the statistical statements of results are statements about groups not individuals.

From a perspective that is not oriented toward policy, the study based on small numbers may be externally valid. Reports of qualitative studies, particularly ethnographic and case studies, are often described as highly readable because they deal with everyday events. Stake (1978) suggests that if the reader of such a study generalizes the results to his/her own experiences, he or she has gained a better understanding of the situation described, for example, a first grade classroom. The findings are not viewed as idiosyncratic to the setting under study but are generalized to similar settings the reader has known. From the point of view of the reader, then, the study is externally valid.

The methods in this chapter have been presented in a way that emphasizes their differences, according to a sometimes artificial distinction between quantitative and qualitative approaches. The approaches are complementary and can be used appropriately and logically to study different aspects of the same general problems. Some researchers are combining methods from both approaches in the same studies, increasing the likelihood that their findings will be reliable and valid from both quantitative and qualitative perspectives.

Despite the variation among their methods, these observational researchers share some common goals: they observe to discover what occurs or whether something occurs in a particular setting, without manipulation or experimentation. They also share an interest in ongoing processes, whether these are developmental or interactive. Developmentalists often observe because children are either unable or unwilling to talk about what they do or think. Those interested in social interaction believe that what people do can differ sharply from what they say or that each participant has a unique point of view. Educators who want to know how learning occurs in classrooms realize that test scores and questionnaires are insufficient to tell us about educational processes. Regardless of the specific phenomena they seek to understand, these investigators all view observation as necessary for the accomplishment of research.

I am indebted to Christine W. Anderson, Kate Bagley, and Stuart Reifel for their valued comments on an earlier draft of this chapter.

References

ALMY, M., and GENISHI, C. *Ways of Studying Children.* Rev. ed. New York: Teachers College Press, 1979.

AMIDON, E. J., and FLANDERS, N. Interaction analysis as a feedback system. In E. J. Amidon and J. B. Hough (eds.), *Interaction Analysis: Theory, Research, and Application.* Reading, Mass.: Addison-Wesley, 1967.

BAGLEY, K. Educational ideologies and classroom orientations. Unpublished doctoral dissertation, University of California, Berkeley, 1982.

BAKEMAN, R. Untangling streams of behavior: Sequential analyses of observation data. In G. P. Sackett (ed.), *Observing Behavior,* Vol. 2. Baltimore, Md.: University Park Press, 1978.

BAKEMAN, R., and BROWN, J. V. Early interaction: Consequences for social and mental development at three years. *Child Development,* 1980, *51,* 437–447.

BARATZ, S. S., and BARATZ, J. C. Early childhood intervention: The social science base of institutional racism. *Harvard Educational Review,* 1970, *40,* 29–50.

BEREITER, C., and ENGELMANN, S. *Teaching Disadvantaged Children in the Preschool.* Englewood Cliffs, N.J.: Prentice-Hall, 1966.

BERREMAN, G. D. Ethnography: Method and product. In C. A. Clifton (ed.), *Introduction to Cultural Anthropology.* Boston, Mass.: Houghton Mifflin, 1968.

BOEHM, A. E., and WEINBERG, R. A. *The Classroom Observer: A Guide for Developing Observation Skills.* New York: Teachers College Press, 1977.

BOGDAN, R., and TAYLOR, S. J. *Introduction to Qualitative Research Methods: A Phenomenological Approach to the Social Sciences.* New York: Wiley, 1975.

BREMME, D. W., and ERICKSON, F. Relationships among verbal and nonverbal classroom behaviors. *Theory into Practice,* 1977, *16,* 153–161.

BRONFENBRENNER, U. *The Ecology of Human Development.* Cambridge, Mass.: Harvard University Press, 1979.

BROWN, R. *A First Language: The Early Stages.* Cambridge, Mass.: Harvard University Press, 1973.

BUSSIS, A. M., CHITTENDEN, E. A., and AMAREL, M. *Beyond Surface Curriculum.* Boulder, Colo.: Westview Press, 1976.

BUSSIS, A. M., CHITTENDEN, E. A., and AMAREL, M. Collaborative research. In S. Madeja (ed.), *The Teaching Process and the Arts and Aesthetics.* Third Yearbook on Research in Arts and Aesthetic Education. St. Louis, Mo.: CEMREL, 1978.

CAIRNS, R. B. (ed.) *The Analysis of Social Interactions: Methods, Issues, and Illustrations.* Hillsdale, N.J.: Lawrence Erlbaum Associates, 1979.

CAREW, J. V. Experience and the development of intelligence in young children at home and in day care. *Monographs of the Society for Research in Child Development*, 1980, *45* (6–7, Serial No. 187).

CAREW, J. V., and LIGHTFOOT, S. L. *Beyond Bias: Perspectives on Classrooms*. Cambridge, Mass.: Harvard University Press, 1979.

CAZDEN, C. B. The acquisition of noun and verb inflections. *Child Development*, 1968, *39*, 433–448.

CAZDEN, C. B., COX, M., DICKINSON, D., STEINBERG, Z., and STONE, C. "You all gonna hafta listen": Peer teaching in a primary classroom. In W. A. Collins (ed.), *Children's Language and Communication*. Hillsdale, N.J.: Lawrence Erlbaum Associates, 1979.

CAZDEN, C. B., JOHN, V. P., and HYMES, D. (eds.) *Functions of Language in the Classroom*. New York: Teachers College Press, 1972.

COHEN, D. H., and STERN, V. *Observing and Recording the Behavior of Young Children*, 2nd ed. New York: Teachers College Press, 1978.

COOPER, C. R., MARQUIS, A., and AYERS-LOPEZ, S. Peer learning in the classroom: Tracing developmental patterns and consequences of children's spontaneous interactions. In L. C. Wilkinson (ed.), *Communicating in the Classroom*. New York: Academic Press, 1982.

CORSARO, W. A. "We're friends, right?": Children's use of access rituals in a nursery school. *Language in Society*, 1979, *8*, 315–336.

CORSARO, W. A. Entering the child's world: Research strategies for field entry and data collection in a preschool setting. In J. Green and C. Wallat (eds.), *Ethnography and Language in Educational Settings*. Norwood, N.J.: Ablex, 1981.

DENHAM, C., and LIEBERMAN, A. *Time to Learn: A Review of the Beginning Teacher Evaluation Study*. Washington, D.C.: National Institute of Education, 1980.

DYSON, A. H. A case study examination of the role of oral language in the writing processes of kindergartners. Unpublished doctoral dissertation, University of Texas at Austin, 1981.

EDDY, E. M. *Walk the White Line: A Profile of Urban Education*. New York: Doubleday, 1967.

EISNER, E. W. On the differences between scientific and artistic approaches to qualitative research. *Educational Researcher*, 1981, *10*, 5–9.

ERICKSON, F. Some approaches to inquiry in school-community ethnography. *Anthropology and Education Quarterly*, 1977, *8*, 58–69.

ERVIN, S. M., and MILLER, W. The development of grammar in child language. In U. Bellugi and R. Brown (eds.), The acquisition of language. *Monographs of the Society for Research in Child Development*, 1964, *29*, (1, Serial No. 92).

FILBY, N., and MARLIAVE, R. S. Descriptions of distributions of A.L.T. within and across classes during the A-B period. Technical note IV-la. In *Beginning Teacher Evaluation Study*. San Francisco, Calif.: Far West Regional Laboratory, 1977.

FLORIO, S., and THE WRITTEN LITERACY STUDY STAFF. What is writing for?: Writing in the first weeks of school in a second/third grade classroom. In L. C. Wilkinson (ed.), *Communicating in the Classroom*. New York: Academic Press, 1982.

GARFINKEL, H. *Studies in Ethnomethodology*. Englewood Cliffs, N.J.: Prentice-Hall, 1967.

GEERTZ, C. From the native's point of view: On the nature of anthropological understanding. In P. Rabinow and W. M. Sullivan (eds.), *Interpretive Social Science: A Reader*. Berkeley: University of California Press, 1979.

GENISHI, C. Code-switching in Chicano 6-year-olds. In R. Duran (ed.), *Latino Language and Communicative Behavior*. Norwood, N.J.: Ablex, 1981.

GIBSON, E. J. Perceptual learning and the theory of word perception. *Cognitive Psychology*, 1971, 2, 351–368.

GLASER, B. G., and STRAUSS, A. L. *The Discovery of Grounded Theory*. Chicago: Aldine, 1967.

GOTTMAN, J. M., and BAKEMAN, R. The sequential analysis of observational data. In M. E. Lamb, S. J. Suomi, and G. R. Stephenson, *Social Interaction Analysis: Methodological Issues*. Madison: University of Wisconsin Press, 1979.

GREEN, J., and WALLAT, C. (eds.). *Ethnography and Language in Educational Settings*. Norwood, N.J.: Ablex, 1981.

GUMPERZ, J. J., and HERASIMCHUK, E. The conversational analysis of social meaning: A study of classroom interaction. In R. W. Shuy (ed.), *Sociolinguistics: Current Trends and Prospects*. Twenty-third Annual Round Table. Washington, D.C.: Georgetown University Press, 1972.

HESS, R. D., and SHIPMAN, V. C. Maternal influences upon early learning: The cognitive environments of urban preschool children. In R. D. Hess and R. M. Bear (eds.), *Early Education: Current Theory, Research, and Practice*. Chicago: Aldine, 1968.

HOLLENBECK, A. R. Problems of reliability in observational research. In G. P. Sackett (ed.), *Observing Behavior*, Vol. 2. Baltimore, Md.: University Park Press, 1978.

HYMES, D. What is ethnography? *Sociolinguistic Working Paper*, No. 45. Austin, Texas: Southwest Educational Development Laboratory, 1978.

Interviewer's Manual, Survey Research Center. Ann Arbor: Institute for Social Research, University of Michigan, 1969.

IRWIN, D. M., and BUSHNELL, M. M. *Observational Strategies for Child Study*. New York: Holt, Rinehart & Winston, 1980.

JENSEN, A. R. How much can we boost IQ and scholastic achievement? *Harvard Educational Review*, 1969, 39, 1–123.

JUEL, C. Comparison of word identification strategies with varying context, word type, and reader skill. *Reading Research Quarterly*, 1980, 15, 358–376.

KERLINGER, F. N. *Foundations of Behavioral Research*, 2nd ed. New York: Holt, Rinehart & Winston, 1973.

LABOV, W. The logic of nonstandard English. In F. Williams (ed.), *Language and Poverty*. Chicago: Markam Publishing, 1970.

LAMB, M. E., SUOMI, S. J., and STEPHENSON, G. R. (eds.). *Social Interaction Analysis: Methodological Issues*. Madison: University of Wisconsin Press, 1979.

LEACOCK, E. B. *Teaching and Learning in City Schools: A Comparative Study*. New York: Basic Books, 1969.

LOFLAND, J. *Analyzing Social Settings*. Belmont, Calif.: Wadsworth, 1971.

McDERMOTT, R. The ethnography of speaking and reading. In R. Shuy (ed.), *Linguistic Theory: What Can It Say about Reading?* Newark, Del.: International Reading Association, 1977.

McGREW, W. C. *An Ethological Study of Children's Behavior*. New York: Academic Press, 1972.

McPherson, G. H. *Small Town Teacher*. Cambridge, Mass.: Harvard University Press, 1972.

Magoon, A. J. Constructivist approaches in educational research. *Review of Educational Research*, 1977, *4*, 651–693.

Marshall, H. H., Weinstein, R. S., Middlestadt, S. E., and Brattesani, K. A. "Everyone's smart in our class": Relationships between classroom characteristics and perceived differential teacher treatment. Berkeley: University of California, 1980 (ERIC Document Reproduction Service No. ED 186 404).

Medley, D. M., and Mitzel, H. E. The scientific study of teacher behavior. In A. A. Bellack (ed.), *Theory and Research in Teaching*. New York: Bureau of Publications, Teachers College, Columbia University, 1963.

Mehan, H. *Learning Lessons: Social Organization in the Classroom*. Cambridge, Mass.: Harvard University Press, 1979.

Mehan, H., and Wood, H. *The Reality of Ethnomethodology*. New York: Wiley, 1975.

Miller, L. B., and Dyer, J. L. Four preschool programs: Their dimensions and effects. *Monographs of the Society for Research in Child Development*, 1975, *40* (5–6, Serial No. 162).

Ogbu, J. U. *The Next Generation: An Ethnography of Education in an Urban Neighborhood*. New York: Academic Press, 1974.

Ogbu, J. U. *Minority Education and Caste: The American System in Cross-Cultural Perspective*. New York: Academic Press, 1978.

Ogbu, J. U. School ethnography: A multilevel approach. *Anthropology and Education Quarterly*, 1981, *12*, 3–29.

Piaget, J. *The Child's Conception of the World*. Totowa, N.J.: Littlefield, Adams, 1965.

Piestrup, A. M. Black dialect interference and accommodation of reading instruction in first grade. *Monographs of the Language—Behavior Research Laboratory*, No. 4. Berkeley: University of California, 1973.

Rist, R. C. Student social class and teacher expectations: The self-fulfilling prophecy in ghetto education. *Harvard Educational Review*, 1970, *40*, 279–300.

Rist, R. C. On the relations among educational research paradigms: From disdain to detente. *Anthropology and Education Quarterly*, 1977, *8*, 42–48.

Rosenfeld, G. *Shut Those Thick Lips*. New York: Holt, Rinehart & Winston, 1971.

Rosenshine, B. Evaluation of classroom instruction. *Review of Educational Research*, 1970, *40*, 279–300.

Rubin, K. H., Watson, K. S., and Jambor, T. W. Free-play behaviors in preschool and kindergarten children. *Child Development*, 1978, *49*, 534–536.

Ryans, D. G. *Characteristics of Teachers: Their Description, Comparison, and Appraisal*. Washington, D.C.: American Council on Education, 1960.

Ryave, A. L., and Schenkein, J. N. Notes on the art of walking. In R. Turner (ed.), *Ethnomethodology*. Baltimore, Md.: Penguin, 1974.

Sackett, G. P., Ruppenthal, G. C., and Gluck, J. Introduction: An overview of methodological and statistical problems in observational research. In G. P. Sackett (ed.), *Observing Behavior*, Vol. 2. Baltimore, Md.: University Park Press, 1978.

Schegloff, E., and Sacks, H. Opening up closings. In R. Turner (ed.), *Ethnomethodology*. Baltimore, Md.: Penguin, 1974.

Schwartzman, H. B. Children's play: A sideways glance at make-believe. In D. F. Laney and B. A. Tindall (eds.), *The Anthropological Study of Play: Problems and Prospects*. Cornwall, N.Y.: Leisure Press, 1976.

SHARP, R., and GREEN, A. *Education and Social Control: A Study in Progressive Primary Education*. London: Routledge and Kegan Paul, 1975.

SHULTZ, J., and FLORIO, S. Stop and freeze: The negotiation of social and physical space in a kindergarten/first grade classroom. *Anthropology and Education Quarterly*, 1979, *10*, 166–181.

SIMON, A., and BOYER, G. *Mirror for Behavior*, Vols. 1–14, with supplements. Philadelphia, Pa.: Research for Better Schools, 1967–1970.

SINGLETON, J. *Nichu: A Japanese School*. New York: Holt, Rinehart & Winston, 1967.

SMITH, L. M. An evolving logic of participant observation, educational ethnography and other case studies. In L. S. Shulman (ed.), *Review of Research in Education*, Vol. 6. Itasca, Ill.: F. E. Peacock, 1978.

SMITH, L. M., and KEITH, P. *Anatomy of an Educational Innovation*. New York: Wiley, 1971.

STAKE, R. E. The case study method in social inquiry. *Educational Researcher*, 1978, *7*, 5–8.

STALLINGS, J. Implementation and child effects of teaching practices in Follow Through classrooms. *Monographs of the Society for Research in Child Development*, 1975, *40* (7–8, Serial No. 163).

STALLINGS, J. *Learning to Look: A Handbook on Classroom Observation and Teaching Models*. Belmont, Calif.: Wadsworth, 1977.

TIKUNOFF, B., BERLINER, D. C., and RIST, R. *An Ethnographic Study of the 40 Classrooms of the Beginning Teacher Evaluation Study Known Sample*. San Francisco: Far West Laboratory for Educational Research and Development, 1975.

TIKUNOFF, W. J., and WARD, B. A. (eds.). Exploring qualitative/quantitative research methodologies in education. *Anthropology and Education Quarterly*, 1977, *8*(2), special issue.

VENEZKY, R. L., and WINFIELD, L. F. Schools that succeed beyond expectations in teaching reading. Paper presented at the annual meeting of the American Educational Research Association, Boston, Mass., April 1980.

WEBB, E. J., CAMPBELL, D. T., SCHWARTZ, R. D., and SECHREST, L. *Unobtrusive Measures: Nonreactive Research in the Social Sciences*. Chicago: Rand McNally, 1966.

WHITING, B. B. (ed.). *Six Cultures: Studies of Child Rearing*. New York: Wiley, 1963.

WILKINSON, L. C., and CALCULATOR, S. Effective and appropriate use of requests in the classroom. In L. C. Wilkinson (ed.), *Communicating in the Classroom*. New York: Academic Press, 1982.

WILSON, T. P. Normative and interpretive paradigms in sociology. In J. Douglas (ed.), *Understanding Everyday Life*. Chicago: Aldine, 1970.

WOLCOTT, H. F. *A Kwakiutl Village and School*. New York: Holt, Rinehart & Winston, 1967.

WRIGHT, H. F. Observational child study. In P. H. Mussen (ed.), *Handbook of Research Methods in Child Development*. New York: Wiley, 1960.

YARROW, M. R., and WAXLER, C. Z. Observing interaction: A confrontation with methodology. In R. B. Cairns (ed.), *The Analysis of Social Interactions*. Hillsdale, N.J.: Lawrence Erlbaum Associates, 1979.

CHAPTER 23

Measurement of Classroom Process

Robert S. Soar
Ruth M. Soar

ALTHOUGH THIS CHAPTER is primarily concerned with measurement of behavior in classrooms, the principles and procedures are applicable to the observational measurement of any behavior. In fact, some of the observation systems have been used in studies of parents with infants, studies in preschools, and, in one instance, with disturbed children on a raft trip down a river.

We will first describe early attempts at measurement of classroom behavior since their failures have implications for more successful procedures. The nature of different kinds of observational procedures will be examined, examples will be presented, and the advantages and disadvantages of each type will be discussed. Since the more recent observational systems typically collect data using relatively narrow items, we will discuss procedures for combining these bits of behavior into composites or measures as well as problems in estimating the reliability of these measures.

A problem that is receiving more and more attention is that of the appropriate unit of analysis—the individual pupil, the classroom, or some larger unit. The results of the study may differ, depending on which level is employed, and there are both methodological arguments and empirical findings which bear on the question.

Finally, we will examine statistical procedures for analyzing relationships between process measures and outcomes. The available methodology has advanced rapidly in recent years, and practice lags.

Development of Classroom Measurement

The Early Studies of Teaching

Early studies of teaching were not very productive, and in retrospect some of the reasons seem clear. For example, a study might have asked whether teacher IQ was related to effective teaching. IQ would have been measured by a standard test of intelligence, but effectiveness of teaching might have been measured by ratings made by supervisors. These ratings seem to have had several problems. It was not clear whether effectiveness referred to skills or competencies that the teacher showed in the classroom or to outcomes which the rater believed had been demonstrated by pupils. If it had to do with teacher skills, it left open to the rater what specific behaviors should be considered.

Even if ratings were not involved, and pupil outcomes were measured (and numbers of studies did relate teacher characteristics such as IQ or degrees held with pupil outcomes), no knowledge was gained about effective classroom practice because the study bypassed what went on in the classroom.

The Presage–Process–Product Model

A major step in the clarification in thinking about classroom studies was made by Mitzel's (1960) presentation of the presage–process–product model. Presage characteristics were defined as characteristics of the teacher which could be measured before the teacher entered the classroom: IQ, degree status, graduate hours in education, years of experience, measures of personality, or marital status. As Mitzel commented, these were admittedly weak as measures of effectiveness, but they were in wide use for hiring and promotion. Process measures were measures of what happened in the classroom: the organization, the atmosphere, the interaction of teachers and pupils. Product measures were pupil outcomes—consequences of the time spent in the classroom.

This model led to a clarification of the focus of measurement and has been widely used as a way of describing studies. Following this scheme there are presage–process studies (relations between characteristics of the teacher and classroom behavior), presage–product studies (relations between teacher characteristics and pupil outcomes), and process–product studies (relations between classroom behaviors and pupil outcomes).

Emergence of Behavioral Classroom Measures

It seems appropriate to identify the beginning of the current era of classroom process measurement with the Observation Schedule and Record (Medley and Mitzel, 1958) and Flanders Interaction Analysis (Flanders, 1960). Most observation systems since then have followed the procedures set by one or the other of these. The major advance in both systems was the identification of specific behaviors, defined with sufficient care that observers would agree relatively well in coding and that those reading their results would know what behaviors were represented in the measures.

The Nature of Classroom Process Measures

Although the distinction is not always clear and there is some overlap in the kinds of measures to which the terms are applied, measures are usefully classified as being of high or low inference. (As we use the word measure, it includes ratings, items, and composites of items).

High-Inference Measures

High-inference measures, which are recorded on the basis of observation, are abstracted or inferred from the behavior but do not record the behavior itself. An example would be the typical five-point rating scale on which the rater describes the effectiveness of a teacher on a scale running from something like hopeless to fantastic. As Medley and Mitzel (1963) suggest, several observers who enter the same classroom at the same time may see different things. Differing interests and value orientations will guarantee this. If, for example, one rater values order and discipline, another values an accepting climate and pupil independence, and a third is primarily concerned with how the teacher presents subject matter, the behaviors which each will notice and remember from the same classroom are likely to be quite different. The anecdote about the six blind men who "saw" an elephant for the first time and their differing reports seems an apt analogy.

   In addition to noticing and remembering the variety of behaviors that occur in any period of observation, the observer must assemble these events into some sort of overall impression—he must sum them in some way. As different observers do this, they are likely to weight the same behaviors differently. For example, if a pupil gets up, crosses the room to get material, and returns to his seat without asking permission, the first two observers would probably use this item of behavior in their overall picture of the classroom, but the third might ignore it if the behavior had nothing to do with the development of subject matter. The first two observers would probably evaluate this item of behavior (the pupil getting materials) differently—one seeing it positively as constructive pupil freedom; the other negatively as a lack of orderly procedure. Of course, since the third observer ignored it, he would not evaluate it. Finally, each would compare his composite picture of this classroom with his conception of the ideal classroom, and arrive at a rating.

   The key issue is that what is recorded is the observer's evaluation of what she has seen. However, the behaviors observed, the weights given to specific behaviors in forming a composite, and the reference standard against which the composite of behavior is compared, all remain internal to the rater and inaccessible to others.

Low-Inference Measures

In this case, specific behaviors are defined with such care that observers will agree on whether they have occurred or not. For example, if a teacher asks a question, gives a direction, hugs a child, or scolds, an item would be checked. The process of observation, then, is one of recording the observed behaviors, but it goes no further than that. The complete observation is simply a record of behaviors that occurred in the classroom during the observation period. Later, the individual items of behavior may be combined into composites following a scoring scheme similar to that for a standardized test or a personality or attitude measure, and this is done by a clerk or a computer rather than by the observer. These composites can then be compared against norms describing a set of teachers, or minimum standards can be employed, and this process, too, is external to the observer. Notice that in contrast to high-inference measures, all of the steps following the initial observation of the behavior are publicly observable and external to the rater. In fact, it is not infrequent that a set of items will be rescored in later research by a different set of keys, a different weighting system.

The terms high and low inference, although described as separate categories, actually are likely to be the ends of a scale of relative abstraction level. For example, asking an observer to rate the competence of a teacher would be at a high-inference level, since the rating provides no indication of the behavior that entered the rating. At an intermediate level of inference, the observer might be asked whether the teacher was warm or enthusiastic, and the range of behaviors would be considerably narrowed. Items such as "asks question," "directs," "scolds" would be of low inference, since specific behaviors are cited. Because of the specificity of the low-inference items, their use in research has increased.

Examples of Low-Inference Observation Systems

Category Systems

Category systems code ongoing behavior into one of a small number of categories as it occurs. The categories are all-inclusive and mutually exclusive—every behavior in the domain being recorded (for example, verbal behavior) is coded into the most appropriate category.

FLANDERS INTERACTION ANALYSIS

An early category system that has exerted a major influence on classroom process research is Flanders Interaction Analysis (Flanders, 1960, 1970). In it, all verbal behavior is coded into one of ten categories: seven for teacher talk, two for pupil talk, and the tenth, a miscellaneous category for silence and confusion. Four of the teacher categories are termed indirect influence in that they tend to support and expand freedom for pupils; three are termed direct influence in that they tend to direct pupils, to restrict freedom, or to convey a negative affective tone.

In the use of the system, an observer writes, at least every three seconds, the number of the category that best describes the verbal behavior at that moment, but if it changes within the three seconds a new category is recorded.

The data of the Flanders system are then tabulated into a two-way table (a matrix) whose rows and columns are the category numbers. The tabulating is done in such a way that each cell represents both the presently occurring behavior and the behavior which immediately preceded it. Although this procedure is not a necessary part of category systems, it retains a one-step sequence of behavior. As a consequence, one hundred sequences of behavior can be identified although the observer had to learn only ten categories. For example, a buildup of frequencies representing teacher question followed by pupil response (one sequence) and pupil response followed by teacher question (another sequence) would represent a drill session. Frequent teacher criticism followed by teacher directions and the reverse would indicate management problems.

The central distinction is between teacher direct influence and indirect influence, by which the teacher's directing the activities in the classroom is contrasted with the teacher's playing a responsive role, accepting or using affect or ideas expressed by pupils. Even though the teacher plays this responsive role, he or she is still able to exert influence through the choice of the pupil statement that is supported. To some degree, substantive focus can be distinguished from affect expression and management, although the distinction is neither clear nor complete.

An Extension of Flanders

The Reciprocal Categories System or RCS (Ober, Bentley & Miller, 1971) extends the Flanders system in two ways. It adds two categories that make additional discriminations among teacher behaviors and extends all the categories to pupils by coding a leading "1" instead of a leading "0". That is, if the teacher expands a pupil idea, it is coded 03, but if a pupil expands someone else's idea (either teacher or pupil), that would be coded 13. As a consequence, the observer still learns only ten categories (plus the teacher–pupil distinction), but 400 sequences are possible, half of which represent pupil behavior.

The RCS has been adapted for use with parents and infants by Gordon and Jester (1972). In it, the nine categories are coded for infants, mothers, and fathers by using 0, 1, or 2 as the leading digits.

Observation Schedule and Record, Form 5, Verbal (OScAR5v)

This is the current revision (Medley, n.d.) of an instrument which has a history beginning in 1958. Without question, the several forms of OScAR and the Flanders system have been the two instruments used by more classroom researchers than any others.

The current revision of OScAR differs sharply from the original. It uses eighteen categories—four for pupil utterances and fourteen for teacher utterances. Since six of the teacher categories are dual-purpose, however, there are in effect twenty for teacher behaviors. The instrument provides for recording interactions by pairs of items that record either pupil utterance and teacher response or teacher question or initiation and the teacher's reaction to the pupil's response.

An interchange is defined differently here than an interaction in the Flanders system. Whereas the Flanders system would code a teacher question and pupil response as an interaction, and the pupil response and teacher reaction as another interaction, OScAR would omit the pupil response and define the interchange as beginning (entry) and ending (exit) with teacher behavior, thus defining a larger sequence.

The fact that both entry to and exit from the interchange may be coded by a number of items means that the number of combinations is large. Although the primary focus of the instrument is substantive, it also records social-emotional behavior and management.

Another version of the instrument has been developed particularly for early school experience (Personal Record of School Experience—PROSE; Medley, Schluck & Ames, 1973).

Sign Systems

In a sign system, a set of specific behaviors is identified and an item is coded if it occurs during a standard observation period, but each behavior is coded only once and neither the frequency nor the sequence of behaviors is recorded. As a consequence of these two changes, it is possible for the coder to use a much larger number of items.

FLORIDA CLIMATE AND CONTROL SYSTEM (FLACCS)

In the use of this 167-item instrument (Soar, Soar & Rogosta, 1971), a coder observes for a standard period of time—two to five minutes—and then scans each column of items, checking those which occurred and leaving blank those which did not.

One side of the instrument reflects classroom management. The first part represents the kinds of groupings that occur. Attention given to pupils and teacher verbal and nonverbal interventions to modify the behavior of pupils are scaled for degree of coerciveness. The second part records pupil behavior: behavior in response to teacher intervention, behavior that takes responsibility for management, and other ongoing pupil behaviors. The second side of the instrument reflects expression of affect, both verbal and nonverbal, positive and negative, teacher and pupil. The instrument distinguishes between affect used in service of control and that which is affect alone.

FLACCS codes only teacher direction of pupil behavior, as distinguished from purely cognitive activity. This distinction was initially made to eliminate overlap with another instrument which coded cognitive activity, but the results indicate that the distinction between management of behavior and development of cognitive activities is an important one (Soar & Soar, 1979).

CLASSROOM OBSERVATIONS KEYED FOR EFFECTIVENESS RESEARCH

This instrument (Coker & Coker, 1979) is a drawing together of the most discriminating items from five widely used observation systems. The major innovation is a procedure for coding sequence in a sign system, which draws heavily on Medley's OScAR at his suggestion and with his close involvement.

The first part is a matrix whose columns are student behaviors (ten items) reflecting a variety of on-task and off-task behaviors and whose rows are teacher behaviors (twenty-seven items) broken down into presenting, questioning, and responding. An interaction in which the teacher presents or questions and a pupil behavior follows is coded row-column; a pupil behavior to which the teacher responds is coded column-row; and each kind of sequence appears in a different section of the matrix.

This matrix permits coding 270 sequences of behavior in compact form, but each sequence is coded only once in a observation period, as is typical of sign coding, so that it is possible for a coder to manage a large number of items. These are coded as classroom interaction occurs. Next, in a second observation period, the observer codes additional items of behavior which are conventional sign items representing teacher management of behavior, learning activities, groupings, and ongoing pupil behavior.

Since this instrument consolidates five others into one, no single aspect of the classroom which was represented on an earlier instrument is as well represented here, but reliabilities in general are not far behind those obtained from the original instruments (Soar & Dixon, 1979), and it is clear that broader coverage is possible with it than with any one of the originals.

Point-Time Sample

This procedure, also called a time sample, is somewhat different from the previous ones. A number of items describing specific behaviors would be developed, but the procedure for collecting data is different. The observer, at regular intervals or at a prescheduled signal, notes the behavior of an individual child or a group and checks off all the items that describe what was occurring at the moment of the signal. An example of a current instrument is the Classroom Checklist (Stallings, 1977). In it, the classroom as a whole is observed, and the adults and the numbers of children engaged in each of a variety of activities are coded. Her term "snapshot" seems very appropriate.

Multiple Coding

In a sense, this observational procedure is an extension of a category system; it could also be thought of as a fusion of a category system and a time sample. In this procedure, a bit of behavior or an occurrence is described by two or more sets of items which record different aspects of it. Flanders (1970) describes some of the added categories which have been used with his system, and a current version of such an instrument which has been used in large-scale data collection is another observational instrument developed by Stallings (1977). In it, each interaction is described by one item from each of four sets: who, to whom, what, and how. The who and to whom items include the teacher, aide, volunteer, child, and various group sizes of children. The what describes whether the interaction was a command or request, open-ended question, response, instruction or explanation, acknowledgment, praise, corrective feedback, and "others." The how describes the affective tone of the interaction, and/or its management function. Items include happy, unhappy, negative, touch, punish, and "others." A final (fifth) code describes whether the interaction was academic in nature or directed at the behavior of pupils.

A Comparison of System Types

Each type of system offers advantages and disadvantages. The major advantage of the category system is that it can preserve a one-step sequence of events. It is possible, for example, to examine the teacher's characteristic mode of responding to pupil behavior in interaction. It seems reasonable, and there is some evidence, that those teacher behaviors that are immediately responsive to pupils are more influential than other behaviors.

On the other hand, items for a category system must be relatively small in number to enable a coder to record with sufficient rapidity to capture all of the ongoing stream of behavior as it occurs. This means, in turn, that each of the items must describe a relatively broad range of behavior. For example, Flanders Category 6, which represents teacher direction giving, includes all classes of directions, substantive and behavioral, gentle, routine, and even those which are given relatively firmly, so long as they do not involve elements of criticism. On the other hand, FLACCS uses twenty items to make differentiations among the kinds of verbal directions given by teachers to reflect the degree of coerciveness involved and whether reasons are given as part of the directions. It seems reasonable, and again there is some evidence, that direction giving that is relatively unobtrusive or routine probably reflects a classroom that is running more smoothly than a classroom in which harsher directions are given. Therefore, the sign system is capable of identifying shadings of meaning or nuances which cannot be distinguished by the small number of items which can be used in category recording. The other side of the coin, of course, is that the sign system offers no way of knowing what event preceded what or which behaviors occurred together in a given incident. For example, when teacher criticism is coded there is no way of knowing what pupil behavior evoked that criticism.

Multiple coding has another set of advantages and disadvantages. An incident is described in a variety of ways, but either the categories must be very broad and few in number or, if they are more numerous, more time will be required by the observer to record an event, and several additional events may occur before the observer is able to observe again. The basic tradeoff appears to be that of collecting more complete information about individual interactions versus that of preserving a one-step sequence of events.

The interaction matrix of Classroom Observations Keyed for Effectiveness Research appears to be another example of a tradeoff. Although it defines a given sequence in some detail, in rapid-fire interactions not all interactions can be coded. It seems possible, however, that the loss of information may not be so great as when a small number of items broad in nature are used. The types of sequences occurring most frequently in a classroom are likely to be recorded, so that perhaps the only loss will be the relatively infrequent sequence. But even then, if observation is carried out over a number of periods, infrequent events are likely to appear in the record. This new instrument appears to be a promising compromise between recording sequence, as category systems do, and collecting more detailed information about each event, as sign systems do.

Other Systems

Hundreds of observation instruments have been developed. The most extensive collection of such instruments, with annotations, is the series of volumes by Simon and Boyer (1967–1970), with another collection reviewing observation instruments for use with younger children (Boyer, Simon & Karafin, 1973).

Observing in the Classroom

The Role of the Observer

The role of the observer will depend on the type of observation system used. With a rating scale, the observer is frequently also an evaluator. But in systematic observation he is ideally not an evaluator but only a recorder. Medley and Mitzel (1963) commented that to the extent that an observation instrument requires judgment on the part of an observer, it is a poor instrument. Observation does require judgment on the part of the observer, but the judgment should be whether a particular behavior fits an item on the instrument. Evaluation of the behavior—a judgment as to whether it is desirable or not—is very explicitly not part of the task.

The observer should abstain as much as possible from involvement in classroom activities to avoid contaminating the data he is there to collect. He or she should avoid interaction and eye contact with pupils. When pupils come to ask what the observer is doing, a short answer such as "I'm here to watch the way you work" will usually be sufficient. It is highly desirable to meet the teacher before beginning observation to set him/her at ease insofar as possible.

The way the observer moves around in the classroom is important. He will need to take his cues from the way the classroom is conducted. If there is considerable movement and activity, he can probably move, too. But if pupils are in rows, the observer should take a seat at the side of the room where he can see and hear both pupils and teacher, and not move about.

The Effect of the Observer

Does the presence of the observer change the nature of the classroom? To some degree, it seems likely that classroom observation is another example of the indeterminacy principle—that the very fact of measuring changes what is being measured. The conventional wisdom is that the presence of the observer makes little difference if the classroom has had time to adapt to his presence. It seems clear that this will vary with the age or grade levels of the pupils and from teacher to teacher. A common experience in the primary grades is that if the observer does not interact with pupils he very soon ceases to exist for them and they go about their activities naturally. However, most of the evidence on which this conclusion is based is anecdotal. An observer in an intermediate grade classroom had observed for a period of time when the teacher left the room. The pupils posted a monitor so they would know when the teacher was returning, and the spitballs and paper airplanes flew. When the teacher returned, the monitor warned the group and pupils were back in their seats working decorously when the teacher entered. The observer had been present and had been ignored during the incident.

We have frequently tape-recorded conversations of primary grade pupils virtually elbow to elbow with them. When they looked up, if we could be seen watching something in the far corner of the room, they would go back to their activities. The conversations we recorded suggested that the pupils assumed that we were paying no attention to them and that they, as a consequence, paid no attention to us.

It is clear that the presence of the observer continues to be more troublesome for teachers. Even with observations at different hours of the day and different days of the week, the same subject matter has appeared with surprising frequency in some classrooms. Some teachers give indications of distress even after several observations; others appear comfortable from the very beginning.

The best study on this question is that of Samph (1968), who collected observation data from teachers when they were both aware and unaware of being observed. The differences were minor. Teachers who knew they were being observed were somewhat more warm and somewhat more indirect (as indicated by the Flanders system), but the changes were on the order of a quarter or a third of a standard deviation. Other measures did not change significantly.

Beyond this evidence, observation studies often collect data on hundreds of items of behavior, and it seems improbable that teachers change a very great proportion of the observed behaviors in response to the presence of the observer.

In summary, the only evidence, and the most reasonable assumption, appears to be that during observation teachers may be warmer to students and perhaps give more freedom, but the changes are neither very great nor very extensive.

Procedures for Combining Items into Measures

Although most observation studies have related individual items to the outcome measures, this does not seem to be desirable. There may be several hundred items to be correlated with each of several outcomes, and if the relations are calculated separately for different classroom activities (for example, teaching reading versus math versus managing behavior) the number of relationships can reach the thousands—and has done so in some studies. At the 5 percent level, one out of every twenty significant correlations will be a chance relationship. The problem of interpreting the large numbers of significant relations is likely to lead to selective emphases based on agreement with the expectations or interests of the investigator. Biased discussion seems very likely under these circumstances, and few readers will go back to the basic correlation tables.

In addition, individual items are likely to be redundant to some degree and less reliable than measures created by pooling items. The question is on what basis the pooling should be done, and there are several possibilities.

Whether or however items are pooled, an important first step will be to transform the item scores so as to make their distributions normal and equally variable. Observational data are frequently grossly nonnormal, which may distort correlations, and are likely to have widely different variabilities, which will result in quite different weights when items are pooled.

Rational Composites

Often, an instrument itself implies rational groupings of items. For example, the Flanders system, in its contrast of indirect and direct teacher behavior, suggests combining the indirect items and the direct items. FLACCS, by its use of degrees of coerciveness in teacher management behavior and of expression of affect, implies ways of pooling items. To the extent that an instrument is developed on a rational basis, such groupings of items seem to be a reasonable way initially to represent the rationale on which the instrument was constructed.

Alternatively, items may be grouped rationally on some basis other than the instrument rationale, or it may be that the instrument is an eclectic one which does not have a rationale. Or, composites may combine items across instruments of quite different theoretical orientations; an example is reported in Soar (1973).

Once individual items have been coded in classrooms, different scoring schemes can be used later if research or a changing theory suggests that a different scoring scheme would be useful. The present concern for teacher competencies suggests that competencies might be scored using instruments originally developed with quite different orientations.

Whatever the pooling procedure, it is important that the internal consistency of the composites be verified statistically by item analysis. However reasonable a rational system may seem, it is surprising how often one or more items will be unrelated to the composite. Our understanding, our theory, is apparently too limited to be dependable. Evidence for this will be reported in a later section.

Empirical Composites

Another approach is to group the items on the basis of their intercorrelations, without theory or rationale. Factor analysis and cluster analysis are procedures for doing this. Factor analysis will create dimensions in such a way as to maximize the relationships between items within dimensions and simultaneously minimize relationships between dimensions. Dimensions (factors) group items in such a way as to retain as much of the variance of the original items in as few dimensions as possible. That is, there is internal consistency within dimensions and independence across dimensions. Each subject (teacher, classroom, family, infant) is then given a score (a factor score) for each dimension, based on performance on the items that entered the factor.

There are advantages and disadvantages to this procedure. A major disadvantage is that factor analysis is a least squares procedure and will "overfit error." That is, it will capitalize on idiosyncratic variation that appears in a particular sample. This problem is serious when the number of subjects is small and the number of measures is large, and it is at its worst when the number of measures approaches the number of subjects—a situation which is common in observational research. Some factor analysts set a minimum of 100 subjects for the use of factor analysis, with 200 or 300 being more desirable, but this is not a requirement often met in our field.

One of the questions to be answered in the use of factor analysis which does not have a satisfactory analytic solution is that of how many factors to rotate. In our experience, some of the usual rule-of-thumb criteria suggest rotating more factors than appear to have the clearest interpretation in observational data. Probably the best estimate is obtained from the "scree test" in which the eigenvalues from factor extraction are plotted against factor numbers, with the assumption that the factor at which the curve appears to level off is the point at which no more reliable variance is being extracted. Rotating the number suggested by the scree test ± 1 has typically produced an interpretable set of factors. In general, fewer rather than more factors than indicated have been preferable.

Once a rotated factor structure has been decided upon, the next question is how to represent each teacher (classroom, child) on each factor—how to calculate factor scores. Glass and McGuire (1966) have argued that anything other than complete factor scores in which every item receives a weight on every factor is an unsatisfactory procedure. They base this conclusion primarily on the fact that other methods of creating factor scores are likely to result in correlations among the factors. However, Horn (1965) points to the problem of "fitting error" and suggests that validity shrinkage on cross-validation would be expected to be extensive for complete factor scores. He suggests that this problem should be less severe with incomplete factor scores in which the items on each factor which load above some cut-off are summed with equal weights (giving negative signs to items with negative loadings in bipolar factors). Morris (1975) has demonstrated that under a variety of conditions incomplete factor scores show higher cross-validation validities than complete factor scores, although the differences are small.

More recently, Kukuk and Baty (1979) have argued in favor of using the total number of measures (items) rather than reducing them to factor scores, if the data are subsequently to be used in multiple regression, arguing that valid variance is lost in the factoring process. In contrast, Morris (1980) has found that factor scores were significantly better predictors than the original items; that incomplete factor scores were superior to complete scores; and that the superiority of factor scores increased as samples were smaller. These findings are consistent with those of Dawes (1979), who summarizes evidence that, in general, the use of differential weights is not likely to improve predictive accuracy over the use of unweighted composites.

One of the advantages of using factor analysis is its occasional heuristic value. That is, it may point out patterns of organization in behavior which were previously unsuspected but which seem very reasonable when identified. For example, we had assumed that teachers who were not coercive in management style would be similarly noncoercive in both verbal and nonverbal behavior. However, factor analysis indicated that there was a dimension of gentle verbal behavior and one of gentle nonverbal behavior, but these two were essentially independent of each other. A further surprise was that the teachers' use of the face to communicate nonverbally was placed in the verbal rather than the nonverbal dimension. After the fact, this made sense, but we would not have placed the item there on a rational basis.

If small numbers of cases and large numbers of measures are likely to produce undependable results, the heuristic value of factor analysis is logically limited to hypothesis formation. The procedure can also be helpful in creating internal consistency of the measures, but with small samples this is not completely dependable.

Although factor analysis may sometimes have heuristic value, it may also group items in a way which makes interpretation of the factor difficult or which makes understanding the relation of the factor to an outome difficult. For example, data from a set of fifth grade classrooms produced a factor which reflected both expression of positive affect and physical movement of both teacher and pupils, with no evidence of task involvement. The factor was negatively related with pupil achievement gain, and our interpretation was that it was because of the lack of task involvement. But that left uncertain the role played by the positive affect—a rather unsatisfactory circumstance. When the factor was rationally broken up into two subscores, one reflecting positive affect and the other reflecting freedom of movement, the two scores correlated .57, showing considerable independence from each other and permitting them to relate differently with an outcome measure. In fact, free movement was related significantly negatively with gain while positive affect was related negatively but not significantly.

A more complicated situation emerged from the factor that accounted for most of the variance in that analysis. It was originally titled negative control versus orderly classroom, with the items with positive loadings reflecting negative affect and teacher harsh control along with much pupil freedom, and with the items with negative loadings indicating a warm emotional climate, order, and task involvement. The pattern appeared to be a reasonable one—ranging from disorderly classrooms with harsh teachers to warm, orderly task-oriented classrooms—but there appeared to be at least four subsets of behaviors. When they were scored and interrelated separately, the findings of Table 23–1 resulted. Relationships among subsets of behaviors are not consistently strong, and the meaning of the relation of factors to outcomes is not clear, nor is it clear what recommendations should be made.

Although this is a troublesome set of difficulties, a relevant question appears to be "Compared to what?" Rational groupings typically pool some items that are unrelated or that may even be negatively related. Apparently, our understanding of the nature of classroom behavior is very weak. And although the typical observation study has too few subjects to produce a stable factor structure, this is only one of several problems. Teachers and pupils are not assigned together randomly, and the characteristics of pupils at the beginning of the school year are correlated with the classroom behaviors observed at mid-year (Soar & Soar, 1975). Teaching behaviors probably change across grade levels; and different schools and school systems favor different styles of teaching so these value differences may reasonably create differences in the classroom interaction. All of these would presumably make a difference in the factor structure identified by the analysis. That is, there probably are real differences in the patterns of behavior at different locations, and the problems inherent in factor analysis may be a minor part of the total set of difficulties. Even under ideal conditions for the analysis, the resulting structure probably could not be generalized to other locations or grade levels.

Rational-Empirical Procedures

A procedure which may integrate some of the better features of both previous procedures is to begin with a set of items which, on a rational basis, represent a nar-

TABLE 23–1. Correlations of Subsets of Items Within a Factor

	Negative Behavior	Pupil Freedom	Order, Interest
Negative Behavior	—		
Pupil Freedom	.35	—	
Order, Interest	-.70	-.57	—
Warm Emotional Climate	-.31	.37	.16

row domain (for instance, emotional climate) and then to examine the structure of those items by factor analysis. The process would be repeated for as many domains as there are present.

As mentioned earlier, if rational measures are used, it is obligatory to test internal consistency, just as it would be in the development of a standardized test. If internal consistency were tested using item analysis, it might be clear either that some items should be dropped or that the entire composite was too unreliable to be retained. But it might not be clear that the item set could be broken up into two or more measures, each of which would be internally consistent. Factor analysis would provide this information.

In a recent project (Soar & Soar, 1980), we proposed several rationally derived domains, based on a subjective integration of previous factor analyses of several data sets and interpretation of the relations of those factors with student outcomes. When items comprising these rationally derived domains were separately factored, every one of the domains broke up into at least two factors. After the fact, these factors often seemed to point up distinctions which we had not made but which seemed useful. For example, the teacher's use of high-cognitive-level interaction with pupils (broad questions) broke up into two factors. One was called guided discovery backed up by facts, in which the teacher encouraged the pupils to go beyond the facts given but required them to test and evaluate the new ideas. The other factor was called guess or hypothesize (no evaluation); like the first, it encouraged pupils to suggest new and different ideas, but unlike the first, it did not require testing, evaluating, or backing up with facts. We found ourselves characterizing it as "loose and sloppy" in the sense that any answer would be right and there was no hard thinking required. Perhaps "brainstorming" would have been a better term, an activity which has its value, but the thinking process must go beyond this to be rooted in reality. Parenthetically, it may be that some of the negative relationships between high-cognitive-level interaction and pupil learning which have been reported in teacher effectiveness studies may be a function of interaction of this sort which did not prepare students to answer abstract questions in which there were right or wrong answers. After the fact, this distinction seems important, but we did not make it until the factor analysis made it for us.

The use of factor analysis within rational groupings may mitigate some of the difficulties of factor analysis mentioned earlier. First, problems of interpretation will not occur, since the item pool was assembled on a rational basis. Second, although the number of subjects may be smaller than desirable, the problem of overfitting error is somewhat less severe since the number of items would be only a fraction of those which would have been factored had the entire item set been analyzed together. The tradeoff is that measures from different domains may be correlated, sometimes strongly. For example, in the analysis just described, a measure of teacher negative affect from one domain was correlated .91 with a factor from another domain, teacher strong control. Although the measures were logically separable, empirically there was no justification for using them separately. So a final step of intercorrelating factors across domains seems necessary, followed by pooling those whose correlations are high.

Implications for High-Inference Measures from Aggregating Low-Inference Items

The difficulty of creating rational dimensions without empirical verification raises serious questions about using five-point rating scales for assessing classroom behavior and in particular for current attempts to assess teacher competencies using these scales. Rationally derived dimensions seldom survive analysis without breaking up. An examination of internal consistencies of sets of items representing competencies defined by a teacher group (Soar, 1976) showed this effect. This study and the earlier cited (Soar & Soar, 1980) do raise questions about the dependability of any measure that has not been tested for internal consistency. Since the behaviors that enter a high-inference rating are not even identified and therefore cannot have their internal consistencies checked, ratings seem to be fatally flawed.

In addition to the internal consistency problem just cited, such rating scales may raise validity problems by producing misleading results. For example, a scale of emotional climate which runs from warm to cool probably oversimplifies. Research suggests that there is a positive affect dimension and a negative affect dimension and that the relationship between the two is low. Negative affect is typically negatively related to pupil learning but positive affect shows mixed results (Medley, 1977). To simplify, if positive affect is unrelated and negative affect is negatively related, and if the rating scale runs from warm to cool and does not distinguish positive affect from negative affect, the use of the scale may be misleading. Frequent use of both kinds of affect would be recorded toward the middle of the scale, but so would little of either. Yet, the classroom described and the implications for pupil growth would be quite different. Or, if the rater were more concerned about one kind of affect than the other, this could bias the rating.

There are probably instances in which nothing better can be done and in which high-inference rating scales might be usable for research purposes. Where it is possible to use low-inference items, the weight of the evidence seems clearly to support their use rather than the use of high-inference measures.

A qualification needs to be made at this point. Although it is generally true that five-point rating scales are of high inference and individual items are of low inference, that is not always the case. A five-point rating scale could be developed with each point reflecting increasing numbers of pieces of children's art displayed in the classroom. Such a measure would clearly be of low inference. On the other hand, an individual item such as "enthusiastic" or "friendly" is clearly not low-inference in the same way as "teacher smiles" or "gives a direction." Some of the onus may be taken off high-inference items by the fact that they are not used alone as measures, but rather are likely to be pooled with other, low-inference items in creating measures.

Reliability of Process Measures

The question of reliability of observation is usually answered by the use of observer agreement. The typical procedure is to count the number of items for which two observers agreed (either checked or not checked) and express that as a percentage of the total number of items. This is usually all that can be done during observer training, and it is customary to set a limit on the number of disagreements permitted. Frick and Semmel (1978) have discussed a number of issues of reliability during observer training.

But percent of agreement is not a satisfactory index of reliability for research purposes for two reasons. First, percent of observer agreement is calculated for an entire observation schedule, whereas subsets of items are usually pooled to create measures to be used in later analysis or individual items are used. It is obvious that an index of reliability for the total instrument cannot be generalized to subsets of items or individual items; in fact, Soar (1973) found that reliabilities for factors from the same instrument ranged from approximately zero to the high nineties. Second, percent of agreement does not reflect the ability of an instrument or a measure to discriminate between teachers or the consistency with which that discrimination is made. As an extreme example, Medley, in a personal communication, points out that the easiest way to get a high percent of observer agreement is to include many items that never happen, such as "teacher levitates." Observers are likely to agree 100 percent that a teacher did not levitate, but since it is probable that no teacher among those observed levitated, the measure would fail to discriminate. Following this line of thought, it will be clear that both frequently occurring items and infrequently occurring items are likely to contribute to percent of agreement but are likely to do little to discriminate between teachers.

Procedures for Estimating Reliability

Medley and Mitzel (1963) proposed three useful indices of reliability, all of which use the same correlational procedure. For the first, which they call observer agreement (not percent of agreement), two coders observe a number of teachers on the same occasions for each of the measures to be used in subsequent analysis. For the second index, called stability, the same coder observes a number of teachers on two or more occasions. The third index is the one to which they restrict the term reliability and which they recommend, perhaps with additional use of the others. The data for that index are collected by having different coders observe the teachers on different occasions.

Each of these procedures asks a different question. Observer agreement asks whether the differences from observer to observer for each teacher are smaller on the average than the differences from teacher to teacher. Stability asks whether differences from occasion to occasion for each teacher are smaller, on average, than differences from teacher to teacher. Reliability asks whether differences between occasions and observers are smaller, on average, for each teacher than differences from teacher to teacher. Medley and Mitzel suggest that the last index is the most realistic estimate of reliability, since differences in teacher behavior from occasion to occasion (stability) are likely to be greater than differences in the way two observers code the same occasion (observer agreement) and that this index of reliability treats both differences across occasions and differences across observers as error.

This last procedure also has the practical advantage that teachers will be observed on twice as many occasions as will be true if two observers are present on each occasion to permit assessment of observer agreement. If teacher behavior varies more across occasions than across observers, as McGaw, Wardrop, and Bunda (1974) agree, then extending the number of occasions is highly desirable in order to obtain a more representative sample.

Statistical Analysis of Reliability Data

It seems clear from the arguments presented earlier that a correlational measure is more desirable than the measure of percent of observer agreement. Although the usual product-moment correlation is a major step in the right direction, it is still not the best analytic procedure for these data. To illustrate the point, assume that two observers each count the number of expressions of negative affect emitted by each of a number of teachers, and assume further that the counts they obtain put the teachers in highly similar rank orders. But assume that Observer A is more sensitive to these behaviors than Observer B, so his scores are regularly higher. Product-moment correlation is sensitive to differences in the shape of profiles across teachers, but not to differences in level. The fact that Observer B regularly records a lower score will not affect the correlation. Yet, it will be clear that unless every teacher is seen an equal number of times by each observer, the score the teacher obtains will depend on the coder who observed as well as on the behavior of the teacher. To the degree that there are differences between coders, the reliability estimate should be lower.

An analysis which recognizes this source of error is the intraclass correlation. To the extent that the average difference across observers and occasions for each teacher is less than the average difference across teachers, the intraclass correlation will be higher. But as differences between occasions or observers are greater, the intraclass correlation will be lower. Sums of squares from standard analysis of variance computing procedures provide the necessary information for estimating this statistic, and details of the procedure under different circumstances are available in Rowley (1976) and in Bartko (1976), with a critique by Algina (1978).

It should be clear that the size of the reliability coefficients as defined by Medley and Mitzel will generally be lower, and probably much lower, than the usual observer agreement statistic. It is to be expected that teachers and pupils will be engaged in different behaviors on different occasions, and to the extent that this is true, reliability will be lowered. It even seems reasonable that the more competent the group of teachers being studied, the lower the reliabilities would be, since each teacher's behavior would probably be more varied. It is not unusual to find reliabilities on the order of .5 to .6; indeed, in a study of ours, a measure with a reliability of only .38 was one of the most powerful in terms of accounting for pupil gain.

It seems clear that procedures for estimating reliability are a case in which existing knowledge is far ahead of practice and that practice needs to be upgraded.

Number of Observations

A perennial question is how many observations ought to be conducted in each classroom. In a sense, that question has no general answer, since the more reliable the measures being obtained, the fewer the number of observations required. But as a practical answer, some studies using about twelve to eighteen five-minute observations across one or several days have produced meaningful results. Others have collected as much as thirty hours of observation data in each classroom, and Flanders (1970) has commented that matrices from his system stabilize by the time six hours of interaction have been coded.

Rowley (1978) has approached the question somewhat differently. He has shown that for the same total amount of observation time, a larger number of brief observations will produce more reliable results than a smaller number of longer observations. This seems quite reasonable on two counts—with sign systems, the more observations that are made, the greater the possible range of scores; and with any observation system, the more occasions that are sampled, assuming they vary by hour of the day and day of the week, the more representative the result will be.

A related question is the tradeoff between the amount of observation data to be collected for each classroom and the number of classrooms that can be observed. In most research settings, the purpose is not to describe with maximum reliability the behavior of an individual teacher but rather to assess the effects of a program or to study the relations between different styles of teacher behavior and differences in pupil outcome. In these cases, leaning toward greater numbers of classrooms, rather than greater time in each classroom seems desirable to permit the idiosyncracies of the behavior of individual teachers to be averaged out. This appears to be a question for which hard and fast answers do not exist, but these issues merit consideration in allocating observation time—always a scarce and expensive resource.

The Unit of Analysis

An issue which is emerging with some frequency in the literature is the question of what the unit of analysis should be—individual pupils, classrooms represented by means, pupils within classrooms, classrooms within school, or some higher level. One of the basic issues is the question of independence of observations which is assumed by most statistical analyses. That is, using individual pupils as the unit of analysis in a test of the effect of different programs assumes that pupils are independent observations—that pupils within classrooms are not more alike than pupils in general. (The same problem arises in studies of both parents interacting with the same child.) Independence does not appear to be a reasonable assumption in either situation, and a number of methodologists have argued against it in the classroom setting (Peckham, Glass & Hopkins, 1969; Wiley & Bock, 1967; Rim & Coller, 1978; Raths, 1967). Glendenning and Porter (1974) suggest procedures for testing the assumption of independence but recommend against using it to decide whether to analyze data ignoring classroom grouping, and recommend the use of class means whenever independence might be in doubt.

One of the most thorough treatments of this issue is that of Cronbach (1976) who argues that most educational research data are improperly analyzed. He argues further that data should be analyzed identifying relationships within classroom, after partialing out the effect of classroom membership. He suggests circumstances in which relationships within classrooms may be quite different from relationships between classrooms and that analyses in general—process–product relationships, item analyses, and factor analyses—should be carried out both at the classroom level and at the within-classroom level.

It may be hard to visualize that relationships may differ even in direction from within group to between groups. Perhaps the clearest example is that of Vynce A. Hines in a personal communication who suggests that the relationships between mental age and chronological age are likely to be quite different within grade level than across grade level. Within grade level, the relationship is likely to be a moderate negative one, since the less able pupils are likely to have been held back and are therefore the older pupils within grade. In contrast, the correlation between mental age means and chronological age means across grade levels will be positive and high.

A different kind of example might be the relationship between anxiety level and achievement for individual pupils within classroom considered in relation to the mean level of anxiety across classrooms. It would not be surprising if the anxiety-achievement relationship were negative within classrooms where mean anxiety is high and positive in classrooms where mean anxiety is low. This would be an example of an interaction between the classroom level measure and the individual level measure in determining an outcome.

Cronbach (1976) argues that analyses of this sort should routinely be carried out to exploit the maximum of information available from the data, and he illustrates this with reanalyses of several major data sets. The procedure which he followed was to express each pupil's score on the dependent variable as a deviation from the classroom mean for that variable, so that classroom level variance was partialed out in the analysis of within-classroom variability.

Soar and Soar (1980) have reanalyzed two sets of classroom observation data in relation to pupil outcomes, using regression procedures within a split-plot design. Relationships between classrooms were examined, the remaining variance due to classrooms was partialed out, and relationships within classrooms were examined. This appears to be a different analysis procedure for attaining the same end suggested by Cronbach. The relative strength of each variable would be parallel, but percentages of variance accounted for would differ.

In the latter analyses, the proportions of variance accounted for by pupil level analyses within classrooms were not large, although they sometimes approached those of the classroom level analyses. This comparison is complicated by the fact that the base on which proportions of variance are calculated for the between and within sums of squares is different. Classrooms accounted for from roughly 8 to 25 percent of total variance, depending on outcome, so changing from one base to the other had a major effect on the proportion (Soar & Soar, 1980, p. 56). Within-classroom statistical interactions between classroom behavior and individual pupil characteristics as they predicted outcome were probably conservative, since the classroom process variables were available only at the classroom level. That is, a classroom level variable describing behavior was used to interact with a pupil-level characteristic, such as socioeconomic status or anxiety level, in predicting outcome. To the extent that teachers interacted differently with individual pupils within classrooms, that variance was not available, so relationships were probably conservative. As an example of such a statistical interaction, pupils high in reading pretest gained significantly more in vocabulary in classrooms where the teacher was high in the use of a gentle, noncoercive management style than did pupils who were low in pretest reading (Soar & Soar, 1980, p. 64).

The earliest example of data analyzed at multiple levels is that of Medley and Mitzel (1959), in which they report that process–product relationships at the classroom level were quite different when school level variance was held constant than when it was not. The implication of these studies appears to be that large-scale analysis ought to be done between schools, between classrooms partialing out school effects, and within classrooms partialing out classroom level effects.[1]

Analyses of Process–Product Relationships

The typical analysis of process–product relationships in the past has been carried out by calculating the matrix of product-moment correlations between all of the process measures and all of the outcome measures. This is a quick, easy analysis to carry out and answers a large number of questions in one analysis. But this analysis oversimplifies and misses important relationships.

Two of the sorts of relationships it misses are nonlinear and interactive. Nonlinear relations often appear for measures representing teacher structuring of learning tasks for complex outcomes, with evidence that an intermediate level is best and that pupil achievement decreases with either greater or lesser structuring. Product-moment correlation assumes that if some of a behavior is good, more

---

[1] Since this was written, another helpful methodological source (Burstein, 1980) and other reports of such analyses have appeared. Clearly, it is a developing area of work.

is better, without limit. Stated in this way, the assumption does not seem probable in very many instances. If a product-moment correlation is used instead of a nonlinear one when a nonlinear relation exists, the degree of relationship is understated and may even appear to be zero.

Evidence of nonlinearity has been found in all of four data sets by Soar and Soar (1976), and in the Rim and Coller (1979) reanalysis of the Stallings and Kaskowitz data (1974). The latter findings modified earlier interpretations of the results. For example, the Stallings-Kaskowitz report is often cited as evidence of the importance of time on task for achievement gain, but the reanalysis showed that in classrooms where time on task was highest, gain was sometimes less than where time on task was lower.

Another possibility missed by product-moment correlation is that of inter-action effects among classroom process variables or between process variables and pupil characteristics. The importance of pupil characteristics in determining the most functional classroom behavior is illustrated in the Medley review (1977). In cases in which the same process variable was significantly related to outcome for both high and low socioeconomic status pupils, the direction of the relation was reversed about two-thirds of the time.

It also seems reasonable that classrooms are a complex network of interrela-tionships in which the effect of one behavior is likely to be moderated by the level of another behavior, and tests of interactions examine such possibilities. Such rela-tions were found by Soar and Soar (1973, 1980), and it was not unusual to find sig-nificant interaction effects between variables when neither one alone was related significantly to the outcome measure.

Product-moment correlation may mislead by not recognizing collinearity (interrelationship) among independent variables. Consider a possibility: product-moment correlations indicate that both expression of positive affect and degree of structure of the learning tasks are positively related to pupil achievement gain. Are both important to pupil learning? What if the positive affect is found pri-marily in the high-structure classrooms? If some classrooms follow contingency management teaching procedures (Skinnerian conditioning principles) and use praise as a structuring and management procedure, and other classrooms do not, positive affect and structure would be expected to occur together. That is, they would be collinear. In an analysis which recognized this collinearity, only one of these variables might be found to be related to outcome, while the other would have its relationship reduced or perhaps even reversed. A realistic indication of the relationship of each could be obtained only if the two were independent of each other (not collinear), but an analysis which at least makes one aware of the prob-lem is desirable. Otherwise, one might conclude positive affect is an effective vari-able in teaching, when in fact it may appear to be so only because it is collinear with structure, which may be the truly effective variable. (See the discussion of suppression effects in Cohen & Cohen, 1975.)

In contrast to the deficiencies of product-moment correlation, multiple re-gression (or the general linear model) is an analysis which can test for nonlinearity and interaction effects and which recognizes collinearity. It is now being recognized that this analysis is able to answer the kinds of questions that were formerly asked of analysis of variance and that it offers material advantages when the independent variables are continuous. For example, consider testing the interaction of the variable "teacher central" (the frequency with which a teacher is front and center in learning activities) and the variable "broad questions." If each were measured by systematic observation, a continuous measure would be available reflecting differences across teachers on each of these dimensions. To test the interaction of these two variables by analysis of variance would require breaking each of the measures up into subgroups on each variable, and sorting teachers into a two-way table. If a 3 by 3 ANOVA were used, classrooms would need to be sorted into the nine cells of the table and one would need a relatively large number of classrooms to assure a minimum of two classrooms per cell. Unless unequal numbers of cases per cell are used (which raises difficulties), a considerable amount of expensive data would have to be omitted from the analysis to make frequencies in all cells equal. Worse yet, the information available on each measure would have been reduced to a three-level category system, and a large number of degrees of freedom is required to test the hypothesis—eight degrees of freedom to test both main effects and the interaction. Multiple regression would require only three, since any continuous variable (the interaction is also a continuous variable) requires only one degree of freedom. The practical problems of sorting cases into cells and of minimum or equality of numbers would not arise.

Relatively brief discussions of the advantages of multiple regression are available in Cohen (1968) and in Walberg (1971). More detailed discussions presenting both conceptual understanding and operational details are available in Kerlinger and Pedhazur (1973) and in Cohen and Cohen (1975).

Several statistical program libraries are available for carrying out these analyses. Testing a nonlinear relationship or an interaction requires the addition of only one program statement, so the procedure is straightforward. The problem of collinearity is dealt with as an integral part of the analysis.

Analysis of data at different levels of aggregation (unit of analysis) is dealt with efficiently by the general linear model (GLM) available in SAS (SAS Institute, 1979). Although not a simple, straightforward procedure, it is not unreasonably time-consuming, given the requisite knowledge of the program. The major advantage of this approach in its various forms over product-moment correlation is that these analyses better represent the complexity of the interrelationships, whereas the simpler analysis does not. The phenomena of classrooms are exceedingly complex, and using a simple method of analysis fails to deal with that complexity, risks serious loss of information, and may be misleading. When the data are as scarce and as expensive to collect as observational data are, the loss is particularly damaging.

A Concluding Comment

This chapter has traced the methodology of classroom observation, describing the development of observation instruments, the advantages and disadvantages of different types, and the apparently fatal flaws of one popular type of instrument. It has reviewed procedures for combining items into measures, again with advantages and disadvantages, and has suggested procedures different from the ones commonly used for estimating reliability. We discussed methods for analyzing the relations of these observational measures with outcome measures, and we suggested to capitalize on information which the most commonly used procedure may miss. The level or unit of analysis was cited as a critical emerging methodological issue which may mislead if managed inappropriately or yield a richer harvest of information if recent procedures are employed.

The procedures we have recommended have not emerged suddenly; rather, they are the result of slow development during some twenty years of intensive investigation of the classroom process. What is more, the problems and recommendations are applicable to any observational measurement of behavior, whether in families, preschool groups, or day camps.

References

ALGINA, J. Comment on Bartko's "On various intraclass correlation reliability coefficients." *Psychological Bulletin*, 1978, 85, 135–138.

BARTKO, J. J. On various intraclass correlation reliability coefficients. *Psychological Bulletin*, 1976, 83, 762–765.

BOYER, E. G., SIMON, A., and KARAFIN, G. R. *Measures of Maturation*, 3 vols. Philadelphia: Research for Better Schools, 1973.

BURSTEIN, L. The analysis of multilevel data in educational research and evaluation. In D. C. Berliner (ed.), *Review of Research in Education*, Vol. 8. Washington, D.C.: American Educational Research Association, 1980.

COHEN, J. Multiple regression as a general data-analytic system. *Psychological Bulletin*, 1968, 70, 426–443.

COHEN, J., and COHEN, P. *Applied Multiple Regression/Correlation Analysis for the Behavioral Sciences*. New York: Wiley, 1975.

COKER, J. G., and COKER, H. Classroom observation keyed for effectiveness research. P. O. Box 1017, Carrollton, Ga. 30117, 1979.

CRONBACH, L. J. Research on classrooms and schools: Formulation of questions, design, and analysis. Stanford, Calif.: Stanford Evaluation Consortium, Stanford University, 1976 (ERIC Document ED 135 801).

DAWES, R. M. The robust beauty of improper linear models in decision making. *American Psychologist*, 1979, 34, 571–582.

FLANDERS, N. A. *Teacher Influence, Pupil Attitudes, and Achievement*. Minneapolis: University of Minnesota, 1960.

FLANDERS. N. A. *Analyzing Teacher Behavior*. Reading, Mass.: Addison-Wesley, 1970.

FRICK, T., and SEMMEL, M. I. Observer agreement and reliabilities of classroom observational measures. *Review of Educational Research*, 1978, 48, 157–184.

GLASS, G. V., and MAGUIRE, T. O. Abuses of factor scores. *American Educational Research Journal*, 1966, 3, 297–304.

GLENDENNING, L., and PORTER, A. C. The effects of correlated units of analysis: Violating the assumption of independence. Washington, D.C.: National Institute of Education, 1974 (unpublished working paper).

GORDON, I. J., and JESTER, R. E. Instructional strategies in infant stimulation. *JSAS Selected Documents in Psychology*, 1972, 2, 122.

HORN, J. L. An empirical comparison of various methods for computing factor scores. *Educational and Psychological Measurement*, 1965, 25, 313–322.

KERLINGER, F. N., and PEDHAZUR, E. J. *Multiple Regression in Behavioral Research*. New York: Holt, Rinehart & Winston, 1973.

KUKUK, C. R., and BATY, C. F. The misuse of multiple regression with composite scores obtained from factor scores. *Educational and Psychological Measurement*, 1979, 39, 272–290.

McGAW, B., WARDROP, J. L., and BUNDA, M. A. Classroom observation-schemes: Where are the errors? *American Educational Research Journal*, 1972, 9, 13–27.

MEDLEY, D. M. *Teacher Competence and Teacher Effectiveness*. Washington, D.C.: American Association of Colleges for Teacher Education, 1977.

MEDLEY, D. M. A Manual for Coding OScAR 5v. Charlottesville, Va.: University of Virginia, n.d.

MEDLEY, D. M., and MITZEL, H. E. A technique for measuring classroom behavior. *Journal of Educational Psychology*, 1958, 49, 86–92.

MEDLEY, D. M., and MITZEL, H. E. Some behavioral correlates of teacher effectiveness. *Journal of Educational Psychology*, 1959, 50, 239–246.

MEDLEY, D. M., and MITZEL, H. E. Measuring classroom behavior by systematic observation. In N. L. Gage (ed.), *Handbook of Research on Teaching*. Chicago: Rand McNally, 1963.

MEDLEY, D. M., SCHLUCK, C. G., and AMES, N. P. *The Personal Record of School Experience*. Charlottesville: University of Virginia, 1973.

MITZEL, H. E. Teacher effectiveness. *Encyclopedia of Educational Research*, 3rd ed. New York: Macmillan, 1960.

MORRIS, J. D. A comparison of regression prediction with data-level variables versus factor scores. Unpublished doctoral dissertation, University of Florida, 1975.

MORRIS, J. D. On the predictive accuracy of full-rank variables versus various types of factor scores. *Educational and Psychological Measurement*, 1980, 40, 389–396.

OBER, R. L., BENTLEY, E. L., and MILLER, E. *Systematic Observation of Teaching*. Englewood Cliffs, N. J.: Prentice-Hall, 1971.

PECKHAM, P. D., GLASS, G. V., and HOPKINS, K. D. The experimental unit in statistical analysis. *Journal of Special Education*, 1969, 3, 337–349.

RATHS, J. The appropriate experimental unit. *Educational Leadership*, 1967, 25, 263–266.

RIM, E. D., and COLLER, A. R. Research methologies pertinent to the study of schooling effects: A synthesis. Philadelphia: Research for Better Schools, 1978 (unpublished report).

RIM, E. D., and COLLER, A. R. In search of nonlinear process-product functions in existing schooling effects data: A reanalysis of the first grade reading and math data from the Stallings and Kaskowitz Follow Through Study. *JSAS Catalog of Selected Documents in Psychology*, 1979, 9 (ms. no. 1956).

Rowley, G. L. Reliability of observational measures. *American Educational Research Journal*, 1976, *13*, 51–59.

Rowley, G. L. The relationship of reliability in classroom research to the amount of observation: An extension of the Spearman-Brown formula. *Journal of Educational Measurement*, 1978, *15*, 165–180.

Samph, T. Observer effects on teacher behavior. Unpublished doctoral dissertation, University of Michigan, 1968.

SAS Institute, *SAS User's Guide*. Raleigh, N. C.: SAS Institute, 1979.

Simon, A., and Boyer, E. G. (eds.) *Mirrors of Behavior: An Anthology of Classroom Observation Instruments*. Philadelphia: Research for Better Schools, Vols. 1–6, 1967; Vols. 7–14 and summary, 1970.

Soar, R. S. *Follow Through Classroom Process Measurement and Pupil Growth (1970–71), Final Report*. Gainesville: Institute for Development of Human Resources, University of Florida, 1973 (ERIC Document Reproduction Service No. Ed 106–297).

Soar, R. S. Validity of two sign systems based on inductively derived teacher competencies. In H. Coker (chairman), *Classroom Observation and Teacher Competency*. Symposium presented at the Annual Meeting of the American Educational Research Association, San Francisco, 1976.

Soar, R. S., and Dixon, G. M. One instrument from four: Gains and losses. Paper presented at the Annual Meeting of the American Educational Research Association, San Francisco, April 1979.

Soar, R. S., and Soar, R. M. Classroom behavior, pupil characteristics, and pupil growth for the school year and for the summer. Gainesville: Institute for Development of Human Resources, University of Florida, 1973. Also in *JSAS Catalog of Selected Documents in Psychology*, 1975, *5*, 200 (ms. no. 873).

Soar, R. S., and Soar, R. M. An attempt to identify measures of teacher effectiveness from four studies. *Journal of Teacher Education*, 1976, *27*, 261–267.

Soar, R. S., and Soar, R. M. Emotional climate and management. In P. L. Peterson and H. J. Walberg (eds.), *Research on Teaching: Concepts, Findings and Implications*. Berkeley, Calif.: McCutchan, 1979.

Soar, R. S., and Soar, R. M. Setting variables, classroom interaction, and multiple pupil outcomes. *JSAS Catalog of Selected Documents in Psychology*, *10*, 1980.

Soar, R. S., Soar, R. M., and Ragosta, M. Florida climate and control system. Gainesville: Institute for Development of Human Resources, University of Florida, 1971.

Stallings, J. A. *Learning to Look*. Belmont, Calif.: Wadsworth, 1977.

Stallings, J. A., and Kaskowitz, D. H. Follow Through classroom observation evaluation. Contract OEC–0–8822480–4633(100) from Office of Education, Dept. of Health, Education, and Welfare to Stanford Research Institute, Menlo Park, Calif., 1974.

Walberg, H. J. Generalized regression models in educational research. *American Educational Research Journal*, 1971, *8*, 71–91.

Wiley, D. E., and Bock, R. D. Quasi-experimentation in educational settings: Comment. *The School Review*, 1967, Winter.

CHAPTER 24

Methods of Evaluating Program Outcomes

Jacqueline M. Royce
Harry W. Murray
Irving Lazar
Richard B. Darlington

EVALUATION HAS ASSUMED increasing importance in early childhood education as program accountability has become a dominant theme in all areas. Funding agencies at local and federal levels require data for planning and demand effective, equitable programs at reasonable cost. Federally funded programs in health, human services, and education now mandate evaluation reports (see, for example, *Head Start Program Performance Standards*, 1975).

Inevitably, evaluation of early childhood programs occurs in a turbulent setting because it deals with value systems. All programs operate in social, political, and economic contexts, and the process of evaluating these programs shares the same milieu. The sometimes conflicting values and belief systems of evaluators, program planners, administrators, and the families of children in the programs make the process of program design and evaluation a political activity. As in any political arena, all interests must negotiate their own perceptions of program needs and compete for resources and credibility. For example, program effectiveness is a highly salient value in outcome evaluation. Program effectiveness must, however, compete for influence on program decision making with other considerations, such as the political acceptability, feasibility, and ideology of the program. The political process involves accommodation and negotiation between these competing values in the research design and in the use of the findings of evaluation studies.

Since the 1960s, evaluators of early education programs have been concerned primarily with children poorly served by the traditional schools—low-income children, minority children, or children with special needs. As soon as children graduated from the first summer Head Start programs in 1965, national evaluations of Head Start were planned. The data now available from early childhood education programs such as Head Start, Follow Through, Home Start, and Title I programs are voluminous. Reviews and bibliographies of these data have also accumulated (Brown, 1978; Mann, Harrell & Hurt, Jr., 1976; Bronfenbrenner, 1974; Gotts, 1973; Rivlin & Timpane, 1975). A new field of meta-analysis has evolved in an attempt to integrate and make sense of findings from diverse studies (Pillemer & Light, 1980; Light & Smith, 1971; Cook & Levitan, 1980; Glass, 1978).

Beginning in the early 1960s, a number of early childhood investigators independently conducted early childhood programs for research and demonstration purposes. Their infant and preschool programs, designed for low-income children, had diverse curricular approaches and were located in both urban and rural sites. Some programs were home-based, others were center-based, and some combined a center program with home visits. In 1975, partly in response to the negative findings of the Westinghouse Report (Cicirelli, 1969), the investigators formed a collaborative research group—The Consortium for Longitudinal Studies—in order to study the long-term effects of their early childhood programs. Members of the Consortium were: E. Kuno Beller, Richard Darlington, Cynthia and Martin Deutsch, Robert E. Jester, Irving Lazar (chair), Susan Gray, Merle Karnes, Phyllis Levenstein, Louise B. Miller, Francis Palmer, David Weikart, Myron Woolman, and Edward Zigler. Ira J. Gordon was an active member until his death in 1978. The members pooled the data they had collected independently before 1975 and then conducted two common follow-up studies: the first in 1976–1977 when their subjects were 9 to 19 years old, and the second in 1979–1980. The group members delegated the coordination of the collaborative follow-up studies of 1976 and 1979 and the analysis of pooled data to investigators at Cornell who had no vested interest in a particular early childhood education approach. The authors of this chapter, along with other colleagues, form the Cornell group.

The pooled analyses of the Consortium for Longitudinal Studies have demonstrated long-term positive effects in cognitive and noncognitive areas (see Consortium, 1977, 1978, in press; Darlington et al., 1980). Consortium investigators have published reports individually as well.

Our work with the Consortium for Longitudinal Studies used primarily traditional methods of outcome evaluation. In this chapter, we will discuss the outcome evaluation approach in the broad context of evaluation research, describe the basic tasks in conducting traditional program outcome evaluations, and then focus on certain methodological issues. These issues include (1) selection and scheduling of outcome measures; (2) establishing comparisons (selection, recruitment, and assignment of subjects); (3) hypothesis testing and estimation; (4) validity, power, and generalizability; (5) the nature of conclusions; (6) randomization and statistical control of group differences; and (7) attrition problems.

Overview of Evaluation Research

The process of evaluating social programs in variously termed evaluation research, policy research, action research, field research, applied research, program evaluation, or simply evaluation. Numerous textbooks and anthologies are available (Caro, 1977; Cook et al., 1978; Coursey et al., 1977; Glass, 1976; Guttentag & Saar, 1977; Schulberg & Baker, 1979; Sechrest et al., 1979; Suchman, 1967; Weiss, 1972; Wholey et al., 1970), and journals with titles such as *Evaluation* and *Evaluation Quarterly* have proliferated. A comprehensive handbook for the application of measurement and evaluation to early education was recently published by Goodwin and Driscoll (1980). Campbell (1979) sees this as the emergence of a new discipline involving participants from many backgrounds, including economics, sociology, political science, education, and psychology, in addition to specialists from human service professions. Currently, evaluators are deeply involved in defining their unique area of expertise.

Evaluation can be broadly defined as the process of making judgments about social programs based on systematic data collection and analysis. The overall purpose of program evaluation is to inform policy at various levels of program management, planning, and development. It is intended to be of practical use in decision making and policy formulation, but it may extend beyond the immediate programmatic level to basic theoretical concerns about the role of certain kinds of experiences in child development. Evaluation data may thus affect conceptualization about the developmental process (Evans, 1974).

Evaluation research differs from other research in its emphasis on making judgments and its relationship to decision making. Research questions for evaluation are derived from the program itself rather than from a theoretical concern. In a sense, then, evaluation research begins with the independent variable (the program), whereas other research typically begins with the dependent variable (an area of interest). Another distinguishing aspect of evaluation research is that it attempts to apply research methods in an "inhospitable action context" (Weiss, 1972). It involves mostly open systems with multiple causation and a search for unbiased estimators of program effects in a setting that is not "noise-free" (Cook & Campbell, 1979). Thus, the evaluator can expect logistical problems, interpersonal conflicts, and methodological compromises to an extent not seen in other research.

Purposes of Program Evaluation

Organizations require information to maintain effective internal operations and an effective relationship with the external environment. Depending on the level of organizational development and the resources (time and money) available, an evaluation serves several overlapping functions. First of all, evaluators can focus on collecting information on the internal operation of a program for system resource management. A second function might be to collect data on service delivery in order to improve client use of the program. A third focus might be on treatment effects on clients or community impact effects. In addition, evaluation studies can have a dissemination function to replicate programs and a theory-building function to evaluate the assumptions underlying programs (Attkisson & Hargreaves, 1979; Coursey et al., 1977).

The two major types of evaluation research, outcome and process evaluations, primarily serve two distinct purposes. Outcome evaluations are designed for "summative" purposes; process evaluations are designed for "formative" purposes (Scriven, 1967). Formative (process) evaluations focus on programs in operation and feed back into the cycle of program development; summative (outcome) evaluations judge a program at the end or at a critical decision point.

Evaluation data are expected to influence policy decisions. The most commonly held expectation is that evaluation will be instrumental in drastic decisions such as whether a program should continue or be terminated. It is ironic, as Weiss (1972) and others have pointed out, that although evaluation methods may be appropriate for this type of decision making, they are rarely used to terminate a program unless the decision serves political ends (Datta, 1976, 1980; Zigler & Valentine, 1979). In the case of the outcome evaluation completed by the Consortium for Longitudinal Studies, positive findings played a role in the congressional decision to increase the appropriations for Head Start (Comptroller General, 1979) and in the federal budget decision making for fiscal year 1982 (Raines, 1981). In general, evaluations are used more often to aid in decision making about improving program practices or achieving better allocation of resources among program strategies.

The purpose of the evaluation study determines the design and methodological approach that will be used in an evaluation. In the next section, we present a brief overview of evaluation models, so that the outcome model can be placed in the context of alternative perspectives.

Evaluation Models

The evaluation literature offers many typologies of research approaches. Indeed, there are probably as many listings of evaluation models and research strategies as there are authors on the topic. A typical listing might include seven evaluation models: the outcome model, the system analysis model (Wildavsky, 1979), cost analysis model, descriptive and quality assurance model (outside review), program planning/management model, the Goal Attainment Scaling model (Kiresuk & Lund, 1979), and legal adversary model (Levine & Rosenberg, 1979). Other authors would provide different typologies (see, for instance, Goodwin & Driscoll, 1980; Guba, 1977). The variety of evaluation models reflects on ongoing methodological debate between the mainstream "outcome" or "goal" model view of program evaluation and alternative perspectives.

The goal model to be discussed in this chapter involves the following activities: program goals are determined, the primary goals are translated into measures to indicate goal achievement, and collected outcome data compare a treatment to a control group or compare the treatment group to a certain standard. This approach attempts objectivity; it assumes that programs are designed to achieve specific ends, that success can be measured by the extent to which ends are achieved, and that policy decisions will (or should) be made according to objective data provided by evaluation (Wergin, 1976).

Critics argue that the goal model ignores organizational issues. In addition to their official goals for children or parents, programs are organizations that must adapt to their social, political, and economic environment and acquire the resources necessary to continue the program. To tap these other functions, "goal-free" evaluation models have been proposed. These alternatives to the goal model, termed process or system models, use other criteria to judge the effectiveness of an early childhood program, such as success of a program in acquiring resources. The naturalistic approaches of Stake (1967, 1975), Guba (1978), Stufflebeam (1968), Guttentag (1979), and Scriven (1967, 1974) have received wide attention as alternatives to the outcome model. Goodwin and Driscoll (1980) provide a good summary of various evaluation frameworks and note their application to early childhood education. Although we feel that process models and naturalistic methods have an important place in evaluation research, in this chapter we will focus on the use of quantitative methods in outcome studies such as the Consortium study.

There are few rules to guide an investigator in the selection of appropriate research strategies. There is obviously no one best way, and as Weiss (1972) points out, a compromise must be found between the ideal and the feasible, given the program and situational constraints of time, place, people, and money. A basic research primer such as Selltiz et al. (1976) is a good source for general research design rules. Maynard-Moody and McClintock (1981) provide an exploratory attempt to study the appropriateness of evaluation designs and methods. They suggest that awareness of the organizational context, particularly the degree of uncertainty about program goals and the level of causal knowledge in a given program area, can provide guidance in choosing an evaluation strategy.

The particular model and methods used in program evaluation depend on the purpose and scope of the study and also on the orientation of the evaluators. At every stage of the study, the underlying research paradigms play a strong role. Two major paradigms, the qualitative and the quantitative, have divided the evaluation field into two camps. The labels "quantitative" and "qualitative" imply both specific data collection techniques and a particular conceptual framework or set of assumptions (Reichardt & Cook, 1979). The quantitative paradigm comes from the experimental tradition in physical sciences and psychology. Quantitative research is outcome-oriented, assumes a stable reality, uses an objective "outsider" perspective, collects "hard" replicable data, and is concerned primarily with reliability and generalizability. The alternative approach, qualitative evaluation research, derives primarily from social anthropology in response to dissatisfaction with quantitative approaches. Qualitative research is process-oriented, dynamic, and humanistic, uses a subjective "insider" perspective, collects "real and rich" naturalistic observations, and is concerned mostly with validity. Qualitative research is characterized by the single case study which is not generalizable.

Some evaluators have chosen to view the two approaches as incompatible. Others, however, advocate the use of a wide array of conceptual and methodological tools from both qualitative and quantitative approaches, depending on research needs. Recently, bridges instead of walls have been under construction between the two approaches (Campbell, 1979; Filstead, 1979). For example, the naturalistic and holistic attributes of the qualitative paradigm can be combined with characteristics of the outcome model from the quantitative paradigm. Only tradition may prevent a researcher from mixing and matching qualitative and quantitative attributes to find the most appropriate approach for a research problem (Reichardt & Cook, 1979).

Combining qualitative and quantitative approaches serves several purposes. First of all, evaluation research usually has multiple purposes and thus a variety of methods is appropriate. Second, the two approaches can build on each other to offer more complete insights. Third, because all measures have biases, multiple techniques enable a researcher to "triangulate"; that is, to converge on understanding the same event with different methods (Denzin, 1970).

We turn now to some general methodological issues, beginning with the basic tasks that are required for outcome evaluation.

Basic Tasks in Outcome Evaluation

The traditional goal model approach to outcome evaluation involves a basic set of tasks. The first task is to determine the general program goals and the specific program objectives. From these, the primary goals for study are selected and then operationalized into outcome measures. Another major task is to identify an appropriate population to test the hypothesis of program effectiveness. From this population, subjects are selected, recruited, assigned, and maintained in the program and, usually, in control groups. A data collection system must be designed to estimate both immediate and later program effects. Data collection instruments and procedures are selected to obtain valid and reliable indicators of baseline, intervening, and outcome measures. Procedures to ensure protection of subjects' rights must be instituted. Actual data collection must be monitored for consistency and accuracy. The characteristics of early childhood programs in operation must be specified and then monitored to determine if the program is implemented as planned. Analyses of the outcome data compare measurements influenced by the program with measurements not influenced by the program in order to ascertain the program's effect. Results are disseminated to sponsors of the study, and application of the findings is expected. In practice, the order in which these tasks are performed varies from study to study, as does the amount of control the evaluator actually has over the tasks.

In this chapter, we will address some of the issues involved in conducting such an outcome evaluation. The topics we have selected are, for the most part, ones which have concerned us in the course of our Consortium study. For instance, we will not discuss documenting program implementation despite its obvious importance for outcome evaluation. Each of the projects was carefully implemented and documented before our participation; our role in the Consortium did not begin until long after the actual programs had ended. Thus, our Consortium experience gave us little new insight into this particular issue. The issues we will cover include: selection of measures; creation of comparisons; hypothesis testing and estimation; validity, power, and generalizability; the nature of conclusions; randomization; and attrition.

Measures

Perhaps the most politically sensitive and controversial aspect of evaluating program outcomes is what to measure and how to measure it. Regardless of the evaluation model or strategy chosen, appropriate indicators must be agreed upon to describe and understand the relationship between programs and outcomes. When a goal model approach is selected, the theoretical constructs underlying program goals need to be operationalized in order to create outcome measures.

Specifying Program Goals and Outcome Criteria

Specification of goals and of the criteria used to judge success creates problems because both goals and outcome criteria are value statements. Consensus can be difficult because of the diversity of vested interests with conflicting values and priorities. There is some evidence that the very act of specifying outcome criteria can have an influence on program implementation such as when the goal of teaching becomes improving the test scores themselves (see Campbell, 1979, for examples of corrupting effect of quantitative indicators).

The goals of early childhood programs are value statement reflecting differing educational philosophies and theories of learning. Thus, each philosophical viewpoint or paradigm has characteristic goals for children. For example, early childhood programs with a development-interaction paradigm might specify their outcome goals in terms of fostering psychological development; personal autonomy and self-reliance; and integration of thought, feeling, and action (Evans, 1974). The short-term objectives might focus on attentional responses, task orientation, and motivation to learn. The long-term global aim might be to encourage a positive attitude toward learning. This viewpoint would caution against concentration on academic goals as ends in themselves at the expense of genuine intellectual growth.

Follow Through evaluation provides an example of an outcome evaluation study that focused on specified program goals (Stebbins et al., 1978). The Follow Through evaluation studied twenty-two program models which probably reflected twenty-two different viewpoints of developmental psychology. The stated goals and objectives of the program models were used to classify the diverse programs along two dimensions: first, the models were differentiated in terms of amount of emphasis placed on learning basic skills, cognitive conceptual skills, or self-esteem and sense of control; and second, the models were classified according to the degree of structure (low to high) in the curriculum.

Head Start provides an example of the evaluation problems created by multiple goals. The original program goals of Head Start included efforts to meet the health and nutritional needs of children from low-income families, to involve their parents and the community in fostering children's development, and to provide a happy transition from the home to a group setting. Emphasis was placed on the children's personal and social development, curiosity, motivation, trust in others, and independence (Datta, 1976). In order to sustain widespread support from varied constituencies, Head Start had a multiplicity of objectives—a "glorious goalfulness." In addition to its goals in child development, Head Start was also designed to be an employment program and a community action agency. The problem for Head Start evaluators became which goals had highest priority and which outcome criteria would be the "best" measure of Head Start's effectiveness.

Types of Outcome Measures

The selection of measures to assess outcomes of early childhood programs is both critical and difficult. Costs, benefits, and negative effects are important outcomes to assess. The task of the investigator is to link the implementation of the early childhood program (inputs) to some later observation (outcomes). In evaluation research, both the treatment (cause) and observation (measure of effect) are complex products of many determinants. Stated more formally, measures are imperfect indicators with random error and systematic bias. Like other research, evaluation research involves the philosophical issue of causality and methodological issues of validity (Cook & Campbell, 1979). Evaluation research is particularly constrained by what is feasible to measure and what is meaningfully related to goals of early childhood programs.

Early education programs for low-income children typically have as one of their goals the stimulation of cognitive development and the subsequent improvement of children's later school performances. Standardized intellectual tests are usually selected to measure these outcomes (Horowitz & Paden, 1973). Despite advantages of reliability, validity, and ease of administration, the use of standardized measures has been heavily criticized. Intelligence tests in particular have been attacked for cultural bias and as an inadequate sampling of the skills and abilities of low-income children (Kamin, 1974). Zigler and Trickett (1978) criticize the use of intelligence tests scores alone as relatively uninformative and, at worst, misleading. They propose instead a social competence index that includes both individual intelligence tests and molar social expectancy variables, such as school attendance and incidence of juvenile delinquency. Bronfenbrenner (1979) notes that outcome measures such as standardized intelligence and achievement tests are ecologically constricted, measuring a narrow range of behavior. He has described developmental psychology as the "science of strange behavior of children in strange situations with strange adults for briefest possible periods of time" (1979, p. 19). Moreover, the validity of standardized measures depends on the extent to which the children share the experimenters' definition of the specific testing situation. Measurements are "ecologically valid," according to Bronfenbrenner, only insofar as the environment experienced by the subject has the same meaning as that assumed by an investigator (1979, p. 29).

Interviews and tests have also been criticized because they intrude as a foreign element into the natural setting, elicit atypical roles and responses, and are limited only to subjects who cooperate. Some researchers have advocated the use of unobtrusive measures, such as archival or written records, as an alternative strategy for gathering information (Webb et al., 1966). Such measures are also termed "nonreactive" because they do not contaminate the response.

Whether a measure is reactive or nonreactive depends on the specific actors in the setting: a particular measure is not inherently reactive or nonreactive. For example, data on assignment to special education classes collected from school records constitute a nonreactive measure vis-à-vis the children who participated in an early education program. Similarly, these data are nonreactive vis-à-vis the school if they are used to evaluate an early education program which was distinct from the school. However, if this measure is used to evaluate a program within the school making the assignments, the data could be reactive vis-à-vis the school; if school officials know they are being evaluated on this measure, this knowledge may alter either the pattern of assignment to special education or the manner in which they record assignment.

Tests and interviews are always reactive relative to the subject since they depend on the subject's reaction to the testing interview situation. These measures may also be reactive relative to the program being evaluated. If, for example, program personnel know their program will be evaluated by the Stanford-Binet IQ test, they may include the Stanford-Binet items as part of the curriculum. Thus, for each proposed measure, the evaluator must judge the extent of reactivity for the subjects, for the program being evaluated, and for the person or agency that actually records the measure.

In addition to cognitive goals, many programs have goals for children's personal and social development, such as enhancing self-esteem, increasing achievement orientation, and facilitating the transition into the peer group and the classroom setting. In this area, there continues to be a lack of well-constructed and well-validated instruments to measure noncognitive outcomes (for suggested sources, see Goodwin & Driscoll, 1980).

Another criticism of early education program evaluations, implicit in Bronfenbrenner's (1979) model for experimental ecological research, is the restriction of outcome measurements to attributes of the child. In order to be truly indicative of development, measures should assess the program's impact on the multiple contexts in which the subject lives, such as his/her family, school, and community.

Multiple Measures

Most authors recommend the collection of multiple measures at several time points for a number of reasons. First of all, we know that our measurements are only indicators of an unmeasured underlying construct. Multiple measures, perhaps both quantitative and qualitative, provide additional confirmation of observations and raise our level of confidence in our findings. The various measures can supplement and cross-validate each other—the process termed "triangulation" (Denzin, 1970). Collecting multiple measures of the same construct also provides an opportunity for creating indices. An additional reason for assessing several outcomes is that programs can have multiple objectives and effects.

We used four types of measures in the Consortium data. First, we used IQ tests individually administered by the project. These tests were reactive for both the subject and the program, but they had the advantage of being well-known standards for judging success. Second, we collected data on assignment to special education and grade retention from school records. These data were nonreactive for the children, because collecting this information required no reaction by subject to researcher; for the early education program, this criterion was not chosen until after program termination; and the schools were not being evaluated. School record data were more ecologically valid than test scores since they indicated the ability of the child to meet the minimal demands of his/her school. School success was thus measured in a visible and meaningful way in the child's own ecological context. In addition, because of the crucial impact school actions may have on a child, these records were also important as a reflection of the interaction between the child and the school. Comparisons across school systems should not be used for detecting individual differences because they may primarily reflect school policy differences.

For our third measure, we used scores of school-administered achievement tests collected from school records. These proved extremely difficult to analyze for several reasons: different schools and projects used different tests; identification of the test was incomplete; and different types of scores (grade equivalent, percentile, standard score) were recorded in different schools. In general, our experience suggests that for evaluation purposes, standardized test data should come from tests specifically administered for the evaluation rather than drawn from school records. Garfinkel's (1967) observation that good administrative record keeping is very different from good research-oriented record keeping seems to apply here. The fourth measure we used was data from interviews with both the mother and the youth. Interestingly, we found that some subjects gave responses that differed from school record information (for example, on high school graduation). Multiple data sources improved our confidence in the accuracy of our measures. The multiple measures we collected enabled us to assess various domains of cognitive and noncognitive functioning.

Scheduling of Measurements

Another important consideration in the selection of outcome measures is the timing of the assessments. The effects of early education programs can be investigated at multiple time points. Ideally, evaluators should use multiple reporting schedules: early measurement, immediately following program participation; at a subsequent intermediate time, to test the reliability of early estimates; and a later assessment to test the long-range effects (Bernstein, 1976).

As Cook and Campbell (1979) suggest, the scheduling of outcome measures can be one of the most important tools for detecting effects and for attributing effects to the treatment. The formulation of the research question and the theoretical link between the program and its effects helps to determine the appropriate postprogram time(s) to measure outcomes. Planning for short-term before/after evaluations as well as long-term assessments can satisfy the needs of both policy makers who require quick reporting of results and evaluators who prefer more certainty. Long-term evaluations are rarely possible, but they can prove surprising (see Nagel & Neef, 1979, for an example of positive effects of the New Deal on farmers who were observed thirty years later). In our case, the Consortium was fortunate to be able to follow subjects into high school and beyond and found long-term positive effects in contrast with disappointing earlier assessments.

Establishing Comparisons

Evaluation is essentially a matter of comparison. A program can be evaluated only in relation to something else. This "something else" is usually either another program or "what would have happened without the program." Successful program evaluation depends, first, upon the conceptualization of a theoretically relevant comparison, and, second, upon the creation of an empirical comparison that accurately reflects the conceptual comparison.

In order to make inferences about whether a program caused certain outcomes, an evaluator must compare a set of outcome measurements to at least one other set of measurements. The purpose of evaluation design is to create an empirical comparison for which the observed differences can be said to have been caused by the program under study. In other words, the evaluation design should attempt to create sets of measurements that are comparable in all respects except that one set was influenced by the program and the others were not. This is done by systematically eliminating rival explanations for observed differences between the comparison sets of measurements or, alternatively, by eliminating rival explanations other than program failure for a lack of differences. This elimination of alternative explanations allows the evaluator to say with reasonable certainty that the program caused the differences. Alternative explanations are often referred to as "threats to validity" (Campbell & Stanley, 1966; Cook & Campbell, 1979).

The two major methods of eliminating or minimizing alternative explanations are (1) the selection-assignment procedure; and (2) the statistical procedures for controlling measured nonprogram-related differences. The former operates to ensure the comparability of the sources of the sets of measurements; the latter functions to adjust the measurements themselves for other measured differences in the sources. Often, both methods are used in conjunction. The next section focuses on selection-assignment procedures; other sections will address related methodological issues.

Selection-Assignment Procedure

In the Consortium study, the present authors were not involved in designing the procedures for selection and assignment. At the time the Consortium was formed, the constituent projects had already completed posttest evaluations of their participants and had published reports. Our exposure to the selection-assignment process was from an entirely different perspective: our task was to analyze the procedures used in each of the fourteen original projects in order to determine to what extent the results could be pooled across the projects. In effect, we performed a post-hoc comparison of fourteen selection-assignment procedures. Such comparisons are relatively rare (one was performed for randomized field experiments by Conner, 1978), but they can be a very useful way to discover the problems of evaluation design. Our analysis led us to conclude that published evaluation reports rarely describe the selection-assignment procedure in sufficient detail to enable a reader to understand the procedure and make a fair judgment about its validity. This may be due to two factors: (1) a general reluctance on the part of both journal editors and readers to devote much space to the mundane topic of sample creation; and (2) a belief that a few sentences can adequately summarize the entire selection-assignment procedure. Here, we will attempt to treat the procedure as a whole, using some of the insights we derived from our analyses and the reflections of the Consortium project staff members about their own procedures.

The goal of the selection-assignment procedure is to create two or more sources for sets of measurements in such a way that these sources are equivalent in all respects except exposure to the program. Usually, these sources are two groups of people, although in some designs the sources can be different points in time from the same group of people (for example, the single group pretest–posttest design or, more generally, the single group repeated-measures design). The first topic to consider, then, are the relative advantages and disadvantages of using only one group of subjects as the source of measurements.

A one-group design involves only the children who participate in the program. The children may be assessed both before and after the program (a one-group pretest–posttest design) or assessed only at the end of the program (a one-group after-only design). The after-only design is the simplest of all, but it has the obvious disadvantage that there is simply nothing with which to compare outcomes. If a group of third-grade children are reading at fourth-grade level at the end of the program, how do you know that they weren't simply an exceptional group of children and that their outstanding performance has nothing to do with their participation in a preschool program?

One-group pretest–posttest designs control for this obvious source of error by providing a pretest comparison to the posttest. Unfortunately, they also have a number of weaknesses. A difference between pretest and posttest scores might be caused by any number of factors, including:

1. *External events unrelated to the program.* A new and highly effective educational television program might begin about the same time as the experimental program. Or, if the experimental program is only one of several programs in a public school, some other school program might improve dramatically at the same time. These are just two examples; the variety of external events and their possible effects on measured program outcomes are virtually infinite.

2. *Consequences of time.* For programs lasting weeks or months, the major factor in this category is maturation of the children involved. For programs of a few hours, time might have a negative effect: increased hunger or fatigue between pretest and posttest might result in impaired performance. For programs of a few days, adaptation to the program environment might substantially increase scores from pretest to posttest.

3. *Effects of pretest.* The experience of taking the pretest can affect scores on the posttest. Positive effects may include practice and elation; negative effects may include fatigue, boredom, or embarrassment.

4. *Unintended effects of the experimental program.* It may become clear to the subjects during the program that they are part of an experiment; this can stimulate either improved or decreased performance on the posttest.

5. *Instrumentation changes.* Instruments used to assess subjects at posttest might differ from those used at pretest, even if they have the same name. Even if one uses the same standardized IQ or achievement test, this test may have different items and be standardized on different samples at the time of the posttest in comparison to the pretest. Thus, instruments may not measure the same traits at both time periods.

Numerous other alternative explanations of pretest–posttest differences for a single group can be advanced; a thorough discussion of such factors is available in Cook and Campbell (1979). Many, although by no means all, of these alternative explanations can be eliminated by comparing separate groups of subjects: one that participated in the program and one that did not. For the remainder of this section, then, we will focus on establishing comparisons between at least two groups of subjects.

Discussions of the selection-assignment process usually focus only on the procedures used to assign subjects to groups. However, particularly in the case of program evaluation, the selection-assignment procedure as a whole must be evaluated in terms of whether it produces comparable groups. As used here, the selection-assignment process will refer to the entire process by which comparison groups are created: selection for the study, recruitment, refusal or acceptance, assignment to groups, and attrition. In most discussions, these procedures are categorized according to the type of assignment used (random versus nonrandom). This emphasis is appropriate because the assignment procedure is the most important component of the entire process for ensuring comparability of groups. At the same time, many researchers mistakenly conclude that the selection-assignment procedure can be adequately conceptualized and reported by a description of the assignment; but type of selection, methods of recruitment, response of potential subjects to recruitment, units used in assignment, and attrition of subjects during the evaluation period must also be taken into account in ascertaining whether a given selection-assignment procedure has provided comparable groups of subjects.

This almost exclusive emphasis on assignment can be traced to the historical origins of evaluation research. Evaluation research designs were adopted from the research designs used in agricultural and psychological laboratory experiments where proper assignment procedures generally were sufficient to ensure comparability. With few exceptions, subjects entered and remained in the groups to which they were assigned. Corn did not refuse to be treated with certain chemicals; rats did not refuse to be subjected to certain types of stimuli. Even when human beings were the subjects of an experiment, they usually entered and remained in their assigned groups because (1) they had volunteered for the experiment and did not perceive any of the treatments as having great positive or negative value for them relative to any of the others; or (2) they were a captive pool of subjects whose position permitted them no choice (in a prison, mental hospital, or the armed services). Thus, the models of the selection-assignment process were developed under conditions in which assignment by the researcher basically assured the composition, and hence the comparability, of the groups.

The situation in most program evaluations is quite different. Programs are usually perceived by potential subjects as important; therefore, they will have an interest in whether they are placed in a group receiving the program or in a no-program control group. Furthermore, the ultimate decision to participate in a program lies with the subject. For most early education programs, the parents of subjects can refuse to have their child enter the program. Such a decision is influenced by many factors, including the perceived desirability of the program and the manner of recruitment. Obviously, responses could differ, depending on whether the subject was asked to participate in a program or in a no-program control group. Thus, the actual selection-assignment experiences of the program evaluator do not always conform to a model in which subjects enter and remain in the groups to which they have been assigned.

Evaluators have responded to this challenge by identifying and categorizing such threats to validity. Cook and Campbell (1979) list a total of thirteen possible threats to the internal validity of the design. Seven of these threats result directly from the perceived importance of the program to the subjects and/or the participation choices of the subjects.

1. Different types of people can enter different groups if they are free to choose groups or if they are specifically recruited for different groups.
2. Different types of people can drop out of different groups during the evaluation period.
3. If there are particular types of people in the different groups, external factors can affect each group in a different way. For example, if most of the program group is on welfare and most of the control group is not, a change in welfare policy during the course of the evaluation could affect one group but not the other.
4. Subjects in the control group might receive some of the benefits of the program by contact with subjects in the program group.
5. Some or all of the control subjects may participate in a similar program offered by another source—perhaps offered in response to the program under study.
6. Control subjects may be motivated to perform better than usual because they know they are being compared to a group receiving a special program.
7. The performance of controls could be depressed by resentment that they were not assigned to the program group.

Obviously, specifying the assignment procedure does not rule out these threats. Such threats may also exist in laboratory experiments; however, they are less likely to occur and less likely to be important in laboratory experiments. The question is: for a given study, at what point do such threats become important enough that they must be dealt with specifically at every stage of the process?

The selection-assignment process can be divided into three types of action taken by the researchers: selection, recruitment, and assignment. Although some type of selection must precede the other actions, recruitment for the program can occur either before or after assignment. Any recruitment or assignment action calls for a response by the subject to participate or not. We will describe each type of action in general and then illustrate how these actions can interrelate in a selection-assignment process.

Selection requires the definition of a target population or populations. The selection process is concerned more with generalizability of results than with comparability of groups. Evaluations rarely use a random sampling design from any population to select the subjects; hence, most generalizations extending evaluation results to wider populations are "common sense" rather than statistically based generalizations, built on perceived similarities between the population under study and a wider population. Nonetheless, these selection procedures are relevant to the comparability of groups if different selection procedures are used for the groups, for example, if a preschool group is compared to a group selected from the first grade classroom of the preschool graduates.

Recruitment is the actual contact with subjects for the purpose of convincing them to participate in some phase of the evaluation research. Recruitment may be the most neglected action in the research design literature and in reports of actual evaluations. Recruitment actions can be classified in several ways: (1) in terms of technique: public advertisement, door-to-door canvassing, and letters sent to a preselected group (usually followed by personal contact); (2) in terms of the reason given for recruitment: for a one-shot assessment, for a series of assessments, for participation in the program, for a chance to participate in the program, for delayed participation in the program, or for participation in another program not under study and not expected to affect the relevant outcomes; (3) by timing: are the program and control groups recruited at the same time or at different times?

Assignment is the process of placing specified subjects in specific groups. The major distinction in assignment is between random and nonrandom assignment (nonequivalent control groups). The advantages and disadvantages of random assignment have been described in detail elsewhere (Cook & Campbell, 1979; Boruch, 1978; Conner, 1978). Types of nonrandomized assignment include assignment by need, by ability, by age, by first-come/first-served, by personal connection, or by geographic area. Types of assignment are also distinguished by unit. Often, the unit is the individual subject, although it is sometimes an already constituted classroom (treatments assigned by classroom) or a geographic area, in which certain blocks, neighborhoods, or towns are assigned to program or control conditions. A final distinction sometimes made is whether or not the assignment procedure is completely specified or known to the evaluator (Cook & Campbell, 1979).

To show how these actions can be combined to form a selection-assignment process, we will give a few hypothetical examples for early education programs. All will involve random assignment; hence, the statement, "The program and control groups were formed by random assignment," would apply to all examples.

1. Public advertisements of a program are made in a given area. Applicants come to an office where they are told that the space is limited and that their names will be entered in a lottery to see if they will get into the program. They are asked to participate in a control group (that is, to agree to periodic assessments) if they do not get into the program. The pool of applicants who agree to participate in either the program or control group are randomly assigned to either group and then notified of their assignment. A few potential control subjects may drop out of the assessment process due to the disappointment that they did not get into the program.

2. A list of preschool-age children is obtained from a local hospital or school district. Names on the list are randomly assigned to program or control groups. Program children are contacted and asked to participate in the program. Controls are asked to participate in a series of assessments and are not told about the program. Some parents of program children may refuse because they do not want outsiders to interfere with the raising of their children. Some parents of control children may refuse to participate because they feel that the assessments are a nuisance and will not benefit them or their children.

3. Subjects are recruited door-to-door for a child health screening program involving periodic assessments. The subjects who volunteer for this program are randomly assigned to either program or control conditions. Those assigned to the

program group are recruited for the early education program; those assigned to the control condition have already agreed to participate in the assessments for the health screening program and need not be recruited again.

All three examples involve random assignment at some stage. However, all three will not necessarily result in equally comparable groups. In the first example, those who agree to participate regardless of whether they get into the program are likely to be rather unusual, and this may lower generalizability. However, if all subjects participate as agreed, regardless of assignment, the groups should be comparable. On the other hand, despite their previous agreement to participate in the study, some subjects may drop out in disappointment at being assigned to the control group. If refusals occur in the control group after assignment, a biased comparison could result; that is, the effect of the refusals could provide an alternative explanation for explaining results. In the second example, the groups are comparable at assignment (before recruitment). However, since the groups are recruited for different purposes (one for the program, the other for assessment only), people in one group may respond differently from people in the other group. Certain types of people may consent to participate in an early education program but not in assessments, and vice versa. Hence, an alternative explanation for results may be that the groups were not equivalent after recruitment because of a selection effect in which a differential response to recruitment for different purposes destroyed the prerecruitment equivalence of the groups. In the third example, the groups are comparable at assignment, after recruitment for the health screening program, but before recruitment for the early education program. If all those recruited for the early education program accept, the groups are still comparable. One of the advantages of this design is that even if certain subjects refuse the early education program, they will still be given assessments as part of the health screening program and their data will still be available to test for biases caused by their refusal.

It should be clear from the above examples that the assignment procedure alone does not ensure comparability. Although random assignment was used in all three examples, they may differ greatly in whether the groups that actually agreed to enter the evaluation design were comparable. Again, these examples emphasize that the assignment procedure should be regarded as one part of a total process leading toward group comparability rather than as the sole criterion.

Hypothesis Testing and Estimation

The ideal of traditional outcome evaluation is to create a comparison between two or more sets of measurements in such a way that any differences observed between the groups are attributable to the program(s) being evaluated. The comparison is then used to determine: (1) the effect of the program on selected outcomes; and (2) an estimate of the size (magnitude) of the effect of the program on the outcome measures. In order to obtain this information, the evaluation usually employs statistics. These two types of information correspond to the basic types of statistical methods: hypothesis testing and estimation.

When an investigator attempts to determine whether a program has affected a given outcome, he or she is testing the hypothesis that the program has had no effect on the outcome. If this hypothesis is disproved, one can say that the program had some effect on the outcome. By convention, the no-effect, or null, hypothesis is said to be disproved if the observed difference has less than a 5 percent probability of occurring by chance.

In attempting to determine the size of an effect, an evaluator can use various statistical estimation techniques. Evaluators generally compute single-point estimates of effect size in terms of a percent, a mean, a median, or a regression coefficient. For example, an estimate of the magnitude of the effect can be the mean gain in IQ points or a difference in the percent of subjects assigned to special education classes. A simple, available technique would estimate a range of values within which it is likely that the true effect of the program will fall. This can be done by computing a confidence band. Although this technique is found in most elementary statistics texts, it has been underused in evaluation studies.

The hypothesis testing/estimation dichotomy concerned the Consortium study, as it does all evaluation studies, in terms of whether to emphasize the statistical significance or the size of effects. Statistically significant differences can result from very small effects—with a large enough sample. A one-point IQ score difference can be statistically significant even if it is educationally meaningless. On the other hand, a large effect may not be statistically significant, due to small sample size or other considerations. Our solution to the dilemma was to interpret results in terms of both statistical significance and size of effect.

Validity, Power, and Generalizability

Program evaluators can make three types of errors: they can conclude that the program is effective when in fact it is not (a Type I error); they can conclude that the program is ineffective when it really is effective (a Type II error); or they can apply the results of the evaluation to other situations for which the results do not hold. Stated positively, the ability of the design to avoid these errors can be conceptualized respectively as validity, power, and generalizability. In thinking about some apparent problem with an evaluation design, it is always important to decide whether it affects validity, power, or generalizability.

Validity essentially means the likelihood that the design will not find a significant difference between groups when the program has no effect. Design characteristics that lower validity make it more likely that an evaluator will find significant differences when none exist. The convention in statistical decision making is to reject the no-effect hypothesis when the probability of making this type of error is .05 or less. Validity, as used here, is a more restricted concept than as used by Campbell and Stanley (1966) or Cook and Campbell (1979). Here, it applies only to what the results of the evaluation will be when there is no real program effect.

Power refers to the likelihood that the design will find a significant difference when the program really has an effect. Design characteristics that lower power make it harder to find significant differences when real differences exist. Other considerations being equal, a reduction in sample size always lowers power. Cohen and Cohen (1975) demonstrate techniques for calculating power for a particular sample size.

Generalizability means that the findings of the study can be validly applied to other subjects, conditions, or programs that are similar but not identical. This is essentially what Campbell and Stanley (1966) refer to as external validity.

In our pooled Consortium analyses, we chose to maximize validity at the expense of power. In order to establish credibility in the post-Westinghouse Report era, we felt that every analysis decision should be made according to the criterion of minimizing the probability of finding a significant result unless the program effects really existed. In many cases, these conservative decisions increased the probability that we would not find a significant result even if a true effect existed. But this approach ensured that those results we found were genuine program effects.

The issue of generalizability has also arisen in the Consortium study, particularly with respect to whether the Consortium results can be generalized to Head Start. Since the Consortium programs were not a random sample of Head Start programs (in fact, only one of the projects was a Head Start program), our results are not statistically generalizable to Head Start. Our findings are still relevant to Head Start, however, since many Head Start programs were modeled after the Consortium programs, and the subjects would all have been eligible for Head Start. One might say the Consortium results show that Head Start can work, but not that Head Start does work.

Nonsignificant Results

The crucial dilemma of what to report when results are not significant can be approached by applying the concepts of power and validity within the framework of hypothesis testing and estimation of the magnitude of the effect.

A nonsignificant difference between experimental and control groups cannot be interpreted as "proving" or even "confirming" a null hypothesis of no difference between groups, because the data are also consistent with the hypothesis that there is a small but nonzero true difference between groups. Especially when a difference is nonsignificant, it is useful to calculate a confidence band on the true difference in order to make some statement about how large the actual difference might be.

One dramatic example of this involved a treatment designed to prevent blindness in certain premature babies. It was established beyond reasonable doubt that the new treatment was at least partially successful in preventing blindness, but the question remained whether babies given the new treatment had a higher mortality rate than other babies. In a study cited by Day et al. (1979), twelve out of forty experimental-group babies died, and nine out of forty-five control-group babies died. The difference was not significant ($p = .28$, two-tailed), so the treatment was approved for use. It was later found, however, that the new treatment did increase death rates, and it is no longer used. A confidence band calculated from the same data that yielded the nonsignificant difference suggests that the difference between mortality rates of the two treatments could be as large as 28 percent. If this figure had been calculated at the time, it might have suggested that more study was needed before adoption of the new treatment.

An alternative procedure, calculating the power of the analysis, is sometimes used when reporting nonsignificant results. The argument for this procedure is that the nonsignificant result should not be accepted unless the power analysis shows that the sample size was large enough to have detected a difference of important size. Power analysis may be appropriate before data collection; but after data collection, we prefer to use the confidence band rather than power analysis. The confidence band incorporates the data actually collected into the conclusions, whereas the power analysis is based entirely on a hypothetical analysis of what might have happened.

This difference between the two methods of analysis can perhaps be explained better if we introduce a word that is useful generally in discussing statistical results: consistency. We can describe the ordinary p from a hypothesis test as a measure of the consistency between the data and the null hypothesis. The smaller p is, the less consistent the data are with the null hypothesis. A confidence band can then be defined as the range of values consistent with the data, in the sense that the p measuring consistency would be over .05. A power analysis essentially shows what hypotheses are consistent with *some* nonsignificant result, while a confidence band can show what hypotheses are consistent with the *particular* nonsignificant result that was observed.

It is also important to remember that if a sample size is large, a difference between two programs may be statistically significant, but may still be too small to be of practical importance. This is an important reason for reporting the size of effects or differences as well as their statistical significance.

The Nature of Conclusions

A final set of concepts related to interpreting the results of hypothesis tests is important but rarely stressed. This set of concepts concerns making a distinction between "accepted conclusions" and "demonstrated conclusions." If you find a significant difference between a program group and a control group, you have demonstrated a difference between the two groups. This does not mean that you have proved that the difference exists beyond all possibility of doubt; after all, statistical principles tell us that the probability was .05 that the difference may have occurred by chance. But you have still demonstrated the difference in an important sense. On the other hand, suppose one finds no significant difference between the two groups. As most statistics books assert, this does not mean that you have demonstrated that there is no difference. After all, the true difference might have been a small one, so that there was little chance of finding a statistically significant difference with your sample size. But we can say that the data are consistent with the hypothesis that there is no difference between the two programs. Furthermore, the hypothesis of no difference is simpler or more parsimonious than the hypothesis that there is some difference. Thus, the hypothesis of no difference is the most parsimonious hypothesis consistent with the data. This is a very important notion in statistics and in science generally. Following Popper (1959), the eminent philosopher of science, we can never say we have proved a hypothesis. However, we can say that a certain hypothesis is the most parsimonious or simplest hypothesis consistent with the data we have observed so far. We thus tentatively "accept" that conclusion, knowing that we may well change our conclusion after more data are collected. Thus, we will say that a nonsignificant result leads to an "accepted conclusion" of no difference while a significant result leads to a "demonstrated conclusion" that a difference exists. In other words, a demonstrated conclusion is one arrived at by a formal test of a hypothesis, whereas an accepted conclusion is one that has not been finally tested but that is the most parsimonious hypothesis consistent with the data. The distinction is particularly important in evaluation research since evaluators are often pressured to make statements about which they cannot test a hypothesis. Thus, most questions of generalizability of results can be answered only as "accepted conclusions" because evaluation designs rarely incorporate a sampling strategy that permits statistically valid generalization.

Another application of this distinction would be the use of parametric statistics with ordinal scales. In much evaluation research, the measure of program success is an ordinal scale (such as a five-point Likert scale) rather than an interval variable (such as height or weight). Thus, questions are frequently raised about the validity of comparing the mean score of children in an experimental group with the mean score of children in a control group. How can we usefully compare means if they are not valid measures for ordinal scales? One answer to this question makes use of the distinction introduced between accepted conclusions and demonstrated conclusions. When a scale is genuinely interval in every sense and when the mean of a program group is significantly higher than the mean of a control group, we can say we have demonstrated that the program is better than the control treatment. In other words, we have a demonstrated conclusion. On the other hand, if the scale is merely ordinal, this same conclusion is merely an accepted conclusion. But it is still a valid conclusion, and because there is a significant difference between the two means, it is the simplest or most parsimonious conclusion consistent with the data. We have not demonstrated that the program is better than the control treatment, but to conclude otherwise would require an assumption for which there is no evidence: that the ordinal scale is distorted in such a way that it produces a significant difference between means even though the program is no better than the control treatment. Thus, it is reasonable to draw conclusions from differences between two means even if the scale used is ordinal.

Randomization and Statistical Control of Group Differences

Randomization has received a great deal of attention in the evaluation literature (Campbell & Stanley, 1966; Cook & Campbell, 1979; Boruch, 1978; Conner, 1978). There has been some confusion in the field, however, about what randomization is and how it fits into the evaluation design as a whole.

First, we must distinguish between random assignment and random selection. If you make a list of all the children in a school, use a random number table to choose thirty children for a study, describe two programs to the children, and let each child choose the program he or she wants, you have used random selection. On the other hand, if you allow thirty children to volunteer for your study and then use a random number table to place some of them in an experimental program and some of them in a control group, you have used random assignment.

Curiously, most statistics textbooks discuss random selection repeatedly but hardly ever mention random assignment. However, for most evaluation studies, random assignment is far more useful than random selection. Furthermore, although both are difficult to achieve, random assignment is often easier to implement than random selection. If the population from which to select is not even carefully counted—for instance, the population of the United States—random selection is virtually impossible.

Achieving random assignment in a field setting is a very difficult task. It is frequently difficult to obtain cooperation from subjects who know they are being randomly assigned to treatments, especially if one "treatment" is simply a control group which receives no special program. The problem is alleviated substantially if the only random assignment is between two or more attractive programs. Also, random assignment may be presented in a more acceptable manner to applicants if there is more demand for participation than can possibly be satisfied. Wortman and Rabinowitz (1979) found that a group of college students considered random assignment to be the fairest method of choosing subjects for programs in comparison to assignment on the basis of need, merit, or first-come/first-served. The investigator might also watch for situations in which random processes occur naturally or at least without intervention by the investigator. For instance, Staw (1974) studied attitude changes among young ROTC men who had or had not been selected by the draft lottery in 1970 (Cook and Campbell, 1979, p. 372). Conner (1978) and Cook and Campbell (1979) list useful ideas about implementing random assignment designs.

Ordinary statistical methods are valid in the presence of random assignment, even without random selection. The nature of the conclusion, however, is changed somewhat. For instance, suppose you are given permission to conduct a research project in a nursery school with ten children. These ten children probably do not even approximate a random sample from any larger population; they might simply be the ten children in that neighborhood whose parents both work. But suppose you randomly assign five of these children to an experimental group and five to a control group, and after several weeks you find that all the children in the experimental group score higher on a vocabulary test than any of the children in the control group. It can be shown that the probability that this would happen by chance is about .004. That is, if the experimental program had no effect on vocabularies, then the probability is about .004 that the five children with the highest vocabularies would be assigned to the experimental group. This is because there are 252 ways that ten children can be divided into two groups of five children each. Only one of these 252 possible ways involved putting the five children with the highest vocabularies in the experimental group. Thus, the probability this will happen by chance is 1/252, or about .004.

The population referred to by the significance test consists of the 252 possible ways of assigning ten children to two groups of five children each. In other words, the population is not a population of children at all, but rather a population of possible assignment patterns. Thus, the justification for the significance test is quite different from the justification given in most elementary statistics texts, but it is a real justification nonetheless, and it is far more relevant to most evaluation research.

If you have used random assignment without random selection and you find a significant difference between programs A and B, then you have proved quite rigorously that there is some difference between the effectiveness of the two programs for these children. It is then a matter of judgment to guess whether this difference applies to a broader population of children; but you have used statistical methods to show formally that there is some difference between the two programs. To put the matter in terms of validity and generalizability, random assignment is important for validity, and random selection is important for generalizability.

The distinction we established between demonstrated and accepted conclusions is useful in discussing the difference between studies using only random assignment and studies using both random selection and random assignment. In both cases, a significant result means you have demonstrated that there is some nonchance difference between two programs. If you used random selection from some broader population as well as random assignment, you also have a demonstrated conclusion that there is a difference in average effects of the two programs for the population as a whole. If you used random assignment without random selection, you can still have an accepted conclusion that there is a difference in effectiveness of the two programs for the population as a whole. You have demonstrated that there is a nonchance difference between programs for the sample you studied. Thus, the most parsimonious hypothesis about the population as a whole, consistent with this piece of data, is that the same difference you observed in your sample also applies to the population as a whole.

We have discussed at some length how random assignment differs from random selection, and how this difference affects conclusions. Now let us focus on random assignment itself, and ask why it is important. To do this, we must first introduce the term "covariate." A covariate is a variable on which two groups may differ which is unrelated to the effectiveness of the programs being studied. For instance, if you let children choose which program they will enter, then it may be that the children who chose program A are more intelligent or more highly motivated than the children who chose program B. If this occurs, then intelligence and motivation must be regarded as covariates and their effects must be accounted for in evaluating the relative outcomes of the two programs.

There are several statistical methods for controlling covariates: partial correlation, analysis of covariance, and multiple regression. A much simpler method of control is matching of distributions. For instance, suppose you find that children who chose program A come from families with higher socioeconomic status (SES), on the average, than children who chose program B. SES is a covariate. Suppose you allowed all children to participate in the programs for which they volunteered. When you analyze the relative effectiveness of the two programs later, you may delete from the statistical analysis some of the higher SES children who chose program A, and some of the lower SES children who chose program B, to make the distributions of SES similar for the two programs. This is a fairly simple way to improve the validity of your analysis. Its obvious disadvantage is that the deletion of subjects makes it harder to find a significant difference between the two programs; that is, it lowers power. This is the major advantage of the statistical methods of control, such as multiple regression, over matching. Nevertheless. we wish to discuss some problems that arise with any methods of control, and for simplicity we shall assume for the moment that you have used matching of distributions.

If there is no random assignment, then differences between groups A and B can arise in many ways. Regardless of whether the children themselves volunteered, their parents chose which group they would participate in, or some other process was used, there might be differences between groups A and B.

Suppose you match the distributions on IQ scores in order to eliminate that potential source of invalidity in your research design. A critic might still say that perhaps the two groups differ on SES, so you might match on that. Then another critic might say that perhaps the two groups differ on motivation, so you might match on that. In principle, critics could keep naming potential covariates indefinitely; it is impossible to match on all of the covariates or even to measure them satisfactorily. Thus, no matter how complete and careful your matching, a critic can always point to other variables on which there was no matching or control.

How does the situation differ from this when you have used random assignment? After all, even with random assignment, differences between the two groups can still arise by chance. In fact, we know that the probability is .05 that, just by chance, there could be a significant difference between groups A and B on IQ. There is also a probability of .05 that there is a significant difference between the two groups on motivation, and another .05 for SES. A critic might argue, therefore, that it is virtually certain that the two groups will differ on some covariate. So what has been gained by random assignment? The answer to this question is found in the basic meaning of statistical significance. Even though it is almost certain that the two groups will differ on some trait just by chance, the probability is only .05 that they will differ on the dependent variable. This is true even when you have used no matching or control of covariates at all. In a study using random assignment in which no covariates were controlled by other means or even measured, there is better control of covariates than in the most carefully matched study without random assignment, all other things being equal.

This does not mean that with random assignment, there is no need for matching or other methods of controlling covariates. Suppose we have a design with random assignment, and we are wondering whether to match groups on covariates such as IQ and SES. Although we have argued that random assignment gives us good validity even without matching, it can be shown that matching can substantially increase power. That is, matching can substantially improve the chance of finding a significant difference between programs if a difference really exists. The same is true of the more complex methods of controlling covariates, such as multiple regression. Therefore, these methods are still useful with random assignment, but their major contribution is to raise power rather than validity.

Attrition

Some subjects drop out during the course of any longitudinal study. Some may move; some may become disatisfied with the program and drop out; some may refuse to be assessed a second time; some may even die. This process of attrition may be either random or systematic (caused by some aspect of the program or of the evaluation process).

For an evaluation design to be valid, groups must be comparable at the time that they are being analyzed. A design could have comparable groups at the beginning, but due to systematic attrition they are no longer comparable at posttest. Attrition always affects power, but it may also affect validity or generalizability.

Attrition was a major concern in the Consortium study because the first Consortium follow-up in 1976 was generally conducted about a decade after subjects had left the early education programs. When the Consortium was formed, no one was certain whether we could find enough subjects to make a valid study. We addressed this problem on two levels: first, each project staff attempted to find all possible subjects; and second, the Cornell staff (the authors) designed a system of analyses to detect attrition-related biases. Although the latter form the basis of our discussion, it was the former—the determination of the project staff members—that enabled the Consortium to overcome the problem of attrition.

In the Consortium study, this problem was in one respect greater but in another respect smaller than what one would anticipate for an evaluation involving only a posttest administered immediately after the program. Attrition was a greater concern for the Consortium in that finding the subjects after a lapse of several years was often extremely difficult. On the other hand, attrition was less of a concern because the factors that made a subject difficult to find several years later were more likely to be similar for program and control subjects than were the factors involved at immediate posttest. Attrition at immediate posttest is more likely to be caused by a reaction to the program (for example, dropping out because of problems with the program); hence, the attrition rate is more likely to be different for the two groups. Such differential attrition is a greater threat to the validity of an evaluation than is sheer amount of attrition.

Although attrition has long been recognized as a major problem in longitudinal research, comparatively little thought has been directed to analyzing the attrition process and even less to what to do if attrition is discovered. In this section, we will discuss some definitional problems with attrition; delineate several types of attrition; discuss each type in terms of its effect on validity, power, and generalizability; and suggest some approaches to addressing the problem in the analyses of program outcomes.

Types of Attrition

Attrition is not a single phenomenon, the presence or absence of which can be determined by a single analysis. Rather, there are several types of attrition which can affect validity, power, or generalizability. Different rates of dropout between treatment and control groups constitute attrition; a difference between the dropouts and the final sample on some important characteristic also constitutes attrition. For the Consortium study, we developed five specific questions designed to detect different types of attrition:

1. Rate of attrition. What percentage of the original sample was recovered in the follow-up?
2. Differential rate of attrition. Were there different rates of attrition for program and control groups?
3. Main attrition effect. Did the final samples differ from the dropouts on some important characteristic?
4. Differential attrition effect. Are different kinds of children selectively retrieved in program versus control groups?
5. Equivalence of final groups. Did final program samples differ from final control samples on some important characteristics?[1]

The first four questions ask to what extent the final sample accurately represents the original sample and reflect four distinct types of attrition. The usefulness of such information hinges primarily on the initial equivalence of the program and control groups. If the groups were equivalent initially, analyses of attrition can assess the extent to which they remained equivalent. The fifth question, although not an attrition question per se, directly addresses the question of the equivalence of the final preschool and control groups. Thus, differences found in answer to the fifth question are not always attributable to attrition, but may be caused by differences in the original groups.

---

[1] A very similar scheme was developed by Jurs and Glass (1971).

Rate of Attrition

The question of attrition rate asks what percentage of the original sample was recovered. Rate of attrition, by itself, affects only power. If a large percentage of subjects have dropped out, but no other attrition effects have been discovered, then it is reasonable to conclude that attrition was a random process that will not affect validity or generalizability. This question is not susceptible to tests of inferential statistics since it does not involve a specific null hypothesis.

Differential Rate of Attrition

Differential rate of attrition poses the question of whether different proportions of treatment versus control children dropped out of the sample. In an experimental design, a differential rate of attrition is a distinct possibility during the experiment: the treatment children would have more incentive than the controls to report for evaluation if they perceive the treatment as beneficial; therefore, they may have a lower dropout rate during the treatment than the control group. After termination of the treatment, there is less reason to hypothesize a differential rate of attrition since the treatment group no longer has an added incentive to be available for evaluation.

A differential rate of attrition indicates that different attrition processes were occurring for program and for control subjects; hence, it poses a threat to validity as well as to power. If the rates of attrition are quite different for program and control groups, it becomes doubtful that the groups are still comparable, even if no difference between the groups emerges on any measured variables.

The appropriate test for differential rates of attrition is a chi-square statistic from a 2 by 2 cross-tabulation of program/control status by dropout status for each project. We used the uncorrected chi-square for all 2 by 2 tables (see Fienberg, 1978).

Main Attrition Effect

Main attrition effects pose the question of whether the dropouts differed from the final sample on some important characteristic. The existence of a main attrition effect does not affect the treatment-control comparison for the final sample, but it does mean that one cannot extend this inference to the original experimental sample. For instance, if the final sample was found to be of lower SES then the dropouts (the higher SES families had moved out of the area and could not be located), then any treatment/control differences found at follow-up would hold true only for the lower SES subjects and not necessarily for all subjects. Thus, a main attrition effect changes the referent population to which the findings can be generalized and lowers power as well.

To test for a main attrition effect, one must first identify preprogram variables on which it is important to know if the dropouts differ from the final sample. For the Consortium study, we focused on preprogram IQ score, mother's education, and socioeconomic status. Each of these variables becomes the dependent variable in a 2 by 2 analysis of variance in which program/control status and dropout status are the factors. The significance level of the dropout main effect in this ANOVA determines whether there is a main attrition effect. A simple analysis would be a *t*-test between dropouts and final sample on each preprogram variable. We used the ANOVA approach because (1) it removes any variance attributable to a program-control difference; and (2) the single ANOVA gives the information necessary for both this question and the following one.

Differential Attrition Effect

The question of differential effects is the most complex attrition question we have posed: it asks whether different kinds of children were selectively retrieved in treatment and in control groups. More specifically, is the difference between the preschool dropouts and final sample significantly different from the difference between the control dropouts and the final sample? This could occur if for some reason only the "best" experimentals and the "worst" controls were retrieved. Alternatively, one could find that the initial "best" treatment subjects had dropped out of the follow-up assessment program, while only the "best" control subjects were motivated to continue assessments. The differential attrition effect question investigates this type of effect by comparing four groups: treatment dropouts, treatment final sample, control dropouts, and control final sample, on selected characteristics. A differential attrition effect threatens both validity and power. It indicates that groups that were originally comparable on a specific variable are no longer comparable. The appropriate test for differential attrition effects are the significance levels of the program status (treatment/control)–dropout status (found/not found) interaction in the 2 by 2 ANOVAs described above.

Equivalence of Final Groups

As noted previously, the question of the equivalence of final groups is not an attrition question per se. It asks whether the final treatment group was equivalent to the final control group on important background measures rather than whether the final sample was equivalent to the original sample. Differences between final treatment and control groups cannot be ascribed automatically to attrition, because such differences may reflect only differences between the original treatment and control groups. Therefore, any differences must be explored further to ascertain whether they are caused by attrition or by differences in the original sample.

Nonequivalence of final groups, like nonequivalence of initial groups, poses threats to both validity and power. One can test for equivalence of final groups by using t-tests between the final sample program and control groups on the preprogram variables used in the main attrition effect and differential attrition effect analyses.

These five questions provide a framework for detecting the effects of attrition. As can be seen, not all types of attrition distort the program-control comparison. Loss of subjects alone only lowers power. Certain types of systematic attrition can operate equally in program and control groups, producing a main attrition effect which makes the final sample different from the dropouts but which does not alter the internal validity of the program–control comparison in the final sample. The other types of attrition—differential rates of attrition and differential attrition effect—indicate that the program–control comparison for the final sample may be biased. As a last step, the final sample group should be tested for equivalence on preprogram variables, since nonequivalence here, for whatever reason, will produce biased results.

This set of analyses will reveal a great number of the problems caused by attrition. However, the evaluator should be aware of the limitations of these attrition analyses. First, they are limited to the background variables collected. If there was differential attrition with respect to an unmeasured variable, it will remain undetected. Second, since the attrition analyses are an attempt to prove the null hypothesis, at most one can arrive only at an accepted, rather than demonstrated, conclusion that there was no attrition effect.

Stronger conclusions may be possible if the rate of attrition is small and the outcome variable is dichotomous. If a child drops out and has no posttest data, it would seem that the investigator has no choice but to delete him or her from the analysis. Surprisingly, however, there is an alternative.

Suppose that the dependent variable on which the child is to be evaluated after the program is dichotomous—for instance, "successful" or "unsuccessful" at a certain skill taught by the program. Assume that each child was placed in the category that would make the program look least effective; specifically, assume that children who dropped out of the experimental group were placed in the "unsuccessful" category and children who dropped out of the control group were placed in the "successful" category. As an example, suppose that forty children completed the experimental program and another forty completed a control program, and that thirty of the experimentals and ten of the controls are measured as "successful" at the end of the program. Now suppose that three children had dropped out before the completion of each program. Assume that if they had continued, the three from the experimental program would have been unsuccessful and the three from the control program would have been successful. Then the frequencies for the experimental program would have been thirty successful and thirteen unsuccessful; and frequencies for the control program would have been thirteen successful and thirty unsuccessful. The difference in success rates is still significant at the .00025 level (two-tailed) even after these subjects have been placed as they were. This is a very conservative procedure which of course is lacking in power if the number of missing subjects is at all large. Furthermore, its use with a continuous dependent variable might be unfeasible because in order to ensure complete validity, the missing subjects in the experimental group should be placed at the bottom of the range and those in the control group should be placed at the top. This would entail an extensive reduction in power. To use this procedure with a continuous dependent variable, it may help to dichotomize it in order to avoid too much loss of power.

In effect, this technique establishes a "worst case" program effect by showing what the effect would be if calculated on the assumption that all dropouts had outcome scores unfavorable to the program. Obviously, if there is a large percentage of dropouts, then the "worst case" would produce a negative program effect. If, however, the program effect is calculated in this way, one has set a lower limit on the program effect.

A final technique could be used if there is differential attrition or nonequivalence of final groups on a certain preprogram variable. This technique would be to delete the dropouts from the analysis and to use the troublesome preprogram variable as a covariate in all outcome analyses. This would adjust for the measured bias, although it would systematically underadjust for the "true bias" due to measurement error in the covariate (Campbell & Erlebacher, 1975; Cook & Campbell, 1979). It would not adjust for the loss of power.

These techniques are only partial solutions to problems of attrition. The only effective way to minimize attrition effects is to make every effort to assess all possible subjects during posttest data collection.

Summary

We have presented an overview of issues in research methodology that can be applied to studying the outcomes of early childhood education programs. These concepts are relevant to experimental and quasi-experimental studies such as our investigation of the long-term effects of Consortium early childhood programs. The outcome evaluation approach was placed in the context of evaluation research in general, and the basic tasks in conducting program outcome evaluations were described. We then discussed some general research design issues and applied them to outcome evaluation using examples from early childhood education evaluations, particularly the research of the Consortium for Longitudinal Studies.

We considered several methodological issues that we felt were most relevant to studying program outcomes. The first topic we considered was the selection of suitable measures, the specification of program goals and outcome criteria, and the scheduling of measures. We next addressed the issue of comparing outcome measures to other sets of measurements and offered suggestions for minimizing alternative explanations through appropriate selection, recruitment, and assignment procedures. The weaknesses of one-group pretest–posttest designs were considered in the section on establishing comparisons. In the next section, we discussed the use of statistics in judging whether the program had a measurable effect and in estimating the magnitude of the effect (hypothesis testing and estimation).

We then discussed the ability of evaluation designs to maximize validity, power, and generalizability, and examined the value of calculating confidence bands when results are nonsignificant. The nature of conclusions and the distinction between accepted and demonstrated conclusions were discussed and applied to ordinal scales. We also discussed randomization and the statistical control of group differences. Finally, we described types of attrition and offered approaches to addressing attrition problems.

We are grateful to our Cornell colleagues Ann Bell, Chia-Ying Chang, Ruth Hubbell, Daniel Koretz, Paula Massengill, Marilyn Rosché, Ann Snipper, Reuben Snipper, Judy Vopava, and Marjorie Wikerd for their generous contributions; to Consortium members for their vision and cooperation; and to Bernard Brown and Edith Grotberg of the Administration for Children, Youth, and Families for their encouragement. Our work was supported by OHDS, DHEW grants Nos. 90-C-1311 and 18-76-07843, Maternal and Child Health grant No. MCT-004012-01-0, and by the William and Flora Hewlett Foundation.

References

ATTKISSON, C. C., and HARGREAVES, W. A. A conceptual model for program evaluation in health organizations. In H. C. Schulberg and F. Baker (eds.), *Program Evaluation in the Health Fields*, Vol. 2. New York: Human Sciences Press, 1979.

BELLER, E. K. Research on organized programs of early education. In R. Travers (ed.), *Handbook of Research on Teaching*. Chicago: Rand McNally, 1973.

BERNSTEIN, I. *Validity Issues in Evaluating Research*. Beverly Hills, Calif.: Sage Publications, 1976.

BORUCH, R. F. On common contentions about randomized field experiments. In G. V. Glass (ed.), *Evaluation Studies Review Annual*, Vol. 1. Beverly Hills, Calif.: Sage Publications, 1978.

BRONFENBRENNER, U. *A Report on Longitudinal Evaluations of Preschool Programs. Vol. 2: Is Early Intervention Effective?* DHEW Publication No. (OHD) 74-25, 1974.

BRONFENBRENNER, U. *The Experimental Ecology of Human Development*. Cambridge, Mass.: Harvard University Press, 1979.

BROWN, B. *Found: Long-Term Gains from Early Intervention*. Boulder, Colo.: Westview Press, 1978.

CAMPBELL, D. T. Assessing the impact of planned social change. *Evaluation and Program Planning*, 1979, 2, 67–90.

CAMPBELL, D. T., and ERLEBACHER, A. How regression artifacts in quasi-experimental evaluations can mistakenly make compensatory education look harmful. In E. L. Struening and M. Guttentag (eds.), *Handbook of Evaluation Research*, Vol. 1. Beverly Hills, Calif.: Sage Publications, 1975.

CAMPBELL, D. T., and STANLEY, C. *Experimental and Quasi-Experimental Designs for Research*. Chicago: Rand McNally, 1966.

CARO, F. G. (ed.). *Readings in Evaluation Research*, 2nd ed. New York: Russell Sage Foundation, 1977.

CICIRELLI, V. G. *The Impact of Head Start: An Evaluation of the Effects of Head Start on Children's Cognitive and Affective Development.* Washington, D.C.: National Bureau of Standards, Institute for Applied Technology, 1969.

COHEN, J., and COHEN, P. *Applied Multiple Regression Correlation Analysis for Behavioral Sciences.* Hillsdale, N.J.: Laurence Erlbaum Associates, 1975.

Comptroller General of the United States. Early childhood and family development programs improve the quality of life for low-income families. A report to the Congress. Washington, D.C.: General Accounting Office, February 6, 1979.

CONNER, R. F. Selecting a control group: An analyis of the randomization process in twelve social reform programs. In T. Cook, M. Del Rosario, K. Hennigan, M. Mark, and W. Trochim (eds.), *Evaluation Studies Review Annual,* Vol. 3. Beverly Hills, Calif.: Sage Publications, 1978.

THE CONSORTIUM ON DEVELOPMENTAL CONTINUITY. *The Persistence of Preschool Effects.* Washington, D.C.: U.S. Government Printing Office, 1977.

CONSORTIUM FOR LONGITUDINAL STUDIES. *Lasting Effects after Preschool.* Washington, D.C.: U.S. Government Printing Office, 1978.

CONSORTIUM FOR LONGITUDINAL STUDIES. Lasting effects of early education. *Monographs of the Society for Research in Child Development,* in press.

COOK, T. D., and CAMPBELL, D. T. *Quasi-Experimentation: Design and Analysis Issues for Field Settings.* Chicago: Rand McNally, 1979.

COOK, T. D., DEL ROSARIO, M. L., HENNIGAN, K. M., MARK, M. M., and TROCHIM, W. M. K. (eds.). *Evaluation Studies Review Annual,* Vol. 3. Beverly Hills, Calif.: Sage Publications, 1978.

COOK, T. D., and LEVITAN, L. C. Reviewing the literature: A comparison of traditional methods with meta-analysis. *Journal of Personality,* 1980, *48,* 449–472.

COURSEY, R. D., SPECTER, G. A., MURRELL, S. A., and HUNT, B. (eds.). *Program Evaluation for Mental Health: Methods, Strategies and Participants.* New York: Grove & Stratton, 1977.

DARLINGTON, R. B., ROYCE, J. M., SNIPPER, A. S., MURRAY, H. W., and LAZAR, I. Preschool programs and later school competence of children from low-income families. *Science,* 1980, *208,* 202–204.

DATTA, L. The impact of the Westinghouse/Ohio evaluation on Project Head Start. In C. Abt (ed.), *The Evaluation of Social Programs.* Beverly Hills, Calif.: Sage Publications, 1976.

DATTA, L. Goosing the system: Some federal purposes for demonstrations. In J. M. Love (chair), The Role of Educational Demonstrations in Shaping Public Policy. Symposium presented at the Annual Meeting of the American Educational Research Association, Boston, 1980.

DAY, M. C., and PARKER, R. C. (eds.). *The Preschool in Action: Exploring Early Childhood Programs,* 2nd ed. Boston: Allyn & Bacon, 1977.

DAY, R. L., DELL, R. B., DARLINGTON, R. B., and FLEISS, J. On statistical nonsignificance and retrolental fibroplasia. *Pediatrics,* 1979, *63,* 324–344.

DENZIN, N. *The Research Act.* Chicago: Aldine, 1970.

DEUTSCH, M., TALEPOROS, E., and VICTOR, J. A brief synopsis of an initial enrichment program in early childhood. In S. Ryan (ed.), *A Report on Longitudinal Evaluations of Preschool Programs,* Vol. 1. Washington, D.C.: Office of Child Development, DHEW Publication No. (OHD) 74-24, 1974.

EVANS, E. D. *Contemporary Influences in Early Childhood Education*, 2nd ed. New York: Holt, Rinehart & Winston, 1974.

FIENBERG, S. *The Analysis of Cross-Classified Data.* Cambridge, Mass.: M.I.T. Press, 1978.

FILSTEAD, W. J. Qualitative methods: A needed perspective in evaluation research. In T. D. Cook and C. S. Reichardt (eds.), *Quantitative and Qualitative Methods in Evaluation Research*, Vol. 1. Beverly Hills, Calif.: Sage Publications, 1979.

GARFINKEL, H. "Good" organizational reasons for "bad" clinic records. In H. Garfinkel (ed.), *Studies in Ethnomethodology.* Englewood Cliffs, N.J.: Prentice-Hall, 1967.

GLASS, G. V. (ed.), *Evaluation Studies Review Annual*, Vol. 1. Beverly Hills, Calif.: Sage Publications, 1976.

GLASS, G. V. Standards and criteria. *Journal of Educational Measurement*, 1978, *15*, 237–261.

GOODWIN, W. L., and DRISCOLL, L. A. *Handbook for Measurement and Evaluation in Early Childhood Education.* San Francisco: Jossey-Bass, 1980.

GORDON, I. J., GUINAGH, B., and JESTER, R. E. The Florida parent education infant and toddler programs. In M. C. Day and R. K. Parker (eds.), *The Preschool in Action: Exploring Early Childhood Programs*, 2nd ed. Boston: Allyn and Bacon, 1977.

GOTTS, E. E. Head Start research, development, and evaluation. In J. L. Frost (ed.), *Revisiting Early Childhood Education: Readings.* New York: Holt, Rinehart & Winston, 1973.

GRAY, S. W., RAMSEY, B. K., and Klaus, R. A. *From Three to Twenty: The Early Training Project in Longitudinal Perspective.* Baltimore, Md.: University Park Press, 1981.

GUBA, E. G. Educational evaluation: The state of the art. Paper presented at meetings of Evaluation Network, St. Louis, Missouri, September 1977.

GUBA, E. G. Toward a methodology of naturalistic inquiry in educational evaluation. C.S.E. Monograph Series in Evaluation. No. 8. Los Angeles: Center for the Study of Evaluation, University of California, 1978.

GUTTENTAG, M. A decision theoretic approach to evaluation research. In H. C. Schulberg and F. Baker (eds.), *Program Evaluation in the Health Fields*, Vol. 2. New York: Human Sciences Press, 1979.

GUTTENTAG, M., and SAAR, S. (eds.). *Evaluation Studies Review Annual*, Vol. 2. Beverly Hills, Calif.: Sage Publications, 1977.

HOROWITZ, F. D., and PADEN, L. Y. The effectiveness of environmental intervention programs. In B. M. Caldwell and H. R. Ricciuti (eds.), *Review of Child Development Research*, Vol. 3. Chicago: University of Chicago Press, 1973.

JURS, S. G., and GLASS, G. V. The effect of experimental mortality on the internal and external validity of the randomized comparative experiment. *Journal of Experimental Education*, 1971, *40*, 62–66.

KAMIN, L. *Science and Politics of IQ.* New York: Wiley, 1974.

KARNES, M. B., ZEHRBACK, R. R., and TESKA, J. A. Conceptualization of the GOAL (game-oriented activities for learning) curriculum. In M. C. Day and R. K. Parker (eds.), *The Preschool in Action: Exploring Early Childhood Programs*, 2nd ed. Boston: Allyn & Bacon, 1977.

KIRESUK, T. J., and LUND, S. H. Goal attainment scaling: Research, evaluation, and utilization. In H. C. Schulberg and F. Baker (eds.), *Program Evaluation in the Health Fields*, Vol. 2. New York: Human Sciences Press, 1979.

LEVENSTEIN, P. The mother–child home program. In M. C. Day and R. K. Parker (eds.), *The Preschool in Action: Exploring Early Childhood Programs*, 2nd ed. Boston: Allyn & Bacon, 1977.

LEVINE, M., and ROSENBERG, N. S. An adversary model of fact finding and decision making for program evaluation: Theoretical considerations. In H. C. Schulberg and F. Baker (eds.), *Program Evaluation in the Health Fields*, Vol. 2. New York: Human Sciences Press, 1979.

LIGHT, R. J., and SMITH, P. V. Accumulating evidence: Procedures for resolving contradictions among different research studies. *Harvard Educational Review*, 1971, *41*, 429–471.

MANN, A. J., HARRELL, A., and HURT, M., JR. *A Review of Head Start Research since 1969*. Washington, D.C.: Social Research Group, George Washington University, 1976.

MAYNARD-MOODY, S., and McCLINTOCK, C. C. Square pegs in round holes: Program evaluation and organizational uncertainty. In D. Palumbo, S. Fawcett, and P. Wright (eds.), *Evaluating and Optimizing Public Policy*. Lexington, Mass.: Lexington Books, 1981.

MILLER, L. B., and DYER, J. L. Four preschool programs: Their dimensions and effects. *Monographs of the Society for Research in Child Development*, 1975, *40*(5–6, Serial No. 162).

NAGEL, S., and NEEF, M. What's new about policy analysis research. *Society*, September/October 1979, *6*(6).

PALMER, F. H., and SIEGEL, R. J. Minimal intervention at ages two and three and subsequent intellective changes. In M. C. Day and R. K. Parker (eds.), *The Preschool in Action: Exploring Early Childhood Programs*, 2nd ed. Boston: Allyn & Bacon, 1977.

PILLEMER, D. B., and LIGHT, R. J. Synthesizing outcomes: How to use research evidence from many studies. *Harvard Educational Review*, 1980, *50*, 176–195.

POPPER, K. R. *The Logic of Scientific Discovery*. New York: Basic Books, 1959. (Originally, *Die Logik der Forschung*, 1935.)

RAINES, H. Reagan won't cut seven social programs that aid 80 million. *New York Times*, February 11, 1981.

REICHARDT, C. S., and COOK, T. D. Beyond qualitative versus quantitative methods. In T. D. Cook and C. S. Reichardt (eds.), *Quantitative and Qualitative Methods in Evaluation Research*, Vol. 1. Beverly Hills, Calif.: Sage Publications, 1979.

RIVLIN, A. M., and TIMPANE, P. M. *Planned Variation in Education*. Washington, D.C.: Brookings Institution, 1975.

SCHULBERG, H. C., and BAKER, F. (eds.). *Program Evaluation in the Health Fields*, Vol. 3. New York: Human Sciences Press, 1979.

SCHWEINHART, L. J., and WEIKART, D. P. Young children grow up: The effects of the Perry Preschool Program on youths through age 15. *Monographs of the High/Scope Educational Research Foundation*, 1980 (No. 7).

SCRIVEN, M. The methodology of evaluation. In R. E. Stake (ed.), *Perspectives on Curriculum Evaluation*. AERA Monograph Series on Curriculum Evaluation, No. 1. Skokie, Ill.: Rand McNally, 1967.

SCRIVEN, M. Evaluation perspectives and procedures. In W. J. Popham (ed.), *Evaluation in Education: Current Applications.* Berkeley, Calif.: McCutchan, 1974.

SECHREST, L., WEST, S. G., PHILLIPS, M. A., REDNER, R., and YEATON, W. (eds.). *Evaluation Studies Review Annual,* Vol. 4. Beverly Hills, Calif.: Sage Publications, 1979.

SELLTIZ, C., WRIGHTMAN, L. C., and COOK, S. W. *Research Methods in Social relations,* 3rd ed. New York: Holt, Rinehart & Winston, 1976.

STAKE, R. E. The countenance of educational evaluation. *Teachers College Record,* 1967, *68,* 523–540.

STAKE, R. E. To evaluate an arts program. In R. E. Stake (ed.), *Evaluating the Arts in Education: A Responsive Approach.* Columbus, Ohio: Merrill, 1975.

STAW, B. M. Attitudinal and behavioral consequences of changing a major organizational reward: A natural field experiment. *Journal of Personality and Social Psychology,* 1974, *29,* 742–751.

STEBBINS, L. B., ST. PIERRE, R. G., PROPER, E. C., ANDERSON, R. B., and CERVA, T. R. An evaluation of Follow Through. In T. D. Cook, M. L. Del Rosario, K. M. Hennigan, M. M. Mark, and W. M. K. Trochim (eds.), *Evaluation Studies Review Annual,* Vol. 3. Beverly Hills, Calif.: Sage Publications, 1978.

STUFFLEBEAM, D. L. Evaluation as enlightenment for decision-making. Mimeo. Columbus: Evaluation Center, Ohio State University, 1968.

SUCHMAN, E. *Evaluation Research.* New York: Russell Sage Foundation, 1967.

U.S. Department of Health, Education and Welfare; Office of Human Development Services; Administration for Children, Youth and Families; Children's Bureau, *Head Start Program Performance Standards,* 1975.

WEBB, E. J., CAMPBELL, D. T., SCHWARTZ, R. D., and SECHREST, L. *Unobtrusive Measures.* Skokie, Ill.: Rand McNally, 1966.

WEISS, C. H. (ed.). *Evaluating Action Programs: Readings in Social Action and Education.* Boston: Allyn & Bacon, 1972.

WERGIN, J. F. The Evaluation of Organizational Policy Making: A Political Model. *Review of Educational Research,* 1976, *46,* 75–115.

WHOLEY, J. S., SCANLON, J. W., DUFFY, H. G., FUKUMOTO, J., and VOGT, L. M. *Federal Evaluation Policy.* Washington, D.C.: The Urban Institute, 1970.

WILDAVSKY, A. The self-evaluating organization. In H.S. Schulberg and F. Baker (eds.), *Program Evaluation in the Health Fields,* Vol. 2. New York: Human Sciences Press, 1979.

WOOLMAN, M. Learning for cognition: The micro-social learning system. Report to the New Jersey State Department of Education, 1971.

WORTMAN, C. B., and RABINOWITZ, V. C. Random assignment: The fairest of them all. In Sechrest et al. (eds.), *Evaluation Studies Review Annual,* Vol. 4. Beverly Hills, Calif.: Sage Publications, 1979.

ZIGLER, E., and TRICKETT, P. K. IQ, social competence, and evaluation of early childhood education programs. *American Psychologist,* 1978, *33,* 789–798.

ZIGLER, E., and VALENTINE, J. (eds.). *Project Head Start: A Legacy of the War on Poverty.* New York: Free Press, 1979.

Name Index

Subject Index